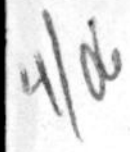

THE AUDIO DICTIONARY

THE AUDIO DICTIONARY

Glenn D. White
and
Gary J. Louie

Third Edition, Revised and Expanded

University of Washington Press
Seattle and London

Printed in the United States of America
12 11 10 09 08 07 06 05   5 4 3 2 1

University of Washington Press
PO Box 50096
Seattle, WA 98145-5096
www.washington.edu/uwpress

Library of Congress Cataloging-in-Publication Data

White, Glenn D., 1933–
The audio dictionary / by Glenn D. White and Gary J. Louie.—3rd ed., rev. and expanded.
p. cm.
Includes bibliographical references.
ISBN 0-295-98498-8 (pbk. : alk. paper)
1. Sound—Recording and reproducing—Dictionaries. I. Louie, Gary J. II. Title.
TK7881.4.W48 2004
621.389'3—dc22   2004029425

The paper used in this publication meets the minimum requirements of American National Standard for Information Sciences—Permanence of Paper for Printed Library Materials, ANSI Z39.48-1984.

This edition contains several entries from Larry Blake's Glossary of Film Sound terms. The complete version of which is only available on his Swelltonelabs website <www.swelltonelabs.com>.

To Naomi Pascal,
who first suggested that I write this book,
and who, with characteristic enthusiasm and good humor,
inspired me to finish it.
—G.W.

Contents

Preface to the Third Edition

Although the second edition of *The Audio Dictionary* is enjoying healthy sales, friends, acquaintances, and strangers have asked me now and then when a third edition would be published. When my good friend Naomi Pascal, now Editor-at-Large at the University of Washington Press, who inveigled me to write the book in the first place, asked me the same question, I decided it was time. I realized at once that putting a new edition together would be a daunting task to tackle because of the new audio-related technologies such as the explosion of the home theater systems market, and the upgrades in motion picture sound. I asked Gary Louie, who gave me many suggestions and lots of information when I was preparing the first two editions, if he would like to cowrite this new edition. Gary, a longtime friend and crack audio/video electronics technician, experienced recording engineer, and avid collector of audio memorabilia and arcana, agreed, and the present volume is the result.

Gary and I were amazed at the magnitude of changes the audio industry has undergone in the last ten years. This third edition contains over 400 new entries, the second edition entries and appendices have been thoroughly gone over and in some cases enlarged and brought up to date, and two new appendixes have been added.

Glenn White
2005

Introduction

"Lexicographer, n. A pestilent fellow who, under the pretense of recording some particular stage in the development of a language, does what he can to arrest its growth, stiffen its flexibility, and mechanize its methods."—From Ambrose Bierce, *The Devil's Dictionary*

Throughout the years of teaching acoustics and audio-related courses at the university level, we have felt the need for a book covering the terminology and basic concepts in the fields of sound recording, sound reinforcement, and musical acoustics. The marginal emphasis on audio education by our schools and universities has permitted a large body of folklore to exist. This book is aimed at dispelling some misinformation and is intended to supplement textbooks for courses in these areas and also to serve as a source of information for the general reader who has an interest in reproduced music and/or musical acoustics. The dictionary format was chosen primarily for ease of cross-referencing as well as ease of locating specific information. Definitions of fundamental principles and standards are included, as well as entries on more abstract and subjective concepts. The areas of basic acoustics, elementary electroacoustics, digital audio, electronics as applied to audio, and some topics within the areas of psychoacoustics are covered.

A diligent attempt was made to keep the text free of mathematics and to present the material in a framework of familiar and comfortable territory to the nonspecialist. At the same time, oversimplification was avoided as much as possible. It might be argued that some concepts, such as decibels, cannot be adequately described without mathematics, and this is no doubt true; however, the underlying concept of logarithmic ratios can be explained without resorting to mathematical symbols. This approach to the subject via intuitive principles is used consistently.

There is a certain amount of repetition of some concepts as they are discussed in various contexts. In these cases, we have tried to make the approaches different enough to increase the understanding by the nonspecialist. There is included in the definitions a significant amount of information in anecdotal form, but we have tried to keep personal opinions out of the dictionary proper. In the back of the book are eleven appendixes that discuss certain topics in more detail, and we confess that here a certain amount of personal bias may have crept in.

It is expected that this treatment will allow the book to appeal to a broad audience, from the nontechnical stereo set owner to the semiprofessional who needs a ready source of information. We hope that the former may be stimulated to dig deeper into the subject, and the latter may find that the intuitive approach will increase understanding. The appearance of a capitalized word within an entry signifies another entry with that heading. Thus, one may be led in a zigzag path through the dictionary by looking up unfamiliar words as they are encountered.

THE AUDIO DICTIONARY

A

AAC, Advanced Audio Coding A high-quality perceptual audio coding technology appropriate for many broadcast and electronic music distribution applications. Coding efficiency is superior to that of MP3, providing higher-quality audio at lower bit rates. Developed and standardized as an ISO/IEC specification by four industry leaders (AT&T, Dolby Laboratories, The Fraunhofer Institute for Integrated Circuits, and Sony Corporation), AAC is supported by a growing number of hardware and software manufacturers as the logical successor to MP3. It was declared an international standard by MPEG in April 1997. It is used by Apple Computer for their music downloading service begun on April 28, 2003.

A Battery The low-voltage battery that supplied current for the tube heaters of early radios. One of the earliest types of A battery was the No. 6 dry cell, which gave 1.5 VOLTS. Later, 6-V lead-acid storage batteries were used, which of course were rechargeable. Standard automobile batteries of the day would work, but special radio A batteries were said to provide smoother current! The first power supplies to provide heater current from the AC line were called "A eliminators" and had to have very effective filtering to avoid 60-HERTZ HUM.

ABS, ABS-Time, A-Time, Absolute Time Most digital recorders provide a means for recording a time count along with the audio. Recorders such as DAT and ADAT will start the time count at 00:00:00 at the beginning of the tape, and advance in real time as the recording is made. CD-Rs have a similar method of timing using a pre-made signal groove, known as ATIP, for Absolute Time In Pregroove. The first generation of DAT recorders did not have A-Time implemented, thus a tape recorded on such a machine will not show A-Time. A-Time is not the same as SMPTE time code, although some machines can work with A-Time in an SMPTE environment.

Absolute Phase A sound system that preserves the actual POLARITY of the original sound waves being recorded. In other words, care is taken that there is no polarity reversal anywhere in the recording/reproducing chain. Thus, a compression wave at the recording session is reproduced as a compression wave at the listener's location, rather than a rarefaction. There are those who claim there is no audible difference if the polarity of both channels is reversed and others who claim there is a vast difference. In any case, the term should be ABSOLUTE POLARITY.

Absolute Pitch Some people, not necessarily musicians, on hearing a sound have the ability to accurately identify its position or note on the musical scale. Absolute pitch is simply an accurate pitch memory, and persons who have it almost always acquire it at an early age. Nobody is born with it, but there may be a genetic factor that facilitates its learning. It is also sometimes called "perfect pitch."

Persons with absolute pitch vary in their precision, and some have been shown to be remarkably accurate. Such a person can tell immediately what key a particular piece is being performed in, and whether it is sharp or flat. These people usually insist on having a phonograph turntable with variable speed so they can adjust it to the exact pitch desired.

Many musicians have the ability to recognize musical intervals very quickly, and this is called "relative pitch." It does not seem to be related to absolute pitch.

Absolute Polarity A condition where the POLARITY of a musical signal is not reversed no matter what devices are used in the signal path. When a musical sound reaches the ear, the first sensation the ear will feel will be either a compression or a rarefaction of the sound wave. An example is a bass drum. If you are situated facing the side of the drum that is struck by the heavy drumstick, the onset of the audible sound will be a rarefaction of the air pressure since the drum head initially moves away from you when struck. This is called a negative polarity at the instant of the sound's arrival at the ear. However, if you were on the other side of the drum, your first arriving sound will be a compression, or a positive polarity. There is some controversy about whether the human hearing mechanism can tell the difference between positive and negative initial polarity, and under what conditions. One faction says the initial polarity of music must be preserved in music reproduction systems. This means the polarity of the audio signal would have to be maintained throughout the path from the microphone through preamplifiers, cables, signal processing equipment, the delivery medium, the playback amplifier, loudspeakers, and the loudspeaker wires. Even more important, the relative polarity between the stereo channels must be the same in order to maintain directional realism (a condition sometimes referred to as being "in phase"). It is generally agreed that a positive pressure into a microphone will produce a positive voltage at its output connector, but there is no guarantee that all audio devices maintain absolute polarity in themselves.

Absorption Coefficient A measure of the relative amount of sound energy that will be absorbed when a sound strikes a surface. It is a pure dimensionless number ranging from 0 to 1, and is represented by the Greek letter α (alpha). The actual percentage of sound absorbed by a surface is equal to the surface area multiplied by the absorption coefficient and is expressed in units called SABINS, after the well-known Harvard professor and acoustician Wallace Sabine.

An absorption coefficient of one means that all the energy striking the absorber will be absorbed and none reflected. An open window has an absorption coefficient of one. If the absorption coefficient is equal to zero, then all the sound would be reflected and none absorbed. This is never possible in practice, for all materials absorb some sound energy. The absorption of any material will vary with frequency; that is, a material will have a different absorption coefficient for different frequencies.

In order to predict the REVERBERATION time of a room, the engineer must know the total absorption of all the inside surfaces of the room, and for this reason, many common materials have been measured and the absorption coefficients have been published for a wide frequency range. The measurement of alpha is not simple, and there are several techniques recognized by various standards organizations and carried out by approved testing laboratories.

A-B Stereo A-B stereo is a method of recording whereby two OMNIDIRECTIONAL microphones are spaced several feet apart and placed in front of the sound source. This was the system used by Harvey Fletcher in his historic demonstration of STEREOPHONIC reproduction of a symphony orchestra in 1933. It is also known as spaced microphone stereo or spaced omnidirectional microphones.

Two omnidirectional microphones placed in front of an orchestra provide the stereo listener with differences in LOUDNESS, differences in arrival time (or PHASE), and to a certain extent, differences in spectral content, or TIMBRE, between the two channels. These cues are used by our hearing mechanism to detect the locations of sources of sounds.

The exact placement of the microphones in an auditorium is very important to obtaining the best balance of direct and reverberant sound. No amount of EQUALIZATION or other SIGNAL PROCESSING can correct for poor microphone placement.

A-B stereo recording generally has more AMBIENCE, or room sound, than other methods of recording, and if well done, has a musically satisfying perspective. It is especially successful when done in an auditorium with excellent ACOUSTICS. *See also* STEREOPHONIC.

A-B Testing A-B testing is the comparison of one AUDIO device with another by switching between the two while listening to the same signal being processed by the devices.

A-B testing is thought by many to be a valid way of evaluating audio components, but it is fraught with pitfalls. One problem in comparing one device with another is that the test can say nothing about how accurate either device actually is. In comparing two loudspeakers, for instance, one should compare each with reality, i.e., with live music. This is not completely possible because the LOUDSPEAKER must be used in conjunction with other components (AMPLIFIERS, recorders, MICROPHONES) in order to reproduce music, and it is impossible to isolate the effects of each link in the chain. Over the years, various live-vs.-recorded comparisons have been staged, with interesting if not conclusive results. A great deal of effort is required to make such a comparison useful.

Another problem with A-B tests is that the volume levels of the two sounds being compared must be identical. Otherwise, the louder one will generally be judged to be better, or at least as having a wider FREQUENCY range.

ABX Test A type of listening test where a person attempts to differentiate between two or more audio devices such as COMPACT DISC players or AMPLIFIERS. The test involves use of the so-called ABX box, a device from ABX Corporation, first invented in 1977 by Arnold Krueger and Bern Muller (of the famous Southeastern Michigan Woofer and Tweeter Marching Society or SMWTMS), later refined and marketed by David Clark and his ABX Corp. [For complete details see David L. Clark, "High-Resolution Subjective Testing Using a Double-Blind Comparator," *J. Audio Eng. Soc.*, Vol. 30, No. 5, (May 1982): 330–38.][1] The device assigns the letters A and B to the two devices to be compared and the letter X to one of the devices. In a series of trials, the box randomly assigns X to be either A or B. The subject then listens to A, B, and X and tries to determine whether X is the same as A or B; the box keeps track of the answers. During each trial, the subject can listen to A, B, and X as many times as needed before answering. Over a long series of trials, the listener can be expected to achieve a 50% correct score simply by guessing. If a score is significantly better than 50%, then one can say that the listener is in fact able to tell the two components A and B apart for a certain percentage of trials.

The ABX test is quite popular and is generally a trusted way to compare audio products, but the statistical interpretation of the results of any given series of tests is not as simple and straightforward as might be imagined. It is not easy to distinguish between known correct responses (i.e., correct responses based on actually hearing a difference) and correct guesses, especially if the percentage of correct answers is not too far from 50%. Therefore, care must be exercised in the interpretation of the results. This is an example of double blind testing, since the person giving the test also does not know which device is X.

AC *See* ALTERNATING CURRENT.

AC-1 The first Dolby digital audio coding system was AC-1 and was introduced in 1984. A refined form of adaptive DELTA-SIGMA MODULATION, it was intended for applications such as direct broadcast satellite systems at a time when digital signal processing "horsepower" was very costly. AC-1 featured a comparatively complex encoder, relatively few of which would be needed by broadcasters, and simple, inexpensive decoders that could be readily incorporated into mass-produced consumer receivers.[2]

AC-2 A Dolby adaptive audio coder that combines professional audio quality with a low bit rate, substantially reducing the data capacity required in such applications as satellite and terrestrial links. The algorithm uses a multiband approach to take advantage of psychoacoustic masking, while a partially adaptive bit-allocation scheme keeps codec complexity relatively low. It is used by recording studios and postproduction facilities for such purposes as remote monitoring and dialogue rerecording (looping) sessions.[2]

1. Thanks to Dennis Bohn, Rane Corp.
2. From Dolby Laboratories literature.

AC-3 The audio coder capable of a large amount of data compression used in Dolby Digital™ audio was called Audio Coder 3, or AC-3. Dolby Laboratories defines AC-3 thus: "AC-3 is the technical name for the digital decoding technology upon which Dolby Digital is based. The terms AC-3 and Dolby Digital are generally used interchangeably, and the company now usually refers to AC-3 by its trademarked name, 'Dolby Digital'."

It is used in NTSC DVDs, some laserdiscs, and certain special CDs for 5.1 multichannel home theater use and has been adopted for ATSC HDTV broadcasting. AC-3 competes with DTS Consumer.

The AC-3 codec has been designed to take maximum advantage of human auditory masking in that it divides the audio spectrum of each channel into narrow frequency bands of different sizes optimized with respect to the frequency selectivity of human hearing. This makes it possible to sharply filter coding noise so that it is forced to stay very close in frequency to the frequency components of the audio signal being coded. By reducing or eliminating coding noise wherever there are no audio signals to mask it, the sound quality of the original signal can be subjectively preserved. In this key respect, a coding system like AC-3 is essentially a form of very selective and powerful noise reduction. Additional features include the transmission of METADATA, that can control playback parameters such as dialogue-keyed playback level, and the ability of two-channel decoders to down-mix multichannel soundtracks.

AC Bias *See* BIAS.

Accidental In a musical scale, the accidentals are the extra sharp and flat notes that are not part of the diatonic series. In the key of C on a piano, the accidentals are the black keys.

It is surprising that these notes are called "accidentals," so important are they to music. In no way can one say that they exist simply by accident. *See also* Appendix 8.

Acetate In the making of phonograph records, the first step is called "mastering," and this consists of recording the audio signal onto a metal disc coated with a thick lacquer made of cellulose nitrate with some castor oil added as a plasticizer. This disc, either before or after recording, is often called an "acetate," which is a misnomer since it is not made of acetate. Subsequent discs, or PRESSINGS, are replicated from the master record. It consists of a 14-inch diameter aluminum disc, which is coated with a special formulation of cellulose nitrate. The MASTER TAPE is played while connected to a RECORDING LATHE, which has a CUTTERHEAD that cuts the groove in the nitrate material. The disc is then electroplated with several layers of silver and pure nickel.

Finally, the nickel plating is carefully stripped away from the disc, a procedure requiring considerable skill and experience, and becomes a "negative" replica of the original disc. It can be used as a STAMPER to press records, or it can be subjected to further plating in THREE-STEP PROCESSING, if many hundreds or thousands of records are to be pressed. The acetate is also commonly referred to as the "lacquer master."

Cellulose acetate is one of the older magnetic tape base materials, and has been largely replaced by polyester material with the trade name MYLAR in professional applications. Cellulose acetate is a little unstable under changing humidity, becoming brittle when very dry.

Acousta-Voice™ A trademark owned by the Altec Lansing company for the first commercial one-third octave EQUALIZER designed for sound system equalization. It was a graphic equalizer and was introduced in about 1967. Since then, many other similar units have appeared on the market.

Acoustic Feedback Acoustic feedback refers to the introduction of acoustic energy from a sound system back into the same system.

One form of acoustic feedback is the disturbance of a record player system by the sound produced by the system. For example, if a turntable playing a record is placed directly on top of a loudspeaker cabinet, vibration from the cabinet caused by the sound being reproduced will be picked up by the cartridge and amplified along with the music. If the GAIN is sufficiently high, the level of the feedback sound will increase, finally causing the AMPLIFIER, LOUDSPEAKER, or both to be overloaded. The result is a loud rumble, or low-frequency tone.

Even before the feedback signal becomes regenerative, that is, before it begins to increase in AMPLITUDE, the reproduced sound will be colored by the feedback, causing "muddiness" in the low-frequency range. For this reason, turntables must be very well isolated from vibration and should be a relatively long way from the loudspeakers.

Another form of acoustic feedback is familiar to most people as the "howl" of a sound reinforcement system when the volume control is set too high. The amplified sound enters the MICROPHONE where it is amplified again, making repeated trips around the loop and becoming louder and louder. Acoustic feedback is the limiting factor in the gain of a sound system, and much effort has been expended in developing techniques to reduce it. Sound system EQUALIZATION is one such technique.

Even if the gain is not high enough to cause a continuous howl, the FREQUENCY RESPONSE of the sound system will be distorted when the gain nears the feedback point, and the apparent REVERBERATION will be increased also.

Acoustic Labyrinth A type of loudspeaker BAFFLE popular in the 1950s in which the rear of the WOOFER cone is coupled to a folded duct about 6 to 8 feet long. The inside of the duct is lined with sound-absorbing material to reduce the tendency for the duct to resonate, and to absorb the energy radiated from the back of the cone. The labyrinth acts as a load on the loudspeaker, providing some control over the cone motion at the low-frequency resonance. Reasonably good low-frequency performance can be obtained from a well-designed system of this type, but it will be rather more bulky than an INFINITE BAFFLE of comparable performance.

Acoustic Lens An acoustic lens is a device sometimes placed in front of a high-frequency HORN loudspeaker to spread out the sound wave in order to make it less directional. In this way, the angular coverage of the LOUD-

SPEAKER is increased. Acoustic lenses sometimes cause problems, such as reflecting some energy at particular frequencies back into the loudspeaker and causing a somewhat rough FREQUENCY RESPONSE.

Acoustic Radiation Pressure The steady state pressure exerted upon a surface exposed to a sound wave. This pressure is very small, but LORD RAYLEIGH, a prominent investigator in the nineteenth century, used the phenomenon to construct an instrument to measure sound level. It consisted of a small, extremely lightweight disc suspended on a fine filament, and the sound radiation pressure would cause the disc to twist the filament in proportion to the magnitude of the pressure.

Acoustic Recording An early recording where no electrical energy is used to cut the record grooves is known as an acoustic recording.

Edison's phonograph was a purely acoustic device, i.e., all the energy needed to emboss the tin foil on the CYLINDER was supplied by the sound waves entering the RECORDING HORN. All recordings made before 1925 were acoustically powered. Many acoustic recordings sound surprisingly good, and the first electrical recordings were thought by many to be inferior. This is probably true, considering that the acoustic method had been highly perfected by this time and the first electrical apparatus was by comparison somewhat crude.

Acoustics Acoustics is the study of sound and its interaction with the human hearing mechanism.

Physical acoustics is the scientific discipline dealing with measurable objective parameters of sound and its behavior in any medium. Audio people are interested in the acoustics of air, but underwater acoustics is a very large field under abundant study. One of the most famous of the physical acousticians was LORD RAYLEIGH, the nineteenth-century British scientist who wrote a monumental book on sound (*The Theory of Sound*).

PSYCHOACOUSTICS is the second major branch of acoustics; it is concerned with the interaction of sound with the human hearing system. Because mental impressions are difficult or impossible to measure objectively, psychoacoustics deals with subjective responses to objectively measured phenomena. Psychoacoustics had its beginnings in the work of Hermann von Helmholtz, a well-known nineteenth-century German physician and scientist, who wrote a book titled *On the Sensations of Tone,* which covers the beginnings of psychoacoustics and also goes deeply into musical acoustics. Psychoacoustics is a rich field for study. A great deal of the twentieth-century work in psychoacoustics was done by the Bell Telephone Laboratories. Musical acoustics is a subset of both physical acoustics and psychoacoustics and deals with how musical instruments work, how and why music is perceived, performance techniques of musical instruments, and the acoustics of rooms. The oldest surviving work on acoustics is contained in the *Ten Books on Architecture,* by Vitruvius, a Roman architect who lived about 79 B.C. Vitruvius discusses in some detail the acoustics of Greek and Roman theaters. He makes the curious suggestion that certain large urns, or "sounding vessels," will, if placed in strategic locations about the audience area of a classical theater, improve the acoustics.

Acoustics has been called the most basic of the sciences, everything else being a branch of it. This may be an exaggeration, but it is true that energy is transferred from the interior of the sun to its outer surface by acoustic waves. Without them, we would not exist. Also, it has been postulated that the most basic of the particles of which matter is made may be in the form of tiny "super strings" that vibrate at their natural or resonant frequencies. The strings vibrating at different frequencies correspond to the different energy levels that the various subatomic particles are observed to possess. This theory is a simplification of the quantum theory of physics. More basic than this, it is difficult to get.

Acoustic Suspension A design for a low-frequency LOUDSPEAKER BAFFLE where most of the restoring force on the CONE is the result of the elasticity of the air in the sealed cabinet. *See also* WOOFER.

Active An AUDIO device that requires a power source, such as from the AC line or a battery, is called active, as opposed to a PASSIVE device. Sometimes amplifying components such as TRANSISTORS or INTEGRATED CIRCUITS are called active CIRCUIT elements.

Active Crossover An active crossover is a CROSSOVER NETWORK that is designed to be placed before the power amplifiers in a BIAMPLIFIED or TRIAMPLIFIED loudspeaker system. Active crossovers are often designed so the CROSSOVER FREQUENCIES can be varied, and they have advantages such as better control of parameters and eliminating passive crossovers that rob some of the power from the amplifier.

Active Noise Canceling A method of reducing acoustic noise by adding a polarity-inverted noise signal to cancel it. Some headphones are available that work well in noisy environments such as airplanes. A small microphone on the headphone receives the noise, inverts it, and adds it to the headphone signal that partially cancels or reduces the level of the noise heard in the headphones. It is also possible to perform noise cancellation at very low frequencies in small, enclosed spaces using loudspeakers to add the inverted noise, obviating the need for headphones. An example is helicopter cockpits.

Adaptive Decorrelation™ A DIGITAL SIGNAL PROCESSING (DSP) circuit found in Dolby Digital 5.1 decoders for use in home theater sound systems that takes the surround signal, which may be monaural, and derives two signals to feed the surround speakers. The decorrelation process adds diffusion to the sound field to prevent its being localized at the speaker locations, which would occur if the monaural signal were fed directly to the surround speakers. If the surround channels are in stereo, the decorrelation circuit is automatically disabled. Adaptive Decorrelation is a registered trademark of THX LTD.

ADAT, Alesis Digital Audio Tape Recorder A digital audio recording system developed by Alesis that allows 8 independent CD-quality tracks to be recorded on S-VHS video cassettes.

In the ADAT system, the tape is "formatted" (an operation that can be done before or during recording) with a proprietary Alesis time code that is much more accurate than SMPTE, and it time-stamps the tape to the single-sample accuracy; that is, 1/48,000th of a second. Because of this tight synch, multiple ADATs are virtually free of incoherent phase between tracks playing on different machines. This means that if you lock 2 or more ADATs together, you create the equivalent of one large digital tape recorder and one very wide, seamless piece of tape.

The ADAT was somewhat of a landmark product; it accelerated the home and project studio market with affordable digital multitrack recording capability. It and others like it are sometimes described as Modular Digital Multitracks (MDM).

ADC, or A/D Converter Abbreviation for ANALOG-TO-DIGITAL CONVERTER.

Additive Synthesis The generation of complex musical WAVEFORMS in electronic music SYNTHESIZERS by the linear addition of SINE WAVE components whose frequency relationship is a HARMONIC SERIES.

The first musical instrument to use additive synthesis was the ill-fated TELHARMONIUM of Thaddeus Cahill. The idea was very successfully exploited by Laurens Hammond with the introduction of the first Hammond Organ in the early 1930s. A limitation of the Hammond scheme was that the sine wave components added together were taken from an equally tempered musical scale and, other than the octave components, are not precisely in tune with a harmonic series. This gives the Hammond Organ a particular TIMBRE that is easily recognized and, in some cases, highly prized.

The advent of the digital computer has greatly expanded the possibilities of using additive synthesis with precisely controlled frequencies of the components. However, FM SYNTHESIS is more economical of hardware, and although somewhat more limited in the range of waveforms generated, it is much more commonly used than additive synthesis in electronic music synthesizers.

Ader, Clement A Parisian engineer who, in 1881, filed a patent in the German Imperial Patent Office covering "Improvements of Telephone Equipment for Theaters." This is no doubt the world's first patent having to do with two-channel transmission of sound. In fact, it essentially covers a BINAURAL sound system for listening from the comfort of one's home to a musical performance taking place in a remote auditorium. Ader states in his patent: "The transmitters are distributed in two groups on the stage, a left and a right one. The subscriber has likewise two receivers, one of them connected to the right group of microphones and the other to the left. Thus, the listener is able to follow the variations in intensity and intonation corresponding to the movements of the actors on the stage. This double listening to sound, received and transmitted by two different sets of apparatus, produces the same effects on the ear that the stereoscope produces on the eye."

The apparatus was demonstrated in the Paris opera house as a part of the 1881 Paris Exposition. This was a remarkable achievement, for it occurred only five years after the invention of the telephone and almost twenty years before the invention of the AUDION amplifier.

ADR Short for Automatic Dialog Replacement, or Additional Dialog Replacement. This is the technique of adding or replacing dialogue in a motion picture by recording the appropriate voice in the studio after the film is shot and adding the resulting dialog recording to the sound track of the film. It is often used when the original dialogue recording cannot be used due to noisy conditions on the set, etc. There are many techniques used, including devices that operate automatically and can space the recorded words afterward to fit the LIP SYNCH.

ADR, Astra Digital Radio A European satellite system that is the largest provider of satellite broadcasting of television and radio. It is said to offer near CD-quality music.

ADSR Short for Attack Decay Sustain Release. It is the time constants associated with signals generated by electronic music SYNTHESIZERS. The attack time is the time it takes the signal level to rise from zero to its maximum value. The decay time is the time required for the level to fall to the sustain value, and the sustain time is the time it remains at this value. The release time is the time it takes for the level to fall to zero after the sustain time is elapsed. These times are all adjustable to allow a wide variety of dynamic possibilities in synthesized signals. The ADSR actually defines the envelope of the generated signal.

In a typical keyboard-controlled synthesizer, the ADSR sequence is initiated each time a key is pressed, and that particular envelope will be

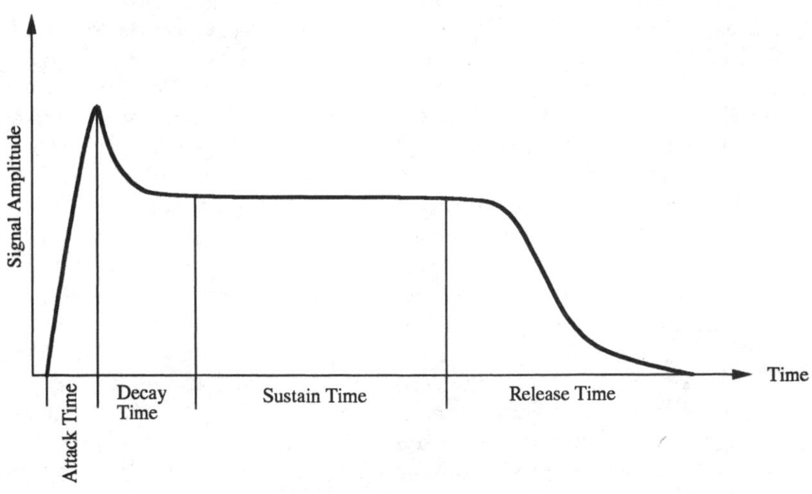

ADSR

impressed on the generated note. The sustain part of the envelope can be set to be as long as the key is held down, providing an organ-like TIMBRE to the signal. The shape of the envelope has a great deal to do with the timbre of the signal, even if the WAVEFORM of the signal is the same. The ADSR is also called an envelope generator.

Advance Ball A small highly polished ball, usually made of sapphire, which is mounted on a CUTTERHEAD assembly of a cutting lathe used in the cutting, or "MASTERING," of vinyl records. The advance ball rests on the uncut surface of the rotating ACETATE disc during the cutting process. Its purpose is to control the depth of cut of the stylus. It must be kept scrupulously clean to avoid damaging the disc surface, and it is usually polished with a small leather pad before each cut is begun.

Not all cutterheads use an advance ball and instead control the depth of cut with an electronic servomechanism.

Advance Head *See* PREVIEW HEAD.

AES The Audio Engineering Society is a worldwide professional society of audio people somewhat analogous to the Society of Motion Picture and Television Engineers in the U.S. It was formed in 1947 in the U.S. and its headquarters are in New York City. The AES is active in the setting of standards, research, and education. The RIAA DE-EMPHASIS curve was originally formulated by the AES, and was known as the AES curve before record manufacturers agreed to standardize. The standard de-emphasis curve for 30 IPS ANALOG tape recorders is from the AES.

AES3 Interface A digital audio transmission standard created by the AES and standardized by the American National Standards Institute (ANSI S4.40-1985) and the IEC (IEC 60958-4). AES3 transmits two channels of digital audio data on a single twisted-pair 110-ohm balanced cable using XLR-3 (IEC 268-12) connectors. An unbalanced configuration also exists. Previously known as the AES/EBU digital interface, a term which is still commonly used. The consumer version is called S/PDIF.

AES/EBU, Audio Engineering Society / European Broadcast Union. *See* AES3 INTERFACE.

AF, or A.F. Audio FREQUENCY (AF) means having frequencies within the audible range, usually taken as 20 HERTZ to 20 KILOHERTZ. This frequency range is only an average for a large number of people. Many people hear tones below 20 Hz, and some people hear above 20 kHz, although most people are virtually deaf above 15 or 16 kHz. The audibility of a given frequency depends on its level. *See also* FLETCHER-MUNSON EFFECT.

AFL, After Fader Listen A pushbutton sometimes found on older audio mixing consoles. When the AFL button is pressed, the monitor output is affected by the volume control, or FADER.

AGC An Automatic Gain Control (AGC) CIRCUIT adjusts the GAIN of an audio device in inverse proportion to the signal level entering the device. An example is a portable tape recorder that is designed for speech recording. When the talker is close to the MICROPHONE, the gain is reduced so as not to overload the tape. As the level from the talker decreases, for instance because of a greater distance, the gain increases to keep the recorded level the same.

This type of machine is often used for radio interviews, and usually the gain changes can be plainly heard as the background noise rises each time the speaker pauses for a few seconds, only to suddenly fall the moment the next syllable is uttered.

Another use of AGC is in radio receivers, where the gain is adjusted to keep all stations at about the same level even though the signal strength from the transmitter varies widely depending on distance.

AGC is also called AVC, for automatic volume control, or ALC, for automatic level control.

AIM *See* AMPLITUDE INTERMODULATION DISTORTION.

Air Coupler A type of WOOFER system that consisted of a woofer mounted on a wall near the floor or ceiling facing into the wall and centered between two wall studs. About 8 feet below or above the speaker, a rectangular hole was cut into the wall to let the sound out. The system was like a speaker in an 8-foot-long organ pipe, which is resonant at about 30 Hz, giving a pronounced peak in the response at this frequency. The air coupler was popular among some do-it-yourself audiophiles in the late 1950s, but its appeal has mercifully waned.

Air-Motion Transformer A proprietary type of loudspeaker developed by Oscar Heil. The air-motion transformer resembles a miniature accordion-fold door in a strong magnetic field. The folds contain conductors that carry the amplified audio current, and the interaction with the magnetic field causes the folds to alternately squeeze together and move apart, generating a radiated sound wave. The system is said to be quite linear and low in distortion.

Aliasing Aliasing refers to the production of spurious FREQUENCY components in a DIGITAL audio system due to the presence of frequencies in the SIGNAL that are higher than one-half the SAMPLING frequency.

Visual aliasing can sometimes be seen in motion pictures, especially westerns. If a wagon is moving at a speed where the spokes in a wheel are passing by faster than the frame rate of the camera (24 frames per second), the spokes will be seen to move backward, or forward at an incorrect speed. This is also the principle of the stroboscope, which is a quickly flashing light used to examine rotating machinery. When the lamp flashes at the correct rate, corresponding to the RPM of the machine, the moving parts will appear stationary.

Alignment Adjustments of various characteristics of AUDIO devices are loosely grouped together and called alignment procedures. Alignment is somewhat analogous to "tuning" a car engine. Some of the steps in the alignment of an analog tape recorder are properly adjusting the head AZIMUTH angle and adjusting the playback DE-EMPHASIS and record PRE-EMPHASIS and BIAS level circuits for optimum response.

Alignment Tapes The adjustment of an analog tape recorder's many calibration controls is a painstaking and delicate job if the best results from the machine are to be realized. To assist the technician in this procedure, specially recorded and standardized tapes are used. Not only does this allow optimum results from the machine, but it also ensures that tapes can be freely traded between properly aligned machines with similar results on each. Some of the parameters that have been standardized are operating level and playback EQUALIZATION, although there are many standards in existence.

The alignment tape is made under carefully controlled laboratory conditions to ensure accuracy. One of the tones on the tape is a high-frequency AZIMUTH alignment tone, usually at 16 KILOHERTZ. While this tone is replayed, the head azimuth is adjusted so that a maximum SIGNAL level at the high FREQUENCY is attained, and the signals from any two tracks are as nearly as possible in PHASE. For STEREO recording, the phase response of the two channels should be the same.

There will then be a series of tones at various frequencies, all at standardized levels. The playback equalization is adjusted until all the tones are at the same level as the tape is played. The tape machine is now said to have FLAT FREQUENCY RESPONSE in the playback mode.

Next, there will be a tone of 700 or 1,000 HERTZ (usually 400 Hz in the case of cassettes) recorded at the standardized REFERENCE LEVEL. The playback gain control is then adjusted to give the standardized output level, usually 0 DECIBELS on the tape recorder meter.

When the first American tape recorder standards were being formulated by manufacturers in the late 1940s, the state of the art of tape manufacture was not very advanced. The reference level was defined as that record level that produced 1% third-HARMONIC DISTORTION or sometimes, total harmonic distortion (THD). The maximum level used for signal to noise measurements was typically defined as the level that produces 3% distortion. This meant that the reference level was not the same for all tapes because of variations in the tape manufacture. For practical reasons this level was carried on as a FLUXIVITY, regardless of the DISTORTION produced. This standard flux level was measured as 185 NANOWEBERS per meter (nW/m) at 700 Hz, which became known as Ampex Operating Level. Note that fluxivity changes at different frequencies.

By the 1970s and 80s, tapes were available with much greater capacity for high recorded levels at low distortion, and the 185 nW/m reference level is seldom used. The European DIN standard uses 320 nW/m, which is 4.7 dB higher than 185 nW/m. The method of flux measurement prescribed by DIN has traditionally been thought to result in about 1 dB less output than the American (ANSI) standard. Thus, a tape played on a DIN-aligned machine will be about 1 dB higher in level than when played on an ANSI-aligned machine. This discrepancy has been refuted recently, and for practical reasons it is difficult to attempt to adjust most fluxivities with excessive precision. *See also* OPERATING LEVEL.

Alkaline Cell A type of cell used for powering small tape recorders, radios, etc., similar in appearance to the LECLANCHE CELL but using a zinc

ANODE and a steel CATHODE with an alkaline ELECTROLYTE. The alkaline cell can be recharged if done slowly and has almost twice the capacity of a similar-sized LeClanche cell. It also has better REGULATION than the LeClanche cell, delivering most of its current capacity at over 1 volt.

Alligator Clip An alligator clip is a TERMINAL for the end of a wire that is designed like a small spring-loaded clamp with serrations along the edges. It resembles the jaws of an alligator, hence the name. Alligator clips are used to connect test equipment such as OSCILLOSCOPES and voltmeters, etc., to various places in a CIRCUIT.

All-Pass Filter An all-pass filter, or all-pass network, as it is often called, is an electrical CIRCUIT with a uniform AMPLITUDE response versus FREQUENCY (also called FREQUENCY RESPONSE), but it has a PHASE SHIFT that does not vary in a LINEAR relationship with frequency. (A pure time delay device will have a phase shift that is directly proportional to frequency, i.e., its phase shift increases at a constant rate with frequency.)

Complex FILTERS often have significant phase DISTORTION because they are not phase linear, and an all-pass network can be designed to correct the phase anomalies without affecting the amplitude response. Sometimes all-pass networks are used in PSYCHOACOUSTIC research to investigate the audibility of phase distortions of various types. *See also* GROUP DELAY and GROUP VELOCITY.

Alternating Current An alternating current, or AC, is an electric CURRENT that periodically reverses its direction, as opposed to a DIRECT CURRENT, or DC, which maintains a single direction. The rate of alternation is called the FREQUENCY and is measured in cycles per second, or HERTZ (Hz).

We are all familiar with normal house current, which alternates at 60 Hz in the U.S., Canada, and Mexico. AUDIO signals are, of course, always alternating, the frequency corresponding to the frequencies of the sounds the signals represent.

AM *See* AMPLITUDE MODULATION.

Ambience Ambience refers to the acoustical qualities of a listening space. REVERBERATION, ECHOES, background noise, etc., are components of ambience. On most music recordings, some of the acoustical characteristics are recorded along with the music and are to a certain extent reproduced in the listening environment. For instance, an organ in a cathedral will be recorded with a good deal of reverberation included, and this helps to provide the proper acoustic "atmosphere" when heard in playback.

The true acoustical qualities of the source cannot, however, be very effectively recorded and reproduced, mostly because the REVERBERATION in the source room is diffuse, coming from all directions. This helps to give the concertgoer a sense of ENVELOPMENT. This directional realism is not preserved in a STEREO recording, regardless of any advertising to the contrary. One of the promises of QUADRAPHONIC SOUND was the preservation and reproduction of the ambience of the hall where the original recording was made, but it fell far short, a fact that contributed to its rapid demise.

Ambisonics Ambisonics is a system for the reproduction of a three-dimensional sound field, something that QUADRAPHONIC SOUND systems promised and failed to provide. It uses two or more transmission channels and four or more LOUDSPEAKERS. Ambisonics is the result of research efforts of the British Technology Group, formerly the National Research Development Corporation, in England. The late Michael Gerzon (1945–1996), of Oxford University, was responsible for most of the theoretical work that led to its development.

According to Gerzon, all the information to re-create a sound field in three dimensions can be transmitted by four independent AUDIO channels, and only three channels are needed to reproduce SURROUND SOUND in two dimensions. These channels are not simply SIGNALS from microphones, but are derived by suitable mixing, or "matrixing," and PHASE SHIFTING of several microphone signals. Imagine three FIGURE EIGHT microphones and one OMNIDIRECTIONAL microphone all occupying the same point in space. The figure eights are orthogonal, i.e., they are angled 90 degrees from each other. One is oriented "front-back," one is "left-right," and the third is "up-down." The up-down signal is only needed if vertical localization is desired in the reproduced sound field. These four signals are called "B-format" signals, and there is one compound microphone made by Calrec which synthesizes them directly from four closely spaced TRANSDUCER elements.

These signals are fed into an Ambisonics decoder which suitably matrixes and phase shifts them to obtain signals that are fed to AMPLIFIERS and then to loudspeakers. The loudspeaker array may be of several different configurations, with four or six loudspeakers. The Ambisonics decoder can be adjusted to supply these different signals, depending on the requirements and bank account of the listener.

In order to record or broadcast these B-format signals, they can be encoded into two channels in several ways similar to techniques formerly used for quadraphonic recordings. The one chosen by the Ambisonics design team is the Universal HJ system designed by the BBC. The UHJ composite signal is of either two or three channels. The two-channel version is suited to recording on stereo records or cassettes, and the three-channel version could be easily accommodated by COMPACT DISC with suitable modifications.

Once transmitted and received (or recorded and reproduced), these signals are able to feed loudspeakers for conventional MONAURAL or STEREO reproduction. To recover the surround-sound information, a UHJ decoder is used to recover the B-format signals, which are fed to the Ambisonics decoder. In other words, the UHJ encoding system converts the B-format signals into a form compatible with mono and stereo playback.

All this sounds very impressive on paper, but it is quite another thing to bring it to commercial fruition. Unconventional mixing and recording techniques are required for initial production, and a good deal of added equipment is needed.

Ambisonics research can be said to have started with Alan BLUMLEIN, chief engineer for the BBC, in the 1930s. Interestingly enough, nearly all the subsequent research and development has also occurred in Britain.

Ampere, abbr. Amp or A The ampere is the SI unit of electric CURRENT; it is defined as that current that, if existing in two parallel wires 1 meter apart, will cause an attractive force between them amounting to 0.2 millionths of a newton per meter of length. The ampere is also equal to a current of 1 COULOMB of charge per second, or 6.2414 million million million electrons flowing past a point in 1 second. Incidentally, one should not speak of the "flow of current." The current exists; the charge flows. This is analogous to the current in a river, which consists of the flow of water.

The mathematical symbol for current is I. The relationship between current, VOLTAGE, and IMPEDANCE is quite complex for ALTERNATING CURRENT, but for DIRECT CURRENT it is a simple proportion. The current I is equal to the voltage V divided by the RESISTANCE R. *See* OHM'S LAW.

Amplifier A device for increasing the amplitude of the VOLTAGE, CURRENT, IMPEDANCE, or POWER of a SIGNAL. An amplifier is an ACTIVE device and strictly speaking should always increase the power of a signal (some amplifiers, such as certain distribution amplifiers, may only reduce the impedance level of the signal for the purpose of driving long lines).

The amount of amplification that an amplifier provides is called its GAIN. The gain is a ratio of its input signal level to its output signal level and is simply a multiplier or a pure number. For instance, an amplifier that doubles the voltage of its input signal is said to have a voltage gain of 2. If its output current is 10 times its input current, its current gain is 10, etc. An amplifier may have almost any combination of voltage gain, current gain, or power gain, and some of these quantities may be negative—some power amplifiers can have a negative voltage gain but a large current gain and thus a large power gain.

Amplifier gain is also commonly expressed in DECIBELS, or dB, and this causes some potential (and actual) confusion because dB always expresses a power ratio by definition, and one should not express the voltage gain of an amplifier in dB unless the input and output impedances are equal. The confusion arises because the voltage gain of a typical amplifier is not related to its power output capability. For instance, if an amplifier has a voltage gain of 10, one is tempted to say the amplifier has a gain of 20 dB because it actually would raise the power level of a signal by 20 dB if the input and output impedances were the same. In practice, however, this is very seldom the case, and the true power gain is usually very much different from what would be predicted by the voltage gain. For instance, a power amplifier could have a 1.6-megohm (MΩ) input impedance and could deliver 400 watts (W) to a 4-ohm load. Its output and input voltages could be the same, leading one to say it had a voltage gain of 1, or 0 dB. But its voltage output is 40 volts (V) when delivering 400 W into 4-ohm, and its input voltage is also 40 V. The 40 V of input delivers only 1 milliwatt (mW) to the input (40^2 divided by 1,600,000), so the power gain is actually 400 divided by .001, or 400,000. This is a true gain of 56 dB.

For another example, consider a microphone PREAMPLIFIER with a voltage gain of 1,000, an input impedance of 100 ohms, and a 1-mV signal. The input power is $.001^2$ divided by 100, or one ten-millionth of a watt. Its output will be 1 V, and when connected to a 10,000-ohm load, will deliver .1 mW. Its true power gain is .0001 divided by .00000001, or 10,000, which is 40 dB, and its voltage gain of 1,000 would imply 60 dB of gain.

To reduce the confusion in practice, one says the voltage gain of the first amplifier is 0 dB and the voltage gain of the second one is 60 dB, but we believe it would be preferable to express voltage gains simply as pure numbers and let the original definition of the much-beleaguered decibel stand.

Amplitude Amplitude is the strength of a SIGNAL or a sound, without regard to its FREQUENCY content. Amplitude measurements of audio signals generally refer to signal VOLTAGE rather than POWER, which is proportional to voltage squared. The amplitude of a sound is usually measured in decibels of SOUND PRESSURE LEVEL. It is possible to define and measure the SOUND POWER, but this is seldom done in audio work.

It is important not to confuse SOUND PRESSURE LEVEL with SOUND INTENSITY, which has a very specific definition.

Amplitude Intermodulation Distortion This is the conventional INTERMODULATION DISTORTION as distinguished from PHASE INTERMODULATION DISTORTION.

Amplitude Modulation, abbr. AM In AM radio transmission, the AUDIO signal is combined with a very high frequency SINE WAVE called a CARRIER, in such a way that the strength or amplitude of the carrier is varied in exact response to the amplitude and FREQUENCY of the signal. This is called amplitude modulation of the carrier. The modulated carrier is then transmitted at high power by the transmitter and the broadcast antenna, where it is later received by radio sets that are tuned to the carrier frequency. The modulated carrier is then demodulated by a process called DETECTION, and this recovers the original signal. The process of modulation and demodulation of the carrier permits the transmission of the signal information over long distances with relatively high efficiency, and allows many

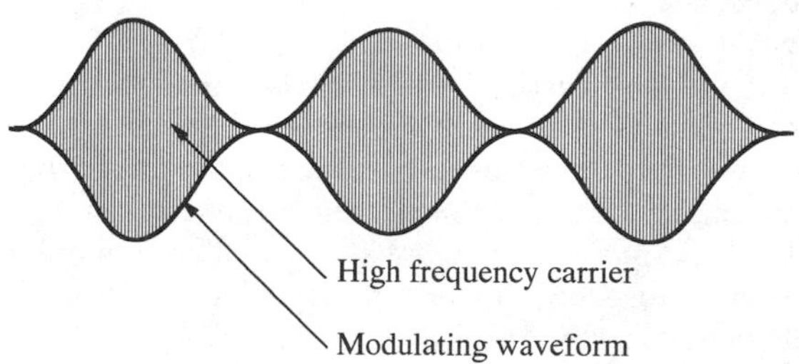

Amplitude Modulation

radio stations to broadcast different programs simultaneously because the carrier frequencies are different. The different carriers are easily separated by the tuning CIRCUITS in the receiver set.

Strictly speaking, the carrier wave is not actually varying in strength, but new frequencies, above and below the carrier frequency, are generated in the modulation process. In typical AM broadcasting, these sidebands extend in frequency 10 KILOHERTZ on either side of the carrier frequency, while the carrier frequency will be between about 500 kHz and 1.5 MHz.

AM transmission is capable of high quality if the received signal strength is adequate, but interference from lightning and other electrical disturbances can cause noise in long-distance reception. *See also* AM STEREO

AM Stereo AM Stereo was actually the first stereophonic broadcast technology to be ready for widespread use. Engineers such as Leonard Kahn developed and tested AM Stereo systems in the late 1950s that worked well and might have made a very satisfactory solution for AM Stereo broadcasting at the time. The Federal Communications Commission (FCC) approved use of FM Stereo, but did not allow AM Stereo to be broadcast, presumably because the proposed systems required greater bandwidth than the existing 10 kilohertz allowed for each AM station.

Meanwhile, AM Stereo had not been forgotten. Engineers continued to work on it and perfect its performance and sound quality. Various companies, including Motorola, developed their own systems for transmitting AM Stereo.

As the 1980s approached, the FCC decided to take another look at AM Stereo. There were five different AM Stereo systems being proposed by different suppliers, and the FCC struggled with the decision of which one to choose as the standard.

At first, the FCC decided to select one of the systems, designed by Magnavox, as the standard. As you can imagine, the proponents of the four other systems complained, saying that their systems worked better than Magnavox's and that the FCC should do some more research before trying to decide a single standard again.

In 1993, the FCC chose the Motorola "C-Quam" system as the standard, which was already the standard for all other countries in the world that were broadcasting AM Stereo. C-Quam stands for Compatible Quadrature Amplitude Modulation. The AM CARRIER being broadcast is accompanied by another AM carrier of the same frequency, but it is 90 degrees out of phase with the regular carrier. This is called a quadrature carrier, and its main advantage is that it does not increase the bandwidth the station uses to transmit its signal. The stereo information in the music signal is used to modulate the quadrature carrier, while the normal carrier is modulated by the sum of the two stereo channels. The system is compatible with monaural receivers because the receiver does not sense the stereo carrier because of the 90-degree phase difference.

Today (2003) there are several hundred AM Stereo stations in operation in the United States, and thousands more in the rest of the world.

AM Suppression The ability of an FM tuner or receiver to reject AMPLITUDE MODULATION of the received signal. Ideally, the receiver would only be sensitive to FREQUENCY MODULATION, but some FM DETECTORS are also sensitive to AM. Much of the interference and noise in broadcasting appears as amplitude modulation, so a tuner with good AM suppression will have less distortion and noise than a tuner with poorer suppression.

Analog An AUDIO signal is an electrical replica, or analog, of the WAVEFORM of the sound it represents. The VOLTAGE of the signal varies up and down (negatively and positively, in electrical terminology) the same way as the SOUND PRESSURE varies up and down at the MICROPHONE.

As long as the signal is in this form, i.e., a voltage that varies directly with the sound pressure, it is an analog, and audio devices that use such signals are analog devices. The majority of audio devices are analog in nature, though DIGITAL devices are rapidly catching up in popularity.

An analog audio device need not be electrical; the Edison mechanical phonograph was an analog device, the groove depth being an analog of the sound pressure at the recording diaphragm.

Analog-to-Digital Converter, ADC or A/D In DIGITAL audio systems, the audio SIGNAL (ANALOG) must first be converted to digital form before it can be further processed. This entails SAMPLING the signal at very short successive time intervals, and converting the height of each sample to a digital word, which is simply a BINARY number indicating the AMPLITUDE of the WAVEFORM at that instant.

The output of the A/D converter is a series of digital "words," or samples, expressed in binary form, at a rate of 44,100 samples per second for linear PCM such as on compact discs. Each word in CD digital audio is 16 bits, or binary digits. Other digital audio formats may have different word sizes and sample rates. Before the signal can be fed to a common analog amplifier so it can be heard, it must undergo digital-to-analog conversion. This recovers a replica of the original audio signal from the digital words.

ADCs are subject to certain errors, as follows:

1. Absolute accuracy: The difference between the ADC's actual input voltage and the equivalent VOLTAGE value of the resultant output digital code.

2. Conversion rate: The maximum rate at which the ADC can perform valid conversions.

3. Conversion time: The time interval between the application of the convert command and the output of a valid digital code.

4. Differential linearity: Any deviation in the ADC's measured step width, which is ideally exactly one least significant bit (LSB).

5. Linearity: A measure of any departure from a LINEAR transfer function, expressed in percent of full-scale range, or as a fraction of one LSB.

6. Offset error: The mean value of the input voltage to set the output code to zero.

7. Resolution: The amount of input voltage change required to change the output by one LSB.

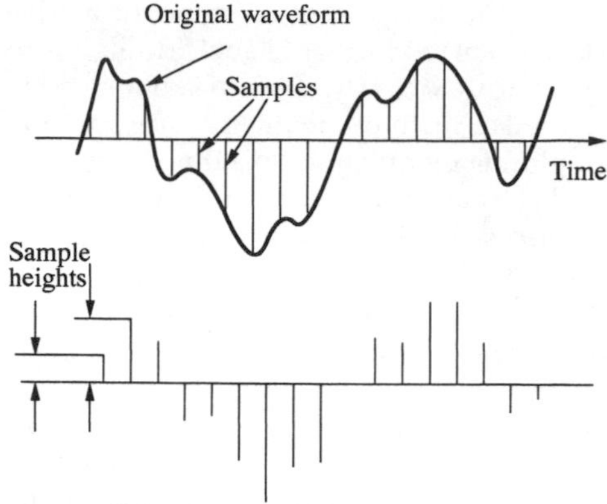

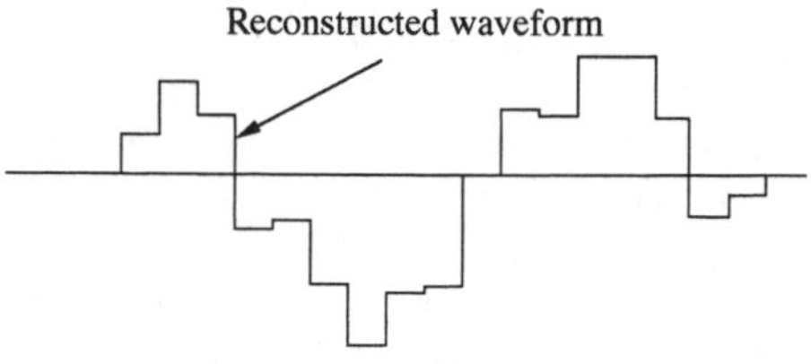

Analog-to-Digital Conversion

8. Scale error: The departure of the actual input voltage required to attain a full-scale output code from its design value.

Analytic Signal An analytic signal is by definition a signal that has two parts—the so-called real part, that is the same as a conventional signal, and an imaginary or "quadrature" part that is always 90 degrees out of phase with the real part. The analytic signal is very useful in several types of signal analysis. For instance, a conventional signal is represented by its waveform, which is simply a graph of the signal amplitude vs. time. The waveform (and the signal itself) has positive and negative parts, and for this reason it cannot be graphed on a logarithmic or decibel scale since logarithms of negative numbers are not defined. The waveform can be viewed on an oscilloscope to see its overall shape, but it is difficult to see very small components of the signal. However, the analytic signal can be transformed by squaring the real and imaginary amplitudes, adding the squared values together, and then taking the square root of the result. This is the RMS value of the signal vs. time, and is always positive. It is called the magnitude of the signal, and can be expressed in a decibel scale, where extremely small components and variations in the signal can be easily seen. The analytic signal is also used in plotting the so-called HEYSER SPIRAL.

Anechoic Literally, without echo. An anechoic room, or chamber, as it is usually called, is designed to have as short a REVERBERATION time as possible. This means the sound in the room will disappear as soon as the source of sound is stopped. It is impossible to build a completely anechoic chamber because there is no perfect sound absorber, but at high frequencies, nearly anechoic conditions can be obtained. Low frequencies present a much greater problem because the absorption of a surface is WAVELENGTH dependent. The absorber must be at least as thick as one-half wavelength to be effective. The wavelength at 100 HERTZ is about ten feet, so the problem is obvious: it takes a very large chamber to accommodate low-FREQUENCY absorbers.

Anechoic chambers are useful for the testing of LOUDSPEAKERS and MICROPHONES where reverberation would confuse the measurement. For low frequencies, a good pseudo-anechoic environment is a parking lot on a Sunday morning, provided no buildings or trees are nearby. This is actually a semi-anechoic space because of the reflecting surface of the pavement, but it can still be useful if the test object is placed at the pavement level so no delayed reflections will be measured. The effect of the so-called ground plane is predictable and can be subtracted from the data.

Anhysteretic Literally, without HYSTERESIS. In analog magnetic tape recording, the hysteresis inherent in the process of magnetizing the tape represents a large nonlinearity, and this causes harmonic DISTORTION. The use of BIAS in the recording process reduces the effect of the hysteresis (makes the magnetization anhysteretic) and reduces the distortion.

Anode The anode in any electronic component, such as a silicon DIODE or a vacuum TUBE, is the ELECTRODE normally connected to the positive VOLTAGE or, in a battery, the positive terminal. In vacuum tubes, the anode is often called the PLATE, and its positive charge attracts electrons emitted by the CATHODE or negatively charged element.

ANSI The American National Standards Institute (ANSI) is an organization engaged in the establishment of standards.

Anti-Aliasing Filter Before a signal is subjected to the process of A/D conversion, it must be passed through a LOW-PASS FILTER to remove any components that are higher in FREQUENCY than one-half the SAMPLING frequency. This is because it requires at least two samples per cycle to determine the existence and strength of a frequency component, that is, it would require at least one hundred samples per second to encode a tone of 50 HERTZ. The A/D process will create spurious signals, called aliased components, if this rule is not followed.

The frequency corresponding to one-half the sampling rate is sometimes called the NYQUIST FREQUENCY, and the requirement to limit signals into an A/D to below this frequency is sometimes called the NYQUIST CRITERION.

In order to affect the audible signal as little as possible, an anti-aliasing filter is designed to be very steep, having an extremely rapid fall-off above the upper frequency limit. Such filters are complex, and they of necessity suffer from PHASE SHIFT, which under some conditions may be audible. There are those who believe they can detect a certain "harshness" in DIGITAL audio systems that might be caused by this phase shift, and some experiments have been reported where signals with and without phase shift were directly compared. Most people are able to tell a difference in the sounds, but it is another matter to tell reliably which one is the phase-shifted and which one is not.

Anti-Imaging Filter In a DIGITAL audio system, in order to recover the SIGNAL from the digital words, a D/A converter is used. The output of this is a stair-step type of WAVEFORM which contains a great deal of high-FREQUENCY energy called "images." To reconstruct a smooth replica of the original signal, the stair-step is passed through a steep low-pass filter called an anti-imaging filter. It is similar, or even identical, to the ANTI-ALIASING FILTER found at the input of the A/D converter, but its purpose is quite different.

Antinode A place of minimum SOUND PRESSURE LEVEL in a STANDING WAVE, as opposed to a node, which is a maximum in level.

Antiphase Signals are said to be in antiphase if they are of opposite POLARITY, or 180 degrees out of phase with each other.

Antiskating Device The antiskating device on a record player tonearm tends to force the arm toward the outer edge of the record to counteract the SKATING FORCE, which forces the arm toward the center.

The magnitude of the antiskating force is dependent on the STYLUS vertical tracking force and must be adjusted accordingly.

Aperiodic Aperiodic means "without period" and refers to a signal or WAVEFORM that does not repeat at a fixed time interval. An example of an aperiodic waveform is random noise. *See also* PERIODIC.

In reference to mechanics the term is sometimes applied to a system with a high degree of DAMPING such that it no longer oscillates, or resonates. For instance, a loudspeaker is said to be aperiodic if its mechanical resonances are at least critically damped. Advertising claims aside, true aperiodic behavior in a loudspeaker is rare, if not nonexistent.

Aperture Time Errors In an ANALOG-TO-DIGITAL CONVERTER, the SAMPLE AND HOLD circuit would ideally take zero time to determine the level of the signal WAVEFORM and to hold this level until the next sample is called for. However, it takes a finite time to charge the "holding" CAPACITOR in the sample and hold, and this is called the aperture time. Because the time required to establish a new value of charge depends on the amount of change in the SIGNAL level from one sample to the next, the aperture time will vary with the rate of change in signal level, increasing for high-level, high-frequency signals.

The starting time of the sampling aperture is also slightly uncertain, and this is called JITTER. In other words, lack of precision in the sampling time leads to AMPLITUDE errors in rapidly changing signals. The errors involve aperture time, uncertainty in aperture time, and jitter. The result is DISTORTION of the sampled signal which rises with FREQUENCY.

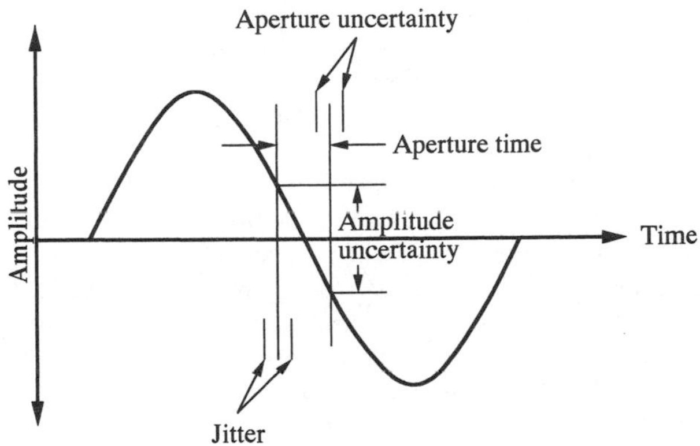

Aperture Time Errors

Aphex Aural Exciter A trade name for a device that adds even-order HARMONIC DISTORTION to a SIGNAL for the purpose of making it more audible in the presence of other sounds. The Aphex system is used in multitrack popular music recording, generally on only one or two signals. Voice tracks are commonly so treated. The added even harmonics make the signal a little brighter and crisper, with minimal change in LOUDNESS. Vocal lines stand out more from the rest of the "mix."

It is interesting that even-numbered harmonics have this effect, while odd-numbered harmonics cause a closed-in, or "covered," sound.

Apodize Literally, "to remove the foot." To apodize is to remove a sharp discontinuity in a structure, a SIGNAL, or a mathematical function.

One example of apodization is the rounding of the edges and corners of loudspeaker cabinets to reduce the DIFFRACTION of sound waves from them. Diffraction in this case results in a reflection of the wave, and the reflected wave will interfere with the direct wave from the LOUDSPEAKER cone, causing irregular FREQUENCY RESPONSE. The first proposed cabinet apodization was probably by Harry F. Olson, of RCA Research Labs. Other forms of cabinet apodization are the placement of sound-absorbing material on the cabinet front around the speaker CONE, especially helpful in the case of TWEETERS.

Another example of apodization is the system of absorbing-wedges on the walls of an ANECHOIC chamber, which eliminate the effect of the acoustic boundary at the walls.

In mathematics, the smoothing of discontinuities in a CURVE is called apodization. The Hanning window, used to smooth the ends of the time record in an FFT ANALYZER, is a form of apodization.

Arc The phenomenon of electricity jumping across a gap is called an arc, even though its path may not be shaped like a true arc. A spark is a very short-duration arc.

When electric switches carrying significant CURRENTS are opened, a momentary arc is formed, and this accounts for the eroding of the switch contacts. Arcing in electronic equipment is never desired, and effort is expended on suppressing it.

One example of a useful application of an arc is the carbon arc lamp, one of the first types of electric light to be built. It predates the incandescent electric light bulb and was used extensively for street lighting in the nineteenth century. The arc between two carbon ELECTRODES emits a very bright, almost pure white light, and it is still used in some commercial motion picture projectors. More modern projectors use xenon lamps, which are actually arc lamps enclosed in quartz bulbs. The electrodes are of tungsten and the arc occurs in an atmosphere of xenon gas.

Arm The moving contact in a POTENTIOMETER is sometimes called the arm.

Armature The moving part of an electric motor or a magnetic transducer such as a phono CARTRIDGE.

Armed When a channel of an audio recorder is set so it will record when the machine is placed in record mode, it is said to be "armed." In multitrack recorders, the channels can be armed independently in any combination. The unarmed channels will not be recorded while the armed ones will be. Some machines call this "safe" (unarmed) and "ready" (armed).

ASA, Acoustical Society of America An organization founded by Harvey Fletcher of the Bell Telephone Laboratories in 1929. The ASA sponsors yearly meetings where investigators in all areas of acoustics gather and deliver papers on current research. The Journal of the Acoustical Society of America (JASA) is a very important forum for workers and students in the extremely complex world of acoustics.

Also, the American Standards Association (ASA) was founded in 1928 by renaming and reorganizing the American Engineering Standards Committee (AESA) which had been founded in 1918. Then, in 1969, the ASA was renamed ANSI, for American National Standards Institute. The sensitivity of photographic film was formerly rated by so-called ASA numbers, but ISO also published a standard for film speed, and all film manufacturers conform to it. The speed numbers are almost identical with the old ASA numbers. ASA film speed numbers had nothing to do with the Acoustical Society of America.

ASCII Acronym for American Standard Code for Information Interchange. This is the standard digital code used first by teletype technology and later for communication of text between computers.

Asperity A small irregularity or imperfection in the surface of a MAGNETIC TAPE is called an asperity. Some gross asperities are visible on inspection of the tape, but most are not. Asperities are numerous in all tapes and produce ASPERITY NOISE in tape-recorded signals. The author, in a previous life working in a data analysis lab at a well-known airplane company, heard a loud low frequency "burp" when listening to a reel of ½-inch-wide tape with vibration data recorded on it. There was a relatively well-preserved and well-flattened mosquito embedded in the oxide surface! The name of the tape manufacturer is withheld at the request of the American Anti-Agony Society.

Asperity Noise Low-frequency noise in analog magnetic tape recordings caused by ASPERITIES in the surface of the tape. Asperity noise is a type of MODULATION NOISE.

Assemble Editing Editing of an audio or video program by making a master copy of the various takes, rather than physically splicing the pieces of tape together. Virtually all digital editing is done this way.

Assigns Push buttons on the input modules of a control console (audio mixer), that connect, or assign, that particular input to any of the output busses of the console.

Asymmetrical Limiter A special type of LIMITER that is used mostly in AM broadcasting to reduce the DISTORTION caused by overmodulation. The asymmetrical limiter limits the negative-going peaks of the audio WAVEFORM more than the positive-going peaks, and this helps to prevent the degree of modulation from going below zero. In amplitude modulation, there is no theoretical limit to positive-going peaks, but there can be no modulation below zero carrier amplitude. Any attempt to modulate more than this results in hard CLIPPING and gross distortion. This distortion is sometimes called "splatter," which is quite descriptive of what it sounds like.

Asymmetrical Response This refers to the spectral shapes of the boost and cut response curves of certain equalizers. Usually, the cut response curves are quite a bit sharper than the boost response curves. The purpose of symmetrical response is to improve the subjective quality of the equalizers in question.

ATIP, Absolute Time In Pregroove All CD-R and CD-RW discs have a pre-embossed spiral groove that wobbles slightly. The groove keeps the laser assembly tracking properly, and the wobble (sinusoidal with a frequency of 22.05 kHz) provides timing information to the recorder. The wobble is frequency-modulated with a +/-1kHz signal, which creates an absolute time clocking signal, known as the Absolute Time In Pregroove. In addition, the ATIP area has other encoded data, which purports to contain the CD-R manufacturer, length of disc, and dye strategy.

ATRAC™, Adaptive Transform Acoustic Coding A lossy, split band PERCEPTUAL CODING and compression scheme, invented by Sony, for reducing the amount of data to be written on a MiniDisc. ATRAC offers a 5 to 1 data reduction ratio in the case of MiniDisc, employing the equivalent of 52 filter bands for spectral analysis and re-quantization. Later versions of ATRAC vary the size of the sample blocks dynamically between 11.6ms and 1.45ms according to the input signal to allow for temporal masking.

ATRAC compresses compact disc audio to approximately ⅕ of the original data rate with virtually no loss in sound quality.

ATRAC2 is a new version released by Sony that can compress digital audio by a factor of 10 "without sacrificing audio quality," according to Sony. ATRAC3 and ATRAC3plus are further developments of ATRAC2 designed especially for audio transmission over the internet. ATRAC3plus achieves a compression ratio of 20 to 1, again without loss of sound quality, according to Sony.

ATSC, Advanced Television Systems Committee The Advanced Television Systems Committee Inc. is an international, nonprofit membership organization developing voluntary standards for the entire spectrum of advanced television systems.

ATSC is working to coordinate television standards among different communications media focusing on digital television, interactive systems, and broadband multimedia communications. ATSC is also developing digital television implementation strategies and presenting educational seminars on the ATSC standards.

ATSC was formed in 1982 by the member organizations of the Joint Committee on InterSociety Coordination (JCIC): the Electronic Industries Association (EIA), the Institute of Electrical and Electronic Engineers (IEEE), the National Association of Broadcasters (NAB), the National Cable Television Association (NCTA), and the Society of Motion Picture and Television Engineers (SMPTE). Currently, there are approximately 170 members representing the broadcast, broadcast equipment, motion picture, consumer electronics, computer, cable, satellite, and semiconductor industries. ATSC incorporated on January 3, 2002.

When the DTV Standard was first adopted by the ATSC in 1995, the ATSC was strictly a United States organization with approximately fifty members, although Mexican and Canadian organizations played a significant role throughout the entire Advisory Committee process in developing what was always expected to be a standard for all of North America, at least. In January 1996, the ATSC modified its charter to become an international organization, and the ATSC began to work with a variety of countries around the world to explore the possibility of using the ATSC Standard for their DTV services. Since that time, the ATSC DTV Standard has been adopted by the governments of Canada (November 8, 1997), South Korea (November 21, 1997), Taiwan (May 8, 1998), and Argentina (October 22, 1998), and many other countries are now considering the ATSC Standard for possible use in their countries. Today, the ATSC has approximately 170 members from a variety of countries in North America, South America, Europe, Asia, and Australia.

Attack Time Attack time is the time it takes for a COMPRESSOR or LIMITER to reduce its GAIN after a strong signal is applied to it.

TRANSIENT SIGNALS that are shorter than the attack time of the device will not be affected by the gain reduction, so it is important that the attack time be as short as possible. In the case of COMPANDER systems, the attack time of the compressor and the expander must be exactly the same in order to preserve accurate dynamics of the signal. In this case, these times are selected for minimum audibility of noise PUMPING.

Attenuation Reduction in AMPLITUDE or level of a SIGNAL is called attenuation. It is usually measured in DECIBELS. RESISTANCE in transmission line wires, among other things, causes attenuation of signals. Sometimes signal attenuation is desired, and ATTENUATORS are used to achieve it.

Attenuator An attenuator is a device for reducing, or attenuating, the AMPLITUDE of a SIGNAL. A common example is the volume control. Many times, attenuators are specially designed to reduce signals by various numbers of DECIBELS. Such attenuators may be either fixed or variable. Inexpensive attenuators can affect the FREQUENCY RESPONSE of a signal under some conditions, and high-quality attenuators are never cheap.

Attenuators are sometimes called PADS, or loss pads. We have wondered

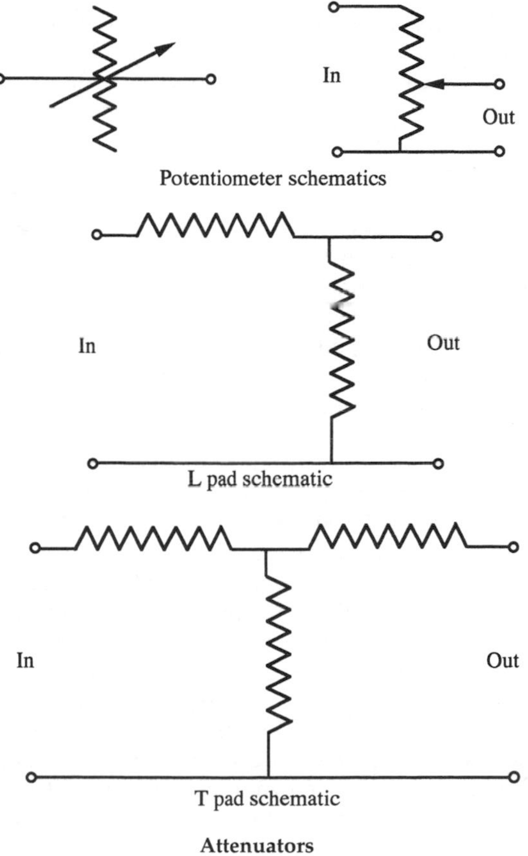

Attenuators

for many years why the term "pad" came to be used to describe an attenuator, but we haven't discovered the source of this usage.

Audio Literally, "I hear" in Latin. The term pertains to any SIGNAL, sound, WAVEFORM, etc., that can be heard, as distinguished from ULTRASONIC sound, RADIO-FREQUENCY signals, or VIDEO signals. In some people's minds, audio is nearly synonymous with STEREO, or hi-fi.

Audio Analgesia A technique, introduced in the 1950s, for reducing sensitivity to pain in dental patients. The patient wore a headset that reproduced a specially equalized PINK NOISE signal at a relatively high level. Usually, stereo music was added to the noise signal to further distract the listener's attention from the violence being done in his mouth. The theory, according to Dr. J. W. Gardner and Emory Cook, two of its developers, was that the nerves carrying the pain impulses to the brain were effectively "jammed" by the music and noise. The audio analgesiac, as it was called, enjoyed some temporary popularity among dentists, but the novelty apparently soon wore off, as did the analgesia.

Audiometer An audiometer is a device for measuring the hearing acuity of a person. It actually measures the auditory threshold at various frequencies, usually from 100 HERTZ to 8 KILOHERTZ. The resulting FREQUENCY RESPONSE curve is called an audiogram. There are several accepted ways to measure hearing threshold, the most common using calibrated earphones. *See also* HEADPHONES.

Audion Audion is the name given the first TRIODE (three-element vacuum TUBE) by its inventor, Dr. Lee DeForest in 1906, the year of the invention. In an article on the history of the electronic age that DeForest wrote for the fiftieth-anniversary issue of *Popular Mechanics* magazine (January 1952), appears the following paragraph: "As a growing competitor to the tube amplifier comes now the Bell Laboratories thermistor, a three-electrode germanium crystal of amazing amplification power, of wheat-grain size and low cost. Yet its frequency limitations, a few hundred kilocycles, and its strict power limitations will never permit its general replacement of the audion amplifier."

The "thermistor" is of course the TRANSISTOR we know today. This shows again the futility of trying to predict the future, even by so knowledgeable an authority as Dr. DeForest. That 1950s issue of *Popular Mechanics* makes fascinating reading today.

Audiophile Audiophile stems from Latin and Greek roots and means, literally, a "lover of hearing." There are many vernacular synonyms for audiophile, including hi-fi nut, audio weenie, sound freak, etc.

The true dyed-in-the-wool audiophile is interested in the (real or imagined) perfection of the reproduction of music. The music itself is of minor importance; it serves merely as a vehicle for the apparatus. (In fairness, it must be said that there are many music lovers and musicians who qualify as audiophiles.) In contrast, many musicians are not extremely concerned with the accuracy of the reproduction of the sound, but are able to listen to the music "through" the medium. I have been frequently amazed that some musicians can put up with gross distortions of sound from their sound systems.

Audio Taper A type of POTENTIOMETER designed for use as a volume control in audio equipment. Its resistance varies more in a logarithmic, rather than linear, fashion with rotation of the knob. This gives a better correlation between control rotation and subjective loudness of the signal.

Auditory Perspective A phrase used by the Bell Telephone Laboratories engineers in the early 1930s meaning STEREOPHONY. According to John Frayne, who was one of the engineers at the Western Electric company at the time, the term *auditory perspective* was thought too cumbersome for commercial use, and Western Electric held a contest among its employees to coin a better term. Someone suggested *stereophony* and *stereophonic,* and these names have been accepted usage ever since.

Auralization The use of computer modeling to simulate the sound field in a virtual space. The result is the ability to hear, via special headphones, the acoustical properties of an auditorium that has not been built, allowing architects and sound system technicians to make changes in proposed designs and hear the results. Some auralization programs are quite sophisticated, and allow the modeling of different types of sound systems and different locations in virtual rooms of varying designs. A very important feature of these programs is the simulation of binaural sound in the earphones in order to gain a semblance of directional realism.

Autocorrelation Function, or ACF A measure of how much a signal resembles a delayed version of itself. It is a function of time delay and can vary from 1 to -1, always having a value of 1 for zero delay.

The ACF of music is a significant statistical parameter, especially the time delay required for a given selection to decrease to one-tenth of its maximum value. This is called the effective duration of the ACF. Music with a short effective duration of ACF requires a relatively short reverberation time to maintain clarity, whereas music with a long duration of ACF (such as organ music) sounds better with long reverberation times. Speech has a short ACF, and this explains why intelligibility is reduced when it is heard in very reverberant spaces.

Some years ago there was a single-pass noise reduction unit on the market called an autocorrelator. It was actually a DYNAMIC FILTER and had nothing to do with autocorrelation. This was an unfortunate and misleading use of terminology.

Automated Mixdown, Automation *See* MIXDOWN.

Auto Reverse Tape recorders that can play a tape in either direction, eliminating the need to flip the tape to play the other side. Virtually all recent automobile cassette players are auto reversing. The mechanisms that evolved could be quite interesting. Some machines used dual capstans, some a central capstan. Separate heads were usually used for each side, although some machines moved one head and some simply have one head with cores for all tracks. Some machines sensed the end of a side by the application of a metal foil to the ends of the tape, sensed by an electrical contact. Some machines used a photocell and looked for clear leader tape. Some cassettes simply sensed the tension of the end of the tape. Professional tape machines never record on 2 sides and thus are never auto reverse.

Autotransformer A TRANSFORMER which has only one WINDING. The winding will have taps along its length as well as TERMINALS at each end. Autotransformers are used in some multiple-LOUDSPEAKER sound systems to couple the individual loudspeakers to a wire coming from the AMPLIFIER. Selection from the various taps determines how much power the speaker will accept from the line. The autotransformer does not provide electrical isolation between the input and output signals as does a conventional transformer, and cannot be used where this is required, such as MICROPHONE PREAMP input transformers.

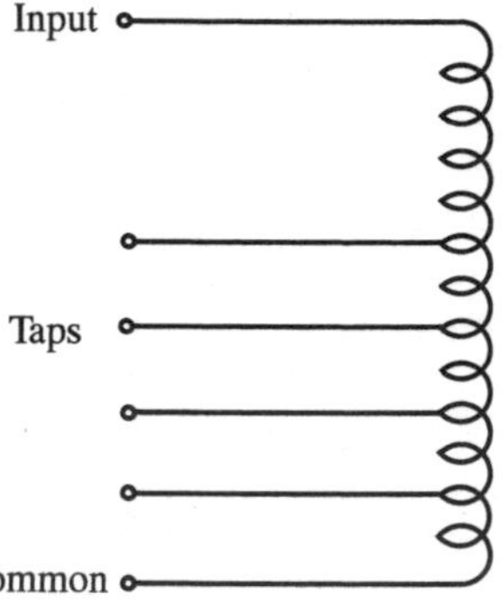

Signal input is usually across the entire winding, and output is taken from intermediate taps

Autotransformer

Aux, Auxiliary Generally refers to an input connector in a preamplifier or integrated AMPLIFIER which is not specifically designed to accept a phono cartridge output. The auxiliary input has no DE-EMPHASIS or other special EQUALIZATION and accepts line level signals.

Aux Send *See* SEND.

Avalanche Diode *See* DIODE; ZENER DIODE.

AVC *See* AGC.

AVI, Audio Video Interleaved A Microsoft multimedia file format, similar to MPEG, used by Video for Windows. In AVI, audio and video elements are interleaved (stored in alternate segments) in the file.

A-Weighting A-weighting is an EQUALIZATION curve first applied to SOUND LEVEL METERS in an attempt to make their measurements correspond better to perceived LOUDNESS of sounds. It decreases the SENSITIVITY of the meter to frequencies below 1,000 HERTZ in a way that approximates the Fletcher-Munson curve of equal loudness of 40 PHONS. (*See* FLETCHER-MUNSON EFFECT.) If a sound level meter is measuring sound levels corresponding to loudness levels of about 40 phons (the LOUDNESS of a 1,000 Hz tone at 40 DECIBELS SPL), then it makes sense to use the A-weighting filter. At greater loudnesses, however, the contours of equal loudness are more uniform with FREQUENCY, and a different CURVE would be required. To build a sound level meter that approximates the sensitivity of the human ear at all frequencies and loudnesses would be impossible due to the complexity required.

Even though A-weighting is not suited for measuring loud sounds, it has been used so much in the past, and there is so large a database of A-weighted measurements, that its continued use is almost mandated. Most standards for noise measurement, both American and European, call for A-weighting.

There is one advantage to makers of noisy products in using A-weighted levels: they give smaller numbers than nonweighted measurements would, giving the impression of less subjective noise to the uninitiated.

AWG Acronym for American Wire Gauge, also known as the Brown & Sharpe wire gauge. A numerical code, from 0000 to 40 is used to indicate the diameter of electrical wire. The higher the gauge, the smaller the wire diameter.

Azimuth In an ANALOG tape recorder, the angle that the gap in the record or playback head makes with the direction of tape travel is called the azimuth angle, and it must be precisely 90 degrees to ensure proper high-frequency performance. To adjust the azimuth, an ALIGNMENT TAPE is put on the machine and the output SIGNAL level is monitored while the azimuth adjustment is slowly moved back and forth. The azimuth is correct when the highest level signal is obtained and the signals from the top and bottom tracks are in PHASE.

The FREQUENCY recorded on the tape is usually 16 KILOHERTZ. Of course the accuracy of this adjustment relies on the accuracy of the alignment tape.

The narrow tracks of quarter-track machines require less precise adjustment than the wider tracks of half-track or full-track tape recorders to attain correct high-frequency response.

B

Back Coat Back coat is an electrically conductive coating on the "back" or nonrecording side of recording tape, for the purpose of preventing static electricity from collecting on the tape and improving tape handling by providing a bit of friction on the normally smooth plastic. It is only seen on open reel tapes, and always black in color from the conductive carbon particles.

Back EMF A VOLTAGE that is induced in a LOUDSPEAKER VOICE COIL due to the coil's motion in the magnetic field. The back EMF is in opposite POLARITY to the voltage driving the coil, and so opposes that voltage. *See also* MOTIONAL IMPEDANCE.

Back Plate The surface behind the diaphragm in a CONDENSER MICROPHONE. The exact spacing, configuration, and features of the back plate, such as vents, determine many of the microphone's characteristics.

Baffle An enclosure, or a large panel, into which a LOUDSPEAKER is mounted in order to improve its low-frequency efficiency is called a baffle.

Originally, the baffle was simply a flat panel of wood that effectively separated the radiation coming from the front of the speaker CONE from the rearward radiation, preventing cancellation at low frequencies. An ideal flat baffle would be of infinite size so none of the rear wave would reach the front regardless of the FREQUENCY. This would be a true "infinite baffle." A practical infinite baffle is a totally closed box that isolates the rear radiation, although it also raises the low-frequency RESONANCE of the speaker. This effect can be used to advantage in certain loudspeaker designs.

There are a great many different designs for loudspeaker baffles, and it seems that several new ones are patented each month. Many of these designs are popular for a while and then rapidly fall into disfavor, but some, such as the BASS REFLEX, ACOUSTIC SUSPENSION, and HORN, and their variations, have endured for a long time.

Balanced, Balance Balanced refers to AUDIO lines in which the SIGNAL current is not carried by the SHIELD.

To transmit information electrically, whether by telegraph, telephone, or an audio signal, two wires, or conductors, are needed. The CURRENT is in the opposite direction in the two conductors. In most audio circuitry and in interconnecting cables, one conductor of the signal is connected to the CHASSIS, or GROUND. This configuration is called "single-ended." The chassis thus carries signal current. Wires interconnecting audio devices are commonly shielded, with the shield grounded, or connected to the chassis. The shield prevents electrostatic fields from inducing noise voltages in the inner conductor. The shield carries audio current in such a cable.

The problem with this arrangement is that any noise induced in the shield will be added to the signal. Typically such noise is 60-HERTZ HUM induced by magnetic fields produced by power lines, and it is troublesome in audio cables that are more than a few feet long.

The way to prevent this type of noise interference is to use two conductors for the signal and enclose them together in a shield, with neither conductor connected to the shield. This is called a balanced configuration, and the shield carries no audio current. The conductors in the shield are also twisted together, which helps in reducing magnetically induced hum. The wires change places every half-twist, and this reverses the direction of the induced current, causing it to effectively cancel itself over the length of the cable.

Also, any hum induced in a balanced CIRCUIT will be equal in the two conductors, i.e., in PHASE, whereas the signal currents will be out of phase in the two conductors. This in-phase noise induced in the two conductors is called a COMMON-MODE current, while the signal current is called differential. At the receiving end of the cable, it is not desirable to pick up the common-mode current, so a DIFFERENTIAL AMPLIFIER is used. It is sensitive only to the difference in VOLTAGE between the two conductors, and rejects the common-mode part of the signal. This characteristic of differential circuits is called "common-mode rejection."

Most long audio cables are balanced. Probably the most familiar examples are MICROPHONE cables. One way to balance an audio circuit is to use a TRANSFORMER at each end because the transformer is not sensitive to the common-mode currents. This is the usual practice for microphones. It is also possible, by using differential SOLID-STATE amplifiers and audio OPAMPS, to construct balanced circuits without using transformers.

Sometimes the CENTER TAP of the input transformer primary is grounded, which does not affect the balance. If it is not grounded, the circuit is said to be "floating and balanced." *See also* DIFFERENTIAL AMPLIFIER and Appendix 6.

Balanced Line *See* Appendix 6.

Balanced Power Mains AC power supplied to power audio equipment that is configured as a transformer secondary with a center tap grounded. Such a powering scheme can reduce power line induced noise by isolating the audio equipment from the power line ground. While the "neutral" conductor supplied by the power line is technically grounded, it can have a lot of different kinds of electrical noise riding on it, and this noise can become audible in audio systems. The U.S. National Electrical Code (NEC) recognizes the scheme, but it is somewhat obscure and requires knowledgeable installation.

Ballistics The dynamic behavior of the needle in a meter such as a VU meter is called the meter's ballistics. Such things as the time it takes for the meter to read full scale after a 0 VU SIGNAL is applied, the distance the needle will overshoot the 0 VU mark, and the time it takes to fall back when the signal is removed are examples of ballistic specifications.

The ballistics of a meter are very important because music and speech are such irregular signals, having large PEAKS lasting only short times. Meters with different ballistics will read quite different levels of such signals. It is interesting that American VU meters have different ballistics from similar meters on European equipment. Even the reaction of nonmechanical level indicators may have their response described as ballistics. *See also* PPM.

Balun A transformer connecting a *bal*anced circuit to an *un*balanced circuit. The Balun was originally used to connect radio transmitters to their antennas. A common use is to connect a 75-ohm antenna coaxial cable to a 300-ohm TWINLEAD TV or radio receiving antenna input. They are also often used to connect balanced audio lines to unbalanced lines or audio components, although the term is seldom heard in this application. Nowadays, they mostly consist of solid-state circuitry rather than transformers, although the transformer is often superior if complete electrical isolation is required, such as to solve a ground problem.

Banana Plug, Banana Jack A banana plug is an electrical connector designed to join wires such as speaker wires to BINDING POSTS, or special jacks called banana jacks. The metal part of the plug resembles a small banana, hence the name. A common configuration of banana plugs is two of them molded together and spaced ¾-inch apart. Such plugs allow fast engagemant and disengagement, and can carry reasonably high currents.

This assembly is also called a "GR" plug, after the General Radio Corporation, which introduced it many years ago. Banana jacks are often found as terminals on older test equipment such as VOMS, VTVMS, OSCILLOSCOPES, and OSCILLATORS, etc., but they are essentially obsolete for this application. They are sometimes found as output connectors on power amplifiers.

Band An extent along the FREQUENCY dimension in which a SIGNAL exists is the band. For instance, an OCTAVE BAND is a band one octave wide, while a one-third octave band is one-third octave wide. The AUDIO band, encompassing the frequency range of human hearing, is usually regarded to be 20 HERTZ to 20 KILOHERTZ.

Band-Limited A SIGNAL is said to be band-limited if its FREQUENCY content is restricted to a particular frequency range. A band-limited signal can be made with a BANDPASS FILTER, but some signals are band-limited by their nature. For instance, the output signal of a COMPACT DISC player is band-limited to 20 KILOHERTZ by the ANTI-IMAGING FILTERS built into the player.

Bandpass Filter A bandpass filter is a filter which has a BANDWIDTH. Bandpass filters can be "broad," having a wide bandwidth, or "narrow," having a narrow bandwidth. They may be fixed in frequency and bandwidth, or variable in either frequency and/or bandwidth. *See also* SOUND EFFECTS FILTER; TONE CONTROL.

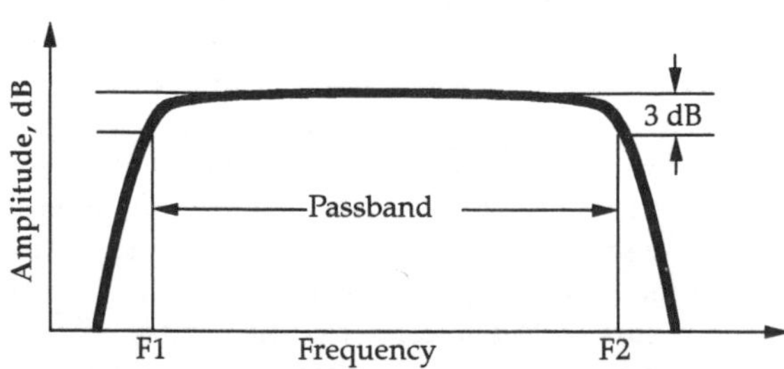

Bandpass Filter Frequency Response

Bandpass Filter

Band Reject Filter A FILTER that discriminates against signals in a specific frequency band. The most common band reject filters reject a very narrow frequency band, and they are usually called NOTCH FILTERS.

Bandwidth The bandwidth of a BANDPASS FILTER is the upper CUTOFF FREQUENCY minus the lower cutoff frequency. It is thus the extent, in HERTZ, of the frequency range, or BAND, passed by the filter.

Bandwidth is literally a frequency span, and is not necessarily connected to the specification of a filter. For instance, the human voice can be transmitted with good intelligibility if the FREQUENCY RESPONSE of the transmission chain extends from about 100 Hz to about 3,000 Hz. Thus, a 2,900-Hz bandwidth is needed to transmit voice. This is about what a standard telephone system attains. The audio bandwidth, however, is generally considered to be about 20 KILOHERTZ.

The information-carrying capacity of any communication channel is determined by its bandwidth, although there are many ways to encode signals within the bandwidth. Information theory is the study of how bandwidth and encoding schemes affect the transfer of information. The most significant work in the field of classical information theory was done by Claude Shannon, of the Bell Telephone Laboratories.

Bar Originally defined as the average air pressure at sea level and 45 degrees latitude, which is equivalent to 10.1325 newtons per square centimeter. The SI system has redefined it as 10 newtons per square centimeter, or 10 PASCALS, simplifying some calculations.

The reference pressure for the SOUND PRESSURE LEVEL scale used to be based on the bar, but is now based on the pascal.

Barkhausen Effect The Barkhausen effect is the tendency of the magnetic elements, or "domains" as they are called, to influence one another and to become magnetized in one direction or another as a group rather than individually. This means that a magnetic medium, such as recording tape, has a "graininess" in its magnetic makeup, which is what causes most background noise or "tape hiss" in magnetic recordings.

MODULATION NOISE, which is only present in conjunction with a recorded signal, is also caused by the Barkhausen effect, and is sometimes called "Barkhausen noise." The term comes from the name of the discoverer of the effect.

Barney A soft, heavy fabric zip-up cover designed to be placed over a motion picture camera to reduce its noise output so sound can be recorded while filming. *See also* BLIMP.

Barometer "An ingenious device that indicates what kind of weather we are having."—A. Bierce

Base The control ELECTRODE in a bipolar TRANSISTOR is called the base. It is analogous to the GATE in a FIELD-EFFECT TRANSISTOR and to the GRID in a vacuum TUBE. Base is sometimes used to designate the plastic portion of recording tape onto which the magnetic coating is applied.

Basilar Membrane The part of the cochlea in the inner ear that contains the hair cells that generate the nerve impulses sent to the brain. Sound striking the ear drum is transmitted through the middle ear to the cochlea, where it causes the basilar membrane to vibrate. This vibration excites the hair cells, which emit impulses into the auditory nerve.

Bass Bass is that portion of the audible FREQUENCY which encompasses the lower PITCHES. The bass range is generally considered to be from 30 HERTZ or so up to about 200 Hz. Sometimes frequencies around 200 to 300 Hz are called "mid-bass."

Bass Intermodulation, or BIM Bass Intermodulation is a type of DISTORTION caused by the MODULATION of AUDIO frequencies by SUBSONIC NOISE. The term is not universally recognized, but the effect is real.

Examples of low-frequency noises that cause BIM are FLUTTER, WOW, and TONEARM RESONANCE. It might be thought that noises that are below the FREQUENCY range of human hearing should be of no concern, but this is far from the case. If an audible signal is AMPLITUDE MODULATED by a subsonic WAVEFORM, the modulation will add SIDEBANDS to the signal, and they are closely spaced in frequency to the signal. In some cases, these sidebands can be as little as 10 DECIBELS lower than the signal itself. This constitutes 30% distortion.

Tonearm resonance can be a major offender, for the AMPLITUDES of the CARTRIDGE response due to it are frequently at levels comparable to the actual signal level from the record. If the phono PREAMP is not LINEAR in this low-frequency region, BIM will occur. The audible effect is a general "muddying" of the sound and an imprecise or "smeared" STEREO image.

Bass Management A function built in to many surround-sound processors in home theater systems that route the low-frequency content of the program to the SUBWOOFER. If the system has no subwoofer, the bass management function can be adjusted to route the bass to the full-range speakers in the system.

Bass Reflex™ The term *bass reflex* was a trademark of the Jensen company in the 1930s and referred to a type of LOUDSPEAKER enclosure that was sealed except for a rather large hole, or "port," below the speaker itself.

Such enclosures are now called "vented" systems, and the theory behind their operation has been thoroughly investigated by two workers named Neville Thiele and Richard Small. In essence, a vented enclosure is a resonant box (a HELMHOLTZ resonator), even without the loudspeaker in it. The loudspeaker will also have a low-frequency RESONANCE, caused by the springiness of the CONE suspension and the mass of the cone and VOICE COIL assembly. Each one of these resonances results in a PEAK in the FREQUENCY RESPONSE. If the two resonant frequencies are made the same and then are coupled by mounting the speaker in the box, an odd thing happens: the two resonances effectively cancel each other and two more resonances appear, one higher in FREQUENCY and one lower in frequency than the originals. The lower of these two peaks helps to extend the response of the system to a lower frequency than it would achieve without the resonance.

What actually happens is that the air in the port is moving out of PHASE with the speaker at the original resonant frequency, partially canceling its output. Below this frequency, the air in the port is in phase with the cone motion, adding to the output and extending the lower limiting frequency downward.

An important characteristic of such a system is the DAMPING, because if it is under-damped, the lower resonance will cause the response to hang on after the signal stops. Some under-damped early Bass Reflex systems were called "boom boxes" for good reason. An example of a "boom box" is the juke box, popular in the 1950s. *See also* HANGOVER; THIELE-SMALL PARAMETERS.

Bass Trap A bass trap is a low-FREQUENCY sound absorber specially designed to reduce the effects of STANDING WAVES in recording studios. It is a "tuned" absorber, and may have a narrow or wide range of frequencies over which it operates. It usually consists of resonant wood panels with absorptive material behind them, or suitably shaped slots in a wall or ceiling.

Battery A device for storing electrical energy and making it available for powering electrical devices. Strictly speaking, a battery is two or more electric cells connected in SERIES. Thus, a flashlight "battery" is really only a CELL.

There are many types of batteries available, and the variety can be bewildering to the uninitiated. The least expensive type uses carbon and zinc as the active elements, but the more common alkaline cell provides more power and longer life at a somewhat higher cost. Lithium cells provide very high energy density at high cost.

Many batteries are rechargeable, the most common of which are nickel-cadmium (NiCad or NiCd) or nickel-metal hydride (NiMH). The NiCad battery can be damaged if it is recharged when less than completely discharged, although this has been disputed. To best prolong its useful life, it should periodically be completely discharged and then fully charged. The NiCad battery, even when fully charged, does not contain as much electrical energy as the alkaline battery, so if the application requires long continuous use between replacements, the alkaline battery is a better choice. Under high power draw conditions, the NiMH battery can deliver even more energy. Lithium Ion batteries are rechargeable and have very high energy capacity, but are tricky to handle safely.

Baud The speed of digital data transmission is measured in baud. One baud roughly corresponds to one-half dot cycle per second in Morse code, or one BIT per second in a train of BINARY signals.

In the case of a modem, where DIGITAL data are modulated onto a CARRIER for transmission over a telephone line, the baud rate may be different from the bit rate. In such a situation, the baud rate is equal to the reciprocal of the shortest modulation element duration in seconds, and thus may be faster than the actual bit rate if the bits have variable spacing.

The term comes from Baudot, a French engineer who devised a five-level code for telegraphs.

Baxandall Tone Controls A type of bass and treble tone control CIRCUIT invented in Britain by Peter Baxandall in the 1950s. Baxandall tone controls work by inserting variable frequency-selective elements in the NEGATIVE FEEDBACK loop of an amplifier stage. To achieve TREBLE boost, the FEEDBACK at high frequencies is reduced, and to achieve treble cut, the high-frequency feedback is increased. The action is similar for low frequencies. Baxandall circuits were very popular for many years, but they are not ideal. The variable feedback causes the DISTORTION to vary with the tone control settings, and the inevitable noise added to the SIGNAL is higher than with some other circuits and has a spectrum that varies with tone control settings.

Baxandall tone controls can be easily realized using circuits based on OPAMPS and are still used.

B Battery The relatively high voltage battery used to supply the tube PLATES in the radios of the 1920s was called the B battery. At first, B batteries were made of a series of small 1.5-V LECLANCHE CELLS, but later, rechargeable B batteries became available. Usually these consisted of 60 or so EDISON CELLS in test tubes connected in series. Every so often, the cells needed to be refilled with distilled water, which was no small bother. Few people today realize the difficulties involved in listening to the radio in the 1920s. It was in 1938 that Robert Eichberg asked: "Is the radio listener of today as happy as the fan of yesteryear? I doubt it, for though programs have improved with the equipment, the old thrill is largely gone. No more does one wonder, every time the set is switched on, whether it will actually work! Perfection has replaced chance in radio reception" (*Radio Craft* magazine, March 1938).

The nomenclature lingers on, however, for we still call the power supply voltages in modern audio equipment the "B+" and "B–." *See also* B PLUS.

BBC Over the years, the British Broadcasting Corporation (BBC) has been responsible for much research, innovation, and improvement in the quality of broadcast AUDIO, from the days of Alan BLUMLEIN, to DIGITAL audio and the AMBISONICS system.

Beam Bottle Amateur radio operators' slang for BEAM POWER TUBE.

Beam Power Tube A type of TETRODE vacuum tube in which a set of plates is so arranged that the electron stream from the CATHODE forms two beams directed at the PLATE of the tube. The effect is to increase the efficiency of the tube, increasing its power output for a given size of tube. One of the first beam power tubes, and also the most commercially successful, was the 6L6. All the modern power output tubes, such as the EL-34, EL-84, KT-66, KT-88, 6550, and 5881, are derived from the 6L6 design. Incidentally, the "KT" in the British type designations stands for "kinkless tetrode," ostensibly because of a relatively smooth CHARACTERISTIC CURVE.

Beats When two periodic SIGNALS or sounds are less than 30 HERTZ or so apart in FREQUENCY, and if they are mixed together, the AMPLITUDE of the combined signals will fluctuate as they alternately reinforce and cancel each other. These amplitude fluctuations cause LOUDNESS fluctuations and are called beats. They can most easily be heard when two sounds of equal strength are mixed.

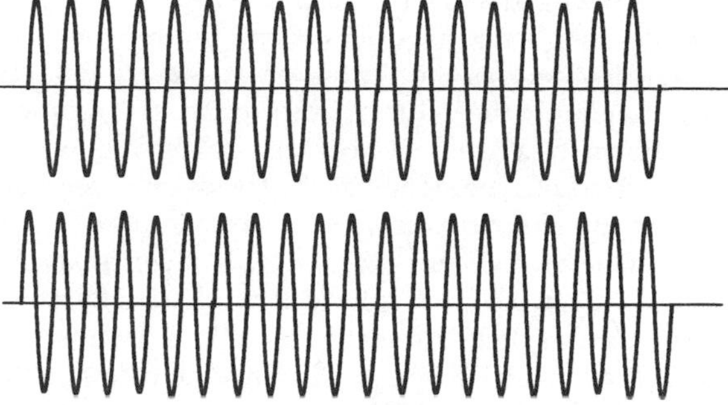

Two components added together to form a complex wave

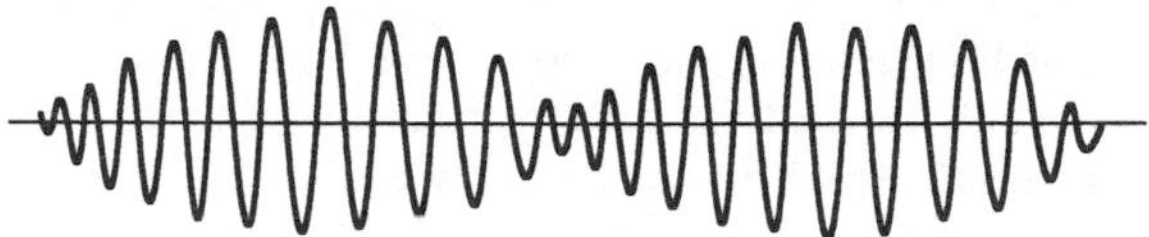

Amplitude fluctuations at a rate equal to the difference in frequency between the two components

Beats

The beat frequency is equal to the difference in frequency between the two signals. When the difference in frequency rises to 30 Hz or so, the beats are so fast that they are heard more as a roughness of the sound rather than as distinct beats. Beats are audible in most musical instruments, and are very useful in the tuning of instruments, for they will disappear when two sounds being tuned together have the same frequency. When complex sounds are mixed, the various PARTIAL components may beat at different rates, giving rise to several simultaneous beat frequencies. It is easy to hear this in the sound of the piano.

Beats are a physical phenomenon, and occur in air when sounds are mixed; they also occur when electrical signals are mixed. In addition, there are subjective beats, which are sometimes heard when a tone of one frequency is heard by one ear and one of a different frequency is heard by the other.

Bessel Crossover, Bessel Filter A type of crossover utilizing low-pass filter design characterized by having a linear PHASE response (or maximally flat phase response), but also a monotonically decreasing PASSBAND amplitude response (which means it starts rolling off at DC and continues throughout the passband). Linear phase response (e.g., a linear plot of phase shift vs. frequency produces a straight line) results in constant time-delay (all frequencies within the passband are delayed the same amount). Consequently the value of linear phase is it reproduces a near-perfect step response, i.e., there is no overshoot or ringing resulting from a sudden transition between signal levels. The drawback is a sluggish roll-off rate. For example, for the same CIRCUIT complexity a Butterworth response rolls off nearly three times as fast. This circuit is based upon Bessel polynomials; however, the filters whose network functions use these polynomials are correctly called Thompson filters [W.E. Thomson, "Delay Networks Having Maximally Flat Frequency Characteristics," *Proc. IEEE,* part 3, vol. 96 (Nov 1949): 487–490]. The fact that we do not refer to these as Thompson crossovers demonstrates, once again, that we do not live in a fair world.[3]

Beta The second letter of the Greek alphabet, β. The current GAIN of a BIPOLAR TRANSISTOR is called the beta. A beta of 100 means that X amount of BASE current will result in 100 times X of collector CURRENT in a transistor.

Beta Hi-Fi Beta Hi-Fi is a method of recording high-quality STEREO sound on Beta format video recorders. The technique was introduced by the Sony Corp., using the same platform as the Sony BETAMAX video recorder system. The signal is companded (*see* COMPANDER) and frequency modulated onto a CARRIER that is recorded in a gap in the BANDWIDTH between the "chrominance" and "luminance" portions of the video signal. The specifications for Beta Hi-Fi are similar to those of most digital systems, offering more than 90 DECIBELS SIGNAL-TO-NOISE RATIO and no WOW or FLUTTER, etc., even though it is entirely ANALOG. The system was developed as an improvement to the original linear audio tracks on videotape.

A similar but incompatible system was developed for the VHS video format recorders invented by JVC. It is called VHS Hi-Fi.

Betamax The first popular method of home video recording, introduced by Sony, now abandoned. *See also* BETA HI-FI.

Biamplification Some LOUDSPEAKER systems with multiple DRIVERS do not contain a CROSSOVER NETWORK, and they require a separate AMPLIFIER for each FREQUENCY range. Such a system is called a biamplified loudspeaker, and the technique is called biamplification.

Because each amplifier in a biamplified system is called on to amplify only a limited frequency range, it will generate less INTERMODULATION DISTORTION, and the system can sound cleaner than a conventional loudspeaker with internal crossover. The biamplified system still requires a crossover network, but it precedes the amplifiers and does not handle the power amplifier output. It thus can be of higher IMPEDANCE and can be made variable in its crossover frequency. This allows a choice of crossover frequency to optimize the performance of the speaker system. Most high-

3. Thanks to Dennis Bohn, Rane Corp.

power commercial sound systems use biamplification. *See also* ACTIVE CROSSOVER.

Bias Bias can be either a small direct VOLTAGE applied to a tube GRID or FIELD EFFECT TRANSISTOR gate along with the signal or a small direct current applied to the BASE of a bipolar TRANSISTOR along with the SIGNAL. The bias moves the operating point on the CHARACTERISTIC CURVE of the device to a more LINEAR portion so as to reduce DISTORTION. The bias must be carefully adjusted to the proper value for optimum effect.

In an ANALOG magnetic tape recorder, bias is an ULTRASONIC signal (usually about 100 kHz) that is mixed with the audio signal and applied to the recording head. The level of the bias is several times as high as the signal level, and its purpose is to reduce distortion by achieving ANHYSTERETIC magnetization of the tape. As the tape passes by the gap in the record head, the high-level bias causes the magnetic domains to be magnetically saturated first in one direction and then the other at the bias FREQUENCY. In so doing they rapidly traverse their nonlinear magnetic HYSTERESIS curve. The audio signal is very much lower in frequency and lower in level than the bias, and it appears to the magnetic particles between the head gap to be a nearly constant magnetic level. As the tape passes the edge of the gap, the effect of the bias is gradually weakened, and the magnetic particles are alternately magnetized as before, but at gradually reduced peak magnetization levels. This gradual reduction in the extremes causes the domains to experience ever-smaller hysteresis curves and leaves the tape magnetized at the slowly varying level of the audio signal. This is the process of AC bias, so named because the bias current is alternating.

The level of the bias must be carefully adjusted for optimum effect. Too little bias increases the distortion, and too much bias reduces the recorded signal level and reduces the high-frequency response of the tape recorder. Adjusting the bias is an important part of tape recorder alignment. *See also* OVERBIAS.

It is possible to use a direct current bias in the tape head along with the signal, and it does reduce the distorting effect of magnetic hysteresis, but it is relatively noisy and results in a relatively small DYNAMIC RANGE. This is called DC bias and has been used in the past in some tape recorders.

Bias Beat A high-frequency whistle is sometimes heard in recordings when two ANALOG tape recorders are connected in order to simultaneously record the same SIGNAL. The beat is the difference in FREQUENCY between the two BIAS frequencies of the two machines. To prevent bias beat, the bias OSCILLATORS must be synchronized so they have the same frequency. This capability was provided in most commercial analog tape recorders.

Bias Trap A special FILTER in the output of a tape recorder to remove any residual BIAS from the signal output when the recorder is actually recording is called a bias trap. The bias, being of a very high FREQUENCY and at a high level, can cause DISTORTION and overload problems in subsequent AUDIO devices if there is no bias trap. When playing an already-recorded tape, the bias OSCILLATOR is not operating, and no bias reaches the output.

Bidirectional Microphone *See* VELOCITY MICROPHONE.

BiFET A type of integrated circuit opamp that has a differential pair of FIELD EFFECT TRANSISTORS as the input stage. They are capable of very low noise levels and very high input impedances and high SLEWING RATES.

Bifilar Winding A method of winding TRANSFORMERS with the primary and secondary coils wound together in one coil. The wires of the primary and secondary are simultaneously wound side by side in the coil. This greatly increases the magnetic coupling between the two circuits and correspondingly reduces the LEAKAGE inductance in the transformer. The output transformers of high-quality vacuum tube power amplifiers are sometimes bifilar wound.

Biflex *See* WHIZZER CONE.

Bifurcate To divide or split into two parts. Many audio connectors use a separable pin and cup contact arrangement, where the spring-loaded bifurcated cup is designed to separate in half slightly when the pin is inserted to maintain firm electrical contact for many use cycles.

BIM *See* BASS INTERMODULATION.

Binary A binary number system uses only two digits, as opposed to the decimal system, which uses ten. Binary numbers consist of a series of ones and zeros, and are easy to implement in computer systems because the presence of a voltage can indicate a 1, while the absence of a voltage indicates a 0.

All DIGITAL audio systems use binary numbers to encode the SIGNALS.

Binaural Literally, "having two ears." Because we have two ears spaced apart by the width of our head, our hearing mechanism can make use of several cues to allow us to determine the direction from which a sound is coming. This ability is called "localization." The localization cues depend on the fact that the two ears hear somewhat different sounds. These differences can be categorized as AMPLITUDE differences, arrival time (PHASE) differences, and spectral (FREQUENCY RESPONSE) differences. If a sound is heard with greater loudness, at an earlier time, or with a greater high-frequency content in one ear than the other, the sound will be localized as coming from that side of the head. The greater the magnitude of the differences, the farther to that side the sound will seem to originate. If there are no differences, the sound will seem to be coming from directly in front of the head.

All three localization mechanisms operate simultaneously. The distance between the ears causes the phase differences, and the shading effect of the head and the shape of the PINNAS cause the amplitude and spectral differences.

Binaural hearing is a very complex phenomenon and is not completely understood. It is one of the topics of PSYCHOACOUSTIC research, which is actively being carried out by several laboratories around the world.

Binaural Dissimilarity The opposite of INTERAURAL CROSS-CORRELATION. A measure of the degree to which the sounds heard by the two ears are different. Listeners tend to prefer environments where the sound has a high binaural dissimilarity rather than low.

Binaural Recording A system of sound recording where the BINAURAL localization cues are preserved, and the listener is able to achieve localization of sounds as if he were actually at the site where the recording was made. Advertising hype notwithstanding, stereophonic techniques, especially two-channel stereo, do not come close to sounding as realistic and natural as properly made binaural recordings.

A binaural recording system consists of a dummy head, complete with PINNAS, with MICROPHONES at the entrances to the ear canals. These microphones are sensitive to the differences in level, arrival times (phase), and spectral content that a person's ears would sense if at the same location. The microphones are connected to a two-channel recorder in the same manner as if a stereo recording were being made. When listening to the resulting recording, each ear must hear only the sound picked up by the corresponding microphone in the dummy head, and for this reason HEADPHONES are used.

The effect of listening to a true binaural recording is completely different from listening to a stereophonic or monophonic recording via headphones. Stereo through headphones gives a greatly exaggerated sense of spaciousness and reverberation that is quite unnatural. A monophonic recording heard via headphones sounds like it originates inside the head instead of in front of the head. Binaural recording has neither of these defects.

It has been found that a binaural recording and reproducing system must have the two channels identical in frequency response and particularly phase characteristics within very narrow limits, especially over the midrange of frequencies from about 500 Hz to 3 kHz. It has also been found that noise reduction systems (see COMPANDER) such as Dolby A, Dolby B, Dolby C, and dbx degrade the localization ability because of slight variations in GAIN, noise, and frequency response between the two channels due to mistracking. Cassette recorders do not provide very good binaural effects because they rely on noise reduction techniques to achieve a satisfactory signal-to-noise ratio. A good digital recorder, with a minimum of signal processing devices between the microphones and the recorder, probably provides the best available medium for true binaural recording. The headphones used must also be extremely well matched if the effect is not to be compromised.

There have been many attempts to convey the binaural effect by using stereophonically recorded material, with varying degrees of success. The STER-BIN developed by Benjamin Bauer was probably the first of these. It was further refined by Martin Thomas and others. These systems reduce the exaggerations present in stereo recordings when heard via headphones but do not eliminate the basic incompatibility of stereo and binaural techniques.

Likewise, there have been many attempts to provide binaural hearing using LOUDSPEAKERS as reproducers rather than headphones. These systems are sometimes called "transaural." A transaural system must compensate for the fact that with loudspeaker listening, each ear hears both speakers rather than just the one it should hear. To do this, a specially equalized and delayed signal is fed to the right speaker in opposite POLARITY to cancel the sound the right ear would hear from the left speaker. The same is done in the other channel. The initial research in this technique was done by Manfred Schroeder in the early 1960s. In the late 1970s, the JVC Corporation produced their BIPHONIC system, which used these results. The Biphonic system sounded quite convincing, but the listener had to be in the SWEET SPOT, a precisely equal distance from the two loudspeakers, for the cancellation to work properly. JVC also experimented with a four-channel system called Q-Biphonic, which used two extra loudspeakers behind the listener and two dummy heads for the original recording.

Others, including Cooper and Bauck, have demonstrated similar systems, and have reported exceptional results when listening in an ANECHOIC environment. The reverberation of the listening room inevitably degrades the signal cancellation in the two ears and compromises the binaural effect.

The first consumer-oriented transaural processor was the Lexicon CP-1 developed by David Griesinger. It was a digital system and had several programs for simulation of different types of acoustical conditions.

Supersonix was a binaural sound system for motion pictures first demonstrated in early 1989 in New York. It used a dummy head for original recording, and each member of the audience wore a binaural headset that could be plugged into phone jacks or could use an infrared link that transmitted the signal to the headsets.

Binaural Synthesis A type of recording-playback system where the BINAURAL microphone dummy head is replaced by two microphones appropriately spaced. The microphone signals must be specially processed to simulate the frequency-dependent time delays that would occur between the ears of a true dummy head.

Binder Binder is the flexible plastic material in which the magnetic particles are embedded in the coating of MAGNETIC TAPE. It must be tough enough to withstand wear and yet remain flexible to allow proper head-to-tape contact in the tape recorder.

Binding Post A binding post is a type of TERMINAL which allows wires, such as LOUDSPEAKER wires, to be connected to the output of an AMPLIFIER. Binding posts usually are designed so they can accept ALLIGATOR CLIPS and BANANA PLUGS as well as bare wires. They are almost always color coded, the black one being the common, or GROUND, and the red one being the "hot" terminal. They are sometimes called five-way binding posts, although one might be hard-pressed to come up with all five ways.

Biphonic An early experimental TRANSAURAL STEREO system, using a dummy head for recording, developed in the late 1970s by JVC. Several years later, JVC extended the system to four channels and called it Q-Biphonic. Neither system was commercialized.

Bipolar Electrolytic A type of ELECTROLYTIC CAPACITOR that does not need a direct polarizing voltage across it to operate properly. It is actually two regular electrolytic capacitors connected back-to-back. Bipolar electrolytics are commonly used in passive LOUDSPEAKER CROSSOVER NETWORKS because they are physically small for their capacitance value and are relatively inexpensive. They will be marked NP (nonpolarized), or have no + or - mark denoting a polarization.

Bipolar Transistor *See* TRANSISTOR.

Birdies Extraneous, high-pitched whistles sometimes heard in tape-recorded signals where the high-frequency content of the signal causes beats with the bias signal. The term is also used to refer to high-pitched interference in AM radio reception.

Biscuit The soft, hot piece of vinyl compound that is placed in an ANALOG record press and from which the record is formed. A biscuit is also stage-hand-speak for a Clear-Com brand intercom box, which had a model number beginning with KB, for King Biscuit.

Bit Depth The size of the digital word used for the audio samples in PCM audio. The bit depth of the CD system is 16 bits. Some devices can operate at 20 or 24 bits, and some reduced FIDELITY formats use 8 bits.

Bite A subjective term for the sharp onset or attack of a musical instrument, especially brass instruments. Bite is usually desired in recordings of such instruments; however, excessive bite can result from positioning microphones too close to the instrument or from DISTORTION caused by a momentary overload.

Bit Rate The time rate at which bits are transmitted in a digital system, expressed in bits per second (bps). The bit rate of the COMPACT DISC is 4.3218 million bps.

Bits Binary digits, abbreviated "bits," are the numbers used in the binary number system. The reason the binary system is used in computers and in DIGITAL AUDIO is that only two numbers, 0 and 1, are needed. This simplifies the electronics system, for a 0 can be represented as the absence of a voltage, while a 1 can be represented by the presence of a voltage. Bits are commonly divided into groups of eight, which are called binary words, or BYTES.

Bitstream A general term for the flow of data in a digital data channel. Also, a system for playback of COMPACT DISCS developed by Philips that performs 256 times OVERSAMPLING (i.e., the sampling rate is 256 times the normal 44.1 kHz rate) using 1-bit words. The normal digital word length in CDs is 16 bits, and to encode the same information with 1-bit words a technique called pulse density modulation is used, with the bits either +1 or –1 and a bit rate of 11.2 megahertz. Pulse density modulation is somewhat similar to DELTA MODULATION. The output of the sampler is a series of pulses, either positive or negative, of equal height and equal width (as opposed to the pulse width modulation technique, which varies the width of the pulses to encode the signal). The average value of the adjacent +1s and –1s is equal to the value of the signal WAVEFORM at that instant. To recover the audio signal, all one needs to do is to average the pulses; this is accomplished with a simple ANALOG low-pass filter of moderate slope, which minimizes any phase shift problems that occur in conventional ANTI-IMAGING FILTERS.

The Bitstream system is more LINEAR than conventional DIGITAL-TO-ANALOG conversion, especially at very low signal levels, and the DISTORTION plus noise is said to be at least 106 dB below the maximum signal level.

Biwire or Bi-wire Biwiring amounts to having a passive LOUDSPEAKER system with the inputs to the high-pass (going to the tweeter) and low-pass (going to the woofer) sections of the crossover separated; they appear at separate terminals on the rear panel. Normally, there are shorting bars across them, in which case the speaker works conventionally (attaching speaker wires to either section drives them both). BUT, if you want, you can remove the shorting bars and attach a pair of wires separately to the two filter inputs. This means that you can select the wiring for each section of the speaker according to their sonic needs (ha!). Similarly, three- and four-way systems can use triwiring or quadwiring. With these systems, you have further options possible in terms of which portions of the system you leave strapped together, and/or you wire (and possibly drive) them separately.

At the AMPLIFIER end, you have other options, depending upon the depth of your pocketbook, or the volume of your bank vault.

1. You can just parallel the wires again and drive them from the same amplifier.

2. You can buy a second (or third or fourth if you are triwiring or quadwiring) power amp, parallel its input with your existing amplifier, and drive each section of the speaker from its own amplifier. You'll note that both amplifiers are operating full range, just that one is not loaded at the high frequencies and one is not loaded at the low frequencies. I don't think that anyone has figured out that you stand to gain more if you filter the inputs to the power amps first. Of course, that would probably interfere with the internal crossovers anyhow but it would still be beneficial even if the filters were somewhat removed from the internal crossover frequency. By eliminating the unneeded signals from the amplifier's input you minimize a potential source of intermodulation distortion.[4] *See also* BIAMPLIFICATION.

Black Box An electronic CIRCUIT of unknown or secret design is sometimes called a black box.

Black Vinyl Black vinyl is a pseudonym for the LP stereo record, sometimes used to distinguish it from the COMPACT DISC. Vinyl need not be black, but it hides bubbles and flaws that might otherwise bother the consumer.

Bleeder A large RESISTOR connected across the big power supply capacitors in audio amps. The bleeder draws current from the supply and prevents the capacitor charging current from climbing too high. In tube

4. Thanks to Rick Chinn, Uneeda Audio.

amplifiers, it prevents the capacitor from suffering over-voltage before the tubes warm up and start drawing current.

Bleedthrough Synonymous with CROSSTALK.

Blimp A soundproof solid cover for a motion picture camera to silence it when shooting on a sound stage. *See also* BARNEY.

Blocked Impedance The electrical IMPEDANCE of a dynamic LOUDSPEAKER measured when the CONE is held or "blocked" so it cannot move. If the cone is allowed to move, the measured impedance will include the mechanical components of the system as well as the electrical impedance.

Blooper Slang term for an early regenerative radio receiver. *See also* REGENERATION.

BL Product The arithmetic product of the length of the wire in a VOICE COIL (*L*) and the strength of the magnetic field (*B*) in the gap in which the coil is immersed. The BL product determines the MAGNETOMOTIVE FORCE that the voice coil experiences for a given coil current and is a measure of the efficiency of the loudspeaker.

Blumlein, Alan The chief engineer at EMI in London in the early 1930s and British pioneer in the study of STEREOPHONIC sound, Alan Blumlein probably made the world's first two-channel phonograph records in 1931. (Bell Telephone Laboratories were experimenting with stereophonic recording in the thirties also, but there seems to be no evidence of any communication between them and Blumlein.) The early Blumlein discs used the two sides of the groove to record the two channels independently, as is done today in modern stereo records. They were thought of as a laboratory curiosity at the time, and no attempt was made to commercialize them. (This was also the case with the Bell Labs recordings.)

Blumlein also did fundamental work in the theory and practice of using COINCIDENT MICROPHONES for stereo recording. He showed that a stereophonic pickup can be achieved from a single point. An interesting and detailed account of his findings can be found in his British patent No. 394325, issued in 1931.

BNC A type of coaxial connector mostly used on test equipment such as oscillators, oscilloscopes, etc., and professional video and digital signals. It is a bayonet type rather than a screw-on type and was invented by Paul Neill and Carl Concelman of the Bell Telephone Laboratories, hence the name BNC (bayonet-Neill-Concelman). Its threaded counterpart is the TNC, but it is less often used although it is a superior connector. 75- and 50-ohm designs are available.

Larry Blake reminds us that BNC also means Blimped Newsreel Camera, the 35 mm Mitchell Camera model BNC that was the industry standard for over thirty years.[5]

Board The control or "mixing" console of a recording studio or sound reinforcement system is often called a board, even though it is generally a very

5. This entry copyright © 1999–2003 by Larry Blake is reprinted with permission.

complex piece of equipment, containing MICROPHONE preamplifiers, volume controls, EQUALIZERS, etc. The lighting control console in theaters is also often called a board. Sometimes PRINTED CIRCUIT BOARDS and CARDS are called boards. Not to be confused with BREADBOARD.

Boom A type of MICROPHONE stand that has a horizontal element to hold the microphone at a distance from where the base of the stand touches the floor. Small units of this type are called "baby booms."

The long poles used to support microphones for recording of motion picture sound are also called booms, or "fishpoles." Portable booms held by sound technicians are designed to be light in weight. Studio booms on SOUND STAGES and TV studios can be quite large and complex, allowing the boom operator to sit on it and to physically zoom and rotate the microphone in order to point it toward the source of the sound being recorded.

Boom is also a derogatory term for the response of low-frequency LOUDSPEAKERS that are poorly DAMPED. *See also* BASS REFLEX.

Boom Box Some poorly designed BASS REFLEX loudspeakers might be called "boom boxes," but there is also a commercial device with this name. It is actually a subharmonic synthesizer, dividing the lowest OCTAVE of the signal input FREQUENCY by two to generate a SIGNAL one octave lower. This signal is then either mixed with the input signal at the output of the device or is sent to a separate AMPLIFIER and then to a SUBWOOFER.

The boom box, of course, has nothing to do with accuracy of sound reproduction and is meant to add another octave to the bass response of a sound system. It has been used to good advantage in some movie theater sound systems, where it can make sound effects such as explosions more convincing. Also a portable stereo, AKA "ghetto blaster."

Boomy The subjective effect of excessive bass response or lack of low-frequency DAMPING in a LOUDSPEAKER system. Some early (and some present-day) resonant loudspeaker systems were called BOOM BOXES because of this effect.

Boost Boost refers to an increase in AMPLITUDE, usually within a specific FREQUENCY or frequency range. Boost/Cut EQUALIZERS, the most common of which are TONE CONTROLS, cause an amplification (boost) or a reduction (CUT) of selected frequency ranges.

Bootstrap A clever arrangement where the apparent IMPEDANCE of a CIRCUIT element is reduced by applying an appropriate FEEDBACK voltage to it. Bootstrapping can improve the LINEARITY of a circuit and thus reduce DISTORTION. It is especially useful in circuits that are required to carry a very wide range of power or voltage levels. Bootstrapping is also sometimes used in EQUALIZATION circuits. Probably the term "booting" a computer comes from the early computer improvement of being able to start by itself, by its own bootstraps, so to speak.

Bottle Slang term for a vacuum tube, especially power output tubes used by amateur radio operators.

Bottoming The mechanical striking of the moving parts of a LOUDSPEAKER or other TRANSDUCER against the magnet structure as a result of too high a drive level. Bottoming, or "bottoming out," can quickly damage a speaker, so care must be taken to prevent it. The acoustic load on a speaker has a great deal to do with how easy it is to bottom and is therefore a factor in the protection of the system. WOOFERS in infinite BAFFLES, for instance, are effectively loaded at very low frequencies, whereas woofers in vented cabinets are not and are thus more prone to damage from very low frequency signals or transients.

Bounce On a multitrack recording device, to re-record mixes of certain tracks onto other tracks, thus freeing tracks for other use.

Boundary Microphone *See* PZM.

B Plus, or B+ In the early days of radio, receiving sets were battery-powered, and the batteries were called by different code letters depending on their function. The "A" battery was a low-VOLTAGE, high-CURRENT battery that was used to supply current to the TUBE heaters. The "B" battery was a high-voltage, relatively low-current battery used to supply the positive voltage for the tube PLATES. The "C" battery was of low voltage and low-current capacity, and supplied the BIAS voltage for the tube grids.

Nowadays, with tubes rarely used and battery-powered tube equipment seldom used, these terms are obsolete. AUDIO equipment still requires electric power and this is obtained from the AC line via a power supply, which is a group of CIRCUITS that generate and regulate various voltages for use by the device. The main voltage, which is used to supply current to the transistors, is called the B+ as a holdover from the old days. The plus means it is positive with respect to GROUND.

Many AMPLIFIERS and other devices also need a voltage that is negative with respect to ground, and this is called B–. A power supply that makes both B+ and B– is called a "bipolar" supply. This is not to be confused with bipolar TRANSISTOR. Sometimes the B+ and B– are called supply rails.

Breadboard A breadboard is an experimental electronic CIRCUIT, put together temporarily to test a particular configuration, or TOPOLOGY. The term comes from the early days of radio when experimenters supposedly used the family breadboard as a base on which to construct such things as CRYSTAL SETS.

The term is also used as a verb; to "breadboard" is to make a breadboard circuit.

Break Before Make A type of selector switch in which the movable contact, or "wiper," breaks the connection with one CIRCUIT before it makes a new contact with the next selected circuit. Most audio applications call for "make before break" switches to reduce clicks and pops when switching.

Breakdown Voltage The REVERSE VOLTAGE that, when applied to a semiconductor junction, causes a sudden increase in REVERSE CURRENT. The junction is then said to be operating in the avalanche condition.

Breakout Cable Any form of cable adapter that converts a multiconductor connector into many separate cables. Since many products are too small to physically mount all the connectors needed, a breakout cable converts the multiple contacts of a small connector into several cables with normal connectors. Another example is a MICROPHONE cable breakout, a multiple-wire flexible cable containing several microphone lines that is connected to the microphone inputs of a mixing console with a multi-pin connector and terminates in several microphone input connectors (usually XLR-3 female) at the far end. These breakout cables, also commonly called "snakes," are often used in recording studios and sound reinforcement venues, and they are much more convenient to deploy and use than a similar number of individual microphone cables. Multichannel cables that do not employ a multi-pin connector at the end are usually called SNAKES.

Breakup *See* CONE BREAKUP.

Breathing The audible variation in the background noise level of a sound system that has some type of NOISE REDUCTION is called breathing, or "noise pumping." *See also* COMPANDER.

Brickwall Filter Some LOW-PASS FILTERS have such a steep cutoff slope that they resemble a "brick wall." Brickwall filters are of several design types, and are used for ANTI-ALIASING and ANTI-IMAGING filters.

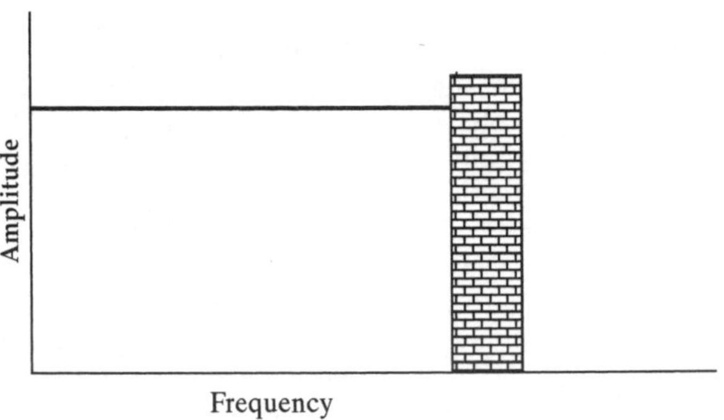

Brickwall Filter

Bridge Disc A COMPACT DISC that contains information that can be read by CD-ROM/XA drives and also CD-I players. The specifications for the Bridge Disc were released in the "White Book" in 1991. The Kodak Photo CD is an example of a Bridge Disc, and it can be played on a Photo CD player, a CD-I player, and a CD-ROM/XA player.

Bridging In a sense, bridging is the opposite of MATCHING. When the input of an AUDIO device is connected to the output of another device, it is a bridging connection if the second device does not appreciably LOAD the previous device and essentially no power is transferred. The second device is sensitive to the output VOLTAGE of the first device, and this is maximized when the loading is minimized. This is an example of deliberately mismatching the IMPEDANCES. Most audio connections are bridging, although in systems involving very long lines (e.g., telephone systems), the impedances must be matched to prevent reflections of the SIGNAL at the ends of the line from causing an audible echo.

Generally, a CIRCUIT is said to be bridged if the LOAD IMPEDANCE is at least five or ten times the OUTPUT IMPEDANCE.

Another use of the term bridging is in the connection of two power amplifiers in such a way as to give one double the power output. To do this, the signal is fed to one AMPLIFIER normally, but it is inverted (its POLARITY is reversed) before sending it to the other amplifier. This puts the amplifier outputs out of PHASE with each other. The load is then connected between the high, or "hot," terminals of the two amplifiers. The effective voltage swing seen by the load is thus doubled and the current carrying capacity is unchanged, so the power output is doubled. STEREO amplifiers are sometimes "bridged" in this way to make mono amplifiers of more power.

Bridging Transformer An AUDIO transformer with a relatively high IMPEDANCE primary that is designed to operate when connected to a low-impedance CIRCUIT so as to prevent any LOADING of the circuit. Bridging transformers permit connection of several circuits, such as lines, to a single circuit without affecting its impedance. Usually a bridging transformer is made by simply adding series RESISTORS in the primary circuit. The output, or secondary, of the bridging transformer is not able to supply any significant power to its load. The bridging transformer is an example of a case where impedances are deliberately mismatched.

Broadband Broadband means encompassing or consisting of a wide band of frequencies, as opposed to NARROWBAND, which contains a relatively small BANDWIDTH. Almost all music is considered a broadband SIGNAL. Some EQUALIZERS, such as TONE CONTROLS, are broadband in action because they affect a large bandwidth of the signal.

A high-speed internet connection, such as DSL (digital subscriber line) or a cable modem is also called a broadband connection.

Brute Force *See* REGULATION.

Bucket Brigade The bucket brigade, also called a charge transfer device (CTD) or a CHARGE-COUPLED DEVICE (CCD), is a type of time delay INTEGRATED CIRCUIT for sampled signals. It consists of a series of small capacitors and a switching circuit whereby the charge from one capacitor is transferred to the next one and to the next, etc., in response to a series of timing pulses. The charges move along the line much like the buckets of water in a firefighters' bucket brigade. It is important that the size of the charge does not change as it passes from one storage capacitor to the next, for otherwise the SIGNAL will become distorted as it is passed down the line.

The bucket brigade is actually a specialized form of shift register, but it is not a digital device, for the charges are analogs of the magnitude of the sampled signal. If the signal has been digitized before entering the delay line, then the amplitude accuracy of each charge is not important, because each charge simply represents a BINARY digit, or BIT, rather than an instantaneous magnitude of the signal itself. For this reason, shift registers are much better at delaying digital data than analog data.

Bucket brigades are used in some relatively inexpensive audio delay devices such as reverberators.

Bucking The cancellation of one SIGNAL or FREQUENCY component of a signal by another signal with equal AMPLITUDE but opposite POLARITY is called bucking. *See also* HUM BUCKING; PHASING; FLANGING.

Buffer A temporary location in a computer's or digital signal processor's memory for temporarily storing digital data that is being processed or transmitted.

Bulk Eraser *See* DEGAUSSER.

Burst A burst is a test signal that lasts only a short time, typically a few milliseconds. A burst of a SINUSOID is called a TONE BURST, and a burst of WHITE or PINK NOISE is called a noise burst.

The term burst has a special meaning in television systems. The NTSC "color burst" is a short burst of a high-frequency CARRIER that is included as a part of the video signal. It is modulated with the color information.

Burst Error In the reading of the individual BITS from a COMPACT DISC (CD) or a digitally encoded tape, two types of erroneous readings can occur. Individual bits can be misread at random; these are called bit errors and are caused by tiny imperfections on the CD or tape surface. Errors that occur in groups of adjacent symbols are called burst errors. They are caused by dirt and scratches in the medium.

Error correction schemes in DIGITAL tape and CD systems depend on knowing the data adjacent to the burst. The "maximum correctable burst error" is a very important specification for such an error-correction method.

Bus A bus is a point in an electronic CIRCUIT where many connections are brought together. For instance, a GROUND bus is a common connection for all the grounds in a device. The bus will then be connected to the CHASSIS at one point, usually near the SIGNAL input connector. A mixing bus is the point in an audio mixer where the various signals from different MICROPHONE preamps are connected. It is the point at which the mixing is actually done.

Sometimes the term is used for a bundle of wires that are not connected but are used for parallel transmission of DIGITAL data, sometimes in two directions. This is called a data bus.

Butterworth Filter A multiple-section FILTER designed in accordance with the so-called Butterworth polynomials.

The Butterworth filter is usually an RLC filter, meaning it contains RESISTORS, CAPACITORS, and INDUCTORS, although it can be realized as an ACTIVE filter using capacitors, resistors, and amplifying stages. Because of its lack of any peak in its response CURVE, it is sometimes called a "maximally flat" filter. It usually contains more than two sections and is made with up to twelve POLES, or six sections. It is suitable for use as an ANTI-ALIASING filter in DIGITAL audio devices. It was named after S. Butterworth, a British engineer who first described it in his paper "On the Theory of Filter Amplifiers," *Wireless Engineer*, vol. 7 (1930): 536–41.

Butt Splice A type of tape splice used in EDITING where the ends of the two pieces of tape to be joined are cut at a 90-degree angle and then butted together and fastened with splicing tape. The butt splice results in an instantaneous transfer from one "take" to the other and frequently adds a transient, or click, to the sound. For this reason, butt splices are seldom used, and the tape is usually cut at an angle, such as 30 or 45 degrees, so the transition is more gentle.

In the case of DIGITAL editing, which is usually all electronic, one SIGNAL is rapidly FADED out while the other is faded in. This is called a "cross-fade." If the digital splice is instantaneous, it is then still called a butt splice, even though no actual splicing of the tape is performed.

BWF (Broadcast Wave Format) A digital audio file format introduced by the EBU in 1996 to facilitate professional editing and file exchange. It is a special case of Microsoft's WAV format, but adds extra information deemed important for professional use such as titles, date, time, origination, editing data, etc. It is increasingly used on DAWS and digital recorders.

BWF only carries linear PCM and MPEG audio. Its filename extension is not .bwf as one might expect, but .wav, as it is merely considered a subset of .wav. *See also* WAV.

Byte In DIGITAL systems, the binary BITS are grouped into words. A byte is a binary word of eight bits. The information-storage capacity of digital systems is measured in bytes or kilobytes. The astute reader may assume that a kilobyte consists of 1,000 bytes, but this is not true, for a kilobyte actually contains 1,024 bytes! This is because 1,024 is a power of 2, whereas 1,000 is not. Learning such irregularities is one of the keys to becoming proficient in the domain of digital systems and computers. *See* Appendix 10.

C

Calendering In order to reduce the ASPERITIES in the surface of magnetic tape, the tape is squeezed between giant polished metal rollers. This process is called calendering, and is derived from the paper industry, that uses a similar process of the same name to make very smooth shiny paper.

Cakebox When ordering bulk quantities of blank CD-R discs or other optical storage media, they often are packed on a spindle and covered with shrink-wrap plastic. These units are called "cakeboxes," although they usually are rather tall and thin compared to a standard edible cake unless they are packed fifty discs or fewer at a time.

Cans Slang for HEADPHONES.

Cannon Connector, Cannon Plug Literally any connector made by Cannon, but popular usage usually means an XLR-3 connector, a type that was introduced by Cannon. This is the most common connector used on MICROPHONE cables. XLR-3 connectors are made by many manufacturers and are a worldwide standard. *See also* XLR CONNECTOR.

Cantilever The tiny rod, usually of light tubular metal, that holds the STYLUS in a phonograph CARTRIDGE and couples its motion to the sensing elements that generate the output signal. The cantilever must be very light and stiff to ensure that it has a resonant frequency above the audible range. *See also* CARTRIDGE.

Cap Short for CAPACITOR.

Capacitance Capacitance is the quantitative measure of the electrical effect of a CAPACITOR, and its unit is the farad (in honor of Michael Faraday, the brilliant English investigator who studied electrostatic effects), abbreviated F. Capacitors are able to store electric charge; the amount of charge is the VOLTAGE across the capacitor times the capacitance in farads. 1 volt would impress 1 COULOMB of charge on a capacitor of 1 farad.

The farad is a very large unit, and the more convenient microfarad (μF, or one millionth of a farad), and picofarad (pF, or one million millionth of a farad) are commonly used in practice.

Capacitors react to alternating currents in a somewhat complex way, and this characteristic is called CAPACITIVE REACTANCE.

Capacitive Reactance Capacitive reactance is the part of IMPEDANCE that is due to CAPACITANCE in a CIRCUIT. Capacitors have some RESISTANCE, and the CURRENT in this resistance obeys OHM'S LAW, but the current in the capacitive portion of the capacitor does not. The current in a capacitor is equal to the capacitance times the rate of change of VOLTAGE across it. In other words, at a constant voltage, as FREQUENCY goes up, the current in a capacitor also rises. (This is the opposite of what happens in an INDUCTOR.)

Because the capacitor has an impedance that varies with frequency, it can be (and is) used in EQUALIZERS. The value of capacitive reactance is calculated as follows:

$$X_C = \frac{1}{2\pi f}$$

where Xc = Capacitive Reactance,
and F = frequency in hertz

The capacitor passes very rapid changes in current with ease but has difficulty in passing very slowly changing currents and will not pass DC at all. The voltage across a capacitor lags behind the current by 90 degrees; i.e., the capacitor has 90 degrees of PHASE SHIFT.

Capacitor An electronic component that has CAPACITANCE. It used to be called a CONDENSER, but modern usage favors the more accurate term.

Some capacitors, however, still use the old terminology, such as CONDENSER MICROPHONE and TUNING CONDENSER.

Capacitors accumulate electrical CHARGE according to the law that says the charge Q equals the VOLTAGE V times the capacitance C. *See also* CAPACITIVE REACTANCE.

There has been a great deal of raising of eyebrows (an exercise much practiced in the audio industry) about the relative merits of different types of capacitors for use in audio circuits. On the surface, it seems that a capacitor is a capacitor, and as long as its capacitance and voltage ratings are correct for an application, it will do its job perfectly; many people adhere to this view. After all, it only has to separate AC signals from direct voltages in most applications, or in some cases its variable reactance with frequency is utilized. However, if one looks more closely, the capacitor is subject to a host of potential problems. For instance, capacitors that are made by rolling up strips of conducting foil with the DIELECTRIC in between will also have some INDUCTANCE, and this can cause problems, mostly at high frequencies. Many such capacitors will actually resonate by themselves, as if they were wired in an LC CIRCUIT. *See also* Q. Some capacitors also exhibit nonlinearity in the sense that their capacitance and LEAKAGE current vary a little with the signal level.

Another type of nonlinearity possessed by some capacitors is nonsymmetry, meaning their capacitance is different for positive and negative swings of the signal. These nonlinearities add DISTORTION to the signal, especially if the offending capacitor is in a FEEDBACK loop of an AMPLIFIER.

Capstan In a tape recorder, the rotating part that drives the tape past the heads is the capstan. Usually, the tape is squeezed between the capstan and a rubber wheel known as the PINCH ROLLER or PUCK.

One would expect the tape speed to be equal to the surface speed of the capstan, but this is not exactly true. If the capstan has a small diameter, so that the tape makes a significant curve where it makes contact, it will actually move faster than the surface speed due to the "belting" action of the tape. Furthermore, thick tapes will move faster than thin ones. The effect is quite small, but can be measured. This means that a tape with a splice in it will move faster as the splice goes over the capstan, causing a slight rise in pitch. This change in speed can be heard in some recordings, especially if very thin tape is used.

Capstan Drive Motor A motor drives the capstan in a tape recorder. Most professional-quality tape recorders will have a separate motor to turn the capstan, traditionally an AC synchronous motor, which means its speed is determined by the line frequency rather than the voltage. Thus, it will run at a constant speed regardless of voltage fluctuations. Most modern tape recorders use DC motors, which are servo-controlled, to drive the capstan, and this facilitates varying the speed. *See also* VARI-SPEED.

Capstan Idler Synonymous with PINCH ROLLER, or PUCK.

Capsule The business end of a CONDENSER MICROPHONE is sometimes called a capsule. The capsule is the TRANSDUCER, and it contains all the microphone's elements except the PREAMPLIFIER. In some MICROPHONES, the capsule is removable and interchangeable with others having different directional characteristics.

Some manufacturers use the term "cartridge" for the same device, but CARTRIDGE is more commonly used for a phonograph transducer.

Capture Ratio The ability of an FM receiver to lock onto, or "capture," a broadcasting station in the presence of an interfering signal near the same FREQUENCY. Capture ratio is expressed in DECIBELS, and the smaller the number, the better. A capture ratio of 1.5 dB means the receiver will lock onto a signal only 1.5 dB stronger than the unwanted one.

Carbon Microphone The carbon microphone was one of the earliest types of MICROPHONE to be devised and is still widely used in older telephones. It consists of a metal diaphragm, one side of which makes contact with some small carbon granules contained in a small receptacle. When the diaphragm moves in response to SOUND PRESSURE, the granules are alternately compressed and relaxed, and their combined RESISTANCE to an electric CURRENT changes. This causes the current to vary in response to the sound pressure WAVEFORM, and this constitutes the signal from the microphone. This arrangement is not a perfect TRANSDUCER, and it suffers from noticeable DISTORTION and noise compared with most modern microphone types. However, the carbon microphone is very well suited to telephone usage because its sensitivity increases with sound pressure level. This makes it more sensitive to a nearby voice and much less sensitive to background sounds in the room. This peculiar effect has been called a "serendipitous nonlinearity" by our friend John Bareham.

The carbon microphone was developed by Thomas Edison while he was under contract with Alexander Graham Bell, who patented the design. It was also used in the early days of radio broadcasting, but it has long been obsolete in this application.

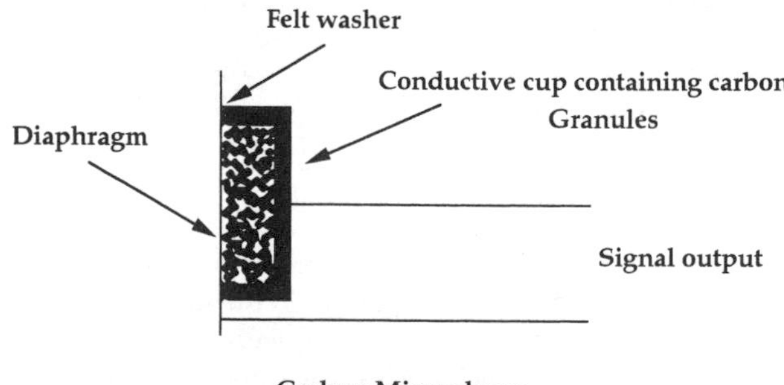

Carbon Microphone

Card A small PRINTED CIRCUIT BOARD is often called a card, from its similarity in size and shape to a playing card. Cards are often designed so they plug into a socket, which may be mounted on another circuit board. This larger board is called a "MOTHER" board, and the cards are then called "daughter" boards. (This may be an example of the essential lack of sexism in the audio world.)

Cardioid Cardioid literally means "heart-shaped," and any MICROPHONE that has a heart-shaped POLAR PATTERN is called a cardioid microphone. The cardioid is most sensitive to sounds arriving from the front, is 6 DECIBELS less sensitive to sounds from 90 degrees to the sides, and, theoretically, is completely insensitive to sounds coming from the rear. In practice, the directional qualities of a cardioid are not fully realized due to reflected sounds from room walls and ceiling entering the sensitive area of the microphone.

The most important attribute of the cardioid is its ability to discriminate between direct sounds (coming from the direction in which the microphone is pointed) and REVERBERANT sounds, which are coming from all other directions at random. Compared to an OMNIDIRECTIONAL microphone, the cardioid will give a direct-to-reverberant ratio about 4.5 dB higher. That is, the direct sound will be about 4.5 dB stronger than the reverberant sound, and this improves the subjective clarity of the received sound.

Another way to state the same fact is that a cardioid may be placed 1.7 times as far from a sound source in a room as an omni and it will give the same subjective ratio of direct and reverberant sound. This is an advantage when the microphone should not be seen, such as in motion picture recording, etc. In most real cases, however, an omni microphone can be placed about two-thirds as far away as a cardioid, and not only will the reverber-

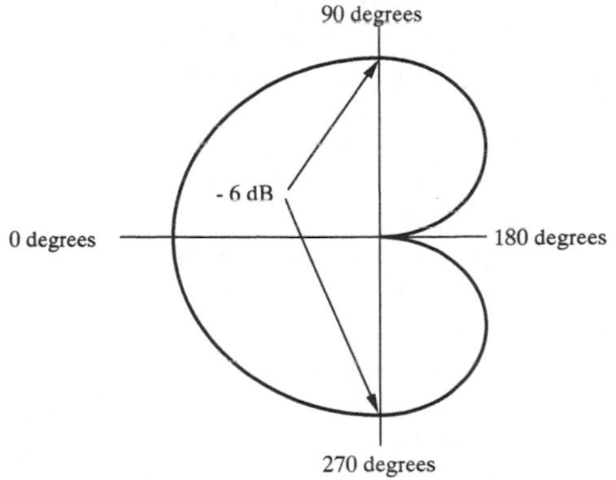

Sensitivity vs. angle for a cardioid microphone (the curve is more flattened if plotted in decibels)

Cardioid Polar Pattern

ant balance be the same, but the quality will usually be better because omni microphones are usually smoother and have a wider sound range than cardioids. Also, cardioids suffer from PROXIMITY EFFECT when they are near sound sources, while omni microphones do not.

One of the most important uses of cardioid microphones is in sound reinforcement, where the directivity allows the system GAIN to be higher without generating acoustic FEEDBACK. *See also* SUPERCARDIOID; HYPERCARDIOID.

Carrier The high-frequency SIGNAL transmitted by a radio or television station after having been AMPLITUDE MODULATED or FREQUENCY MODULATED by the audio or video signal. Theoretically, the carrier could be any frequency, and in broadcasting the carrier frequencies are chosen based on considerations of ease of generating high power output, required antenna size, etc. In the U.S., the AM radio band has carriers between 550 and 1650 kilohertz, and the FM and television bands use frequencies between 54 and 806 megahertz.

The carrier itself does not transmit any information; all the intelligence is in the modulation SIDEBANDS, which are in a band of frequencies on either side of the carrier frequency. The carrier is used by the receiver to aid in the DEMODULATION, or DETECTION, of the signal.

Some signals, such as FM STEREO, involve more than one carrier to encode the information. The lower frequency carrier is called a subcarrier, and it is mixed with certain parts of the audio signal and used to modulate the main carrier. In the receiver, the subcarrier is recovered by demodulation of the main carrier, and it is then demodulated to recover its signal.

Cart Machine Broadcasters' slang for "tape cartridge machine," which is a playback machine that uses endless loops of tape in plastic cartridges. Commercials and announcements are recorded on carts, and some of the playback machines can handle a dozen or so of them, something like a record changer. Now obsolete, they were replaced by MINIDISCS and other digital storage systems.

Cartridge, Phono Cartridge The cartridge is the TRANSDUCER that converts the motion of the phonograph STYLUS into an electrical VOLTAGE. This voltage is the output SIGNAL of the cartridge.

There are several kinds of phono cartridge, but the MOVING MAGNET and MOVING COIL types are the most common. In the moving magnet cartridge, a very small magnet is made to vibrate in response to the MODULATION of the record groove. This motion induces a current in two nearby coils of wire, one for each stereo channel. The moving magnet cartridge is characterized by relatively high output voltage and relatively low cost, although some good-quality examples are quite costly. Almost all such units are made to operate correctly when connected to a 47,000-ohm LOAD. Virtually all phono PREAMPS thus have an INPUT IMPEDANCE of 47,000 OHMS.

The moving coil cartridge contains two tiny coils of wire, which are made to vibrate in accordance with the record groove modulation. They are in the magnetic field of a small stationary permanent magnet; thus a signal current is induced in them. Moving coil cartridges are characterized by relatively high prices, very low output voltages, and very low output impedance, in some cases as low as a few ohms. This means they require either a TRANSFORMER or a PRE-PREAMP between them and the phono preamp.

As usual in audio, there is some controversy over which is the best type of cartridge, and it is difficult to present objective data that clearly favor either one. Some comments may be appropriate, however:

The moving coil types have very low mass, and thus very high RESONANCE frequencies, sometimes as high as 60 KILOHERTZ or so. Even though this is above the audible range, it can cause subtle DISTORTION of the sound. This resonance is very difficult to DAMP, and as a result, the output of the cartridge rises very much at high frequencies. This means the preamp (and pre-preamp) are subjected to high levels of ULTRASONIC noise from the record surface, and this can cause INTERMODULATION distortion in the audible range. This means that an expensive moving coil cartridge used with a mediocre-quality preamp usually sounds worse than an inexpensive moving magnet with the same preamp. Also, the very low output voltages can lead to SIGNAL-TO-NOISE RATIO problems unless the pre-preamp is very quiet. On the other hand, they tend to be more LINEAR, and the HARMONIC DISTORTION of moving coils is lower than that of moving magnets.

The moving magnet cartridges are somewhat easier to use than the moving coils because of their higher output and the wide availability of phono preamps with the correct input characteristics. They also generally have user-replaceable stylus assemblies, whereas moving coils usually do not.

CAS Cinema Audio Society, an honorary group of people in the motion picture sound industry.

Cathode The negatively charged terminal of a COMPONENT such as a DIODE or battery is called the cathode. CURRENT, which is defined as a flow of CHARGE, was thought by Benjamin Franklin to be in the direction from ANODE to cathode. Franklin, who established many of our conventions regarding ELECTRICITY, thought the charged particles which constitute electric current were positively charged, but today we know that they are negatively charged (electrons). So the actual current is in the direction from cathode to anode, although many old-timers (the writers included) still cling to the old convention of "positive charge." As long as one is consistent, there is no problem with this.

Cathode Bias A method of applying BIAS to a vacuum TUBE by placing a resistor between the CATHODE and GROUND. The CURRENT in the resistor forces the cathode to be at a higher potential than ground, and the GRID, if referenced to ground, will be at a negative potential with respect to the cathode. Cathode bias provides a certain amount of negative FEEDBACK around the tube, along with some reduction in GAIN. If the cathode resistor is shunted by a large CAPACITOR, called a bypass capacitor, the AC gain is restored and the feedback reduced.

Cathode Follower If the PLATE of a vacuum TUBE is connected to a positive VOLTAGE supply without a series RESISTOR, and if the CATHODE has a series resistor to GROUND, the cathode will vary in its VOLTAGE in the same manner as the GRID. This arrangement is called a cathode follower. It is characterized by a very high INPUT IMPEDANCE, a very low OUTPUT IMPEDANCE, a voltage GAIN of less than 1, and a very high current gain. It also has very low DISTORTION, and is used as an impedance MATCHING device for driving long lines, such as between PREAMPLIFIERS and power AMPLIFIERS.

With the general adoption of SOLID-STATE equipment, the cathode follower is essentially obsolete. Similar techniques are used in solid-state circuits to achieve low impedances.

Cathode Ray Tube, or CRT Traditionally the active display device in an OSCILLOSCOPE, the "picture tube" in a television set, and the display for a computer, often called simply CRT. Newer technologies such as liquid crystal and plasma displays are replacing the CRT.

The CRT was invented by Dr. Vladimir K. Zworykin of RCA laboratories in the 1930s. An evacuated glass tube contains an "electron gun," which emits a stream of electrons, and a fluorescent screen on which the electrons impinge. On their way from the gun to the screen, the electrons are accelerated by a high-VOLTAGE electric field, and they are deflected in their path by voltages applied to deflection plates adjacent to the gun in the case of the oscilloscope, or by magnetic fields from a deflection yoke of wire coils placed around the neck of the TV picture tube. Electrons have very little mass and are easy to deflect even though they are moving very fast. This ability to rapidly deflect the beam makes the CRT useful for looking at the instantaneous voltage of a changing WAVEFORM, as in the oscilloscope. When the electrons hit the screen, they are rapidly decelerated, and in so doing, they emit a certain amount of X-ray radiation. The amount depends

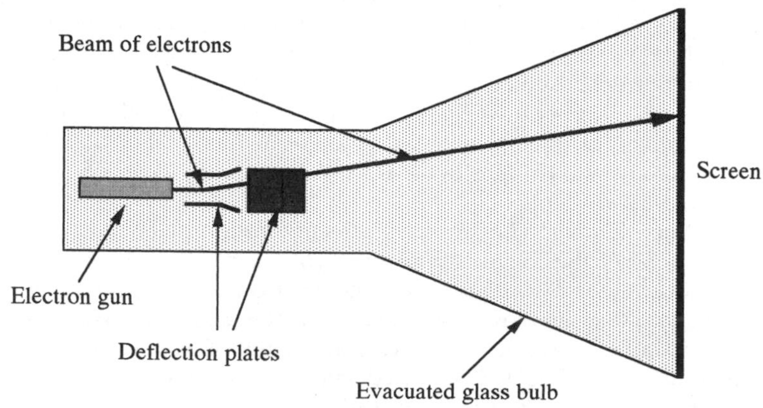

Cathode Ray Tube

on the accelerating voltage used in the CRT, so large CRT computer screens and TV screens make X-rays that would be harmful to computer users and TV watchers. To prevent X-ray exposure, the glass in the business end of the CRT contains a fairly large quantity of lead, which is a good X-ray absorber. The larger the screen, the more lead required, and this causes large-screen TVs and large CRT computer screens to be inordinately heavy for their size.

Cat's Whisker *See* CRYSTAL SET.

CAV, Constant Angular Velocity When a phonograph or laserdisc maintains a constant RPM, the LINEAR VELOCITY at the pickup decreases as the diameter gets smaller. The problem with a phonograph disc is that since the actual speed of the disc surface past the stylus is faster at the outer edge of the disc and much slower at the inside of the disc, the FREQUENCY RESPONSE declines and DISTORTION increases as the record is played. In the case of the LASERDISC (Laser Video Disc, LVD), this is not a problem, and CAV refers to an original formatting of the disc that places each video field on exactly ½ of the diameter no matter where on the disc. This design simplified slow motion and stop frame effects on early players with electromechanical control. It also limited playing time to 30 minutes per side, so a constant linear velocity laserdisc was introduced with an hour of playing time per side. The introduction of digital video buffer memory allowed decent still frame and slow motion effects on CLV discs. *See also* CLV.

C Battery In the early days of radio, receiving sets were all battery powered if they were not crystal sets. The low-VOLTAGE, high-current A battery supplied power to the tube heaters, and the high-voltage, low-current B battery supplied the voltage for the tube plates. An addition in the mid-1920s was the C battery, which supplied a low voltage at very low current to provide BIAS to the tube GRIDS. The bias reduced the distortion considerably, but most set owners thought the major benefit of the C battery was to reduce plate current, allowing the B battery to last much longer.

CCD *See* BUCKET BRIGADE.

CCIR CCIR was an international organization concerned with the setting of standards and practices for audio and broadcast equipment. CCIR stood for Comité Consultatif International Radio and was analogous to the National Association of Broadcasters (NAB) in the United States. The CCIR joined the ITU in 1992 and became ITU-R, the division dealing with radio communications and standards. CCIR standards are generally now IEC standards.

Many European tape recorders use CCIR-designed PRE-EMPHASIS and DE-EMPHASIS curves; tapes made on them are incompatible with ones recorded in the United States. It is interesting to note that a good case can be made for the idea that U.S.-made tapes are more suited to CCIR EQUALIZATION, while European tapes are better optimized by the NAB curves. This is an example of the Law of Probabilistic Adversity.

CD, Compact Disc. The original 120 mm DIGITAL optical disc format invented by Sony and Philips in 1982. It is fully specified in the RED BOOK, and all other CD formats are derived from it. It was originally known as CD-DA for Compact Disc-Digital Audio.

CD-DA, Compact Disc Digital Audio The original name of what we know today as simply the CD, or COMPACT DISC.

CD Horn EQ *See* CONSTANT DIRECTIVITY HORN.

CD+G A special COMPACT DISC format that allows simple graphics and text to be stored in the SUBCODES of an audio CD. A special player is needed to display the data, such as a special karaoke player.

CD-I Acronym for Compact Disc–Interactive. A digital disc system for storing video, audio, and graphics information in such a way that the user can control the presentation of the various media. The CD-I standard was released by Philips and Sony in the "Green Book" in 1987.

CD-MIDI A CD format that stores MIDI information in the SUBCODE area.

CD-R, Compact Disc Recordable A recordable optical disc with the same physical dimensions as the normal COMPACT DISC. CD recorders are common in computers, and many stand-alone units are available for home use. CD-Rs can be used for recording music or recording computer data as in CD-ROMS. CD-R audio recorders for home use usually require a special "music" CD-R that has a special code on the blank. Extra fees for music CD-R blanks go to a music industry fund.

CD-ROM Acronym for Compact Disc–Read Only Memory. The COMPACT DISC medium modified to store computer information rather than audio. This is analogous to a magnetic hard drive in a computer, except the storage is by optical means and once created, the CD-ROM can only be read from and not written to. The CD-ROM must be used in conjunction with a computer to retrieve the data.

CD-ROM XA A CD specification defined in 1988 by Philips, Sony, and Microsoft as an extension of the Yellow Book standard. The XA stands for Extended Architecture. The format shares many traits of the CD-I.

CDS *See* CINEMA DIGITAL SOUND.

CD-Single A small COMPACT DISC that can record 20 minutes of STEREO music. It is 80 mm in diameter. The record industry will sometimes make a standard size CD with one or two songs on it and call it a CD single.

CD-V Acronym for Compact Disc-Video. The COMPACT DISC medium modified to record video signals as well as digital stereo audio signals. The video information is recorded in ANALOG form rather than digital. The system was compatible with the LASERDISC system and is similarly obsolete. Not to be confused with Video CD, which is a digital audio/video format compatible with many DVD players.

CEDAR, Computer Enhanced Digital Audio Restoration CEDAR Audio began as a research project between the British National Sound Archive and Cambridge University in the mid-1980s for restoring the sound of old media such as discs, cylinders, and film. Now a commercial enterprise, they manufacture CEDAR noise reduction products and offer "denoising" and restoration services on existing recordings.

Cell A single unit of an electrical battery is a cell, even though cells are often called batteries, as in "flashlight battery." Various types of cells produce VOLTAGES between 1 and 3 V depending on the chemicals involved; most are around 1.5 V.

Centering Device The flexible mounting that allows the VOICE COIL of a CONE-type LOUDSPEAKER to move in and out of the magnetic gap but prevents it from striking the sides of the gap. *See also* SPIDER.

Center Tap The center tap is an electrical connection to the center of a TRANSFORMER winding. The VOLTAGE at the center tap will be midway between the voltages at the two ends of the winding, and this is often the GROUND potential in an AUDIO device. Frequently, center taps of audio transformers are connected to the CHASSIS of the device. This has the effect of reducing the 60-HERTZ, COMMON-MODE voltages in the CIRCUIT and thus reducing the HUM and noise.

In the case of the PHANTOM POWER of MICROPHONES, the center tap of the input transformer primary winding is usually used as the point where the phantom voltage is applied.

Cents Besides 1/100th of a dollar or a Euro, musical cents are frequency increments of 1/100th of a SEMITONE. Some audio devices with variable speed can be adjusted in cents. One cent is a frequency ratio of the 1200th root of 2, or about 0.06 percent.

CF, Compact Flash A format of SEMICONDUCTOR memory package. Often used as storage for digital cameras, higher capacity has led to use in digital audio recorders.

Channel An independently processed or recorded SIGNAL is called a channel. A tape recorder able to record two simultaneous signals is a two-channel machine, and so on.

Channel Bit Rate The actual BITS being read from a DIGITAL tape or COMPACT DISC (CD) are much greater in number than would theoretically be required to encode the AUDIO. This is because ERROR CORRECTION and synchronization bits, etc., are added to the audio code.

In the CD, the audio bit rate is 1.41 million bits per second. The channel bit rate is actually three times as high, or 4.32 million bits per second.

Channel Separation Channel separation refers to the CROSSTALK between the channels of a multichannel system. It is the inverse of inter-channel crosstalk, measured in DECIBELS. A small amount of crosstalk is equivalent to a large channel separation.

Channel Strip On an inline mixing console, each input and its controls, such as sends, EQs, and fader, is arranged vertically, and is known as a channel strip.

Characteristic Curves It is convenient to present the electrical characteristics of a TUBE or TRANSISTOR in terms of graphs or curves that relate the various VOLTAGES and CURRENTS at the inputs and outputs of the devices. The most important curves for a tube are probably the plate characteristics, which are a family of curves made by plotting plate current versus plate voltage at various values of grid voltage. Similarly, the collector characteristics of a bipolar transistor are a family of curves that plot collector current versus collector voltage at various values of base current. By referring to these curves, an engineer can predict the performance of different circuit designs.

Charge Charge is a measure of the quantity of electricity, and its unit is the COULOMB, named after the famous French physicist Charles Augustin de Coulomb. In an electrical CIRCUIT, charge consists of negative charges, or electrons. A positive charge can be thought of as simply an absence, or deficiency, of electrons. The electron is the smallest possible quantity or unit of charge. Charge is what is moving in an electric current; the electric CURRENT exists, but does not itself flow. (By analogy, the current in a river is a flow of water and the current exists but does not flow.) Use of the phrase "flow of current" should be discouraged.

Positive charges exist in the form of protons, which are one of the fundamental particles from which all matter is made, but they do not take an active part in electrical circuits.

The symbol for charge is Q.

Charge-Coupled Device, or CCD Often referred to as charge transfer device. *See* BUCKET BRIGADE.

Chase-Lock A type of controller for a video or audio recorder that will "listen" to the SMPTE TIME CODE signal from another device and will adjust its own speed to find the correct time and then will lock into synchronization with the external time code.

Chassis (Pronounced "chassey.") The metal mechanical structure that houses electronic CIRCUITS and shields them from external magnetic and electric fields is called the chassis. It is always connected to GROUND and to the SHIELDS of audio cables. Many times one of the two wires carrying the SIGNAL is also connected to the chassis. *See also* Appendix 6.

Chebyshev Filter A multiple-POLE, low-pass FILTER designed according to Chebyshev polynomials is a Chebyshev filter. It has a steeper CUTOFF than does the BUTTERWORTH FILTER, but it has irregularities in its FREQUENCY RESPONSE, called RIPPLE.

The Chebyshev is called an overcompensated filter in that it has peaks in its PASSBAND. These peaks are collectively called ripple, and a ripple of 1 DECIBEL means the response remains within 1 dB of flat in the passband. The filter trades ripple depth for cutoff steepness; the steeper the cutoff, the deeper the ripple. The Butterworth filter can be considered a ripple-free Chebyshev filter. Chebyshev filters can be used as ANTI-ALIASING FILTERS in DIGITAL audio devices. Pafnuty Lvovich Chebyshev, also spelled Tschebyscheff and Tchebysheff, (1821–1894) was a Russian mathematician, best remembered for his work on the theory of prime numbers.[6]

Chip During the MASTERING of an ACETATE, the cutting stylus removes a hairlike filament of the acetate material as it cuts the groove. This is called the chip and, in most mastering setups, is removed by a vacuum in a small

6. Thanks to Dennis Bohn, Rane Corp.

metal pipe beside the cutterhead. The cutting stylus is heated with a small coil of resistance wire, and because the chip is flammable care must be taken that it does not catch fire on contact with the heater. In Britain, the chip is called the swarf.

The term chip is also used to mean an integrated CIRCUIT, probably because a small "chip" of silicon is the basis of the device.

Choke, Choke Coil Obsolete term for INDUCTOR. The term probably stems from the idea that an inductor "chokes" ALTERNATING CURRENTS in proportion to their FREQUENCY. The most common usage of the word has been and is in connection with power supply inductors, which are used to reduce RIPPLE. Otherwise, inductors are generally so called.

Chorus An electronic music effect that modifies the sound of a single instrument to simulate a large group of the same instruments, for example, a vocal chorus or a string section. The subjective effect of a real chorus is caused by the fact that the many sound sources being mixed together all have slightly different frequencies and also do not have precisely steady frequencies. The mixture becomes extremely complex as the relative PHASES of the signals cause partial cancellation and reinforcement over a broad frequency spectrum.

The synthetic chorus effect was first attained by subjecting the input sound to a series of very short time delays and mixing the delayed sounds. The delays were then randomly varied, or "modulated," to increase the uncertainty of the combined PITCH. This could be called the "time domain" chorus synthesis and can be quite expensive if enough delay times are used to ensure a satisfactory result. Another type of chorus device operates in the frequency domain and is somewhat simpler and at the same time more convincing. The signal is split into many frequency bands by a series of bandpass filters, and each band is randomly varied in phase and AMPLITUDE, after which they are recombined.

Chromium Dioxide Tape Chromium dioxide can be used as a magnetic medium in recording tapes, in addition to the usual OXIDES of iron. Chrome tape, as it is sometimes called, has better high-frequency performance and less noise than iron oxide tape. It is especially useful with very short recorded WAVELENGTHS, i.e., when the tape speed is low, as in cassettes.

It requires more BIAS current than conventional tapes, and a different PRE-EMPHASIS curve; therefore, cassette decks designed for chrome tape will have a switch to change these parameters, or the machine may do the switching automatically via standardized slots in the cassette shell.

Some specially formulated iron oxide tapes are similar in their characteristics to chrome tape and are called "chrome compatible." Although DuPont owns the patent for chromium dioxide and the tradename, CROLYN, the IEC has a standard for chrome and chrome-compatible tapes and calls them Type II cassette tapes. They contain cobalt-doped gamma ferric oxide, which has similar magnetic characteristics, but avoid using any chromium dioxide.

Cinema Digital Sound A system of digitally recording motion picture sound onto the film via a laser beam, that reportedly combines the dynamic and FREQUENCY ranges and low distortion of the COMPACT DISC on six discrete channels. It was a joint project between the Eastman Kodak company and Optical Radiation Corporation of Azusa, California. Five channels encompass the full audio BANDWIDTH, and the sixth is designated a SUBWOOFER channel and contains only the lowest frequencies. The CDS-encoded film was capable of being shown with conventional stereo optical sound but required a special sound system to reproduce the six channels digitally. The 1990 feature *Dick Tracy* in 70-mm format was the first production to use CDS. The system succumbed to other digital cinema sound systems.

CinemaScope™ The trademark of the first true stereophonic motion picture sound system that had the sound tracks on the same film with the picture. The system was developed and introduced by 20th Century Fox, and the first film to use the process was *The Robe,* in 1953. The process used a wide screen with a 2.35 to 1 aspect ratio. The image was compressed sideways by a factor of 2 to 1 onto the film by a special cylindrical lens and was then expanded to full width by a similar "anamorphic" lens on the projector. (This system could be thought of as an optical COMPANDER!)

The first CinemaScope movies were produced with full stereophonic three-channel sound, with a fourth channel for ambience effects reproduced from LOUDSPEAKERS in the rear and sides of the theater. This proved to be very expensive in practice, and later films had stereo music but dialogue and sound effects PANPOTTED to the various channels from a monaural source. The early CinemaScope movies were very painstakingly made and had a three-dimensional audio realism that was quite remarkable in 1953, and is seldom exceeded today!

There were four independent magnetic sound tracks on the film, two on each side of the rows of sprocket holes. To accomplish this, Fox reduced the width of the holes to allow enough space for the mag tracks. This meant that special sprockets had to be installed in the projectors (sometimes called "Fox-hole sprockets"), but these new sprockets were still usable with standard non-CinemaScope films, and virtually all projectors have them today.

Cinerama™ A motion picture format introduced in 1952 that used three separate synchronized 35-mm projectors simultaneously to produce three images that fused on the screen into one very wide panorama. The sound system consisted of five channels of AMPLIFIERS and LOUDSPEAKERS (later seven channels) and five or seven magnetic sound tracks on a separate 35-mm magnetic film. The synchronization of the projectors and sound reproducer was quite complex and entailed precise threading of the machines.

The sound system was capable of very high quality results for the time, but the problems in producing five- or seven-channel stereophonic sound tracks were formidable and turned out to be prohibitively expensive, as was the production of three simultaneous 35-mm picture films.

Circuit An arrangement of electronic COMPONENTS for performing a particular task is called a circuit. Literally, a circuit is a path through which the signal CURRENT exists. The circuit path is always in the form of a LOOP, although it may be very convoluted. Most AUDIO circuits are formed on etched circuit boards, where the "wires" consist of a copper plating on the fiberglass board.

Circuit Board *See* PRINTED CIRCUIT BOARD.

Circumaural A circumaural headset has a large cushion that surrounds the ear and makes contact with the head. Such headsets exclude external noise, unlike SUPRAAURAL designs.

Clapboard *See* SLATE.

Class A, Class AB, Class B, Class C, Class D, Class G, Class H *See* POWER AMPLIFIER.

Click Track A click track records a series of clicks, like a metronome sound, on one channel of a multitrack tape recorder. The click track is used to synchronize the recording of subsequent tracks by playing it back via HEADPHONES to the musicians while they are playing for the added tracks. A MIDI sequencer is sometimes used to generate clicks. This has the advantage of easy on the spot editing and control over such things as varying tempo.

Clipping If a signal WAVEFORM is passed through an AMPLIFIER or other device that cannot accommodate its maximum VOLTAGE or CURRENT

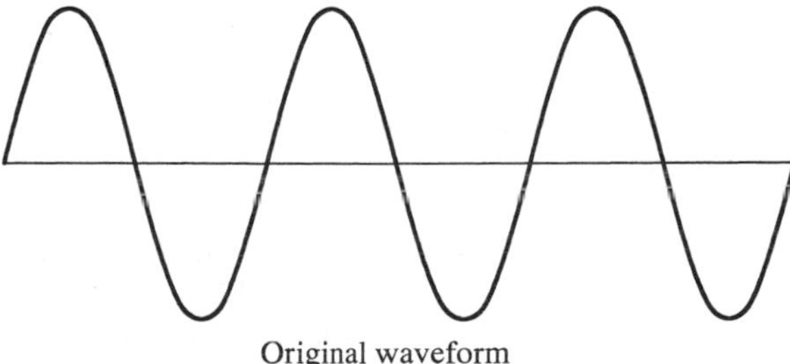

Original waveform

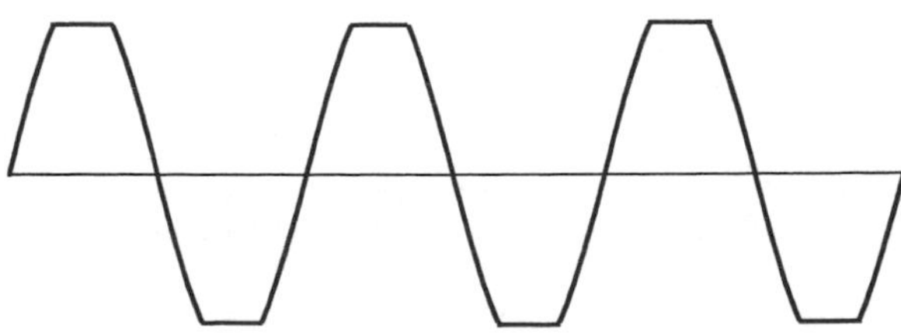

Clipped waveform

Clipping

requirements, the waveform is sometimes said to be clipped, because it looks like it has had its peaks clipped by a pair of scissors. A clipped waveform contains a great deal of HARMONIC DISTORTION and sounds very rough and harsh. Clipping is what typically happens when an AUDIO amplifier output is overloaded or its input STAGE is overdriven. The clipping point of an amplifier is defined as the maximum SINE-WAVE signal level which, when viewed on an OSCILLOSCOPE, shows no signs of flat-topping to the trained observer.

It is interesting that clipping does not usually reduce the intelligibility of speech signals; in fact, it has been shown that clipped speech is easier to understand than normal speech in noisy environments. Probably the reason for this is that clipped speech has much greater high-frequency content due to the added distortion, and this is easier to hear under noisy conditions. *See also* HARD CLIPPING; SOFT CLIPPING.

Clock, Clock Frequency A high-FREQUENCY signal, usually generated by a CRYSTAL-controlled OSCILLATOR, which is used as a master timer to control the events in a digital system. For instance, the SAMPLING frequency, even though it is lower in frequency, is determined by the master clock frequency.

It is important that the clock is accurately controlled in frequency. If a signal is sampled at one frequency during recording and at a slightly different frequency at playback, the resulting musical pitch of the signal will be different. Also, the clock must have a very high degree of stability in frequency to reduce sampling errors due to JITTER.

Closed Circuit Television A television system where the SIGNAL is routed through coaxial cables from the camera or cameras to the monitor(s) rather than being broadcast.

Closed Loop An AMPLIFIER or amplifier STAGE is said to be operating in the closed-loop mode if it has FEEDBACK around it. *See also* OPEN LOOP.

Closed-Loop Tape Drive A drive system for the tape in a magnetic tape recorder in which the tape is pinched between a CAPSTAN and a PUCK on each side of the TAPE HEADS. This double-capstan arrangement is capable of excellent control of the tape motion and can result in very low values of FLUTTER and WOW. Sometimes only a single capstan is used, and the tape is looped around and is forced against the opposite side of the capstan by a second puck.

Close Miking The placement of a recording or broadcast MICROPHONE extremely close to a vocalist or a musical instrument for the purpose of eliminating as much extraneous sound as possible is known as close miking. Close miking rarely provides a natural-sounding pickup of the instrument or voice, but accuracy may not be desired in many instances. *See also* JOLLY GREEN GIANT EFFECT.

CLV Acronym for Constant Linear Velocity. The COMPACT DISC is an example of a medium whose rotational speed (rpm) is varied depending on what part of the recording is being played. It runs fastest at the inner part, and gradually slows down towards the outer part as the disc is played so as to achieve a constant translational velocity to the laser pickup beam. The purpose of CLV is to conserve disc space. The laser videodisc can also utilize CLV as well as CAV.

CMRR Acronym for Common-Mode Rejection Ratio. *See* COMMON MODE; Appendix 6.

Coaster A popular term for a damaged recordable audio CD, named after the round object you rest your drinking glass on so that it doesn't mark the table.

Coaxial Loudspeaker A coaxial loudspeaker is a two-way system (WOOFER and TWEETER) combined into one unit such that their centers are in line. Coaxial literally means "coincident axes." The tweeter in a coaxial speaker is usually a HORN-loaded unit with the throat of the horn formed by boring out the center of the woofer magnet. The advantage of the coaxial arrangement is that at the crossover frequency, the PHASE irregularities are minimized.

One manufacturer some time ago introduced a three-way loudspeaker in one unit and called it "triaxial," literally, "with three axes," but this did not describe the loudspeaker in question—an example of the misuse of language.

Cockpit Trouble Often problems with recording or reproducing equipment are not actually in the equipment but are caused by an inept user. This is referred to by some professionals as cockpit trouble, sometimes also called "a short between the earphones."

Cocktail Party Effect A PSYCHOACOUSTIC effect that allows us to localize the sources of sounds around us. It arises because we have BINAURAL hearing. When a person is in a sound field where sounds are arriving from many directions at once, it is possible to direct one's attention in a particular direction and ignore sounds from all other directions. For instance, at a crowded cocktail party, one can concentrate on a talker at a certain location in the room to the exclusion of all the others; the other voices merge into amorphous background noise. If, on the other hand, a single-channel (MONAURAL) recording is made at the same party, it is not possible to isolate individual voices in the playback. A binaural recording and playback restores the ability.

The effect contributes greatly to the sonic clarity one experiences in listening to live music in an auditorium and explains why monaural recordings must be recorded to exclude much of the reverberation of the room to help increase the clarity of the playback. Stereophonic recording restores part of the localization ability, but only a true binaural recording is completely effective.

The cocktail party effect was investigated and so named by Irwin Pollack and J. M. Pickett in 1957. They reported it in an article in the *Journal of the Acoustical Society of America* in February 1958.

Code In DIGITAL audio devices, the SIGNAL exists in the form of BINARY "words," and this digital information is called code. The ANALOG audio signal is sometimes said to be encoded. The set of instructions that make up a computer program is usually in cryptic form, and this is also often called code.

Codec Abbreviation for Code-Decode. In the audio world, a codec is a software application that encodes a digitized audio signal file into a different format, often for the purpose of reducing its size. This process is also called data compression, or simply compression. The encoded file must be decoded to recover the original audio file, a process one might expect to be called decompression, but we have not heard this term used in practice. An example of a familiar codec is PKZip.exe that encodes any computer file into a "Zip" file that is smaller than the source file. The file can then be stored in its compressed form and then "unzipped" to recover the file in its original form. Such a codec is called "lossless" because no information is lost in the coding-decoding process. Another example of a lossless codec is used by ANALOG-TO-DIGITAL CONVERTERS (ADCs) and DIGITAL-TO-ANALOG CONVERTERS (DACs), used to encode and decode the audio signal to be recorded onto a COMPACT DISC. Since there are usually errors in writing and reading coded audio, some people think it should not be called lossless. Elaborate ERROR CORRECTION and ERROR CONCEALMENT schemes are used in CD players for this reason. Some codecs do not recover the original signal exactly, and they are called "lossy." An example of a lossy codec is Dolby AC-3, which uses PSYCHOACOUSTIC principles to remove parts of the signal that cannot be heard by the human ear due to MASKING by louder sounds, a technique called "perceptual coding." This allows the coded files to be more compressed, resulting in much smaller coded files than are possible with lossless coding. Other examples of lossy codecs are the ATRAC system on MiniDiscs, audio MP3, and video MPEG2.

Codecs have been around for a long time—Samuel F. B. Morse's so-called Morse Code for telegraphy is a codec, as are all secret codes for communication.

Coercivity Coercivity is a measure of a magnetic material's resistance to being demagnetized. Coercivity is an important specification of MAGNETIC TAPE. Tapes with low coercivity are easily demagnetized, meaning they can become erased if exposed to relatively small magnetic fields. Units of coercivity are OERSTEDS.

Cogging Uneven torque as a function of rotation produced by an electric motor because of the finite number of poles in the motor. Cogging in direct-drive turntable motors or tape recorder spooling motors can cause FLUTTER unless the motors are carefully designed to reduce the effect.

Coherer A type of DETECTOR invented in 1892 by the Frenchman Edouard Branly after a discovery by D. E. Hughes of England and used in very early radio receivers that received SIGNALS from spark gap TRANSMITTERS. The coherer consisted of a small insulating cylinder containing zinc and silver filings with a contact wire on each end. The RF signal received by the antenna, or "aerial," caused the particles to "cohere," or stick together, and to detect the signal. The Russian experimenter Popoff added a small hammer, actuated like the hammer on an electric doorbell, which rattled the particles around, breaking them apart and readying them for the next spark reception. It was called, obviously enough, the "decoherer."

Coil Literally, a coil of wire. Coils abound in AUDIO devices; most LOUDSPEAKERS have VOICE COILS as active elements; transformer PRIMARIES and SECONDARIES are coils; a phono CARTRIDGE contains coils in which the signals are induced.

A coil has electrical INDUCTANCE, the amount of which is determined, among other things, by the number of turns of wire in the coil. The inductance of a coil is not linearly related to the number of turns, however, but is proportional to the square of the number of turns. Thus, two coils whose turns differ by a factor of 2 will have inductances differing by a factor of 4.

Coil Former The cylindrical structure on which the VOICE COIL of a dynamic LOUDSPEAKER is wound is called a coil former or simply a former. The design of the coil former has a great deal to do with the performance of the loudspeaker. In olden days, it was made of paper impregnated with varnish or shellac, but such a voice coil is not very tolerant of heating at high signal levels. A former made of metal, such as aluminum, is much better from a temperature tolerance standpoint and also conducts the heat away from the coil, but it is also an electrical conductor, so it behaves as a "shorted turn," or the secondary of a TRANSFORMER with the voice coil as PRIMARY. Its motion in the magnetic field would also be greatly impeded by EDDY CURRENTS induced in it. To reduce these effects, a metal former must be slotted so it does not make a complete turn.

In some loudspeakers, especially TWEETERS, the voice coil is simply glued together without a former. This saves space in the magnetic gap, eliminates eddy currents in the former, and increases the sensitivity or efficiency of the speaker.

Coincident Microphones In the recording of INTENSITY STEREO, where all the directional CUES are caused by differences in LOUDNESS of the SIGNALS in the two channels, the two MICROPHONES must be at the same place to avoid RESPONSE differences between the two signals. This is impossible in practice, but the microphones are placed as close together as possible and they are called coincident microphones. They must be directional microphones if each is to pick up its side of the STEREO image, and they are usually CARDIOIDS or BIDIRECTIONAL microphones.

In a special case of intensity stereo one of the coincident microphones is a bidirectional (FIGURE 8), and the other one is an OMNIDIRECTIONAL, or CARDIOID. By combining the outputs of the two microphones in various ratios, the apparent width of the stereo image can be changed. This is called MS STEREO standing for mid-side stereo: the bidirectional microphone is the side and the cardioid the mid.

Coloration Coloration is a term for subtle DISTORTION that results in a change in the TIMBRE of a sound, without that sound being noticeably distorted.

If the same SIGNAL is routed to various LOUDSPEAKER systems, the resulting sounds will be easily discerned as different, although it may be difficult to determine which is the most accurate reproduction of the original. Each speaker is said to possess its own coloration.

Colortek A four-channel discrete optical motion picture sound system invented by John Mosely and introduced in 1977 with the movie *A Bridge Too Far*. Its full name is the Colortek Optical Stereophonic Sound Film System, and was the successor to "Quintaphonic Sound," which was an obscure two-track optical film sound system. The innovative design of the system employs, as a sound reader, a charge-coupled-device scanner (CCD scanner) and applies video technology to the readout of soundtracks. It scans the four soundtracks transversally at 10 MHz, resulting in a CCD frame rate of 40 kHz, as the tracks pass longitudinally at the normal speed of 24 film frames/s (457.2 mm/s) through the sound reader. In 1978, Colortek was modified and reborn as "Kintek Stereophonic Sound," only to be reincarnated in 1980 with further modifications as "Cinesonics." One feature that seems to have been retained throughout this metamorphosis is the use of the DBX COMPANDER system. *See also* Comtrak.

Column Loudspeaker A column loudspeaker, also called a "line array," is a LOUDSPEAKER system with the DRIVERS arranged in a vertical column, usually from three to six feet long, and six to eight inches wide. This configuration causes the system to have a narrow vertical coverage angle; the longer the column, the narrower the angle. The horizontal coverage is the same as that of the individual drivers. The value of this arrangement is that in an auditorium with a sound reinforcement system it is important that the loudspeakers cover only the area where the audience is, for any other coverage simply adds to the REVERBERANT sound, decreasing clarity and speech intelligibility.

The column effect is WAVELENGTH dependent, and this means a given column will become more and more directional as the FREQUENCY goes up. For this reason, some manufacturers make two-way systems where the highest frequencies are fed to a shorter column and the mid and low frequencies to a longer column, with a CROSSOVER NETWORK dividing the SIGNAL between them.

The column speaker was introduced in the 1950s and since that time has almost revolutionized sound reinforcement, especially in the case of relatively small systems. It is important to note that the column speaker must be mounted vertically to achieve its benefits. A natural position for one is above the proscenium in an auditorium.

Comb Filter A comb filter is a FILTER that has a series of very deep notches, or dips, in its FREQUENCY RESPONSE. The spacing of the notches along the FREQUENCY axis is at multiples of the lowest frequency notch, so they look evenly spaced along a graph plotted on a linear frequency scale. On the more common LOGARITHMIC frequency scale, the notches become closer together on the paper as frequency increases.

A comb filter is produced when a SIGNAL is time-delayed and added to itself. Frequencies where the time delay is one-half the PERIOD and multiples of these frequencies are canceled when the signals are combined because they have opposite POLARITY. If the signals are of equal strength, the cancellation is perfect and the notches are infinitely deep on a DECIBEL scale. *See also* FLANGING.

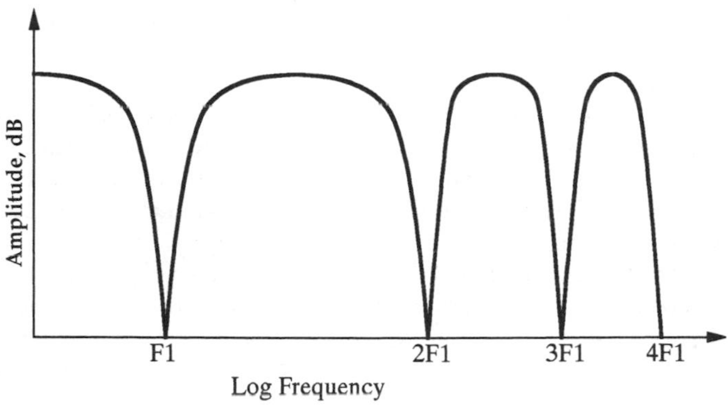

Comb Filter

Combination ¼-inch-XLR Jack A clever dual female connector that incorporates two jacks in one space—a ¼-inch stereo phone jack and a 3-pin XLR jack. The ¼-inch jack hole is nestled between the 3 holes for the XLR pins. Also known as a TRS/XLR jack.

Common Mode Common mode refers to equal VOLTAGES induced in the two wires of a signal-carrying pair.

In a BALANCED audio CIRCUIT, the SIGNAL voltages are of opposite polarity in the two signal wires. Any voltage that appears with the same POLARITY on each wire is called a common-mode voltage. Usually noise, such as 60-HERTZ hum, is induced in AUDIO cables equally and in the same direction, and so is a common-mode voltage. If the signal is connected to a DIFFERENTIAL AMPLIFIER input, the common-mode voltages will cancel, while the signal voltages, being of opposite polarity on each input terminal, will add together. This is the reason why balanced lines are less prone to induced noise from external influences.

Common-Mode Rejection Ratio *See* COMMON MODE; Appendix 6.

Compact Cassette The official name for the ubiquitous audio cassette. The name and the detailed specifications for the compact cassette recording and playback system were established and patented by Philips many years ago, and they will grant licenses to make cassette equipment only if the specifications are precisely followed, ensuring compatibility among equipment and tapes from various manufacturers.

Compact Disc The compact disc system, also sometimes called the DAD, for digital audio disc, or CD-DA, for compact disc-digital audio, was the first truly DIGITAL audio system to be widely available for home use. It is an outgrowth of the LASERDISC technology, although the laserdisc is not a digital system (It would later gain digital audio capabilities).

The system consists of a fast-rotating, variable-speed, aluminized disc with a very fine spiral pattern of extremely small "pits" in its surface, which are detected by a laser beam. The pit depth is one-quarter WAVELENGTH of the laser light. The spiral is oriented as it is "played" from the inside out. The disc is scanned by a low-power laser focused onto its surface and a photodetector, which receives the reflected light. The existence of a pit will cause the reflected laser light beam to be delayed by one-half wavelength (one-quarter wavelength each way), causing cancellation. (For this system to operate, the distance between the laser and the disc surface must be very closely controlled. This is done by a special SERVO system that continuously adjusts the position of the laser lens.) The pattern of the pits in the disc corresponds to the digital BITS of the encoded audio signal, which consists of the audio signal and a series of extra bits that are used in the decoding process for ERROR CORRECTION. In playback, the coded series of bits is decoded with a complex program that checks the recovered digital signal from the disc for errors caused by mistracking, scratches, or foreign material on the disc surface and corrects the errors if they are not too severe. The error-corrected digital signal is then passed through a DIGITAL-TO-ANALOG CONVERTER to recover the original audio signal WAVEFORM.

All optical storage systems for digital information use a laser beam to read the data. The beam is generally a small gallium arsenide SEMICONDUCTOR laser. To read the information, the laser beam is focused on the spiral track consisting of microscopic pits. The laser light is reflected in different ways by the pits and the surface land between the pits. On striking a pit, the light is diffracted while light striking the land is reflected back to the laser and is detected by a photo detector. To do its job, the laser must be focused down to a tiny circular spot. The pits are 0.6 microns wide and 0.12 microns deep. (A micron is one millionth of a meter!) The length of the pits and lands can vary between 0.833 microns and 3.56 microns, and the track density on the disc is about 16,000 tracks per inch. The length of the track on a compact disk is about 4 miles. To illustrate what these figures mean, if the diameter of a CD were enlarged to 120 meters (about the size of a baseball diamond), the tracks would still be less than 0.5 millimeters wide!

Compactron A multiple-purpose vacuum TUBE introduced by the General Electric company in 1960. Some types had as many as three separate tubes in one small glass envelope. The advent of the INTEGRATED CIRCUIT and the increasing popularity of the transistor doomed the compactron.

Compander A shortened version of compressor-expander. A compander is a device for reducing noise in AUDIO devices such as tape recorders and is actually a type of LOSSLESS CODEC. The compander will reduce the dynamic range of the SIGNAL, or "compress" it, before sending it to be recorded. The compression makes the softer passages louder so the dynamic range recorded on the tape is less than it would be if it were not compressed. Then, on playback of the tape, the signal is "expanded"; that is, the softer passages, which are too loud on the tape, are reduced in volume to match the original signal to restore its DYNAMICS.

In the expansion, which is similar to a fast-acting automatic volume control, the noise introduced by the tape-recording process is effectively reduced. This is because the music, when loud, MASKS the noise, and during the soft passages, the volume is turned down, making the noise that much less loud.

The effectiveness of a compander system is dependent on the ability of the music to mask the noise during loud passages. If it is not able to do so, the action of the compander will cause the audible noise level to fluctuate up and down with the signal level. This is annoying and is called noise pumping or BREATHING. Signals that have relatively strong high-frequency content suffer less under a compander than do simpler signals.

There have been many designs for companders over the years, with the Bell Telephone Laboratories taking credit for the earliest ones. The first commercially successful compander system in recent times was the Dolby A system, which was widely used commercially in ANALOG recording studios and in Dolby Stereo optical movie sound tracks. This system divides the

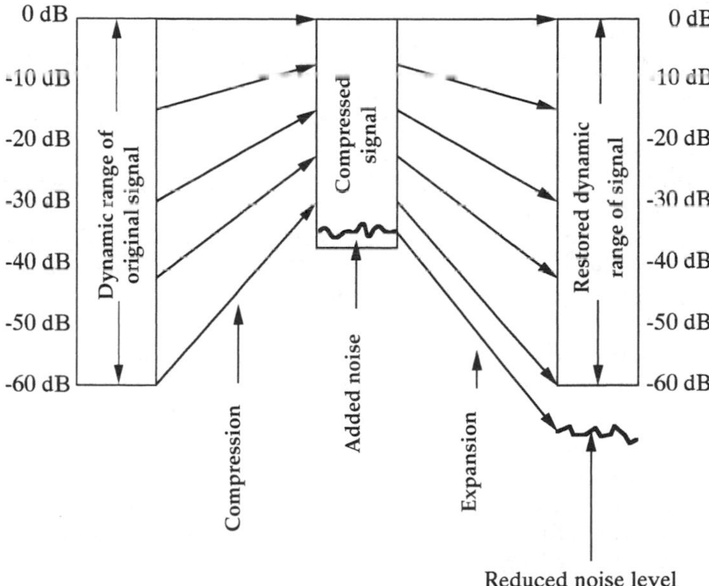

Compander

audio BANDWIDTH into four FREQUENCY bands and independently compresses and expands each one. This reduces the possibility of low-frequency signals causing noise pumping in the high-frequency range and makes the system much less audible than it otherwise would be. The Dolby A system has been simplified for use with home cassette recorders, where it is called Dolby B and Dolby C. These systems operate in the high-frequency range only, where tape cassettes are noisiest. Dolby C offers about 20 dB of noise reduction above 1 kilohertz (kHz), and Dolby B will provide about 10 dB above 4 kHz.

No doubt, the highest development of the analog compander is the Dolby SR (for SPECTRAL RECORDING), system. The Dolby SR system has also been simplified for use with cassette recorders, where it is called the Dolby S system. It provides 24 dB of noise reduction at high frequencies and 10 dB at low frequencies.

The dbx noise reduction system is a "linear" compander in that it compresses and expands the signal equally at all frequencies. It employs high-frequency PRE-EMPHASIS and DE-EMPHASIS to reduce the effect of noise pumping.

Compatibility Usually the term compatibility is used to mean stereo-monaural compatibility, which has several manifestations. STEREO recordings are said to be mono compatible if they can be played over a MONAURAL sound system without DISTORTION or loss of tonal balance. This is one of the concerns of FM radio broadcasters, who have no control over the type of receivers the listeners may be using.

One of the design criteria of the stereo tape cassette medium was that it be mono compatible. This means the stereo tracks are placed next to each other in such a way that if played on a monaural cassette machine, the SIGNAL from both channels will be heard equally.

QUADRAPHONIC records, which were released in the 1970s, were designed to be compatible with two-channel stereo playback.

In former times, after the introduction of stereo records, some were designed to be compatible with the old monaural playback cartridges. This meant reducing the stereo separation between the channels, especially at low frequencies. Virtually all playback CARTRIDGES made today are designed for stereo, so this is no longer a requirement.

Audio devices are also said to be compatible with one another if they operate correctly when connected together. Often this involves the signal levels and IMPEDANCES of the inputs and outputs of the devices. If recorded media play properly on other machines, the machines are also said to be compatible. *See also* IMPEDANCE; MATCHING.

Complementary Symmetry Complementary symmetry is a CIRCUIT configuration, or TOPOLOGY, which uses a PNP and an NPN TRANSISTOR connected in a PUSH-PULL arrangement. It is often used in the output stage of AUDIO power amplifiers.

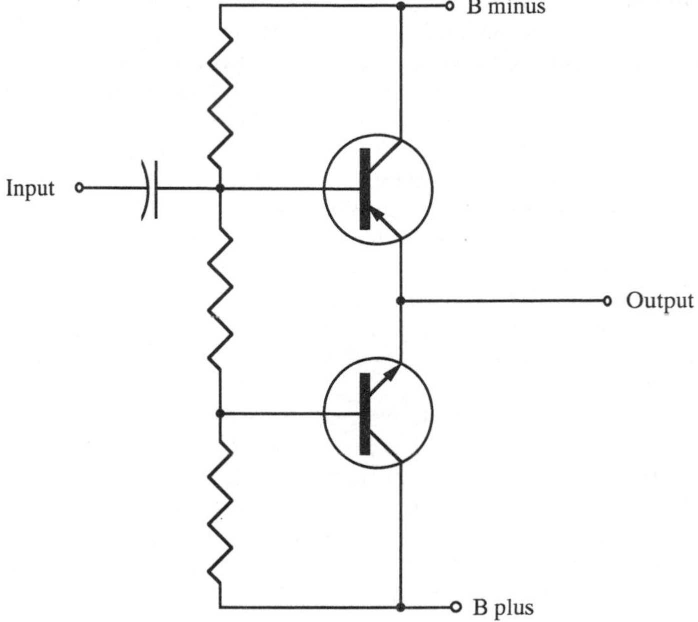

Complementary Symmetry

Complex Impedance The total IMPEDANCE, taking into consideration the MAGNITUDE and the PHASE is called the complex impedance. Sometimes the NYQUIST PLOT of the impedance, which is the real part plotted versus the imaginary part, is called the complex impedance plot. For more detail, *see* Appendix 11.

Complex Wave A sound or an electrical SIGNAL that consists of more than one SINE WAVE is a complex wave. It may be thought of as a combination of a number of sine waves, in accordance with the FOURIER theorem.

This should not be confused with complex numbers, which involve the imaginary unit, or square root of –1. *See* Appendix 11.

Compliance Compliance is the reciprocal of stiffness. It is a measure of the ease with which a mechanical structure can be deflected. The greater the compliance, the less the stiffness.

Compliance is an important specification of the STYLUS cantilever in a phonograph CARTRIDGE, and is measured both vertically and laterally. Too much compliance results in too low a FREQUENCY for the TONEARM RESONANCE, and will cause problems in tracking.

Sometimes one hears about the compliance of the CONE in a LOUDSPEAKER. This relates to the low-frequency resonance of the speaker. Cone compliance is one of the THIELE-SMALL PARAMETERS.

Component An element of an electronic CIRCUIT, such as a RESISTOR, CAPACITOR, TRANSISTOR, or DIODE, is called a component.

Component Video A method of handling video signals where the picture information is separated into three components. One method separates the picture into Red (R), Green (G), and Blue (B), and is known as RGB. The other method usually associated with the term separates the picture into the mathematically equivalent luminance (Y), and two color-difference signals, Red minus Y (R-Y) and Blue minus Y (B-Y). Whether processing, editing, or conveying the picture, the three components are processed separately and do not interfere with one another, hence higher picture quality is retained. S-VIDEO is similar, but only separates chrominance and luminance.

Component video has many variations and notations, often used incorrectly. One may see references to Y/R-Y/B-Y, Y/U/V, $Y/P_B/P_R$, $Y/C_B/C_R$, and others.

HDTV uses a wide-BANDWIDTH version of component video.

Component video transmits the highest quality picture available to the consumer. *See also* COMPOSITE VIDEO.

Composite Video An ANALOG video interconnection scheme that combines the chrominance (color) with the luminance (brightness signal, Y) and the synch into one signal. Composite video is available on almost all consumer video devices. On consumer devices, it usually uses a single RCA JACK with a yellow insert, and is patched with a yellow ended cable. The yellow cables should be 75-OHM video cables. Industrial devices may also use a BNC connector, or on some old devices, a UHF connector. The quality of composite video is better then that of video over RF, which has to be demodulated to recover the video signal and also contains the sound information. Composite video cables and connectors are usually good for digital audio connections, such as S/PDIF. Early digital tape recorder systems would encode the bitstream into a composite video signal and use ordinary video recorders. *See also* DAT.

Compound The mixture of polyvinyl chloride and additives used to make ANALOG phonograph records.

Compression A DYNAMIC RANGE problem that occurs in LOUDSPEAKERS caused by nonlinearity under conditions of high input power levels. It is sometimes called power compression. As the power input to a loudspeaker is increased, the sound power output should increase by the same amount. This will be true at low and moderate power levels, but at very high levels, the acoustic output increases more slowly or ceases to increase altogether as the input power is increased. Not only does the acoustic output fail to increase as it should, but DISTORTION is produced and the FREQUENCY RESPONSE curve is usually also different at very high levels. In a multidriver system, each DRIVER will begin to compress at different power levels, and the overall frequency response of the system therefore becomes dependent on the level.

Compression is a characteristic of all loudspeakers, but the better designs begin to compress at power levels well above those that are generally encountered (or should be encountered) in music listening. It is rare to find a discussion of compression in the specifications provided by loudspeaker makers.

Compression also refers to the use of a COMPRESSOR.

Compression Driver A special type of DYNAMIC loudspeaker designed to fit onto the small end of a HORN. The horn acts like an acoustical TRANSFORMER, with the driver providing a relatively high sound pressure at the throat of the horn, and the mouth of the horn providing a large area of low pressure to radiate the sound efficiently into the air.

The compression driver was developed by the Bell Telephone Laboratories people in the early 1930s, and their basic designs are still used with very little change. The voice coil is directly connected to a small metallic dome, or "diaphragm," whose inside surface radiates the sound into the horn throat. One of the design problems for such a unit is how to ensure that sounds from all parts of the diaphragm arrive at the throat at the same time in order to prevent PHASE cancellation at certain frequencies. The

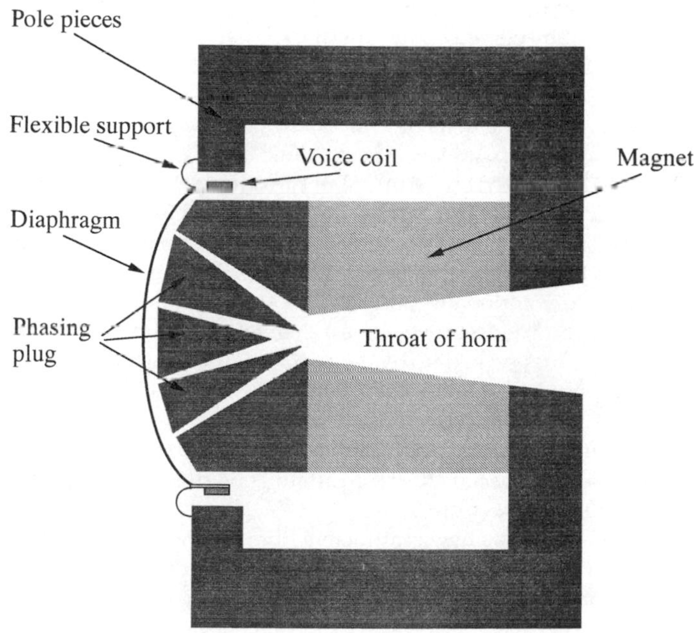

Cross section of a compression driver

Compression Driver

diaphragm must be large enough to handle high power levels but must be small enough to avoid the phase problems. The solution is the "phasing plug," which consists of a series of annular or tangential slits through which the sound passes.

In high-power compression drivers, it is possible to attain such high sound pressure levels in the throat of the horn that nonlinearities in the compression of the air are introduced. This causes very significant harmonic DISTORTION and is partly responsible for the objectionable sound of some high-power horn systems.

Compressor An audio device that reduces the DYNAMIC RANGE of a SIGNAL. The compressor is the first part of a COMPANDER.

The effect of the compressor is to make the loud parts of a signal softer and to make the very soft parts louder. Compressors are frequently used in recording popular music and in radio broadcasting, where very soft passages may be lost in the background noise of the listening environment. For instance, when music is playing on the radio in a car, the car's noise level will easily mask the quieter musical passages.

The LIMITER acts something like a compressor but operates only at the top end of the DYNAMIC range. The subjective audibility of a compressor depends strongly on its TIME CONSTANTS, and they are selected with care to minimize obvious "pumping" of the volume. To restore the original dynamics to a compressed signal, a VOLUME EXPANDER can be used, but great care must be taken that the time constants match those of the compressor.

COMTRAK According to its developer, the late John Mosely, COMTRAK stood for Combined Academy Monophonic and Compatible Four-Track Stereophonic Photographic Sound Track. Among the myriad of audio-related acronyms and abbreviations this is surely the most obscure.

The COMTRAK system was a form of optical motion picture sound track that provided four independent stereo channels (left, center, right, and surround) plus a conventional VARIABLE AREA monaural track. The STEREO channels were recorded alongside the monaural track and were of constant area and so were not picked up by the standard photocell in a conventional projector. A special reproducer that looks at only the edge of each track was used to recover the stereo information. In addition to the four stereo tracks, there was a control track that could be FREQUENCY MODULATED with very low frequencies for special effects. To attain good dynamic range, the four channels were COMPANDED.

The COMTRAK system was attractive from several standpoints, not the least of which was that it was compatible with the then-widespread conventional monaural theater sound. It also provided four independent channels of audio, whereas other SVA systems used matrixing to encode four channels onto two. COMTRAK was developed in the late 1970s and was never used commercially. Mr. Mosely lamented that acceptance and commercialization of the system was a classic chicken and egg situation. *See also* COLORTEK.

Condenser Condenser is the old-fashioned name for the CAPACITOR. It is interesting that some uses of the term have lingered on, such as CONDENSER MICROPHONE.

Condenser Microphone One of the earliest types of microphone to be invented after Dr. Lee DeForest invented the AUDION amplifier in 1906 was the condenser microphone. Thomas Edison is sometimes credited with its invention, but this seems to be in doubt. At any rate, Wente, of Bell Telephone Labs, designed a condenser microphone in 1917 and introduced it commercially in 1931.

The condenser microphone is a very simple mechanical system, with almost no moving parts compared to other microphone types. It is simply a thin stretched diaphragm held very close to a metal disc called a BACK PLATE. This arrangement is an electrical CAPACITOR, and it is given an electric CHARGE by an external VOLTAGE source or a permanently charged ELECTRET material. When sound acts on the diaphragm, the pressure variations cause it to move slightly in response to the sound WAVEFORM. This causes the CAPACITANCE to vary in like manner, and because the charge is fixed, the voltage on the back plate will vary according to the laws governing the capacitor. This voltage variation is the SIGNAL output of the microphone. The condenser microphone has extremely high OUTPUT IMPEDANCE, and must be placed very near a PREAMPLIFIER to avoid loss of the signal.

In its simplest form, the condenser microphone is a PRESSURE MICROPHONE, sensitive to sound pressure variations. It behaves like a very high speed barometer, sensing instantaneous variations in atmospheric pressure. The pressure exerted by a sound is independent of direction, and so a pressure microphone is nondirectional, or OMNIDIRECTIONAL. It is generally agreed that the highest quality microphones are condensers.

It is possible by special treatment of the back plate and by combining several microphone elements to attain various directional patterns, including BI-DIRECTIONAL, CARDIOID, and SUPER-CARDIOID.

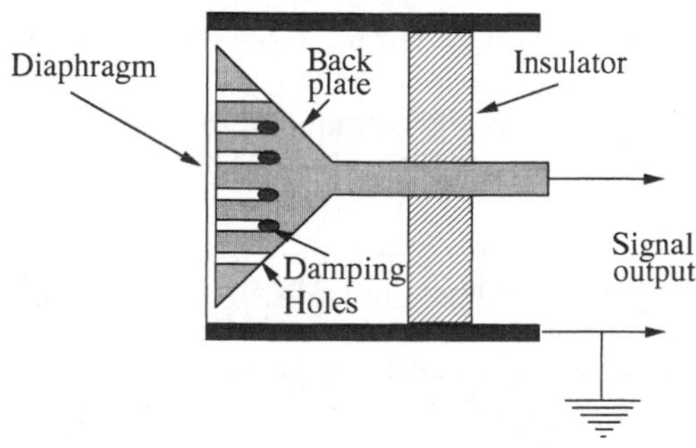

Condenser Microphone

Conductance The reciprocal of RESISTANCE, or electric CURRENT divided by VOLTAGE. The traditional unit of conductance was the mho, which is OHM spelled backward. The SI metric unit is the siemens, named after the German inventor who made the first moving-coil dynamic loudspeaker. *See also* TRANSCONDUCTANCE.

Cone The surface, usually conical in shape, which actually radiates the sound in a DIRECT RADIATOR loudspeaker is called the cone.

The traditional material for speaker cones was paper, and most cones today are made of a paperlike material that has added fillers for DAMPING of resonances. Recently, the plastic polypropylene has been used for cones, and it has excellent characteristics for this use. It has very high internal damping and is strong.

Cone Breakup The motion of a loudspeaker CONE in different modes of vibration such that it no longer moves as a solid piston.

It is desirable to operate a LOUDSPEAKER only at frequencies below that of the first mode of vibration, but this is difficult to achieve in practice. Operation at frequencies of the higher modes causes nonuniform radiation with rough FREQUENCY RESPONSE and POLAR response of the speaker. DAMPING can be applied to the cone to reduce the effects of breakup, and this adds mass and reduces the first resonant frequency, which is not necessarily undesirable.

Confidence Head Some tape recorders have extra hardware that allows playing the actual recorded signal moments after the fact, during the recording process. If the signal thus played sounds OK, one has some confidence that the recording is proceeding correctly. The term is primarily used with DAT recorders. Open reel and cassette recorders with such systems are referred to as "three head."

Console In studio parlance, a mixing console, or in Britain, a desk.

Consonant Literally "sounding together." Musical tones that are consonant sound harmonious or "in tune" when sounded together rather than discordant or harsh. Musical intervals composed of tones that have relatively simple frequency ratios are more consonant than ones with more complex ratios. The most consonant interval is considered to be the OCTAVE, which has a frequency ratio of 2 to 1. *See also* Appendix 8.

Constant Directivity Horn, CD Horn Conventional horn-loaded, high-frequency LOUDSPEAKERS have a directivity pattern, or Q, which varies with FREQUENCY. Typically, the HORN becomes more sharply directional as the frequency rises. In recent years, designs have been introduced which combine the operating principle of the COLUMN LOUDSPEAKER and the horn. To do this, the horn has two shapes, although the rate of area expansion (flare rate) is constant over its length. The first section of the horn will be narrow and flat, terminating in a vertical slot. This slot is connected to another horn that will flare both vertically and horizontally and has a square mouth. Such a horn will distribute the high-frequency energy more uniformly in the horizontal direction, but at the expense of ragged frequency response, which is compensated for by special equalization called CD Horn EQ.

Constant Displacement *See* CONSTANT VELOCITY.

Constant Q *See* EQUALIZER and Q.

Constant Velocity A magnetic phonograph CARTRIDGE is sensitive to the velocity of tip motion, and will produce the same output VOLTAGE at any FREQUENCY if this velocity is held constant. Records are cut so that the velocity of the STYLUS is constant over a certain frequency range, and at a given RMS velocity, as frequency rises, the stylus displacement decreases, and conversely, as frequency goes down, the displacement increases. If this constant velocity were maintained down to low frequencies, the displacement of the grooves would be so much that they would have to be too widely spaced on the record, and the maximum recorded time would be too short. (*See also* VARIABLE PITCH.) Therefore, below a certain frequency, called the TURNOVER frequency, the recording is made at constant displacement. In order to achieve flat FREQUENCY RESPONSE, the low frequencies must be boosted to compensate for the reduced velocity. This is accomplished by the RIAA EQUALIZATION curve built into the PREAMPLIFIER.

The RIAA PRE-EMPHASIS and DE-EMPHASIS also involves a high-frequency boost in cutting the record and a high-frequency cut in reproducing it in order to reduce the effect of high-frequency surface noise.

Contact Microphone Strictly speaking, a contact microphone is not a MICROPHONE at all, but is a vibration TRANSDUCER that generates an electric SIGNAL proportional to the vibration of the surface to which it is applied. Such a device can be used as a microphone, although the signal produced will not generally resemble the signal an air microphone would produce from the same instrument. Nevertheless, contact microphones are often used for sound reinforcement and recording of musical instruments. The primary advantage of contact microphones is that they are not sensitive to the ACOUSTICS of the room, and they do not pick up the sounds from other adjacent instruments.

Continuous Wave One of the important innovations in early radio transmission was the use of a continuous carrier SIGNAL modulated by the audio signal. The technique was first perfected around 1902 by Reginald Fessenden, the great American pioneer of early radio. Before Fessenden, radio transmission was by damped-wave carriers, which were the result of using a spark gap to generate the radiated signals. Spark gap transmitters transmitted telegraph messages. Fessenden wanted to be able to transmit speech rather than telegraph messages by radio, and he knew the damped-wave technique would not allow this. The first continuous wave (CW) transmitters used a carbon ARC as part of the resonant transmitter CIRCUIT and were quite inefficient and noisy. Fessenden later used a high-frequency alternator, or AC generator, to create the carrier signal, and this became the standard of the day.

Control and Display (C&D) Symbols *See* SUBCODES.

Control Track One track of a multitrack magnetic tape recorder used for recording special signals that provide control information to the recording console during automated MIXDOWN. Also, VCRs and some VCR-based digital audio recorders record a linear track of timed pulses to synchronize the tape speed and helical scan head tracks, which is called a control track.

Control Voltage A direct VOLTAGE, usually varying, used in electronic music SYNTHESIZERS to control various parameters of the signal being produced. Control voltages are used for envelope control, FREQUENCY control, and filter bandpass and cutoff frequency control, etc. Suitable control voltages can be generated in various ways, one of the most straightforward of which is by a standard keyboard.

Convolution In any LINEAR system or device, the output SIGNAL is a function of the input signal and the characteristics of the device. The interaction between the input and the device is described by a mathematical infinite integral called convolution. The output is the input convolved with the IMPULSE RESPONSE of the device. The mathematical operation of convolution is complex, and it is not generally easy to ascertain the characteristics of a device by looking at the output signal directly. However, a fortunate circumstance is that the Fourier transform converts the convolution into a simple multiplication. This is why spectrum analysis is used so much in audio measurements. The spectrum of the output of a device is simply the spectrum of the input multiplied by the frequency response of the device. The Fourier transform is easy to implement with modern FFT ANALYZERS. *See also* DECONVOLUTION.

Copper Loss A loss of power in a CIRCUIT because of heating due to the resistance of the wire. The term is most commonly used in conjunction with power TRANSFORMERS and power supplies.

Copy Code A technique, proposed by CBS in 1982, that puts a narrow deep notch at 3.8 kHz in the FREQUENCY RESPONSE of COMPACT DISCS and a CIRCUIT in R-DAT recorders to sense the absence of signal at this FREQUENCY. If any signal exists at this frequency, the DAT machine will not enter the record mode. The idea was to prevent the unauthorized copying of CDs. CBS claimed that the notch was inaudible, which of course was nonsense, and no one ever adopted the system. *See also* SCMS.

Core The magnetic material in a TRANSFORMER around which the coils are wound. The cores of most audio transformers are made of thin laminations of a high-PERMEABILITY material such as iron or MUMETAL. The central metal part of a magnetic TAPE HEAD is also called the core.

Corner Frequency The frequency at which the response of an EQUALIZER or other audio device is reduced by 3 dB. This is also sometimes called the "half-power point" and can refer to both low-pass and high-pass response curves. The term probably comes from the appearance of the FREQUENCY RESPONSE graph, which bends or turns a corner near this point.

Cosine Pattern The POLAR RESPONSE CURVE of certain LOUDSPEAKERS and MICROPHONES can be expressed mathematically as a polar plot of the trigonometric cosine function. This curve consists of two circles if plotted in linear units. The responses of audio devices are usually plotted in DECIBEL units, and the cosine curve plotted this way looks like two distorted circles.

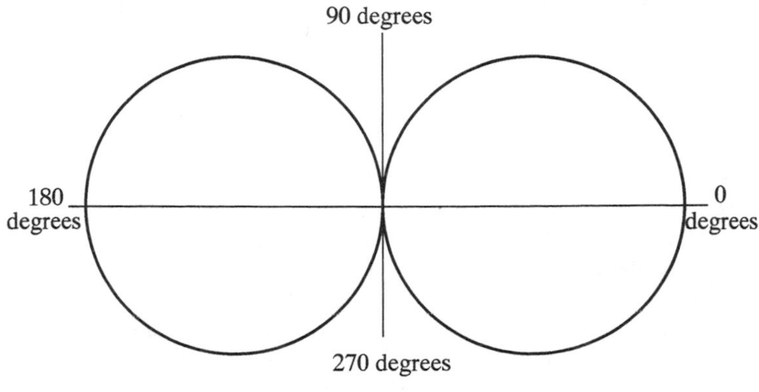

Cosine in linear units

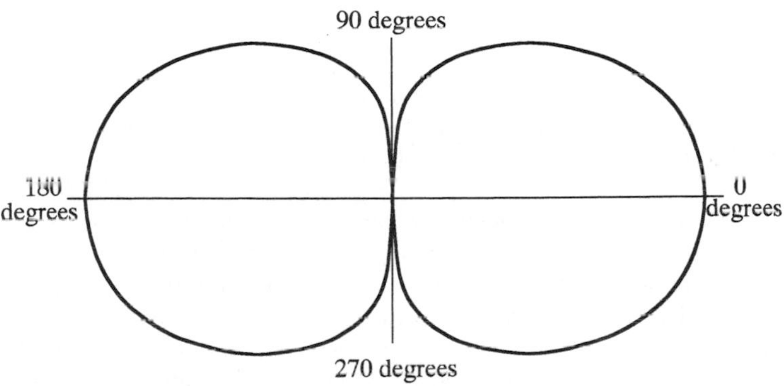

Cosine in logarithmic (Decibel) units

Cosine Pattern

Cough Button A push-button usually placed within reach of a radio announcer that disconnects his microphone in case he has to cough, hiccup, fart, etc.

Coulomb The coulomb is the unit of electric CHARGE, abbreviated C, and is the quantity of electricity transferred in 1 second by a CURRENT of 1 AMPERE. It is named after C. A. de Coulomb, a French physicist who worked in electrostatics.

Coupling In an AUDIO device with more than one STAGE of amplification, the stages are connected, or "coupled" together. Frequently a CAPACITOR is used to transfer the AC signal and to block any DC component. This is called capacitive coupling, and the capacitor is called a coupling capacitor.

In a TRANSFORMER, the COILS are said to be magnetically coupled, although there is no direct electrical connection between them. The amount of coupling can vary depending on the physical arrangement of the coils on the CORE. Coils that are close together or even interleaved are said to be tightly coupled, and this increases the efficiency of the transformer action.

Magnetic coupling can become a source of unwanted NOISE, especially 60-HERTZ HUM. Stray magnetic fields from power transformers or from wires carrying large amounts of 60-Hz CURRENT can induce 60-Hz noise in SIGNAL wiring. *See also* BALANCED.

CRAP Completely Ridiculous Audio Performance. According to Dennis Bohn of the Rane Corp., a favorite acronym describing poor quality sound equipment.

Crescendo A gradual increase in LOUDNESS of a musical sound. In conventional music, a crescendo is usually attained by gradually increasing the number of instruments sounding. In electronic music, a crescendo may be achieved by simply increasing the VOLUME of the generated music signal.

Crest Factor Crest factor is the ratio of the PEAK level of an AUDIO signal to its RMS value, usually measured in DECIBELS. For instance, a SINE WAVE has a peak value of 1.4 times its RMS value. This is a crest factor of 1.4, which in decibel notation amounts to 20 log 1.4, or 3 dB.

Musical WAVEFORMS are never smooth and uniform, but are rough and "peaky." TRANSIENTS, such as the beginning attacks of percussive sounds, have high instantaneous levels, but fall rapidly to a much lower continuous level. Speech sounds have short-duration transients as well, especially if the MICROPHONE is close to the source of the sound. The conventional way of measuring the level of an audio signal is the venerable VU meter, which responds to the average value of the signal, but this does not tell very much about the peak level, and it is the peak level that causes OVERLOAD of audio devices and consequent DISTORTION. The crest factor is a measure of how peaky the signal is, and the greater its value, the greater the HEADROOM needed in the audio chain. *See also* MODULOMETER.

Critical Band In hearing, the critical band for LOUDNESS is that FREQUENCY band within which the loudness of a band of NOISE of constant SOUND PRESSURE LEVEL is independent of its BANDWIDTH. If the noise bandwidth exceeds the critical band, the loudness will increase.

The critical band is somewhat less than one-third OCTAVE wide over much of the audible frequency range. It acts something like a one-third octave FILTER whose center frequency can be anyplace along the audible frequency axis. The loudness of several tones, if they lie within one critical band, can be predicted by summing the power of all the components. If, however, the several tones are in different critical bands, then each one will have a particular loudness, and these loudnesses will sum to arrive at the combined loudness. Thus, components more widely spaced will sound louder than if they are close together in frequency.

The measurement of the width of the critical band is difficult, and different methods give different answers. One of the earliest investigators into the critical band was Harvey Fletcher, who was working in the 1920s and 1930s.

Critical Distance In a reverberant space, the sound perceived by a listener is a combination of direct and reverberant sound. The ratio of direct to reverberant sound is dependent on the distance between the source and the listener and upon the REVERBERATION time. At a certain distance, the two will be equal (the direct-to-reverberant ratio will be 1). This is called the critical distance, and the concept is useful to designers of sound reinforcement systems, where the sound heard by the listener must not be too reverberant if clarity and intelligibility are to be maintained.

The critical distance depends on the sound source: a source that is directional in its output will have a longer critical distance than a nondirectional source because less of the room's reverberation will be excited. For this reason, directional loudspeakers are used in sound reinforcement systems.

Critical Frequency The highest RADIO FREQUENCY that will be reflected from the earth's ionosphere to allow reception at great distances from the transmitter. The ionosphere is a complex and constantly changing area in the upper atmosphere. It reflects frequencies lower than the critical frequency and transmits higher ones to outer space. For any particular atmospheric condition and depending on the time of day, the season of the year, and the sunspot activity, there will be a maximum usable frequency, or MUF.

Crolyn™ A trademark and patent of DuPont for their formulation of CHROMIUM DIOXIDE recording tape.

Cross-Correlation Cross-correlation is a mathematical measure of how much a SIGNAL resembles another signal. Two signals that are identical will have a cross-correlation of 1, and two signals that are completely different from each other will have a cross-correlation of 0. The cross-correlation between two signals is also a function of the time delay between them.

Cross-correlation can be used to measure the accuracy of an AUDIO component, or series of components. If, for example, the input VOLTAGE to a LOUDSPEAKER is correlated with the output of a precision MICROPHONE in the room, the cross-correlation should be 1 for the time delay equal to the transit time of the signal through the air, neglecting REVERBERATION. Any inaccuracy in the loudspeaker (and any reverberation or noise added by the room) will cause the cross-correlation to be less than 1. *See also* INTERAURAL CROSS-CORRELATION (IACC).

Cross-Fade In EDITING of recorded material, it is possible to more or less rapidly FADE one signal out while the other is faded in. This is called a crossfade. *See also* BUTT SPLICE.

Cross-Feed *See* STER-BIN.

Cross-Field Head The cross-field head is a type of MAGNETIC TAPE head for applying high-frequency BIAS to the tape during recording of a SIGNAL.

It is on the back side of the tape opposite the audio recording head, and applies the bias field through the plastic backing.

Normally, the bias is mixed with the signal and applied to the record HEAD. This configuration causes SELF-ERASURE of high frequencies due to the strong bias field in the record head gap. The cross-field method reduces this tendency, and allows the recording of higher levels of high frequencies. One disadvantage is that the position of the head is somewhat critical, and different tape thicknesses result in different effective bias levels.

Crossover Distortion Crossover distortion is a type of distortion present in some AMPLIFIERS that increases for low-level SIGNALS. In many amplifiers, the output devices (usually TRANSISTORS) are so connected that one of them is active during the positive half of the WAVEFORM and the other one is active for the negative half. There is thus a region near zero CURRENT where the signal is transferred from one to the other. If this is not done smoothly, there will result a small discontinuity in the output waveform. This discontinuity causes high-order HARMONIC DISTORTION, and, being constant in value, it is more noticeable with low-level signals than with stronger ones.

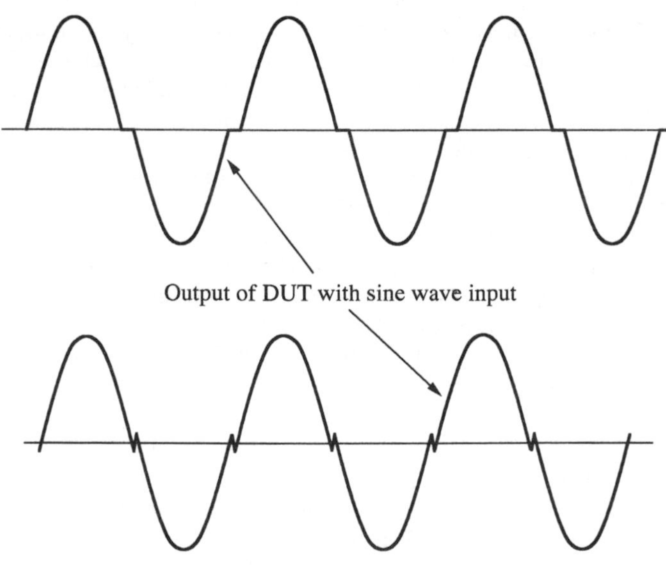

Two types of crossover distortion

Crossover Distortion

The phenomenon is reduced by application of NEGATIVE FEEDBACK around the output stages of the amplifier, and by proper BIAS current in the transistors. Modern amplifiers are nearly free of the effect, but early SOLID-STATE amplifiers were plagued by it.

Crossover Frequency *See* CROSSOVER NETWORK.

Crossover Network In multiple-driver LOUDSPEAKERS where a different speaker is used to cover each of several FREQUENCY ranges, some means is needed to allocate the frequency bands to the appropriate DRIVERS. This is the crossover network, which is actually a type of FILTER. It varies in sophistication depending on the number of drivers used and on their type.

In a two-way system, the signal for the low-frequency driver will pass through a LOW-PASS FILTER, which attenuates signals above a certain frequency, and the high-frequency unit will be fed from another filter, which attenuates frequencies below that frequency. This frequency is called the crossover frequency, and at that frequency, both drivers will receive the same amount of energy. The two filters will typically have 3 DECIBELS of ATTENUATION at the crossover frequency so the sound output of the system is flat over the crossover region.

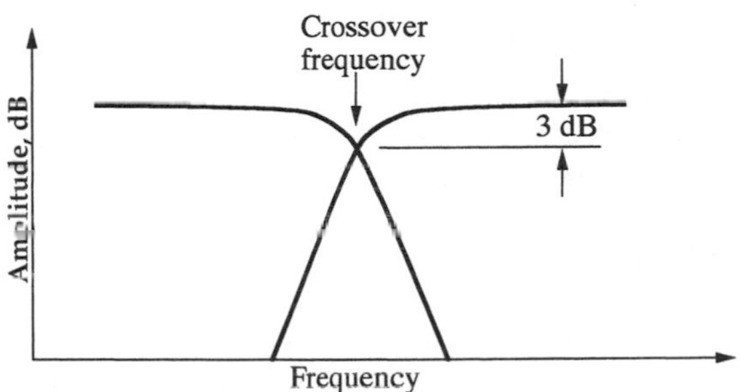

Frequency response curve of crossover network

Crossover Network

The high- and low-pass filters of a crossover network may have various rates of attenuation outside their PASSBAND, and values of 6, 12, and 18 dB per OCTAVE are common. The larger rates of attenuation are generally required for speaker systems using HORN-loaded, high-frequency drivers rather than DIRECT RADIATORS because horn-loaded units will not handle very much power below their CUTOFF FREQUENCY.

Crossover network design is somewhat complicated because filters cannot be designed that have the needed FREQUENCY RESPONSE characteristics without also having significant PHASE SHIFT near the crossover frequency. This prevents the sounds from the individual drivers from adding together to form a coherent sound. This PHASE nonlinearity can be heard in many speaker systems, especially those with crossover frequencies near the middle of the ear's most sensitive range of about 1,000 to 4,000 HERTZ.

The crossover network is usually built into the speaker system, where it must handle the entire power output of the AMPLIFIER. It is then called a "passive" crossover. It also may be placed before the amplifier, in which case a separate amplifier is needed for each frequency range and driver. This is called an ACTIVE CROSSOVER. Such a system is often called bi-amplified, or triamplified in the case of a three-way system. Such a crossover need handle only very small signal levels, and many units of this type use active electronic components (TRANSISTORS or INTEGRATED CIRCUITS), which is why they are called active crossovers. Many of them are able to provide variable crossover frequencies to tailor the response to suit various different loudspeaker configurations.

Crosstalk In multichannel AUDIO transmission systems, such as tape recorders, record players, or telephone lines, a SIGNAL leaking from one channel to one or more of the others is called crosstalk. The term comes from early telephone company usage.

Crosstalk is almost always measured as a power ratio and is expressed in DECIBELS, dB. CHANNEL SEPARATION in stereo systems is the inverse of crosstalk and is also expressed in decibels. Channel separation of 30 dB is the same as saying the crosstalk between the channels is minus 30 dB. Phono CARTRIDGE performance is ordinarily stated this way. Crosstalk usually varies with FREQUENCY, so a simple number does not tell the whole story. Crosstalk can be reduced by using BALANCED lines, proper SHIELDING, and correct equipment design.

In a STEREO music system, there is not a great need for extremely low crosstalk, for crosstalk of less than –20 dB or so cannot be heard because of the similarity of the two channels and because of MASKING of each channel by the other. But if the adjacent channels carry different programs, such as is the case with quarter-track tape recordings that are recorded in both directions, the crosstalk must be much lower to be inaudible, on the order of –60 dB or better.

CRT *See* CATHODE RAY TUBE.

Crystal The frequency-determining device in radio or television transmitters and digital clocks is a small vibrating PIEZO-ELECTRIC crystal, usually of quartz. Small pieces of such crystals will naturally vibrate at a certain frequency when an alternating voltage is applied across them. The frequency of vibration can range from kHz to GHz, and it depends on the size and dimensions of the crystal. All digital audio systems use a crystal to generate the high-frequency "clock" signal used to time the events involved in ANALOG-TO-DIGITAL CONVERTERS and DIGITAL-TO-ANALOG CONVERTERS. *See also* CRYSTAL SET; CRYSTAL SYNCH.

Crystal Set An early type of radio receiver, known as a crystal set, used a small crystal of galena, or lead sulfide, as a DETECTOR. The galena crystal acted as a SOLID-STATE rectifier, or DIODE, to recover the AUDIO signal from the radio wave. To achieve suitable sensitivity, the listener had to carefully place a small wire, the cat's whisker, at various places on the crystal while listening to the program over headphones. It is interesting to note that the first radio receivers were of solid-state design, although most people think of solid state as a recent development.

Crystal Synch Crystal synch is a method of running the tape recorder and camera in a motion picture production setup at precisely constant speed to ensure that they will remain synchronized when combined into the edited sound film. No interconnection between camera and recorder is needed.

A quartz crystal is used as a FREQUENCY standard and the camera drive motor is controlled by this stable SIGNAL. The tape recorder used for the audio recording also contains a crystal, which records an accurate frequency on the tape along with the audio. When the tape is reproduced, this frequency is sensed and the speed of the machine is controlled to hold it constant, or to keep it in synchronization with the movie projector.

The advent of the SMPTE TIME CODE has made crystal synch obsolete.

CSA Acronym for Canadian Standards Association, which is loosely analogous to the National Institute of Standards and Technology (NIST) in the United States.

CTD Acronym for charge transfer device. *See* BUCKET BRIGADE.

Cue To position a recording at the start of a recorded selection or to position a playback STYLUS at the beginning of a record cut is to cue or cue up the selection. Cuing is one of the most important activities that a disk jockey performs, although the skill is different today with digital media.

The signal sent to the MONITOR loudspeakers for studio musicians to listen to is sometimes called a cue mix. The monitor speaker is also sometimes called the cue box.

Current In electrical and electronic CIRCUITS, the SIGNAL consists of electric currents, and these are the flow of electrical CHARGE. Audio signals are always ALTERNATING CURRENTS, meaning the current reverses direction each time the signal WAVEFORM passes zero. The current from a BATTERY, in contrast, is a DIRECT CURRENT, meaning it always has the same direction.

Electric current does not "flow" in a circuit; it is the electric CHARGE that flows, and the flow of charge constitutes the current.

Curve A curve is a graphic representation of the relationship between two quantities, called the independent and the dependent variables. The dependent variable is said to be a function of the independent variable.

In a FREQUENCY RESPONSE curve, the response (dependent variable) is plotted vertically as a function of the FREQUENCY (independent variable), which is plotted horizontally. In this case, the best curve is not curved but straight, as in FLAT RESPONSE.

Frequently in audio, the variables are not plotted directly, but their LOGARITHMS are plotted. In frequency responses, it is almost always the case that the horizontal axis will be log frequency, and the vertical axis will be DECIBELS, which is a log AMPLITUDE scale.

Cut A reduction in AMPLITUDE of a SIGNAL level, usually referred to a specific FREQUENCY or frequency range, is a cut. EQUALIZERS, such as the common TONE CONTROLS, cause cuts and BOOSTS of selected frequency ranges.

The making of an ACETATE master record is often called a cut. Sometimes in recording studios, the recording of a tape is called a "cut," probably because of earlier usage in record cutting. One individual song on a record may be called a cut.

Cutoff Frequency In a HIGH-PASS or LOW-PASS FILTER, the cutoff frequency is where the AMPLITUDE response is 3 DECIBELS below the response in the PASSBAND. This is also sometimes called the half-power point. The response of the FILTER falls off more or less rapidly above or below the cutoff frequency depending on its design.

Cutterhead In the making of an ACETATE master record, a tiny, pointed, chisel-shaped STYLUS is used to cut the groove, and this stylus is moved in response to the audio SIGNAL by the cutterhead. To cut a STEREO record, the stylus must be moved in two ORTHOGONAL directions at once. Each motion is directed to cut one side of the groove, and the motions are 90 degrees from one another. The stylus is driven by two small VOICE COILS attached to the stylus lever arm. The two coils operate like miniature LOUDSPEAKERS without CONES and they must be designed so that each one drives the stylus in one direction only and does not interfere with the other motion imparted by the other coil.

The stylus assembly in a cutterhead is very stiff, and it takes considerable power to drive the coils, typically several hundred WATTS. Most of this power is dissipated as heat, and the cutterhead must be cooled, usually by blowing helium around the coils.

To ensure a smooth and noise-free cut, the stylus itself is heated by a small coil of resistance wire wrapped around it.

CW *See* CONTINUOUS WAVE.

CX A type of COMPANDER noise reduction system for stereo records, introduced with much ballyhoo by CBS in the early 1980s. The system works by compressing the DYNAMIC range on the record and expanding it on playback to restore the musical dynamics to the original levels. The expansion on playback effectively reduces the background noise added by the record medium. CX works in a manner similar to that of the dbx system except CX operates on only the upper 40 dB of the input signal dynamic range, providing 20 dB of noise reduction. Signal levels below -40 dB are not altered. To properly decode the recorded signal, the decoder has to be matched in level to the recorded signal level. This level-matching requirement is similar to that of the Dolby noise reduction systems. To achieve this level matching, decoder manufacturers provide a small record containing a reference tone to be played into the decoder in order to set the gain to the proper value. About fifteen manufacturers were initially licensed to produce decoders.

At the time of its introduction, CBS made the claim that even though the CX-encoded records are not compatible with conventional playback, the degradation of sound when playing them undecoded was not significant for most records or most listeners, even though the upper 40 dB of musical dynamics were compressed into only a 20-dB range. This, of course, was preposterous, and the system died an early death in the marketplace.

The CX system found success in the audio tracks on laser video discs, and most video disc players included the necessary decoders.

Cycles per Second, cps Until 1948, the accepted unit of frequency. In 1948 HERTZ, abbreviated Hz, was adopted as the standard unit of frequency.

Cylinder The first commercial PHONOGRAPH, built by Thomas Edison, recorded on a hollow cylinder of wax; the records are called cylinders. Cylinder records had the advantage of a constant speed of groove with respect to STYLUS, in contrast to the disc record, whose relative speed decreases as the groove nears the center of the record. This fact convinced Edison that the disc record would never overtake the cylinder. The deciding factor was, of course, that the disc requires much less storage space for a given playing time. The reduced stylus velocity is, however, a real disadvantage, along with the curvature of the groove, which causes TRACKING ERROR.

C-Zero An empty tape cassette shell that is to be loaded with tape as the tape is being recorded in a high-speed tape duplication machine.

D

DA See DISTRIBUTION AMPLIFIER.

DA-88 The first in a family of modular digital multitrack tape recorders introduced by Tascam in 1993. It uses Hi-8 video tape cassettes to record 8 tracks of PCM digital audio, and units can be added to create up to 128 tracks. DA-88 and its siblings, the DA-38 and DA-98, are also called DTRS™ for Digital Tape Recording System. The format was also offered by Sony, and is considered a competitor to the similar but incompatible Alesis ADAT system.

DAC Abbreviation for DIGITAL-TO-ANALOG CONVERTER.

DAD Short for Digital Audio Disc, also known as CD-DA, for Compact Disc-Digital Audio. *See* COMPACT DISC.

Damp, Damping Damping is the addition of friction to a RESONANCE to remove energy from it and thus reduce its magnitude. For example, a clock pendulum is a resonant system with very little friction. If it is placed in a jar of molasses, it will no longer vibrate because of the frictional damping of the molasses.

Almost all mechanical systems have resonances, and they tend to vibrate, or "ring," at the resonant frequencies. This is desirable in a bell, but not in a LOUDSPEAKER or phono CARTRIDGE, which should not contribute any sound of its own to the music. Therefore, speakers and cartridges have frictional damping added to them, sometimes without complete success.

The electrical ANALOG of friction is RESISTANCE, and it is used to damp resonating electrical circuits, such as CROSSOVER NETWORKS and FILTERS. *See also* Q.

Dampen To add water to something, to "make damp." This has nothing to do with DAMPING, and it is surprising how often the term *dampening* is used when *damping* is intended.

Damping Factor The damping factor refers to the ratio of the rated LOAD IMPEDANCE of an AMPLIFIER to the actual OUTPUT IMPEDANCE of the amplifier. It is the ability of the amplifier to control the motion of a LOUDSPEAKER cone after a SIGNAL disappears. An amplifier with a high damping factor looks more like a "short circuit" to the speaker, reducing its vibration when the signal stops. This is because the speaker acts like an electrical generator when the CONE is moving, and the low impedance of the amplifier absorbs the energy from the generated signal, damping the cone.

Damping factors above 15 to 20 are not significantly better than those slightly lower because the resistance of the loudspeaker wires must be added to the output impedance of the amplifier, reducing the effectiveness of damping. There is a common misconception that the impedance of the VOICE COIL of the speaker also must be added to the amplifier output impedance when calculating the effect of the damping factor, but this is not true. Voice coils of higher impedance generate greater VOLTAGES, which are correspondingly reduced more by the low impedance of the amplifier. For the same reason, loudspeakers connected in series will experience the same damping when connected to an amplifier as they do when connected in parallel.

The damping factor of an amplifier will vary with FREQUENCY, and sometimes a manufacturer will publish a CURVE of damping factor versus frequency. The effect of high damping factors is most audible at low frequencies, where the primary resonance of the WOOFER cone is reduced in level.

DAO Disc At Once, a method of writing an audio CD-R where all information on the disc is written in one pass, without the writing laser ever being interrupted. *See also* TAO.

DAP *See* DIGITAL ACOUSTICS PROCESSOR.

DASH Short for Digital Audio Stationary Head. DASH is one standard format for DIGITAL multitrack studio recorders that use stationary, rather than rotating, heads. The open reel format covers a wide range of versions, such as from 2 to 48 tracks and tape speeds from 12 to 76 cm per second, and was agreed on by such manufacturers as Sony and Studer. A competing, and similar but incompatible system called ProDigi was promoted by Otari, AEG, and Mitsubishi.

DAT Generally, any Digital Audio Tape recorder, but more commonly, a standardized 4mm cassette format for recording digital AUDIO on MAGNETIC TAPE with a rotating head. Originally designed for consumers, the standardized DAT cassette format became widely used by professionals instead. The same cassette format is used for data recording, but should be called DDS (Digital Data Storage) in that application and not DAT. DDS tapes are functionally the same as audio DATs, however, they are labeled in tape length in meters rather than time, and come with some data formatting already recorded. The 60 meter DDS tape is equivalent to the 120 minute audio DAT, and many people find the lower price of the DDS and equal performance attractive. Longer DDS tapes are not recommended for audio use as the tape and coating is thinner, and the audio transport is not designed to accommodate that. However, it is one way to get 3 or more hours on an audio DAT if one is careful.

The first consumer digital audio tape recorders were actually adapters to allow audio recording on videocassette recorders. Examples are the Sony PCM-F1 processor and the dbx 700 system. In these devices, the SIGNAL must be formatted so it resembles a video signal (in other words, broken up into "frames" so the recorder will accept it). This also puts certain constraints on the SAMPLING RATE.

There are two general DAT technologies: the R-DAT, which uses a rotating head assembly similar to a VCR; and the S-DAT, which uses a stationary head. The R-DAT records diagonally across the tape while the S-DAT records several linear parallel tracks of DIGITAL signals. The R-DAT is more complex mechanically and the S-DAT requires more electronics. The EIAJ first issued a standard for R-DAT and later issued one for S-DAT. The R-DAT standard includes a four-channel format that would permit recording of AMBISONICS, although it is seldom seen. The standard 4mm DAT format utilizes the rotating head system, and is always called simply DAT instead of R-DAT. S-DAT systems are usually referred to by their trademark format such as DASH or ProDigi.

DAW Acronym for Digital Audio Workstation. A DAW consists of a computer with a large amount of disc storage space and specialized software for editing and modifying digitized audio signals. It usually also includes high-quality ANALOG-TO-DIGITAL and DIGITAL-TO-ANALOG CONVERTERS. DAWs vary in their complexity and capabilities, and the best (and most expensive) ones can perform many modifications to audio signals such as editing, noise reduction, frequency equalization, adding reverberation and/or echo, dynamic range compression and expansion, etc. on many tracks. DAWs can be assembled from personal computers, or can be bought as a manufactured product.

dB *See* DECIBEL.

dBA Sound pressure level measured using an A-WEIGHTING filter. *See also* A WEIGHTING.

dBf Literally, decibels referred to 1 femtowatt, or 10 to the minus fifteenth power watts. The dBf is used to specify SIGNAL levels at the RF inputs to FM tuners.

dB FS The absolute digital SIGNAL level referenced to full scale on a digital level detector.

dBk The signal level in DECIBELS referred to 1,000 watts. dBk is most often used in radio and television transmitting stations.

dBm Literally, DECIBELS referred to 1 milliwatt. The term dBm is now obsolete, and was replaced by dB (mW). Strictly speaking, the 1 milliwatt must be dissipated in a LOAD of 600 OHMS. The dB (mW) is used in stating power levels of signals in broadcast, recording consoles, and in tape recorders. 1 dB (mW) into 600 ohms will result in .775 VOLTS RMS. This causes some confusion. The dB (mW) is a power level and only results in .775 V when the LOAD IMPEDANCE is 600 ohms. *See also* DECIBEL.

DBS, Digital Broadcast Satellite A digital satellite system that uses geosynchronous earth satellites to broadcast more than 200 channels of high quality audio and television programming to home subscribers using small dish antennas. Both DISH® Network and DIRECTV® use the DBS system.

dBu Formerly the signal level in DECIBELS referenced to one microwatt into an impedance of 600 ohms. The term has been redefined in recent years to the signal voltage level referenced to 0.775 Vrms with no load impedance specified. The new dBu (perhaps as in dB unterminated) is equivalent to dBv with a lower case v. The use of dBv is discouraged due to likely confusion with dBV.

dBμ The signal level in DECIBELS referred to 1 microwatt.

dBv *See* dBu.

dBV Literally, DECIBELS referred to 1 VOLT RMS. This is an unfortunate usage because decibels cannot properly compare simple voltages unless their impedances are the same. *See also* DECIBEL.

dBW Literally, DECIBELS referred to 1 WATT. Power amplifier output levels are sometimes specified in dBW, a 100-W AMPLIFIER is then 20 dBW. Power rating in dBW is numerically equal to ten times the common LOGARITHM of the power output in watts. *See also* DECIBEL.

DC Short for direct current (*see also* ALTERNATING CURRENT). Direct current always has the same direction, namely, from the positive terminal (anode) to the negative terminal (cathode). This convention of describing electricity flowing from positive to negative was established by Benjamin Franklin, who hypothesized that charge consisted of tiny units of positive electricity, and the convention has been retained to the present day. However, it has been known for a very long time that an electric current usually consists of a flow of electrons, which are negatively charged and move from negative to positive. Sometimes in a SEMICONDUCTOR the current can consist of positive charges, called "minority carriers" or "holes," and in these cases, Franklin's convention was right. In any case, it would be inconvenient to reverse the convention, for all the shortcuts engineers like to use, such as "right-hand rules" would have to be changed.

DC Amplifier An AMPLIFIER whose frequency response extends all the way to zero frequency, or to DC. Such an amplifier is also called "direct coupled," meaning there are no CAPACITORS in the signal chain. An example of a DC amplifier is an OPAMP in its raw state with no input or output capacitors. Some audio power amplifiers are direct coupled, and it is true that a

DC amplifier will not have any PHASE SHIFT caused by the low-frequency ROLLOFF that capacitive coupling provides. However, if the BANDWIDTH of an AC amplifier extends to sufficiently low frequencies, this phase shift is negligible.

DC Bias *See* BIAS.

DCC *See* DIGITAL COMPACT CASSETTE.

Dead In ACOUSTICS of rooms, the effect of very little REVERBERATION is called a dead room. A dead recording is one with very little or no recorded reverberation or AMBIENCE of the space where the recording was made.

Debouncing The removal of noise and multiple making and breaking of switch contacts used for voltage-controlled switching. Switches, especially push-button switches, do not usually make a clean contact when they are closed but tend to "bounce," causing ambiguous or erroneous signals to be sent to the controlling elements. Debouncing can be as simple as shunting various combinations of RESISTORS and CAPACITORS across the switch or can become quite complex with the use of pulse-forming and shaping INTEGRATED CIRCUITS.

Decade A frequency ratio or interval of 10 to 1, as opposed to an octave, which is a 2 to 1 ratio. Sometimes the ROLLOFF of a filter or EQUALIZER is expressed in DECIBELS per decade rather than in decibels per octave. A rolloff of 20 dB per decade is equal to a rolloff of 6 dB per octave. The decade interval has no musical significance.

Decay Time Decay time is a synonym for REVERBERATION TIME, or the time it takes a sound to decay to one millionth of its former strength. This is a 60-DECIBEL reduction in level.

Decca Tree A three-MICROPHONE array for two-channel stereo recording originally devised by Decca Records in England. The microphones used are omnidirectional, making the Decca tree a special case of spaced omnis, or A-B STEREO. The right and left microphones are spaced about 2 meters apart, and the third, or center, microphone is on the center line between the other two but is located about 1.5 meter in front of them. The signal from the center microphone is mixed into both of the stereo channels. The forward location of the center microphone distinguishes the Decca tree from more conventional AB placement. The location results in the center microphone picking up sounds from the center of the stereo field slightly earlier than the side microphones, and this tends to emphasize centrally located sources due to the HAAS EFFECT, essentially eliminating the "hole in the middle" sometimes exhibited by AB recordings.

Decibel, or dB Literally, one tenth of a bel. The bel is named after Alexander Graham Bell, and the number of bels is defined as the common LOGARITHM of the ratio of two powers. Thus, two powers, one of which is ten times the other, will differ by 1 bel; 10 WATTS are 1 bel higher in level than 1 watt. A 360-horsepower car is 1 bel more powerful than a 36-horsepower motorcycle. Any power ratio may be expressed in bels, and it is important to note that only power ratios are allowed. A bel is a pure number with no dimensions.

Decibel

The bel had its origin in the Bell Telephone Labs, where workers needed a convenient way to express power losses in telephone lines as power ratios. Because the bel is a power ratio of 10, and this is a rather large ratio, it is convenient to divide it into tenths of bels, or decibels, abbr. dB. Ten dB is 1 bel; thus the decibel is ten times the common log of the ratio of two powers. The decibel was originally called the "transmission unit," or TU, by the Bell Labs people.

Because of the properties of logarithms, it is easy and convenient to form some "rules of thumb" about decibels. The common log of 2 is .301, so a power ratio of 2 is 3.01 dB, normally taken as 3 dB. Therefore, any two powers differing by a factor of 2 will be 3 dB apart, and this applies to any type of power whatever, so long as it is power. Two light bulbs of 100 W and 50 W differ by 3 dB, just as electric motors of 1 horsepower and 2 horsepower differ by 3 dB. So, any time a power is doubled, it is increased by 3 dB. An increase of 6 dB represents two doublings of power, or a power ratio of 4. If an orchestra increases its SOUND PRESSURE LEVEL by 3 dB, its acoustic power output will be doubled.

Another rule of thumb that is useful to remember is that 10 dB is a power ratio of 10. Any time a power is increased tenfold, it is increased by 10 dB; thus, a 200-W power amplifier will put out 10 dB more electrical power than a 20-W amplifier, and its sound power output will also increase by 10 dB.

Another way to think of decibels is to think in terms of percentages. We all know what 10 percent means, and nobody thinks of percentages as being quantities of anything. A decibel is nothing more than a power change of 27 percent, 3 dB is a power change of 100 percent, and 10 dB is a power change of 1,000 percent.

Decibels have caused untold confusion among AUDIO people, and most of this is due to the failure to realize that decibels are not quantities of anything and can represent only power ratios. The trouble starts when we measure audio signals in volts rather than watts. If we note that power is proportional to the square of VOLTAGE, then a power ratio would be the same as a ratio of two squared voltages. Then, because the log of a squared ratio is twice the log of the simple ratio, we can see that the number of decibels is twenty times the log of the voltage ratio between two signals. Therefore, we can still measure in volts and express power ratios in decibels simply by multiplying the log of the voltage ratio by 20 instead of 10. Thus,

$$dB = 10 \log_{10} \frac{P_1}{P_2} = 20 \log_{10} \frac{V_1}{V_2}$$

Because we usually measure voltages in audio circuits instead of power, we need some more rules of thumb for voltage ratios. Here they are: a doubling of voltage is a 6-dB increase, or a power factor of 4. A tenfold increase in voltage is a 20-dB increase, or a power factor of 100.

In the decibel equation, we could replace the power in the denominator with a fixed amount of power. Then, dB would represent the power in relation to this reference. For instance, if P_2 in the equation above is always 1 milliwatt, then the decibel level will represent a specific amount of power. In other words, 3 dB would be 2 mW, 10 dB would be 10 mW, etc. This is commonly done, and if the reference power is 1 mW, the measured quantity is in dB(mW); dB(mW) = 10 log P_1/.001 W. The reference power could be any value, and sometimes different values are used, for instance dBW uses a reference of 1 W. Thus X dBW is X dB above 1 W, and 3 dBW is 2 W, etc.

Decibels are also used in measuring SOUND PRESSURE. Because sound pressure squared is proportional to sound power, sound pressure in decibels is equal to 20 times the pressure ratio. If a reference pressure is chosen, then we can measure actual sound levels in decibels, and this is done. The reference pressure is 20 micropascals (μPa), 1 Pa being a pressure of 1 newton per square meter; 20 μPa is about the threshold of hearing at 1,000 Hz for most people, so it is a convenient reference. In any case, it has been agreed upon by all international standards. A sound pressure level in decibels is always referred to this standard sound pressure.

The GAIN of an AMPLIFIER commonly is expressed in decibels, and this can lead to further confusion: an amplifier with 3 dB of gain literally means it doubles the power in the signal, and an amplifier with 60 dB gain would be expected to increase the power one million times. This would be true if the IMPEDANCE of the input and output of the amplifier were the same, but this is seldom the case in practice. For instance, a power amplifier typically has a high INPUT IMPEDANCE and a very low OUTPUT IMPEDANCE for driving a LOUDSPEAKER. The true power gain of such an amplifier is very high because the input signal has essentially no LOAD and thus supplies almost no CURRENT or power. This power gain could be correctly expressed in decibels if the actual input and output powers were taken into consideration. This, however, is rarely done; it works out correctly only if the two impedances are the same, as is sometimes the case in amplifiers used in broadcasting and some sound systems. The impedance of such units is usually 600 OHMS.

When amplifier gains are expressed in decibels, what is usually meant is VOLTAGE GAIN, and as we have seen, a simple voltage ratio cannot be expressed in decibels by the definition of the decibel. The formula used to calculate amplifier gain is dB (gain) = 20 log [V(output)/V(input)], and again, it would be correct only if the impedances at the input and output were the same. It is small wonder that decibels cause so much confusion!

Decilog, Del, dL A logarithmic ratio of two numbers, defined as 10 times the common logarithm of the quotient of the numbers, i.e., $dL = 10 \log A/B$. The decilog differs from the DECIBEL in that the quantities A and B can be any numbers. Whereas the decibel is defined only as the logarithmic ratio of two powers, the decilog can express the ratio of any two quantities, such as the relative sizes of two bank accounts, populations, etc.

Decoherer *See* COHERER.

Deconvolution A mathematical process for separating two SIGNALS that have been convolved (combined by the process of CONVOLUTION). Convolution is a mathematical operation involving an infinite integral, and it describes how certain acoustic, electrical, and vibration signals combine in linear systems. For instance, the human voice is a complex signal consisting of an acoustic input from the vocal cords that is modified by the complex, variable resonances of the vocal track. These resonances accentuate certain frequency ranges and attenuate others to produce the sounds we know as vowels. The vocal track modifies the input signal by impressing its own characteristics on that signal. Mathematically, the input signal is said to be convolved with the IMPULSE RESPONSE of the vocal track. Once this convolution is done, it is not an easy task to separate the various contributors to the final sound, but it is theoretically possible by mathematical deconvolution. It is also sometimes possible in practice and can be accompanied by certain postprocessing steps in a dual-channel FFT ANALYZER. Also, if the input signal is accurately known, the deconvolution can be done mathematically with a computer program.

It is frequently desirable to measure the characteristics of an audio system, such as a sound system in a building, but it is difficult to separate the effects of the input signal, the system itself, the reverberation of the room, and the characteristics of the measurement system (MICROPHONE). When the impulse response of the sound system–room combination can be measured directly, it is easy to calculate the FREQUENCY RESPONSE, for it is simply the Fourier transform of the impulse response. The FFT ANALYZER does this handily. One way to determine the impulse response of the sound system (or any other audio device) is to input PSEUDORANDOM NOISE, or a MAXIMUM-LENGTH SEQUENCE signal, and then record the resulting output signal. A deconvolution can then be done on this signal, which gives the impulse response.

Decoupling Decoupling is the presence of FILTERing at the power supply RAILS of amplifiers. The filtering is between GAIN stages of the AMPLIFIER to prevent some stages from modulating the supply VOLTAGE and affecting the amplification of other stages.

Improper decoupling can cause an amplifier to be an OSCILLATOR, or at least to be unstable and begin to oscillate under certain SIGNAL conditions. Decoupling must be effective at both high and low frequencies to effectively isolate the amplification stages from each other. Decoupling is usually done with series RESISTORS between the supply rails and the gain stages and shunt CAPACITORS from the stage to ground, but using voltage regulator circuits for each stage is another way to do the same thing. Digital circuit ICs will also commonly have small decoupling capacitors on their power leads.

Decrescendo A musical term indicating a gradual reduction in loudness. The opposite of CRESCENDO.

DED Dark Emitting Diode, the inverse of the LED. DEDs are said to be used by the CIA and other clandestine operatives for power-off indicators in their electronic equipment.[7]

De-emphasis The complementary EQUALIZATION that follows PRE-EMPHASIS is called de-emphasis. The RIAA phono equalization CURVE is a de-emphasis. *See also* PRE-EMPHASIS.

De-esser A de-esser is a special type of COMPRESSOR that operates only at high frequencies, usually above 3 or 4 KILOHERTZ. It is used, especially in the broadcast industry, to reduce the effect of vocal SIBILANT sounds, which are normally too strong when singers and announcers use very close-up MICROPHONES. When the high-frequency energy exceeds a preset threshold, the compressor starts to operate to reduce the high-frequency response. Low-level high-frequency sounds are not reduced.

De-essers are not used for nonvocal music.

Degausser Degaussers are used to erase tape recordings and to demagnetize metallic objects such as tape recorder CAPSTANS and tape guides and heads; syn., demagnetizer. Magnetized components such as these will add noise to tape recordings, although modern tapes have sufficient COERCIVITY that they are not so sensitive to the effect as were older formulations.

Degaussers consist of a COIL of wire wound on an iron core. The coil is designed to accept the 120 VOLT line, and this produces a strong magnetic field pulsating at 60 times per second, which corresponds to the 60 HERTZ line frequency. This pulsating field alternately magnetizes the part being degaussed in one direction and then the other. As the degausser is pulled away from the part, the field strength gradually diminishes and the part is left with no net magnetization. There is a battery-operated degausser that contains an OSCILLATOR to supply the pulsating field. It is used for degaussing cassette recorder heads.

A tape degausser (or bulk eraser) usually takes the form of a box with a very large and powerful coil/core assembly inside. Tape reels or cassettes are passed over the field and are erased while leaving the field. These degaussers are very strong and can erase wide tapes (up to 2 inches), and come with warnings to avoid use if wearing a pacemaker. They also affect wristwatches, possibly magnetizing mechanical watches and affecting their accuracy, or affecting the stepping motor on electric watches. Purely digital watches are not affected. A tape recorder head degausser takes the form of a wand where the core extends out to form a tip and the hand grasps the encapsulated coil.

It is possible to erase tape by passing it over a strong permanent magnet. This saturates the magnetization of the tape in one direction, wiping out any remnant of the recording. This is actually a "gausser" rather than a degausser, and it results in a relatively high BARKHAUSEN noise level on the tape.

Deglitcher When a DAC is called upon to move from one VOLTAGE state

7. Thanks to Dennis Bohn, Rane Corp.

to another, it sometimes introduces an undesired excursion due to nonsimultaneous operation of the ANALOG switches involved in the conversion. This is a gross nonlinearity and is called a glitch. An external CIRCUIT which reduces the effect is called a deglitcher.

A deglitcher can be made by following the DAC with a SAMPLE AND HOLD circuit, which disconnects the DAC from its output and holds it at the previous level while the transition occurs. The sample and hold must be very fast and have low control feedthrough; in other words, its transitions must not introduce significant disturbances in the output signal.

Delay Line An audio signal processing device, called a delay line, is used to simulate the effect of an acoustic ECHO or to simulate REVERBERATION. Delay lines are usually DIGITAL processing devices, but there exist ANALOG delay lines as well. The first delay lines were made by using tape recorders to record a signal while playing it back on the same machine. The distance between the record and reproduce heads causes a time delay. This technique is called "tape delay."

Delta-Sigma Modulation Delta-sigma modulation is an analog-to-digital conversion scheme rooted in a design originally proposed in 1946, but not made practical until 1974 by James C. Candy. Inose and Yasuda coined the name delta-sigma modulation at the University of Tokyo in 1962, but due to a misunderstanding, the words were interchanged and taken to be sigma-delta. Both names are still used for describing this modulator. Characterized by oversampling and digital filtering to achieve high performance at low cost, a delta-sigma A/D thus consists of an analog modulator and a digital filter. The fundamental principle behind the modulator is that of a single-bit A/D converter embedded in an analog negative feedback loop with high open loop gain.[8]

In the simplest form of delta modulation, only the direction in which the signal must go to arrive at the next sampled level is encoded. In other words, if the next sample is higher than the previous one, the code is a 1, meaning increase in level. If the next sample is lower, the code is a 0, meaning decrease in level. The rate at which the level moves is fixed, and the resulting encoded WAVEFORM looks like a series of sawteeth, zigzagging up and down in an approximation of the signal shape.

It would seem that this is a very inaccurate way to encode a signal, and this is true unless the sampling frequency is extremely high. In one such early system, made by the dbx company, the sampling frequency is 700 KILOHERTZ, compared to conventional PCM, which usually uses 44 to 48 kHz. But the digital words needed for each step contain only 1 BIT, rather than the 16 or more usually required. Thus delta-sigma modulation trades word size, with its inherent complication, for sampling rate. The bit rate in each system is about the same, meaning the BANDWIDTH required to record the encoded signal is nearly the same.

An advantage of delta-sigma encoding is that it provides 1-bit infor-

8. Thanks to Dennis Bohn, Rane Corp.

mation at a very high rate and in a format that a digital filter can process to extract higher resolution (such as 20-bits) at a lower sampling rate.

Dematrix To separate signals that have been combined by MATRIXING. Generally, dematrixing is actually another form of matrixing.

Demodulation See DETECTION.

Demodulator A demodulator is a device that recovers the audio signal from a modulated WAVEFORM. It is also called a DETECTOR. *See also* AMPLITUDE MODULATION; FREQUENCY MODULATION.

Depth In stereophonic reproduction of music, depth refers to the apparent distance between the listener and the various instruments in the sonic image. The perceived depth also has to do with the high-frequency content of the instrument in question as well as relative time delays between it and other, nearer instruments. Also important is the perceived size of the reproduced ensemble, a small group seldom exhibiting a large amount of depth and vice versa.

Derating The reduction in a theoretical rating, such as power-handling capacity, due to some environmental factor such as high ambient temperature. For instance, a 1-watt resistor may be derated to .5 watt if it is used at an elevated temperature.

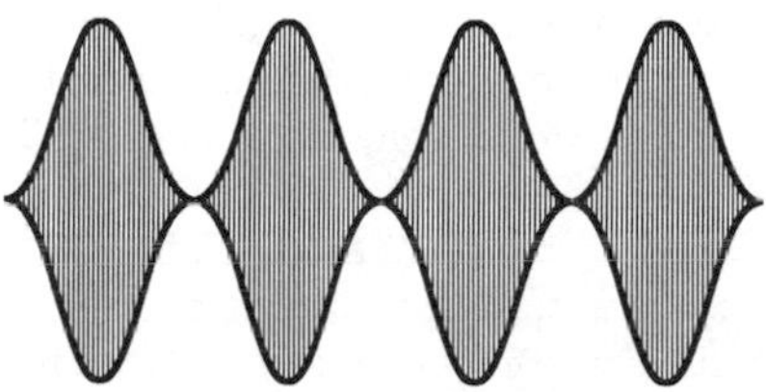

Amplitude Modulated Waveform

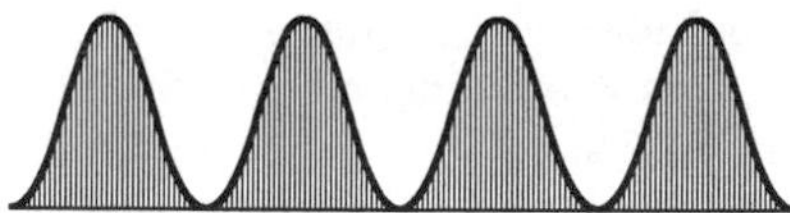

Waveform after rectification

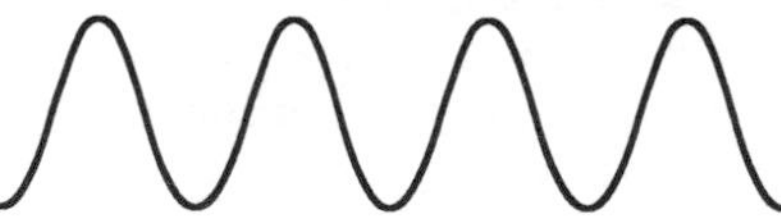

Recovered audio waveform

Detection

Desk British terminology for a recording console, or BOARD; also called a mixing desk.

Detection, Detector The process of recovering the audio WAVEFORM from a MODULATED CARRIER is called detection or demodulation. In the case of AMPLITUDE MODULATION, simple rectification followed by some smoothing is all that is needed.

Detection of a FREQUENCY MODULATED waveform is more complex. Some FM detector types are the ratio detector, slope detector, and frequency DISCRIMINATOR.

Deutlichkeit Deutlichkeit (pronounced Doyt-lish-kite) is the German word for "clarity," and is a measure of the relative energy in early REVERBERATION of sound in a room compared to later-occurring reverberation; literally, the ratio of the sound pressure squared and integrated over the first 50 milliseconds to the pressure squared averaged over all time. *See also* ENVELOPMENT.

DI *See* DIRECTIVITY INDEX. *See also* DIRECT BOX.

Dial Cord A length of strong string that connects the tuning knob on a radio or tuner to the station indicating needle and the actual tuning CONDENSER that selects the station. Dial cord has been used since the introduction of commercial radio broadcasting, but is becoming obsolete on higher quality products due to the proliferation of digital tuning controlled by push buttons and indicated with digital displays.

Dialnorm Dialog Normalization. In digital television broadcasting and receiving using Dolby audio coding, dialog normalization is a method to automatically adjust the sound volume of received TV programs so that the level of speech is relatively uniform from program to program. In the U.S., the Federal Communications Commission (FCC) mandates that digital television broadcast stations encode their signals with sound volume information so that the home television sets can read it and adjust the sound volume accordingly.

The reason this is needed is illustrated by this example: The dialog of a typical news broadcast does not require very much HEADROOM because sound effects that could be much louder than the dialog are generally not used in such broadcasts. The listener adjusts the volume to a comfortable level in her living room. Then, if the next program is a motion picture, the sound track will have music and sound effects that might be momentarily much louder than the dialog, and the broadcast signal will have to be reduced in level to avoid excessive loudness. The result is that the dialog will be too soft, and the listener will have to raise the volume to compensate. Dialnorm adds the headroom information to the sound track so the Dolby decoder can vary the volume automatically. However, it is suspected that the Dialnorm system is usually turned off during commercials! *See also* METADATA.

Diatonic A musical scale of eight notes spanning one OCTAVE, consisting of an ascending pattern of two whole steps, a half-step, three whole steps, and another half-step. The familiar "do re me fa sol la ti do" is a diatonic scale. Most Western music is built on diatonic scales, but there are many other possibilities, such as the pentatonic scale with five tones in an octave used in some Chinese music.

DI Box *See* DIRECT BOX.

Dichotic Dichotic refers to HEADPHONE listening where each ear hears a different SIGNAL, as opposed to DIOTIC, where the same signal is presented to both ears. BINAURAL listening is an example of DICHOTIC presentation. These terms are used mostly by researchers into PSYCHOACOUSTICS.

Dielectric An electrical insulating material, as opposed to an electric CONDUCTOR. The term is most commonly used to mean the material between the plates of a CAPACITOR, where it serves as a spacer/insulator and increases the capacitance of the capacitor. The relative amount the capacitance is increased by using a dielectric between the plates rather than by placing the plates in a vacuum is called the dielectric constant of the material, and this can vary from about 2 to over 50 for various materials.

The dielectric strength of a material is the highest electric field the material can stand without breaking down, and this determines the highest VOLTAGE that a given capacitor will tolerate before shorting.

Difference-Tone IMD *See* TWIN-TONE.

Differential Amplifier Normally, one of the SIGNAL input terminals of an AMPLIFIER is connected to the CHASSIS of the amplifier; in common parlance, it is "grounded." This is sometimes called a "single-ended" connection. The amplifier is then sensitive to the VOLTAGE existing between one input terminal and GROUND.

It is possible to build an amplifier that has neither input terminal grounded and is sensitive to the difference in voltage between the two input terminals. This is called a differential input, and the amplifier is called a differential amplifier. Before the advent of INTEGRATED CIRCUITS, differential amplifiers were made by adding a TRANSFORMER to the input and not connecting either side of the primary to ground; this is still done in the case of some MICROPHONE PREAMPLIFIERS.

Integrated circuit differential amplifiers without transformers are commonly available. They allow BALANCED configurations to be easily built at lower cost than using a good transformer.

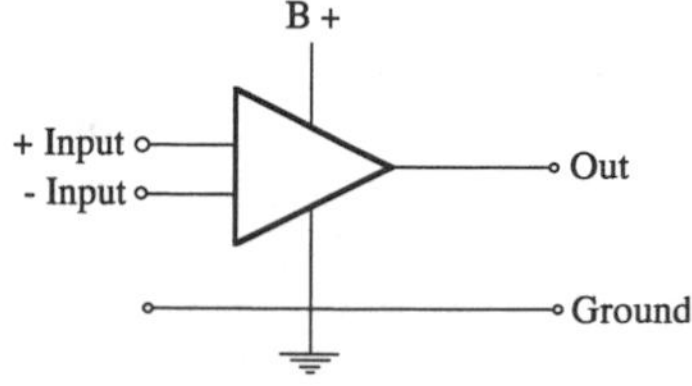

Differential Amplifier

Diffraction The bending of a sound wave around an obstacle and the reflection of a sound wave from a discontinuity in its path are called diffraction. It is WAVELENGTH dependent. Where the wavelength is short (relatively high FREQUENCIES) compared to the obstacle, reflection will occur as well as bending of the wave front. When the wavelength is long (lower frequencies) with respect to the obstacle, little reflection will occur and the bending will be more pronounced.

The diffraction of light is analogous to that of sound, although it is seldom seen because of the extremely short wavelengths of light.

Digital *See* DIGITAL AUDIO; Appendix 7.

Digital Acoustics Processor, DAP A consumer audio device that attempts to simulate the acoustics of an auditorium or other room by adding suitable digital time delays and synthetic reverberation to recorded signals. It is the latest in a long line of ANALOG devices that began with the STEREOPHONER designed by the Viennese orchestra conductor Hermann Scherchen in the 1950s and the XOPHONIC made by Radio Craftsmen in the U.S. in the 1960s. The Xophonic had multiple outputs for feeding SURROUND loudspeakers and came with preprogrammed delay settings to simulate certain existing concert halls. DAPs are often used to process the stereo audio signals from prerecorded video tapes and video discs to enhance the illusion of ambience. Illusion is the proper word, since DAPs do not produce very accurate simulations of actual acoustical spaces.

Digital Audio The application of digital computer-based technology to the recording and reproduction of music is somewhat loosely called digital audio. For an overview of the techniques, *see* Appendix 7; and for a discussion of test measurements on digital devices, *see* Appendix 5.

Digital Audio Broadcasting, DAB As an alternative to AM and FM broadcasting, several types of digital audio broadcasting have been proposed. One promising system is known as Eureka 147. Its audio quality is said to be comparable to that of the COMPACT DISC, and it does not suffer from fringe area fading or MULTIPATH DISTORTION. It is broadcast by earth-bound transmitters and requires much less radiated power from the station than conventional broadcasting does (only about 1,000 watts, compared with up to 50,000 watts for AM and up to 100,000 watts for FM), and 16 different programs can be broadcast from a single 1,000-watt station, greatly reducing hardware costs to the broadcasters. The Eureka 147 system was developed by the Eureka 147 Project, an international consortium of broadcasters, network operators, consumer electronic industries, and research institutes. The promotion and marketing of the system worldwide was taken over in the year 2000 by an independent group called WorldDAB.

While the Eureka 147 system has emerged as clearly superior in laboratory and field tests carried out by CEMA (Consumer Electronics Manufacturers Association), the National Association of Broadcasters (NAB) made public on January 23, 2003, its opposition to the adoption of Eureka 147 in the U.S. This opposition is based on lack of new spectrum, dislike of sharing transmitters in the multiplex, and concerns that DAB would introduce new competition.

The iBiquity Digital Corporation has now developed a more limited in-band solution (originally named IBOC, for In Band On Channel, but now trademarked HD Radio™), utilizing existing FM and AM transmitters. *See also* IBOC.

DAB signals can also be broadcast by satellites, and two such competing systems named SIRIUS and XM are now in operation.

These systems are not compatible with one another, and each requires a special receiver to pick up its signals.

Digital Compact Cassette, DCC A consumer recording format announced by Philips in 1990 that either failed in the marketplace or was never adequately marketed, depending on how you look at it. DCC was an interesting system designed to compete with the R-DAT format and allow compatibility with ANALOG cassettes. The DCC was a tape cassette the same size as a standard analog compact cassette, and its tape speed was the same. It utilized several linear (as opposed to helical scan in the R-DAT) digital tracks in each direction to encode the audio signal at a sampling rate of 44.1 kHz, the same as used in the COMPACT DISC. The DCC was quite similar to the S-DAT format.

This system had some interesting characteristics. Since it used the same sampling rate as the CD, it could be used to make direct digital copies from CDs without going through digital-to-analog conversion. It contained a version of SCMS to prevent unauthorized proliferation of digital copies. The system also allowed for the recording and playback of analog cassettes as well as DCCs on the same machine. A major advantage of the DCC format was that it allowed high-speed duplication of prerecorded cassettes, which would have reduced production costs. The system used Precision Adaptive Sub-band Coding (PASC) to reduce the recorded bit rate compared with the CD format. The PASC is a European standard for digital radio broadcasting. The dynamic range was said to be 110 dB although the audibility of the bit rate reduction could be questioned. The DCC has been discontinued.

Digital Dubber A motion picture sound post-production term for a specialized multitrack audio recorder with removable media used to mix film sound tracks. Older analog dubbers usually used 35–mm sprocketed FULLCOAT.

Digital Equalizer An EQUALIZER that operates in the "digital domain"; that is, it operates on signals that have undergone analog-to-digital conversion and uses DIGITAL SIGNAL PROCESSING techniques. The first commercially available unit of this type was the Yamaha DEQ7, introduced in 1987.

Digital Signal Processing, or DSP The manipulation and modification of signals in the digital domain (after having undergone analog-to-digital conversion). A great many electronic music instruments use DSP, as do certain test equipment types such as the FFT ANALYZER. DSP devices have a MICROPROCESSOR inside them to do most of the work.

Digital Time Delay A DIGITAL device that provides an adjustable time delay. Time delays are used in artificial REVERBERATION systems, for special ECHO effects in music recording, and to provide delayed sound to certain LOUDSPEAKERS in some SOUND REINFORCEMENT SYSTEMS. Before the advent of digital delays, the only way the effect could be achieved was by TAPE ECHO, or by placing a loudspeaker at one end of a long tube and a MICROPHONE at the other. This gives a delay of about 1 millisecond per foot of length, and it becomes bulky when long delays are needed.

Digital-to-Analog Converter, DAC, D/A The component within a digital AUDIO device that converts BINARY digital words into an ANALOG signal that can then be amplified and sent to a LOUDSPEAKER, etc. The DAC is the last link in the digital chain, just before the ANTI-IMAGING FILTER.

When the COMPACT DISC system was first commercialized, 16-bit DACs with sufficient linearity for use in high-quality audio were pushing the state of the art in SOLID-STATE electronics. Like the ADC, the DAC is subject to certain inaccuracies, as follows:

1. Absolute accuracy: The difference between the actual analog output and the correct output expected from a given DIGITAL code word.

2. Differential linearity error: The deviation from the ideal output change of one LSB when the input goes from one value to the adjacent value.

3. Feedthrough: Undesirable signal coupling around switches or other components that should be turned off.

4. Gain drift: A change in the DAC's full-scale VOLTAGE output caused by a change in temperature of the device.

5. Linearity: A measure of the deviation of the actual transfer function CURVE from the ideal curve.

6. Offset drift: The actual change in DAC output voltage with variation in temperature with all BITS in the input digital word equal to zero.

7. Settling time: The time required for the DAC's output voltage to stabilize to its final value, measured from the time the digital input code changes.

Because DACs are costly, many less expensive compact disc machines use only one DAC which is time-shared between the two STEREO channels. This may cause degradation of sound quality because of the increased number of GLITCHES in the output signal due to the switching involved. (The fact that one channel is time-offset by one-half the SAMPLING period in this scheme is of no audible consequence. It is simply equivalent to moving one of the loudspeakers by a fraction of an inch.)

Digitization The process of analog-to-digital conversion. *See* ANALOG-TO-DIGITAL CONVERTER.

Diminuendo Synonym for DECRESCENDO.

DIN Acronym for Deutsches Institut für Normung, which is the German standards organization roughly equivalent to the American NIST, formerly the National Bureau of Standards. The DIN determines standards for almost all types of products and procedures for making measurements. In many cases, the corresponding DIN standard is different from the American standard, and care must be used in comparing specifications of audio equipment specifications made in the two countries.

DIN Hub Also known as a CCIR/DIN hub, which is a recording tape reel style used in Europe. American machines use the NAB style hub on their large tape reels.

Diode A diode is a CIRCUIT element that will pass CURRENT in one direction only, from the ANODE to the CATHODE.

The first diode was an Edison light bulb with a second electrode enclosed in the bulb. Electrons boiled out of the filament and migrated to this PLATE when it was connected to the positive POLE of a battery. The cat's whisker of the old CRYSTAL SET radio was a SOLID-STATE diode, which served as a DETECTOR of the received radio waves.

Today, most diodes are made of silicon and are used as rectifiers to change the alternating household current to direct current for powering all manner of audio devices. Some diodes, called signal diodes, are very fast-acting, and are used as detectors for radio signals.

A special type of diode called a ZENER, or avalanche, diode is designed to operate in its "avalanche" mode, in which it conducts current in the opposite direction from normal. An avalanche diode will have a constant VOLTAGE across it regardless of current through it, and it is used as a voltage regulator circuit.

Diotic Literally, "with two ears." Diotic generally refers to HEADPHONE listening whereby the two ears hear the same signal, as opposed to MONOTIC, where only one ear hears the signal. *See also* DICHOTIC.

Dipole With reference to radio or television antennas, a dipole is simply two metal rods extending out from a common point where they are connected to the transmission line.

In LOUDSPEAKER designs, a dipole radiator is a system that radiates forward and rearward with equal energy but with opposite POLARITY. Examples of dipole radiators are ELECTROSTATIC loudspeakers and planar loudspeakers. Some CONE-type speakers have been arranged so they form dipole radiators. For a dipole radiator to have adequate low-frequency response for full-range music reproduction, it must be quite large to prevent the rear wave from canceling the front wave. Also, the dipole radiator must not be placed close to and parallel to a wall; it will work best when not near reflecting surfaces.

Direct Box The direct box is an adapter to allow connecting an instrument pickup, instrument preamplifier, or power amplifier directly to the mic or line input of a recording or sound reinforcement console. This avoids having to use a MICROPHONE for acoustic pickup, or offers a different sound quality. Electric guitars, basses, and keyboards are typical candidates for this treatment. Such boxes can offer several attenuation options to accommodate this wide range of signal inputs. They can also be passive, usually with a small TRANSFORMER, or active, typically with a FET input to minimize any loading of a pickup that might affect the sound. Sometimes called simply a DI (pronounced "dee-eye") as in direct input or direct inject.

Direct Coupling A connection between two devices that allows both direct current (DC) and alternating current (AC) between them. Direct coupling is by a simple wire rather than through a series CAPACITOR. *See also* DC AMPLIFIER.

Direct Current, abbr. DC An electric CURRENT that is always in the same direction, such as the current supplied by a BATTERY, is called direct current. In classic ELECTRICITY theory, the direction of the current was thought to be from positive to negative. It has since been learned, however, that current almost always constitutes a flow of negative charges, or electrons, and they flow from negative to positive.

Thomas Edison was the great champion of power distribution to homes via direct current, and he built up such a power distribution network, some of which is still in use in some eastern cities. It seems he never was convinced that this was a mistake—one of his few lapses of judgment. DC power has many disadvantages compared to ALTERNATING CURRENT, one of the most important of which is that DC VOLTAGE cannot be changed by the use of TRANSFORMERS.

Nicola Tesla, the famous Yugoslavian-born physicist, was convinced very early that AC was the only practical way to distribute power, and of course history has proven him correct.

Directivity Factor A measure of the directionality of the sound output from a LOUDSPEAKER. *See also* Q.

Directivity Index, DI A measure of how directional a particular LOUDSPEAKER is, as compared with a completely omnidirectional one. To determine DI, an omnidirectional loudspeaker connected to an AMPLIFIER and variable-FREQUENCY signal source is placed in a FREE FIELD. The SOUND PRESSURE LEVEL is measured at a fixed distance as a function of frequency. Then the DUT is put in the same place and its input power adjusted so its SOUND POWER output is the same as that of the omnidirectional speaker. The DUT is aimed directly at the measurement microphone. Because it is directional, the resulting measured SPL will be higher by a certain number of DECIBELS, and this number is the directivity index for that loudspeaker as a function of frequency. Accurate measurement of DI is quite involved and time-consuming. Certain highly directional speakers, such as high-frequency horns, may have DIs of 15 dB or so. For another definition of loudspeaker directivity, *see also* Q.

Direct Radiator A LOUDSPEAKER that does not have a HORN between the moving element and the air is called a direct radiator. Most loudspeakers for home use are direct radiators, and most commercial loudspeakers for sound reinforcement are horn-loaded types. Direct radiators generally provide smoother, more uniform response, while horns are much more efficient, providing greater output level for a given power input. Also, horns are more directional, which is desirable in sound reinforcement systems.

Direct-to-Disc Direct-to-disc is a type of vinyl LP disc MASTERING in which a master tape is not used. The signal directly from the control console is used to cut the original ACETATE disc. This means a direct-to-disc recording cannot be edited in the sense of making a better performance by splicing several performances together. The recording is made "live."

There are audio people who think the tape is a weak link in the audio chain, and that significantly better quality can be attained by eliminating it. However, there are many problems with direct-to-disc mastering. Increased stress on the musicians is only one. The mastering engineer has no way of knowing in advance just how loud a performance will be and must set the volume controls by educated guesswork. A single note that causes an overload means the disc must be rejected and the whole process started over. Mastering from a tape is thought to be an art by many, and direct-to-disc mastering must be more so.

Disc Any disc that stores music or data in optical or mechanical form is spelled with a *c* as in COMPACT DISC or PHONOGRAPH disc. *See also* DISK.

Discrete Refers to a 1:1 relationship of recorded tracks on a movie and the resulting number of speaker channels. For example, a 5.1 digital mix will be reproduced through six channels—left-center-right-LFE-left surround-right surround—in the theater. Obviously each of the surround channels, and possibly the LFE channel, will have more than one speaker. Discrete playback is often contrasted with 4:2:4 matrix encoding/decoding.[9]

Discrete Circuit An electronic CIRCUIT that uses individual TRANSISTORS as active elements rather than INTEGRATED CIRCUITS (IC). It is thought by many that ICs, especially IC OPERATIONAL AMPLIFIERS, do not lend themselves to high-quality AUDIO applications. They are used extensively because of their relatively low cost and ease of use. In almost all cases, a discrete circuit will be superior if well designed.

Discrete Operational Amplifier The somewhat poor performance of early INTEGRATED CIRCUIT OPAMPS led to the design of an operational AMPLIFIER using discrete components. The best known of these is the JE990, designed by the late Deane Jensen. It has been optimized for audio use and is generally credited with outperforming all IC opamps and most other discrete amplifier designs.

Discriminator One type of DETECTOR in an FM radio receiver is the FREQUENCY discriminator, a CIRCUIT invented by Major Edwin Armstrong, the originator of FM broadcasting. One disadvantage of the discriminator is that it is sensitive to AMPLITUDE MODULATION as well as FREQUENCY MODULATION. It is therefore sensitive to radio interference unless it is preceded in the circuit by LIMITERS that remove the AM from the signal.

The discriminator is actually a specific circuit, but any FM detector is often called a discriminator.

Disk The spelling "disk" is used for disks that store data or music magnetically as in a computer floppy disk rather than optically. *See also* DISC.

Dispersion Usually refers to the ability of a LOUDSPEAKER to radiate sounds over a wide angle—synonymous with angular coverage. This usage is

9. This entry is copyright © 1991–2003 by Larry Blake and is reprinted with permission.

unfortunate because dispersion actually means the variation in speed of sounds of different frequencies. In air, all frequencies travel at the same speed (luckily), but some media are dispersive. *See also* GROUP VELOCITY.

Dissipation The absorption of energy and its conversion to heat, analogous to DAMPING. LOUDSPEAKERS are limited in the amount of energy they can dissipate because of temperature limitations of the voice coil assembly. Sometimes the descriptive specifications for a loudspeaker will include its maximum power dissipation in watts. The less efficient a loudspeaker is, the more dissipation it will have. The SURROUNDS of loudspeaker cones, however, are designed to have relatively high dissipation to help prevent CONE BREAKUP and spurious resonances. As Gilbert Briggs, of the Wharfdale Wireless Works, once said, dissipation appears to be better for audio products than for their producers.

Dissipation Factor Is the reciprocal of the Q-value of a CAPACITOR.

Dissonant The opposite of CONSONANT.

Distortion Theoretically, any addition or modification to a SIGNAL caused by any type of equipment could be called "distortion," but the term has come to be somewhat more restricted in its use.

Distortion may be conveniently grouped into six types.

1. NONLINEAR distortion, manifested as HARMONIC DISTORTION and INTERMODULATION DISTORTION. For many years, engineers have struggled to formulate an objective measure of the subjective effects of nonlinear distortion, but this has proved to be a nearly impossible task. Low-order harmonic distortion, for instance, does not sound unpleasant to most listeners and in fact adds a certain "richness" or "brightness" to music. Similar percentages of intermodulation, however, are much more objectionable.

2. FREQUENCY distortion, the unequal amplification of different frequencies. This relates to the frequency response of audio devices. It has been shown that differences in FREQUENCY RESPONSE curves amounting to less than 1 DECIBEL can be distinguished by the human hearing mechanism. It is also very important that the frequency response of a device is the same for all signal levels. Audio TRANSFORMERS are sometimes the cause of response variation with output level.

3. PHASE distortion, an effect caused when PHASE SHIFT in an audio device is not a linear function of frequency. In other words, different frequencies experience different time delays. This changes the WAVEFORM of the signal, and is especially injurious to transients.

4. TRANSIENT distortion, including TRANSIENT INTERMODULATION DISTORTION. Many experiments have shown that the beginning and ending transients on musical sounds are largely what determine their TIMBRE, rather than their harmonic, or OVERTONE, content. An audio device that passes steady-state signals perfectly well may distort the transients, causing audible COLORATION of music. Low transient distortion means a device must have wide frequency response, no phase distortion, and no HANGOVER.

5. Scale distortion, or volume distortion. Because the human ear has a

sensitivity that varies with frequency and with LOUDNESS level (*see* FLETCHER-MUNSON EFFECT), a musical ensemble must be reproduced at the same loudness as the listener would experience at the actual event if frequency distortion is not to occur. For example, if a symphony orchestra is reproduced at 70 PHONS loudness level, whereas the concertgoer in a seat in the auditorium would experience 90 phons, the apparent bass response will be decreased by about 10 dB. On the other hand, if the reproduced level is above that of the original, the bass (and to a lesser extent, the extreme treble) will be too loud.

6. FREQUENCY MODULATION distortion. Examples of this are FLUTTER and WOW, and DOPPLER distortion caused by the motion of loudspeaker cones.

There are other factors that cause music reproduction to be untrue to the original, but are not considered distortion. An example is background NOISE. Another is lack of directional realism and proper AMBIENCE due to the use of too few channels of reproduction.

There have been many subjective terms used for describing the sound of reproduced music, some of which are summarized below:

Frequency range	
Extreme lows:	below 40 HERTZ
Lows:	40 to 300 Hz
Mid-range:	300 to 4,000 Hz
Highs:	4,000 Hz to 10,000 Hz
Extreme highs:	10,000 Hz to 20,000 Hz
Distortion	
Nonlinear:	dirty, strident, rough, metallic, harsh
Intermodulation:	thick, bassy, fuzzy, wiry, brittle
Noise:	frying, sizzle, popping
Transient distortion:	hangover, loose, slow
General terms	
Source size:	live, broad, dead, flat, compressed
Detail:	veiled, transparent, clear, opaque, focused
Realism:	presence, canned, natural, thin, muddy, dead

Distribution Amplifier, DA A distribution amplifier is a device designed to feed one signal to many different outputs, such as to a series of headsets or to several remote audio lines. The DA outputs are usually individual amplifiers all fed from the single input, although gain is usually not a primary purpose. Instead, the benefit is that many outputs can be had without overloading the source, and if an output is short-circuited accidentally, the source and other outputs are not affected.

Dither In order to reduce the effect of QUANTIZATION noise and DISTORTION in DIGITAL AUDIO systems when the SIGNAL level is very low, a

BROADBAND random noise with an AMPLITUDE of about ½ quantizing step is added to the signal. This causes the signal to vary in level and to make the quantizing process more LINEAR, reducing distortion. The dither actually increases the noise content of the signal, trading wideband noise for quantization noise and distortion, but the improved accuracy in the quantization results in a subjective improvement in noise performance of the system. Dither noise is usually WHITE NOISE, at low level; quantization noise contains much greater quantities of lower-frequency components and is much more audible.

To fully attain the advantage of using dither, the signal must be averaged in time after being converted back to ANALOG. In the case of a low-level SINE WAVE, averaging over several seconds allows the recovery of a virtually undistorted signal. Music, however, does not wait for us to do this averaging, especially with short TRANSIENT sounds, and the ear in any case is not able to do a long time-average, so the improvement, while significant, is not ideal.

"Aside from being a funny sounding word, dither is a wonderfully accurate choice for what is being done. The word 'dither' comes from a twelfth-century English term meaning 'to tremble.' Today it means to be in a state of indecisive agitation, or to be nervously undecided in acting or doing, which, if you think about it, is not a bad description of noise. Dither is one of life's many trade-offs. Here the trade-off is between noise and resolution. Believe it or not, we can introduce dither (a form of noise) and increase our ability to resolve very small values; values, in fact, smaller than our smallest bit."[10]

Diversity Receiver In some WIRELESS MICROPHONE systems, a special receiver is used which has two separate antenna systems. The receiver senses which antenna can supply the best quality SIGNAL, and switches to that one. If the signal starts to fade in this channel, the receiver will switch very quickly to the other antenna. As the transmitter is moved around within the reception area, the receiver constantly evaluates both receiving antenna signals and switches back and forth as fast as necessary to always receive the least noisy signal.

Diversity receivers have greatly increased the reliability and quality of wireless microphone systems, which used to be notorious for picking up interference from various other transmissions and for picking up noise due to poor signal levels at the receiver.

Dividing Network See CROSSOVER NETWORK.

dL *See* DECILOG.

DMM A trademark standing for Direct Metal Mastering, which is a process whereby the PHONOGRAPH record master is cut into a disc of copper instead of ACETATE. The advantage of the process is said to be better high-frequency response and less noise in the final records. The copper master is used as

10. Thanks to Dennis Bohn, Rane Corp.

a MOTHER to make STAMPERS, simplifying the normal THREE-STEP PROCESSING.

The copper is much harder than the acetate, and the groove cut in it is more precise. It does not develop HORNS at the top of the groove, and the STYLUS is made with sharper edges. This reduces the DISTORTION that builds up in the inner grooves of records. Up till now, most metal mastering has been done in Germany.

DMM also stands for digital multimeter, which is a MULTIMETER with a digital readout.

Dolby *See* COMPANDER.

Dolby A *See* COMPANDER.

Dolby Digital® Dolby's name for its format for the digital soundtrack system for motion picture playback. It utilizes their AC-3 system of LOSSY digital compression. When used in 35mm motion pictures, the digital signal is optically printed between the sprocket holes. Now being found in home theater installations on DVDS, Dolby Digital may use any number of primary audio delivery and reproduction channels, from 1 to 5, and may include a separate bass-only effects channel. The designation "5.1" describes the complete channel format. Surround decoder systems with Dolby Digital automatically contain Dolby Pro Logic processing to ensure full compatibility with the many existing program soundtracks made with Dolby Surround encoding.

Dolby® Digital EX™, Dolby® Digital Surround EX™ provides a third surround channel on Dolby Digital movie soundtracks. The third surround channel can be decoded at the cinema's or home viewer's option for playback over surround speakers located behind the seating area, while the left and right surround channels are reproduced by surround speakers to the sides. To maintain compatibility, the back surround channel is matrix-encoded onto the left and right surround channels of an otherwise conventional 5.1 mix, so no information is lost when the film is played in conventional 5.1.

Dolby NR Any of Dolby Labs' ANALOG noise reduction systems. *See* COMPANDER.

Dolby, Ray Ray Dolby, founder and Chairman of Dolby Laboratories, Inc, was born in Portland, Oregon, in 1933. Between 1949 and 1952 he worked on various audio and instrumentation projects at Ampex Corporation where, from 1952 to 1957, he was mainly responsible for the development of the electronic aspects of the Ampex video tape recording system. In 1957 he received a B.S. degree from Stanford University, and upon being awarded a Marshall Scholarship and a National Science Foundation graduate fellowship, he left Ampex for further study at Cambridge University in England. He received a Ph.D. degree in physics from Cambridge in 1961.

Dolby is a fellow and past president of the Audio Engineering Society and a recipient of its Silver and Gold Medal Awards. He is also a fellow of the British Kinematograph, Sound, and Television Society and an Honorary Member of the Society of Motion Picture and Television Engineers, which in the past has also awarded him its Samuel L. Warner Memorial Award, Alexander M. Poniatoff Gold Medal, and Progress Medal. The Academy of Motion Picture Arts and Sciences voted him a Scientific and Engineering Award in 1979 and an Oscar in 1989, when he was also presented an Emmy by the National Academy of Television Arts and Sciences. In 1986 Dolby was made an honorary Officer of the Most Excellent Order of the British Empire (OBE).

In 1997 Dolby received the U.S. National Medal of Technology, the IEEE's Masaru Ibuka Consumer Electronics Award, and the American Electronic Association's Medal of Achievement. That year he also received an honorary Doctor of Science degree from Cambridge University, and in 1999 he was awarded an honorary Doctor of the University degree by the University of York. He holds more than 50 U.S. patents and has written papers on video tape recording, long wavelength X-ray analysis, and noise reduction.[11]

Dolby Stereo Dolby Stereo is an ANALOG matrix 4 channel sound system

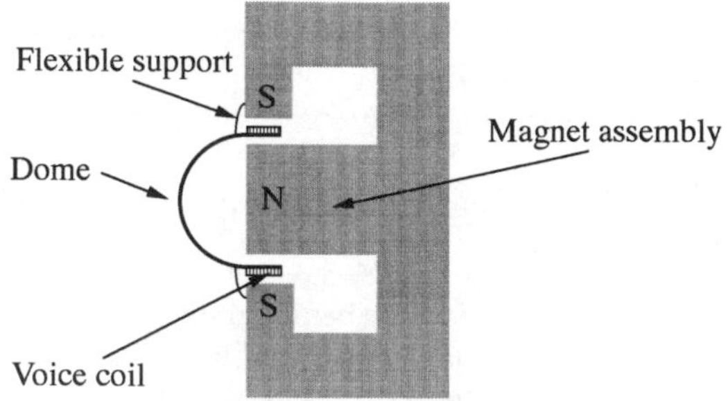

Cross section of a dome tweeter

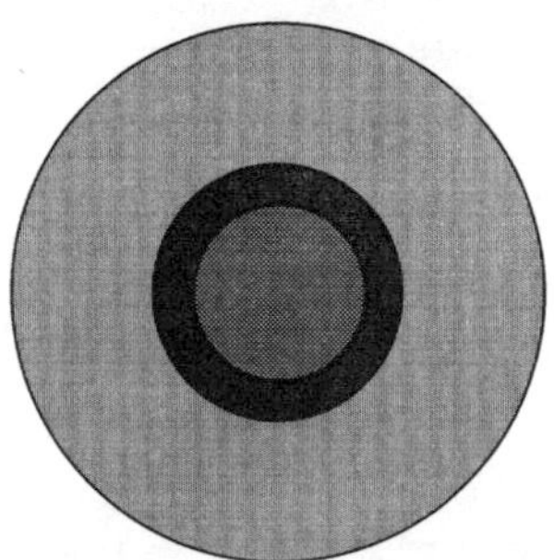

Front view of dome tweeter

Dome Tweeter

11. From Dolby Labs. literature.

for movie theaters that produces three channels of sound in the front (left and right for music and effects and center for dialog) and a surround channel for effects. It was introduced in the late 1970s and effectively revolutionized motion picture sound. The film sound track consists of two optical channels that have the original 4 channels matrixed into them, somewhat similar to the QS and SQ matrixing systems used in the "quadraphonic" systems sold in the early 1970s.

Dome Tweeter A high-frequency LOUDSPEAKER that uses a small hemispherical dome as a radiating surface is called a dome tweeter. It was introduced by Acoustic Research Inc. and has been widely used by others since the 1960s.

It is characterized by smooth FREQUENCY RESPONSE and relatively wide-angle DISPERSION. It suffers from quite low efficiency and so is not suited for large auditorium sound systems. The dome may be made of different materials such as aluminum, titanium, cardboard, or coated textile and so may be called hard or soft dome. Each has unique characteristics.

Dome tweeters are often covered with a protective metal grill, which degrades their performance by reflections.

Dongle A small device that must be plugged into a computer communication port to allow certain software to run. It contains a small amount of Read Only Memory (ROM) that contains code that authenticates the legality of the software. It is very effective in preventing software piracy. Sometimes any small device or adapter with a short cable may be called a dongle.

Doppler Distortion The Doppler effect, named after a German physicist, is the apparent change in the pitch of a sound when the source of the sound is moving with respect to the listener. A car horn sounds higher in pitch as the car approaches and lower in pitch after the car passes us. If a LOUDSPEAKER cone is reproducing both low and high frequencies at the same time, the low frequencies will cause the CONE to move alternately toward and away from the listener. While the cone is moving toward the listener, the high FREQUENCY will rise in pitch, and when the cone is moving the other way, the high frequency will fall in pitch. This is actually a FREQUENCY MODULATION of the high frequency by the low frequency, and it is called Doppler distortion.

In cases where small cones are producing the full range of music, Doppler distortion is audible as a general muddying of the sound, but in multi-speaker systems, where low, mid, and high frequencies are produced by different DRIVERS, the effect is very small. Some loudspeaker designers, notably the late Paul Klipsch, are very much concerned about Doppler distortion, while others seem to pay little attention to it.

Doppler Effect *See* DOPPLER DISTORTION.

Double System Sound Any of several methods of producing sound motion pictures where the sound track is recorded on a magnetic tape recorder that is synchronized with the movement of the film in the camera. The synchronization is done by recording a special tachometer signal on one track of the tape. This "synch" signal is generated by the camera and is 60 Hz when the camera runs at 24 frames per second. When the tape of the sound track is played back, the synch signal, or "pilot" signal, is sensed by a device called a "resolver," which adjusts the speed of the tape player to exactly match the speed of the movie projector. In this way the playback of the track will always be at the correct time to match the action in the picture. There have been many different types of systems to do the synchronization, but the one most commonly used until the advent of CRYSTAL SYNCH and the SMPTE TIME CODE system was the "Neopilot" system invented by Stefan Kudelski, maker of the Nagra tape recorders. SMPTE time-code synchronization of audio recorders and cameras is almost universally used today.

Doublet A LOUDSPEAKER system with both sides of the transducers open to the air, such as an electrostatic or planar speaker. Also sometimes called a DIPOLE radiator. *See also* LOUDSPEAKER.

Double Tracking Originally, double tracking meant the recording of a vocal track on one tape recorder track, then listening to this while recording another similar track. The two tracks are combined and re-recorded into a single track, which will sound more diffuse due to slight differences in the two original tracks. Double tracking gives a slight "chorus" effect to voices, and is frequently used in recording popular music.

In the 1980s double tracking could be done with DIGITAL signal processors, which introduce small randomly varying time delays to one signal and then combine it with the original signal.

Doublet Response Literally, the imaginary, or quadrature, part of the IMPULSE RESPONSE. The impulse response is a time-dependent function and can be either positive or negative in value. Its phase increases uniformly with time. Another function can be created by simply adding a 90-degree phase shift to the impulse response. This process is called the Hilbert transform, after the mathematician David Hilbert, and the new function is called the doublet response. If the doublet response is squared and added to the square of the impulse response, and the square root of the sum is extracted, this quantity will always be positive, and thus it can be expressed on a logarithmic, or DECIBEL, scale. This is called the magnitude of the impulse response and is also known as the ENERGY-TIME CURVE. The log conversion allows a much greater dynamic range to be visible on a graph.

Doubling If a LOUDSPEAKER is driven too hard in its low-frequency range, it will produce second HARMONIC DISTORTION, sometimes with greater AMPLITUDE than the FUNDAMENTAL. This is called FREQUENCY doubling, or simply "doubling."

The doubled frequency sounds one OCTAVE higher than the fundamental and is therefore not musically annoying to the casual listener, greatly easing the task of the loudspeaker designer.

It may also refer to a studio technique of playing a track twice in a multitrack recording and using both in the final mixdown. One musician can make a sound like two bass players or two singers, etc.

DPDT Acronym for Double Pole Double Throw. This refers to a switch that simultaneously routes each of two independent inputs to one of two outputs.

DPST Acronym for Double Pole Single Throw. This refers to a switch that turns two independent current paths off or on.

Drain One of the terminals of the FIELD EFFECT TRANSISTOR, the other two being the SOURCE and the GATE.

In some AUDIO cables, the SHIELD is in the form of an aluminum-coated MYLAR wrap which surrounds the SIGNAL conductors. This plastic material cannot be effectively connected to other CIRCUIT elements, so a bare wire is enclosed inside the shield for the connection. This is called a "drain wire."

DRAW Acronym for Digital Read After Write (we have also heard "Direct Read After Write"), which applies to an erasable COMPACT DISC that can be re-recorded. The CD-RW (Compact Disc–Read Write) is the commercial implementation of the idea. The term DRAW is seldom used except for some digital tape systems that offer the ability to monitor the actual recording quality during recording.

Driven Shield A technique by which the SHIELD of an audio cable is not grounded but rather is connected to an audio VOLTAGE that is essentially the same as the SIGNAL being carried by the cable. By "driving" the shield at the signal voltage, the effective shunt CAPACITANCE between the signal conductor and the shield is much reduced, allowing much longer lines to be used without high-FREQUENCY attenuation. Driven shields are sometimes used for low-level high-IMPEDANCE circuits, such as the output of magnetic tape heads when the AMPLIFIER is some distance from the head assembly.

Driver Individual LOUDSPEAKERS are often called drivers, especially if they are in a system where several are used. Also, in the case of a horn-type loudspeaker, everything except the HORN is called the driver.

In an audio AMPLIFIER, the STAGE before the power output stage is called the driver.

DRM Digital Rights Management. The sale of music is poised for change as distribution changes from physical formats such as CDs to online files distributed over the internet. Integral to the change is some way to protect the rights of the music performer or owner, and the needs of the consumer. Digital rights management schemes encoded in the files provide various ways of reducing unauthorized copying while allowing fair use by the consumer.

Drop-Frame Time Code This code is a version of the SMPTE TIME CODE and is used for color video recording. The original time code labeled each frame of a motion picture or videotape with a precise time. The frame rate of movies is 24 per second and that of black and white television is 30 per second in the U.S. With these formats, the time code follows real time; that is, it runs in synch with the clock on the wall. The introduction of NTSC color television required the frame rate to be changed to 29.97 frames per second to prevent the color carrier from interfering with the video and sound carriers, which were fixed in FREQUENCY. This means there are 108 extra frames in a 1-hour color program, and the time code frame count would add up to 3.6 extra seconds of time in the hour. To avoid this, the drop-frame time code was introduced to drop two frames at the beginning of each minute, except at the beginning of every tenth minute. This gets rid of the extra 108 frames, and the frame times run in synch with the wall clock. The term may be abbreviated DF or DFTC. If a sound RECORDIST on the set does not properly set his time code for DF or non-DF, his synch will be audibly off. The editors might be able to fix it in post-production, however.

Dropout In ANALOG MAGNETIC TAPE recording, the quality of the recorded SIGNAL depends on the uniformity of the magnetic coating of the tape. If its SENSITIVITY varies from place to place on the tape, the signal level will be reduced periodically, and these reductions in level are called dropouts.

A dropout seldom is complete, causing only a few DECIBELS of signal reduction, but the combined effect of small dropouts is an increased noise level in the reproduced signal. Newer recording tapes are much more free from dropouts than older tapes were.

In DIGITAL recording, dropouts cause momentary loss of data and would result in very strong noises in the audio if it were not for ERROR CORRECTION schemes, which either correct the error or make an approximation or prediction of what the data would look like if they were there. A serious digital dropout may simply mute the audio.

Dry Lacking in reverberation; DEAD.

DSD Direct Stream Digital™, a proprietary audio CODEC developed by Sony and Philips for use in the Super Audio Compact Disc (SACD). DSD bandwidth is normally 2.8224 Mb per channel (64 times 44.1 kHz), with optional sampling rates of 32 or 128 times 44.1 kHz. DSD uses a delta-sigma ADC to generate a 2.8224 MHz, 1-bit SIGNAL, a rate chosen as a simple multiple of the lowest common high-FIDELITY PCM sampling rate, 44.1 kHz. The 1-bit data stream is recorded directly to disc, inherently improving the resultant audio quality by doing away with anti-imaging BRICK WALL FILTERS, and simplifying ERROR CORRECTION. Sony claims that the sampling rate is so high that it more nearly approximates the original ANALOG signal, allowing EQUALIZERS and other effects processors to better simulate analog effects. A number of DSP algorithms are available that allow the optimization of either bandwidth or dynamic range.

The delta-sigma DIGITAL-TO-ANALOG CONVERTER uses a negative FEEDBACK loop to accumulate the audio WAVEFORM. If the input waveform, accumulated over one sampling period, rises above the value accumulated in the negative feedback loop during previous samples, the converter outputs a digital "1." If the waveform falls relative to the accumulated value, a digital "0" is output. As a result, full positive waveforms will be all 1s. Full negative waveforms will be all 0s. The zero point will be represented by alternating 1s and 0s. Because the instantaneous amplitude of the analog waveform is represented by the density of pulses, the method is sometimes called Pulse Density Modulation (PDM).

DSD is probably an updating and refinement of the Philips BITSTREAM technology of the 1980s.

DSP *See* DIGITAL SIGNAL PROCESSING.

DTMF Abbreviation for Dual-Tone Multifrequency. DTMF techniques are used for sending coded information over transmission channels. In designing such a system, care must be taken that distortion in the transmission channel will not interfere with the signals. The frequencies are chosen to be noncommensurate with each other so harmonics of one tone cannot be confused with the other tones. The most common example of DTMF signals are the "touch tones" generated by modern telephones. The term "Touch Tone" was filed as a trademark owned by AT&T in 1960, but the trademark was canceled in 1984. The term is apparently now a trademark of a series of percussion mallets!

DTS A company, Digital Theater Systems, and their products. DTS was originally developed for the film industry and is a 5.1-format theater surround-sound system that uses 6 discrete channels and a perceptual encoding scheme for digital surround-sound on a CD-ROM interlocked with a time code to a movie projector. They also have similar systems for LASERDISC, DVD, and CD. A special DTS decoder is always required for playback. A DTS CD carries 6 channels of digital audio in 5.1 format with 20-bit words at a 44.1 kHz sample rate and a compression ratio of about 3:1. One major difference of DTS on film over DOLBY DIGITAL is that the film itself does not carry the digital sound track, only a time code. DTS was first used in 1993 in the film *Jurassic Park*.

DTV, Digital Television The standard for digital broadcast television in the U.S. including HDTV and SDTV, formulated by ATSC (Advanced Television Systems Committee).

Dual Capstan Some tape recorders have two CAPSTANS, one on either side of the head assembly. This is sometimes called a closed-loop drive, and the motion of the tape is very well controlled with such a system. Perturbations in speed due to supply reel or take-up reel disturbances are minimized. *See also* CLOSED LOOP TAPE DRIVE.

Dub A copy of a recorded tape is called a dub, and the process of making the copy is called dubbing.

Ducker A special device used in paging/PA systems and some radio stations to reduce the volume of the broadcast SIGNAL in the presence of another signal, usually an announcer's voice. The ducker enables the voice to be heard clearly over the background regardless of the former strength of the background.

The ducker develops a control VOLTAGE from the voice signal and uses this to control the GAIN of a voltage-controlled AMPLIFIER through which the background signal is passed. The voice signal is then mixed with the reduced-level background signal, and the mixture is broadcast.

Ducted Port A modification of the BASS REFLEX loudspeaker system where a tube, or "duct," is placed internally over the hole in the cabinet. The purpose is to reduce the FREQUENCY of the HELMHOLTZ RESONANCE, allowing a smaller cabinet than a standard bass reflex would require. However, the ducted port has a higher Q, i.e., it has less DAMPING, and can therefore sound more "boomy" than a conventional bass reflex. In some ducted port systems, the air velocity is quite high, and it can produce audible sound, called PORT NOISE.

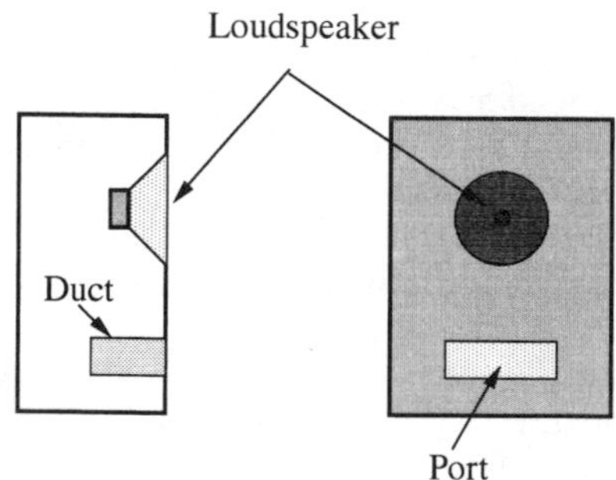

Ducted Port Loudspeaker

Dummy Head *See* BINAURAL RECORDING.

Dummy Load For convenience in POWER AMPLIFIER testing, the LOUDSPEAKER is usually replaced with a noninductive resistor capable of dissipating the full power output of the amplifier. This resistor is called a dummy load. The resistive dummy load is a poor simulation of an actual speaker load, however, due to the complex impedance of a real speaker.

Dust Cap A circular, usually dome-shaped, piece of lightweight cardboard, aluminum, or similar material that is glued to the center of LOUDSPEAKER cones to protect the voice COIL from dust and iron filings. Note that the diameter of the dust cap has nothing to do with the diameter of the voice coil that it covers. Besides covering the area, the cap is also decorative, and perhaps it contributes to the piston action of the cone. Small dents in the cap are unlikely to be detrimental and can often be simply pulled out with sticky tape.

DUT Electronic technicians' shorthand for "Device Under Test."

DVD Originally an abbreviation for Digital Video Disc, then gradually changed to Digital Versatile Disc, and now stands for . . . nothing, just DVD. The DVD has the same dimensions as a regular music CD, but it can hold about six or more times as much information as a CD. A DVD cannot be played on a standard audio CD player; however, many DVD players can play music CDs and other disc formats. Several standards apply to the DVD.

DVD AUDIO discs can handle digital quantization of 16, 20, or 24 bits at sampling rates of 44.1 kHz, 48 kHz, 88.2 kHz, 96 kHz, 167.4 kHz, and 192 kHz. The DVD is also sometimes called the Multi Media Compact Disc (MMCD) or the Multi-Media Video File (MMVF). The digital audio on a DVD movie is DOLBY DIGITAL® in the countries conforming to the NTSC television standard. Variants of the DVD format for data have been introduced into computers.

DX Slang for "distance" as applied to radio reception. In the early days of radio, hearing a station more than 20 miles away or so was called DX reception.

Dynagroove A proprietary system for adding a certain amount of HARMONIC DISTORTION to signals recorded on ANALOG STEREO records in such a way that the TRACING DISTORTION caused by the playback STYLUS is effectively cancelled out. It was introduced by RCA, but was not very effective because of the lack of standardization in playback stylus dimensions.

Dynamic, Dynamics When applied to MICROPHONES, HEADPHONES, and LOUDSPEAKERS, the term "dynamic" means that the operating principle is a coil of wire moving in a magnetic field. It seems strange that the term has not been applied to MOVING COIL phono CARTRIDGES, which are called "moving coil cartridges."

The magnetic field is nowadays always provided by a permanent magnet, but in earlier times, electromagnets were used, especially in loudspeakers. Such loudspeakers were called electrodynamic.

The term "dynamics" refers to the changes in LOUDNESS in a piece of music.

Dynamic Filter A dynamic filter is a type of single-pass noise reduction system that uses one or two FILTERS whose cutoff frequencies are controlled by the level of the SIGNAL. As the signal level falls during soft passages, the high-FREQUENCY response is reduced (like turning down the TREBLE tone control), and when the signal level is high, the full BANDWIDTH is restored.

The effective operation of such a system depends on the fact that the noise will be MASKED by the signal during loud passages, and this is true in many, but by no means all, cases.

A key element in the design of dynamic filters is the TIME CONSTANTS during which the bandwidth is changing. If they are too fast, DISTORTION will result, and if too slow, the noise will be heard to swish in and out as the signal level changes.

There are several manufacturers making such noise filters. The first one to be placed on the commercial market was H. H. Scott's DYNAURAL system.

Dynamic Headroom The dynamic headroom of a power AMPLIFIER is a measure of its ability to handle short BURSTS of power without overload. Such strong short signals are common in music.

According to the EIA, it is to be measured as the ratio of the level of a 1-KILOHERTZ tone lasting 20 milliseconds, which is at the CLIPPING point, to the average continuous SINE WAVE power output. In other words, it expresses how much more instantaneous power an amplifier will produce compared to its continuous power, and it is expressed in DECIBELS. Amplifiers vary widely in this ability, and ones with high dynamic headroom sound "louder" than similar-sized ones with lower dynamic headroom.

Dynamic Microphone A dynamic microphone consists of a diaphragm with a COIL of wire attached to it such that SOUND PRESSURE moving the diaphragm causes the coil to move in a magnetic field supplied by a permanent magnet. Motion of the coil causes an electric CURRENT to be induced in it, and this is the signal output of the microphone. It is similar to a dynamic LOUDSPEAKER operating in reverse.

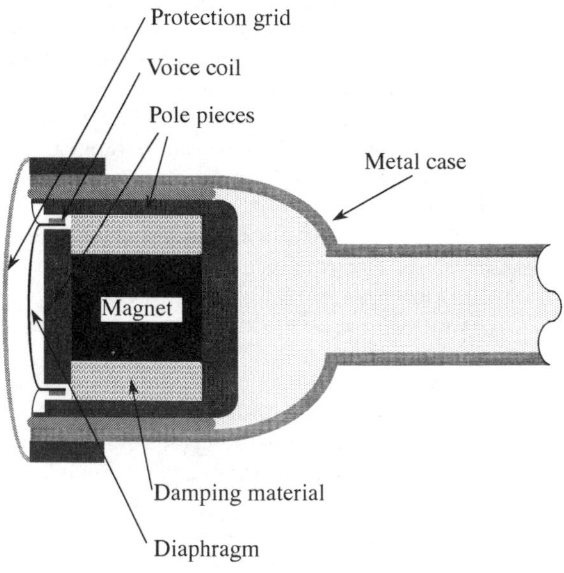

Dynamic Microphone

A dynamic microphone in its simplest form is a PRESSURE MICROPHONE, and so is OMNIDIRECTIONAL in its POLAR RESPONSE curve, but more complex types are made with CARDIOID and SUPER-CARDIOID patterns.

Dynamic microphones were first made by the Western Electric company in the early 1930s, and they had a somewhat irregular response to various frequencies. They were rapidly improved to take their place among other high-FIDELITY types. But a high-quality dynamic microphone is not easy to make, and some of them are more expensive than quality CONDENSER MICROPHONES.

Because the moving parts in a dynamic microphone are relatively massive and quite highly DAMPED, this type of microphone does not respond as readily to TRANSIENT sounds as do condenser microphones, and the result is a certain lack of smoothness. Dynamic microphones are quite rugged and will stand up to a lot of punishment. They are easy to use because no power supply is needed, as contrasted with most condenser microphones.

Dynamic Range The dynamic range of a sound is the ratio of the strongest, or loudest, part to the weakest, or softest, part; it is measured in DECIBELS. A full orchestra may have a dynamic range of 90 dB, meaning the softest passages are 90 dB less powerful than the loudest ones. Dynamic range is a power ratio, and has nothing to do with the absolute level of the sound.

An AUDIO signal also has a dynamic range, which is sometimes confused with SIGNAL-TO-NOISE RATIO. Rarely is the dynamic range of an audio system as large as the dynamic range of an orchestra because of several factors. The inherent NOISE of the recording medium determines the softest possible recorded sound, and the maximum SIGNAL capacity of the system (CLIPPING level) limits the loudest possible sound. Many times an extremely wide dynamic range is not desirable (e.g., in radio broadcasting for listening in cars) and broadcasters frequently use COMPRESSORS and LIMITERS to reduce the dynamic range of the signals before they are transmitted. This type of SIGNAL PROCESSING distorts the music in a more or less noticeable way, symphonic music being the most sensitive to it.

The dynamic range of recorded signals can be increased by VOLUME EXPANDERS, such as the ones made by the dbx company.

Dynaural Dynaural was the trade name for a noise-reduction system introduced by H. H. Scott in the 1940s. It was a DYNAMIC FILTER that reduced the high-FREQUENCY response as the SIGNAL level became lower. Then, in loud passages, full response was restored. The theory of operation is that low-level music does not need as full a range of reproduction because of the FLETCHER-MUNSON EFFECT, i.e., our ears become less sensitive to high frequencies as the level is reduced. The loud passages of the music, which require full range, effectively MASK the high-frequency noise. This type of noise-reduction system is called a dynamic filter, and several others have been marketed in recent years.

The PSYCHOACOUSTIC phenomenon of louder sounds masking softer ones is the basis upon which all noise-reduction systems operate. If the music does not mask the noise during loud passages, then no noise-reduction scheme will work.

Dynaural was what is today called a single-pass system in that the signal was processed only after being recorded. Other systems, such as COMPANDERS, process the signal before and after being recorded in order to reestablish the proper dynamics to the music. One problem with the Dynaural was that its high-frequency reduction was all too audible during softer passages, and the filter could be heard swishing up and down with the DYNAMICS of the music.

E

Earbuds Small, lightweight earphones that fit into the concha at the entrance to the ear canal of the outer ear. They are typically used with portable CD and MP3 players and radios.

Earphones *See* HEADPHONES.

Earth *See* GROUND.

EBU European Broadcasting Union. An international professional society that, among other things, helps establish audio standards. Active membership of the EBU is open to broadcasting organizations or groups of such organizations from a member country of the International Telecommunication Union (ITU) situated in the European broadcasting area.

Echo Commonly used incorrectly to mean REVERBERATION, echo, technically, is a discrete sound reflection arriving at least 50 milliseconds after the direct sound. It also must be significantly above the level of the reverberation at that time.

"Echo chambers" are reverberation rooms, which are carefully designed to be without echoes. If an actual echo is desired in a recording, a DIGITAL TIME DELAY device is used, where the time delay is variable. An ANALOG tape recorder has sometimes been used to add a time delay, the delay representing the time it takes the tape to move between the record and reproduce heads. This was called "tape echo," and is appropriate usage.

Eddy Currents Eddy currents are induced in electrical conductors by fluctuating magnetic fields in the conductors. These currents are localized, and they circulate in rather small areas of the material. Iron, being a reasonably good conductor, as well as having a large magnetic PERMEABILITY, has eddy currents induced in it when it is used as a CORE of a TRANSFORMER. The eddy currents cause the iron to heat due to its electrical resistance, and this represents a power loss—the higher the FREQUENCY and the more rapid the changes in the magnetic field, the greater the loss. To reduce the effect, the transformer core is made up of many layers or sheets of iron, which are insulated from one another. This keeps the eddy currents down to small areas, reducing the power loss from heating and raising the efficiency of the transformer.

Some magnetic materials, such as ferrite, have high resistance, so eddy currents are small in strength. Ferrite is a very efficient material for transformer cores as a result.

There is a type of electric motor, called the eddy current motor, which uses copper rotors in which eddy currents are induced. The magnetic field set up by the eddy currents opposes the magnetic field that generated them, causing the rotor to turn. The eddy current motor was used in some early 78-rpm phonographs, where a mechanical governor controlled its speed.

Edge A subjective impression of a certain roughness in the reproduced sound of a musical instrument. It is usually caused by nonuniform high-FREQUENCY RESPONSE in the LOUDSPEAKER or other audio device.

Edge Slotting Edge slotting is the cutting of small grooves in the surface of an ANALOG tape recorder head where tape edges would otherwise contact a ledge caused by wear. This allows tape to always maintain contact with the head surface in spite of wear or wider than normal tape. As an analog tape recorder head wears, it creates a "trough" in the face of the head surface that is nominally the width of the tape used. The width of tape varies slightly within a tolerance, and it is possible to get a portion of wider than normal tape. When wider tape tries to go through the wear "trough," the edges of the tape may flex or the tape may move away from the surface of the head. Edge slotting alleviates this problem. Inexpensive consumer heads would never be slotted, but use a felt pressure pad to keep the tape against the head. Pressure pads cause many other problems, though. Also known as head slotting.

Edison Cell A type of STORAGE CELL developed by Thomas Edison. It uses nickel and iron ELECTRODES and an alkaline ELECTROLYTE consisting of a solution of potassium and lithium hydroxides. Edison cells are somewhat complex to build but are very rugged and difficult to damage, and they have an energy storage capacity much greater than the same weight of LEAD-ACID CELLS. However, they have a higher internal resistance, making them unsuitable when high CURRENT is required, such as for starting cars. Edison cells found much use as current sources for railroad switching applications and also were sometimes used in early radio B BATTERIES.

Edison Effect The ability of a vacuum DIODE to carry a unidirectional electric CURRENT was originally called the Edison effect, after Thomas Edison, who first investigated the phenomenon. In working with his newly invented light bulb, Edison conducted many experiments to determine why it darkened with use and why the negative end of the filament was always where it burned out. He noted that if another ELECTRODE were introduced into the bulb, and if it were connected to the positive terminal of a BATTERY, a unidirectional current was established. Edison could not explain it, nor did he envision a practical use for it, but, being Edison, he immediately patented it, calling it an "electrical indicator." This patent, issued in 1884, is considered the world's first electronics patent. William Preece, an English investigator, visited Edison and obtained some of his mysterious bulbs. It was Preece who coined the term *Edison effect*. *See also* FLEMING VALVE.

Edit Decision List, EDL When EDITING a sound or video recording or motion picture, the various TAKES are auditioned and a list of the desired ones is created, along with notes telling exactly where the cuts are to be made. This could be done manually written on paper, but today a computerized list of the desired takes is created in the proper sequence, along with information telling exactly where the cuts are to be made and any processing to be done when assembling the entire list. The resulting document is the EDL, which the computer follows to assemble the edited result. Note that one can control ANALOG recorders with DIGITAL edit controllers.

Editing Intercutting of several recordings of a musical selection in order to make an improved apparent performance.

The advent of MAGNETIC TAPE as an original medium for making PHONOGRAPH records allowed recorded performances to be perfected by replacing wrong notes and removing extraneous noises, etc. (Editing of a similar type was possible in the recording of piano rolls, an activity that many well-known pianists engaged in during the early 1900s.)

The technique for editing ANALOG tape is quite simple: the tape is cut at the appropriate point, selected by moving it slowly across the head by hand in order to hear the point, and another section is attached with adhesive "splicing" tape. If one is careful, undetectable splices may be accomplished, and a composite recording can be made with nobody the wiser.

DIGITAL editing is essentially the same technique, but the edited version is a copy made from the takes to be intercut. This is all done electronically rather than mechanically, as the software arranges the takes according to the edit decision list. Early digital tape formats contained an analog track to allow "razor blade editing" like an analog tape, with electronics attempting to compensate for the damage to the data stream at the splice point. This was abandoned as affordable computing power became available. The precision in the timing of digital edits on some early systems was determined by the format of the digital signals. In some digital audio tape recorders, the signal was recorded onto the tape in blocks of data called FRAMES, a video-like format. There are 30 frames per second in the American (NTSC) standard system, and 25 frames per second in the European (PAL/SECAM) video standard. Editing points could most easily occur between frames, meaning the precision in timing of the edit was 1/30th or 1/25th of a second respectively. Today it is easy to edit at any point on the audio WAVEFORM.

Virtually all recorded music is edited, making performing artists infallible in the ears of the record-buying public. (One performer was heard to murmur, on hearing the playback of the edited master tape for a record he was making, "Wow, I wish I could play like that.")

Editing of any kind puts tremendous stress on musicians who appear live before an audience as well as on record, and calls for ever more accuracy and care in performance. This can, it is contended by many, lead to dull, "mechanical" performances, less imbued with spontaneity and musical flexibility. At least one famous critic has said that all the younger pianists sound very much alike, with nowhere near the individual differences heard a generation or so ago among a similar group. (No less an old master than Vladimir Horowitz has said that in any performance he expects to miss several notes, explaining that to avoid this, he would have to play very carefully, without taking any chances, and that the music would thereby suffer.)

EDL *See* EDIT DECISION LIST.

EE, E to E A term more often heard in the video industry, it means monitoring the signal directly through a recorder's electronics (electronic to electronic) and not after the recording has been made via the CONFIDENCE HEAD. Audio people tend to refer to "source" monitoring as opposed to "tape" monitoring during recording.

EE Tape, Extra Efficiency Tape A type of improved open reel recording tape introduced in the 1980s. In a manner similar to the chrome cassette, EE tape offered higher performance but required a machine with a special EE equalization setting, 35 microseconds instead of 50. The system has essentially died along with the use of open reels for home recording.

Effects Specialized audio devices found in recording studios, such as REVERBERATORS, FLANGERS, PHASERS, and DELAY LINES, are called effects, which probably is derived from the "sound effects" of motion picture jargon. Sometimes the abbreviation FX, a shortened version of EFX, is used.

Effects Bus The mixing bus in a recording console used to mix the signal to be sent to the various EFFECTS devices. It is also called the "effects send bus."

Effects Return An input on a mixing console that receives the modified signal from the EFFECTS devices. The effects return inputs usually have volume controls, or FADERS, to control the intensity of the particular effect in use.

Effects Send An output from a mixing console that is connected to the input of an EFFECTS device. The effects send outputs usually have volume controls to set the SIGNAL level the effects device will see, and the overall level of all the effects send outputs may be controlled by an "effects master" control operating from the EFFECTS BUS.

Efficiency A measure, usually applied to LOUDSPEAKERS, of how much of the input electrical energy is converted to sound energy, expressed in percent. The remaining energy is converted into heat. Most DIRECT RADIATOR loudspeakers are about 1 or 2 percent efficient, while HORN-loaded units may be as much as 10 to 20 or even 30 percent efficient.

High efficiency is important in commercial sound systems where high volume levels are desired in order to reduce the AMPLIFIER power output requirements. Also, low-efficiency speakers would be damaged by heat when driven to high power levels.

Efficiency, contrary to some popular opinion, is not related to quality, or "FIDELITY." In fact, a good case can be made for the assertion that low-efficiency loudspeakers, in general, are more accurate than high-efficiency ones. This is because low efficiency implies the existence of more DAMPING, which absorbs energy and makes response CURVES smoother and reduces the effects of RESONANCES.

EFM *See* EIGHT-TO-FOURTEEN MODULATION.

EFX Short for EFFECTS.

EIA Electronic Industries Alliance. Previously called Electronic Industries Association. A private U.S. organization consisting of manufacturers for the purpose of agreeing on industry standards in audio and video equipment. This is the group that standardized the dimensions of the 7-inch tape reel for consumer tape recorders, among many other things.

EIAJ Electronics Industry Association of Japan. This is the Japanese agency involved in the setting of standards, not only for audio equipment, but for video as well. The EIAJ also makes recommendations for test procedures, and published a set of recommended tests for COMPACT DISC players.

Eigentone An acoustical RESONANCE or STANDING WAVE in a room caused by parallel wall surfaces, also called a room mode. Any set of parallel walls will establish a series of standing waves, the lowest one of which has the wall spacing as a half-wavelength. A standing wave causes a nonuniform sound level distribution in a room, with peaks and dips at various locations in the room. Thus, two sound-reflecting walls spaced 16 feet apart would give rise to a resonance at about 30 hertz and at all the harmonic frequencies of 30 Hz. If the surfaces are absorbers of sound, the standing waves are much less pronounced. The lowest FREQUENCY mode between parallel surfaces will produce a sound pressure maximum at each surface and a sound pressure minimum halfway between them. If the surfaces are very reflective at that frequency, the minimum will be very low, and the sound may be almost inaudible at that position.

In a room designed for listening to music, either live or recorded, the length, width, and height dimensions should not be equal, so that the modes between different pairs of surfaces will not occur at the same frequencies and reinforce each other. The relative dimensions should not be commensurate; that is, they should not have a simple arithmetic ratio. The golden ratio, which is about 1:1.62, is sometimes recommended as the ideal proportion for the dimensions of a music room.

In recent years, there has been quite a bit of emphasis placed on the location of LOUDSPEAKERS in rooms to avoid the excitation of certain strong room modes, and it is true that if placed at a minimum for a particular mode, very little energy will be drawn from the speaker at that particular modal frequency. Also, sometimes complex EQUALIZATION of a sound system will be attempted to reduce the effect of modes. But the distribution of sound energy in the room will still be nonuniform, for this is dictated by the modes themselves, not the location of the sound source. The best way to correct such a situation is to eliminate the mode rather than relocate or equalize the loudspeaker.

One way to avoid strong room modes is to avoid smooth hard parallel surfaces. Because low-frequency modes are the most objectionable, a listening room for recorded music should have a fair amount of low-frequency absorption. Another technique for reducing the effects of low-frequency room modes is active cancellation by the introduction of a sound that is of opposite POLARITY to the objectionable room mode sound. This is done by sensing the sound field near a boundary of the room with a MICROPHONE and reproducing this SIGNAL in PHASE opposition with a suitable amplifier and loudspeaker.

Eight-to-Fourteen Modulation, EFM The coding of the BITS in the COMPACT DISC system in order to optimize the process of reading off the disc.

Each 16-bit sample is divided into two 8-bit blocks, which are then expanded to 14 bits each by the addition of certain zeros and ones. The purpose of this is to constrain the pattern and thus reduce the DC content of the code. Three extra bits called "merging" bits are added at the end of the 14-bit code—two to ensure that the code meets the pattern constraint, and one to minimize the power of the bit stream SIGNAL at low frequencies. This procedure forces the pits and "lands" on the disc to be between 3 bits and 11 bits long, and their repetition rate is more nearly optimized to the time constant of the laser detector. Thus, 17 channel bits (14 EFM plus 3 merging) are used instead of the 8 original audio bits for each block.

Eight-Track Cartridge A slim plastic box containing ¼-inch magnetic tape in an endless loop configuration so it could be played continuously if desired. It had four separate stereo pairs of tracks and a moving head played any of the four stereo programs. Performance was not very good, and the endless loop precluded rewinding or fast forwarding, but it was widely used in cars before the advent of the cassette. It was developed by the Lear company, of William Powell Lear, the man who invented a business jet.

EIN, Equivalent Input Noise Also called input referred noise. EIN is how noise is specified on mixing consoles, stand-alone mic preamps and other signal processing units with mic inputs. The problem in measuring mixing consoles (and all mic preamps) is knowing ahead of time how much gain is going to be used. The mic stage itself is the dominant noise generator; therefore, the output noise is almost totally determined by the amount of GAIN: turn the gain up, and the output noise goes up accordingly. Thus, the EIN is the amount of noise added to the input signal. Both are then amplified to obtain the final output signal.

For example, say your mixer has an EIN of -130 dBu. This means the noise is 130 dB below a reference point of 0.775 volts (0 dBu). If your microphone puts out, say, -50 dBu under normal conditions, then the S/N at the input to the mic preamp is 80 dB (i.e., the added noise is 80 dB below the input signal). This is uniquely determined by the magnitude of the input signal and the EIN. From here on out, turning up the gain increases both the signal and the noise by the same amount.[12]

Elastomer A synthetic rubbery substance that has a high degree of DAMPING and high compliance. It is used in phono CARTRIDGES to damp various mechanical resonances. In the old days natural rubber was used for mechanical damping of phonograph moving parts, but it gradually hardened over time.

Elcaset Elcaset was a type of audio tape cassette containing ¼-inch tape and running at 3¾ inches per second tape speed. The standard cassette uses tape only a little wider than ⅛ inch and runs at 1⅞ inches per second.

The Elcaset was introduced in the late 1970s as a high-quality alternative to the COMPACT CASSETTE, and it did have relatively impressive characteristics. However, it was introduced so late that the compact cassette had already been widely accepted as a music recording medium and had been developed to the point of very fine performance. The typical consumer was simply not willing to invest in a different machine and in the higher costs of the Elcasets, and the system died in the marketplace.

12. Thanks to Dennis Bohn, Rane Corp.

Electret Microphone A type of CONDENSER MICROPHONE that does not require a polarizing VOLTAGE. The electret microphone contains on the back plate, or inherent in the diaphragm, a material called an electret, which holds a permanent electric CHARGE. An electret is the electrostatic counterpart of a permanent magnet. Sometimes electret microphones are called prepolarized condenser microphones.

In the electret microphone, there is a slight danger of the charge leaking off the electret due to high humidity or high temperatures. More recent designs have minimized this problem. If the electret loses its charge, the SENSITIVITY of the microphone will gradually decrease, reducing the SIGNAL-TO-NOISE RATIO.

The IMPEDANCE of the electret microphone is very high, as in the condenser microphone, so there must be a PREAMPLIFIER close by. This may consist of a small FIELD EFFECT TRANSISTOR, which is built into the microphone housing. A small battery may be included to power the preamplifier, or it may operate by PHANTOM POWER.

Inexpensive electret microphones costing less than a dollar are found in virtually all consumer electronics with voice input, such as cell phones. High-quality electret microphones found in recording studios can cost several thousand dollars.

Electricity "The force causing all natural phenomena not known to be caused by something else."—Ambrose Bierce. *See also* CHARGE.

Electroacoustics The science that deals with the application of electrical principles and apparatus to acoustical phenomena. TRANSDUCERS, such as MICROPHONES, LOUDSPEAKERS, and PHONO CARTRIDGES, are electroacoustic devices.

Electrode A part of an electric CIRCUIT that conveys CURRENT or VOLTAGE from one section of the circuit to another. Examples are the PLATE, CATHODE, and GRIDS of a vacuum TUBE; the BASE, emitter, and collector of a TRANSISTOR; and the carbon rods in an ARC light.

Electrodynamic Many years ago, certain DYNAMIC MICROPHONES and LOUDSPEAKERS used electromagnets rather than permanent magnets to attain the needed magnetic fields. These devices were thus called electrodynamic. The availability of very strong permanent magnet material has made them obsolete.

Electrolyte Literally, a liquid that can conduct an electric current. It usually consists of water with certain chemicals dissolved in it. Most batteries contain a liquid or paste electrolyte, as do most ELECTROLYTIC CAPACITORS.

Electrolytic Capacitor An electrolytic capacitor is a type of CAPACITOR that must be polarized in order to operate correctly. The name comes from the fact that an ELECTROLYTE is used as one of the conductors. In other words, it must have a direct VOLTAGE placed across it, and moreover, this voltage must be of the correct direction. An electrolytic capacitor will have a very high IMPEDANCE when a positive voltage is placed on it, but will have a relatively low impedance when this voltage is reversed. It acts somewhat like a DIODE and is thus NONLINEAR.

The electrolytic capacitor has a much greater CAPACITANCE for its size and cost than a conventional capacitor and is therefore desirable for use in AUDIO circuits. As long as it has the proper voltage across it (i.e., it is properly "biased"), it works correctly in audio circuits, but if the BIAS is lost, the capacitor will cause HARMONIC DISTORTION in the SIGNAL it is passing.

Electrolytic capacitors are used extensively in audio power AMPLIFIERS, especially for power supply FILTERING, where their very large values of capacitance are needed. Small ones are also much used as coupling capacitors between the stages of amplifiers.

There are available today so-called bipolar electrolytics, which have two capacitors connected in series "back-to-back" in a single housing. They do not need to be polarized and are often used in LOUDSPEAKER CROSSOVER NETWORKS.

Electrolytic Detector The first diode DETECTOR, invented by the American engineer Reginald Fessenden around 1901. Fessenden's detector used a small aluminum cup containing a mixture of acid and water, and a small silver wire that dipped into the acid. This arrangement allows CURRENT to pass in one direction only and thus can be used to RECTIFY, or DETECT, the received radio signal. Dr. Lee DeForest also made an electrolytic detector for his wireless system, and there ensued a legal battle that was finally resolved in Fessenden's favor. All this predates the FLEMING VALVE of 1904, which was the first vacuum diode and was also used as a detector.

Electromagnetic Compatibility, or EMC Audio equipment that is designed to be immune to ELECTROMAGNETIC INTERFERENCE is said to be electromagnetically compatible.

Electromagnetic Interference, or EMI A great many of the unwanted noises heard in audio systems, such as hum, "static," and buzz, are caused by electromagnetic waves that are picked up and amplified by the audio system. Common sources of EMI radiation are fluorescent lamps, power lines, computers, automobile ignition systems, SOLID-STATE light dimmers, AM and FM radio transmitters, and television transmitters. EMI caused by very high frequency transmissions is called RADIO FREQUENCY INTERFERENCE (RFI) and TELEVISION INTERFERENCE (TVI).

EMI can be a major problem under certain circumstances and is usually very difficult to eliminate from audio equipment that is not designed to be immune to it in the first place. Properly designed equipment is said to possess ELECTROMAGNETIC COMPATIBILITY (EMC).

Methods of controlling EMI include SHIELDING of audio wiring and devices, grounding and elimination of ground loops, balancing of audio circuits and twisting of the wires in a balanced line, TRANSFORMER coupling, and the use of bypass CAPACITORS and FERRITE beads in low-level circuits.

Electromagnetism The science of the interactions between electrical and magnetic phenomena.

In the early days of physics, it was not known that there was any connection between electricity and magnetism, and they were studied independently. It was the brilliant Scottish physicist James Clerk Maxwell who in 1873 first postulated the quantitative relationship between electricity and magnetism, and predicted the existence of electromagnetic waves. This theoretical understanding brought about by Maxwell's famous equations led to the development of all the electrical and electronic equipment we know today. *See also* MAGNETISM.

Electron The elementary particle that carries the smallest unit of electric CHARGE is the electron. An electric CURRENT normally consists of a flow of electrons, although in some cases, a current could consist of a flow of positive charges. In a vacuum TUBE, electrons are boiled off the hot CATHODE and are attracted by the positively charged PLATE. They constitute the current through the tube.

The theory of electrostatics says that like charges repel one another and unlike charges attract. Any charge has an electric field around it, and another charge in this field will feel a force. Electric fields in tubes or the SEMICONDUCTORS of TRANSISTORS cause the charges to drift one way or the other, and this constitutes the electric current. In transistors, the current is sometimes thought of as if it consisted of positive charges, but normally it consists of electrons.

Electronic Architecture The physical design of the various interconnections of the components in a DISCRETE or INTEGRATED CIRCUIT are sometimes called its architecture. *See also* TOPOLOGY.

Electronic Crossover *See* ACTIVE CROSSOVER.

Electrosonic *See* INTENSITY STEREO.

Elliptical Equalizer A special EQUALIZER that causes the two channels of a STEREO signal to be more nearly in PHASE at low FREQUENCIES. The purpose is to make the signal easier to cut onto a record.

Large out-of-phase, low-frequency stereo signals result in large vertical motion of the recording STYLUS, sometimes to the extent that the stylus will leave the surface of the record. This means the discontinuity in the groove cannot be tracked by the playback stylus. The elliptical equalizer actually works by introducing CROSSTALK between the channels at low frequencies. Making the signals in phase only at the low end does not appreciably reduce the apparent stereo separation, for our ears rely most on high-frequency CUES for the stereo effect.

The name comes from the path of the cutting stylus, which is more nearly confined to the form of an ellipse than a circle. *See also* MONO COMPATIBILITY.

Elliptical Filter A multiple-element LOW-PASS FILTER that has the steepest possible cutoff slope and a small amount of RIPPLE in the PASSBAND. Its name comes from the fact that elliptical functions are used in its design.

The elliptical filter is a low-pass or bandpass filter with one or more NOTCH filters added to it. The first notch is just a little above the CUTOFF FREQUENCY, reducing the response in this area. At higher frequencies where the notch filter has less ATTENUATION, another notch filter is added, etc.

Elliptical filters are excellent for use as ANTI-ALIASING FILTERS in DIGITAL audio devices, but they are complex and difficult to design.

EMC *See* ELECTROMAGNETIC COMPATIBILITY.

EMF Electromotive Force (EMF) is synonymous with VOLTAGE. The term "BACK EMF" is the usual usage, and it indicates a voltage induced in a VOICE COIL that is in opposition to the voltage applied externally to the coil. The back EMF is a result of the motion of the coil in the magnetic field of the LOUDSPEAKER.

EMI *See* ELECTROMAGNETIC INTERFERENCE. Also Electric and Musical Industries, the diverse British recording company formed by a merger of the Gramophone Company and Columbia Graphophone (sic) in 1931. In the same year, EMI opened the famous Abbey Road recording studio in London, and the chief EMI scientist, Alan Dower BLUMLEIN patented a means of recording stereophonic sound. This remarkable patent foresaw a great deal of future products, such as stereo records using a single groove with the STYLUS recording and playing the left and right channels by two separate motions angled 90 degrees apart—the same basic system as was used worldwide for stereo LP vinyl records first introduced in 1958 by EMI. Blumlein also foresaw the use of stereo sound for motion pictures, and a method for realizing it is covered in his 1931 patent.

The Bell Laboratories in the U.S. were also experimenting with stereo recording at the time, but there is no documentation of any communication between them and EMI.

Emitter Follower A CIRCUIT containing a BIPOLAR TRANSISTOR in such a configuration that its VOLTAGE GAIN is 1. It is a SOLID-STATE version of the CATHODE FOLLOWER. Emitter followers have very high INPUT IMPEDANCE and very low OUTPUT IMPEDANCE, making them suited to driving fairly long audio lines. The emitter follower has a large amount of CURRENT gain and can become unstable unless care is taken in its design. *See also* SOURCE FOLLOWER.

EMT Plate *See* PLATE REVERBERATION.

End-Addressed, End-Fired A MICROPHONE that is positioned so its end is pointed toward the sound source, as opposed to a side-addressed microphone, which is positioned with its side toward the sound source. Condenser microphones may be either end-fired or side-fired, and ribbon mics are almost always side-fired. Generally, what is considered the end or side is merely a function of the shape of the outer housing. The transducer itself, such as a diaphram, points toward the sound source.

Energy Time Curve The energy time curve is the ENVELOPE of the IMPULSE RESPONSE of a device, usually expressed as the common logarithm of the magnitude of the envelope.

If the impulse response of an AUDIO device is examined directly, it is not possible to see any detail where the response is at very low values because it is displayed on a LINEAR amplitude scale. This must be so because the impulse response of any device has both positive and negative values, and negative values cannot be represented on a LOGARITHMIC scale.

The ENVELOPE of the impulse response, however, is always positive, and it can be expressed on a log or DECIBEL scale. In this way, it is possible to see details at low levels that are invisible in the impulse response itself.

It is instructive to investigate the energy time curve of such devices as LOUDSPEAKERS, MICROPHONES, and entire sound-reinforcement systems, including the rooms in which they are placed. Special care must be taken in making energy time curve measurements, especially if FFT techniques are used, or large errors can occur.

Enhancer One of any signal processing devices for use in recordings and performance to add special effects. An example is the APHEX AURAL EXCITER.

In general, enhancers work by adding certain types and amounts of harmonic DISTORTION. The type of distortion (even-order harmonics or odd-order harmonics) added affects the subjective character of the resulting sound. It is interesting that harmonic distortion does not sound unpleasant unless it is present in relatively large amounts. This is because the harmonics are "in tune" with the music itself. This is not the case with some other types of distortion such as intermodulation, which sounds harsh and unpleasant.

Envelope *See* ADSR.

Envelope Delay Another name for GROUP DELAY.

Envelope Follower A device used in electronic music synthesis that will convert the envelope of a musical SIGNAL into a CONTROL VOLTAGE. That is, the output voltage will be low when the signal is soft and high when the signal is loud. This control voltage can then be used to control any number of parameters in the synthesizer.

Envelope Generator *See* ADSR.

Envelopment Envelopment is the characteristic of an auditorium that causes the listener to be surrounded or "enveloped" by sound, and it has been shown to be probably the most important single attribute of GOOD ACOUSTICS. It is related to DEUTLICHKEIT, a term originated in Germany.

A sense of envelopment in a room is caused by the existence of fairly early reflections (within 20 or 40 milliseconds) of sound from the side walls. Early reflections from the ceiling do not provide the same benefit, for they reinforce the direct rather than the reverberant sound, and sometimes give the room a somewhat "dry" and clinical sound. It has been shown that audiences greatly prefer the enveloping sound to come from fairly large angles from straight ahead. This means the room should be designed so the wall reflections move across the room, rather than towards the rear. A room with good envelopment sounds "warm" and agreeable, even if the REVERBERATION is lacking. On the other hand, a room with sufficient reverberation but lacking in envelopment is likely to sound "mushy" or "blurred" and indistinct. One objective measure of envelopment is the INTERAURAL CROSS-CORRELATION, or IACC, which is a measure of the differences in the sounds reaching the two ears. A relatively large value of IACC corresponds to a large subjective impression of envelopment.

Epoxy Patent The epoxy patent is a clever method of avoiding the piracy of proprietary CIRCUIT designs. When someone designs a particularly innovative electronic circuit, it is likely that it will be copied by other designers. To protect the circuit against this, it can be totally encased in opaque epoxy plastic. Then, a would-be pirate would have to destroy the assembly completely in order to get it apart. This procedure is called an "epoxy patent" in the vernacular.

EQ *See* EQUALIZER.

Equalizer, Equalization An equalizer, contrary to what its name implies, alters or distorts the relative strength of certain FREQUENCY ranges of an audio SIGNAL. In a sense, it should probably be called an "unequalizer." However, the first equalizers were used to make the energy at all frequencies equal, or to achieve "flat response," in telephone lines, and this is where the term originated. Another early use of equalizers was in the motion picture sound industry, where they were used to improve intelligibility in film sound tracks. Later on, equalizers were found useful for creating special sound effects in the early days of radio and movies, where they are extensively used to this day. All equalizers are made up of various CIRCUITS called FILTERS, which are frequency-selective networks containing RESISTORS (R), CAPACITORS (C), and INDUCTORS (L). Normally, filters attenuate certain frequency ranges and do not boost them; however, some equalizers that boost the signal are called filters.

The first consumer-type equalizers were the tone controls on radios, the first one of which was simply a variable low-pass filter to reduce "static" and other high-frequency noise. The familiar BASS and TREBLE tone controls came later. Today, equalizers are also used in vast numbers in SOUND REINFORCEMENT systems and in recording and broadcast studios for various purposes.

An equalizer can boost or attenuate a certain frequency band, but in common usage, *equalize* means to boost. The preferred terminology for the actual process is boost/cut rather than equalize/attenuate. In Britain preferred usage is lift/dip.

Equalizers that can have peaks in their response curves (such as parametric and graphic equalizers) are characterized by the relative sharpness of the peaks. The Q of a filter is a measure of this sharpness and is defined as the center frequency divided by the half-power BANDWIDTH. For instance, a one-third OCTAVE filter centered at 1,000 HERTZ will be 232 Hz wide at its half-power points. Its Q is thus 1,000/232, or 4.31. Filters with Q values much higher than this tend to "ring," distorting transients, and call attention to themselves when used in sound systems. *See also* Q.

Some equalizers, such as ⅓-octave graphics, have a constant Q regardless of the amount of boost or cut, and they are sometimes called "constant Q" equalizers. Most parametrics, on the other hand, have higher Q values with high boost or cut levels. These are called "proportional Q" equalizers.

All equalizers cause the signal to be selectively PHASE shifted, and the more sharply defined the equalization, the steeper the phase shift curve will be. For instance, an octave-band filter will have about a 90-degree phase shift spread over the octave band, while a $\frac{1}{10}$-octave filter will have the same 90-degree phase shift occurring in the narrow $\frac{1}{10}$-octave band. These phase shifts distort transient WAVEFORMS, for they really are variable time delays for different frequencies. In general, the more rapidly the phase is changing as a function of frequency, the more audible the effect is.

Many equalizers are integral parts of audio components and are not adjustable by the user. Such equalizers include DE-EMPHASIS, PRE-EMPHASIS, RIAA equalization, SHELVING, and NAB EQUALIZATION. Many other equalizers exist as stand-alone devices, and they can be roughly grouped as follows:

Active and passive equalizers: An active equalizer requires power to operate. It has active components in it such as TRANSISTORS and INTEGRATED CIRCUITS. A passive equalizer does not require any power to operate. Passive equalizers contain resistors, inductors, and capacitors, but no active components. Passive equalizers are essentially noiseless in operation and are very reliable and distortion-free, but they have INSERTION LOSS, which sometimes has to be compensated for by an amplifier. Active equalizers are very popular but suffer from noise, reduced dynamic range, and susceptibility to RFI. Many of the following types of equalizers exist as active or passive.

Rotary equalizer: An adjustable equalizer with several frequency bands with stepped rotary knobs to select the frequency range and the degree of boost or cut. The frequency bands are fixed.

Parametric equalizer: Somewhat like the rotary equalizer but with added control of the center frequencies and bandwidths of the frequency bands. Boost and cut and the other "parameters" are generally continuously variable rather than being stepped. An equalizer that does not allow variable control of all the parameters is sometimes called a quasi-parametric, and some units with slide controls rather than rotary are called para-graphic. Some parametrics allow cut only and are then called notch equalizers, band-reject equalizers, or cut-only equalizers. The Q values of most parametric equalizers increase at high boost or cut levels. Sometimes these equalizers are called proportional Q equalizers.

Graphic equalizer: A multiband variable equalizer that consists of a series of parallel filters, usually of the same bandwidth, that are capable of boosting the signal or cutting it. Each filter band is controlled by a slider knob, and these are arranged on the front panel of the equalizer so their positions show, at least approximately, the overall response curve for each setting. The band center frequencies are fixed for each band and are spaced proportionally to the logarithm of frequency. In other words, each filter controls a frequency span encompassing the same musical interval controlled by every other filter, such as octave bands or one-third octave bands. Some graphic equalizers do not have all the filter intervals equal, having the low-frequency bands narrower than the high-frequency ones. This makes a good deal of sense for applications such as the equalization of sound-reproducing systems in listening rooms, where low-frequency anomalies are generally more numerous than high-frequency anomalies.

Probably the most common graphic equalizer has one-third octave bandwidths. It has been shown that filters narrower than this, especially when used to boost the signal, are quite audible because the filters themselves ring. The ringing is less audible for narrowband notch filters.

One-third octave graphic equalizers have a constant Q regardless of the amount of boost or cut. They are sometimes called constant Q equalizers.

If all the knobs on a graphic equalizer are at the same level, one would assume the overall frequency response would be flat, but this is usually not the case. With most such units, a flat curve can be attained only with the knobs set for no boost or cut. A level boost or cut causes "ripple," or peaks or dips at each filter center frequency. For this reason, any graphic equalizer should be operated with the controls as close to the zero boost line as possible.

Transversal equalizer: A special and uncommon type of equalizer that uses a tapped time-delay line as the active element. A signal fed through a time delay and then connected back to the delay input and recirculated through it many times will have peaks and dips in its frequency response curve depending on the delay time and the loop GAIN of the delay line. By selecting many different delay times and judiciously connecting the various feedback loops, many different frequency response curves may be attained. The transversal equalizer is an analog, not a digital, device and can use a BUCKET BRIGADE, charge-coupled device, or an all-pass filter as a delay line. A similar result can be attained with digitized signals. *See* DIGITAL EQUALIZER.

Narrowband filter: Early in the days of sound reinforcement system equalization, very narrow notch filters were used in an attempt to reduce the tendency for acoustic FEEDBACK. The technique was pioneered by C. P. Boner. He used very narrow filters, sometimes as little as 5-Hz wide at the –3dB points, and he used as many as 150 of them, all custom-tuned, at once. It was later realized that the narrowband technique is much more complex than need be and that similar results, without doing as much violence to the signal quality, can be achieved by one-third octave filters.

In the digital domain, including the use of DAWS, all the types of equalization are accomplished by mathematical manipulation of the digitized audio signal, in many cases at much less expense than using analog devices. Digital editing can be more sophisticated than analog editing; for instance, phase shift problems can be tamed by the use of Finite Impulse Response (FIR) filtering which can be implemented to have no relative phase shift as a function of frequency. However, FIR filters do have a time delay that must be compensated for in the overall equalization setup.

Equivalent Circuit An electrical circuit that behaves like an ANALOG of a mechanical or acoustic system is called an equivalent circuit. It is interesting that mechanical quantities such as mass and stiffness can be modeled with electrical quantities such as inductance and capacitance. Theoretically, any mechanical system could be represented by an appropriately designed circuit. The important thing is that the behavior of electric circuits is well predicted mathematically, and the equations can be used to analyze the mechanical system. Generally it is easier to construct and analyze an electrical analog of a mechanical system than to analyze the mechanical system directly.

Erase Head A TAPE HEAD that is used to erase, or demagnetize, the tape before it reaches the record head in an ANALOG audio or video tape recorder. Some audio recorders allowed selective activation of individual erase tracks, some merely erased the entire width of the tape. If erasing the entire tape is acceptable, bulk erasing is usually more efficient and can leave less noise on the tape, but to use this benefit would require turning the erase head off, which is possible but seldom done. Instead, bulk erasing ensures an entirely blank tape, and users put up with the slight increase in erasure noise from the erase head. Note that the R-DAT needs no erase head—data is simply overwritten. *See also* BULK ERASER, DEGAUSSER.

Error Concealment A technique to reduce the audible effect of a digital error in a digital audio system when the error cannot be corrected by the techniques of ERROR CORRECTION. Error concealment usually consists of making a smooth transition from the last good data block before the error to the first good data block after the error.

Error Correction In DIGITAL audio systems, the sampled AMPLITUDES of the signal WAVEFORM are expressed by digital codes in the BINARY number system. The codes are grouped into "words" of eight binary digits (BITS) each. If in the transmission of the digital words some bits are missing, or are incorrect due to tape dropouts, etc., the result will be gross DISTORTION of that portion of the signal when it is reconstructed. Therefore, it is extremely important to provide detection and correction of such digital errors.

In a digital system, error detection is possible if the number of allowed words is less than the maximum. For example, in a two-bit transmission system we might allow only 00 and 11 as possible words. If we receive 01 or 10 at the end of the transmission chain, we know there is an error. We can't correct it, however, because we do not know whether a 00 or 11 was intended.

Things are a little different in a three-bit system. Suppose we allow 000 and 111 as valid words. Then, we can say a received 110 should probably be a 111, and a 100 should have been a 000. Thus we can make the substitutions and correct the information. To enable this, we have added one bit per word, and this is called a "parity check" bit.

COMPACT DISCS are produced with two simultaneous schemes of adding parity bits for error detection and correction. In this system, one set of audio samples is grouped into 32 eight-bit words (or BYTES), four of which are added parity bytes. The second code has a word length of 28 bytes of which four are parity bytes.

Although it is theoretically possible to correct up to four errors per word by fully utilizing this method, it is not done in practice because of the very large amount of hardware required to do it. Instead of error correction, the words with detected errors are replaced by words having intermediate values between the two adjacent correct words. In other words, an interpolation scheme is used. If two or more adjacent words are incorrect, the system simply "mutes" those words, effectively disconnecting the signal for that instant. It is surprising how tolerant the ear is to the presence of this muting—if it occurs infrequently and randomly, it is inaudible to most listeners.

This procedure of detection, interpolation, and muting might be called "ERROR CONCEALMENT" rather than error correction.

ET *See* TRANSCRIPTION.

Etching The process by which PRINTED CIRCUIT BOARDS are made. The boards are covered with copper, and the areas where the conductors will be are covered with an acid-resistant material. Then the board is immersed in an acid bath which etches away the uncovered copper, leaving the conducting paths intact.

Euroblock Connector Short for European style terminal blocks, which are pluggable multiconductor connectors with screw terminals for holding the wires.

Exciter Lamp *See* SOUND HEAD.

Exponential Horn *See* HORN.

F

Fade To gradually change the volume, or LOUDNESS level, of an audio SIGNAL. Fades are often done to end recordings of popular music. Also called a "fade out."

Fade In An inverse FADE, starting from inaudibility and rising to full volume.

Fade Out A fade out is the gradual reduction to zero of the volume near the end of a recording, often used to end popular songs.

Fader Another name for a variable ATTENUATOR, or volume control. PANPOTS are also sometimes called faders, used for "fading" a SIGNAL from one channel to another.

Fanning Strip *See* TERMINAL STRIP.

Fanout An end of an audio SNAKE that has all of the loose, separate conductors and connectors. Fanout also refers to how many electrical devices a given device can effectively drive, or operate. An example is a digital logic gate which can drive 4 other logic gates, has a fanout of 4.

Fantasound™ An early type of stereophonic motion picture sound developed jointly by RCA and the Walt Disney Studio for the Disney movie *Fantasia,* which opened in 1940. Fantasound is often credited as the first commercial stereophonic motion picture sound system, but the Bell Telephone Laboratories had publicly demonstrated a similar system in 1937 in New York and again on a much larger scale at the 1939 New York World's Fair, where it accompanied a stereoscopic movie produced by John Norling. It was said that five million people saw and heard this presentation! *See also* SSFS.

The original recording in Fantasound was accomplished using eight channels of optical recording on two 35-mm films. The first six channels accepted the signals from individual MICROPHONES placed strategically in the orchestra, and the seventh channel was a mix of the first six. The eighth channel was connected to a single microphone placed in the hall for a distant, or reverberant, pickup. For reproduction in the presentation theater, three loudspeaker systems were placed behind the screen, and surround speakers were placed in the sidewalls and rear of the theater. In the first road show presentations of *Fantasia,* the signals from the eight optical tracks were mixed by an experienced operator into the theater's four reproduction channels. This entailed a tremendous amount of skill and equipment and was a very expensive undertaking. Shortly after the initial release, a simplified system was utilized that had a single separate 35-mm film with four optical sound tracks derived from the original eight and a fifth track that acted as a control for the dynamics and placement of the four sound tracks. This control system was called TOGAD, for Tone-Operated Gain-Adjusting Device. The TOGAD was the predecessor of the automated MIXDOWN systems found in modern recording studios.

Even with this simplification, Fantasound was found to be too expensive in practice, and what with the complications encountered with the beginning of World War II, it was not used after 1941. The name Fantasound is still a trademark owned by the Disney Studio.

Faraday Cage An electrostatic SHIELD is sometimes called a Faraday cage, after Michael Faraday, the English scientist who first described its action. Sometimes it is also called a Faraday shield. An example is the braided copper shield over a MICROPHONE cable. The better the conductor (in other words, the less resistance it has), the more effective a shield it will be.

In most audio TRANSFORMERS there is a Faraday shield between the primary and secondary WINDINGS in order to prevent capacitive coupling between them. (*See* CAPACITANCE.) This reduces extraneous noise such as HUM and increases COMMON-MODE rejection.

Far Field If a sound source is operating in an enclosure or room, the SOUND PRESSURE LEVEL will vary with the distance that the measuring MICROPHONE is from the source. At certain close ranges, the levels will obey the INVERSE SQUARE LAW, and at these distances there will exist approximately a FREE FIELD. At greater distances the reduction in measured level with increased distance will be less than predicted by inverse square until finally a region is reached where the level is constant regardless of distance; this is called the REVERBERANT FIELD.

The area between the free field and the reverberant field is called the far field. Its extent is a characteristic of the directionality of the sound source as well as of the ACOUSTICS of the room. *See also* CRITICAL DISTANCE.

Far-Out Field When measuring sound pressure level (SPL) in an enclosed space, it will be found that the measured levels will increase in value near the boundaries of the space. The increase will generally be 6 dB at the boundary surface, and will decline to the reverberant level at a distance of one-half wavelength of the sound. The reason for this is that the sound pressure reflected from the boundary adds to the incoming sound pressure, doubling it at the boundary. The double pressure is a 6 dB rise in level. The region in which this effect occurs is called the far-out field, and its extent depends on the frequency of the sound in question. It is important to take care when measuring sound levels indoors to avoid taking measurements in the far-out field. *See also* FAR FIELD and REVERBERANT FIELD.

Fat Wire System In telephone systems before the advent of digital multiplexing, where several incoming lines were available at one subscriber location, the switching between the lines was done in the telephone itself, usually by push buttons. This required that all the lines be routed to each phone through a 25-pair cable. This is called a fat wire system, as opposed to a slim wire system, in which the switching is done at a central location and each phone has only three or four pairs of wires running to it. Today, it seems that virtually all multiline systems in offices use digital multiplexing.

Faulkner Microphones A pair of figure-8 pattern microphones about 8 inches apart and both facing the same direction. It would seem like the idea was a modification of the classic X-Y STEREO pickup using coincident figure 8s angled 90 degrees apart, but the only difference between the two signals is due to the time difference between a sound's arrival at the two microphones. We suspect two OMNIDIRECTIONAL microphones in the same configuration would sound much better because at least the deep BASS would be natural-sounding, and off-axis sounds would not be attenuated.

FCC The Federal Communications Commission is the government agency that regulates all radio and television transmissions in the United States. Broadcast stations are licensed by the FCC, including hobbyist or "ham" stations, and the FCC maintains surveillance of all broadcast signals to be sure they remain in their allocated FREQUENCY bands. Maximum power output of transmitters is also regulated. Quality standards for broadcast signals were set by the FCC, but in recent years enforcement has been relaxed, to the detriment of the technical quality of broadcasting.

Feedback There are two types of feedback of interest to the audio person: acoustic and electronic.

Acoustic feedback is the condition where a GAIN control is set too high in a sound reinforcement system and the amplified sound enters the MICROPHONE and is re-amplified until a steady howl or whistle is heard. This is sometimes also called regeneration. The remedy is to reduce the volume control setting. Another way to reduce feedback is to equalize the sound system so the response is smoother. The acoustic gain of a system is higher at peaks in the response CURVE, and these are the frequencies where feedback occurs. Also, the PHASE SHIFT in the entire system from microphone through electronics, LOUDSPEAKERS, and the room back to the microphone is important. If this phase shift is a multiple of 360 degrees, the system will be likely to regenerate.

EQUALIZATION for feedback control is tricky, however. The best that one can do is equalize the entire system for a specific microphone and microphone location. The acoustic gain is dependent on the spatial relationship between the loudspeakers and the microphone, and different microphone locations require different equalization curves.

Devices such as the Sabine Feedback Eliminator have been developed that constantly monitor the sound system and quickly activate a notch filter if feedback is detected.

There are also automatic techniques by which a dual-channel FFT ANALYZER is used to determine the system FREQUENCY and phase response using live music as the test signal. Then the proper equalization is determined to optimize the response curve and the equalization is added while the analysis is going on. In this way the system is continually updated and changes in ACOUSTICS due to temperature or humidity variations are compensated for in almost real time during the actual concert.

The other type of feedback important in audio is negative feedback applied to AMPLIFIERS and some other audio devices. Negative feedback is the insertion of a small portion of the output VOLTAGE of an amplifier, that is 180 degrees out of phase with the input, back to the input so as to cancel part of the input signal. This reduces the gain of the amplifier, but also reduces the DISTORTION and NOISE introduced by the amplifier. The lost gain must be made up, but the net effect of the feedback is still to reduce distortion. Negative feedback also reduces the OUTPUT IMPEDANCE of the amplifier, improving its DAMPING FACTOR, and making it more suitable to drive a loudspeaker. There is much controversy in audio design circles about how best to apply negative feedback. It is widely thought that for best results it should be used in small amounts, and around local gain stages rather than "globally" around an entire device.

Negative feedback is of prime importance in electronic designs using operational amplifiers, or OPAMPS, as they are commonly called. An opamp is a device with extremely high gain, and its characteristics can be tailored to various tasks such as microphone PREAMPLIFIERS, voltage amplifiers, active equalizers, etc., by application of proper feedback.

Negative feedback as an improvement in audio amplifiers was invented by a Bell Telephone Labs scientist named Harold S. Black, and was first described in the Bell Labs Technical Review in 1934.

Feedforward A type of CIRCUIT to reduce DISTORTION caused by an active component. The feedforward amplifies the SIGNAL at the input of the component and adds this signal to the output signal of the device so as to cancel the distortion. Feedforward can only be used in conjunction with FEEDBACK and is effective only when the distortion-creating mechanism is well understood.

Feed-through Capacitor A special capacitor, usually of less than 50-pF CAPACITANCE, designed to pass audio SIGNALS through metal partitions or SHIELDS, but at the same time to shunt radio frequency (RF) energy to the CHASSIS. The purpose of using feed-through capacitors is to prevent

RF from either entering or escaping from shielded sections of electronic CIRCUITS in order to prevent or reduce RADIO FREQUENCY INTERFERENCE.

Ferrite According to the OED, a mixed oxide of ferric iron and another metal or metals; specifically, a compound of formula MFe_2O_4 (where M is a divalent metal), many examples of which have magnetic and electrical properties, which make them suitable for use in high-frequency electrical components.

In other words, a nonmetallic composite material that has a high magnetic PERMEABILITY and a low electrical conductivity. The high permeability means that coils that use it as a CORE have a relatively high INDUCTANCE. The low conductivity means it has low losses due to EDDY CURRENTS.

Ferrite is well suited to high-frequency use and is used for the cores of transformers operating at radio frequencies. Its low losses also make it suitable for use in the cores of magnetic TAPE HEADS, especially erase heads. Ferrite "beads," which are small doughnut-shaped pieces of ferrite, are used to reduce the susceptibility of audio devices to RADIO FREQUENCY INTERFERENCE. The beads are placed around the signal-carrying wires near the input terminals of the device, and they increase the series inductance of the wire, attenuating very high frequencies.

Ferrite Bead *See* FERRITE.

Ferro Fluid An interesting material that is a stable colloidal suspension of small magnetic particles in a fluid. In the presence of a magnetic field, the fluid becomes quite stiff, and when out of a magnetic field, it resembles lubricating oil.

Ferro fluid is used in some LOUDSPEAKERS, especially TWEETERS, to conduct heat from the VOICE COIL to the magnet assembly. The fluid is placed around the voice coil in the magnetic gap, and the magnetic field keeps it in there. It is a much better heat conductor than air, and because it keeps the coils cool, more power can be applied to the COIL. The fluid also acts as a DAMPING agent, but this effect is minimal.

FET *See* FIELD EFFECT TRANSISTOR.

FFT Analyzer The Fast Fourier Transform (FFT) is an algorithm for the extraction of a FREQUENCY spectrum from a time WAVEFORM. *See also* FOURIER ANALYSIS.

The FFT analyzer is a digital device that performs the seemingly magical transformation from the time domain to the frequency domain. It does so very quickly, hence the name. The FFT analyzer can be, depending upon its design, an extremely high-resolution analysis device with wide frequency range and DYNAMIC range.

For the highest accuracy under laboratory oconditions it is the analyzer of choice for measuring DISTORTION, SIGNAL-TO-NOISE RATIO, PHASE RESPONSE, FREQUENCY RESPONSE, and FLUTTER and WOW, because it can make the measurements over a wide frequency band simultaneously.

It is also able to measure the TEF curves, familiar from TDS measurements.

The dual-channel analyzer uses the input and output signals from a device and calculates the device's characteristics from them. It measures a system rather than a signal. This means the SIGNAL itself need not be any special type, such as a SINE WAVE. For instance, an ideal signal for measuring the frequency response of a LOUDSPEAKER or tape recorder is music. The FFT notices the difference between the music signal at the speaker's input terminals and the speaker output as sensed by a measurement MICROPHONE and calculates the FREQUENCY RESPONSE based on this difference. It is thus a simple matter to measure response at various levels and with various types of music. It is even possible to measure the entire frequency response of a sound reinforcement system, including the ACOUSTICS of the auditorium, in real time and with live music as a signal. In this way, the system can be equalized while it is being used for a concert, and the audience is unaware that any testing is going on.

Fiddle "An instrument to tickle human ears by friction of a horse's tail over the entrails of a dead cat."—Ambrose Bierce

Fidelity The accuracy with which a music reproduction system will recreate the sound of the original music. True fidelity would be perfect reproduction, which can be considered an ideal to be aimed for.

It is impossible to reproduce at the ears of a listener an exact replica of the sounds they would hear in a concert hall. The greatest discrepancies are probably the lack of directional realism caused by too few independent channels, and the impressing of the local ACOUSTICS of the listening room onto the recorded AMBIENCE of the original recording room. Some multichannel systems address these problems; *see* AMBISONICS.

Luckily (for the sound equipment makers), our ears are not too critical in their evaluation of fidelity and they can be easily trained to accept gross DISTORTIONS as accurate reproduction.

"High fidelity" sound systems are generally designed to please the listener rather than to achieve high accuracy. It has been shown many times over that when the average listener is allowed to adjust the tonal balance of a sound system as he wishes, he will seldom if ever do so in a way that maximizes the accuracy of the system; in fact it seems he will often maximize the deviation from highest fidelity.

Field In NTSC color video, each FRAME lasts 1/29.97 seconds, and is actually composed of two interlaced sequential half pictures consisting of every other horizontal line lasting 1/59.94 seconds. Each such half picture, i.e., the odd-numbered lines and the even-numbered lines, is called a field.

Field Effect Transistor, FET A special type of TRANSISTOR that behaves somewhat more like a TRIODE than a transistor. The FET is symmetrical, and its three terminals are the GATE, the source, and the DRAIN. CURRENT in the FET is from the source to the drain, and the magnitude of this current is determined by the VOLTAGE on the gate.

There is almost no current in the gate, meaning the FET has a very high INPUT IMPEDANCE, similar to that of a triode. The FET is relatively LINEAR in its control of the current by the gate, and it is easier to design low-DISTORTION amplifiers using FETs than using regular, or bipolar, transistors.

FETs are used frequently in the PREAMPLIFIERS in CONDENSER MICROPHONES, where their high input impedance is ideal.

There are two main types of FET, called junction FETs or JFETs and metal-oxide-semiconductor FETs, or MOSFETS. JFETs are the most common and inexpensive. MOSFETs have exceptionally high input impedance and are used where this is important. Either of these can be of one of two classes, called N-channel and P-channel. The N-channel FET requires the gate to have negative BIAS with respect to the source, and the P-channel FET requires a positive bias. MOSFETS have the gate insulated from the drain-source channel, and they are sometimes called IGFETs (insulated gate FETs). They have surpassingly high, nearly infinite, input impedances.

A third type of FET is the unijunction transistor, which behaves like a NONLINEAR resistor. It is used in certain OSCILLATOR circuits.

Dr. Julius Lilienfeld has been credited with inventing and patenting the field effect transistor in the 1920s, before the invention of the bipolar transistor at Bell Labs.

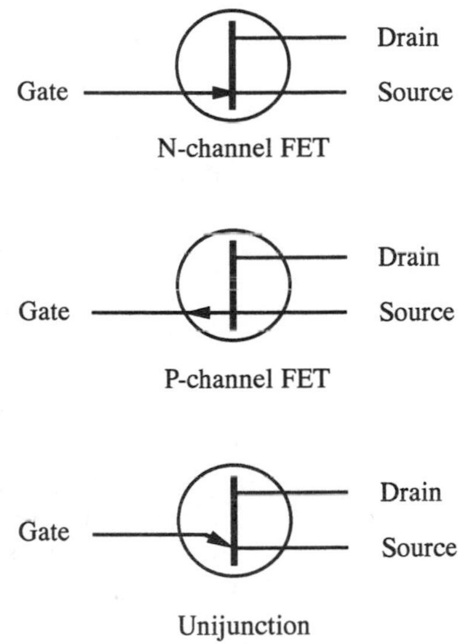

Field Effect Transistor

Field Recording Any recording not done in a studio. The resultant tapes may be called field tapes, although as tapes become obsolete, we may see field coherent laser cubes. *See also* LOCATION RECORDING.

Figure-8 Microphone A microphone whose directional pattern resembles the figure 8, meaning it is insensitive to the sides but has full sensitivity at the front and back. The figure-8 pattern is the shape of the mathematical cosine curve when plotted in polar coordinates, so a figure-8 microphone is also sometimes called a cosine microphone. Historically, the only figure-8 microphones available were RIBBON MICROPHONES, but today many CONDENSER MICROPHONES are made that can be adjusted to provide the figure-8 pattern. *See also* VARIABLE PATTERN MICROPHONE.

Filament The heater in a vacuum TUBE, which heats the CATHODE to induce it to give off electrons, is sometimes called the filament. This is analogous to the filament in a light bulb, although it usually does not get as hot. Typical tubes are heated until the cathode glows red. The major consumers of power in vacuum tube equipment are the HEATERS, and a big advantage of SOLID-STATE equipment is the reduced power consumption and reduced heat output. It has been shown that the failure rate of electronic components approximately doubles for each 10-degree Farenheit temperature rise, and increased reliability is another advantage of the fact that solid-state equipment requires no heaters.

Fill The ambient sound between words in a production track that is used both to replace undesirable noises on the track and to create "handles" extending the track at the beginning and end. Handles enable the re-recording mixer to crossfade smoothly between shots with differing background tones.[13]

Film Chain A device consisting of a motion picture projector and video camera, used to copy films onto videotape or to broadcast them directly. To reconcile the 24 frames per second of the movie to the NTSC television frame rate of a little less than 30 frames per second NTSC video frame rate, some chains use a projector with a five-bladed shutter, which projects each frame of film five times into the video camera. The resulting 120 frames per second are regrouped four-at-a-time into 30 video images per second. *See also* DROP FRAME and 3:2 PULL DOWN.

The film chain is nearly obsolete today, having been replaced by a simpler device known as the "flying spot scanner," wherein the film moves continuously rather than intermittently and is scanned with a tiny spot of light.

Filter A filter is a type of EQUALIZER that is designed to reduce the energy at a certain FREQUENCY or in a certain frequency BAND. Filters always act as subtractive devices, never adding anything to a signal; at least they should not. The most common type of filters are ANALOG filters, which operate on signals directly.

An example of a filter is a subsonic or "rumble filter" found on some record playing equipment. This filter attenuates the very low frequencies, typically below 15 HERTZ or so, and this reduces the effect of noise caused by the mechanical vibration of the turntable.

Analog filters come in many types, but they always use REACTIVE elements in their design, such as INDUCTORS and/or CAPACITORS. Perhaps

13. This entry is copyright © 1999–2003 by Larry Blake and is reprinted with permission.

the simplest filters to build are made of RESISTORS and CAPACITORS, and they are called R-C filters. Some filters use ACTIVE components such as AMPLIFIERS or GYRATORS in their design, and they are called active filters as opposed to passive filters. Some filters use DELAY LINES in FEEDBACK CIRCUITS, and they are called recursive filters.

DIGITAL filters operate on signals that have been digitized. They are purely mathematical, performing a series of arithmetic operations on the digital words. In a sense, digital filters are synthesized filters; digital techniques being used to emulate or simulate analog filters. Digital filters have the advantage of being drift-free. They always do their job in exactly the same way. They can be designed for nearly any desired characteristics in the frequency domain and in PHASE response.

In some digital audio systems, notably some COMPACT DISC players, digital filters are used as portions of the ANTI-IMAGING and ANTI-ALIASING filters. Of course a digital filter cannot work on an analog signal directly; it must first be converted into digital form. This means an analog anti-alias filter is needed before the first SAMPLING of the signal. After this initial digitization, digital filters can be used. *See also* OVERSAMPLING.

FIR, Finite Impulse Response A commonly used type of digital filter. Digitized samples of the audio signal serve as inputs, and each filtered output is computed from a weighted sum of a finite number of previous inputs. An FIR filter can be designed to have LINEAR PHASE (i.e., constant time delay, regardless of FREQUENCY). FIR filters designed for frequencies much lower than the sample rate and/or with sharp transitions are computationally intensive, with large time delays.[14]

FireWire, IEEE 1394 A high-speed serial digital interface bus that supports multiple data formats so that audio, video, MIDI, and control signals may all be sent over a single cable. The fastest current data rate is 800 megabits per second with a 100 meter cable limit, whereas the original FireWire was 400 Mbps with a 4.5m cable limit. Different connectors are used. FireWire can distribute power as well as data, and the system is smart-configuring, permitting hot-plugging of devices. IEEE 1394 is designed to be bidirectional and with the ability to broadcast from a single source to multiple receivers. One of FireWire's important features is its ability to transmit ISOCHRONOUS data such as digital video. FireWire has found wide use in computer and digital audio-video devices. The term "FireWire" was coined by Apple Computer, which invented it and submitted it to the IEEE where it became standardized as IEEE 1394.

First Law of Acoustics A variation on Murphy's law which can be stated, "Never make the same measurement twice, because you will not get the same answer." The complexity and variability of acoustic phenomena make it very difficult to make exactly repeatable measurements.

Fishpole Slang for microphone BOOM.

14. Thanks to Dennis Bohn, Rane Corp.

5.1, 6.1, 7.1 In soundtracks such as those on movies and DVDS, 5.1 means that the soundtracks are recorded with five main channels: left, center, right, left surround, and right surround, plus a low-frequency-effects (LFE) bass channel (called a ".1" channel because it covers only about 10 percent of the frequency range of the main channels).

In his excellent book *5.1 Surround Sound"* (2000), Tomlinson Holman states: "In 1987, when a subcommittee of the Society of Motion Picture and Television Engineers looked at putting digital sound on film meetings were held about the requirements of the system. In a series of meetings and documents, the 5.1-channel system emerged as being the minimum number of channels that would create the sensations desired from a new system, and the name 5.1 took hold from that time, In fact, this can be seen as a codification of existing 70mm practice, which already had five main channels and a low-FREQUENCY, high HEADROOM channel."

Some movie soundtracks use a variation of 5.1 called Dolby® Digital Surround EX™, which can be used via DVDs in home theaters. The Surround EX format matrix encodes a third surround channel onto the left and right surround channels of 5.1 soundtracks, and may be decoded or not at the cinema's or home listener's option due to their inherent compatibility. Because the extra surround information is carried on the left and right surround channels, Dolby Digital Surround EX encoded soundtracks are still regarded as 5.1 soundtracks.

With respect to home playback, the terms 5.1, 6.1, and 7.1 mean that there are five, six, or seven main speakers, plus a subwoofer, in the playback system. (The subwoofer reproduces the LFE channel recorded on 5.1 soundtracks, plus any bass the main speakers cannot handle.) The difference is in the number of surround speakers: two in a 5.1 system, three in a 6.1 system, and four in a 7.1 system.

5.1-channel soundtracks can be played on a 5.1-speaker system, but they can also be played on a 6.1- or 7.1-speaker system. To do this, the two surround signals on the 5.1 soundtrack are spread across the three or four surround speakers. This distribution can be accomplished by a Dolby Digital EX decoder, a THX Surround EX decoder, or other proprietary methods provided in home theater equipment by various manufacturers.

The number (i.e., 5.1) describing the soundtrack does not have to match the number applied to the speaker system. It is even possible to play two-channel stereo content over these multi-speaker systems by using a matrix surround decoder such as Dolby Pro Logic® II. The delivery format and the speaker configuration are independent, and it is the decoder's job to bridge them effectively.

Fixed Bias A circuit arrangement where the BIAS of an active component is supplied by a separate power supply and is thus constant even though the current in the component may vary.

Flag A digital BIT or group of bits that is inserted in a digital code to accomplish a specific task different from that which the code usually does. Originally, flags were put into computer programs at certain points to call the programmer's attention to certain aspects of the program. These flags have no effect on the execution of the program. In digital audio, however, flags may be used to disable the recording circuits of digital tape recorders to prevent unauthorized copying. An example is the anticopy flag found on most CDs.

Flanging A special effect made popular in the 1960s where a delayed version of a SIGNAL is mixed with the signal, creating a "swooshing" sound.

Flanging was first done by recording a signal on two similar tape recorders, playing them back simultaneously, and mixing them together. The record-playback sequence on the tape recorders results in a small time delay of perhaps a tenth of a second. Both output signals are delayed by the same amount if the tape recorders are similar and they add together in the mixer, and the sound heard is essentially the same as the signal at the input to the tape recorders.

To achieve the effect of flanging, one recorder is slowed down a little, increasing its time delay. This is done by pressing one's thumb against the flange of the tape recorder supply reel, hence the name "flanging." When the time delay is different for the two combined signals, there will be frequencies where the PHASE SHIFT is 180 degrees, and the signals will cancel, causing deep dips or holes in the FREQUENCY RESPONSE CURVE. This is called the COMB FILTER effect. As the speed is varied, the frequency of the dips is swept across the frequency range, giving the swooshing sound. Attaining the most desirable effect requires an educated thumb. The best effect is obtained when the signal being flanged contains frequencies over a wide range.

This technique was thought primitive by many, which led to the development of all-electronic flangers. These units contain an electronic DELAY LINE that is adjustable. If the time delay is very short, the effect is called "phasing," and does not sound nearly as convincing as true flanging.

It is interesting to note that a sound similar to flanging is familiar to many people. As a jet airplane passes overhead, the direct sound is heard first, and the sound reflected from the ground, buildings, etc., is heard later. This time delay causes a cancellation of the combined sound at the ear at some frequency, and this frequency varies as the airplane moves and the path lengths change. This is the reason flanging reminds one of the sound of a jet plane.

Flash Excess vinyl compound squeezed out around the STAMPERS when records are pressed. It is removed with a special cutter.

Flat Lower in PITCH, as opposed to SHARP, which means higher in pitch. In reference to musical scales, flat indicates one-half tone lower; for example, B flat is a whole tone lower than C.

Flatbed Editor A machine for editing motion picture film and its sound track. It is essentially a table with several horizontal pairs of reels of film and sprocketed magnetic sound stock. The picture film is routed through an apparatus that projects the image onto a small screen for viewing, and the sound stock is routed through a playback head assembly. The sound and picture films are synchronized to run at the same speed, and this speed is variable so the editor can hear the sound and see the picture at low speeds and in forward or reverse to allow her to select the editing points. Both films are then cut and spliced to maintain synchronization of the sound and picture. Such an editor may be referred to by a brand name such as MOVIOLA or Steenbeck, however, such manufacturers also make other editing products that may also be called by the brand name.

Flat Frequency Response An AMPLIFIER, LOUDSPEAKER, MICROPHONE, etc., is said to have flat frequency response, or "flat response," if its output is at the same level for all frequencies of interest, provided its input also has uniform AMPLITUDE over the same frequency range. In other words, a flat system has the same GAIN or SENSITIVITY at all frequencies of interest. A graph of the gain versus frequency will be a straight line, hence the name. In reality, a tolerance is allowed, typically plus or minus 3 dB. *See also* FREQUENCY RESPONSE.

Fleming Valve A vacuum DIODE patented in 1904 as a DETECTOR for use in wireless telegraphy by the English professor Ambrose Fleming. Fleming did not build the first diode; he made use of the EDISON EFFECT bulbs brought to England in 1884 by William Preece, who had obtained them from Edison. Fleming was working with the Marconi Wireless Company and was trying to find a better detector than the COHERERS then in use. He realized the Edison bulbs would rectify low-frequency AC signals, and he experimented to verify that they could be used at radio frequencies.

When news of Fleming's patent reached Edison, he immediately filed suit because of his 1884 patent of the Edison effect, but the courts ruled, after a prolonged dispute, that Edison's patent did not cover the use of the device as a detector.

It is interesting that Fleming resisted the use of the term *diode* (first proposed by Dr. Eccles of Manchester University in 1919) and insisted that it be called an oscillation valve.

Fletcher-Munson Effect In the early 1930s, Fletcher and Munson undertook to measure the SENSITIVITY of the human hearing mechanism at different frequencies. They first generated sounds at very low levels at many frequencies over the audible range to determine the threshold of hearing, or the softest sound that could be heard. They made a plot of these levels versus FREQUENCY, and found the CURVE was not uniform, but varies drastically with frequency. The most sensitive range of human hearing is between 3 KILOHERTZ and 4 kHz; the sensitivity falls off rapidly at lower frequencies and somewhat more slowly at higher frequencies. In other words, very soft sounds must be more powerful at frequencies lower and higher than 3 to 4 kHz in order to be heard. This result was expected from previous experience, but the effect had not been precisely measured before.

Next, the experimenters chose 1,000 HERTZ as a reference frequency and increased the strength of the softest audible sound at that frequency by ten times (10 DECIBELS). They then generated other tones at lower and higher frequencies and strengths and asked the subjects to judge when these other tones were as loud as the reference tone at 1,000 Hz. The strengths of these tones were plotted on the same graph as the threshold was plotted to form a "contour of equal loudness" and the surprising result was that this curve was not parallel to the threshold curve. It was not as steeply curved, indicating that our ears hear different frequency tones more uniformly in LOUDNESS when they are stronger than the threshold levels. The experiment was repeated with 1,000-Hz reference tones in increments of 10 dB all the way up to 120 dB above threshold.

These equal loudness contours become flatter as the level increases, indicating that our ears have much more uniform sensitivity at high levels than at low levels.

The results of this experiment were widely reported and were thought to be important in understanding how we perceive music. One outcome of this was the so-called LOUDNESS CONTROL found in many music-reproducing systems. The loudness control attempts to compensate for the Fletcher-Munson effect by boosting the lowest and highest frequencies of the music SIGNAL by an amount that increases as the volume is reduced. Thus, as one turns down the volume control, the low and high frequencies are reduced less than the frequencies between 3 and 4 kHz.

The loudness control, however, was not as great a success as the designers expected it to be, and most music listeners ignored it, or used it very little.

The reason for this is a further complexity in the way we perceive complex sounds. The Fletcher-Munson experiment used SINE WAVES, or pure tones, to measure the equal loudness contours, but music never consists of pure tones. All music WAVEFORMS are complex in that they contain energy at many frequencies in a HARMONIC SERIES, and such complex sounds do not obey the equal loudness contours, at least not the ones measured for pure tones. Most rock listeners seem to love the loudness switch, as it greatly boosts the bass and treble, which they associate with rock music.

Floating Floating is a CIRCUIT configuration in which neither wire carrying the SIGNAL is connected to the system GROUND. *See* BALANCED; Appendix 6.

Fluff Either a verb meaning to garble or miss a word or phrase when speaking into a MICROPHONE or a noun meaning the result of this action. Sometimes the word "blooper" is used as a synonym for the noun, but "fluff" is more common.

Flutter In an ANALOG tape recorder, if the tape speed varies, the PITCH of the recorded music will vary. If the rate of variation is fairly high, typically above 5 HERTZ or so, it is called flutter. If the speed varies at rates below several hertz, it is called WOW. Flutter is actually FREQUENCY MODULATION and imparts a tremolo-like or VIBRATO-like character to the music. It is very annoying with certain types of music, such as piano, which never has any natural pitch variation. On the other hand, recordings of stringed instruments are much more tolerant of flutter, string players not being able to sustain a steady pitch.

According to the DIN and IEC standards, flutter is measured by recording a steady 3,150-Hz tone and then passing the resultant signal through an FM DETECTOR. The Japanese standard (JIS) calls for 3,000 Hz rather than 3,150 Hz. The demodulated portion of the signal is then passed through a WEIGHTING filter, which discriminates against frequencies above 15 Hz or so, and then the RMS value may be determined. This is expressed as a percentage and is called the RMS weighted flutter. The DIN standard calls for peak rather than RMS detection and so is more strict than the American standard.

An acceptable value for flutter in a tape recorder is 0.1 percent or less. Record turntables also have flutter, but the speed variations are generally much lower in FREQUENCY and are called WOW. The measurement technique is the same, with a different weighting curve.

It is said that the Flying Karamazov Brothers juggling team has a cat named "Flutter."

Flutter Echo An acoustic effect in some rooms where sound is reflected back and forth between two parallel surfaces, such as opposite walls. In order to qualify as a flutter echo the reflections must be fewer than about 15 or so per second. This happens when the walls are more than about 25 feet apart. Parallel surfaces closer than this give rise to STANDING WAVES that result in a nonuniform distribution of sound between the surfaces.

Flutter echoes are to be avoided in auditoria, and this is usually done by making large wall surfaces nonparallel.

Flutter Roller *See* SCRAPE FLUTTER.

Flux The total number of lines of magnetic induction threading through a surface is called the magnetic flux through the surface. The unit of flux is the weber, abbreviated Wb, which is a relatively large unit. The nanoweber (nWb), which is one billionth of a weber, is used to measure magnetic flux levels that exist in ANALOG recording tape. Before the adoption of the weber, the Maxwell was used, which was one tenth of a nWb. One may see a reference to a fluxivity of 20 milliMaxwells/mm, equal to 200 nWb/m.

A MAGNETIC TAPE head, when replaying a tape, is sensitive to the rate of change of flux in its iron pole pieces, not to the flux itself. *See* TAPE HEAD.

Flux also refers to a cleaning agent used on metals before they are soldered. Rosin is a typical soldering flux and is commonly packaged with the solder as a small core running down the center of the solder wire. This is called "rosin core solder." For soldering heavily corroded metals, an acid flux is often used. Acid core solder is available but is never used in electronics work because the acid is very corrosive and damages electronic circuit components.

Flux Density A measure of the strength of a magnetic field. The unit of flux density is the TESLA, named after Nikola Tesla, the Serbian scientist. In a LOUDSPEAKER, the flux density supplied by the magnet is closely related to the overall quality, transient response, and efficiency of the unit, as well as its cost. The traditional material for loudspeaker magnets has been a cobalt-nickel alloy called Alnico, but in recent years ceramic magnets have been used in large quantities. Some relatively exotic materials such as samarium cobalt and neodymium can produce extremely strong magnetic fields and are sometimes used for high-frequency drivers.

FM *See* FREQUENCY MODULATION.

FM Stereo A method of FM broadcasting that allows stereo receivers to receive the full stereo signal. It is also compatible with MONAURAL FM receivers, which simply sense the sum of the two stereo channels.

The system works by first forming sum (L+R) and difference (L–R) signals from the stereo input signals (L and R). This is sometimes called MATRIXING. It can be shown that all the stereo information resides in the difference signal; in other words, if the difference is zero, then the original signals were identical, and it therefore was not stereo. The L–R signal, which is normally lower in level than the L+R signal, is used to modulate a 38-kilohertz subcarrier, which is then added to the L+R signal and used to modulate the main FM carrier. In addition to this, a low-level 19-kHz pilot signal is added to the composite signal. This pilot, at one-half the frequency of the subcarrier, is used by the receiver to generate a 38-kHz subcarrier with which to demodulate the L–R signal. It is interesting to note that the stereo indicator lights on most FM tuners use the existence of the 19 kHz pilot to identify stereo broadcasts. If the station is broadcasting monaural source material, but the pilot is still transmitted, the resulting audio signal will still be monaural even though the stereo indicator will still light up.

A standard monaural receiver is not sensitive to the subcarrier and simply demodulates the L+R signal. A stereo receiver senses the pilot tone and uses this to demodulate the L–R signal, which is then matrixed with the L+R to obtain the original L and R signals.

The advantage of this system is that it is compatible with existing monaural FM receivers. Its disadvantage is that the subcarrier, which carries all the stereo information, is much more sensitive to signal degradation from MULTIPATH DISTORTION and long-distance reception. This means that good-quality stereo reception is limited to an area relatively near the transmitter.

The 19-kHz pilot signal must also be filtered out of the signal, because it will cause interference with the BIAS frequency of analog tape recorders, causing audible whistles to be recorded. *See also* BIRDIE. It can also confuse noise reduction systems such as Dolby, which is why cassette decks with Dolby NR must have a 19kHz, or "multiplex" notch filter switch.

Over the years, there have been many attempts to broadcast stereo programs, and they competed fiercely for FCC standardization in the late 1950s. Probably the first of these was a system designed by Murray Crosby and William Halstead and experimentally broadcast in 1950 under the call letters KE2XKH in New York City. This system used a 35-kHz subcarrier that was modulated by the second stereo channel, and then this signal was mixed with the other channel, and the combination modulated the main carrier. The system was called Stereosonic, from "stereo using an ultrasonic subcarrier." (*See* STEREOSONIC for another, more common use of the term.)

Later, in 1958, Murray Crosby patented the Crosby multiplex system, which used sum and difference matrixing to achieve compatibility with standard FM mono reception, as in the present-day system. The Crosby system was very well designed, boasting complete compatibility, 15-kHz frequency response on both channels, and no degradation of signal-to-noise ratio. It used a 41-kHz subcarrier to transmit the L–R stereo information. The subcarrier was also used to modulate the main carrier, unlike the present-day system.

Experimental broadcasting was undertaken by WBAL in New York (operating under the call letters KE2XXT) and by KDKA in Pittsburgh.

Many engineers at the time expected the FCC to standardize on the Crosby system because the competing systems were of demonstrably lesser quality, but the FCC chose the system in use today because it allows another channel to be simultaneously broadcast (*see* SCA) with another subcarrier at 67 kHz. The result is the degradation of the SIGNAL-TO-NOISE RATIO of the stereo program and reduced listening range from the station.

Among the competing stereo broadcast systems were the Halstead, which used no matrixing and modulated the 41-kHz subcarrier with the right channel. The left channel modulated the main carrier. This system was not compatible with monaural reception and had differing frequency responses on each channel. The Burden system tried to overcome these difficulties by using sum and difference matrixing in transmission like the Crosby system. However, no de-matrixing occurred in the receiver, presumably to reduce cost. Burden argued that the requisite de-matrixing would occur acoustically in the listening room. How this was supposed to happen was not satisfactorily explained, and the system never saw the light of day. The Phantodyne and Calbest systems were also contenders, but they suffered from poor frequency response and were not taken seriously.

It is interesting to note that in 1958, three-channel stereo was broadcast experimentally in Boston by WGBH-TV, WGBH-FM, and WBUR-FM. The center channel was carried by the TV station, and the two FM stations broadcast the other two channels. The listener needed a TV set and two FM sets to hear the full effect, and it was said to be very convincing.

Stereo broadcasting was also done experimentally in England in the 1950s and as early as 1926 using two AM stations. An interesting note is that the BBC, in its two-station broadcasts in 1958, reasoned that it had no control over the POLARITY of the sound output of the receivers in use and that there was only a 50% chance that the phasing would be correct. Applying impeccable British logic, it reversed the phase of one channel halfway through each program, ensuring that each listener would hear the program under the proper conditions half the time!

FM Synthesis The generation of complex SIGNAL WAVEFORMS in electronic music by FREQUENCY MODULATION of one or more SINE WAVE signals by other sine waves. This method is an alternative to ADDITIVE SYNTHESIS.

FM synthesis as a method of generating complex musical waveforms was pioneered by John Chowning of Stanford University, and he has shown that an extremely wide variety of waveforms may be made this way. The method also requires significantly less hardware than other methods, such as additive synthesis.

One of the first commercial synthesizers to use FM synthesis was the Synclavier, produced by New England Digital Corp. There are now many other such units available.

FMX A proprietary system of FM transmission and reception to improve the SIGNAL-TO-NOISE RATIO in stereo broadcasting. FMX was developed by the now-defunct CBS Technology Center in the mid-1980s. It is well known that FM stereo reception is much noisier than MONAURAL reception in low-signal, or "fringe," areas. This is a result of the method by which the stereo information is encoded on the transmitted signal (*see* FM STEREO). CBS claimed that quiet FMX stereo reception extends as far from the transmitter as quiet monaural reception of conventional FM. This more than doubled the area in which stereo could be received from a given station.

FMX added another subcarrier to the transmitted signal that was 90 degrees out of PHASE with the stereo subcarrier. This new subcarrier was said to be in quadrature with the main subcarrier. The stereo information in the input signal, consisting of the L–R, was compressed and used to modulate the new carrier. In the FMX receiver, the quadrature carrier was sensed and demodulated, and the L–R signal expanded to restore the dynamics of the original signal. In order to properly restore the quadrature L–R signal, the receiver used the level of the stereo L–R signal from the standard subcarrier as a reference. Even though this signal may be noisy, its level was indicative of the amount of stereo separation in the original signal. The quadrature L–R signal was then used, after expansion, to restore the original stereo signal.

FMX was compatible with regular FM stereo because a standard stereo receiver does not detect the quadrature subcarrier. There was some controversy over whether the FMX system would work properly in the presence of multipath reception. MULTIPATH DISTORTION in FM is analogous to ghosts on television, and is especially severe for stereo transmission.

FOH, Front Of House. The location within the audience area of an auditorium or arena for the mixing console and its operator that controls the sound the audience hears, or the "house sound." In many cases, especially in large arenas, there will be another control console location at one side or the other of the stage. This console is called the monitor mixer, and controls the sound into the MONITOR speakers through which the performers hear themselves. Both the FOH and the monitor mixer inputs will be connected to all the MICROPHONES on stage for maximum flexibility. The signal fed to the stage monitors is usually not the same as is sent to the house sound reinforcement speakers. This is because the performers may want to emphasize certain microphones, such as vocals, so they can better hear themselves.

Foil The copper conducting path on a PRINTED CIRCUIT BOARD.

Foldback Foldback is the general term for the part of a sound reinforcement system in an auditorium that supplies amplified sound to the performers so they can hear themselves. Foldback LOUDSPEAKERS are often placed on the stage in front of the performers, although they may be above or behind the performers. They are commonly called "monitors" by the performers. Another use of the term is the "foldback" earphone often used by so-called "talking head" television personalities. The earphone allows the person to hear his own voice along with directions from a technician or producer. *See also* IFB.

Folded Horn A type of HORN loudspeaker where the horn is folded or "wrapped" around itself to save space. Mostly, folded horns are used for low frequencies, but there are some high-frequency folded horns.

There have been many designs for folded horns over the years, some which use a corner of a room as an extension of the horn itself. The "Klipschorn," patented by Paul Klipsch in the 1940s, was of this type. It is interesting to note that the first commercially available EXPONENTIAL HORN reproducer was a folded horn. This was the Orthophonic Victrola acoustic phonograph introduced in 1925. The exponential horn was first described by A. G. Webster of the Bell Telephone Laboratories in his article that appeared in the *Proceedings of the National Academy of Sciences* in 1919 titled "Acoustical Impedance and Theory of Horns and Phonograph."

This was one of the key papers in the early history of sound reproduction, introducing the concepts of acoustical and mechanical IMPEDANCE and noting the similarities to electrical impedance.

Foley Effects Sound effects in a motion picture or video tape that are produced by various mechanical devices operated by hand and other sounds such as footsteps. Examples are slamming doors and creaking floors and hinges. The recording of Foley effects is carried out in a dedicated studio called a Foley stage. Some of the contraptions used for Foley effects are quite complex and ingenious. Purportedly named after an early practioner of these effects, Jack Foley.

Foley Stage *See* FOLEY EFFECTS.

Foley Walkers Foley technicians that work on a Foley stage to record Foley effects. They use a variety of objects and/or surfaces to generate realistic sound effects. On-screen footsteps are one of the most commonly used effects, hence the term "walkers."

Follower An ACTIVE circuit element, such as an OPAMP or a TUBE, which is connected so that its output VOLTAGE will be the same as its input voltage. In other words, it will have a GAIN of 1. Followers act as IMPEDANCE converters, and this is the reason they are used. A follower will have a high INPUT IMPEDANCE (sometimes extremely high) and will have a low OUTPUT IMPEDANCE. It is thus suited to driving long lines, or low-impedance circuits, while it does not act as a significant LOAD on the device connected to its input. One use of the follower is the first stage in the preamplifier for a CONDENSER MICROPHONE. *See also* CATHODE FOLLOWER; EMITTER FOLLOWER.

Forensic Audio The practice of techniques that analyze recordings for validity. This is often done for legal reasons, such as to determine if a wiretap recording is genuine or altered. A famous instance of forensic audio was the analysis of the gap in the Watergate tapes.

Formant A frequency BAND in the SPECTRUM of a voice or musical instrument that contains more energy or amplitude than the neighboring area. Formants are the distinguishing characteristics of the vowel sounds of the human voice and, for any vowel, are relatively fixed in frequency, even though the pitch of the voice may be changing, as in singing. The overall shape of the spectrum of a musical or vocal sound is called the spectral envelope, and may not change much as different pitches are sounded. The formants determine this shape in large part.

A musical instrument has a definite set of formants, and it is they that impart its tone color, or TIMBRE. The fact that the timbre does not change too much as the instrument sounds different notes allows us to recognize the instrument regardless of the pitch being played. It is interesting that our hearing mechanism is very sensitive to formants, no doubt because speech intelligibility depends heavily on recognition of vowels. If the sound of any musical instrument is prolonged without changing the pitch—for instance, if it is recorded on a tape loop—it soon begins to lose its subjective timbre and begins to sound like a buzzer. It is the unvarying formant frequencies in the presence of the varying pitch of the instrument that allow us to recognize the timbre.

If a sound-reproducing system has peaks in its frequency response, these peaks will be heard in the presence of music as a definite timbre or "coloration" in the sound. Such a sound system can be said to have a tone color of its own that it impresses on the music. The same thing happens with many other audio devices, especially MICROPHONES and LOUDSPEAKERS. This is why peaks in the response curve of any device are to be avoided.

However, the great adaptability of the human hearing mechanism is such that if one listens for a long time to a particular sound system, one will become habituated to that particular sound. This is the reason so many people put up with very poor quality sound systems and seemingly don't mind. This is also the reason one should compare the reproduced sound of a system with the actual sound itself, rather than trusting to memory, when evaluating components such as loudspeakers.

Former *See* COIL FORMER.

Forward Resistance The actual RESISTANCE of a DIODE or other SEMICONDUCTOR junction when conducting CURRENT in its normal direction. The forward resistance of a semiconductor junction is not as simple and LINEAR as normal, or so-called ohmic, resistance, but depends on the voltage across the junction and the current through it, especially at low values of voltage and current. *See also* REVERSE RESISTANCE.

Forward Voltage Drop The VOLTAGE across a DIODE or other SEMICONDUCTOR junction when it is passing a CURRENT in the normal direction. Most SOLID-STATE junctions will have a nearly constant forward voltage drop regardless of the current. For silicon junctions, it is about 0.7 volt.

Foster-Seeley Detector A type of FM DETECTOR developed to provide rejection of AMPLITUDE MODULATION so it would be less susceptible to RADIO FREQUENCY INTERFERENCE. It was an improvement over its predecessors but not as good as the RATIO DETECTOR.

Fourier Analysis Baron Jean Baptiste Joseph Fourier was a gifted nineteenth-century French engineer who developed the mathematical techniques to allow the "transformation" of a mathematical function from one "domain" to another domain. Fourier did this, interestingly enough, while working on problems of heat transfer in artillery for Napoleon. The "Fourier transform" allows a function that represents an AUDIO signal (SIGNALS are in the "time domain" because they exist in time) to be transformed to another function that represents the same signal in the "frequency domain." The signal in the time domain is called a WAVEFORM, and the same signal in the frequency domain is called a SPECTRUM.

The Fourier transform performs a FREQUENCY analysis, assigning periodicities in the waveform to specific frequencies in the spectrum. For instance, a waveform that repeats itself 100 times per second is said to be periodic at 100 repetitions per second. This periodicity means that the spectrum of the signal will have a component at a frequency of 100 HERTZ, or 100 cycles per second. Similarly, other periodicities will correspond to other frequencies in the spectrum. No information is lost when transforming to the frequency domain from the time domain, and in fact the inverse transform may be applied to go back to time from the frequency domain.

Sometimes the spectrum is called the FREQUENCY RESPONSE function, but this is not exactly rigorous, for the frequency response is a transfer function and is a characteristic of a device, whereas a spectrum is simply a signal expressed in the frequency domain. *See* FREQUENCY RESPONSE.

The reason we want to transform a signal from the time to the frequency domain is that our hearing mechanism seems to do a similar thing. We tend to analyze signals into their frequency components, which are related to musical pitches. (*See* PITCH.) When we look at a waveform on an OSCILLOSCOPE, it is very difficult to predict what it will sound like. It is almost impossible to tell the pitch of a complex signal by looking at the waveform, but when it is transformed into frequency we know that specific frequencies correlate (in a fairly complex way) to pitch sensations. The spectrum is like looking at the signal from another angle, which reveals detail not otherwise visible.

Fourier did the mathematics but he did not build a spectrum analyzer. In fact, it was not until 1967 that a technique (called the "Cooley-Tukey algorithm," after the discoverers) was devised that permits a digital computer to perform the Fourier transform at a very high speed. (It probably should be called the Lanczos algorithm, for it was actually described by Cornelius Lanczos much earlier.) This rediscovery led the way to the digital "fast Fourier transform," or FFT, analyzers that are common today.

There are many far-reaching consequences of Fourier analysis, one of which is that any repeating (i.e., PERIODIC) waveform can be represented by only a FUNDAMENTAL frequency and a series of HARMONICS. The fundamental frequency is the reciprocal of the period of the wave, and the harmonics occur at integral multiples of this frequency. For instance, a signal whose period is 100 milliseconds will have a repetition rate of 100 Hz, and will also contain energy at 200 Hz, 300 Hz, 400 Hz, etc.; no matter what the shape of the wave is, it will still consist of only this fundamental and harmonics. The level and PHASE of the harmonics will vary with the waveform.

Fourier Transform *See* FOURIER ANALYSIS.

Fox-Hole Sprockets *See* CINEMASCOPE.

Frame In motion pictures or video, a frame is one complete picture. The standard frame rate in sound movies is 24 pictures per second, and in NTSC television in the United States, it is 29.97 frames per second. Special effects such as slow motion are filmed at higher frame rates, and the frame rate for silent movies was around 16 per second, although it varied widely.

In DIGITAL audio, a frame is a "slice" of digital information. In the COMPACT DISC, a frame covers six SAMPLING periods, or 136 microseconds. Each frame ends with a synchronization code. When digital audio was recorded onto a video tape recorder, the digital frame was fitted into a video frame, hence the name. The synch pulses of the video format were then used to synchronize the digital audio data. It was found to be technically convenient to use a SAMPLING rate of 44.05594 kHz to fit the data into the video signal.

The European standards for video (PAL/SECAM) of 625 lines and 25 frames per second are different from the American standards (NTSC) of 525 lines and almost 30 frames per second.

Free-Cone Resonance The FREQUENCY at which the cone of a dynamic LOUDSPEAKER will resonate when in free air; that is, when not mounted in a BAFFLE or cabinet. The free-cone resonance is the mass of the cone assembly resonating with the springiness of the cone SURROUND and SPIDER and is always lower in frequency than the mounted resonance. It is one of the THIELE-SMALL PARAMETERS.

Free Field A sound source radiating into three-dimensional space where there are no reflecting surfaces is said to be radiating under free field conditions. The SOUND PRESSURE LEVEL as measured at various distances from the source would obey the INVERSE SQUARE LAW precisely. There is no such thing as a true free field, but it is approximated in the ANECHOIC chamber.

Because all rooms have at least a small amount of REVERBERATION, the sound field from a source is always contaminated with reflected sound. This makes accurate measurements of sound levels difficult because the MICROPHONE is not able to discriminate between the direct and reflected sounds. This is the reason that anechoic rooms are used for much acoustical testing—the reflected sound is of sufficiently small AMPLITUDE that it is negligible for most work.

For certain small sound sources in large rooms, the sound field fairly close to the source will approximate a free field, but as the distance increases, the reverberation becomes relatively stronger. The sound field closer to the source than about one WAVELENGTH of the sound is not a free field, but is referred to as the NEAR FIELD; meaningful measurements this close to a sound source are very difficult to accomplish. *See also* FAR FIELD.

Free-Field Microphone A type of OMNIDIRECTIONAL microphone that is designed to have FLAT RESPONSE when in a FREE FIELD and pointed at the source of sound, as opposed to a true PRESSURE MICROPHONE, which will have an increased high-frequency SENSITIVITY under the same conditions.

The true pressure microphone has a rising high-FREQUENCY response due to reflection of sound from the microphone diaphragm, which causes a pressure increase. The effect is due to the disturbance of the sound field by the microphone itself, and only occurs when the WAVELENGTH is short compared to the diameter of the microphone. The free-field microphone corrects its response for the disturbance it introduces.

Free-field microphones are useful when recording is done at close range to the sound source, where they will give FLAT FREQUENCY RESPONSE. Pressure microphones are better suited to more distant pickups, where the rise in high-frequency response helps to compensate for high-frequency losses due to absorption by the air. Most measurement microphones, as found on SOUND LEVEL METERS, are of the free-field type.

Free-Field Response The frequency response of a microphone in a free acoustic field. Manufacturers will make omni microphones with various response curves at different angles of incidence to satisfy market demands. The free-field responses at different angles will accurately compare the characteristics.

Frequency Frequency, in its simplest form, is a measure of how often (how "frequently") an event repeats itself. A sound source, such as a tuning fork, which vibrates back and forth 1,000 times per second, is said to have a frequency of 1,000 HERTZ.

Frequency used to be stated in cycles per second, or cps, but there has been international agreement that hertz (Hz) will be used to indicate frequency. The term is in honor of Heinrich Hertz, a German pioneer in the transmission of radio waves.

Most sounds are complex and cannot be described by a single frequency. The sound of a bell or a cymbal, for instance, contains very many frequencies at the same time. The best we can do is to perform a FOURIER ANALYSIS on the SIGNAL and thus determine what individual frequencies are present in the complex sound.

Frequency of a signal in large part determines its subjective PITCH, although the correlation is not one-to-one, especially for simple tones. Complex tones that are periodic, i.e., that repeat their WAVEFORM over and over, do have a rather precise correlation between frequency and pitch although the pitch will vary somewhat with the AMPLITUDE of the sound. Such a sound will consist of many component frequencies arranged in a HARMONIC

SERIES, but it is usually said to have the frequency of the lowest, or FUNDAMENTAL, component. For instance, an oboe sounding a tone repeating at 440 times per second will sound like A above middle C, and we say it has a frequency of 440 Hz, even though it has energy at many higher (harmonic) frequencies as well.

Frequency Deviation *See* MODULATION INDEX.

Frequency Discriminator A type of FM DETECTOR. *See* DISCRIMINATOR.

Frequency Doubling An effect sometimes heard with low-frequency LOUDSPEAKERS where the second HARMONIC DISTORTION becomes as strong or stronger than the fundamental. The effect is that the bass sounds an OCTAVE higher than it really is. Frequency doubling is usually the result of overloading a speaker.

Frequency Extender A device used to extend the usable frequency range of a telephone line by about two OCTAVES. A standard telephone line has a frequency response extending only from about 300 to 3,300 HERTZ. This lack of low-frequency response can be troublesome and results in most male voices sounding thin, or "tinny." The frequency extender uses the frequency shifter principle to shift all frequencies up by 250 Hz on the sending end and back down at the receiving end. This extends the response down to 50 Hz on the low end and sacrifices only the upper 250 Hz on the upper end.

Frequency Modulation, FM Frequency modulation is the instantaneous changing of the frequency of a CARRIER in response to a modulating SIGNAL, usually an audio WAVEFORM. As the signal VOLTAGE varies up and down as it follows the waveform, the frequency of the carrier varies up and down from its nominal unmodulated value. In commercial FM radio broadcasting, the carrier frequency is in the BAND from 88 MHz to 108 MHz. The FM receiver is tuned to the carrier frequency, and the received signal, after suitable conditioning, is applied to a special CIRCUIT called an FM DETECTOR, or DISCRIMINATOR, which recovers the audio signal.

FM transmission is relatively quieter than AM transmission because the discriminator is not sensitive to AMPLITUDE variations caused by atmospheric interference, and it permits wider FREQUENCY RESPONSE because the FCC has allocated wider BANDWIDTHS to be transmitted in the FM band than in the AM band. The bandwidth of AM transmission is limited to 10 KILOHERTZ to prevent adjacent stations from interfering with one another, whereas a bandwidth of 100 kHz is allocated in each FM channel.

In music, VIBRATO is a form of frequency modulation because it is a periodic variation in frequency. FM is also used in the synthesis of musical tones in some forms of electronic SYNTHESIZERS. It is possible to achieve a very wide range of HARMONIC and nonharmonic effects by this means.

Frequency modulation DISTORTION is a type of distortion produced by a loudspeaker. *See* DOPPLER DISTORTION.

Frequency Response Frequency response is a shortened way of stating the AMPLITUDE response versus FREQUENCY characteristic. It is a complex function that describes the way in which the GAIN and PHASE of a system or a device vary with the frequency of the stimulus. Frequency response is usually presented as a graph or plot of the output of a device on the vertical axis versus the frequency on the horizontal axis. In audio work, it is common to use the logarithm of frequency as the horizontal axis and to use the DECIBEL scale for AMPLITUDE in the vertical axis. This is sometimes called a "log-log" plot, and it correlates better than a linear plot with our hearing mechanism. The frequency response consists of two parts, called the MAGNITUDE and the PHASE. The magnitude is the part most often seen.

Another way to graph the frequency response is to divide it into "real" and "imaginary" parts. This presentation includes the phase information as well as the magnitude. The real and imaginary parts are simply the projections of the complex function onto two orthogonal axes, which are arbitrarily called real and imaginary. There is nothing imaginary about the "imaginary" part, and it is also sometimes called the quadrature part, indicating that it is a projection on an axis 90 degrees (a quarter circle) from the real part. The magnitude is the square root of the sum of the squares of the real and imaginary parts.

It is important to realize that frequency response is defined to be a characteristic of a system or a device, not a characteristic of a SIGNAL.

Frequency Shifter A device that linearly shifts all the frequencies of a complex input signal. The amount of shift can be varied, and the shift can be up or down in frequency. Also sometimes called a spectrum shifter.

The key word here is *linear,* which means all the frequency components are shifted by the same number of HERTZ, in contrast to a PITCH change caused by changing the speed of a tape-recorded signal. In such a pitch change, all the frequency components are shifted by a constant percentage, and therefore, high frequencies are shifted proportionally more than lower ones. A pitch shift by speed change thus preserves all the musical intervals between the components. A true frequency shifter, on the other hand, destroys the harmonic relation between the components. The sound of a consonant musical tone becomes dissonant or bell-like or harsh, depending on the amount of shift. Frequency shifters are used in electronic music synthesizers for special effects that would be almost impossible to attain otherwise.

Some years ago, it was conjectured that if a small amount of frequency shift was added to the amplified signal in a sound reinforcement system, the result would be a reduction in the tendency for acoustic FEEDBACK, because the amplified sound picked up by the MICROPHONE comes out of the loudspeaker at a higher frequency. Small amounts of frequency shift, about 4 or 5 hertz or so, are not very audible with speech sounds. Frequency shifters for this use were made and sold in the 1960s. Unfortunately, the theory did not hold in practice, and where there was feedback before, there were little "chirps" at the ends of the words instead. This proved to be about as annoying as the feedback!

Frequency-to-Voltage Conversion *See* PITCH TRACKING.

Fringe Area A location, remote from the transmitter, where radio or television reception is marginal due to low signal strength and high noise level.

Sometimes a special high-gain antenna can pull in weak stations in fringe areas.

Fringing Fringing is a rise in the level of low frequencies when a recording is replayed by an analog TAPE HEAD with a narrower track width than the one used to record the tape.

The replay head is sensitive to the magnetic flux on the tape that is outside the actual track width of the head. Therefore, FLAT FREQUENCY RESPONSE is only maintained when the recorded track is the same width as the reproduce head track. The effect only occurs at low frequencies, where the recorded WAVELENGTH is long compared to the dimensions of the head.

Frontal-Incidence Microphone A microphone having an essentially constant sensitivity over a wide FREQUENCY range when in a free acoustic field and pointed at the source of the sound. Also known as FREE-FIELD MICROPHONE.

Front End In a radio receiver, the amplification stages before HETERODYNING takes place are collectively called the front end. The front end must amplify signals from the antenna that cover a wide FREQUENCY range and a very wide DYNAMIC RANGE. It is common to experience front-end OVERLOAD with very strong stations at close range, and this causes DISTORTION and tuning difficulties.

Fullcoat Motion picture film, either 16 mm or 35 mm wide, that is coated with magnetic material instead of a photographic emulsion. It is also known as magstock. It is used for magnetic recording of film sound tracks, and because it has sprocket holes, it can be easily synchronized with the picture when the final sound track is assembled. *See also* DOUBLE-SYSTEM SOUND.

Full Duplex A communications channel, such as a telephone line, that allows simultaneous transmissions in both directions is called a full duplex channel.

Full Track An analog TAPE HEAD configuration in which the entire width of the tape is used for the recorded track. This, of course, applies to MONAURAL recorders only. Full-track recording achieves about 3 DECIBELS better SIGNAL-TO-NOISE RATIO than HALF-TRACK recording.

Fundamental The lowest FREQUENCY component in a complex periodic WAVEFORM. Any sound waveform that is perceived as having a musical PITCH is periodic, i.e., it has a shape that repeats itself. This sound will have a series of HARMONICS, sometimes called OVERTONES by musicians. (Actually, the first overtone is the second harmonic, etc.) The lowest of these harmonics, called the "first harmonic," is also called the fundamental. The musical pitch of such a sound generally is determined by the fundamental frequency.

An interesting PSYCHOACOUSTIC effect of our hearing mechanism is that we perceive the pitch of a complex wave as being that of the fundamental, even if the fundamental is actually missing. In other words, as long as the higher harmonics are present, the ear will reconstruct the missing fundamental. It does this by sensing the difference in frequency between the successive harmonics. This difference frequency will be constant because the harmonics are all at integral multiples of the fundamental frequency. This phenomenon is called "fundamental tracking," and is very important to our subjective appreciation of music.

Most low-pitched musical instruments, such as the bassoon, bass viol, tuba, etc., produce very little energy at the fundamental frequencies of the lowest tones. It is easy to see how this must be, simply by the physical size of the instruments. To radiate significant energy, a sound source usually must be large compared to the wavelengths involved. For instance, low A on the piano has a frequency of 27 HERTZ, whose fundamental has a WAVELENGTH of over 30 feet, and negligible energy is produced at this frequency. The same is true for most instruments, although the organ is a notable exception. There are specially designed pipes in most organs that do produce large amounts of very low frequency energy, and this is the reason the organ can cause noticeable vibration of floors and walls in buildings.

This fundamental tracking allows us to perceive satisfying bass notes emanating from relatively small instruments, and it also eases the demand on sound reproducing systems. This explains the difficulty of reproducing the sound of the organ at realistic levels. Fundamental tracking also allows us to enjoy music reproduced from very small LOUDSPEAKERS and still hear the bass tones. The sound of a symphony orchestra reproduced on the three-inch speaker in a transistor radio bears very little resemblance to the original wide-range sound; yet we are able to perceive the musical pitches very well. Of course, we will recognize the fact that the low pitches are weak and the sound is "thin," but the pitches are still heard correctly.

Fundamental Tracking *See* FUNDAMENTAL.

Fuse A protective component for an electrically operated device, often consisting of a glass-enclosed wire that will melt, or "blow," and break the electrical connection if the CURRENT through it is higher than its rated value. There are many types of fuses, and they are rated for their current-carrying capacity as well as the speed with which they will open up when overloaded. A "fast-blow" fuse may blow in 1 ms, whereas a "slow-blow" fuse may take many seconds to open up with a small overload current.

Fuses operate because they have a relatively high RESISTANCE compared with the rest of the CIRCUIT they protect, and they are NONLINEAR devices, whose resistance changes with temperature. Some LOUDSPEAKER systems are protected by fuses, usually slow-blow types, and they can affect the DAMPING of the system as well as increase the DISTORTION.

Fusion In stereophonic music reproduction, sounds from two or more LOUDSPEAKERS can be perceived to be coming from some point between the speakers. The multiple sounds are sometimes said to "fuse" into a single sonic image. Probably the most common example of this fusion is the apparent location of a solo instrument or voice in the center between two speakers. The precision of the image location has a great deal to do with the uniformity and similarity of the loudspeakers.

Fuzz Box A device that makes a virtue of DISTORTION. It consists of a PREAMPLIFIER that is overdriven to produce CLIPPING and consequently large amounts of harmonic distortion. It is used as an EFFECTS device, most often with electric guitars.

Fuzzy Distortion A type of DISTORTION first described by Prof. Malcolm O. J. Hawksford, fuzzy distortion is caused by the fact that only a very few electrons will enter a TRANSISTOR'S base and contribute to SIGNAL transmission when amplifying very low level signals. This is analogous to QUANTIZATION distortion in DIGITAL systems. It may be minimized by certain circuit TOPOLOGIES.

FX Short for "effects," meaning any form of audio signal processing or a device to produce reverb, delay, chorusing, ECHO, FLANGING, PHASING, etc.

G

Gaffer An electrician working on a film or video stage is called a gaffer.

Gaffers Tape A very strong cloth adhesive tape used to temporarily secure things such as cables to the floor. Gaffers never refer to this as duct tape. There are a surprising number of opinions about the best characteristics of such tape.

Gain The amount of increase in the power of a signal by an AMPLIFIER is called the power gain. It is simply the ratio of the output power to the input power and is conveniently expressed in DECIBELS.

An amplifier also usually increases the VOLTAGE and/or the CURRENT of a SIGNAL, and these increases are called voltage gain and current gain, respectively. They should be expressed in decibels only if the input and output IMPEDANCES of the amplifier are the same, but this is seldom the case in practice. Voltage and current gains should properly be referred to as simple numbers, that is, a voltage gain of 10 or 100, etc. Nevertheless, most engineers express voltage gains of various types of amplifiers in decibels regardless of the fact that the input and output impedances are very different. As long as they understand that the true power gain cannot be expressed this way, no confusion seems to result. For more information, *see* DECIBEL.

A PASSIVE device, such as a TRANSFORMER, can have voltage gain or current gain (but not both), even though it cannot amplify the signal.

Gain Bandwidth Product A figure of merit for certain active electronic devices such as OPAMPS. It is a numerical multiplication of the gain times the bandwidth.

Gain Riding Gain riding is the variation in the volume control setting while making a recording in order to prevent OVERLOAD and DISTORTION at loud levels and to avoid noise problems at low levels.

If the GAIN is adjusted to maintain the SIGNAL level near the top of the DYNAMIC RANGE of the recording device, the SIGNAL-TO-NOISE RATIO will be maximized, but the DYNAMICS, or LOUDNESS variations naturally present in the signal, will be minimized. For most music, this is undesirable, but gain riding still must be done to some extent in order to avoid overloads.

LIMITERS, COMPRESSORS, and automatic gain controls are devices that perform gain riding in specific ways without operator intervention.

It is important to note that gain riding will not prevent signal overloads that can occur in circuit components that precede the gain control. A common place of signal overload in recording consoles is the input stage of the MICROPHONE PREAMPLIFIER. Well-designed recording consoles have overload detection circuitry built in, and red LED's in each channel warn the user of overloads in the preamplifiers. The user must adjust the microphone preamplifier so it is not overdriven, usually with a control that attenuates the signal to the preamp. Any amplifier can also have this problem, and the solution is always to attenuate the signal to not overdrive the amplifier, or reduce its gain.

It is also worth noting that the terms GAIN and VOLUME CONTROL or ATTENUATION are often used interchangeably, as the effect often seems the same.

Gain Structure The settings of all of the sequential amplification (gain) stages in a device or system. A single device such as a mixer may have many sequential gain stages within it, although some may not be user adjustable. A large sound system may have many separate audio processors in its chain, and each may be considered a gain stage in itself. Good gain structure is the result of the analysis and setting of all gain stages in a device or system to ensure that the system has full DYNAMIC RANGE, that no stage distorts from CLIPPING (overloading), and is high enough above the noise floor for good SIGNAL-TO-NOISE RATIO. If a power AMPLIFIER and speaker is the end of the chain, the amplifier must have its sensitivity adjusted so that full power is available without noise from excess sensitivity (gain). In a multicomponent audio system that has its gain structure adjusted correctly, if you put a signal in at its input and gradually raise the level of that signal, all the gain stages in the system will reach their clipping level at the same time.

Gain structure also refers to a device's internal gain stages that are part of its design and not user adjustable.

Gang To mechanically couple two or more controls, such as POTENTIOMETERS, FADERS, or variable CAPACITORS, is to gang them. The combined assembly is then called a ganged fader, and so on. For example, a stereo volume control consists of two ganged single-channel potentiometers.

Gap Scatter In ANALOG tape recorder HEADS with more than one track, the gaps associated with the tracks are positioned as nearly as possible in a straight line, which ensures that the tracks are recorded and reproduced at the same time. This is important in stereo recording to preserve localization of sound sources.

Any deviation from perfect alignment is called gap scatter, and can be measured by recording the same SINUSOIDAL signal on both tracks of the tape. The tape reels are then reversed and the tape reproduced backward. The PHASE difference between the two reproduced signals is an indication of the magnitude of gap scatter. For this test to be accurate, the head must be in perfect AZIMUTH alignment.

Gassy A condition resulting from an imperfect vacuum that can afflict vacuum TUBES, reducing their performance. When operating, a gassy tube will usually show a purplish glow in the neighborhood of the PLATE. A gassy tube is also said to be "soft" or "flat."

Gate A CIRCUIT that performs like a switch, allowing a SIGNAL either to pass or not, is called a gate. The position of the gate (open or closed) is controlled by an applied VOLTAGE, which can come from a number of different places. If the level of the signal itself determines the gate opening, it is a NOISE GATE, closing when the signal level is so low that the noise would be audible.

One of the three terminals of the FIELD EFFECT TRANSISTOR is also called the gate. The VOLTAGE on the gate acts as a control and determines the CURRENT through the FET.

Gauss A unit of magnetic flux density, equal to one ten-thousandth of a TESLA. Many LOUDSPEAKER manufacturers use this unit in their specifications, but the tesla is more often used by the scientific community. The gauss was named in honor of the famous eighteenth-century German mathematician and physicist Karl Friedrich Gauss, who investigated magnetism.

Getter A small metal tray or cup placed inside a vacuum tube and containing a small quantity of metallic barium. When the tube is evacuated, the barium is heated and it quickly combines with the residual oxygen to make barium oxide. This prevents the oxygen from gradually oxidizing the hot elements in the tube, especially the heater.

Gibson Girl *See* SPLICER.

GIGO, Garbage In, Garbage Out A slang term meaning defective or noisy data sent to the input of a device will result in defective or noisy output from the device.

Glass Master A glass disc with a light-sensitive coating, whose surface is to be etched with pits by a laser beam that is modulated by digital data that represents the audio signal. This surface is then plated with a coating of silver, and is then used as a master for the stampers from which CDs are eventually pressed.

Glitch An undesired VOLTAGE excursion found in a DAC. *See* DEGLITCHER.

Gnat's Nut A vanishingly small distance or quantity.

GND Abbreviation for GROUND.

Gobo A movable panel or baffle used in a recording studio to isolate certain instruments from others in a group. The gobos are usually about three or four feet high and may be made of wood with fiberglass on the surfaces, or sometimes they are of solid foam polyurethane plastic.

Golden Ear A so-called "Golden Ear" is a person to whom is ascribed (usually self-ascribed) the ability to discern and appreciate subtleties and to identify defects in recordings and sound systems that ordinary people find elusive. Generally, Golden Ears are forever modifying and changing their sound systems, much to the delight of the equipment industry. We have been in search of the true Golden Ear for many years, and numerous candidates have come to light. Alas, they have all come up short when put to the test. For instance, many such have failed to tell the difference between STEREO and MONAURAL, or failed to detect when the channels were reversed in a stereo presentation, etc.

This is not to denigrate the importance of careful and critical listening, for our ears are truly marvelous measuring instruments when properly trained and accustomed to evaluating sound. For instance, it has long been known that objective measurements on sound systems may not correlate with what one hears—an AMPLIFIER may seem nearly perfect when measured and still sound faulty. Also, components that look identical to measuring instruments often sound quite different. For this reason, measurement techniques are constantly being refined, and new types of DISTORTION are being discovered all the time. It is generally agreed that no measurement technique thus far discovered can match the well-trained ear in sensitivity to certain types of distortions.

The human hearing mechanism operates quite differently from MICROPHONES and SIGNAL analyzers, and its physiological and psychological aspects are far from being fully understood.

Good Acoustics *See* Appendix 4.

Gooseneck A flexible, spiral, metal pipe about 14 inches long used to attach a MICROPHONE to a microphone stand. The gooseneck allows the microphone to be oriented in almost any direction. It would be nice if goosenecks would allow the microphone to be moved without introducing any noise, but they generally squeak when bent.

Gradient Microphone A gradient microphone is sensitive to the pressure gradient (or variation in pressure over a distance) of a sound field. The RIBBON MICROPHONE is an example. Gradient microphones have a POLAR PATTERN resembling a figure 8. This CURVE is the polar plot of the mathematical cosine curve, and gradient microphones are sometimes called cosine microphones. *See also* FIGURE-8 MICROPHONE.

Grain A subtle type of DISTORTION found in some audio devices, mostly digital devices but sometimes also power AMPLIFIERS. *See also* GRANULATION.

Grammy A recording industry award presented by the Recording Academy, also known as the National Association of Recording Arts and Sciences, NARAS.

Gramophone The Gramophone was the first recorder-reproducer to use a flat disc rather than a CYLINDER as the medium. It was invented by Emile Berliner and commercially produced in 1893.

The Berliner disc introduced important differences from the Edison cylinder phonograph. It used lateral rather than vertical modulation, and the discs were recorded with a STYLUS scratching through a soft wax layer on a zinc disc, reducing the work the stylus had to do. The groove in the disc was then formed by acid etching. These techniques increased the AMPLITUDE of modulation, making the records sound louder than Edison's. The introduction of the disc meant also that records could be easily mass-produced by stamping, which was much cheaper than the complex mold-ing procedure Edison used to reproduce cylinders. No doubt the explosive growth of the recording industry was due to the Berliner innovations.

The first Berliner discs "sounded like a partially educated parrot with a sore throat and a cold in the head," according to Eldridge Johnson, founder of the Victor Talking Machine company.

Granulation DISTORTION in a DIGITAL audio system due to the uncertainty in the level of the samples is known as granulation; also called QUANTIZATION distortion.

If the SAMPLING RATE is an exact multiple of the input tone FREQUENCY, granulation results in HARMONIC DISTORTION, i.e., the distortion components are at multiples of the input FREQUENCY. If not, the granulation resembles random NOISE, with a broad nondiscrete spectrum, in which case it may properly be called quantization noise.

Gravitation "The tendency of all bodies to approach one another with a strength proportional to the quantity of matter they contain, the quantity of matter they contain being ascertained by the strength of their tendency to approach one another. This is a lovely and edifying example of how science, making A the proof of B, makes B the proof of A."—A. Bierce

Gravity Cell An essentially obsolete type of VOLTAIC CELL that uses zinc and copper ELECTRODES and copper sulfate and zinc sulfate as the ELECTROLYTE. The cell is arranged with the copper electrode on the bottom surrounded by a concentrated solution of copper sulfate, and the zinc electrode on the top surrounded by the lighter solution of zinc sulfate. Gravity keeps the two sections of electrolyte from mixing, hence the name "gravity cell." The zinc electrode usually looks like a crow's foot, so the cell is also sometimes called a "crowfoot" cell. The gravity cell is unusual in that it becomes discharged when no CURRENT exists through it but does not become discharged under full-current conditions. For this reason, it is called a "closed circuit" cell and is kept with a shorting strap across it when not in use. It was very well adapted for use in telegraphy, and this is where it saw most of its use.

Green Book *See* RED BOOK.

Grid In a TUBE, the element that controls the electric CURRENT is the grid. It is usually made as a series of fine wires, and is placed between the CATHODE, or emitter of ELECTRONS, and the PLATE, or collector of electrons. A tube may contain several grids, but normally only one, called the control grid, actually controls the amount of current in the tube. *See also* AUDION.

Grip A stagehand working on a film or video stage is called a grip.

Groove Guard™ The result of shaping the cross section of stereo records so the groove area is somewhat protected by raised edges and centers. If records are stacked one on top of another, as is the case with a record changer, the groove areas are prevented from coming into contact.

RCA Records invented and trademarked the term Groove Guard.

Ground In an AMPLIFIER or other audio component, the metal CHASSIS is called the ground, whether or not it is connected to the actual ground. One of the SIGNAL leads is usually connected to ground, as is one of the power supply leads. Ground is therefore sometimes called a "common." In Britain, the term "earth" is used instead.

An electronic chassis is made of metal because metal is a conductor of electricity; the chassis therefore acts as a SHIELD, keeping external electrostatic fields out of the interior. Such electrostatic fields would induce NOISE in the CIRCUITS, and shielding greatly reduces this. The shielding effect of the chassis is extended to the signal wires by using shielded cables, which have an outer conductor completely surrounding the inner conductor. A coaxial television cable is an example. The outer conductor, or shield, is connected to the chassis ground. If two or more components are connected together, such as a PREAMP and an AMPLIFIER, the shield in the cable usually serves to connect the two chassis together, making all the grounds common. If this ground connection is broken, very large amounts of 60-HERTZ noise, or HUM can be introduced. This is because the 60-Hz power lines, which are nearly everywhere, radiate strong electric fields at 60 Hz, just like radio transmitting towers.

Ground Lifter A switch found on some AUDIO adapter boxes, or DIRECT BOXES, interrupts the continuity of the SHIELD connection between the output and input. This disconnects the CHASSIS ground of a device like a guitar AMPLIFIER from the GROUND of the recording console or tape recorder, reducing the possibility of HUM induced by GROUND LOOPS.

Ground Loop *See* SHIELD.

Group Delay The slope of the PHASE-versus-FREQUENCY curve of a FREQUENCY RESPONSE function, i.e., the rate of change of phase of the response as a function of frequency. Group delay is a property of a device or a system.

A pure time delay, equal at all frequencies, gives a constant slope of phase versus frequency. If in an audio component this slope is not constant, but varies with frequency, the component is said to produce group delay DISTORTION. This is equivalent to a time delay that varies with frequency. For instance, an ANTI-ALIASING FILTER will typically have a phase response CURVE that slopes sharply down at high frequencies, which means that the high-frequency components will be delayed longer in their passage through the filter. The audible result is a loss of precision in musical TRANSIENTS; they are spread out, or "smeared," in time, and a more diffuse STEREO image results.

By using an all-pass network, it is possible to correct the group delay distortion of such filters, but this is seldom done in practice. (*See* ALL-PASS FILTER.) The most effective way of measuring group delay is to use the dual-channel FFT ANALYZER, which displays the phase response directly as a function of frequency.

Group Velocity Group velocity is the speed with which a group of waves progresses through a medium.

For some transmission media, it is found that SIGNALS of different frequencies travel at different speeds. Examples of this are ocean waves, where shorter WAVELENGTHS (higher frequencies) travel faster than longer ones; and light waves traveling in glass, where shorter waves travel slower. This phenomenon is called DISPERSION, and such media are called dispersive. Dispersion is what causes a prism of glass to separate the various frequencies of light into a SPECTRUM.

Consider a SIGNAL made up of a short BURST of a single-frequency tone. The tone FREQUENCY will be associated with a relatively short wavelength, while the burst itself constitutes a disturbance of lower frequency. The tone will then travel at a different speed than the burst, and the individual waves of a tone will be seen to move through the burst. This happens with ocean waves; the small waves can be observed as they begin at the rear of the group and peter out at the leading edge of the group.

This, luckily, does not happen with sound waves in air. If it did, music would be aural anguish, even more than some music already is. However, some audio devices are dispersive to electrical signals, and this does cause DISTORTION of the signals. A TRANSIENT, for instance, is necessarily made up of many different frequencies, and if they travel at different rates in a device, the transient will become spread out in time (or "smeared") as it progresses through the device, and it will not sound the same coming out as it did going in. The distortion produced by such a device is sometimes called GROUP DELAY distortion. All FILTERS produce this type of distortion to some extent, although there is no agreement among audio people about the audibility of small amounts of it.

Grunge A rather ill-defined term for a type of DISTORTION in audio equipment that is difficult to quantify and measure. It is also sometimes called mid-range smear, which is at least more descriptive. It is caused by the interaction of the many frequencies present in a music signal. The result is a broad band of NONLINEAR distortion products.

Guard Band A narrow unrecorded area between the recorded tracks of a MAGNETIC TAPE. The guard band reduces CROSSTALK between the channels of the tape recorder. *See also* HALF-TRACK.

GUI Graphic User Interface. A computer operating system that uses symbols on the screen and a pointing device to move objects around and activate and manipulate files without using the keyboard. The Apple Macintosh operating system and the various Microsoft Windows operating systems use GUIs. The principal of the GUI was probably invented by the Xerox Corp., who sold the rights to use it to Apple Computer.

Gyrator A gyrator is a circuit TOPOLOGY that uses only CAPACITORS and RESISTORS along with amplifying stages, but acts like an INDUCTOR.

In some cases it is less expensive to build a gyrator CIRCUIT than to use an actual INDUCTOR, depending on the value of the required inductance.

H

Haas Effect The Haas effect, also called the precedence effect, is related to the localization of the apparent sonic image when the same SIGNAL is presented to the two ears at slightly different times. If a short signal such as a click is presented over earphones to one ear and then to the other ear a few milliseconds later, the human hearing mechanism will judge the sound to be coming from the side of the head where the earliest sound arrived. For no delay between the sounds reaching the ears, the sound is localized straight ahead, or sometimes within the head itself, and as the delay is increased, the image moves farther and farther to the side where the earliest sound occurred. This is true up to about 25 to 35 milliseconds, after which more delay will result in two distinct sounds being heard.

The Haas effect also means that if a sound arrives at a listener's ears from two locations, as is the case with sound reinforcement systems with several LOUDSPEAKERS, the sound will be localized at the loudspeaker that provides the earliest arriving sound, and the other speaker will not be heard at all. This is true even if the delayed sound is stronger than the first sound. The difference in level may be as much as 10 DECIBELS, and the delayed sound will still be inaudible.

The Haas effect is an example of sensory inhibition, where the response to a stimulus causes the response to another stimulus to be inhibited. Sensory inhibition, as the name implies, is a characteristic of other senses besides hearing. The science of psychophysics deals with these phenomena.

Half Normalled *See* PATCH BAY.

Half-Power Bandwidth A standardized method of stating the BANDWIDTH of a BANDPASS or BAND REJECT FILTER. The half-power bandwidth is the higher FREQUENCY where the response is 3 dB lower than the maximum minus the lower frequency where the response is 3 dB lower than the maximum. A 3-dB reduction in level is, of course, a power reduction of one-half. *See* DECIBEL.

Half-Step The musical interval of a minor second in a DIATONIC scale. In JUST INTONATION, the minor second has a FREQUENCY ratio of 15/16, and in the equal tempered scale, the minor second has a frequency ratio of the 12th root of 2, or about 6%. *See* Appendix 8.

Half-Track An analog TAPE HEAD configuration that assigns half the tape width to each AUDIO channel. In MONAURAL recorders, the single channel uses one-half the tape width, allowing the other half to be recorded when the tape reels are flipped over and reversed. Strictly speaking, the track widths are a little less than one-half the tape width. There is a narrow band down the center of the tape that is not recorded in order to reduce CROSSTALK. This is called a GUARD BAND.

Handshaking The initial exchange of BINARY data between two digital devices or systems that establishes proper communications between them. A common example is the noises made by the computer modem when first establishing a link with another modem.

Hamster Switch A control found on professional disk jockey performance mixers that reverses FADER action. For example, if a fader normally is off at the bottom of its travel and on at the top of its travel, then activating the hamster switch reverses this, so off is now at the top and on is at the bottom of travel, or alternatively, it swaps left for right in horizontally mounted faders. It is used to create the most comfortable (and fastest) fader access when using either turntable, and to accommodate left-handed and right-handed performers. Credited to, and named after, one of the original scratch-style crews named The BulletProof Scratch Hamsters.[15]

Hangover When a SIGNAL into a LOUDSPEAKER suddenly stops, as happens with musical TRANSIENTS, sometimes the loudspeaker CONE will continue to move and produce sound. This is called hangover. It is both a low-FREQUENCY and a high-frequency phenomenon, and is reduced by adding DAMPING to the system. One way of doing this is to increase the DAMPING FACTOR of the AMPLIFIER so it has better control of the cone. Hangover causes poorly damped WOOFER systems to sound "boomy," and poorly damped TWEETERS to sound "hissy."

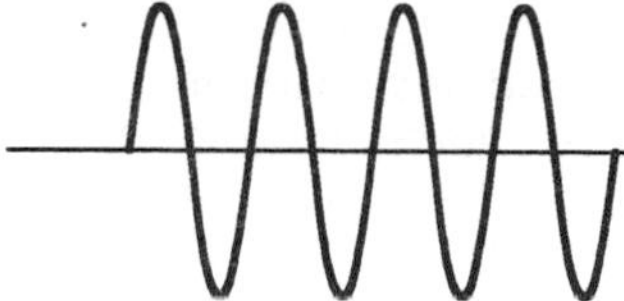

Tone burst input to loudspeaker

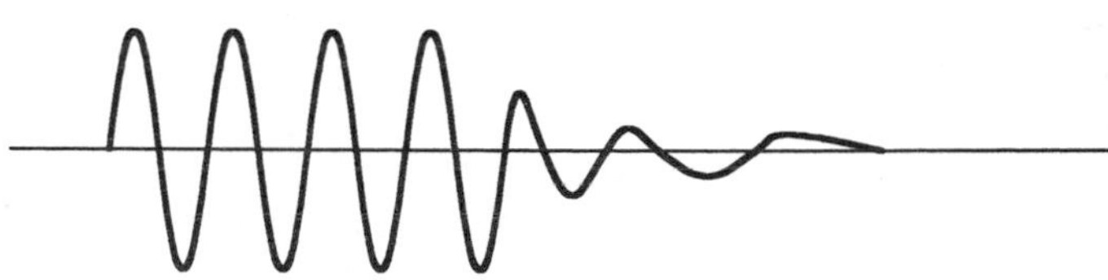

Acoustic response of loudspeaker

Hangover

Hard Clipping CLIPPING where the edges of the WAVEFORM are very sharp, producing the maximum amount of high harmonic content.

Hardware Key *See* DONGLE.

Hard-Wired Permanently connected with wire, rather than being connected by a removable cable or plugs and jacks.

Harmonic Distortion In a perfect AUDIO device, such as an AMPLIFIER or

15. Thanks to Dennis Bohn, Rane Corp.

tape recorder, the output SIGNAL would be a replica of the input signal with no changes except maybe power level. The perfect device does not exist, however, and the output signal will always have some DISTORTION when compared to the input signal. The simplest form of this distortion consists of HARMONICS of the input signal being added to the output signal. This is called harmonic distortion, and is caused by the system not being perfectly LINEAR.

Harmonic distortion is usually measured as a percent. An amplifier putting out 10 VOLTS at 1,000 HERTZ and adding 1 V of 2,000 Hz is said to have 10 percent of second harmonic distortion. Harmonic distortion is best measured with a SPECTRUM ANALYZER, where the amounts of the various harmonics are shown. The summed levels of all the added harmonics is called the total harmonic distortion, or THD, and is usually expressed as a percentage of the level of the signal being measured. This signal is typically a SINE WAVE. The percentage of one harmonic, typically the third, may also be reported by itself, and would be denoted as HDL3 for 3rd harmonic distortion level.

Various devices contribute different types of harmonic distortion; for instance, an ANALOG tape recorder adds odd-order harmonics (primarily third) almost exclusively, while a typical amplifier will add both even- and odd-order harmonics. TUBE-type amplifiers add lower-order harmonics, and TRANSISTOR-type amplifiers tend to add higher-order harmonics. This is at least partially responsible for the differences in "sound" between different types of audio devices. When the THD consists of second harmonics, the sound is "loud" and "brassy." Some amplifiers and preamps cause this type of distortion when overloaded, and this has often been deliberately exploited to increase the "punch" of certain recordings.

Third harmonic distortion, on the other hand, creates a somewhat "covered" sound, generally considered undesirable. *See also* APHEX AURAL EXCITER.

Harmonic Series A harmonic series is a group of frequencies, each one of which is an integral multiple of the FREQUENCY of the lowest one, or FUNDAMENTAL. *See also* OVERTONES.

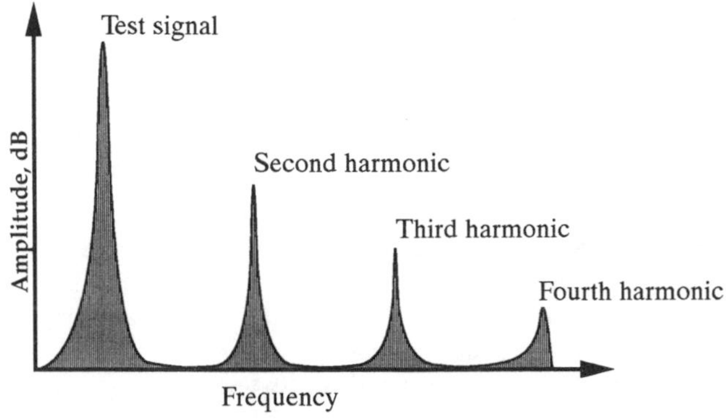

Harmonic Series Spectrum

HATS Head And Torso Simulator, or a DUMMY HEAD but with the torso. It is used to more accurately simulate the acoustics near a human upper body.

HDCD High Definition Compatible Digital. An encode/decode system for music CDS and DVDS that encompasses up to 176.4-kHz SAMPLING rate and 24-bit resolution. The system was introduced by Pacific Microsonics, before it became a subsidiary of Microsoft, and it is compatible with standard RED BOOK CDs. HDCDs can thus be played on conventional CD players and are claimed to attain lower noise levels and somewhat less DISTORTION. It is also claimed that conventional CDs can be played on HDCD players with improved noise and distortion figures.

HDR Hard Disc Recorder. An audio recording device that digitizes the audio and records directly onto a computer-type hard disc. Several configurations are available, usually with multichannel capability. HDRs are often included in Digital Audio Workstations, "DAWS."

HDTV, High Definition Television Television that has about twice the resolution or more of the original ANALOG systems like NTSC, PAL, and SECAM, with multichannel audio. HDTV could theoretically be analog, but consumer HDTV systems are digitally transmitted. Display of the picture can be analog (similar to a computer CRT display) or digital (similar to a digital flat panel computer display). The analog NTSC system transmits pictures of 525 interlaced scan lines, of which about 480 are visible. The ATSC HDTV system has several modes, and includes 1080 INTERLACED SCAN lines (or vertical pixels), called 1080i, and 720 PROGRESSIVE SCAN lines (720p). ATSC can also transmit non-HDTV at 480 lines.

Head *See* TAPE HEAD.

Head Amplifier, Head Amp Synonymous with PRE-PREAMPLIFIER; mostly British usage.

Head Bump A series of irregularities, or "bumps," in the low-FREQUENCY response of ANALOG tape recorders sometimes can be over 2 DECIBELS in

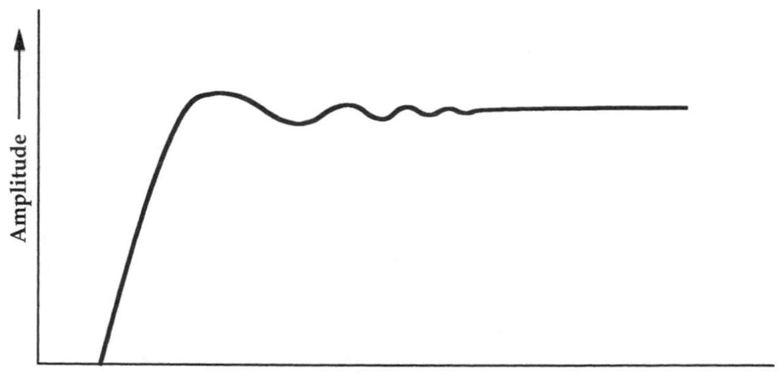

Head Bump Effect

amplitude and are worse at higher tape speeds. They are essentially nonexistent in cassette recorders because of the low tape speed.

Head bumps are caused by the fact that the playback head as a whole responds to very long WAVELENGTHS recorded on the tape, while only the gap in the head responds to the shorter wavelengths. At certain frequencies (corresponding to specific recorded wavelengths), the overall head response will be in PHASE with the gap response, and the overall response is increased. At other frequencies, the two responses will be out of phase and will partially cancel, causing a dip in the overall response. As frequency increases, the effect becomes less and less, and the bumps fade into a smooth FREQUENCY RESPONSE CURVE.

The effect is actually dependent on the recorded wavelength rather than the absolute frequency, and since low tape speeds mean short recorded wavelengths, the effect is only apparent below the audible frequency range. As tape speed increases, the effect occurs at higher and higher frequencies, and can be a real problem at 30 IPS.

Careful head design and attention to the amount of tape "wrap" around the head can reduce the effect.

Headphones Headphones are miniature LOUDSPEAKER-like sound reproducers designed to be worn over the ears for private listening to AUDIO signals. Also known as "earphones" and "headset."

There are many types of headphones, but probably the most common is the DYNAMIC headset, which is similar to a dynamic loudspeaker in operation. Another type is the electrostatic, which is basically similar to the electrostatic loudspeaker. A newer type is the planar dynamic, which uses a perforated magnet assembly and a diaphragm with a metallic conductor embedded in it. It is similar to the "leaf" TWEETERS in operation and can provide very extended, smooth response. Unfortunately, the planar type of headset is seldom seen today, probably because it is expensive to manufacture.

Some headphones require a good seal between the earpiece itself and the head to achieve good bass response. Such a headset is called "circumaural," meaning it fits over the ear. Dynamic headsets are usually in this category. Other units, sometimes called "open air" phones, are designed to rest on the outer surface of the ears and do not require a seal for flat bass response. These sets are often very light in weight and can be of the planar type, or dynamic. This category of headset is called "supra-aural," meaning upon the ear. They do not reduce the interference from ambient noise as do the circumaural units.

It is an unfortunate fact that the FREQUENCY RESPONSE of a headset is a function of the anatomy of the ear on which it rests due to reflections in the ear and variations in the volume of the cavity between the ear and phone. This means each person hears a different tonal balance when listening to the same headset. The effect is measured by inserting a tiny probe microphone next to the eardrum of the listener and performing a frequency SWEEP with various headphones. The variations in frequency response can exceed

10 DECIBELS at certain frequencies. Perhaps this is a reason that various people prefer different types of headphones.

It is interesting that AUDIOMETER testing for hearing loss almost always uses headphones to present the sounds to the subject. The phones are standardized, and must be measured with a specific acoustic coupler with the measurement microphone, but this does not ensure that the subject will have a uniform sound level at the ear drum. This means audiometer testing is subject to at least a 10-dB variation. It would be much better to do audiometer testing under FREE-FIELD conditions; when this is done, almost all subjects have a lower measured hearing threshold.

Headroom Headroom in an AUDIO device is the difference in level between the highest level present in a given SIGNAL and the maximum level the device can handle without noticeable DISTORTION. Music, of course, exhibits very wide variations in level, even within a single selection (except perhaps rock music, which seems to have a dynamic range of 3 DECIBELS or so), and any audio device must handle the maximum expected level in order to sound distortion-free.

Less obvious is that on an instantaneous basis, music WAVEFORMS have short peaks that are much higher in level than the average signal level. This is especially true of percussive sounds in music. These short peaks are not registered by most audio level reading devices, such as the VU meters often seen on ANALOG tape recorders. If a VU meter is used to set the recording level, the temptation will be to set the level too high, allowing the peaks to overdrive the tape, causing distortion. In most audio equipment of high quality, the maximum signal level without overload will be at least 10 dB above the maximum level shown on the meter, i.e., there will be 10 dB of headroom. Nearly all digital recording and signal processing equipment of recent vintage uses SOLID-STATE circuitry with a string of LEDs to indicate the signal level. They usually show the peak level of the signal rather than the average level, and are much better at letting the engineer know how close to overload the signal is. However, there is no agreed-upon standard for the response rise and fall times and peak-hold times of these digital meters, so the engineer must be sure to educate himself in exactly how his meters behave.

Headshell The plug-in holder for a phono CARTRIDGE. The headshell plugs in to the TONEARM and the CARTRIDGE is mounted in the headshell with small screws.

It is a painstaking job to properly mount a phono cartridge and be sure that all the distances and angles are correct for proper tracking of the record groove. Small errors in vertical tracking angle and perpendicularity of the STYLUS cantilever with the record surface will cause significant DISTORTION of the reproduced sound.

The P-MOUNT standard greatly simplifies the installation of cartridges by making everything pre-measured and preset.

Heads Out A reel-to-reel ANALOG tape recording that has been rewound and is ready to play. It is generally considered best for long-term storage to leave recordings in the un-rewound condition (TAILS OUT) for minimum PRINT-THROUGH.

Head Stack The assembly of TAPE HEADS in an ANALOG magnetic recorder. The head stack normally consists of an erase head, a record head, and a playback head. They are mounted close together in a metal housing that provides magnetic SHIELDING for them.

Hear Out To hear, by careful listening, the various PITCH components of a complex tone. It takes a good deal of practice to be able to do this. Also called analytic listening.

Heater In an electronic TUBE, the CATHODE must be heated to a red heat in order to boil electrons out of it. There is a small resistance wire inside it to accomplish this. Sometimes, the heater is the cathode itself; in this case, it is called a directly heated cathode. The first tubes were of this type.

The heaters in a tube-type device are responsible for most of the power dissipation in the device and are the reason the device must be designed for adequate cooling.

Heat Sink A metal structure, usually aluminum, on which power TRANSISTORS are mounted. The heat sink conducts heat away from the transistors, effectively reducing their temperature. The heat sink is actually more of a heat radiator than a true heat sink, and in some amplifiers it occupies a prominent place in the sides or back of the CHASSIS.

Helical Scan A common method of tape recording where a rotating head drum writes and reads slanted tracks of information on MAGNETIC TAPE. This greatly increases the amount of information that can be recorded. The head drum is set at an angle relative to the tape travel, hence would draw a helix, or 3-D spiral. All modern videotape recorders, R-DAT, DTRS and ADAT tape machines use this technique.

Helmholtz Hermann von Helmholtz was a nineteenth-century German physician and acoustician who wrote a fine book on PSYCHOACOUSTICS called *On the Sensations of Tone*. It is still used as a reference today. *See also* HELMHOLTZ RESONATOR.

Helmholtz Resonator A type of acoustical resonator consisting of an enclosed volume of air connected to the atmosphere by a short channel or pipe. The natural springiness of the enclosed air reacts with the mass of air in the pipe, resulting in a sharply tuned resonance, whose FREQUENCY depends inversely on the enclosed volume. Helmholtz resonators are found in some LOUDSPEAKER systems. *See* BASS REFLEX and DUCTED PORT. Hermann von Helmholtz, the great German acoustician of the nineteenth century, invented the Helmholtz resonator to detect the individual component frequencies in complex musical sounds. He made them in a variety of sizes and, by holding them to his ear one after another, was able to "hear out" the harmonics produced by musical instruments and speech. This was probably the first scientific attempt at frequency analysis of sound, although the principle of the Helmholtz resonator was discovered at least as early as 79 B.C. by the Roman architect Vitruvius. *See also* SOUNDING VESSELS.

Hertz, Hz The internationally agreed-upon symbol to indicate FREQUENCY in cycles per second. It is named after Heinrich Hertz, the famous nineteenth-century German physicist who first investigated radio waves.

In 1935, the IEC proposed that hertz (Hz) be used instead of "cycles per second" or "cps," and some European countries did so. In 1948, the General Conference on Weights and Measures adopted the term into the SI metric system. Many people continued to use "cps" into the 1960s.

Heterodyne Another name for AMPLITUDE MODULATION. The process of amplitude modulation is actually the instantaneous multiplication of one SIGNAL by another. This results in the formation of SIDEBANDS that contain the same information as the original signals but translated upward and downward in frequency.

The term *heterodyne* is used for a frequency translation CIRCUIT in AM and FM receivers. The signal from the station is amplified and multiplied by a signal from a "local OSCILLATOR," and this translates the received frequency down to a relatively low frequency called the "intermediate frequency," or IF. This signal is amplified and detected to recover the original audio. By varying the local oscillator frequency, any radio station signal can be translated, or "heterodyned," to the IF, meaning the AMPLIFIERS and DETECTOR need to operate only at this frequency. A receiver using this principle is called a "supersonic heterodyne," or "superhet," receiver. The principle was patented in 1920 by Edwin Armstrong, who also invented the FM DISCRIMINATOR.

Heterodyning is also used in some SPECTRUM ANALYZERS and to a certain extent in electronic music, where it is called frequency shifting.

Heyser Spiral Named for Richard Heyser (1931–1987), who first used TIME DELAY SPECTROMETRY (TDS) for analysis of audio signals. The Heyser Spiral is a graphic representation, or plot, of a so-called ANALYTIC SIGNAL, which is one result of a TEF measurement. The three dimensions of an analytic signal are time, the real part, and the imaginary part of the amplitude in a three-dimensional curve. The Heyser Spiral plot of an analytic sine wave or cosine wave is a constant-diameter spiral, shown below.

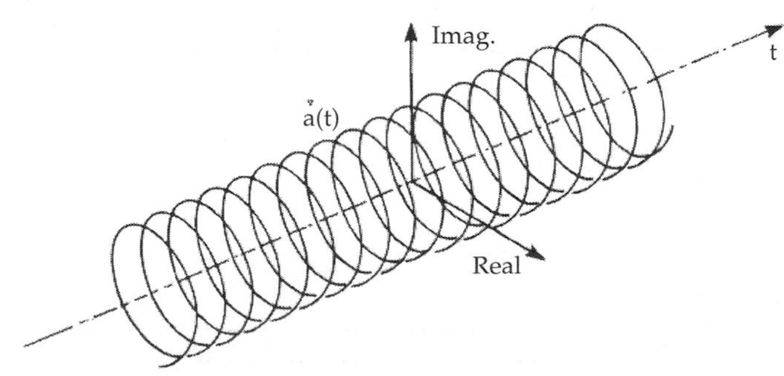

Heyser Spiral Display of a Sine Wave

The same type of plot is often used to visualize the electrical IMPEDANCE of audio devices such as LOUDSPEAKERS. The impedance of most audio devices produces PHASE SHIFT of the audio signal that varies with FREQUENCY, and the actual phase shift angle is decomposed into two parts, the so-called imaginary (or "quadrature") component and the real (or in-phase) component. The Heyser Spiral of an impedance is usually a two-dimensional "polar" plot of the real amplitude versus the imaginary amplitude as a function of frequency. The frequency axis goes through the origin of the plot and is 90 degrees from the plane of the paper. If an audio device has a RESONANCE at a particular frequency, the spiral will show a circle, and if several resonances exist, they will each have a circle in the plot. The size of the circles indicates the strength of the individual resonances.

High-Cut Filter A LOW-PASS FILTER, according to Dennis Bohn, of the Rane Corp.

High End, The The segment of the consumer audio/video industry directed to "hard core" AUDIOPHILES and videophiles is called the high end, possibly in reference to the prices asked for the equipment.

High Fidelity, Hi-Fi A term that became popular in the 1950s meaning a relatively high quality sound system for consumer use. The term *stereo* started to supplant it in the late 1950s.

High-Pass Filter A high-pass filter uniformly passes signals above a certain FREQUENCY, called the CUTOFF frequency. The cutoff frequency is where the filter response is 3 DECIBELS below the nominal response. The response ROLLOFF in the STOPBAND may be gradual or SHARP.

The "rumble" filter found in many record player systems is a high-pass filter. Another example is the bass cut filter on mixing consoles, used to reduce boomyness in certain mics and low-frequency room noise.

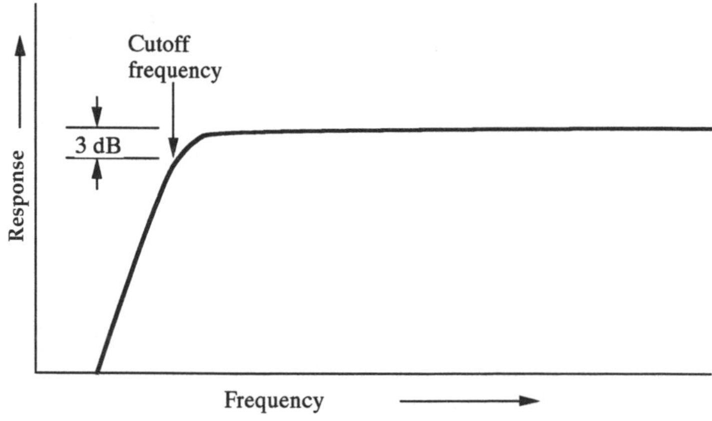

High-Pass Filter

High-Speed Dubbing The copying of ANALOG tape recordings at tape speeds higher than that used for the original recordings. If a tape is played at twice normal speed, all the frequencies will be doubled, and everything will sound an OCTAVE too high as well as twice as fast. If this SIGNAL is recorded onto another tape and then replayed at normal speed, the frequencies all come out correct, but it will take only half as long to make the copy. In like manner, if the original is played at eight times normal speed, it will only take one eighth the time, etc.

When high-speed dubbing is done, it is important that the player and the recorder be able to handle the higher frequencies without DISTORTION, and the PRE-EMPHASIS and DE-EMPHASIS curves must be different from normal-speed machines. Virtually all commercially available cassettes and tapes have been made this way using special dubbing equipment, and the quality can be very good; however, it is thought that the very best quality copies can only be made at the normal speed.

Hill and Dale A descriptive term for vertical, rather than lateral, modulation of the groove on a phonograph record or cylinder. Thomas Edison was the champion of vertical modulation, even though it was well established quite early that lateral modulation results in less DISTORTION because the cutting STYLUS experiences more uniform mechanical resistance when cutting the record. Stereo records, of course, are cut with a combination of vertical and lateral motion.

Hi-Pass Filter Short for HIGH-PASS FILTER.

Hold-Back Tension Also called back tension. The hold-back tension is the tension in the recording tape that holds it in contact with the TAPE HEADS or drum. Hold-back tension can be supplied by simply applying a small braking force to the supply reel on the tape recorder, or it can be imparted by passing some current through the rewind motor, providing a torque on the reel.

The hold-back tension should be fairly constant in any tape recorder to ensure that the tape speed and the tape's contact with the heads will be uniform, but constant torque on the supply reel gives greater tension as the tape pack is reduced in size, causing the tape speed to gradually slow down toward the end of the reel. More sophisticated tape recorders use one of several techniques to provide constant tension regardless of the size of the tape pack on the reel.

Hole in the Middle A phenomenon of two-channel A-B STEREO that causes a performer in the center of the reproduced sound stage to sound farther away than she should. It is caused by the fact that the reproduced level of a centrally located performer is a little too low and a little too reverberant because of relatively longer distances to the two MICROPHONES. The PHANTOM CENTER CHANNEL was an attempt to reduce the effect, but the proper way to do it is to use three independent channels. This was shown conclusively by Harvey Fletcher in his stereophonic transmission experiments in 1933. The effect has also been called the recession of the middle.

Holophonics An acoustical recording and broadcast technology claimed to be the aural equivalent to holography, hence the name. Holophonics is an encode process that occurs during the recording session using a special listening device named "Ringo." It is claimed that "playback or broadcast is possible over headphones or any existing mono or stereo speaker system, with various levels of spatial effect. Optimal effects occur when two tracks (stereo) are played utilizing digital technology over headphones and minimal effect when played over a single mono speaker (two tracks merged into one and played over a single speaker)."[16]

Hookup The interconnection of AUDIO devices is sometimes called the hookup, and the wiring inside the CHASSIS of a device is also called the hookup. Two components in a CIRCUIT that are connected with a wire are said to be "hooked" to each other.

Horn In reference to acoustic phonographs, horns have been used from the start to couple vibrations of the diaphragm to the air; in this, they resemble the ear trumpet.

In reference to LOUDSPEAKERS, a horn is a smoothly tapered tube connecting the loudspeaker diaphragm at the small end to the air in the room at the large end. Most horns of this type have a cross-sectional area that doubles for each unit of distance along its length. Such a horn is said to have an "exponential" flare rate.

Another type of horn is the conical or straight-sided horn, which has an

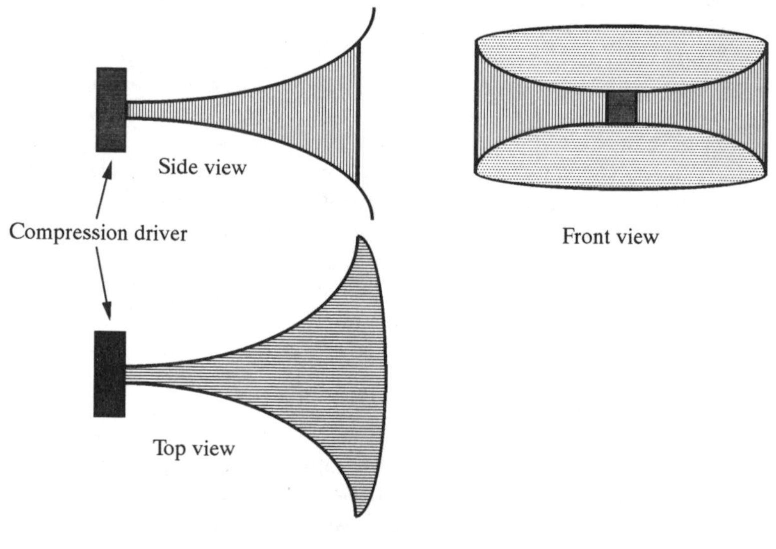

Horn Loudspeaker

16. Thanks to Dennis Bohn, Rane Corp.

area that increases in a linear fashion with distance. Conical horns were sometimes used in old acoustic phonographs. Exponential horns are much more efficient and uniform in their characteristics than conical horns, and although they are more difficult to build, they are the type generally used. The theory behind the exponential horn was first expounded by J. P. Maxfield and H. C. Harrison of Bell Telephone Labs, and was first used in the "Orthophonic Victrola" in about 1925.

High-frequency loudspeakers benefit from the use of horns because the horn acts as an acoustical transformer, coupling the relatively high mechanical IMPEDANCE of the diaphragm to the low acoustic impedance of the air. The horn, by improving the coupling of the diaphragm to the surrounding air, greatly improves the efficiency of the loudspeaker. Such a horn operates well over a FREQUENCY range above a certain frequency called the CUTOFF FREQUENCY, where the horn no longer presents an acoustic LOAD to the diaphragm. Without an acoustic load the diaphragm cannot transfer any energy to the horn, and it is free to move without restriction. The lower the cutoff frequency, the longer and larger the horn must be. This means that for low-frequency loudspeakers (below 300 HERTZ or so) horn loading is seldom used, except in large theater systems. In some cases, the horn may be "folded," or coiled around itself to make it more compact. Various ingenious designs of this type have been introduced over the years, and some are still in use.

Because a horn usually is called upon to radiate frequencies whose WAVELENGTH is short compared to the dimensions of the mouth of the horn, its radiation will be quite directional at high frequencies. This characteristic is desirable in sound reinforcement systems, where the energy must be aimed, or "beamed," at the audience to increase efficiency and to reduce the excitation of the REVERBERATION in the room.

For home use, the high efficiency of horns is seldom needed, and their directionality is usually undesirable, so their use is somewhat limited, although this point is hotly debated by some sound system aficionados. High-frequency horns also do not have quite as smooth a FREQUENCY RESPONSE as do DIRECT RADIATORS, and they produce significantly greater DISTORTION as well, especially at high sound levels.

Another use of the term *horns* is in connection with the making of phonograph records. When the master record is cut into the soft ACETATE of the disc by the hot cutting STYLUS, the slight melting of the acetate gives rise to tiny mounds, or horns, along the sides of the groove. These horns are usually curved over at the top, and they cause difficulty in separating the acetate from the plated metal master or, in the third step, separating the STAMPER from the MOTHER. If left on the stamper, the pressings retain them to some degree. They then often break off, causing debris to be left in the groove, which makes for noisy playback of the record.

There has been a mild controversy going on about what to do about horns. It is possible to remove the horns from the mother by carefully polishing with a cotton ball and a mild polishing agent, but some people in the industry say that a high-frequency loss is the inevitable result. Reducing the cutting stylus temperature will reduce the formation of horns in the acetate, but this also increases the noise. The making of records is as much an art as it is a science.

House Mix An output on a sound reinforcement control console that is used to feed the power AMPLIFIERS for the LOUDSPEAKERS in the main auditorium, or "house." The house mix will typically be quite different from the signal used to feed the stage monitors, or FOLDBACK speakers. *See also* MONITOR MIX.

House Mixer *See* FOH.

House Synch A master timing reference signal used to ensure synchronized operation of timing-sensitive devices such as television equipment and digital audio. Original ANALOG television facilities realized that unless cameras, switchers, effects generators, and so on were all synchronized from a common signal, switching the video signal around between devices would cause a glitch. The solution is a precision signal used by all devices so they all know exactly when the video frame starts, and this is called House Synch because it is used by all devices in the facility, or "house." The format of signal used in the U.S. is usually black burst, which is a composite video (meaning it contains picture, horizontal and vertical sync signals, and the color "burst" or reference waveform) with a black picture.

In the digital world there can be a similar need for synchronization of multiple devices in a facility, as well as more accurate clocking. Audible pops and clicks can result from transfering digital data among devices whose clocks are not quite in sync, and many feel that distortions from clock jitter are exacerbated by multiple reclockings at slightly varying rates. Digital clock devices usually offer several options, such as word clock (the same rate as the sampling frequency in use) and integer multiples of word clock. The old standby, black burst, can also be used.

There is a mild controversy about the term *sync* versus *synch*, and both spellings are seen.

Howlback, Howlround British terms for ACOUSTIC FEEDBACK.

HPS-4000 A multichannel high-powered sound system custom-designed and installed in theaters by John Allen. The system is said to use three-way horn-loaded LOUDSPEAKERS exclusively and many more surround speakers and SUBWOOFERS than are commonly used. The HPS-4000 specifications state each screen speaker will produce 112 dB Sound Pressure Level at 35 feet from the speakers.

HRTF Head Related Transfer Function, a mathematical model of the acoustic response of the human head. It is used for research in sound fields, often using dummy heads or HATS.

HT Acronym for "high tension," which is British usage for "high voltage."

Hub The circular center section of the reel on which magnetic tape is wound; the remainder of the reel consists of the flanges. In recording studios, tape was often purchased wound on hubs without the flanges, resulting in significant savings. *See also* PANCAKE.

Hum A 60-HERTZ or 120-Hz FREQUENCY component in an audio SIGNAL is called hum. One of the most common types of NOISE encountered in audio systems is hum from the 60-Hz power-line FREQUENCY, and its elimination or reduction to inaudible levels is sometimes quite difficult.

Hum is introduced into audio signals by several different mechanisms. The power lines delivering electrical energy around the country behave like giant transmitter antennas and radiate electromagnetic waves at 60 Hz. Sometimes, the strength of these emissions is quite large, especially in locations adjacent to high-VOLTAGE power lines. This radiation induces 60-Hz CURRENTS in audio cables by electrostatic and electromagnetic induction, causing the familiar humming sound at a musical PITCH a little below low B on the piano keyboard. To prevent electrostatic induction, audio cables have an electrostatic SHIELD surrounding them; and to prevent electromagnetic induction, long audio cables are BALANCED and the two signal-carrying wires are twisted together. *See also* Appendix 6.

Another route for hum to enter audio signals is via the POWER SUPPLY found in virtually all audio devices. The power transformer radiates a local 60-Hz magnetic field, which can cause electromagnetic induction, especially into nearby TAPE HEADS or phono CARTRIDGES. Sometimes it is possible to reduce this type of hum by orienting the power transformer in a different direction, for its hum field is not uniform in all directions around it.

The power supply itself must convert the 60-Hz line power into a smooth DIRECT CURRENT for use by the active components in the device, and all traces of RIPPLE must be removed from it. This is done by power supply FILTERING. The ripple caused by faulty power supplies is generally at 120 Hz and higher HARMONICS of 60 Hz rather than at 60 Hz, meaning the audible hum is one OCTAVE higher in pitch than hum directly induced by the power lines. It is thus easy to distinguish between the two simply by listening to the signal.

Another type of hum often heard in audio systems is caused by interference from television broadcast stations and is called TVI, or TELEVISION INTERFERENCE. It is characterized by a buzzing sound rather than a smooth hum, and it changes when the audio cables are moved around.

In most countries outside North America, the power-line frequency is 50 Hz rather than 60, and the resulting hum is correspondingly lower in pitch.

Removal of the various kinds of hum is a constant challenge and frequently a frustration to the audio technician. It is said that a certain technician, when asked by a customer, "Why does my tape recorder hum?" answered, "Probably it doesn't know the words."

Hum Bucking The cancellation of induced HUM in an AUDIO system by the introduction of a 60-HERTZ component equal in AMPLITUDE and of opposite POLARITY to the offending hum.

Hum bucking used to be common practice in the days of the electrodynamic LOUDSPEAKER. The SIGNAL to the VOICE COIL was routed through a hum-bucking coil that was placed by the large coil, which generated the magnetic field in the magnet assembly. The CURRENT in the field coil was not perfectly smooth due to power supply RIPPLE, hence the need for hum bucking.

Hum bucking is often used today in magnetic pickups for electric guitars, and is used in some telephone lines to reduce 60-Hz noise.

Hum Switch A switch found on some audio equipment, such as AMPLIFIERS for musical instruments, which reverses the neutral and "hot" leads of the power cord. The GROUND lead of the power cord remains connected to the CHASSIS.

There is no agreement among manufacturers on which wire is considered the neutral, and in general the CIRCUITS are not perfectly symmetrical with respect to capacitive and magnetic COUPLING from the two sides of the power line. Sometimes reversing the leads on one or more of a series of interconnected pieces of equipment will reduce the noise level, especially hum. *See also* ISOLATION TRANSFORMER.

Hum Tone The sound produced by large, traditional tower bells, such as church bells, consists of many overtones. The lowest, caused by vibration of the whole bell, is called the hum tone and is one octave below the fundamental or prime tone for which the bell is named. It is interesting that the hum tone of a bell is generally not audible at all—the perceived pitch of the bell (called the "strike tone") is one octave higher than the hum tone, and there is no component in the sound spectrum of the bell corresponding to the strike tone.

HVAC Heating, Ventilation, and Air Conditioning. HVAC systems can be major contributors to noise in auditoriums, churches, and other large public spaces.

HX A circuit developed by Dolby Laboratories for use in cassette recorders to reduce the effects of SELF-ERASURE of high-level high-frequency sounds. It involved the reduction of the record BIAS and a change in the high-frequency PRE-EMPHASIS dependent on the signal level. HX has been superseded by HX PRO, which is more effective and simpler.

HX Pro A clever circuit, developed by Dolby Laboratories, found in some cassette recorders. It varies the high-frequency BIAS signal in the record mode to reduce the tendency toward SELF-ERASURE. In MAGNETIC TAPE recording, loud high frequencies in the SIGNAL look like bias to the tape and will tend to erase the signal as it is being recorded. The effect is called high-frequency compression and is a fault of magnetic recorders in general and cassette recorders in particular. The HX Pro system senses the level of the high frequencies and reduces the level of the bias accordingly. It operates only in the record mode, and cassettes recorded with HX Pro can be played on a non-HX machine without any degradation.

Hybrid Amplifier An amplifier that uses a combination of TRANSISTORS and TUBES, supposedly combining the best characteristics of each.

Hybrid Transformer A special TRANSFORMER with the WINDINGS connected in such a way that a receiver can accept SIGNALS from and a transmitter can send different signals down a single transmission line without the signals interfering with each other. If the IMPEDANCES of the CIRCUITS and the transmission line are properly balanced, there is a high degree of attenuation between the two local circuits. Because the hybrid allows one pair of wires to simultaneously carry independent signals in both directions without interference, it is sometimes called a two- to four-wire converter.

The "induction coil" in a standard "old-fashioned" telephone is actually a hybrid transformer, but it is deliberately unbalanced a little to provide "side tone." Side tone is the sound of one's own voice one hears in the receiver when speaking on the telephone. The induction coil in modern phones has been replaced by electronic circuitry.

Hyper-Cardioid The hyper-cardioid is a MICROPHONE with a pattern somewhat like a CARDIOID, but less sensitive at the sides. It is used when it is desired to minimize the reverberant sound picked up when some distance must be maintained between the microphone and the sound source.

The hyper-cardioid will pick up the same direct-to-reverberant sound ratio as an OMNIDIRECTIONAL microphone at twice the distance from the source. Examples of its use are in television and motion pictures, where the microphone must be kept out of sight.

Hysteresis When a device or a system is presented with a stimulus that is increasing in value, the response typically also increases. Then, if the stimulus is gradually decreased, the response also decreases. Ideally, the response at a given stimulus level would always be the same, but in most real systems the response to a rising stimulus is different from the response to a falling stimulus for the same value of stimulus. This effect is called hysteresis and is very common in mechanical, magnetic, and electrical systems. If a graph of response versus stimulus is plotted for a rising stimulus and the plot is continued as the stimulus falls, the resulting curve will be a loop called the hysteresis loop. The area of the loop is a measure of the amount of hysteresis. Friction causes hysteresis in mechanical systems. In ANALOG audio, by far the most important hysteresis effect is that of magnetic materials. In a MAGNETIC TAPE head, the magnetizing force is the CURRENT in the coil, and the amount of magnetization accepted by the tape is always a little lower when the current is increasing than when it is decreasing. The audio signal should magnetize the tape in a pattern that matches that of the coil current, but due to hysteresis, the match is not perfect and the result is DISTORTION of the recorded WAVEFORM. BIAS is used in magnetic recording to reduce the effect of hysteresis. *See also* ANHYSTERETIC.

If the magnetization of the tape is plotted against the coil current, the ideal curve would be a straight line. The actual curve is somewhat S-shaped, and, moreover, it has a slightly different shape when magnetizing in the positive direction than when magnetizing in the negative direction. This difference causes the hysteresis curve to have an enclosed area, and hence it is sometimes called a hysteresis loop. The most desirable magnetic materials have a very small area within the loop, and this area is a measure of the quality

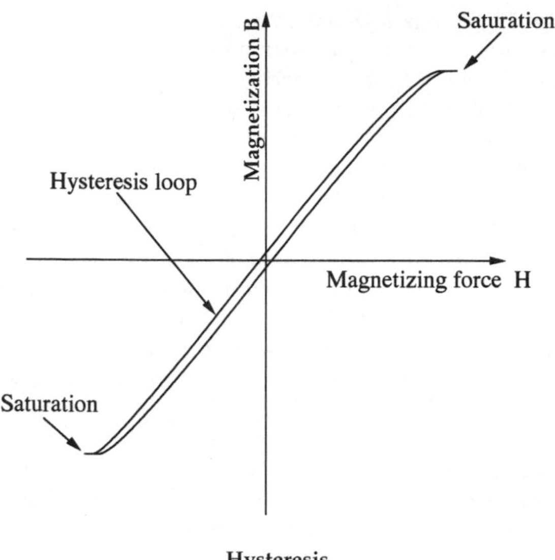

Hysteresis

of a magnetic tape, especially for analog audio recording. DIGITAL and FM audio recording generally magnetize the tape at saturation, and distortion caused by hysteresis does not appear in the demodulated audio output.

Hz *See* HERTZ.

I

IBOC In-Band On-Channel, a system of digital AM and FM radio broadcasting developed by iBiquity Digital Corporation. On October 10, 2002, iBiquity announced that the Federal Communications Commission (FCC) approved the IBOC system for immediate implementation, and the International Telecommunications Union (ITU) has approved In-Band On-Channel (IBOC) as a worldwide digital radio system.

iBiquity calls their version of the system HD Radio™, and on April 24, 2003, Harris Corporation, presumably a licensee of iBiquity, announced that it sold transmitting equipment to ten radio stations in the U.S. under the name of DEXSTAR™ AM/FM High Definition (HD) Radio™ exciters.

It is interesting to note that HD radio is broadcast by existing AM and FM transmitters using existing RF spectrum allocations, and the conventional ANALOG AM/FM signals are also broadcast at the same time, making the system compatible with existing AM/FM receivers.

IC *See* INTEGRATED CIRCUIT.

Idler Any small rotating guide in a tape transport.

Idler Wheel A small wheel made of rubber or similar material that is used in a friction drive system for turntables and some tape recorders. Sometimes also called a PUCK, due to its slight resemblance to a hockey puck.

IEC The International Electro-technical Commission (IEC) is an organization based in Europe that is involved in the setting of standards. The IEC has recommended PRE-EMPHASIS and DE-EMPHASIS curves for tape recorders, and most European models follow the recommendations. *See also* CCIR.

IF Intermediate Frequency. *See* HETERODYNE.

IFB Interrupt Foldback. An addressable, listen-only intercom, often seen as an earpiece worn by television newscasters, that can play the program audio and be interrupted with comments or cues from the director or other off-camera personnel. Also known as a cue system.

IFPI International Federation of the Phonographic Industry is a nonprofit association based in Switzerland that internationally promotes the rights and interests of producers of phonograms and videograms (music videos).

IGFET Insulated Gate Field Effect Transistor, preferred term for the MOSFET. *See also* FIELD EFFECT TRANSISTOR.

IHF, The Institute of High Fidelity The IHF was an organization of U.S. manufacturers engaged in the setting of standard measurement techniques for AUDIO equipment. The IHF merged with Electronic Industries Association (EIA, which is now called the Electronic Industries Alliance) in 1979. The setting of standards in audio has largely been taken over by the Audio Engineering Society (AES).

IIR Filter Short for Infinite Impulse Response Filter. A type of digital filter frequently used in audio applications. It requires fewer DSP calculations than an equivalent Finite Impulse Response (FIR) filter, but is more difficult to design.

IM *See* INTERMODULATION DISTORTION.

Imaging The ability to localize the instruments when listening to a STEREO recording is called imaging, and a great deal of nonsense has been written about it. Accurate imaging of musical instruments on a stage by use of two-channel stereo has been shown to be difficult at best even under the most ideal laboratory conditions. To achieve any kind of accuracy, the channels must have precisely the same GAIN, the FREQUENCY RESPONSE of each LOUDSPEAKER must be identical within 1 DECIBEL or less, and the PHASE response of the two channels must be identical. The listener also must be precisely between the loudspeakers. These conditions are impossible to meet in practice.

Three independent channels have been shown to be the minimum number required for any kind of consistently accurate imaging. The fact is that for most stereo systems, imaging consists of localizing the instruments at one loudspeaker position or the other.

One must take care, however, to discriminate "stereo spread" from accurate imaging. Most stereo systems provide an impression of diffusion and spread of the sound, which can be pleasing to the ear and can lead the listener to think he is correctly imaging the sound sources. The reverberant sound in stereo recordings can sound quite diffused and "spacious," but again this is a far cry from imaging in the true sense.

Impedance In an electric CIRCUIT containing DIRECT CURRENT, the magnitude of the current is determined by the VOLTAGE across the circuit divided by the RESISTANCE of the circuit. This is known as OHM'S LAW.

In a circuit containing ALTERNATING CURRENT, the situation is more complex; the "resistance" presented to the current is a function of FREQUENCY. This "AC resistance" is called impedance and is also measured in OHMS. Impedance is the sum of resistance, CAPACITIVE REACTANCE, and INDUCTIVE REACTANCE. (*See* Appendix 11 for more information on the definition of impedance.) Alternating currents are affected by resistance the same way as direct currents, and Ohm's law can be used for AC if the reactances are zero, that is, if there are no CAPACITORS or INDUCTORS in the circuit.

In AUDIO circuits and components, many different impedances are encountered. A LOUDSPEAKER, for instance, is a low-impedance device, usually about 8 ohms. This means that a given voltage across it will result in relatively large amounts of current in it. The POWER accepted by the speaker is equal to the voltage multiplied by the current. A CONDENSER MICROPHONE, on the other hand, is a very high-impedance device, generally several billions of ohms. The voltage generated by a condenser microphone results in vanishingly small amounts of current because of the high impedance. In general, impedances are relatively low where large amounts of power are being transferred, and are relatively high when power levels are low. An exception to this is found in low-impedance microphones, such as DYNAMIC MICROPHONES, where power levels are also very low.

Low-impedance circuits are less susceptible to electrical interferences such as 60-HERTZ HUM than are high-impedance circuits, and they are used to transmit audio signals over cables. Most audio transmission lines used in the broadcast industry are of 600 ohms impedance, except for speaker lines, which are much lower in impedance. It is interesting that 600 ohms would be chosen as a working impedance for commercial sound and broadcast work.

Four reasons can be stated:

1. Shunt capacitance found in long cables has negligible effect on high-frequency response.
2. Line resistance in long lines is not an appreciable fraction of 600 ohms, so losses are low.
3. Higher impedances are much more sensitive to electrostatic interference, and lower impedances are more susceptible to magnetically induced interference.
4. The capacitors and inductors needed for building equalizers at 600 ohms are of modest size and low cost.

There is a common misconception that impedances of interconnected audio equipment must be "matched," and one is constantly hearing about problems caused by an "impedance mismatch." The fact is that impedances are almost never matched in audio systems. For instance, an AMPLIFIER designed to operate with an 8-ohm loudspeaker will have an OUTPUT IMPEDANCE of a small fraction of an ohm, in fact as low an impedance as the designer can manage. There are two reasons for this, one having to do with efficiency and one with DAMPING FACTOR. If the amplifier driving an 8-ohm load had 8 ohms of output impedance, one half of all the power generated by the amplifier would be dissipated in the amplifier itself and would never reach the load. This is because the output current supplied by the amplifier passes through the amplifier output stage as well as the load, and the same power would be dissipated as in the load. For the same reason, the wires connecting the speaker to the amplifier should be of very low impedance to reduce power loss in them as well. When the output terminals of an amplifier say "8 ohms," this simply means that its maximum current and voltage capabilities are such that it will deliver maximum power to an 8-ohm load. *See* DAMPING FACTOR for a discussion of the other effect.

In radio frequency and video transmission, impedances are matched to avoid signal reflections from the ends of the lines. Such reflections cause double images, or "ghosts." This effect is due to the relatively short WAVELENGTHS of the signals involved. Such reflections could be a problem at audio frequencies if the transmission lines were hundreds of miles long. They were sometimes heard in analog long-distance telephone circuits as an ECHO, but the effect is of no consequence to normal audio circuits. Today long distance telephone lines are almost exclusively fiber optics, and they are not susceptible to this type of echoing. *See also* Appendix 11.

Impulse Response An impulse is a signal or sound that has a very short, in fact, vanishingly small, duration. A true mathematical impulse has zero duration and infinite amplitude, but still a finite amount of energy. Of necessity, the energy in an impulse is spread evenly over a wide FREQUENCY band, and this means that it can be used as a test SIGNAL to measure the characteristics of an audio device. Simply input the impulse to the device and record its output. The resulting impulse response is in the time domain, and it contains all the information about the behavior of the device if the device is LINEAR. Any linear system can be characterized by its impulse response; for instance, the reverberation time of a room is actually its impulse response. The FREQUENCY RESPONSE of the device can be obtained by inputting its impulse response into a spectrum analyzer such as an FFT ANALYZER.

Of course it is impossible to generate a true impulse, and even if it could be done, it would not be a good test signal because its infinite height would overload any device. However, we can produce an approximation of an impulse by generating a very short pulse with amplitude below the overload level of the device being tested. An example of this is a test signal on some special COMPACT DISCS that consists of a single sample at maximum amplitude and all other adjacent samples set to zero. This signal has a perfectly flat frequency and PHASE response from DC to 20 kilohertz.

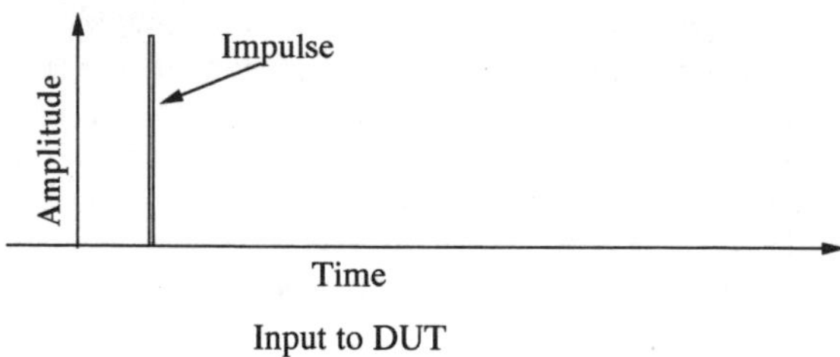

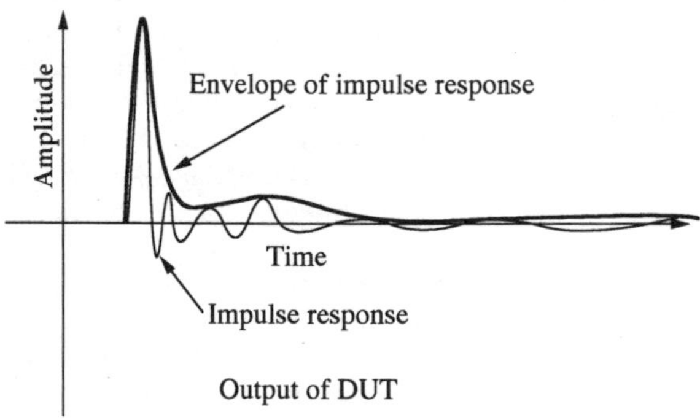

Impulse Response

In general, such impulses are not very good for measuring audio devices because they are so short they contain very little energy, and the SIGNAL-TO-NOISE RATIO is quite poor when making measurements.

The dual-channel FFT analyzer is able to calculate the impulse response of a system from the spectrum of the system input and the spectrum of the system output regardless of what the input signal consists of, and this technique is generally better than true impulse testing because of the improved signal-to-noise ratio. Sometimes music is used as a test signal for this type of measurement. The impulse response can also be calculated by a process called DECONVOLUTION using a small computer program, if the input signal is a perfectly known signal, such as PSEUDORANDOM NOISE. *See also* MAXIMUM-LENGTH SEQUENCE.

In-Band Gain The GAIN, or amplification factor, in the PASSBAND of a device, such as a SUBWOOFER. For instance, in multichannel movie theater sound systems, the standard for adjusting subwoofer response is such that the low-FREQUENCY output of the speaker within its operating range is higher in level than a full-range screen speaker in the same frequency range. The reason for this is to increase the subjective loudness of the subwoofer, whose low frequency output is in the range where human hearing is not very sensitive. All modern digital film sound formats use 10 dB of in-band gain for the subwoofer.

Inductance Inductance is the quantitative measure of the effect of an inductor. The unit of inductance is the henry, after Joseph Henry, a nineteenth-century American physicist. An inductor allows constant electric CURRENT to exist through it, but it resists any change in current in proportion to the value of its inductance. The VOLTAGE across an inductor is equal to its inductance in henrys multiplied by the rate of change in current through it. The current is measured in AMPERES. Since high-FREQUENCY signals have currents that are changing faster than low-frequency ones, an inductor has an increasing IMPEDANCE as frequency rises.

Many types of inductors are used in audio circuits, including EQUALIZERS, CROSSOVER NETWORKS, and FILTERS. Sometimes inductors are called "chokes," especially when they are used to filter out unwanted high-frequency interference. Many interconnecting cables used in computer and some audio equipment have small FERRITE "beads" resembling little doughnuts around them near the connectors. They increase the inductance of the cable, reducing the transmission of radio-frequency interference into the equipment and the transmission of RF energy produced inside the equipment.

Induction The electromagnetic process by which a varying magnetic field causes an electric CURRENT to exist in a CONDUCTOR. The current is called the induced current, and its strength is proportional to the rate of change of the magnetic field. Induction is the basic principle by which magnetic transducers, such as DYNAMIC MICROPHONES and magnetic phono CARTRIDGES, operate. It is also the process by which electricity is generated and by which transformers operate.

Magnetic induction was extensively studied by James Clerk Maxwell, an English scientist of the nineteenth century. He was the first to formulate the precise relationship between electricity and magnetism in his famous "Maxwell's equations," which stand as a major scientific discovery.

Induction Coil *See* HYBRID TRANSFORMER.

Inductive Reactance Inductive reactance is that portion of IMPEDANCE which is due to inductance. Examples of inductors are coils of wire and TRANSFORMER windings. The inductor behaves as if it had "inertia" with respect to electric CURRENT. A current in an inductor resists changes in its magnitude, and to make rapid changes in the current requires rather large VOLTAGES across the inductor.

The defining equation of an inductor says the VOLTAGE across the inductor is equal to the inductance times the rate of change of current. An inductor will have resistance, which behaves in accordance with OHM'S LAW, but with ALTERNATING CURRENTS, the inductance must be taken into account. Inductive reactance is measured in OHMS and is numerically equal to 2 π times frequency times the inductance in henrys.

The impedance of an inductor rises with increasing FREQUENCY, so with a constant AC voltage across it, the current will fall as frequency rises. Therefore, it can be used (and is used) as a frequency-dependent element in EQUALIZERS. An example of this use is in CROSSOVER NETWORKS.

An inductor also establishes the condition whereby the current and voltage are out of PHASE by 90 degrees. The current lags behind the voltage by 90 degrees; therefore, circuits containing inductance exhibit PHASE SHIFT, which can be an unfortunate consequence. In a way this is the opposite of a CAPACITOR, in which the current leads the voltage by 90 degrees.

Inductor *See* INDUCTANCE; INDUCTIVE REACTANCE.

In-Ear Monitors Musicians performing on stage may use earplug-style earphones instead of stage MONITOR speakers. They have the advantage of excellent sound isolation, no possibility of acoustic FEEDBACK, and lower sound pressure levels for the performer than monitor speakers. The disadvantage is that the performer is completely dependent upon the monitor mix and must adapt to performing this way. The system can be damaging to the performer's ears unless careful limiting is used.

Infinite Baffle Theoretically, the infinite baffle is a LOUDSPEAKER mounted in a wall of infinite extent. In practice, it is an enclosure that is totally sealed, so that it completely separates the front sound produced by the speaker from the rear sound. In theory, such an enclosure would have to be infinitely large if it were not to influence the operation of the loudspeaker itself. Fortunately, this is not a requirement, for the influence of the enclosure on the speaker can be beneficial to its operation.

When a loudspeaker is placed in a closed box, its resonant FREQUENCY is raised due to the stiffness of the air in the box. The speaker CONE must alternately compress and rarify this air as it moves in and out. Therefore, a speaker designed for use in an infinite baffle must have a very low resonant FREQUENCY in free air.

The design of infinite baffles was revolutionized in 1954 with the advent of the AR-1 made by Acoustic Research, Inc. This unit was based on an early idea by Harry Olson of RCA Research Laboratories. *See also* WOOFER; BAFFLE; BASS REFLEX.

Infrasonic Refers to sounds or SIGNALS whose frequencies are below the normal human hearing range, generally considered to be 20 HERTZ and lower.

The lowest audible FREQUENCY is not easy to define, for it depends strongly on level. Some experiments have found that hearing can extend to 10 Hz and below at very high SOUND PRESSURE LEVELS. It is a common misconception that infrasonic signals can be ignored because they are inaudible. *See* BASS INTERMODULATION.

Sometimes the term SUBSONIC is wrongly used to mean infrasonic.

Initialization The process of reading the table of contents from a COMPACT DISC after it is inserted into a CD player. The player then displays the track numbers recorded on the disc. Also, most digital recording processes require an initialization step before actual recording can commence. This is somewhat like formatting a disk for storing files in a computer.

Input Impedance The input impedance of a CIRCUIT or device is the IMPEDANCE actually experienced by a SIGNAL that is connected to it. An AMPLIFIER with a 100,000-OHM input impedance looks like a 100,000-ohm resistor to the signal coming into it.

In general in AUDIO work, input impedances of components are several times higher than the OUTPUT IMPEDANCES of the components connected to them. If a device with a relatively high output impedance is connected to a low-impedance input, the signal level will be reduced because the low impedance will effectively SHORT out the signal.

In video systems, impedances of inputs and outputs are the same, or "matched," to avoid signal reflections because of the high frequencies and short wavelengths inherent in the video signal. *See* IMPEDANCE and Appendix 11.

Insert On many mixing consoles, each input channel may incorporate a ¼" TRS jack for the purpose of accessing the signal flow in that channel only, after the mic PREAMP and before the FADER. This allows putting a signal processor, such as a reverberator, in that channel, or accessing the channel output directly. A typical configuration is to use unbalanced wiring with the jack Tip the channel output and the jack Ring the signal return back in. This can create some interesting possibilities when using various Tip/Sleeve and Tip/Ring/Sleeve plugs, depending upon how far they are inserted. A Tip/Sleeve plug inserted to the first "click" will access the signal at the jack Ring contact without activating the switching that would interrupt the signal continuing back through the Return. A Tip/Sleeve plug inserted fully will access the signal normally at the Tip contact and activate the signal interrupt switch, while grounding the Return contact through the plug sleeve. A TRS plug inserted fully accesses the Send and Return normally to allow for an effects loop.

Insertion Loss When a PASSIVE audio device is placed in a sound system, it will, depending on the nature of the device, sometimes reduce the SIGNAL level. This is called insertion loss, and it is measured in DECIBELS.

Insertion loss can be considered the inverse of GAIN. Passive devices that typically have some insertion loss are CROSSOVER NETWORKS and EQUALIZERS. Insertion loss is compensated, or "made up," by additional gain in the AMPLIFIERS.

Integrated Amplifier An audio component consisting of a PREAMPLIFIER and POWER AMPLIFIER all on one CHASSIS.

Integrated Circuit An integrated circuit, or IC, is a miniature one-piece device containing many TRANSISTORS and RESISTORS. Some ICs may contain hundreds of transistors in a space smaller than the head of a pin. Most AUDIO ICs are AMPLIFIERS of various types, especially OPAMPS.

Integrated circuits are far less expensive than equivalent CIRCUITS made from discrete components, and this is the primary reason for their popularity. Early ICs were not optimized for audio use and were not well thought of, but many newer designs are of excellent quality.

Intelligence In the earlier days of broadcasting, the information impressed on the carrier by the process of modulation was called the intelligence. Perhaps the term was more appropriate then than now; in any case, today it is usually called the information.

Intensity Stereo Intensity stereo is an unfortunate linguistic misnomer that has come to mean the recording of STEREOPHONIC signals that are distinguished only by level differences. These level differences have been called "intensity" differences, but SOUND INTENSITY is a specifically defined quantity and cannot be sensed by a simple MICROPHONE, nor would it be valuable in music recording if it could.

The term *coincident microphone stereo* would be a better choice, the two microphones being very close together. This is also called X-Y STEREO, with X and Y representing the left and right channels. In X-Y stereo, the signals in the two channels are in PHASE because the two microphones used are "coincident" or very nearly so.

In localizing sound sources, the human hearing mechanism uses level differences, spectral differences, and time (phase) differences between the signals heard by the two ears. X-Y stereo deprives the listener of spectral and time differences, and results in a sound field that is less spacious and more "compact" than what other stereophonic methods provide.

The first investigator into X-Y stereo was Alan Blumlein, an Englishman who conceived the idea in the early 1930s. He postulated that two FIGURE-8 MICROPHONES angled at 90 degrees to each other and 45 degrees to the centerline of the stage would allow localization of the individual instruments on playback. (*See also* BLUMLEIN, ALAN.) At present, there are at least two microphone configurations that qualify as X-Y stereo. One is the classic Blumlein method with two figure-8 microphones; the other is two CARDIOIDS, each angled at 45 degrees from the centerline. The dual cardioids result in a less reverberant, or "drier," sound because of reduced pickup from the rear of the room. The figure-8 method results in more AMBIENCE from the room. The figure-8 method is also sometimes called the "electrosonic" method, and some people prefer to restrict the term X-Y to crossed cardioids.

Incidentally, Blumlein recorded his two signals on discs in the 1930s, using the same groove format as is used today in stereo records. His technique was all but forgotten when modern stereo records were introduced in 1958. The Bell Telephone Labs also experimented with a similar type of stereo record in the 1930s, but made no attempt to commercialize it.

It has been said that X-Y stereo is easier to cut into a record because there is no out-of-phase information in the signal, resulting in less vertical motion of the STYLUS. This is true, although modern MASTERING and playback equipment can easily handle signals that are out of phase, except perhaps at the lowest frequencies.

It has also been said, mostly by broadcasters, that X-Y stereo is preferable for FM STEREO broadcasters because of MONO COMPATIBILITY. The argument goes that since the two signals are in phase, they will combine with each other without cancellation to form a MONAURAL signal when received by a monaural FM receiver. This is theoretically true, but in practice few listeners with monaural FM radios are concerned with the best quality reproduction. It has also been repeatedly shown that A-B STEREO recordings can be mixed to mono with very little effect on tonal BALANCE. *See also* AMBISONICS.

Interaural Cross-Correlation, IACC The IACC is a measure of the difference in SIGNALS received by the two ears. Its value varies from negative 1, meaning the signals are equal and out of PHASE, through zero, meaning the two signals have no similarity at all, to 1, meaning the signals are identical.

The IACC will be 1 for sound sources directly in front of a listener or located anywhere on the plane bisecting the head vertically. As a source moves laterally from dead center, the IACC decreases from 1 to a minimum value when the angle is about 60 degrees OFF AXIS. It then rises a little as the angle is increased, becoming 1 again when the source is directly behind the listener. The shape of the outer ears (pinnas) and the geometry of the head largely determine the variation in IACC with angle.

The IACC is measured using a DUMMY HEAD that has artificial ears, ear canals, and precision microphones located where the eardrums would normally be. Such a dummy head, also sometimes called "HATS" for head and torso simulator, is placed in the sound field to be measured, and the MICROPHONE outputs are fed into an instrument such as a dual-channel FFT ANALYZER, which measures the CROSS-CORRELATION.

It has been found by several researchers, especially Ando and Schroeder, that small values of IACC correspond to greater degrees of ENVELOPMENT in auditoriums, and that listener preferences are for smaller IACCs. Such findings have important applications in the art and science of room ACOUSTICS.

Intercut An analog MAGNETIC TAPE editing technique where a section of the master tape is physically cut out and replaced with another "take." Adhesive-backed plastic splicing tape is used. Today, most audio tape editing is done digitally, and the original source is not physically cut. The process is still often called intercutting.

Interlaced Scan Video In traditional ANALOG television broadcasting, each video frame is divided into two fields, each having one half of the horizontal scanning lines. The odd-numbered lines are scanned first, then the even numbered lines are added. This is called interlace scanning. NTSC standard color television displays 59.94 interlaced fields per second and is done to reduce visual flicker in the picture. Each pair of fields constitutes one video frame. This means the frame rate of video is 29.97 frames per second, whereas the motion picture frame rate is 24 per second. This complicates the transfer of movies to video (*see* 3:2 PULLDOWN). *See also* PROGRESSIVE SCAN VIDEO.

Inter-Layer Transfer *See* PRINT THROUGH.

Intermodulation Distortion Intermodulation (or IM), as the name implies, is the AMPLITUDE MODULATION of one SIGNAL by another. As an example of how this happens, consider a recording where a piccolo is sounding a steady high-frequency note, and a bass drum is then struck. The loud low-frequency drum tone is added to the piccolo tone, and the combined WAVEFORM has the small fluctuations of the piccolo riding up and down on the relatively slowly changing drum signal. The AMPLIFIER is called on to amplify each tone equally, but if the GAIN of the amplifier varies with signal level (i.e., if it is NONLINEAR), the piccolo will be amplified by different amounts depending on whether the drum signal is near zero or near its maximum excursion. Therefore, the piccolo signal will undergo changes in amplitude at the rate of the drum signal. The drum amplitude modulates the piccolo, and its sound will be heard to "FLUTTER" in the presence of the drum.

Strictly speaking, any two tones A and B when passed through a nonlinear device will give rise to intermodulation tones having frequencies of A plus B and A minus B. These distortion components are sometimes called upper and lower SIDEBANDS. Often the upper sidebands are above the audible range, but the lower sidebands are always in the audible range and are the most objectionable. It is possible, in fact common, to have tones that are ULTRASONIC modulating each other to produce audible sidebands. This is possible with phono CARTRIDGES that have extended high-frequency response. The ultrasonic noise frequencies intermodulate to produce audible DISTORTION if the PREAMPLIFIER is nonlinear at ultrasonic frequencies. This is an example of the fact that audio equipment must be LINEAR over a much wider FREQUENCY range than the audible range if it is to sound as clean as it measures.

There are several methods of measuring intermodulation. The oldest standardized method was devised by the SMPTE, and it consists of passing a mixture of a high and a low frequency tone through the device. The output signal is passed through a FILTER that eliminates the lower tone. The high tone is then amplitude demodulated to recover the sidebands that contain the energy in the modulation, which is then expressed as a percentage of the amplitude of the high tone. Alternatively, the output signal may be examined on a high-resolution SPECTRUM ANALYZER to measure the level of the sidebands independently of the tones.

The SMPTE method was devised many years ago, and it suffers from the disadvantage that only one combination of tones is used as a test signal. A newer and better method uses two tones that are swept through the audible and into the ultrasonic range while their difference frequency is held constant at some low value, such as 50 HERTZ. Intermodulation will cause a tone at the difference frequency to appear in the output, and its level can be plotted as a function of the frequency of the two sweeping tones. The subjective quality of sound equipment is rather well correlated with measurements of this type.

A third way to measure intermodulation is to pass an OCTAVE band of PINK NOISE through the device. The octave band from 10 KHz to 20 kHz may be used. IM components existing between all the frequencies of the noise will appear in the 0 to 10 kHz band, and can be measured with a high-resolution spectrum analyzer such as an FFT analyzer.

IM specifications of audio equipment are meaningless unless the method used is stated. There is no universally agreed-on method, but the SMPTE method is generally regarded as obsolete.

International System of Units, SI In 1960, an international meeting called the Eleventh General Conference on Weights and Measures was held; some small adjustments to the metric system were agreed upon and it was given the new name "Système Internationale," abbreviated SI (the abbreviation was to be used in all languages). In the SI, all physical units are derived from seven primary standards. All electrical units are derived from the meter, the kilogram, the second, and the AMPERE.

In addition to standard measurement units, the SI also recommended a great many other standards, such as nut and bolt diameters, numbers of threads per centimeter, wire sizes, etc.

Perhaps someday the United States will cease to be the last holdout for the picturesque English system and will seriously adopt the SI.

Interpolating Response A term adopted by Rane Corporation to describe the summing response of adjacent bands of variable EQUALIZERS using buffered summing stages. If two adjacent bands, when summed together, produce a smooth response without a dip in the center, they are said to interpolate between the fixed center frequencies, or combine well. [Historical note: Altec-Lansing first described their buffered equalizer designs as combining and the terminology became commonplace. Describing how well adjacent bands combine is good terminology. However, some variations of this term confuse people. The phrase "combining filter" is a misnomer, since what is meant is not a filter at all, but rather whether adjacent bands are buffered before summing. The other side of this misnomer coin finds the phrase "noncombining filter." Again, no filter is involved in what is meant. Dropping the word "filter" helps, but not enough. Referring to an equalizer as "noncombining" is imprecise. All equalizers combine their filter outputs. The issue is how much ripple results. For these reasons, Rane adopted the term "interpolating" as an alternative. Interpolating means to insert between two points, which is what buffering adjacent bands accomplishes. By separating adjacent bands when summing, the midpoints fill in smoothly without ripple.][17]

Interpolation Mathematically, interpolation is the estimation of the unknown values of some variable quantity from the known adjacent values. This is done when plotting a smooth curve from a set of discrete points, for example. In AUDIO, it is the estimation of erroneously read DIGITAL samples in a digital audio system from the adjacent correct samples. *See* ERROR CORRECTION.

Interval The difference in PITCH between any two musical notes. The inter-

17. Thanks to Dennis Bohn, Rane Corp.

val corresponds to a frequency ratio, but intervals are referred to by name and are based on the OCTAVE. For instance, the fifth is the interval between the TONIC and the fifth note of the scale, etc. Some audio frequency response measurements are made in terms of intervals, such as octave bands, one-third octave bands, and one-tenth octave bands. The one-third octave band and one-tenth octave band do not correspond exactly to musical intervals but are defined in terms of frequency ratios.

Intonation The tuning of a musical scale. A musician who plays "out of tune" is said to have poor intonation.

Inverse Feedback *See* FEEDBACK.

Inverse Square Law A small sound or light source radiating energy into three-dimensional space produces an intensity that falls off in inverse proportion to the square of the distance from the observer to the source. This means a reduction of sound pressure of 6 DECIBELS for each doubling of distance if the source is in a FREE FIELD.

A completely free field is never experienced in practice, however, and sound levels in rooms fall off at less than 6 dB per doubling of distance, although in most rooms there will be a range of distances that approximate a free field. *See* REVERBERATION.

Ionophone A type of LOUDSPEAKER invented by the French inventor Sigmund Klein in 1946. A high-frequency electrical discharge ionizes the air in a small quartz tube. The audio signal is applied to the ionized air through a step-up transformer. The ionophone has no moving parts except the air itself. The ionophone was produced commercially for a short time by Electro-Voice as the Ionovac TWEETER. It was capable of excellent high-frequency response, but it was efficient only at very high frequencies and suffered from reliability problems, leading to its demise. Originally called the Ionophone, it was sold under the name of Ionovac by the DuKane Corporation, St. Charles, IL, and IonoFane by Fane Acoustics Ltd., Batley, Yorkshire, England.

IPS *See* TAPE SPEED.

Iron Pejorative term for "outboard equipment" in the context of its effect on sound quality. "He has so much iron in his chain it's a wonder that we can distinguish between men and women on his dialog premix."[18]

ISDN, Integrated Services Digital Network A worldwide digital telephone network that uses standard subscriber lines to telephone exchange buildings and fiber optic lines for long distance communications between exchanges. ISDN provides the subscriber 2 digital channels at 64 kilobits per second BANDWIDTH each. For transmitting stereo audio at high quality, a special modem is used to encode the audio signal with a compression scheme known as MPEG Layer 2. The recipient of the signal needs a similar decoder to recover the stereo signal. The system is capable of near CD quality sound.

Isochronous Literally, having a constant FREQUENCY, such as a clock pen-

18. This entry is copyright © 1999–2003 by Larry Blake and is reprinted with permission.

dulum. In the audio/video world isochronous usually refers to the transmission of a DV (Digital Video) or digital audio stream over FireWire (IEEE 1394). The amount of data is high enough that IEEE 1394 allows a guaranteed BANDWIDTH for the data, which is sent isochronously over the serial bus. The data is thus sent at a continuous rate, regardless of any minor problems such as a data error. This is in contrast to other data communication methods such as synchronous and asynchronous, which typically have request/acknowledge protocols and may wait for enough bandwidth on the bus. This was deemed unacceptable for digital video.

Isochronous may also refer to two or more signals that are transmitted or recorded at the same time and will stay synchronized, such as the sound and video in television broadcasting. If not truly isochronous, the two signals will eventually drift out of synchronization, even if started at precisely the same time. Non-isochronous signals are a problem when attempting to play back audio, video, and/or control signals that require time code–precise alignment for the very accurate long-term synchronization of sound and vision.

Isolation Booth Sometimes shortened to iso booth. A small windowed room or booth within a recording studio where a performer, such as an announcer, soloist, or drummer can be situated with her MICROPHONE(s) while recording and be isolated from the sound made by the other musicians. The microphone(s) in the booth are also effectively isolated from the sound in the studio proper.

Isolation Transformer A TRANSFORMER that is used to isolate an AUDIO system or device from the power line. The third wire in the modern power outlet is the so-called power line GROUND, and is connected to the earth at some point in the power distribution system. This ground wire often carries some CURRENT when many types of equipment are connected to the same power line. Because the wires have resistance, the ground connections at various power outlets in a building will be at different potentials, and GROUND LOOPS will result if various parts of an audio system are plugged in at different places. This can be a real problem, for instance in recording studios, where the control room receives its power from one source and the studio has power outlets from another source. If someone plugs in an electric guitar in the studio and makes a connection between its CHASSIS and a MICROPHONE shield, HUM can very easily be induced.

An isolation transformer breaks the connection from the signal ground to the power line ground, eliminating ground loops.

Audio transformers are frequently used to avoid ground loops between various devices, and they are also called isolation transformers, or REPEAT COILS. *See also* BALANCED POWER.

ISRC The International Standard Recording Code (ISRC) appears on COMPACT DISCS and contains information about the country of origin, the owner, the serial number, and the date of recording. *See also* CONTROL AND DISPLAY SYMBOLS.

ITU International Telecommunications Union. The ITU is an international organization located in Geneva Switzerland. The ITU is the leading publisher of telecommunication technology, regulatory, and standards information. The CCIR was subsumed by the ITU in 1992 and became ITU-R, the division dealing with radio-communications.

J

Jack A female connector, frequently mounted on the CHASSIS of an AUDIO device, that serves as a receptacle for the male connector on the end of an audio cable, such as a MICROPHONE cable, etc. Most commonly used for the one-quarter-inch classic telephone-type receptacles, which are called "phone jacks." One may wonder why it is not called a "Jill."

Jackfield A PATCH BAY in England. *See also* PATCH CORD.

JAES *Journal of the Audio Engineering Society.* A technical journal published by the Audio Engineering Society, which contains research papers on all aspects of the science of AUDIO.

JASA *Journal of the Acoustical Society of America.* A respected technical journal, which publishes the latest research papers on all types of acoustical subjects.

Jewel Box The original hinged plastic container for CDS.

Jitter In an ANALOG-TO-DIGITAL CONVERTER, jitter is uncertainty in the exact timing of the SAMPLING of the SIGNAL. It is also called sampling offset uncertainty. Jitter introduces some DISTORTION to the sampled signal. *See also* APERTURE TIME ERRORS.

JND *See* JUST NOTICEABLE DIFFERENCE.

Johnson Noise Johnson noise, named after John Bernard Johnson of Bell Laboratories, also called thermal noise, is random WHITE NOISE produced by thermal agitation of the charges in an electric conductor. The noise is proportional to the absolute temperature of the conductor. Johnson noise manifests itself in the input circuits of audio equipment such as MICROPHONE PREAMPLIFIERS, where the signal levels are low. The noise power is independent of the resistance of a component, and this means that noise VOLTAGE is proportional to its resistance, and low-IMPEDANCE circuits are thus quieter than high-impedance ones. The Johnson noise level is the limiting minimum noise any circuit can attain.

Jolly Green Giant Effect *See* PROXIMITY EFFECT; Appendix 3.

Joystick Sometimes a special type of PANPOT that divides one input SIGNAL among four output channels is called a "joystick." In a QUADRAPHONIC sound system, a joystick could move the apparent position of a sound from front to back and side to side and in combinations of these moves, all with a single control. The usage probably stems from the control "stick" used to fly an airplane.

Jug Slang for vacuum tube, mostly used by amateur radio operators in reference to power output tubes. *See also* BOTTLE; BEAM BOTTLE.

Just In reference to a musical scale, a just INTERVAL is a frequency ratio determined by the frequencies of a harmonic series of the frequency of the TONIC. Purely tuned just intervals are almost never used in music because of their incompatibility with the OCTAVE, which is the most fundamental of musical intervals. *See* Appendix 8.

Just Noticeable Difference, JND The term is used mostly by researchers into musical perception and PSYCHOACOUSTICS who like to measure JNDs of frequency of tones, LOUDNESS of various sounds, and so on. The methods used for determining JNDs are sometimes quite complex, and there is a certain amount of controversy about their interpretation. For instance, in some cases musicians are able to detect PITCH differences much smaller than JND data predict.

K

KDKA Generally credited as being the first commercial radio station in the U.S., KDKA was built by Dr. Frank Conrad of Westinghouse in Pittsburgh in 1920. Its studio and transmitter were in the upper floors of the Westinghouse building. KDKA was a very innovative and influential station and was the first to broadcast a church service, a presidential inauguration, a remote broadcast of any sort, baseball scores, stock market reports, and time signals.

KEMAR Acronym for a DUMMY HEAD and torso simulator made by Knowles Electronics—the Knowles Electronics Mannequin for Acoustics Research.

Key In music, the key is the PITCH of tonic of the musical scale used. In equal temperament, which is almost universally used today, the same music played in different keys has a different pitch level but all the same intervals. Nevertheless, many musicians, especially those who possess ABSOLUTE PITCH, claim that the various keys have quite different characters, some sounding "bright," some "somber," etc.

Key West Audion An early vacuum DIODE detector, essentially the same as the FLEMING VALVE, independently invented by Lee DeForest about 1906. The name audion was given to it by DeForest's assistant C. D. Babcock. The audion was first used in the Navy's wireless station at Key West, Florida. It was in the same year that DeForest patented the first TRIODE and called it the audion detector. DeForest did not realize at first that the triode could be used as an AMPLIFIER; when he showed it to the engineers at the Bell Telephone Laboratories, they immediately recognized its potential as an amplifier and licensed the rights to use it from DeForest. *See also* TRIODE.

Kilocycle, kc Before 1948, an accepted term for FREQUENCY, representing 1,000 cycles per second. Since 1948, the term kilohertz (kHz) has replaced it. *See also* HERTZ.

Kilohertz, kHz FREQUENCY is measured in cycles per second, and the units are HERTZ, abbr. Hz. One thousand Hz is one kilohertz, abbr. kHz. Sometimes the k is capitalized, but lowercase is correct. Note that it is exactly 1000 Hz, whereas a kilobyte of data is 1024 bytes due to BINARY counting. A recent accommodation for binary counting is reflected in the term Kibibyte. *See* Appendix 10.

Kintek A company affiliated with the dbx company that marketed movie theater sound equipment, and was involved in motion picture sound track experiments including COMTRAK and COLORTEK/QUINTOPHONIC. Sometimes seen as Kintek/Cinesonics.

Klangfarbe Literally, "tone color" in German. This can be considered a synonym of TIMBRE.

Klipschorn A famous design for a full-range LOUDSPEAKER system invented by Paul W. Klipsch in 1941. The low-frequency section of the Klipschorn was an ingenious design for a relatively compact, folded HORN that used the corner of the listening room as an extension of the horn itself. It was capable of low-distortion, low-frequency output down to about 30 Hz, which was nearly unprecedented in those days

The Klipsch company was probably the oldest continuously operating audio manufacturer in the country when Paul Klipsch retired in 1989. He died in 2002, but the company lives on.

Kludge Slang for a poorly executed solution of a problem. It typically refers to a hardware design of any sort that is not very elegant or well constructed and may be composed of oddly designed or "thrown together" subsystems. Sometimes spelled "kluge," and usually pronounced "klooge."

L

L The symbol for INDUCTANCE or inductor, usually used in combination with R and C (for RESISTANCE and CAPACITANCE), as in RLC filter. The unit of inductance is the henry, abbr. H.

Labels Special non-audio information encoded along with the AUDIO in DIGITAL recording systems. They may be used to encode information about the recording session, number of MICROPHONES used, dates, etc. *See also* CONTROL AND DISPLAY SYMBOLS.

Labyrinth *See* ACOUSTIC LABYRINTH.

Lacquer Master *See* ACETATE.

Land The area between the grooves on a phonograph record and between the pits in a COMPACT DISC is called the land. (Actually, there is only one groove on one side of a record.) The name probably comes from analogy with the land between the plowed furrows in a field.

Lapel Microphone *See* LAVALIER.

Laser The light source used in the COMPACT DISC system to read the pattern of pits in the surface of the disc is an aluminum gallium arsenide semiconductor DIODE, which emits light at a WAVELENGTH of 0.78 micrometer. When the beam strikes a LAND on the disc, it is reflected full strength to the DETECTOR, but if it strikes a pit, destructive interference occurs because of the half-wavelength path difference between this and the land reflection. The output of the detector then drops, and thus the detector output is a replica of the land/pit pattern on the disc. Lasers that produce light with shorter wavelengths are used in DVD players because the pits on the DVD are much smaller and closer together than those on a CD. Players designed to play both CDs and DVDs contain two lasers.

The term *laser* is an acronym for "Light Amplification by Stimulated Emission of Radiation." The laser was invented at the Bell Telephone Laboratories.

LaserDisc, LD, Laser Video Disc, LVD, LaserVision Introduced in 1978 as MCA Disco-Vision, the LaserDisc was developed to bring home theater to the masses and compete with the then-emerging videocassette movie with much higher quality. Its technologies would lead to all other optical storage discs such as the CD and DVD, and it is claimed to be the first consumer device to use a laser. The LaserDisc was all ANALOG. A helium-neon gas laser (in a glass tube) would read pits on the 12 inch disc, but these represented an analog FM TV signal (with analog stereo sound) rather than digital data. Later models would use laser DIODES. CAV mode limited playing time to 30 minutes until CLV mode was perfected. Later improvements would add 2 channels of PCM digital audio of CD quality, and the limited introduction of Dolby and DTS digital 5.1 surround sound data streams. Unfortunately, years of early technical problems, the inability to record limited acceptance to all but videophiles, and the DVD finally killed the LaserDisc. It might be said that the LaserDisc gave the original impetus to the concept of the high quality home theater. Pioneer Electronics had bought all the LaserDisc rights in the early 1980s and still administers optical disc patents through its Discovision Associates division.

Laser Rot All but the earliest laser video discs were manufactured of two-playing sides glued together, and after time, many discs were found to develop noise in the picture and/or sound. The blame was placed on reflective coating deterioration, glues, and manufacturing, and likely had little to do with the laser playback system. However, the name was convenient, and it has come to describe deterioration problems with any optical storage disc.

Latency Generally, the time elapsed between a stimulus and a response. Humans have latency between the time they hear something and the time they respond. Computer hardware and software can also have a delay that can affect audio phase and monitoring time.

Lathe, Recording Lathe The recording lathe consists of a powerful turntable, a CUTTERHEAD, and a cutter advancing mechanism that is used to cut the master ACETATE in the first step of producing phonograph records. Recording lathes are built to very high standards of accuracy, to operate with very low FLUTTER and WOW and negligible RUMBLE, all of which, if present, would be recorded onto the record being cut.

Lavalier A small MICROPHONE designed to be worn on a strap around a person's neck. The lavalier has a built-in low-frequency ROLLOFF to improve the intelligibility of speech. It is also sometimes called a lapel or tie-tack microphone and may be clipped to a lapel or other piece of clothing. Pronounced, lav-a-leer by most English speakers. Sometimes called simply a lav for short.

Layback In video editing, layback is transfer of the finished audio mix onto the video edit master. This allows for traditional multitrack audio production techniques while providing a videotape that a TV network can play. In ANALOG days, a special audio recording head with tracks in the videotape's audio track areas would be installed on a multitrack audio recorder and the actual videotape would be loaded and recorded onto. Unfortunately, videotape is somewhat different magnetically from audiotape and this was not optimal, but it was better than the video recorder sound track.

LBR Laser Beam Recorder, the device for making the glass master used to produce metal parts for CD stampers.

LC Circuit A circuit usually found in EQUALIZERS or FILTERS that uses both INDUCTORS (Ls) and CAPACITORS (Cs).

LCD Liquid Crystal Display, a display technology used for computers, watches, and other indicators. Liquid crystals in displays are materials whose light transmission can be changed when an electric current is applied. Filters can provide colors.

LDA, Light-Dependent Attenuator. *See* LIGHT-DEPENDENT RESISTOR.

LDR *See* LIGHT-DEPENDENT RESISTOR.

Lead-Acid Battery An ELECTRIC CELL containing a lead dioxide ANODE, a lead CATHODE, and sulfuric acid ELECTROLYTE.

The common car battery is composed of lead-acid cells. Standard lead-acid cells need to be vented to the atmosphere, for they produce hydrogen when being charged, but some newer types are sealed. An example of the latter is the gelled electrolyte type, whose trademark is GelCell. Such sealed lead-acid batteries are found in emergency lights and uninterruptible power supplies because of relatively high-energy storage capacity, favorable voltage-versus-discharge curves, and good recharge ability. They were also commonly used in devices such as camcorders before the adoption of lithium-ion and NiMH batteries and the greatly reduced power consumption of modern electronics.

Leadering In audio editing, the process of removing the outtakes, count-offs, and noises between takes in a magnetic tape (and by extension, digital) recording. In analog magnetic tape editing, this process also involves inserting LEADER TAPE between songs.

Leader Tape Nonmagnetic plastic or special paper tape that is spliced onto analog magnetic tape between musical selections and at the beginning and end of the magnetic tape. Leader protects the magnetic tape and identifies the beginnings and ends of selections, allowing the recordist to find the appropriate point in the tape when editing or mastering a record. Some leader is "timed," that is, it has marks every 7.5 inches and 15 inches to allow the tape editor to insert the desired time between selections.

Leaf Tweeter The leaf tweeter is a miniature version of a planar LOUDSPEAKER. Its diaphragm is a small sheet of plastic film (the "leaf"), and it has a fine GRID of wires embedded in it. These wires form the VOICE COIL of the tweeter. There is an array of small high-strength magnets in front of and behind the film to provide the magnetic field for the coil to react with.

The leaf tweeter has very extended high-FREQUENCY RESPONSE, sometimes to 40 KILOHERTZ with very little ROLLOFF, and its response is uniform and smooth over its range of operation. It is not effective below 5 kHz or so, and must be crossed over at or above this frequency. Today, it is one of the highest-quality, high-frequency DRIVERS in existence. *See also* CROSSOVER FREQUENCY.

Leakage The pickup of unwanted off-axis sounds by a directional microphone due to the fact that its directional pattern is not ideal, or the pickup of unwanted sounds by microphones that are supposed to be isolated from one another, as in a multitrack studio recording. *See also* ROOM LEAKAGE.

Leclanche Cell The cheapest type of cell. It is used for powering flashlights, radios, small cassette recorders, and so on. It uses a carbon ANODE and a zinc CATHODE with an ELECTROLYTE of ammonium chloride and is commonly called a zinc-carbon cell. Its output voltage is 1.5 V. It does not have a very long shelf life or capacity, especially with heavy loads. Its capacity is greater when used with an intermittent duty cycle. It is capable of limited recharging, but care must be used not to overcharge it or it can explode. The Leclanche cell is essentially obsolete, having been replaced by the ALKALINE CELL.

LED Short for "Light-Emitting DIODE," which is a SOLID-STATE diode that glows a certain color when a CURRENT is passed through it. The emission may or may not be visible light; many LEDs operate in the infrared region of the spectrum. So-called white LEDs actually activate a chemical fluorescence that emits a broad spectrum of light. LEDs are fairly efficient, rugged, and long-lived, and most are inexpensive. Much research has been performed to achieve different color outputs and light levels.

LEDs are frequently used as indicator lights. They can, for instance, be arranged in a series with varying SENSITIVITY so that they will glow in succession as the AUDIO level varies. This assembly can then be used as a substitute for a VU meter or MODULOMETER.

Infrared LEDs are used in a novel system pioneered by Sennheiser to transmit STEREO signals from a transmitter panel to battery-powered receiving headsets in a room such as an auditorium. This permits partially deaf persons to hear a performance at an amplified level and still be free to move about the room with no wires attached.

An example of an LED is the laser diode that provides the beam of light that reads the pattern of the pits in the COMPACT DISC system. *See also* DED.

LEDE™ Short for "Live End, Dead End," which is a commercial trademark used to indicate a particular acoustical design of a recording studio control room. In this design, the area around the MONITOR LOUDSPEAKERS is made acoustically absorbent, or "dead," while the area behind the listener's position is made reflective, or "live." This configuration is said by the designers to increase the accuracy of the reproduction.

Leq Equivalent sound level. The Leq of a sonic event is that constant SOUND PRESSURE LEVEL which has the same amount of energy as the actual event. Thus, the Leq is a long-term average, or integration, of a sound pressure level. Leq is a convenient way of accurately measuring the level of a fluctuating sound. The duration of an Leq measurement can be any amount of time, but usually ranges from a few seconds to several hours.

Leslie Speaker A biamplified speaker-amplifier system for use with an electronic organ where there is a rotating baffle in front of the WOOFER, and where the TWEETER HORNS also rotate. (*See* BI-AMPLIFICATION.)

The Leslie was introduced as an adjunct to the Hammond organ. The rotating parts provide an AMPLITUDE and FREQUENCY MODULATION to the sound in a manner which cannot be duplicated with stationary LOUDSPEAKERS. The effect is a strong VIBRATO. The FM is caused by the DOPPLER EFFECT.

Level The term *level* is loosely used when the magnitude of a SIGNAL is meant, usually VOLTAGE. Strictly speaking, the term should be reserved for the value of a power in DECIBELS when a particular reference power is specified or understood. For instance, two sound pressures can be compared in decibels, but when the reference is 20 micropascals of sound pressure, the number of decibels is called the SOUND PRESSURE LEVEL and is a specific quantity of sound pressure rather than a simple ratio.

Leveler An electronic device used in certain sound systems to maintain the level of background music so it can be heard above the background noise. In a quiet ambience, the music stays at a low volume level, but as the background noise increases, the leveler effectively turns up the volume, increasing the overall sound level, and in many cases, the annoyance level.

Leyden Jar The first CAPACITOR, invented by Pieter Van Musschenbroek, of Leyden, Holland, in 1745. Van Musschenbroek thought that electricity could be bottled and experimented with bottles of water, which he charged to high potentials with friction-induced static electricity. Through a series of experiments, one of which put his assistant in bed for two days, he finally did away with the water, substituting a layer of tinfoil on the inside and outside of the jar. The Leyden jar uses glass as a DIELECTRIC and is capable of storing charges at very high voltages; it has been used in electrostatic experiments for many years.

LFE Low-Frequency Effects, one of the audio channels in motion picture and home theater surround sound, designated by the .1 in 5.1 sound. LFE sounds are routed to the SUBWOOFER in the system, and can consist of sound effects such as thunder and explosions, etc., and also the lowest frequency

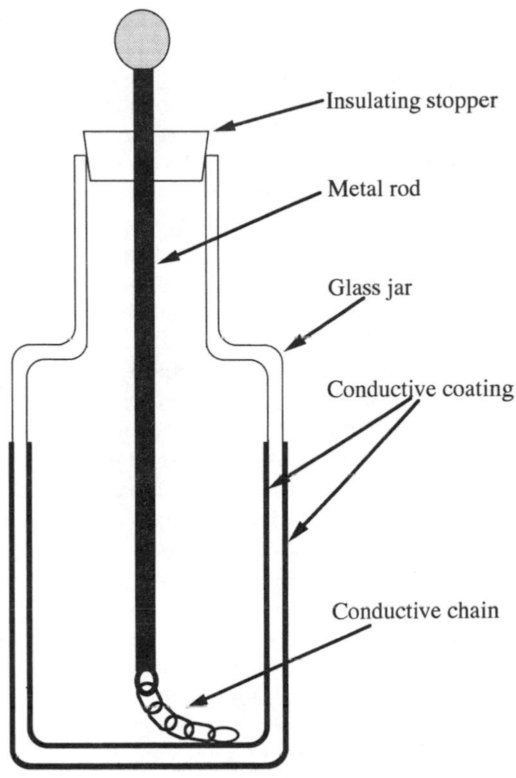

Cross section

Leyden Jar

octave of music. The channel is not capable of full range sound, having only about one tenth of full-range BANDWIDTH.

LFO Low-Frequency OSCILLATOR.

Life "A spiritual pickle preserving the body from decay. We live in daily apprehension of its loss, yet when lost, it is not missed."—Ambrose Bierce

Lifter *See* TAPE LIFTER.

Light-Dependent Resistor, or LDR A type of photocell that has a RESISTANCE that varies with the amount of light striking it. The active element in such a cell is usually cadmium sulfide. LDRs have been used in some audio control consoles as components of ATTENUATORS, which are then called light-dependent attenuators (LDAs). The LDA is operated by a standard POTENTIOMETER, which controls the current through a light bulb that illuminates the LDR. This type of circuit is suited to remote control, where the audio signal does not have to be routed over long cables to the attenuator, and contact noise in the control "pot" is seldom a problem.

LDAs have some disadvantages, including fairly slow response time. It is also difficult to make them track so that several of them controlling various signals provide the same attenuation at all positions of the control potentiometers. To control a stereo signal the channels must track in gain very accurately to preserve the stereo image as a function of volume. The LDR is essentially obsolete. *See also* OPTO-ISOLATOR.

Lightpipe A serial eight-channel multiplexed interface for digital audio transmitted by a single fiber-optic cable, terminating in a proprietary connector. The Lightpipe was invented by Alesis to connect its ADAT MODULAR DIGITAL MULTITRACKS.

Light Valve One type of device used for printing optical soundtracks on movie film. Pairs of metal ribbons in a magnetic field are modulated by the audio SIGNAL, which open and close to vary a light beam which exposes the optical soundtrack on the film. Care must be taken to avoid "valve clash," when overmodulation causes DISTORTION in the valves as the ribbons hit. Another kind of light valve may also be used in additive color film printers. Several types of video projectors often describe their technology as "light valve" type if it involves some sort of transmissive control of a light source.

Limiter A special type of COMPRESSOR that prevents the SIGNAL from exceeding a certain preset level, no matter what the input signal level may be. Limiters are sometimes used for special effects in popular recordings, especially vocals. A vocal with limiting will be essentially at the same level regardless of the effort put out by the singer, from a soft voice to a shout. The shouting will sound subjectively louder, however, because of the increased HARMONIC content of the sound. The DYNAMIC range of a singer at close range to a MICROPHONE is far greater than that of any instrument or musical ensemble, and when recording a vocal with an ensemble without limiting, a great deal of GAIN RIDING must be done to maintain musical balance.

Limiters are sometimes used in front of power AMPLIFIERS in sound reinforcement systems or radio transmitters to prevent unexpected high-level signals from causing overloading and large amounts of DISTORTION.

Line Amplifier Originally, a line AMPLIFIER was a special amplifier designed to amplify telephone signals for transmission over telephone lines. The term is now used to indicate any amplifier with a LINE LEVEL output and an OUTPUT IMPEDANCE of 600 OHMS or so.

Line amplifiers are used in the broadcast industry for sending signals from place to place and in recording studios to send signals between audio devices such as REVERBERATORS.

Linear A system, CIRCUIT, or component is said to be linear if it meets the conditions of proportionality and additivity, that is, if its output level changes smoothly in proportion to input level changes, and if input x causes output X and input y causes output Y, then x + y at the input must cause

X + Y at the output. This is a very important concept, adding predictability to any system. Most tests we employ in AUDIO (FREQUENCY RESPONSE, GAIN, PHASE, IMPULSE RESPONSE, etc.) are based on the assumption of linearity.

Note that this does not imply that the output is identical to the input, or that it even resembles the input. It is a common misconception that linearity implies absolutely faithful music reproduction. Probably this arises from the fact that a ruler-FLAT ("linear") frequency response and a linearly decaying phase of the frequency response mean that the output will be a replica of the input. This is but one of a multitude of possible linear systems. FILTERS, DELAY LINES, REVERBERATORS, rooms, and LOUDSPEAKERS, etc., are all in principle linear, but do not have flat frequency or phase response, and their outputs do not necessarily resemble their inputs. In practice, all these elements possess some nonlinear properties that cause more or less nonlinear DISTORTION, as opposed to linear distortion, caused by nonflat frequency response.

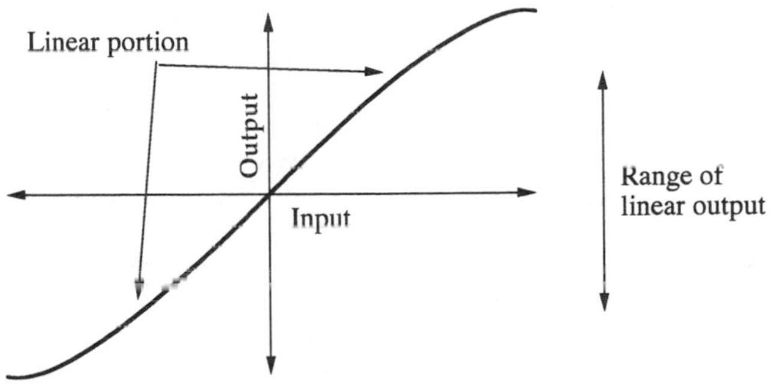

This curve shows input vs output of a tape recorder

Linear

Linear Distortion Any type of DISTORTION that a LINEAR system is capable of producing, as opposed to NONLINEAR distortion. Some types of linear distortion are FREQUENCY RESPONSE errors and time delay errors such as PHASE SHIFT.

Linearity The degree to which a system or device is LINEAR. There is no simple way to express the degree of linearity; it cannot be measured in terms of percentages or any objective quantity. Even though an ideal, perfectly linear system might be said to be 100% linear, it is possible to characterize less-than-perfect linearity only by the various DISTORTIONS that it causes.

Line Array An evolution of the COLUMN LOUDSPEAKER, the modern line array speaker typically consists of modular full-range speaker cabinets that can be attached in a hanging, curved column.

Line Input Any set of input terminals of an audio device designed to accept LINE LEVEL signals, or signals above 25 mV RMS. Most consumer devices are usually intended to work with line levels on the order of 0.5 V rms, and may be marked with terms such as AUX, CD, TAPE PLAY or such. However, they usually work identically, and have flat response. A once common device that did not use line levels was the phonograph CARTRIDGE, which output a few millivolts and required RIAA EQUALIZATION.

Line Level Line level refers to the average audio VOLTAGE level of a SIGNAL at a particular point in an AUDIO system. According to the IHF (now the EIA), line level is any level above 25 mV RMS, but most consumer line level signals are in the neighborhood of 0.5 V rms. How the averaging is done is important to the definition of the level. *See also* VU.

The output level of a PREAMPLIFIER is typically line level, and the input level of a power AMPLIFIER is line level. In commercial audio systems, line level is metered with a VU meter, where 0 VU corresponds to .775 volts rms of signal. The actual line level in these systems may be +4 DBM (1.23 volts rms) or +8 dBm (1.95 volts rms) even though the VU meter reads 0 VU. The 0 VU reference is simply a convenient meter reading to which to adjust the signal when controlling the GAIN. It is especially important to control levels accurately in tape recording and broadcasting to avoid overloads and consequent DISTORTION. Note that nominal line level does not imply headroom figures. The term dates from the early days of telephone engineering usage.

Line Microphone A highly directional microphone that has an acoustical transmission line in front of its active element, which may be of several types, including CONDENSER or DYNAMIC.

Typically, a line microphone will have a fairly long tube (12 to 24 inches long) protruding from its front. The tube will have a series of holes along the side. Sound coming from directly in front of the unit will enter the holes in succession, and each wave coming into a hole will add in PHASE to produce the composite sound reaching the TRANSDUCER. Sounds coming from the rear, however, reach the holes in reverse order, and the phasing is such that they cancel each other out on the way to the transducer, resulting in very little or no output. The longer the tube, the more directional the microphone will be.

In the past, some quite bizarre line microphones have been built. Electro-Voice once made such a microphone that was over 6 feet long. It had a sight, similar to a gun sight, to aid in aiming it, and it was mounted on a tripod with a swivel arrangement. Harry Olson, of RCA Research Laboratories, built some line microphones with a cluster of tubes coming out the front. They were of many lengths and were arranged in a spiral pattern, looking something like a Gatling machine gun with different-length barrels.

Line microphones are sometimes called "shotgun" microphones.

Line Radiator Another name for COLUMN LOUDSPEAKER.

Line Source Loudspeaker *See* COLUMN LOUDSPEAKER.

Line Up The procedure carried out to ensure that recording, editing, playback, amplification, etc. equipment works to the highest possible standard. It consists of systematic adjustment of the equipment according to a schedule and may involve specialized calibration and test apparatus such as a multimeter, tone generator, OSCILLOSCOPE, etc. *See also* ALIGNMENT.

Linked In a multichannel dynamic effects device such as a compressor/limiter, channels may be set to all respond even if only one channel determines the activation of the effect. For example, a stereo compressor can compress both stereo channels the same even if only one channel determines that the compressor should be activated. This maintains a BALANCED sound overall rather than hearing an effect in one channel.

Linkwitz-Riley Crossover An ACTIVE CROSSOVER network that has steep slopes in the STOPBAND, typically 24 dB per octave, and linear PHASE response over the entire audible FREQUENCY range. Moreover, it can be designed to introduce a constant time delay in one or more of the passbands in order to achieve TIME ALIGNMENT of the LOUDSPEAKER system. It was developed in 1976 by Siegfried Linkwitz and Russ Riley.

The fourth-ORDER 24 dB per octave Linkwitz-Riley is probably the most common type of active crossover used in commercial sound systems. Its very steep slopes prevent the high-frequency drivers from being damaged by low-frequency energy, an important consideration with high-power sound systems using high-frequency HORN loudspeakers. The phase response is such that there is no relative phase shift between the channels, and this ensures well-controlled directional behavior of the loudspeaker system at the crossover frequency.

Linkwitz-Riley crossovers are made by cascading BUTTERWORTH FILTERS, and always have an even number of orders, or SECTIONS. Although most such units are fourth order, there has been some experimentation with eighth-order Linkwitz-Riley crossovers, but they may have an audible amount of GROUP DELAY distortion and their transient response is not perfect.

Linkwitz Transform A relatively simple equalization CIRCUIT designed by Siegfried Linkwitz that alters the Q and the low-FREQUENCY resonance of a closed box LOUDSPEAKER. The circuit uses one OPAMP and some RESISTORS and CAPACITORS, and Mr. Linkwitz programmed an Excel spreadsheet that calculates the resistor and capacitor values based on the measured Q and resonance frequency of the speaker in question.

Lip Synch When the dialog accompanying a motion picture or a television program is synchronized with the movements of the actors' lips, the picture is said to be in "lip synch." The process of achieving lip synch in movies can be somewhat complex since the sound is recorded independently of the filming, albeit at the same time. *See also* SMPTE TIME CODE.

The situation can also be complex with television broadcasting, especially when the video and audio are sent across the country via satellite repeaters. The audio and video signals are usually sent over separate channels, and because the distances between the satellites are quite large, the video and audio sometimes arrive at the destination at different times, causing loss of lip synch. The serious viewer is often able to detect this timing problem, much to his discomfort.

Lissajous Jules Antoine Lissajous was a French mathematician of the nineteenth century who described what happens when a graph is created with sinusoidal WAVEFORMS acting at 90 degrees from each other. *See also* SINUSOID.

If two SIGNALS are sent to the horizontal and vertical inputs of an OSCILLOSCOPE, the resulting pattern will be a Lissajous pattern. If the two signals are periodic and the periods are an integral multiple of one another, the pattern will have certain symmetries that can be visually recognized.

One application of Lissajous patterns, and probably the most common, is in determining relative PHASE between two signals. Aligning a multitrack ANALOG tape head is almost always done this way. Some home-type AMPLIFIERS and FM tuners have small oscilloscopes built in for checking phasing. In general, the Lissajous pattern caused by the two channels of a STEREO signal will look like a pulsating round ball of string, while a MONAURAL signal will look like a straight line at a 45-degree angle from vertical. Stereo signals with CROSSTALK between the channels will be somewhere between these two extremes, looking like an ellipse tilted at about 45 degrees. The eccentricity of the ellipse determines the stereo separation. This separation is measured in the electrical sense, and may not predict the audible separation because high-frequency signals are most important in subjective stereo separation, but the oscilloscope is more sensitive to low frequencies. Most digital oscilloscopes are usually not very good at displaying a simple Lissajous figure.

Litz Wire A special type of copper wire that consists of many small strands, each insulated from the others. It has a large surface area and presents relatively low RESISTANCE to very high FREQUENCY signals because of the SKIN EFFECT.

Live-to-Two-Track A method of recording in which the instruments and vocals are mixed and recorded directly onto a two-channel stereo recorder. No remixing is possible; however, the FIDELITY can be excellent since no overdubbing or duplication of recorded tracks is needed. The relatively low cost of direct-to-two-track digital recording has revived the popularity of this medium for making master tapes, especially those intended for release on CDs. Also called direct-to-two-track. *See also* DIRECT-TO-DISC.

Load, Loading An IMPEDANCE connected to the output of an AUDIO device is said to "load" the source. The load is that which accepts the POWER from the source. Without a load, there can be no power transferred. Thus, it follows that the amount of power transferred depends on the impedance of the load. The power is actually absorbed by the "real," or resistive, part of the impedance, and not by the reactive part.

This is true of mechanical and acoustical systems as well as electrical systems. The efficiency of a LOUDSPEAKER, for instance, depends on the acoustic load placed on it. A nondirectional loudspeaker placed in a corner of a room has a higher acoustic impedance connected to it than if it were out in the open, and because it is a "velocity" source, it will radiate more sound power. Likewise, a loudspeaker placed in the throat of a HORN will see a higher acoustic impedance and will radiate more power than if it were radiating directly into the air.

Load Impedance The load IMPEDANCE is the impedance connected to the output of a device. In the case of a power AMPLIFIER, the load impedance is a LOUDSPEAKER, and is usually 4 or 8 OHMS. In most AUDIO devices, the load impedance should be five or more times the source impedance of the device. In some rare cases, the device may be designed so the load impedance should match the source impedance, and this is where the term "impedance matching" comes from. An example of this is in broadcast equipment such as amplifiers for driving telephone lines. The impedances are matched in these cases so signals are not reflected from the amplifier inputs or outputs, causing an ECHO. Sometimes such an echo could be heard on an analog long-distance telephone connection. This audio echo is analogous to a ghost on a television screen, which is caused by reflections of the signal reaching the antenna later than the direct signal.

In audio equipment that does not involve long transmission lines, matching the impedances is not only unnecessary, it is not desirable because signal levels are reduced 6 DECIBELS by the LOADING effect of the added impedance. This would be a disaster in power amplifiers driving loudspeakers, wasting half of the amplifier POWER as heat in the output stages of the amplifier.

Local Feedback NEGATIVE FEEDBACK around a single active circuit component, as opposed to a feedback loop around several such components.

Localization *See* BINAURAL.

Location Cart The sound RECORDIST on a movie or television shoot uses a unique mobile cart to hold his equipment. These can be elaborate rigs, holding several tape recorders, mixers, radio receivers, and so on, all sometimes powered by a large battery system.

Location Recording Any recording not in a studio; for example, an orchestra recorded in their performance hall would be a location recording. In film/TV sound, the recording on the set, usually referring to the dialog. Sometimes called "location sound."

Logarithmic Having to do with the logarithms (abbr. log) of numbers rather than the numbers themselves. In graphs of AUDIO phenomena, frequently the log of AMPLITUDE is plotted versus the log of FREQUENCY.

The common log of a number is the power to which the number 10 must be raised to obtain the number. For instance, 10 to the second power (or 10 squared) equals 100, and this means the log of 100 is 2. Similarly, the log of 1,000 is 3, etc. A log scale is a scale where distances are proportional to the logs of the represented numbers, while a linear scale (like an ordinary ruler) has distances proportional to the numbers themselves.

Logarithmic

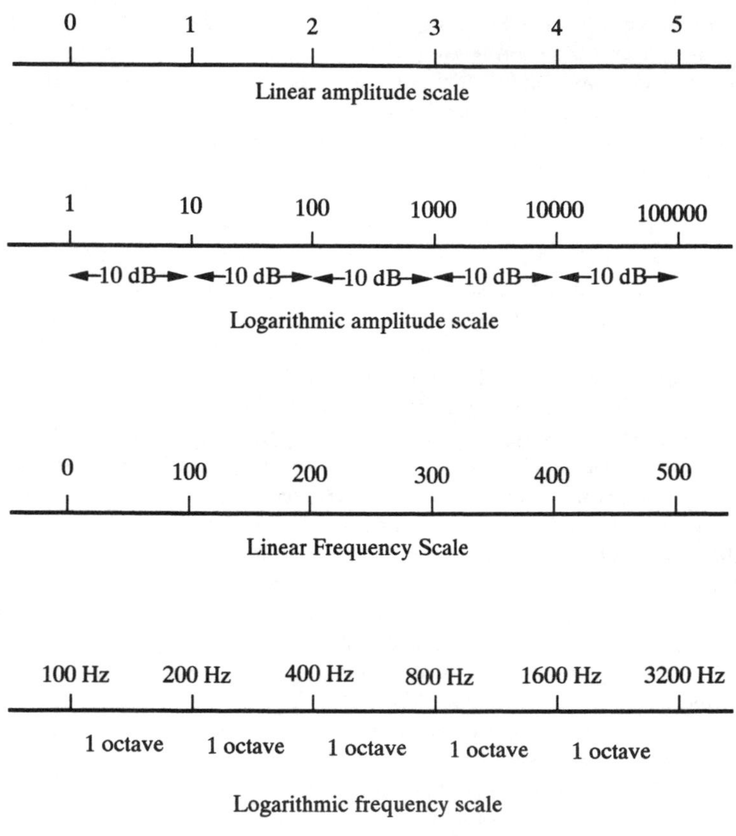

Linear and Logarithmic Scales

The reason we use log scales in audio is because the response of our hearing mechanism is proportional to the logarithm of frequency and approximately proportional to the logarithm of amplitude. As frequency is varied, we perceive the pitch interval of a sound as being proportional to the frequency ratio. For instance, if the frequency is doubled, the PITCH rises one OCTAVE. If the frequency is doubled again, the pitch rises another octave, and so on. A frequency ratio of 2 is always a pitch interval of one octave. In the case of amplitude versus LOUDNESS, we perceive a DOUBLING of loudness for each amplitude ratio of about 3. This is a ratio of 10 in power, or 10 decibels. The DECIBEL scale is a logarithmic scale of power ratios. Thus it takes a tenfold increase in power for us to perceive a doubling of loudness, but another tenfold power increase doubles the perceived loudness again.

The primary reason we use decibel scales in audio is that a relatively small range of numbers represents a very great range of amplitudes of sounds. The DYNAMIC RANGE of the ear is greater than 10 to the twelfth power, or a factor of 1,000,000,000,000. This is easily expressed as 120 dB.

An example of a log relationship outside audio is the behavior of photographic film. To achieve linear increases in density of the negative image requires successive doublings of exposure. This is the reason the shutter speeds on your camera are adjusted so each one is double the preceding one. Likewise, the lens openings are marked so that each f-stop admits twice the light of the adjacent one.

Long Line An ANALOG audio transmission line consisting of copper wire whose electrical length is longer than the shortest wavelength to be transmitted. The wavelength referred to has nothing to do with the wavelength of the equivalent sound in air, for the speed of transmission in a line is very much faster than the speed of sound. The propagation speed depends on the electrical characteristics of the line and can vary from about 180,000 miles per second down to 50,000 miles per second or so; thus the audio wavelengths in long lines are many miles long.

In long lines, care must be taken that the IMPEDANCES are properly matched to prevent the signal from being reflected back and forth from the ends of the line, causing audible echoes or DISTORTIONS. These echoes are analogous to ghost images in television reception.

A long line must also be designed so that the propagation speed of signals is the same for all audio frequencies, and this is done by applying special loading coils, or series INDUCTANCES, along the line. A line with variable transmission speeds at different frequencies is said to be dispersive and causes gross distortion of transmitted signals. Nowadays, long copper lines are seldom used for audio transmission—the task has been taken over by microwave transmission and fiber optics.

Long-Throw A type of dynamic LOUDSPEAKER, often a WOOFER, that is designed to allow the CONE to travel a long distance without encountering nonlinearities in its response.

Looping The process of post-production dialog replacement using identical-length loops of picture, guide track, and record track. The line to be replaced would thus repeat over and over, and the actor would go for a take when they were ready. Also referred to as "virgin looping," when recording onto a blank piece of mag film the same size as the picture and guide loops. When optical sound was used, the recordings were made sequentially on a roll and later manually synched to picture.

Although this process is not used these days—ADR, or Automated Dialog Recording is the standard in the U.S.—the act of replacing dialog is still often referred to as "looping." [19] *See also* ADR.

19. This entry is copyright © 1999–2003 by Larry Blake and is reprinted with permission.

Lo-Pass Filter Short for LOW-PASS FILTER.

Lo-Ro Shorthand for Left only-Right only. Among the many sound formats film sound people must deal with, Lo-Ro is an ordinary stereo left/right audio pair, usually derived from mixing down a multichannel mix or even originally mixed only in two channel stereo. There is no matrixed surround information, thus no derived center or surround is possible, only left and right. Television shows and industrial productions often utilize it. *See also* LT-RT.

Loss The opposite of GAIN. When a signal passes through a CIRCUIT or audio device, if the output power is less than the input power, the circuit or device is said to have loss. It is usually expressed in DECIBELS. *See also* INSERTION LOSS.

Lossless *See* CODEC.

Loss Pad Another term for PAD.

Lossy *See* CODEC.

Loudness Loudness is a subjective attribute of a sound and cannot be quantified, except in a statistical sense. If a large sample of listeners is asked to adjust the strength of two signals so that one is "twice as loud" as the other one, the average POWER difference will be about 10 DECIBELS, and this will be almost independent of the absolute levels of the two sounds. The unit of loudness is the SONE, and a SOUND PRESSURE LEVEL of 40 dB is defined as having a loudness of 1 sone. 2 sones is twice as loud and corresponds to about 50 dB, etc. The use of sones to measure loudness is seldom encountered except in some PSYCHOACOUSTIC research.

The loudness of a sound, especially a complex sound containing many frequencies, has no simple relation to its sound pressure level, and it is hopeless to try to measure relative loudnesses of different sounds by using a SOUND LEVEL METER. Various attempts to build a meter that measures loudness have been made over the years, but with very little success, so complicated is our hearing mechanism. *See also* LOUDNESS LEVEL.

Loudness Control The loudness control is an addition to some AMPLIFIERS or PREAMPLIFIERS that attempts to correct for the reduced sensitivity of our ears for low-FREQUENCY, low-level sounds. *See* FLETCHER-MUNSON EFFECT.

The loudness control is simply a bass-boost CIRCUIT that has a relatively greater effect as the volume is turned down. In some such circuits, the treble is also boosted a little. In other words, as the volume control is turned down, the low-frequency content of the signal is reduced less than the high-frequency content. Early loudness controls tended to overcompensate with the result of too much bass at low levels, but more recent designs are more convincing.

Loudness Level The SOUND PRESSURE LEVEL (SPL) of a 1-KILOHERTZ PURE TONE that has the same LOUDNESS as the sound in question is the loudness level of that sound. The loudness level scale is a DECIBEL scale, and the unit is the PHON. Thus, a sound which is as loud as a 1-kHz pure tone of 60-dB SPL has a loudness level of 60 phons.

Phons are seldom encountered in AUDIO work but are used by researchers in PSYCHOACOUSTICS. *See also* FLETCHER-MUNSON EFFECT.

Loudspeaker The loudspeaker is the TRANSDUCER that converts electrical energy into acoustic energy. The first such transducers were earphones, and the first such unit to make enough sound to be heard in a room was, naturally enough, called a loudspeaker.

The most common type of loudspeaker in use today is called the DYNAMIC loudspeaker, which was invented by a German engineer named Siemens. The dynamic loudspeaker is a moving-COIL device. The motion of the CONE is caused by the force created by an audio signal CURRENT in the coil, which reacts with a stationary magnetic field provided by a permanent magnet. *See also* VOICE COIL.

The most common type of dynamic loudspeaker in use is known as the DIRECT RADIATOR, so called because the sound is radiated directly from the loudspeaker cone, without having a HORN coupled to it.

One of the most important characteristics of a dynamic loudspeaker is its resonant FREQUENCY, which is the frequency at which it will vibrate naturally if perturbed. The resonant frequency will be near the lowest frequency that the speaker will produce well, and is that frequency at which it is easiest to move the cone. The output from the speaker will be at a maximum at this frequency. Therefore, DAMPING must be added to a speaker system in order to reduce this peak in response. The damping may be in the form of acoustic absorption inside the cabinet.

Another important characteristic of a loudspeaker is its EFFICIENCY, which is a measure of how much of the electrical energy it receives is radiated as sound, related to how much is dissipated as heat.

In general, the response from a baffled direct radiator dynamic loudspeaker will be uniform for several octaves above the resonant frequency and will fall off at the rate of about 12 DECIBELS per OCTAVE below the resonance. *See* INFINITE BAFFLE and BASS REFLEX.

There are several other types of loudspeaker mechanisms, that are in relatively limited use but are still important. One of these is the electrostatic loudspeaker, which is a very thin sheet of plastic film suspended between two wire grids or screens. The plastic film is conductive and is charged with a high direct VOLTAGE, usually about 600 volts or so. The grids are connected to the AMPLIFIER output through a step-up transformer, which applies up to 300 alternating volts of SIGNAL to them. The film is alternately attracted to one grid and then the other by electrostatic forces, and the resulting motion of the film radiates the sound.

Electrostatic speakers generally are physically quite large, some standing 6 feet high by 2 or 3 feet wide. They are always direct radiators, and they must be large to attain reasonable efficiency at low frequencies. This is partly because they radiate equal amounts of sound to the front and to the rear, but the two sound waves are of opposite POLARITY with each other and tend to cancel. The radiation pattern of an electrostatic speaker in a FREE FIELD is a COSINE pattern, similar to the sensitivity pattern of a

Loudspeaker

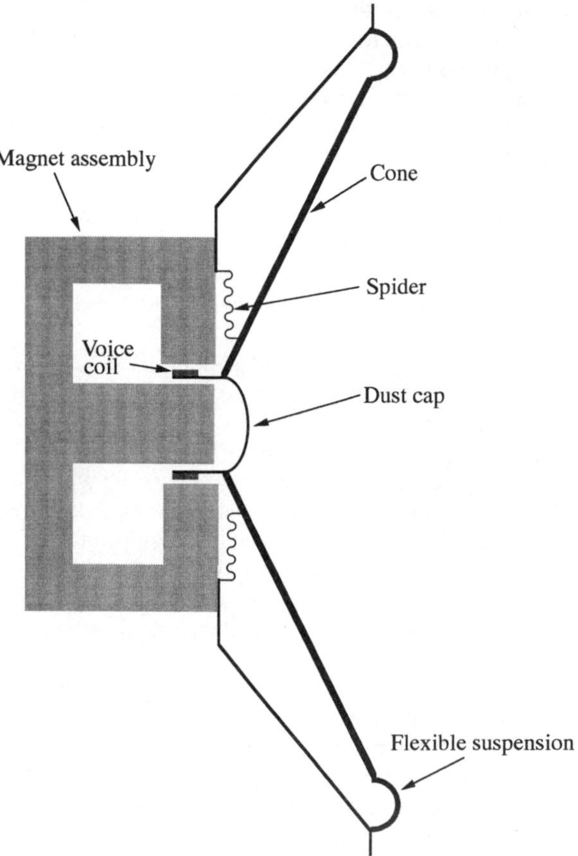

Cross Section of a Dynamic Loudspeaker

FIGURE-8 MICROPHONE. Because of their large size, electrostatics become very directional in the high-frequency range, "beaming" the sound almost like a flashlight. They also have very low electrical IMPEDANCE, which is primarily capacitive, and this presents a problem for some AMPLIFIERS.

Electrostatic loudspeakers, in spite of their disadvantages, can have very low DISTORTION, and careful design can partially overcome the directional problems. They are not capable of extremely high sound levels because the voltages required to permit this would be so large that an ARC would occur between the grids and the film.

Another type of loudspeaker is the so-called planar type, which combines some aspects of the dynamic and the electrostatic designs. The planar speaker consists of a large plastic sheet with conducting wires imbedded in it. The wires are the "voice coil," although they are not coiled up but rather traverse the sheet in a grid-like pattern. Many small magnets in front and behind set up a magnetic field around the sheet, so current in the wires causes a force on it and it moves as a unit, similar to the motion of the electrostatic.

Planar speakers suffer from the same directional problems as electrostatics, but their impedance is more like that of dynamic speakers. *See also* HORN.

Low Bit Rate Coding Digital audio with any data reduction scheme such as MP3. The definition of "low" is not given.

Low-Pass Filter A FILTER that uniformly passes frequencies below a certain FREQUENCY called the CUTOFF FREQUENCY. Usually this is defined as the frequency where the AMPLITUDE response of the filter is 3 DECIBELS below its nominal value.

Many early TONE CONTROLS were variable low-pass filters.

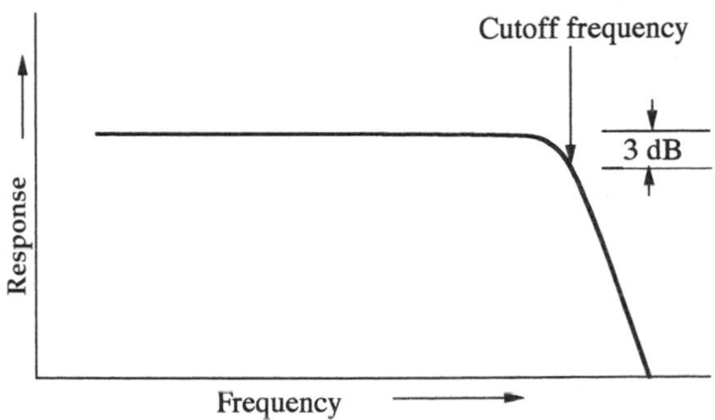

Low-Pass Filter

LP Originally a trademark of the Columbia Broadcasting System designating the then-new (1948) MICROGROOVE long-playing phonograph record. The term was rapidly taken as a generic to distinguish the microgroove 33⅓-RPM record from the 78-rpm standard records.

L-Pad A type of ATTENUATOR typically consisting of two resistors schematically arranged in the form of either an inverted, backward letter L or a capital Greek gamma. The physical layout of the components in an L-pad need not be in the form of a letter L! It can have a fixed amount of attenuation or can be variable, in which case, the two resistors are replaced with POTENTIOMETERS that are GANGED together. The variable L-pad presents either a constant input or a constant output impedance to its associated circuitry regardless of its attenuation setting and is commonly used as a gain control in audio consoles. *See* figure at ATTENUATOR for schematic.

LSB Least Significant Bit refers to the smallest SIGNAL voltage level which an ANALOG-TO-DIGITAL CONVERTER can encode. The term was thought to be nonrigorous mathematically, so it was replaced by the more accurate "quantizing step." Anything below the quantizing step is not recognized by the ADC. The value of the LSB is also equal to the AMPLITUDE resolution of a DIGITAL system. In other words, the minimum difference in level between two successive samples is 1 quantizing step.

The value of the quantizing step is dependent on the number of BITS available for encoding the signal. For example, in a 16-bit encoding system such as is used in the COMPACT DISC, the instantaneous signal amplitude is encoded into one of 65,536 VOLTAGE values. The difference in level between two adjacent steps is 1 LSB.

L-Section A FILTER or part of a filter that consists of two reactive elements, one in series with the signal and one in SHUNT with the signal. The name comes from the schematic diagram's physical resemblance to an inverted letter L. An L-section filter has essentially flat response in its PASSBAND and 12 dB per OCTAVE slope in its STOPBAND.

LSI Large Scale Integration refers to the technology that can produce thousands of TRANSISTORS on an INTEGRATED CIRCUIT. VLSI (Very Large Scale Integration) is common now.

LT Acronym for Low Tension, which is British usage for "low voltage."

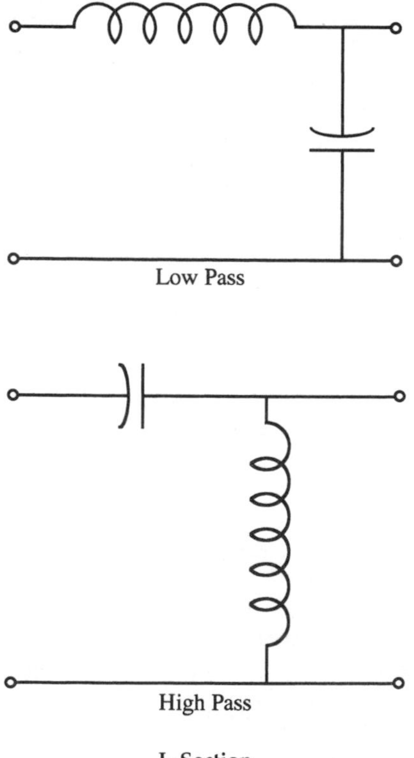

L-Section

LTC Longitudinal Time Code, as opposed to VITC. SMPTE TIME CODE that is recorded linearly like an audio track, although the data is digital. Sometimes spoken as "lit-see."

Lt-Rt Left total–Right total. A 2-track stereo signal that has been matrix encoded with surround channels. *See also* Lo-Ro.

M

Machine Room The room in a motion picture sound mixing facility that held many audio recorders and players using sprocketed magstock. Multi-element sound tracks would be produced in a mixing or dubbing theater with sounds delivered from the machine room.

Macintosh, McIntosh McIntosh is the name of a respected hi-fi manufacturer and the name of an apple variety. Apple Computer calls their computer the Macintosh, a name that originally required permission to use from McIntosh Laboratory, as noted on the Macintosh Plus computer product label of 1986.

MADI Multichannel Audio Digital Interface. A digital audio transmission standard proposed by the AES and standardized by the American National Standards Institute (ANSI S4.43-1991) specifying and controlling the requirements for digital interconnection between multitrack recorders and mixing consoles. The standard provides for 56 simultaneous digital audio channels that are conveyed point-to-point on a single coaxial cable fitted with BNC connectors along with a separate synchronization signal. Basically, the technique takes the standard AES3 (formerly called AES/EBU) interface and multiplexes 56 of these into one sample period rather than the original two. *See also* AES3.

MAF *See* MINIMUM AUDIBLE FIELD .

Magic Eye A small CATHODE RAY TUBE in which the illuminated area of a fluorescent screen varies with the level of an applied voltage. Magic eyes were introduced in the 1930s by RCA for use as tuning indicators in some of their radios. Some inexpensive tape recorders have also used them as volume indicators.

Magnet Something acted upon by magnetism. **Magnetism** Something acting upon a magnet. "The two definitions immediately foregoing are condensed from the works of one thousand eminent scientists, who have illuminated the subject with a great white light, to the inexpressible advancement of human knowledge."—A. Bierce

Magnetic Distortion A type of DISTORTION in DYNAMIC loudspeakers caused by nonlinearities in the interaction between the magnetic field in the gap and the VOICE COIL. Magnetic distortion arises because the voice coil moves in the gap and, in so doing, does not always encounter the same magnetic field strength, causing the force it experiences to vary with its excursion. *See also* OVERHUNG COIL and UNDERHUNG COIL.

Magnetic Tape Magnetic tape generally consists of a plastic base of one type or another that has been coated with a mixture consisting of a flexible BINDER mixed with very fine particles of iron oxide.

Several oxides of iron are used, sometimes along with some small quantities of other elements such as cobalt, and the density of the magnetic particles in the binder has been greatly increased, thus increasing the SENSITIVITY of the recording process and reducing the NOISE.

The first plastic magnetic tapes, made in Germany in the 1940s, were primitive compared to the modern product. The original German recording tapes were made of homogenous magnetic material mixed with the plastic. It worked equally well on either side.

Magnetic tape has been the quality standard for ANALOG audio recording for many years, but now DIGITAL recording and the digital audio COMPACT DISC have proven superior in some ways. Even though tape is still often used as a storage medium in such systems as the DAT, the recording quality is determined more by other factors involving the digital encoding and decoding of the SIGNAL than by the tape itself.

Magnetism The study of magnets and magnetic phenomena. A magnet is a body that attracts iron. It has two ends called poles. The earth is a giant magnet, with poles roughly corresponding to the north and south geographic poles. A bar magnet, if suspended, will orient itself in a north-south direction. One pole is north-seeking, one is south-seeking, and they are commonly called north and south poles. (It follows that the north pole of the earth is actually a south magnetic pole!)

The area of influence around a magnet is called its magnetic field, and its strength is measured in teslas, after Nikola TESLA.

Magnetism relates to AUDIO via the well-known phenomenon of magnetic recording. Magnetic recording is usually thought of as ANALOG recording, but many DIGITAL recordings are also made as magnetic recordings, the BITS of the digitally encoded signal being stored as tiny magnetized areas on either MAGNETIC TAPE or magnetic hard discs. However, optical means of recording are increasing in popularity, such as recording directly onto a blank CD recordable. The original CD-R cannot be edited physically, so the audio signal must be transferred into a computer containing software for digital editing.

Magnetomotive Force The force experienced by a wire in a magnetic field when the wire is conducting an electric CURRENT. The magnitude of the force is proportional to the product of the current, the length of the wire, and the magnetic field strength.

The magnetomotive force is the underlying mechanism for the operation of all LOUDSPEAKERS that use magnets in their construction. *See also* BL PRODUCT.

Magnitude The portion of the FREQUENCY RESPONSE or IMPEDANCE of a device that represents the AMPLITUDE is called the magnitude, as distinguished from the PHASE, which is the other, equally important, part. In most published response and impedance curves, only the magnitude is included, but the phase curve also contains much information about the performance of the device.

Strictly speaking, the term only applies to complex quantities, i.e., quantities characterized by a magnitude *and* a phase. For noncomplex quantities, the term *amplitude* is used. *See also* Appendix 11.

Mag-Optical Print A motion picture film that has both optical and magnetic sound tracks so it can be reproduced in conventional theaters with optical sound equipment and also in houses equipped with stereo magnetic sound. It is now obsolete, with the advent of digital motion picture sound.

Magstock *See* FULLCOAT.

Mains In Britain, the power line has traditionally been called the "mains," and the usage is gradually migrating to the United States. In the U.S., *mains* refers to the 60-HERTZ 115-VOLT power available at wall sockets.

Sometimes the primary output channels of a sound reinforcement system control console are called the "mains," as opposed to the MONITOR output channels.

Make Before Break A type of selector switch that momentarily connects the moving contact, or "wiper," to two of the fixed contacts as it is moved from one position to the next. This is also called a "shorting" type of switch. Most multiposition switches used in audio for step attenuators or for switching between various signal sources, etc., are shorting switches because the output circuit is never left completely disconnected from an input, and no clicks or other noise are induced in the output circuit as the switch is moved.

Marry Unlike videotaping, motion picture sound and picture editing are handled separately. Synchronized viewing during editing is handled by devices that synchronize picture and sound elements. When both elements are done, they are both copied onto film prints that combine the picture and sound into the single film format playable in theaters. It is said that the elements have been married into the release print. *See also* DOUBLE SYSTEM SOUND; MOVIOLA.

Masking Masking is a subjective phenomenon wherein the presence of one sound will inhibit our ability to hear another sound. We all know that we usually don't hear softer sounds in the presence of louder ones, but the precise description of how our ears perform masking is very complex.

At mid-frequencies, a loud PURE TONE of a particular PITCH is much more effective in masking softer high-pitched tones than it is in masking lower-pitched tones. However, at very low frequencies (30 Hz to 60 Hz approximately), such as those produced by certain pipe organ pedal stops, very little masking occurs even though the level of the FUNDAMENTAL may be very high. These stops must be very strong to be heard at all because our hearing threshold is so high at these low frequencies, and this seems to affect the masking phenomenon.

Almost all experimental studies of masking have used pure tones as test signals, and the masking of COMPLEX TONES by other complex tones is a much more difficult and complicated study. It is not necessarily true that one can extrapolate, or sum up, the pure tone masking data and come up with meaningful complex tone masking information. The study of the masking of musical instruments by one another is a wide open field that should be addressed more fully.

It is also possible for a sound to be masked by a sound that occurs slightly earlier than the masked sound, and this is called forward masking, or forward auditory inhibition. The existence of auditory backward inhibition, where an earlier sound is masked by a later-arriving sound, has been reported by Georg von Békésy, but others have had difficulty in reproducing his results.

Master A GAIN control on a sound reinforcement or recording console that controls the level of a mixture of signals whose levels have been controlled by the mixing pots (*See* POTENTIOMETER). A console will have a master gain control for each output signal. The control itself is actually an ATTENUATOR, so it really can only decrease the level of a signal fed into it. The gain, or amplification, occurs before it goes through the control.

Mastering During the time when the vinyl phonograph disc was king, mastering was the common term used for the process of transferring the musical SIGNAL from a MAGNETIC TAPE (usually called a "master tape") to an ACETATE master disc. It is the first step in the manufacture of phonograph records from tapes. Mastering is fraught with pitfalls and complications, and is thought by many to be as much an art as it is a science. The edited tape from which the acetate is cut is called the master tape. It could be an original recording, but more often it is a copy of original tapes. The person performing the task is called a Mastering Engineer.

The advent of the CD has changed the technology and techniques used to record, edit, and make recordings. The work of the modern mastering engineer consists of completing the final changes to the elements in a recording to make a finished product. This can include anything from taking raw separate tracks and mixing, equalizing, limiting, adding reverberation, compressing, etc., into the final product, usually a CD. Many artists rely on famous mastering engineers to create their finished recordings, considering them the final "GOLDEN EARS." *See also* EDITING.

Mastering Lathe A precision turntable and cutting head assembly for the cutting of audio signals onto an "ACETATE" disc, even though the disc is not made of acetate. The movement of the cutting STYLUS over the acetate determines the groove spacing or "PITCH" of the disc. Most records are cut with "variable pitch" in order to squeeze more time on the record. The pitch is larger when loud bass-heavy music is being recorded, and is smaller in softer passages. The depth of the groove on the disc is also adjustable. These functions are performed by the pitch and depth control computer that controls the depth, width, and spacing of grooves being cut. The finished acetate is also sometimes called a "lacquer master," even though it is not made of lacquer either.

Master Tape In the audio business, the master tape is the original medium the SIGNAL is recorded on, while video editors call the master tape the composite edited video, made by intercutting the video from multiple source tapes. It has been said that this is not the only mysterious behavior practiced by video editors.

Matching When one AUDIO device, such as a PREAMPLIFIER or EQUALIZER, is connected to another, they are said to be matched if the resistive part of the OUTPUT IMPEDANCE of the first is equal to that of the other. More correctly, the impedances, not the devices, are matched. (Strictly speaking, it is only the real, or resistive, parts of the impedances that are matched, but in common parlance, the impedances are said to be matched.)

Much confusion exists about IMPEDANCE matching. While it is true that from a theoretical standpoint the power transferred in a CIRCUIT is maximized if the impedances are matched, there are many reasons why this is not desired in practice. The main reason is that efficiency is more important than maximum power transfer.

Consider the flashlight BATTERY, which is not a battery at all, but a CELL. It can be thought of as a VOLTAGE source in series with a RESISTOR; in other words, it has RESISTANCE, just as any electrical conductor has. If a resistor equal in value to the battery's internal resistance (probably less than 1 OHM) is connected across the battery, the power transfer will be maximum. This means the energy per unit time will be maximized. But one-half of the power will be wasted in heating up the battery because of its internal resistance. This means that only one-half of the energy in the battery can be extracted. If, on the other hand, a much larger resistor is placed across the battery, most of the power will be dissipated in the resistor and only a little in the battery because power equals the square of CURRENT times the resistance. Thus, if the resistance ratio is 100, there will be 100 times more energy extracted from the battery than will be wasted in heating the battery. This is the reason batteries are made with the lowest possible internal resistance and they are not designed to have matched loads connected to them. The same argument applies to most audio equipment, especially power AMPLIFIERS.

There are instances where impedances in audio circuits should be matched, but they are relatively uncommon. One example is the transmission of audio over very long lines, such as long-distance telephone lines. The reason is not to maximize the power, but rather to prevent reflections from the ends of the line. If a SIGNAL traveling down a line many hundreds of miles long meets a sudden change in impedance, part of it will be reflected, just as light is partially reflected when it encounters a pane of glass. The reflected signal is then heard at the other end of the line as an ECHO. The signal travels down the line at a speed less than the speed of light, but is still very fast. At audio frequencies, if the line is short, the reflection occurs so near to the time the signal left the source that it cannot be heard or measured at all.

The situation is different with very high frequencies such as television signals. Here, the WAVELENGTH is short compared to the distance traveled, and reflections cause the visual "ghosts" familiar to television viewers. The wavelengths of audio signals on transmission lines are many miles long, so no trouble exists until the lines get comparably long.

In almost all audio equipment, the output impedances are made much lower than the corresponding INPUT IMPEDANCES, and efficiencies are high. There is no valid reason for matching impedances when the distances between devices are short, but there exist engineers (usually from the broadcast or telephone industry) who insist otherwise.

The term matching is also used as a descriptor for the pairing of microphones or loudspeakers with nearly identical characteristics. The pairs are then called "matched pairs," and in many instances are available from manufacturers already matched. Monitoring loudspeakers used in mastering studios should be matched and microphones used for stereo recording should also be matched.

Matrix, Matrixing The LINEAR mixing of two or more SIGNAL channels at specific AMPLITUDES and PHASES to form two or more new signals is called matrixing. These new signals can be combined in similar ways to recover the original signals. The circuit TOPOLOGY used for matrixing is called a matrix.

It is important to note that matrixing is a linear addition, or mixing, of signals, and is not the same as MODULATION. There are many ways in which audio signals are matrixed. One of the most common is the way stereo signals are broadcast over FM radio: the two stereo channels, L and R (for left and right), are added together to form a sum signal L + R. Then they are subtracted to form a difference signal L – R. The sum signal is the MONAURAL or in-PHASE part of the STEREO signal, while the difference is the stereo or out-of-phase portion of the signal. All the directional information is in the difference signal.

In the stereo FM transmitter, the sum signal is used to MODULATE the CARRIER directly. The difference signal is used to modulate a 38-KILOHERTZ "subcarrier," which is then mixed with the sum signal before it modulates the carrier. Thus the carrier is actually modulated with a combination of the sum signal and the 38-kHz subcarrier. If this FM transmission is received by a monaural FM set, the 38-kHz carrier is ignored, while the sum signal (L + R) is recovered. The listener then hears the summation of the two stereo channels. The FM stereo receiver, on the other hand, also recovers the 38-kHz subcarrier and demodulates it to recover the difference signal (L – R), which contains the stereo information. Then, to recover the original stereo signals, the sum and difference signals are matrixed:

$$(L + R) + (L - R) = 2L, \text{ and}$$
$$(L + R) - (L - R) = 2R$$

The purpose of this entire exercise is simply to enable monaural FM receivers to pick up both channels of the stereo signal.

Another example of matrixing is the combination of two rear-channel signals with two front channels for quadraphonic recording. The two rear channels are PHASE SHIFTED, respectively, plus 90 degrees and minus 90 degrees, and are then mixed with the left and right stereo signals. This composite signal is then recorded onto the stereo disc. On playback, the signals are matrixed again with proper phase shifting to recover the rear channels. This technique was used in the so-called QS and SQ quadraphonic systems. Incidentally, the demise of QUADRAPHONIC SOUND had little if anything to do with the matrixing of the signals and consequent lack of "discreteness" of the four signals. *See also* AMBISONICS.

Matrixing is also used to obtain left and right stereo signals from the mid and side channels of the M-S STEREO recording system. A common misconception is that the M-S technique is the only one in which the width of the stereo image can be varied. (This is done by controlling the level of the M (mid) signal compared to the S (side) channel.) Any stereo signal, regardless of which MICROPHONE technique is used, can be manipulated the same way. The sum and difference signals are obtained as in FM broadcasting, and the level of the difference signal is varied before being rematrixed to obtain the left and right signals. As the difference is reduced, the stereo separation, or "width" of the stereo image, will decrease, and vice versa. Incidentally, a CIRCUIT that does this double matrixing and level controlling is sometimes called a shuffler circuit, and it was first described by Alan BLUMLEIN.

In THREE-STEP PROCESSING in the manufacture of records, the MOTHER is sometimes called the matrix.

Maximum-Length Sequence, MLS An electronically generated test signal that has a flat energy-versus-frequency curve over a wide FREQUENCY range. The signal resembles WHITE NOISE in this respect, but it is actually periodic, with a relatively long period, or a very slow repetition rate. The period may be as much as several seconds, and in general, the longer the period, the more uniformly the energy in the signal will be distributed in frequency. Because the signal looks and sounds like random noise, it is sometimes called pseudorandom noise. True random noise has a random distribution of amplitudes as well as frequency, but pseudorandom noise does not; that is, it has a low CREST FACTOR. The maximum-length sequence is generated by a digital process, and the signal looks like a SQUARE WAVE with a random placement of the zero crossings. The name "maximum-length sequence" is a bit of a misnomer, because the actual length of the sequence can be just about anything.

The maximum-length sequence, in conjunction with a two-channel FFT ANALYZER, is often used as a test signal for measuring the FREQUENCY RESPONSE of various devices such as loudspeakers and other transducers. *See also* DECONVOLUTION.

Maximum Output Level, MOL For an audio device such as an ANALOG tape recorder or cassette recorder, the MOL is generally taken to mean the output signal level that results in 3% HARMONIC DISTORTION at low frequencies and usually 3% INTERMODULATION DISTORTION at high frequencies. Any higher signal output than the MOL will result in rapidly increasing DISTORTION. The MOL is not an absolute level in the sense of a known voltage or power level but is a function of the device itself and also a function of frequency. The MOL of a recording device is dependent on the type of tape used, and frequently different tapes are evaluated by comparing their MOLs when used on a particular machine. The shape of the curve of the MOL plotted against frequency is a meaningful characteristic of a device such as a tape recorder, and it depends on many factors, including PRE-EMPHASIS and DE-EMPHASIS. To achieve maximum SIGNAL-TO-NOISE RATIO, a device or system should have an MOL curve with the same shape as the curve of the maximum peak voltage level versus frequency of the signal it passes. The maximum peak voltage level of a music signal depends on the music but generally is lower at high frequencies than at mid and low frequencies. *See also* NAB EQUALIZATION.

MC Phono Input A set of input terminals of a PREAMPLIFIER designed to accept the SIGNAL from a MOVING COIL phono CARTRIDGE is called an MC phono input. This distinguishes it from the previously established ordinary phono input designed for a MOVING MAGNET CARTRIDGE, which takes a much higher input voltage and has a different INPUT IMPEDANCE and capacitance.

MDM *See* MODULAR DIGITAL MULTITRACK.

Mel The mel is the psychological unit of PITCH. One thousand mels is defined as the pitch of a 1,000-HERTZ PURE TONE whose LOUDNESS level is 40 PHONS. A pitch judged "twice as high" would be 2,000 mels, and a pitch "three times as high" would be 3,000 mels, etc.

This unit is completely foreign to musicians, to whom the concepts of "twice as high," etc., are meaningless, and it is seldom used, even by the psychologists!

Mercury Cell A type of dry cell using zinc, mercury, and potassium hydroxide as the active elements. It has a fairly long shelf life and very good voltage REGULATION, that is, its VOLTAGE remains high until it is exhausted. It is likely to explode if recharged.

Metadata Parameters sent along with a particular data transmission, as opposed to the actual data carried in the transmission. These data parameters usually include type of CODEC being used, number of channels, channel format, type of data encryption, etc. In DOLBY DIGITAL, "metadata" specifically refers to the parameters that travel alongside the audio in the Dolby Digital stream as auxiliary data. The metadata here provide scalable decoding information about the audio that can be interpreted in different ways by different receivers, allowing a producer to tailor a program's mix to the playback environment without requiring the medium to store multiple versions, e.g., a 5.1 mix and a stereo mix. Not to be confused with Metadata™, a trademark owned by the Metadata Corp.

Metal Particle Tape A type of magnetic tape, mostly used in the better quality cassettes, that uses microscopic particles of iron rather than iron oxide as the magnetic medium. Metal tape is capable of much better performance than oxide tape, especially at high frequencies, but it requires different EQUALIZATION and BIAS. The improvement in quality is most pronounced at low tape speeds, and this is the reason it is seen most often in cassettes.

Metal particle tape or metal evaporated tape is also used in video recording, such as Hi-8 video cassettes and most digital audio recording.

Meter An audio level indicating device; *see* VU METER and PPM. Also the SI unit of length, equal to the length of the path traveled by light in a vacuum during 1/299,792,458 of a second. In music, meter also means the number of beats contained in each measure.

Meter Bridge The area of a mixing console that holds the audio level indicating devices, usually at the top of the mixer. Meters are sometimes an option; hence, the entire assembly holding the meters may bridge the width of the mixer. Even if the meters are integral, the area is usually called a meter bridge anyway.

Metrology The science of precision measurement. Not to be confused with meteorology, the science of weather.

Mho Archaic term for the unit of CONDUCTANCE. It represents the reciprocal of RESISTANCE, and this is the reason for the spelling—OHM backwards. The modern unit for conductance is the siemens.

Mic Abbreviation for microphone. *Mike* is also seen.

Mic Cable *See* MICROPHONE CABLE.

Mic Flag A little sign containing a network or station identification logo clamped to a microphone used in TV broadcasting and press conferences. Used as a bit of "subtle" advertising.

Microbar Originally, the microbar was defined as a pressure of one millionth of 1 atmosphere, or 1.013 dynes per square centimeter. The standard atmosphere, or BAR, is defined as the average air pressure at sea level at 45 degrees latitude, and is equal to 1.033 kilograms force per square centimeter. The new SI definition sets the bar at exactly 10 newtons per square meter, and thus the microbar became 1 dyne per square centimeter, or .1 pascal.

Microgroove In 1948, the Columbia Records division of the Columbia Broadcasting System introduced the 33⅓-RPM phonograph record, which had grooves designed to be traced with a STYLUS of .001-inch radius. The existing standard at the time was the 78.26-rpm record with grooves of .003-inch tip radius. Columbia established the trademark "LP microgroove" for the system, which quickly set a new standard for the future of commercial recordings. It was not a new idea, however, for the 33⅓-rpm speed had been used for years for radio transcriptions, and Thomas Edison had introduced a long-playing record system with extremely fine grooves before 1929. Edison's LP record played for 20 minutes per side at a speed of 80 rpm!

Microphone An electroacoustic device that delivers an electric SIGNAL when actuated by a sound. A microphone consists of an acoustic system that supplies mechanical (acoustic) energy to a TRANSDUCER, which converts the energy into electrical energy.

Microphones are classified by their acoustical parameters, by their method of transduction, and by their directional characteristics, or POLAR PATTERNS, forming a fairly complex hierarchy. Acoustically, microphones are classed as PRESSURE or PRESSURE GRADIENT or a combination of the two. Within these classes, microphones can have various types of transducing elements, including CARBON, CONDENSER, CRYSTAL, DYNAMIC (or MOVING COIL), and RIBBON.

Microphones of all these classes can have a variety of directional characteristics, or polar patterns. These include OMNIDIRECTIONAL, CARDIOID, FIGURE-8, SUPER-CARDIOID, HYPER-CARDIOID, and SHOTGUN.

For more detail, see each of these headings and also PZM; ELECTRET MICROPHONE; SOUND FIELD MICROPHONE; PARABOLIC MICROPHONE; and LINE MICROPHONE.

Microphone Cable Cable has more than one CONDUCTOR, whereas wire has only one conductor. The common professional microphone cable will have two, three, or four signal wires inside of a SHIELD and then an outer jacket. Good microphone cable should be durable but flexible and have low resistance and capacitance. The wires used should have many fine strands for flexibility and to resist breakage. The insulating materials should resist age, chemicals, and soldering heat. The shield should be tightly braided wires, or one or two spiral layers of wires. Such cable is meant to be flexed and as such, should not have foil shields employed except in fixed cable installations.

Microphone Preamplifier The signal from a microphone is relatively low in level, and the AMPLIFIER that first amplifies it must be carefully designed. One consideration with such small signals is low NOISE level. The preamp usually has a DIFFERENTIAL input able to handle a BALANCED signal to prevent the addition of externally induced noise. This used to be attained by placing an input TRANSFORMER at the preamp input. The transformer allows the line to be balanced, but also allows a step-up in VOLTAGE, giving voltage GAIN without adding significant noise. Most input transformers have a turns ratio of about 10, giving a gain of 20 DECIBELS. This transformer requires careful design also. It should have a large primary INDUCTANCE to prevent loading the microphone unduly at low frequencies, and it must have a wide FREQUENCY RESPONSE. It also must be well shielded against stray magnetic fields to prevent pickup of 60-HERTZ HUM.

Today most high-quality preamps use balanced circuits without transformers and are designed for extremely low noise levels and distortion.

Microphonics Some components in audio devices are sensitive to vibration in the sense that they act like MICROPHONES. An example is some vacuum TUBES, which, when thumped, cause a tinkling sound to be added to the SIGNAL. SOLID-STATE devices are much less prone to microphonics, but TRANSDUCERS, such as phono CARTRIDGES, can be very microphonic. Some AUDIO cables, such as MICROPHONE CABLES, can also add noise to the signal when they are vibrated. Audio cable noise is correctly called triboelectric noise, which is noise induced in a capacitor if the dielectric (insulator) is deformed. Audio cables consist of insulated and shielded wires, and are thus miniature capacitors, making them susceptible to triboelectric noise.

Microprocessor A digital INTEGRATED CIRCUIT, or "chip," that is the heart of a small computer or calculator. Working under the control of a program stored in the digital memory, the microprocessor does all the mathematical operations needed in the computer. Microprocessors are so fast and flexible in operation and so inexpensive that they are used in many audio applications, from the control circuits in CD players to electronic music synthesizers.

The first true microprocessor was the type 4004 made by Intel and introduced in 1972.

MIDI The Musical Instrument Digital Interface is a digital protocol originally designed in 1983 for use between electronic music synthesizers of various manufacture. With MIDI, musical performance information is transferred as computer data commands, rather than transferring actual sound files. There is a long list of commands meant to direct devices to convey nuances of performed music. Since 1983, MIDI has evolved into a diverse tool for creating, editing, and performing music and sounds, and even sound generation for PC games, show control for theatrical devices such as lights, recording studio equipment controllers, and even ring tones for mobile phones.

In the basic music setup, several instruments can be connected on the MIDI, and this can allow the keyboard on one to control the generation of sounds on the others. This was the original purpose for the MIDI. A MIDI-equipped instrument has a MIDI-in and a MIDI-out, each a 5-pin DIN connector. The standard allows for the control of sixteen different devices and functions at the same time. (Actually, the control is not simultaneous, for the MIDI is a serial port, controlling the functions in rapid sequence. But it is fast enough that it sounds like simultaneous control.) The MIDI can also be used to interface certain computers to electronic musical instruments, and can thus be used to transmit voices and musical sequences stored in digital form. It also can be used to transcribe musical notation via the computer, and as such, editing a performance is much like word processing.

The use of a MIDI-controlled synthesizer rather than sampled audio files from a computer has the advantage that far less data need be processed, transmitted, and stored. High-quality audio files, such as .WAV files, require large amounts of disc storage space, however the availability of hard drives with many gibibytes of space instead of mebibytes has partly nullified this advantage. A MIDI-controlled synthesizer usually needs less than 10 kibibytes of code to generate each minute of resulting sound. The MIDI code only needs to tell the synthesizer how to produce the wanted sounds.

The figure below shows a simple three-voice MIDI system. The MIDI Sequencer is a device that stores information about a series of keystrokes and saves it in memory. It then can store similar information about another series of keystrokes, etc. Then, on command, the sequencer will send the information to the synthesizers at the same time resulting in three separate

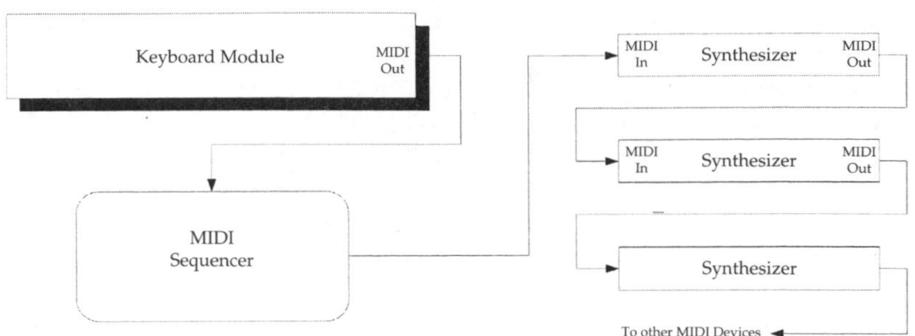

A Three-Voice MIDI System

parts being played at once. More synthesizers and other MIDI-controlled devices can be added to increase the number and complexity of the resulting sounds.

The greater MIDI world is large, diverse, and beyond the scope of this book.

The MIDI Manufacturer's Association, or MMA, is an organization of companies that produce MIDI-controlled devices and is in charge of maintaining and updating the MIDI specification. It has done an impressive job of it over the last 20 years of MIDI existence. The MMA web site <www.midi.org> is a gold mine of information, both technical and practical.

Mid-Range The frequency span of the middle of the audio range. The mid-range is usually considered to be from about 200 HERTZ to 2,000 Hz or so. Most of any music signal is in the mid-range, and because this range is the easiest to reproduce with audio equipment, it is sometimes neglected from the standpoints of DISTORTION and smoothness of FREQUENCY RESPONSE, especially in loudspeaker systems.

Mid-Range Smear A type of sonic degradation in an audio system that is the result of nonlinearities in the equipment interacting with the broad band of frequencies present in music to produce a veil of distortion products throughout the mid-range. It is difficult to test a device for mid-range smear, but the innovative SPECTRAL CONTAMINATION measurement invented by the late Deane Jensen and W. Gary Sokolich seems to correlate well with listening tests.

Mike *See* MIC.

Mil Thousandth of an inch. Recording tape thickness is measured in mils, the most common size being 1½ mils. One-mil tape allows 50 percent more recording time per reel, but suffers from higher levels of PRINT-THROUGH and is not as stable mechanically. Some tapes, most notably those found in CASSETTES, are thinner than 1 mil.

Mil Spec Short for Military Specification, an item that meets official U.S. military contract terms. This is supposed to indicate the highest quality, and is sometimes seen referring to electronic components. Such parts are expensive, and usually not worth it, so commercial grade parts are more commonly used. There are Mil Specs for everything the military uses, from toothbrushes to cheese.

MiniDisc, MD A digital format developed by Sony that uses a 64-mm diameter, magneto-optical rewritable disc in a thin rectangular plastic carrier. Their so-called ATRAC CODEC (Adaptive Transform Acoustic Coding) samples at 44.1 kHz but compresses the data to fit up to 80 minutes of stereo audio onto the small disc. The codec has continued to evolve and is now at "ATRAC3-plus," which also includes reduced FIDELITY LP2 (2X long play, or 160 minutes) and LP4 modes (320 minutes). The format was apparently intended to replace the ANALOG cassette tape. U.S. consumers do not seem to have completely embraced the format, although it is popular in the legitimate theater for sound effects and radio stations. Commercial prerecorded MD releases (rare in the U.S.) use an optical-only playback format and are not recordable. *See also* CODEC.

Minimalist Techniques Term applied to selection of MICROPHONES for classical STEREO recording. A minimalist, or purist, will always use the smallest possible number of microphones to make a recording; this means only two, if at all possible.

The use of multiple microphones for stereo recording has become standard for popular music when there is no desire to reproduce in the listening room the sonic event that happened in the recording studio. The recording is the musical event, and the mixing of microphones and SIGNAL processing techniques is justified.

But for classical music, it is usually desirable to reproduce the sound of a concert hall in the listening room, and this is best done without complex mixing and signal processing. The most natural sounding recordings are usually the ones made with the simplest microphone configuration.

This is not to imply that minimalists agree on what the simplest setup consists of, however. Some recording engineers insist on COINCIDENT MICROPHONES and some swear by spaced-apart microphones. Some insist on directional microphones, whether or not they are coincident or spaced, and some will only use OMNIDIRECTIONAL microphones.

Minimum Audible Field, MAF The same as the THRESHOLD OF HEARING when measured under FREE-FIELD conditions. The threshold of hearing is traditionally measured by presenting the subject with the test sounds via earphones, but it has been found that the differences in the physiology of different subjects result in differing SOUND PRESSURE LEVELS at the eardrum due to unpredictable reflections within the ear canal, PINNA, and earphone. Thresholds measured under free-field conditions are considered more accurate, although much more difficult to determine because of the extremely quiet surroundings required.

Miniplug A common audio plug 3.5 mm in diameter, used for portable stereo headphones and other consumer audio connections. It is a smaller version of the common ¼-inch phone plug. The TRS form is the most common, used for stereo, but TS versions exist. It mates with the minijack.

Mix In the production of a commercial recording, the result of the MIXDOWN is often called the "mix." Also a verb meaning to perform a mixdown.

Mixdown In an ANALOG recording studio, mixdown is the recording of a two-track master tape by mixing the reproduce outputs of several tracks from one or more multitrack tape recorders.

Most studio recordings are made with multitrack recorders to allow the performers and the record producer flexibility. Often each instrument in an ensemble will be recorded on its own track. Then, the relative BALANCE and TIMBRE of the instrument can be manipulated by SIGNAL processing devices while being mixed into the composite, or master, recording.

Frequently as many as twenty-four or more separate tracks are used in a MIX, and it becomes impossible for one person to handle all these volume controls simultaneously while the master is being recorded. In order to facilitate this step, some recording consoles provide automation, or AUTOMATED MIXDOWN, as it is sometimes called. In this type of automation, the volume settings versus time of all the controls are "memorized" by the console and are controlled as the tape is being replayed. The tape may be repeatedly played with different settings to refine the overall effect, after which the master is recorded.

Today (2004) most mixdown is done with DAWS using software such as ProTools, but many engineers still use large format automated consoles (or digital ones).

Mixer Either a device that allows several signals to be combined into a single SIGNAL or a person who operates the console controls during a MIXDOWN.

Portable mixers for combining the outputs of several microphones are common and are used extensively in REMOTE recordings. They will contain a PREAMPLIFIER for each MICROPHONE input, individual GAIN controls for each input channel, a master gain control, and a LOW-IMPEDANCE output CIRCUIT to feed the signal into a control console or recording device. More complex mixing units that also contain EQUALIZATION are usually called recording consoles or "boards."

MLP, Meridian Lossless Packing A lossless audio coding scheme developed by Meridian Audio Ltd. MLP has been selected as the optional coding scheme for use on DVD-Audio, as well as other transmission, storage and archiving applications. It is a true lossless coding technology, in that the recovered audio is bit-for bit identical to the original. Unlike perceptual or lossy data reduction, MLP does not alter the final decoded signal in any way, but merely "packs" the audio data more efficiently into a smaller data rate for transmission or storage. It is simple to decode and requires relatively low computational power for playback.[20]

MM Phono Input A set of input terminals of a PREAMPLIFIER designed to accept the SIGNAL from a MOVING MAGNET phono CARTRIDGE. For many years this was the most common type of phono input on a stereo system.

---

20. Thanks to Dennis Bohn, Rane Corp.

The input IMPEDANCE was standardized at 47 kohms, and RIAA PHONO EQUALIZATION was applied to the signal. GAIN was much higher than on a similar LINE LEVEL input such as aux. *See also* MC PHONO INPUT.

Modular Digital Multitrack, MDM A multitrack digital audio recording system that records digital audio data onto a videocasette using a rotating drum in the same manner as a DAT or video recorder. MDMs are expandable by locking together up to 16 MDM modules for 128 tracks. There are two popular MDM standards: the Alesis ADAT and compatibles which record on S-VHS tape, and the Tascam DA-88 and compatibles, which record on Hi-8 video tape. Other examples of MDMs include the Akai A-DAM, and Yamaha DMR8/DRU8. Also called a modular recorder.

Modular Synthesizer See SYNTHESIZER.

Modulation *See* AMPLITUDE MODULATION and FREQUENCY MODULATION.

Modulation Index In AMPLITUDE MODULATION, the modulation index is the ratio (expressed by a percentage) of the peak AMPLITUDE of the modulating signal to the peak amplitude of the CARRIER. If the modulation index is 100%, the carrier will be turned completely off at the negative peaks of the modulating WAVEFORM.

In the case of FREQUENCY MODULATION, the modulation index is the ratio (again expressed in a percentage) of the frequency deviation to the actual frequency of the modulating signal. The frequency deviation is the difference between the frequency of the unmodulated carrier and the maximum higher or lower frequency it will reach when being modulated.

In each case, the modulation index is proportional to the amplitude of the modulating signal.

Amplitude modulation greater than 100% produces asymmetrical CLIPPING, and large amounts of harmonic distortion. This is sometimes called "splatter" in AM broadcasting.

The frequency modulation index can be much greater than 100%, however, and some electronic music synthesizers use this "deep modulation" to attain complex musical waveforms. One of the first commercial applications of this technique was in the Synclavier, made by New England Digital Corporation.

Modulation Noise Noise that is present only in company with a SIGNAL is called modulation noise. In ANALOG tape recorders, the recording process has a certain "granularity" due to the fact that the magnetic characteristics of the tape are not completely uniform. The magnetic domains are of finite size. A recorded signal has an irregularity that sounds like the addition of noise.

In DIGITAL audio systems, there is also an uncertainty in the level of the signal because of QUANTIZATION in the ANALOG-TO-DIGITAL CONVERTER. This uncertainty also sounds like added noise and is not present if the signal is not present.

Modulation Wheel A modulation wheel is a hand-operated wheel usually at the left side of a keyboard. When rotated, it causes a change in an effect such as VIBRATO. It's effect is programmable by the user.

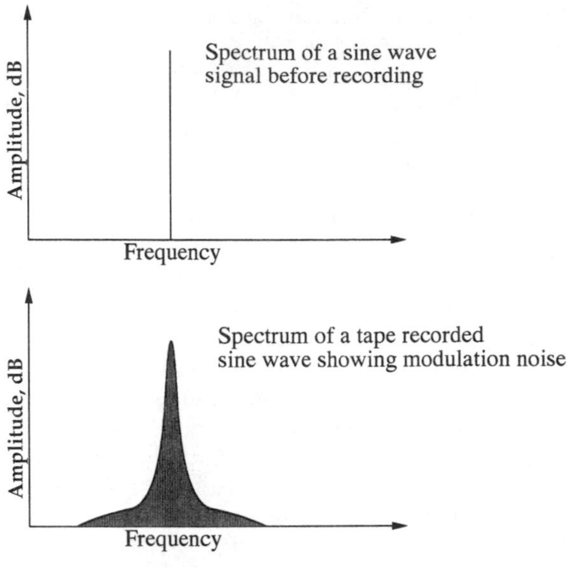

Modulation Noise

Modulometer A meter, similar to the VU meter in appearance, that responds to the PEAK signal level rather than the average level.

The modulometer is a better choice for a tape recorder than a VU meter because short peaks in the signal can easily saturate the tape but still not be detected by the VU meter, which has a much slower response time. This is especially true in DIGITAL tape recorders, where any OVERLOAD, even momentarily, results in hard CLIPPING and DISTORTION.

Many modern metering systems for tape recorders do not have any moving parts at all, substituting instead a series of small lights that provide an animated display of the signal level. Most of these units show the peak level as well as the average level.

MOL *See* MAXIMUM OUTPUT LEVEL.

Mole A large number of small components such as atoms, molecules, electrons, etc. The mole is quantitatively equal to 6.02214×10^{23}, a very large number indeed, which is also known as Avogadro's number. It is defined as the number of atoms in 0.012 kilograms of carbon, which is the number of atoms in a mass of carbon in grams equal to its atomic number. The mole unit is most useful in chemistry, where it simplifies calculations in chemical reactions, but it is sometimes used by computer equipment designers and engineers who talk about moles of bits or bytes.

Monaural Literally, "one hearing." Monaural refers to a sound system with only one channel, regardless of the number of LOUDSPEAKERS used, as opposed to STEREOPHONIC, which must employ more than one independent channel.

Monitor Originally, monitor referred to a LOUDSPEAKER in the control booth of a recording studio or sound reinforcement system that allowed the operators to hear the programs they were controlling.

In more recent times, the term has been used by stage performers to mean the loudspeaker or loudspeakers placed on the stage to allow them to better hear themselves. A better term for this is FOLDBACK.

Monitor Mix A mixed signal in a sound reinforcement console that is sent to the MONITOR speakers on the stage. Because the monitors are near the microphones, this signal is usually highly EQUALIZED to reduce the tendency for acoustic FEEDBACK. A modern mixing console can produce several monitor mixes for use by different performers on stage. Sometimes, a mixing console is dedicated only to monitor mixes. *See also* FOH.

Mono *See* MONAURAL.

Mono Bus A mixing BUS in a recording console that generates a single-channel, or MONAURAL, signal for use with a single-channel tape recorder or a broadcast feed. Most modern consoles have a mono output independent from the regular stereo outputs.

Mono Compatibility The ability of a STEREO musical SIGNAL to be mixed into a single MONAURAL channel without violence to the TIMBRE of the signal. The result of the MIX of two stereo channels would ideally sound like a signal that was recorded with a single microphone.

Mono compatibility is a matter of degree and never can be perfect, for any two signals when mixed will contain FREQUENCY components that will sometimes partially cancel due to the relative PHASE angles between them. Stereo recorded with widely spaced microphones (A-B STEREO) has relatively poor mono compatibility because of the large time differences in the two channels. At low frequencies, these time differences can easily amount to 180 degrees of PHASE SHIFT causing almost complete cancellation when mixed. It might seem that at high frequencies the problem would be worse, but actually the phase differences are so very great and so complex that they are nearly random, and when mixed, the result is very close to the original SPECTRUM.

One way to increase mono compatibility is to arrange things so the lowest frequencies of the two channels are in phase with each other. This can be done by placing the bass instruments in the center of the stereo spread; in other words, making them monaural rather than stereo. Another way is to use COINCIDENT MICROPHONE recording techniques, which automatically prevent large phase differences at low frequencies.

There are several reasons why mono compatibility is desirable. The most important is that the signals are easier to cut onto a stereo phonograph record. This is because out-of-phase signals are represented by vertical motion of the STYLUS, which is limited by geometric considerations. Another reason is for FM broadcasting of stereo in case the listeners have only monaural radios.

The need for mono compatibility is much less today that it was 20 years ago. The COMPACT DISC has no requirement for uniform phase of the signals at low frequencies, and stereo broadcasts are seldom heard over monaural radios, especially where high quality of low-frequency reproduction is attained.

Monotic Literally, "with one ear." Generally refers to a sound presentation where only one ear hears the sound (e.g., sound through a headphone).

MOS Film or video being shot without sound. Legend has it that it stands for "Mit Out Sound," which was supposedly spoken by early German moviemakers in Hollywood. Pronounce each letter separately, EM-O-ESS.

MOSFET *See* FIELD EFFECT TRANSISTOR.

Mother In the three-step processing technique for making phonograph records, the mother (a metal replica of the ACETATE) is the second step, from which the STAMPERS are made. *See* PROCESSING.

Motional Feedback A type of mechanical NEGATIVE FEEDBACK where the actual motion of the CONE of a low-frequency LOUDSPEAKER is used to generate a signal that is fed back to the AMPLIFIER. The motion of the cone itself is then inside the FEEDBACK loop, and DISTORTION can be significantly reduced. The technique was first described and patented by the Englishman P. G. A. H. Voight in 1924. This actually predates the invention of electrical negative feedback in amplifiers by H. Black of Bell Telephone Laboratories. Motional feedback is suited for use only at low frequencies, usually below 500 hertz.

For motional feedback, some method of sensing the cone motion must be used, and this motion must be converted or transduced into a VOLTAGE fed to the amplifier. There are many possibilities here, and many different systems have been tried over the years. Suitable TRANSDUCERS can sense the displacement, the velocity, or the acceleration of the cone. One of the simplest is simply another coil next to or on top of the VOICE COIL. This coil will have a signal induced in it proportional to the velocity of the cone, but it will also have another signal induced in it by transformer action from the voice coil itself. Various schemes have been devised to separate these two components electrically.

Another possibility is the use of a PIEZOELECTRIC accelerometer attached to the cone. This provides a signal proportional to the acceleration of the cone, and this can be converted to a velocity signal by electrical integration. This method is relatively costly and complex, but it has been used commercially.

In all motional feedback schemes, great care must be exercised to ensure that the system is stable. This means that PHASE SHIFT between the drive signal and the feedback signal must be accurately controlled.

Motional Impedance The impedance of a dynamic loudspeaker's VOICE COIL is made up of two parts: the electrical impedance of the coil of wire itself (the BLOCKED IMPEDANCE) and the impedance caused by the motion of the moving parts of the speaker, or motional impedance. As the coil moves in response to an applied VOLTAGE, it will have induced in it a BACK EMF, which opposes the applied voltage. This back EMF effectively increases the electrical impedance, especially when the coil is free to move easily, such as at RESONANCES. It is thus possible to learn a good deal about the moving parts of a loudspeaker by studying the curve of impedance versus FREQUENCY.

Motor Boating A low-frequency oscillation caused by certain types of instability, usually in a POWER AMPLIFIER. The name comes from the characteristic plop-plop sound it produces when heard on a loudspeaker.

Moving Coil Cartridge A phonograph CARTRIDGE that uses two tiny coils of wire connected to the STYLUS assembly as SIGNAL generating elements is a moving coil cartridge. The coils are in a magnetic field, and are caused to move by the motion of the stylus in the groove, this motion inducing the signal VOLTAGE in them.

Some of the earliest types of phono pickups were of the moving coil design, but the MOVING MAGNET types almost completely replaced them when stereo records were introduced. Moving coil cartridges are characterized by very high price, very low output voltage, low DISTORTION, and extended high-FREQUENCY RESPONSE resulting from a very high RESONANT frequency due to light weight of the moving parts. Sometimes this high-frequency response is a negative quality factor because the resonant PEAK in the response, usually at from 30 to 50 KILOHERTZ, effectively amplifies the ULTRASONIC noise present in the record groove.

Although the noise is above audibility in frequency, INTERMODULATION DISTORTION in the preamplifier will result in added noise in the audible range. For this reason, moving coils generally sound worse than other types when used with less than excellent-quality preamps. The old adage that the most money should be spent on the TRANSDUCERS in a sound system is contradicted in this case.

The SENSITIVITY of MC cartridges is usually less than 200 microvolts RMS per centimeter per second of recorded velocity. They should be terminated in less than 10,000 OHMS, sometimes much less.

Moving Magnet Cartridge The most common type of phonograph CARTRIDGE is the so-called moving magnet type. It has a small magnet connected to the STYLUS assembly, and motion of this magnet causes a VOLTAGE to be induced in coils of wire that are nearby. This voltage constitutes the SIGNAL output of the cartridge.

Moving magnet cartridges are relatively inexpensive, and have acceptable FREQUENCY RESPONSE and output signal level, and they have been very popular for many years. Their high-frequency response is somewhat sensitive to the electrical INPUT IMPEDANCE of the PREAMPLIFIER they are connected to. Long cables between the cartridge and the preamp should be avoided also because cable CAPACITANCE will affect high-frequency response as well. MM cartridges usually have a sensitivity of from 0.5 to 2 millivolts per centimeter per second of recorded velocity, and they are meant to be terminated with more than 10,000 OHMS impedance.

Moviola™ The trademarked name of a company that manufactured film editing equipment, and by common usage, their products. In 1924 Iwan Serrurier turned his home movie projector into a personal film viewer for Hollywood editors. The classic upright Moviola that evolved became an industry standard and allowed a film editor to manipulate film and synchronized soundtracks with relative ease. It could hold reels of film and/or soundtracks on vertical reels and the operator could watch a small optical screen while running the reels forwards or backwards. The final evolution of the Moviola was the flatbed editor, where the film sat on horizontal platters on a large table-like mechanism. Today, Moviola deals with digital production products and education, however you can still rent a film Moviola.

MP3, MPEG-1 Audio Layer III, MPEG-2 Audio Layer III MP3 is a general name for a digital audio file encoded to conform to any of several lossy compression standards set forth by the MPEG-1 or MPEG-2 Audio Layer III. The filename extension .mp3 was originally created for software handling MPEG-1 Audio Layer III, and the general name has stuck. Any of several sampling rates and bit stream rates can be used. MPEG-2 Audio Layer III adds functionality to MPEG-1 Audio Layer III and most of it is backward compatible. Lower sampling rate files encoded in MPEG-2 Audio Layer III are also called MP3 files. MP3 files should not be called MPEG-3—there is no such thing. Audio Layers I and II are less complex and not generally suitable for higher quality audio. MPEG-1 Audio Layer III uses sampling rates of 32, 44.1 or 48 kHz and bit rates from 32 to 320 kbits/s, while MPEG-2 Audio Layer III adds 16, 22.05 and 24 kHz sampling rates and bit rates from 8 to 160 kbits/s. Thankfully, the software figures this all out. As a rule, the lower the sampling and bitstream rates, the worse the fidelity. File size savings can be dramatic from normal CD.

MPEG Stands for Moving Picture Experts Group. It is a working group of ISO, and its full name is ISO/IEC JTC 1/SC 29/WG 11 - Coding of Moving Pictures and Audio. Its mission is the development of international standards for compression, decompression, processing, and coded representation of moving pictures, audio, and their combination. MPEG held its first meeting in Ottawa, Canada, in 1988. An MPEG Audio Subgroup concentrates on the audio aspects. The audio layers of the MPEG standards specify decoding standards but leave the perceptual encoding open. Thus, improvements are constantly being made that are completely compatible.

MPEG-2 A term referring to a video and audio digital compression standard created by the MPEG, generally intended for uses such as digital TV and DVDs. The MPEG-2 video CODEC uses variable bit rates to allocate higher bit rates for complex scenes with a lot of motion and lower bit rates for more static scenes. The audio layers include multichannel extensions to the MPEG-1 standards, and the addition of the high-quality AAC (Advanced Audio Coding) system.

MPEG-4 MPEG-4 is a multimedia streaming CODEC aimed primarily at game applications. In addition to streaming video and digital audio, it allows for the transmission of MIDI, facilitates the transfer and playback of DLS-2 files, and incorporates a user-configurable synthesis language. This latter feature is called the Structured Audio Orchestra Language (SAOL), allowing the programmer to specify almost any existing synthesis method and create algorithms at one end, and have the sound played back identically at the end-user's player.

MPSE Motion Picture Sound Editors. An organization of persons who work in the film and TV sound and music editing industry. Members are allowed to use the initials MPSE after their names in credits. *See also* CAS.

MPX Short for multiplex. The letters *MPX* when found on a button on a cassette deck mean the button activates a 19-kilohertz notch filter to eliminate the FM stereo PILOT so it won't cause gain mistracking in Dolby noise reduction systems. The Dolby playback system would sense the pilot and mistake it for high-frequency content of the music. The pilot can also cause audible BIRDIES by beating with the AC BIAS used in tape recorders.

MSB Most Significant Bit; the first (left-hand side) digit in a BINARY number. *See also* LSB.

M-S Stereo M-S is an abbreviation for Mid-Side, or some say Mono-Stereo, and refers to a special type of INTENSITY STEREO invented by Lauridsen in Denmark in the mid-1950s.

The COINCIDENT MICROPHONES used for M-S recording are usually a CARDIOID facing directly to the sound source and a FIGURE-8 MICROPHONE facing sideways. The figure 8 picks up the left half of the source with one PHASE and the right half with inverted phase. When the SIGNAL is added to the signal from the cardioid, the signals from the left side add together, while the signals from the right side subtract due to the phase inversion. The combined pattern of the two microphones is like a cardioid facing 45 degrees to the left. This is one of the stereo output signals from the M-S system. Then, the figure 8 signal is subtracted from the cardioid signal (actually, it is phase-inverted and added), and left sides cancel and right sides add, simulating a cardioid facing 45 degrees to the right. This is the other output signal. This addition of the signals in two ways is sometimes called MATRIXING.

One might well ask why this is done, when two cardioids 90 degrees apart will do the same thing. The only reason is that with the M-S system, the relative level of the cardioid signal can be varied with respect to the figure 8 before matrixing, and this will vary the apparent width of the stereo image. (This is assuming one would rationally want to vary the apparent width in the first place.)

Additionally, it has "perfect" mono compatibility, and assuming one records the individual mic outputs without matrixing (as opposed to recording the decoded stereo), the apparent width can be changed at any time such as in postproduction.

One technical problem with the M-S system is that each output signal is the result of the addition of two MICROPHONE signals, and these microphones cannot occupy the same point in space. Therefore, there will be slight differences in PHASE and AMPLITUDE of the signals being added, causing an added roughness in the FREQUENCY RESPONSE curve of the combined output. The M-S system also assumes that the cardioid and figure-8 microphones have identical frequency responses and POLAR PATTERNS that are constant at all frequencies. Neither assumption is true.

M-S recording has always been more popular in Europe than in the United States, but it seems to be declining in popularity compared to other intensity stereo techniques in both places. *See also* BLUMLEIN, ALAN; INTENSITY STEREO.

MTS, Multichannel Television Sound The method used for broadcasting stereo sound and alternate language channels with ordinary analog NTSC television broadcasting. Added on to the format in 1984, MTS is built into almost all analog NTSC television sets and receiving devices such as VCRs (Video Cassette Recorders).

Muddy A subjective term that describes a type of DISTORTION that reduces the clarity or transparency of the sound of a musical instrument, particularly TRANSIENTS. For instance, the reproduced sound of a collection of sleigh bells should allow the listener to detect the individual bells, each with its sharp attack intact. INTERMODULATION DISTORTION will add new frequencies among the rich collection of natural HARMONICS of the bells and will also add low-frequency components not originally present. The bells sound "thick."

The sound of massed string instruments is extremely complex, for the many harmonics of each instrument are greatly enriched by the fact that all the instruments are not in perfect tune with each other, giving rise to an overall SPECTRUM that is smeared in FREQUENCY rather than consisting of only discrete harmonics of the FUNDAMENTAL frequency. We perceive this smearing as a "chorus" effect, and we say it adds richness to the tone. Intermodulation greatly complicates this spectrum by adding new frequencies that bear no harmonic relation to any of the frequencies originally present. This confuses our ears' pitch-sensing mechanism, and we say the sound is muddy.

Mu-law A nonlinear CODEC, often used for telephone-grade digital audio. It is LOGARITHMIC instead of linear in its quantizing, putting more accuracy into the lower level signals and reducing the word size of samples. Previously supported on many computer platforms, it seems to have been superceded by current popular digital audio compression schemes such as AAC, MP3, RealAudio, and Windows Media. Sometimes seen as u-law.

Mult A connection, usually in the form of an auxiliary box, that shorts two or more signals together. If one or the other or both of the signals are at a low IMPEDANCE, the mult will cause distortion and a reduction in level. The mult must be used with care and should not be used as a substitute for a MIXER. Likely derived from the term, multiple.

Multi-Effects Processor An audio signal processing unit that combines several different audio effects. Originally, effects devices would only have one or two functions such as reverb, phasing, flanging, de-essing, limiting, etc. Modern DSP meant that many effects could be economically done in one device. Some detractors argue that the effects are seldom as good as the best separate units.

Multimeter A piece of test equipment that measures several electrical parameters such as RESISTANCE and AC and DC VOLTAGE and CURRENT. The original multimeter is thought to be obsolete by many technicians due to the introduction of digital multimeters, but there are many die-hards who still like analog multimeters better because when measuring a voltage or current that is varying with time, you can see the variations in real time on the meter. Digital meters present you with a blinking display of different numbers that are not as convenient to interpret. *See also* VOM; DMM; VTVM.

Multipath Distortion Multipath distortion is a type of DISTORTION afflicting FM and television broadcasting. It is the receipt of the transmitted SIGNAL over more than one path due to reflections from hills, buildings, etc. Because the path lengths are different, there is a delay between the various signal arrival times. In analog television, this causes the familiar ghosts, or multiple images, on the screen.

In FM radio, multipath manifests itself as an undesirable distortion of the high frequencies. The effect is most noticeable in a car FM receiver, where the signal will fade in and out very rapidly as the car moves among the reflected signals. This is sometimes called "picket fencing." The effect does not occur in AM broadcasting because of the relatively much longer WAVELENGTHS of the transmitted CARRIER signals.

Multipattern Microphone A microphone that can be adjusted to have several different POLAR PATTERNS is sometimes called a multipattern microphone. Some of the first microphones of this type were the RCA ribbons designed by Harry Olson in the late 1930s. While a ribbon microphone has inherently a figure 8 pattern, Olson was able to modify the design to effectively change the pattern from FIGURE 8 to CARDIOID, and even to OMNIDIRECTIONAL. These microphones enjoyed a long life in radio broadcasting, recording, and motion picture sound applications, and many are still in use today.

The most common multipattern microphone found today is a type of CONDENSER MICROPHONE based on a German design by von Braunmuhl and Weber. The active element in this microphone is the cardioid condenser capsule, which is a condenser microphone with a perforated BACK PLATE and a sound entrance to the back plate. Sound reaching the microphone from the rear is delayed by the back plate on its way to the back of the diaphragm. The same sound is delayed by DIFFRACTION on its way to the front of the diaphragm, and therefore the pressure on the diaphragm is the same on each side, and no output results. This means that the microphone is dead for sounds coming from behind. Sounds from the front reach the front of the diaphragm unimpeded, but are delayed first by diffraction and then by the delay in the back plate so that they arrive at the rear of the diaphragm out of PHASE, causing a greater differential pressure on the diaphragm. This

Multipattern Microphone

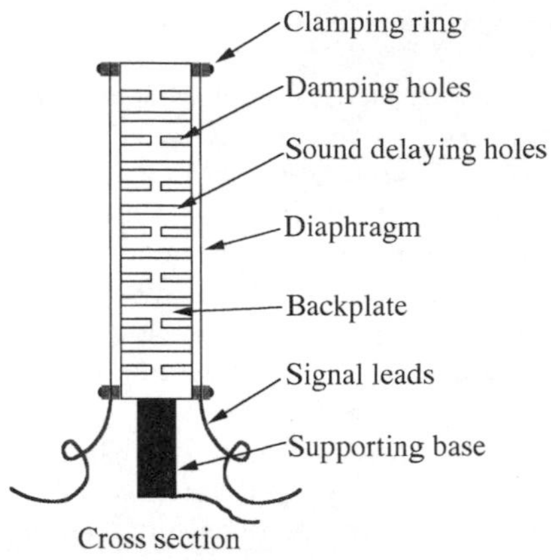

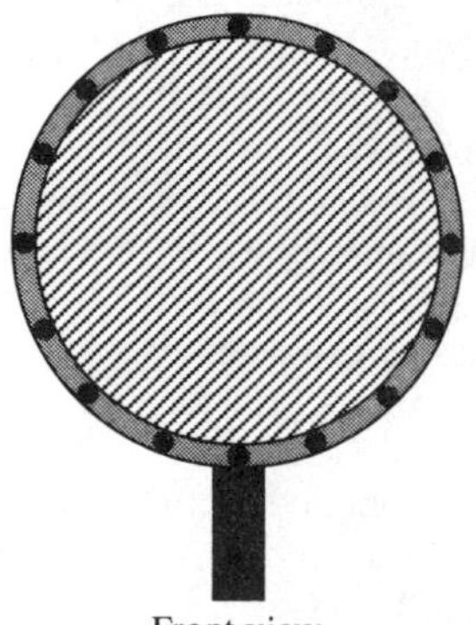

Multipattern Microphone

results in a relatively large output SIGNAL for sounds coming from the front. (This is a refinement of the design of the dynamic UNIDYNE microphone invented by Benjamin Bauer much earlier.)

A double microphone can be made by mounting a diaphragm on each side of the back plate, resulting in two cardioids back-to-back. When the output signals are added, the result is an omnidirectional. If the outputs are added out of phase (i.e., if they are subtracted), the response will be a figure 8. If only one output is used, it is a cardioid. Thus, three patterns are available from a single unit, or, if the responses of the two microphone elements are adjustable in SENSITIVITY, the pattern can be continuously varied from one shape to another.

This type of microphone was introduced commercially by Neumann in 1953 as the model M-49. Other manufacturers have taken up the idea, and the microphone is very popular in recording studios. Its primary disadvantage is that its active elements are somewhat large, causing problems in uniformity of output due to diffraction effects. The ideal microphone would be small compared to the shortest WAVELENGTH of sound it is to reproduce. The wavelength of a sound of 20 KILOHERTZ is about 0.5 inch, and it is difficult to make a microphone this small with sufficient sensitivity to ensure a good SIGNAL-TO-NOISE RATIO.

Multiple Pass In ERROR CORRECTION in DIGITAL audio devices, the multiple pass scheme uses the same hardware many times.

Multiplex Adapter An external device used with a MONAURAL FM tuner to allow it to demodulate FM STEREO broadcasts, common in the early 1960s when stereo broadcasting was getting started. The device that decodes an SCA broadcast is also sometimes called a multiplex adapter.

Multiplex Graphophone Grand A special type of cylinder record player built by the Columbia Phonograph Company around 1898. It had three separate styli and three separate reproducing horns. It therefore was undoubtedly the first pseudo-stereophonic record player, although it was not advertised as such. Its advertising brochure extolled its "intensity of volume and sweetness and richness of tone which seem almost beyond belief." This is probably also the first use of the term *multiplex* in reference to audio, although with a different meaning than it has today.

Multiplexing When signals are combined in such a way that they can later be separated, they are said to be multiplexed together. A multiplexing device is called a multiplexer, abbreviated mux. There are many schemes for multiplexing. Probably the most common is the FREQUENCY multiplexing used for broadcasting STEREO signals over FM. In this technique, the signals are added together to form a "sum" SIGNAL, and are subtracted to form a "difference" signal. The sum signal is used to modulate the FM CARRIER, and this is what is heard if a MONAURAL receiver is used. The difference signal is used to modulate a 38-KILOHERTZ SUBCARRIER, and this modulated carrier is mixed with the sum signal so it also modulates the FM carrier. A monaural receiver is not sensitive to the difference signal because it is translated in frequency above the audible range by the 38-kHz subcarrier.

Multitrack A recorder, usually a tape recorder (either analog or digital) having more than two independent recording tracks. Two-track recorders are merely considered stereo recorders. Multitracks generally must have the capability to enable and disable recording on any track, and to perform selective synchronization. The first multitrack tape machines were analog recorders, and had three tracks using ½-inch-wide tape, and it was not long before 4- and then 8-track machines using 1-inch-wide tape were available. The introduction of the Dolby A noise reduction system allowed the track widths to be narrower without too much penalty in SIGNAL-TO-NOISE RATIO. This brought forth machines with 24 and 32 tracks on 2-inch-wide tape and 4-tracks on ¼-inch tape.

It is interesting to note that the first multitrack audio recorders were optical recorders on motion picture film. The Bell Laboratories produced a 4-track optical sound system using 35-mm film in the mid-1930s, and the Disney studio introduced FANTASOUND with the movie *Fantasia* in 1941.

Mumetal™ A metal with extremely high magnetic PERMEABILITY—that is, in which it is easy to establish a magnetic field. Mumetal is used as a magnetic SHIELD for such low-signal devices as magnetic TAPE HEADS and microphone input transformers. It was invented in the 1920s in England as a loading material for submarine telegraphic cables. By wrapping the insulated copper wire with Mumetal, the INDUCTANCE of the cable was increased, reducing the signal attenuation and increasing the word-handling capacity. The name is derived from the Greek letter μ (mu), which is the symbol for magnetic permeability.

The formulation of Mumetal was patented in 1930, and the name is still a trademark registered by Telcon Metals Ltd., of Crawley, Sussex, England.

Munchkin Effect A sound effect produced by pitch-shifting speech upwards to create a comical, high-pitched voice, presumably named after the effect used in the motion picture *The Wizard of Oz*.

MUSICAM An acronym for Masking pattern adapted Universal Sub-band Integrated Coding And Multiplexing, a perceptual audio CODEC invented by CCETT, Philips, and the IRT. It was a precursor to the MPEG-1 Audio Layer I and II. Due to the oddities of international trademark law, in the United States it refers to a company that markets licensed Layer II products. The original MUSICAM algorithm is not used anymore, and the term should not be used when referring to MPEG-1 Audio Layers.

Musicasting One type of SCA broadcasting by FM multiplex of a music signal designed as background music for subscribers such as supermarkets. It uses a separate 67-kHz SUBCARRIER to FREQUENCY MODULATE the main carrier of the FM station. Musicasting was authorized by the FCC in 1955 and was quite popular for several years.

MUT, Make-Up Table A motor-driven device designed to load and rewind motion picture film to and from platters. 35-mm film is shipped on 2000-foot reels, yet theaters often use platters where all reels have been spliced together into one 18,000-foot roll on a moving horizontal turntable. The projectionist uses the MUT to assemble the whole film, and to take it apart again to fit onto 2000-foot reels for shipping it back.

Mute A button found on some recording consoles that, when pressed, silences the input or other signal it is associated with. Some audio recorders also have mute buttons.

Muting A CIRCUIT in an FM tuner that disconnects the SIGNAL output (or shorts it to GROUND) when the tuner is tuned between stations is called muting.

When an FM receiver is not receiving a CARRIER, its output will be very noisy. This noise level can be greater than the signal level of most broadcasts, and the result is a loud burst of noise when the dial is moved from one station to another. Interstation muting removes this noise, reconnecting the signal in the presence of a carrier. Walkie-talkies and communications radios refer to this as "squelch." *See also* NOISE GATE.

Muting of the signal also occurs in some types of ERROR CORRECTION in DIGITAL audio systems.

Mutual Inductance The property that exists between two coils of wire, as in a TRANSFORMER, when the magnetic lines of force generated by current in one coil induce a current in the other coil. Mutual inductance governs the amount of current in one coil caused by a changing CURRENT in the other one.

Mylar™ A plastic material used for recording tapes. Mylar is the registered trademark of the DuPont company, which first made the plastic. Later, others started to make it, and the generic term became "polyester."

Mylar is a tough plastic that is much stronger than cellulose ACETATE, which is the traditional tape material. However, Mylar will stretch a long way before breaking, and a stretched tape cannot be repaired. The better-quality polyester tapes are "prestretched" to reduce this unfortunate tendency. (Acetate tape will break with the force required to stretch Mylar, but the break can be spliced back together.)

N

NAB The National Association of Broadcasters is an American trade association representing over-the-air radio and TV broadcasters. Formed in 1922, TV interests were included in 1951 with a name change to NARTB (National Association of Radio and Television Broadcasters). In 1958, they changed their name back to NAB. They established various standards for radio and television broadcasting, analogous to the BBC in England. The first standards for magnetic tape recorders were established by NAB/NARTB, and they included tape speed standards (15 ips for commercial and broadcast use and 7.5 ips for less demanding requirements), and the equalization curves for the recording and playback circuits of the recorders. *See* NAB EQUALIZATION.

NAB Equalization In 1954, the National Association of Radio and Television Broadcasters (NARTB) established a standard DE-EMPHASIS curve for use in professional tape recorders operating at 15 inches per second, and it is still in use today. A few years after the 15 ips standard, tape recorders had improved enough to allow the 7.5 ips tape speed to achieve high-FREQUENCY RESPONSE to 15 kHz, and the same de-emphasis was adopted as the standard reproduce curve. This equalization CURVE was designed to take advantage of the tapes existing at the time, but tape has undergone much improvement, especially in high-frequency SIGNAL handling capacity, since 1954. The standard, therefore, does not exploit the capabilities of modern tape; on the other hand, if the standard were changed, a great many existing tape recordings would be obsolete. If a new standard were adopted, there could be at least a 10-DECIBEL improvement in high-frequency SIGNAL-TO-NOISE RATIO, meaning a 10-dB reduction in tape hiss. *See also* NAGRAMASTER.

In 1958, NARTB simplified its name to National Association of Broadcasters (NAB), and so followed the name of the curve. More recently, the IEC has recognized the curve as a standard along with others such as CCIR. CCIR turned over their tape standards to the IEC in 1970 and CCIR became ITU-R in 1992. Original IEC EQs are now called IEC1 (neé CCIR), and NAB EQs are called IEC2.

NAB Hub The center hub of a 10½-inch diameter professional reel of recording tape is of a standardized size, and is called the NAB hub (after the National Association of Broadcasters, which established the standard). It is a 3-inch diameter hole as opposed to the EIA-style hole of 5⁄16 inch. A larger hub aids tape handling.

Tape can be bought wound on NAB hubs without reel FLANGES, and is called a "pancake." Care must be taken in using pancakes on a tape recorder to avoid spilling the tape off the hub. Generally, the tape is wound off the hub once and onto a reel, and is not usually rewound onto the hub. This is the reason many NAB hubs could be found in the trash behind recording studios. *See also* DIN HUB.

NAB Reel A 10½-inch diameter aluminum or plastic tape reel incorporating an NAB HUB used on professional analog tape recorders.

Nagra A Swiss line of professional portable tape recorders originally designed to record on-location synchronous sound for motion pictures. They were the industry standard for thirty years, owing to the quality and ruggedness of the recorders. They used ¼-inch-wide tape and were generally equipped with a CRYSTAL SYNCH generator, or later, SMPTE TIME CODE. The Nagra model III (mono) and IV-S (stereo) were portable, designed for use while being carried, and were superior in performance in the areas of FLUTTER and WOW, SIGNAL-TO-NOISE RATIO, and DISTORTION compared to high-end studio recorders. These analog models have been discontinued, and the digital Nagra model V (stereo onto hard disk) and model D (multitrack onto ¼-inch-tape reels) are available as portable recorders.

Nagramaster An EQUALIZATION CURVE developed by NAGRA for use in analog tape recorders that uses a larger high-frequency PRE-EMPHASIS during recording and DE-EMPHASIS during playback to increase the audible SIGNAL-TO-NOISE RATIO at 15 ips by about 10 dB. It is not compatible with any other tape equalization such as NAB or IEC.

Nano Nano is a prefix meaning one billionth.

Nanoweber The weber is the unit of magnetic FLUX, but is much too large to be useful in measuring the recorded flux on recording tape. The nanoweber (nWb) is equal to 10 to the minus ninth power webers, or one billionth of a weber. The recorded level is expressed in nanowebers per meter of tape track width to normalize the measurement as a flux density.

The standard reference level, which results when the tape recorder meter is reading 0 VU with a mid-frequency signal, has changed over the years as tapes have become better. The standard originated by Ampex in the 1950s, known as Ampex Operating Level, was 185 nWb per meter; 250 nWb per meter is more common today. Some European recorders use as much as

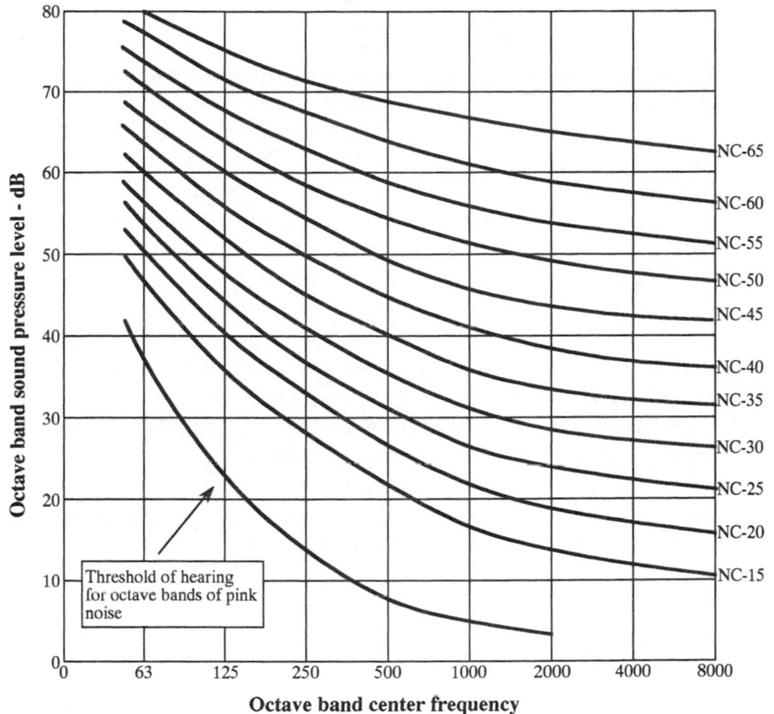

NC Curves

520 nWb per meter as a reference for 0 VU. The higher the reference level, the greater the SIGNAL-TO-NOISE RATIO will be, but the DISTORTION will also be greater and the HEADROOM will be reduced, so a compromise is required. The exact measurement of tape fluxivity is somewhat complicated, so many variations of these numbers are seen for various reasons.

Narrowband A relatively short FREQUENCY span, defining a SIGNAL or FILTER that encompasses a small BANDWIDTH. Filters sharper than one-third OCTAVE are generally considered narrowband filters.

NARTB Short for National Association of Radio and Television Broadcasters, and was the name for the NAB from 1951 to 1958.

NBS Short for the U.S. National Bureau of Standards, whose name was changed in 1988 to the National Institute of Standards and Technology, abbreviated NIST.

NC Curve, NC Contour NC stands for "Noise Criterion," and refers to the ambient or background noise in an auditorium or room.

Because our ears are relatively insensitive to low levels of low-FREQUENCY noise due to the FLETCHER-MUNSON EFFECT, relatively greater amounts of low-frequency noise are allowed in auditoriums and recording studios, etc. In an attempt to relate the apparent noisiness of such a room to an objective measure, the NC curves were developed. These curves are essentially contours of equal LOUDNESS; they are spaced apart by about 5 DECIBELS (they are not quite parallel due to the complex response curves of our hearing mechanism); and they are numbered. NC-15 represents a very quiet environment—so quiet that the average person would not be aware of any background noise at all. NC-20 is noticeably noisier, and NC-25 is considered about the limit for a good auditorium for music listening, although many think NC-25 is too noisy.

To determine the NC value of a room, it is only necessary to measure the background noise with a sensitive SOUND LEVEL METER that has an OCTAVE BAND FILTER, and plot the measured levels on a graph of NC curves. If the measured points are all below the NC-20 curve, for example, the room is said to meet the NC-20 requirement.

Most of the noise in an auditorium, assuming adequate isolation from external noise sources such as airplanes and freeways, etc., is caused by the ventilation system, and, unfortunately, the cost of such systems rises dramatically with decreases in noisiness. Low-frequency noise is the most difficult to control, so it is somewhat lucky that our ears are not very sensitive to it at low levels.

N Curve *See* ACADEMY CURVE.

Near-Coincident Pair A spaced-pair MICROPHONE set-up that uses DIRECTIONAL MICROPHONES placed approximately 7 inches apart, or the average spacing between ears on a human head. This allows for some amount of phase difference in the two SIGNALS, but not enough to lose mono compatibility. ORTF is the most common near-coincident arrangement, but others include NOS, and the FAULKNER MICROPHONE array.

Near Field The sound field very close to a source of sound is called the near field. By very close is meant less than one WAVELENGTH at the FREQUENCY of interest. It is difficult if not impossible to make meaningful SOUND PRESSURE LEVEL measurements, such as with a SOUND LEVEL METER, in the near field because the nature of the field itself is very complex. Frequently the acoustic energy is moving across the surface of the source, or maybe there is a large air velocity near the source. STANDING WAVES are also present in many cases if the source is deeply convoluted. In any case, it is not possible to predict the sound level in the far field from measurements in the near field, so when measuring sound pressure level, a sound level meter must always be at least one wavelength of the lowest frequency of interest from the source.

Near-Field Monitor A LOUDSPEAKER designed to be heard relatively close, such as a person sitting at a mixing console with monitors on the other side of the console.

Necessory An indispensable, or "needed" accessory, such as an audio cable between a PREAMP and an AMPLIFIER.

Needle-Drop A recording of a music passage usually purchased from a music archive that will be used in a movie or video production soundtrack.

The name comes from the prior use of phonograph records to archive musical selections.

Needle Scratch Synonymous with NEEDLE TALK.

Needle Talk The direct acoustic output of the STYLUS assembly of a phonograph CARTRIDGE is called needle talk, from the days when the stylus was called the "needle."

Modern cartridges, which use very low tracking forces, produce very little needle talk, but in the days of the 78-RPM record, the needle talk could often be heard in the room above the sound of the LOUDSPEAKER.

Negative Feedback If a portion of the output SIGNAL of an AMPLIFIER is mixed with the input signal in an out-of-PHASE condition, it will partially cancel the input signal and the GAIN of the amplifier will be reduced. This is called negative feedback, and its amount is measured by the amount of gain reduction. If the gain is reduced by 10 DECIBELS, then it is said to have 10 dB of feedback.

It so happens that DISTORTION (both HARMONIC and INTERMODULATION) caused by the amplifier will be reduced more than the signal will because they are not in the input signal in the first place. The feedback has the effect of reducing anything that the amplifier adds to the signal, which is a reduction of distortion, or in other words an improvement in LINEARITY. Feedback also reduces the amplifier's OUTPUT IMPEDANCE, increasing its DAMPING FACTOR. The FREQUENCY RESPONSE of an amplifier can be made flatter with proper feedback.

If care is not taken in the design of a feedback amplifier, serious problems can occur. If the amplifier has large amounts of PHASE SHIFT at some frequency, the feedback becomes positive rather than negative, and the amplifier will become unstable and will oscillate. Also, large amounts of feedback can cause TRANSIENT INTERMODULATION DISTORTION (TIM).

Neodymium A rare-earth metal element, atomic number 60, used in making strong magnets. Such magnets are often used in DYNAMIC MICROPHONES and LOUDSPEAKERS.

Neopilot A system for the synchronization of a motion picture camera with the tape recorder recording the sound. The Neopilot system uses a clever way to superimpose a 60-hertz signal generated by the camera or by a crystal-controlled OSCILLATOR on the full-track tape in such a way that it is not sensed by the normal full-track playback head, and so is not heard with the recorded sound. This is done by using a special record head with two narrow tracks near the center of the tape. One track records the 60-Hz signal with one polarity, and the other track records the same signal with inverted polarity. These two low-frequency signals cancel each other out in the full-track playback head. The 60-Hz pilot signal is played back by a narrow-track head that encompasses just the width of one of the recorded 60-Hz tracks. The recovered signal is used to control the speed of the tape recorder in playback so the sound remains in "synch" with the picture. This process is called resolving.

The Neopilot system was developed by Stefan Kudelski for his famous

Nagra portable tape recorders, and it revolutionized the recording of motion picture sound. Before then, there were many other systems for synchronization, most of them using large heavy studio-type recording equipment. The advent of stereo recorders with room for a synch track on the tape obviated the need for Neopilot. *See also* CRYSTAL SYNCH; SMPTE TIME CODE.

Neutrodyne A special CIRCUIT developed and marketed by the Hazeltine Corporation starting about 1923 for decreasing the tendency for TRF radio receivers to oscillate. The Neutrodyne used a special trimmer capacitor between the GRID and PLATE of each tube in the RF section to neutralize the interelectrode CAPACITANCE. It is said that the Neutrodyne was the first receiver that could be "logged"; that is, the same station would usually come in on different days at the same place on the dials! It made a great sensation among radio buffs of the day. *Radio Craft* magazine, in its March 1938 issue, stated: "If you didn't have a Neutrodyne, you were such a social outcast that your very dog hid under the bed at your approach and looked at you reprovingly, because the dogs of Neutrodyne owners wouldn't associate with him."

NFB Short for NEGATIVE FEEDBACK.

Nibble *See* NYBBLE.

NICAM 728 Short for Near Instantaneous Companded Audio Multiplex. This mouthful is a DIGITAL system designed by the BBC in the early 1980s for the transmission of six different audio programs from London to the transmitter sites in various parts of Great Britain. The sampling rate is 32 kHz with 14-bit coding, which corresponds to the European Broadcasting Union (EBU) standard. The meaning of 728 is that 728 kilobits per second comprise the raw data.

The NICAM system uses an interesting scheme for reducing the BIT rate of the transmission, called NICAM-3. The audio programs are converted initially into 14-bit linearly coded samples. They are then compressed to 10 bits for transmission. At the receiving end, a digital expansion process expands the signals in a way complementary to the way they were compressed. This is thus a COMPANDER system operating entirely in the digital domain. As in all companders, the noise level varies with the SIGNAL level, increasing as the signal level increases. Ideally, the noise is at a low enough level that it is MASKED by the program, and the BBC has done very careful listening tests to ensure that this is the case with NICAM-3. To help in this, the signals are subjected to a PRE-EMPHASIS before being encoded and a complementary DE-EMPHASIS after decoding at the receiving end.

Nickel-Cadmium (NiCd) Battery A common type of rechargeable BATTERY, consisting of NiCd cells. They use cadmium oxide as an ELECTROLYTE and nickel as the ELECTRODES, and they are capable of many discharge-recharge cycles if used properly. NiCd cells have a terminal voltage of 1.2 VOLTS and retain this voltage well while they are being discharged. They do not have as much capacity as a similar-sized ALKALINE CELL but are more economical in the long run if recharged many times.

Nicads are losing popularity due to better chemistry cells such as

Lithium-Ion (Li-Ion) and Nickel-Metal Hydride (NiMH) and the toxicity of cadmium to the environment.

Nickel Metal Hydride Cell (NiMH) A common type of rechargeable CELL that has superior performance over NiCd cells. They have a much higher capacity than NiCd, especially under high CURRENT draw, while retaining a flat VOLTAGE during discharge and no memory effect. They are popular for applications such as digital cameras, unless the even better but expensive and demanding Lithium-Ion cells are used.

NIST, National Institute of Standards and Technology The successor to the old National Bureau of Standards. The name change occurred in 1988. NIST is responsible for the maintenance of all types of scientific standards and units of measurement in the United States.

Noise Noise can be defined as any unwanted sound that is not related to the wanted sound (if it is related, it is called DISTORTION), and this definition suffices for most uses; but in electronics, noise is specifically defined as a more or less WIDEBAND addition to a SIGNAL by any electronic or mechanical component.

Additions to a signal that are integrally related frequency-wise to the signal are generally called distortion of one type or another. The most common type of noise is sometimes called "random noise" because it is unpredictable from moment to moment, and contains a continuous distribution of energy spread over FREQUENCY. True random noise sounds like a hissing, and has no detectable PITCH. An example of random noise is the sound heard in FM receivers when tuned off-station.

Unfortunately, just about anything you do to a signal adds some noise to it, and there is no such thing in nature as a noise-free signal. PREAMPLIFIERS add noise, POWER AMPLIFIERS add noise, tape recorders add noise, phono CARTRIDGES add noise, and LOUDSPEAKERS add noise. In copying an analog tape recording, for example, the copy will have at least 3 DECIBELS more noise than the original, no matter how good the tape recorder is.

An important measure of the quality of a signal is the SIGNAL-TO-NOISE RATIO, measured in decibels. The signal-to-noise ratio provides information on how much more powerful the signal is than the noise that inevitably rides along with it. Signal-to-noise ratio is sometimes confused with DYNAMIC RANGE, to which it is loosely related at best.

Ambrose Bierce defines noise as "a stench in the ear. Undomesticated music. The chief product and authenticating sign of civilization."

Noise Cancelling Headphone *See* ACTIVE NOISE CANCELLING.

Noise Cancelling Microphone A specially designed DYNAMIC microphone that has both sides of the diaphragm exposed to the sound field so that sounds coming from a relatively large distance are cancelled because the sound pressure causes no net force on the diaphragm. For sound originating very close to the microphone, such as when someone holds the microphone up to the mouth when talking, the rear of the microphone is effectively shaded from the sound field, and the diaphragm does receive the sound pressure. Noise canceling microphones are used in high-noise areas where clear communication is important, such as airplane cockpits, etc.

Noise Figure The ratio between the theoretical JOHNSON NOISE, or thermal noise of a device, and the actual measured noise is called the noise figure and is expressed in decibels.

Noise Floor The noise floor of an audio device is the noise power generated by the device in the absence of any input SIGNAL. It is generally measured in DECIBELS referenced to a particular power. Sometimes the noise floor is measured in terms of RMS VOLTAGE rather than power, and this makes sense in the case of devices such as voltage amplifiers or tape recorders.

In any case, the measurement is useless unless the BANDWIDTH of the measurement and the WEIGHTING NETWORK used (if any) are specified.

Noise Gate A noise-reduction device through which an audio SIGNAL is passed. When the signal level is very small, the noise gate will "close," eliminating any residual noise that may be riding on the signal. In the presence of a signal, the noise gate will open, allowing signal and noise to pass through. Under these conditions, the noise is MASKED by the signal. When the signal is interrupted, the noise is audible (or more audible), having no signal to serve as a masking source.

A noise gate is actually a special type of EXPANDER with an infinite expansion ratio below a preset threshold. The setting of this threshold is adjustable, so as not to cut off too much of low-level signals.

Noise gates are sometimes used with electronically amplified musical instruments such as guitars to reduce background noise when the instruments are not being played. Their effectiveness is in large part determined by the TIME CONSTANTS associated with the GAIN reduction. Often, the background noise can be heard switching on and off with the signal.

Noise Generator Sometimes it is desirable to use a random SIGNAL that contains all frequencies at the same time as a test signal for AUDIO equipment. This signal is called WHITE NOISE or PINK NOISE, and is produced with a noise generator. A good quality noise generator is not a trivial device. It must have a very uniform output versus FREQUENCY and it must be stable in level over a long time.

One use of a noise generator is in the measurement of FREQUENCY RESPONSE of AUDIO devices. The noise is input to the device, and the output is measured with a SPECTRUM ANALYZER, which averages the output VOLTAGE for a time period. If the noise spectrum at the input is flat, then the spectrum of the output noise will be the frequency response of the device. It is important to average the output over some time because the noise signal is random and is only flat in frequency on a statistical basis.

Another use of noise as a test signal is in the measurement of the frequency response of a room-LOUDSPEAKER combination. PINK NOISE input to the loudspeaker and a one-third OCTAVE band analyzer connected to a measurement microphone are used to analyze the acoustic signal. The system may be equalized to attain a specific frequency response. This is often done in setting up sound reinforcement systems. *See also* EQUALIZATION.

Noise Reduction *See* COMPANDER; DYNAURAL.

Noise Shaping In OVERSAMPLING COMPACT DISC players, DIGITAL filtering is used. By a special technique of inverting unneeded bits from one sample and adding to the next sample, the average QUANTIZATION error for slowly varying signals (i.e., low frequencies) will be reduced. This changes the shape of the spectrum of the quantization noise, increasing its high-FREQUENCY content while reducing its low-frequency content. The increased high-frequency content is reduced by the ANTI-IMAGING FILTER.

Non-Fill When a record is pressed, soft vinyl plastic is pressed between the two STAMPERS, which are heated by steam. Sometimes, especially if the heat is too little, the vinyl will fail to flow completely around the grooves, and a large amount of noise is the result. Records with non-fill can be identified visually, and are normally rejected by quality control at the pressing plant before being placed in jackets.

Nonlinear Literally, not on a line. In a nonlinear audio device, the output VOLTAGE is not predictable from a knowledge of the input voltage for all signal levels. For instance, a typical AMPLIFIER with a GAIN of 10 would put out 20 volts with 2 volts input, and put out 30 volts with 3 volts input. The implication is that 50 volts input would produce 500 volts output, but this is impossible with most amplifiers.

There is a point at which the amplifier gain is reduced as the input level is increased. This is the nonlinear region of the amplifier. All devices have local peculiarities or deviations from linearity at specific signal levels.

Nonlinearity produces certain types of DISTORTION, such as HARMONIC and INTERMODULATION DISTORTION. *See also* LINEAR.

NoNoise™ The trade name of a single-pass noise reduction system made by Sonic Solutions. NoNoise is a sophisticated digital signal processing system that analyzes the digitized signal and senses transient noises, such as clicks and pops, and continuous noises, such as TAPE HISS and mains HUM. It removes the transients and makes a substitute signal based on the actual signal immediately before and after the transient. After analyzing the signal for a while, it can distinguish continuous noise from the varying signal and then digitally removes the noise.

Its primary use is in the restoration of old recordings such as analog tapes and rare old records for release in CD form.

Normalize To boost the highest sample of a digital soundfile to the maximum amplitude the system is capable of encoding, short of CLIPPING (0dBFS), and then raising all other samples by the same proportion. In effect, raising the volume of the sound file so it is as loud as possible without going into overload. This maximizes resolution and minimizes certain types of noise. It is not, however, a substitute for compression, limiting, and other DYNAMIC range treatment to make a signal seem louder. Because of the time involved in examining every sample, some software will use shortcuts with varying amounts of accuracy.

Normalled Connection A connection, typically on a MIXER or patch panel, where the signal path is continuous into the signal chain with no plug inserted in the jack. Usually normalled connections are made via TRS jacks. The use of normalized patch panels reduces the number of patch cords one has to have on hand if they represent the most often used connections. A disadvantage of normalized patch bays is that it is not intuitively obvious what the normalization connects. *See also* PATCH BAY.

Norvalizing Hollywood slang for the act of playing a sound effect at a lower level in a vain attempt to hide the fact that it is not in sync.[21]

NOS Acronym for Nederlands Omroep Stichting, which is the Netherlands Broadcasting System. The NOS has developed a method for STEREO recording that uses two CARDIOID microphones placed 30 cm apart and angled at 90 degrees from one another. The method is said to provide more AMBIENCE than COINCIDENT MICROPHONE techniques and fewer PHASE problems than widely spaced microphones. *See also* A-B STEREO; ORTF; M-S STEREO; and INTENSITY STEREO.

NOS also refers to New Old Stock, i.e., a replacement part that is old, but unused and in new condition. Similar to NIB, New In Box.

Notch Filter A FILTER that rejects a narrow band of frequencies; also sometimes called a band-reject filter, although a notch filter usually has maximum ATTENUATION at one FREQUENCY only.

Notch filters are used to remove specific frequencies, such as 60-HERTZ line-induced HUM from AUDIO signals. If a notch filter is sufficiently sharply tuned, it will have minimal effect on the SIGNAL, other than removing the offending frequency. The maximum attenuation of a notch filter can be quite large, typically 60 DECIBELS or more.

One example of a notch filter is the "whistle filter" in some AM tuners. This filter is tuned to reject 10 KILOHERTZ, which is the frequency that separates AM stations on adjacent channels. This puts an effective limit on the FREQUENCY RESPONSE of AM broadcasts at a little below 10 kHz.

When the FCC allocated frequencies for AM broadcasting many years ago, they never anticipated the requirement for FREQUENCY RESPONSE above 5 kHz, and they spaced the allowed carrier frequencies 10 kHz apart.

Noy One noy is the noisiness of a noise for which the perceived noise level is 40 PNdB (PN stands for perceived noise). The noisiness of a noise that is judged by a subject to be *n* times that of a 1-noy noise is *n* noys.

This definition is from PSYCHOACOUSTICS, and practitioners of this discipline seem to be the only ones who use it, let alone understand it. The noy is the result of an attempt, first by psychologists and later by psychoacousticians, to establish a simple scale of perceived noisiness. *See also* MEL.

NPN Short for Negative-Positive-Negative, which refers to a type of TRANSISTOR that is constructed of three layers of semiconducting material. The type of impurity doping in the semiconducting materials determines whether the resulting SEMICONDUCTOR is P or N type. In a CIRCUIT, the

21. This entry is copyright © 1999–2003 by Larry Blake and is reprinted with permission.

emitter is usually a negative VOLTAGE with respect to the collector. A small positive base CURRENT results in a large negative collector current. *See also* PNP; SEMICONDUCTOR.

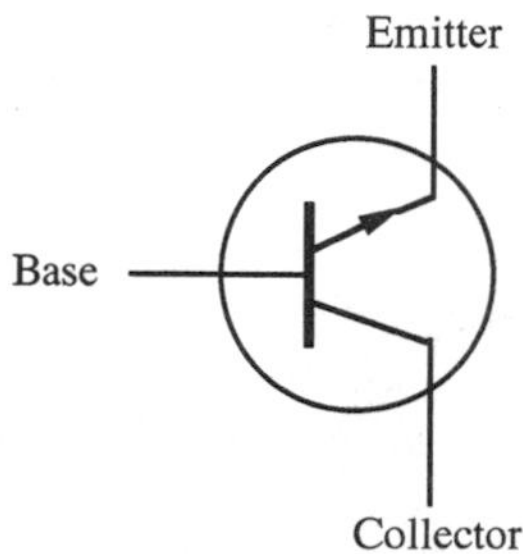

NPN Transistor

NR Short for NOISE REDUCTION.

NRC Acronym for National Research Council. This is an organization established by the Canadian government for the purpose of establishing standards. The NRC is also engaged in wide-ranging research, which is conducted at several well-equipped laboratories in Canada. A good deal of basic research into PSYCHOACOUSTICS and sound reproduction has been conducted at these laboratories.

NSA National Sound Archive, which contains a large collection of recorded material, including over 750,000 records and 50,000 tapes, administered by the British Library in London. The NSA is also actively involved in the restoration and preservation of old recordings, and it, along with Cambridge University, developed a computer-based system for sound restoration called CEDAR (Computer Enhanced Digital Audio Restoration) that is somewhat similar to the NONOISE system. One of the goals of the NSA is to find a permanent storage medium for sound that will last at least 500 years without deterioration.

NSRC The National Stereophonic Radio Committee, which was set up by the Electronics Industries Association (now the Electronic Industries Alliance, EIA) in the U.S. in 1958. The purpose of the NSRC was to study the various proposed systems for FM STEREO broadcasting and to make recommendations to the FCC for standardization. It made its report in 1960, recommending the Crosby system as capable of the highest quality results, but the FCC chose an inferior system, in use to the present day, because it had the capability of SIMULCASTING.

NTSC The National Television Systems Committee (NTSC) is the body that determined the American standards for the transmission of the original analog television broadcast signals. Also known as "Never The Same Color."

Null Test A deceptively simple test for detecting DISTORTION in power AMPLIFIERS, wherein the input signal is subtracted from the attenuated output signal. The difference is the distortion and would be zero in a perfect amplifier. The signal can be anything, such as noise, sine waves, or music.

The problem with this test is that it cannot distinguish relatively benign LINEAR errors such as very small FREQUENCY RESPONSE errors and time delays from nonlinear distortions that cause sonic degradation. Some linear errors, such as overall time delay, are inaudible, and very small frequency response errors are also inaudible, but both show up strongly in the null test.

Nuvistor A miniature type of metal vacuum TUBE introduced by RCA in 1960. Nuvistors were made in several types, including TRIODES and a TETRODE. The nuvistor was not much bigger than early TRANSISTORS and was capable of excellent performance. It is regarded as the highest development of the vacuum tube.

NXT A special process developed by the Agfa company for restoration of old analog audio tape recordings. When some magnetic tape ages, the binder holding the magnetic oxide material in the tape coating undergoes chemical changes that cause the coating to become soft and to slough off onto the heads as the tape is played. The tape plays poorly because it sticks in the mechanism, and playing also further damages the tape. The NXT process is a treatment that stabilizes the coating and allows the tape to be played without further damage. The process does not effect a permanent cure, and the tape soon reverts to its previous state. For this reason, an NXT-treated tape should be copied just after treatment. *See also* STICKY SHED.

Nybble One half of a BYTE, consisting of a group of four BINARY digits. Presumably, it is spelled with a *y* because of the similar spelling of byte.

Nyquist Frequency One-half the SAMPLING frequency in a DIGITAL system. In such a system, the original SIGNAL must be SAMPLED at a certain rate per second before the individual levels can be converted into numerical values for further processing. Obviously, the sampling rate must be high enough to adequately encode the highest FREQUENCY of interest. It was shown by Nyquist that a sampling rate of two times the maximum signal frequency is just sufficient to describe that highest frequency without ambiguity. This is called the Nyquist criterion.

Strictly speaking, the Nyquist criterion is correct, and two samples per cycle are enough to describe a SINE WAVE. However, in order to reconstruct the original sine wave from so meager a quantity of samples, time averaging must be used. In other words, you have to look at a sampled signal for a certain time to decide exactly what the frequency and AMPLITUDE are; there are ambiguities in both for short intervals of sampled WAVEFORMS. The problem is, music is not a steady-state continuum of sound, but is constantly changing in time, sometimes very rapidly indeed, and our ears do not perform the time averaging required to reconstruct the unambiguous signal from the reconstructed output of a DIGITAL-TO-ANALOG CONVERTER.

An analogous condition arises when a signal is present in random noise. Time averaging can extract the signal, but the ear, having a short integration time, hears the noise as well as the signal. This phenomenon is sometimes called the Perman doctrine after André Perman, an engineer working for Brüel & Kjaer who studied the effect.

Nyquist Plot One format for plotting the FREQUENCY RESPONSE function and the IMPEDANCE function, where the real part of the function is plotted against the QUADRATURE part. The Nyquist plot is useful for identifying RESONANCES in circuits or systems, and it is therefore sometimes used to represent the impedance of a LOUDSPEAKER. *See* Appendix 11; HEYSER SPIRAL.

OBU Outside Broadcast Unit. A British term for a team of technicians responsible for remote recording or broadcasting. Also known as "on location" production.

Octave An octave is a FREQUENCY ratio of 2 to 1. An octave BAND consists of all the frequencies within an octave. There is one octave between 100 HERTZ and 200 Hz, and also between 1,000 Hz and 2,000 Hz. Octaves are perceived as equal PITCH intervals, even though the true BANDWIDTH in hertz varies with the frequency level of the octave.

The name arises from the musical practice of defining the eight notes of the scale within a DOUBLING of the frequency. To our ears, two frequencies an octave apart sound like the same note.

It is interesting that our ears obey a precisely LOGARITHMIC law when assigning subjective pitches to frequencies. Even though an octave is strictly speaking a subjective judgment, it is so closely equal to a frequency doubling (no matter where one is in frequency) that it has been defined as an objective measure. (With SINE WAVES, or PURE TONES, the ear does not have this precision of assigning subjective octaves to frequency doublings, but pure tones are never found in nature.) FILTERS having one OCTAVE of bandwidth are called octave-band filters. *See also* Appendix 8; ONE-THIRD OCTAVE FILTER.

Octothorpe According to our friend Dennis Bohn of Rane Corp., the official name for the symbol # is octothorpe. The name was coined by the Bell Telephone Laboratories when they added the # and the * symbols to telephone keypads and the "octo" comes from the eight points the symbol has, and "Thorpe" is the name of an engineer who was instrumental in getting the # on the telephone keypad. Of course, in musical notation the # means "sharp" and in common English # represents "number" or "pound sign." Octothorpe is only proper usage in regard to telephone keypads.

OE, Operator Error A failure in any mechanical or electronic system caused by inappropriate action on the part of the humans setting up or operating the system. Also known as "cockpit trouble" and a "short between the head-set."

OED, Oxford English Dictionary The unimpeachable source of several definitions found herein.

Oersted The oersted is the unit of magnetic field strength (abbreviated Oe) and is named for Hans Christian Oersted, a Danish physicist born in 1777. Oersted discovered the relationship between electric CURRENT and a magnetic field by noting that a compass needle will be deflected when near a wire carrying a current.

Off Axis Not directly in front of a MICROPHONE or a LOUDSPEAKER.

Off-Axis Coloration A dull or colored effect on sound sources that are not placed within the acceptance angle of the MICROPHONE. To avoid off-axis coloration, the user places mics so that they are aimed at sound sources that put out high frequencies, such as cymbals, when miking a large source. In addition, one should use a microphone that has a FLAT FREQUENCY RESPONSE over the recording field, i.e., has similar polar patterns at mid-range and high frequencies. In general, large-diaphragm mics have more off-axis coloration than smaller mics with ¾-inch diaphragms or under.

Offset Angle In a record playing system, the angle that the CARTRIDGE HEAD SHELL makes with the TONEARM is called the offset angle, and it is designed to minimize the angular tracking error of the STYLUS in the record groove. The optimum offset angle is dependent on the length of the tonearm, and the tonearm pivot must be the correct distance from the center of the record as well.

Ohm The ohm (abbreviated Ω , the Greek letter capital omega) is the unit of electrical resistance; it is that which opposes an electric CURRENT in a conductor. *See also* OHM'S LAW.

Ohm's Law The mathematical relationship between electrical VOLTAGE, CURRENT, and RESISTANCE was first formulated by the German scientist Georg Simon Ohm, and it is named after him. Ohm's law says the current in an electric conductor is directly proportional to the voltage across it and inversely proportional to its resistance. In other words, the voltage and current in a conductor exhibit a LINEAR relationship.

Ohm's law works for direct voltages and currents, and also is correct for ALTERNATING CURRENTS if the resistance is a pure resistance. However, if the resistance has any reactive components (INDUCTANCE or CAPACITANCE), the current depends on the FREQUENCY as well as the voltage. *See also* IMPEDANCE.

Most electrical conductors obey Ohm's law very precisely for small current levels, but some materials, most notably the SEMICONDUCTORS used in TRANSISTORS and DIODES, have a much more complex NONLINEAR voltage versus current relationship.

An easy way to remember Ohm's law is illustrated in the figure, where V indicates voltage in volts, I indicates current in AMPERES, and R indicates resistance in ohms. To find the value of any quantity in terms of the others, simply cover its symbol up with your finger. For instance voltage is equal to current times resistance, IR, and current is equal to voltage divided by resistance, V/R.

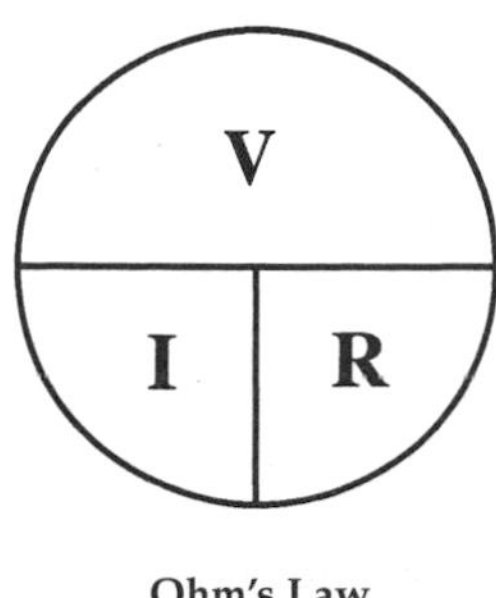

Ohm's Law

OL Abbreviation for OVERLOAD. Often an LED is used to indicate when a circuit is close to or into overload, and will be marked OL.

OMFI, Open Media Framework Interchange A file format first proposed by Avid to allow for digital audio data interchange among digital dubbers, editorial workstations, and hard disk editors.

Omnidirectional Literally, "from all directions." Omnidirectional microphones are equally sensitive to sounds coming from all directions. Paradoxically, such a MICROPHONE is also called nondirectional.

For a microphone to be truly omnidirectional over the entire audible range, it must necessarily be physically small, at most a half-inch or so in diameter. When the WAVELENGTH of the sound being picked up becomes small compared to the dimensions of the microphone, the microphone becomes directional in its response, that is, more sensitive to sounds coming from the front and less sensitive to sounds coming from the sides and rear. Real microphones thus are always more directional at high frequencies, which can be an advantage. When such a microphone is at some distance from a sound source, for instance while recording an orchestra in an auditorium, the rising high-frequency characteristic helps to compensate for the loss of high frequencies due to air absorption. Some microphones with relatively large diaphragms use two diaphragms back-to-back to decrease directionality at high frequencies, but they attain FIGURE-8 directional patterns at high frequencies, which can be undesirable.

On Axis Directly in front of a LOUDSPEAKER, or in the direction of maximum SENSITIVITY of a MICROPHONE.

By convention, FREQUENCY RESPONSE curves of loudspeakers are measured "on axis," usually with the measurement microphone at 1 meter from the cabinet front. This generally gives the flattest frequency response. Microphones also usually have the most uniform frequency response when used "on axis."

One-over-f ($^1\!/_f$) Noise A type of electrical noise that occurs in SEMICONDUCTORS and is inversely proportional to FREQUENCY. It has a "burbling" sound and is caused by the fact that the current in semiconductors is not perfectly smooth, as if the charges clump together.

One-third Octave Filter A BANDPASS FILTER whose BANDWIDTH is almost exactly 23% of its center FREQUENCY. Such a filter will have a bandwidth that spans a musical interval of about a minor third, and this led to its name. One-third octave filters have been used for many years for frequency analysis of acoustical signals, and their shapes (i.e., their frequency response curves) have been standardized by various standards organizations such as the International Standards Organization (ISO) and ANSI. This is to ensure that filters made by different manufacturers will give the same answer when used to analyze the same sound. Their center frequencies have also been standardized for the same reason.

Because the one-third octave filter has a bandwidth proportional to its center frequency, it is a type of proportional bandpass filter. This means its bandwidth becomes greater and greater as its center frequency becomes higher and higher. In other words, its resolution decreases with rising frequency. The reason such filters are useful for analyzing acoustical signals is that this proportional response is similar to the response of the human ear. We sense equal frequency ratios as equal musical intervals, so proportional filters have a constant subjective, or musical, bandwidth as frequency is varied. Moreover, it has been shown by many experiments that the so-called CRITICAL BANDS within which the ear sums energy to determine LOUDNESS are about one-third octave wide over much of the audible range. For this reason, a frequency analysis need not have a greater resolution than one-third octave in order to correlate quite well with our perceived loudness of a sound. *See also* OCTAVE.

Many REAL-TIME ANALYZERS consist of a bank of one-third octave filters, and they may be analog or digital filters.

Opamp, or Op-Amp Short for "operational amplifier," a term originally used for high-GAIN amplifiers in ANALOG computers. An operational AMPLIFIER theoretically has a gain of negative infinity, but practical designs only approximate this ideal. If the amplifier has infinite gain, and proper FEEDBACK is placed around it, the characteristics of the amplifier will depend only on the feedback and not the amplifier.

In recent years, opamps have been produced in the form of INTEGRATED CIRCUITS and with DIFFERENTIAL inputs. They are extensively used in AUDIO circuits. For an opamp to be good for audio use, it must have a wide BANDWIDTH, and must be very fast in its ability to change its output VOLTAGE. *See also* TRANSIENT INTERMODULATION DISTORTION.

Opamps are convenient to use in circuits because they are available in integrated circuit form and are relatively inexpensive. Many opamps are available which have been optimized for audio use.

Open Abbreviation for "open circuit," which denotes no electrical connection between two devices or two components within a device.

Some components, such as TRANSISTORS and RESISTORS, etc., are said to be open if no CURRENT will pass through them. The open is a common failure mode for CIRCUIT components and is generally less destructive to the rest of the circuit than the SHORT.

Open-Circuit Voltage Rating The output voltage of a MICROPHONE with no LOAD, i.e., with infinite resistance such as in an open circuit, or when driving a resistive load at least twenty times the microphone's internal impedance. One of the standard specifications of microphones.

Open Loop An AMPLIFIER without FEEDBACK is said to be operating in the open-loop mode, or to be an open-loop amplifier. The feedback around the amplifier "closes the loop."

The performance of an amplifier with feedback depends a great deal on the GAIN of the amplifier without feedback, i.e., on the open-loop gain, and this is something that is part of the specification of audio OPAMPS.

Open Microphone A microphone that is connected to a broadcast or recording system. A "live" microphone.

Operating Level In ANALOG tape recorders, the operating level or reference level is a signal level near the maximum possible for the recorder but low enough to ensure acceptably low DISTORTION. The difference between operating level and the maximum possible level is known as HEADROOM, and is measured in dB. The operating level is typically about 10 dB below the level that causes 3% third harmonic distortion (or sometimes total harmonic distortion or "THD") at mid-frequencies (around 400 Hz to 1 kHz). Operating level then gives approximately 10 dB of headroom before severe distortion, but this is dependent on several factors such as tape speed and frequency. Often, very high level signals are compressed by saturation and have high distortion, but for brief signals, this may be acceptable. In practice, it is difficult to record program material and precisely achieve the maximum SIGNAL-TO-NOISE RATIO. For the original American tape recorders of the 1950s, the operating level for analog tape recorders was generally accepted by the industry as a level at which a tone of 400 hertz would produce 1 percent third harmonic distortion (or THD), essentially the same in this case, as the predominant distortion in a tape recorder is 3rd harmonic. Maximum level was considered 3% distortion, and the headroom was 6 dB. Later, a fluxivity of 185 nanowebers/meter on the tape was established as the operating level, which was often referred to as "Ampex Operating Level" after the originator of the American tape recorder. This level was lower than the 1% distortion level, hence there was more headroom, and a little less signal to noise ratio. Referencing a fluxivity was easier than measuring distortion. A test tape with a known fluxivity of 185 nWb/m could be played back and the tape recorder adjusted so 0 dB showed on the VU meter. When recording, the operator knew that signals near 0 dB were good for signal-to-noise and that 6 dB of headroom was available for louder peaks.

Later improvements to analog tape led to increased operating levels, in approximately 3 dB increments. Thus, a major improvement in tape in the

1960s, often called "low noise/high output," could use a reference level of 250 nWb/m with the same distortion as the old tape, and enjoy a 3 dB improvement in signal to noise ratio. This was called a "+3" or elevated operating level. More tape improvements led to +6 dB (370 nWb/m) and even +9 dB (520 nWb/m) operating levels. If you had a 185 nWb/m test tape and wanted to have a 250 nWb/m operating level, the recorder would be adjusted so that the test tape would play at an indicated –3 dB on the VU meter. Engineers were certainly free to trade signal to noise improvement for less headroom and use a +6 reference level on a tape designed for +3, or do the opposite and reduce signal to noise for more headroom. The electronics in some tape recorders were not designed to handle elevated levels and would produce unacceptable distortion. Some other recorders, such as the Swiss Nagra, used special circuitry to cancel third harmonic distortion to allow very high operating levels with good headroom and low distortion.

VU meters are only marked 3 dB above 0, so some signals may still be recorded with reasonable distortion even though the meters are PEGGED. The skillful operator can juggle various factors such as the spectral content of the signal, musical dynamics, tape speed, and recorder characteristics to achieve a good balance between low distortion and low noise.

European methods for measuring fluxivity differ from the American, so the numbers will be slightly different. A standard European (IEC/DIN) test tape at 320 nWb/m is about equal to the American (ANSI) fluxivity of 290 nWb/m at mid-frequencies, thus about 1.3 dB higher than an American 250 nWb/m tape. Research by John McKnight in 1998 indicated that this difference was due to measurement errors and is not real.

Because there are so many variables, fluxivities may vary a bit in specifications. Carefully recorded test tapes can be purchased with known fluxivities to enable adjustment of a recorder's operating level. When exchanging tapes with others, it is important to note the reference level used along with the other tape data. With analog cassettes, operating levels are not well standardized, although 0 dB levels of 145–200 nWb/m are common. The lack of standardization is likely due to wide variations in cassette tape and recorder performance and the desire to simplify operation for consumers. *See also* REFERENCE LEVEL.

Operational Amplifier See OPAMP.

Optical Sound Track The method for photographically recording sound on film for reproduction in the theater. Optical sound tracks were introduced in theaters in the United States about 1930. *See* VARIABLE AREA, VARIABLE DENSITY, and SVA for details. With the introduction of digital sound in motion pictures, Dolby developed a system of optical printing of the digital code beside the existing optical analog sound track. At about the same time, DTS (Digital Theater Systems) was introduced and uses a relatively simple code printed with the optical sound track to synchronize the film motion to the multitrack digital sound that is recorded on a CD-ROM to be played in concert with the film.

Optimum Source Impedance The optimum source impedance is that source IMPEDANCE connected to the input of an active device that results in the minimum noise added to the signal. The OSI depends on the type of device but is independent of the INPUT IMPEDANCE and independent of the circuit configuration. FIELD EFFECT TRANSISTORS have an OSI of several megohms, whereas most bipolar TRANSISTORS have an OSI of several thousand ohms.

Opto-Isolator A SEMICONDUCTOR device that contains a light source, usually in the form of an LED, and a light-sensitive device such as a phototransistor or light-dependent resistor. Current in the LED causes it to emit light (usually infrared), which increases the conductivity of the light-sensitive element. Opto-isolators are commonly used as replacements for relays and switches and sometimes can replace mechanical ATTENUATORS. They are also sometimes called opto-couplers. The advantage of the opto-isolator is that its input circuit has no electrical connection to its output circuit, and such complications as GROUND LOOPS can thus be easily avoided.

Orange Peel When records are pressed, the STAMPERS are placed between the platens of the record press, which applies a force of about 150 tons. If the surface of the platens is not perfectly smooth, the irregularities in its surface will be impressed in the record through the stamper, which is quite thin metal. A regular pattern of tiny bumps is the usual effect, and it is called orange peel because of the resemblance of the record surface to the skin of an orange. Orange peel causes an increase in low-FREQUENCY noise. Records with orange peel can be identified by looking at light reflected from the smooth surface between the inner grooves and the label. Any departure from a mirror-like smoothness is bad news.

The constant heating and cooling of the press platens causes the crystalline structure to roughen the surface, so they must be removed and ground flat periodically, which is an expensive operation.

Order In discussing FILTERS, the number of POLES a certain filter possesses is called the "order" of the filter. Thus a T-section is a third-order filter and an L-section is a second-order filter, etc. The slope, in decibels per octave, of the filter response in its STOPBAND is equal to 6 times the order.

ORTF Acronym for Office de Radiodiffusion—Television Française, the French national broadcasting system. The French have designed a MICROPHONE configuration for STEREOPHONIC recording that is known as the ORTF method.

The method calls for two CARDIOID microphones to be spaced 17 centimeters apart and placed at an angle of 110 degrees. The microphones are thus each 55 degrees from the centerline. The 17-cm separation is to simulate normal human ear spacing, and the 110 degrees is to simulate the directional pattern of the ears.

Recordings made in accordance with the ORTF method sound more open and spacious than those produced by the X-Y method of recording, and are quite well suited to HEADPHONE listening; but they do sound somewhat "dry" and lacking in warmth due to the directional patterns of the cardioids, which pick up little ambient room sound. Because of the close spacing of the microphones and the resultant similarity in PHASE, ORTF does provide MONO COMPATIBILITY, that elusive quality broadcasters are forever seeking.

Orthogonal Two phenomena are said to be orthogonal to each other if they can exist in the same medium at the same time and not interfere with one another. The two motions of the STYLUS in a STEREO record groove are an example.

Orthophonic Victrola The Orthophonic Victrola was a new type of acoustic phonograph introduced by the Victor Company in 1925. This was the year that Victor introduced the first electrically recorded records, and the new player was sold as the ideal reproducer for them. The Orthophonic Victrola had many design innovations, and surely was the best acoustic phonograph ever produced. Its design was based on research conducted at Bell Telephone Labs, and it contained the first EXPONENTIAL HORN, which was folded in the lower part of the cabinet. The horn mouth was about 18 inches by 30 inches, and the low-frequency reproduction from it was much better than any player made earlier.

The stylus-diaphragm assembly was also very different from traditional designs, having much greater flexibility and introducing the "spider" to couple the stylus lever to the diaphragm at several points instead of just at the center. This also improved the bass response. The Orthophonic Victrola used a spring-wound turntable motor, although many other phonographs had electric drive motors by this time.

It is interesting that the first electrical recordings sounded worse than the current acoustic ones. In several cases, an acoustic and an electrical recording were made of the same performance, and the listener could choose (as is sometimes the case today, when we can choose between a STEREO record and a COMPACT DISC of the same performance). An example we have heard is Paul Whiteman's orchestra playing Gershwin's *Rhapsody in Blue.* The acoustic recording sounds less distorted and generally smoother than its electrical counterpart.

The Orthophonic Victrola sold for $350 in 1925. It greatly outsold the contemporary Brunswick Panatrope, which was the first all-electrical phonograph.

Oscar The name of the first BINAURAL microphone system, made in about 1932 by Harvey Fletcher and the other engineers at the Bell Telephone Laboratories. The original Oscar was a tailor's DUMMY HEAD with microphones where the ears would normally be, and it was used in experiments in binaural transmission of music in the Academy of Music in Philadelphia.

Oscillator An electronic device that generates a periodic SIGNAL of a particular FREQUENCY, usually a SINE WAVE, and sometimes a square wave or other WAVEFORM. Oscillators are common in audio devices, and are also extensively used as test signal generators.

Oscilloscope The oscilloscope ('scope, for short) is a common instrument that displays the instantaneous VOLTAGE of a SIGNAL versus time on the face of a television-like screen. In other words, it displays the WAVEFORM of a signal. It does so by means of a special device called a CATHODE RAY TUBE (CRT), in which a beam of electrons races toward the screen after being deflected in the vertical and horizontal directions by voltages applied to deflection plates in the tube. The electrons impinge on the phosphor coating on the inside of the screen, causing the phosphor to emit light and trace out the path of the beam. A television picture tube is a cathode ray tube.

The oscilloscope is probably the most useful of the arsenal of test equipment available today. It can be used to estimate the FREQUENCY and PHASE of a signal, to see DISTORTION in some cases, and to measure the instantaneous voltage of very rapidly changing signals. *See* CRT.

Some of the newer designs of oscilloscopes use LCD screens (analogous to screens used in most laptop computers) instead of CRTs. These scopes use digital signal processing, and there is sometimes a noticeable time delay between a change in the signal and the change on the screen. This delay means they are not very good at displaying changing LISSAJOUS FIGURES.

OSI *See* OPTIMUM SOURCE IMPEDANCE.

Ossicles The three tiny bones (the smallest bones in the body) that transmit vibration of the eardrum to the inner ear, or cochlea. They are sometimes called the hammer, the anvil, and the stirrup.

OTL Short for Output TransformerLess. OTL refers to a type of POWER AMPLIFIER using vacuum tubes but having no output transformer. Usually, an OTL amplifier will have several output TUBES connected as CATHODE FOLLOWERS and acting in PARALLEL to attain a sufficiently low OUTPUT IMPEDANCE. In the case of amplifiers designed for driving ELECTROSTATIC LOUDSPEAKERS, it is relatively easy to design an amplifier with no output transformer because the loudspeaker itself has very high INPUT IMPEDANCE, making it a natural to be driven by tubes.

TRANSISTOR amplifiers, of course, do not need or use output transformers because of their inherent low impedance, and the term OTL is reserved for tube amplifiers.

Outboard Any audio equipment that is not contained within another device. Separate EFFECTS devices such as reverbs and equalizers that are apart from the mixing console would be one example, whereas the equalizers built into the mixer are not considered outboard.

Out of Phase A condition where two signals have a phase difference. If the difference is 180 degrees, or one-half cycle, it should be called "out of POLARITY," phase being a continuous variable rather than discrete.

Output Impedance The output impedance of a device is the actual IMPEDANCE at the output terminals. A PREAMPLIFIER with 600 OHMS output impedance means the output signal appears to be in series with a 600-ohm RESISTOR. Thus, if a 600-ohm resistor is connected across the output, the signal VOLTAGE will be cut in half; one-half appearing across the load resistor, and one-half appearing across the internal impedance.

The internal resistance of a BATTERY also can be considered to be an output impedance, with the battery voltage in series with it. Under no LOAD (i.e., no CURRENT being drawn), the voltage will be at its maximum value, but it will be reduced under load because the current causes a voltage drop across the resistance in accordance with OHM'S LAW. The same thing happens with an audio AMPLIFIER—the lower the output impedance, the less the output voltage will vary with load.

A POWER AMPLIFIER may have a rated impedance of 4 or 8 ohms, but this does not mean the true output impedance is that value. The rated impedance is simply that impedance into which the amplifier will deliver its greatest power. The amplifier is capable of a certain maximum voltage output, determined by the internal power supply. It also has a certain maximum current output, usually determined by the output TRANSISTORS. This maximum voltage at the maximum current can only be delivered to a specific impedance, according to Ohm's law, and this is the rated impedance of the amplifier. *See also* DAMPING FACTOR.

Output Transformer A type of audio TRANSFORMER mostly used in tube-type POWER AMPLIFIERS that couples the output tube PLATES to the LOUDSPEAKER load. The output transformer in such a power amplifier is a very important and critical part of the amplifier, and much effort has been expended over the years to perfect its design.

Outro The opposite of "intro," used in popular music to designate the ending of the piece.

Outtake In a recording session where several TAKES of each selection are recorded, the ones not used in the final master tape are called outtakes.

Overbias The use of more BIAS current in an analog magnetic recorder than is required for maximum sensitivity. Normally, the bias is adjusted so that a test tone will be recorded at maximum level as read on the output VU meter. If the bias is increased above this value, the recorded level will go down. If the GAIN reduction amounts to, say, 2 dB, the recorder is said to have 2 dB of overbias. The overbias will reduce the DISTORTION and the sensitivity to DROPOUTS but will also reduce the high-frequency response, so the record EQUALIZATION control must be adjusted to compensate. The frequency of the test tone depends on the tape speed and the record head characteristics and typically is 5 kHz at 7½ ips tape speed and 10 kHz at 15 ips.

The proper adjustment of the bias in a tape recorder is a compromise because bias affects the noise, distortion, frequency response, and dropout sensitivity in a complex way.

Overdrive To input a SIGNAL to an audio device in such magnitude that an OVERLOAD occurs is to overdrive it.

Overdub In analog tape recording, if a tape is copied from one machine to another and if another SIGNAL is added to the copy at the same time, then the copy is called an overdub, and the process is called overdubbing, or sweetening.

Successive overdubbing can create the effect of a great many different musical lines all playing simultaneously. One disadvantage of overdubbing is that it involves repeated copying of the various tracks as new ones are added, and this adds NOISE at the rate of 3 DECIBELS per copy. A better, although more expensive, way to achieve the same effect is to use a multiple-track tape recorder, and record the tracks one at a time, each time while listening to the previous tracks. This is called SEL-SYNC in Ampex parlance, although it is still informally referred to as overdubbing.

Overdubbing can also be performed in the digital domain in an editing work station or DAW, and this does not add the 3 dB of noise with each successive addition of another track. The repeated digital mixing and processing does add some DISTORTION, although probably not very much.

Overhung Coil In a dynamic LOUDSPEAKER, the VOICE COIL can be made to be longer than the magnetic gap in which it resides. It is then called an overhung coil, because the ends of the coil "overhang" the gap. The raison d'être of the overhung coil is to decrease the nonlinear DISTORTION of the loudspeaker for a given power output. This is accomplished because the coil, as it moves in and out of the gap, maintains a constant number of turns of wire in the magnetic field, so the force on the cone is not dependent on the position of the cone.

There is a trade-off, however, for the turns of the coil that are not in the gap do not result in any force on the cone, and they simply add RESISTANCE to the voice coil IMPEDANCE, which wastes amplifier power. This reduces the EFFICIENCY of the speaker, but many designers, especially of small "bookshelf" systems, believe the lower distortion is more valuable than high efficiency. *See also* UNDERHUNG COIL.

Overload An overload is said to occur when the input SIGNAL level in an AUDIO device is so large that it drives the device out of its LINEAR range and into DISTORTION or CLIPPING. Overload may be continuous or may occur only on short peaks in musical WAVEFORMS. The latter condition is common with certain waveforms, such as sharp percussive sounds that have a peak value much greater than their average value. This "peak clipping," as it is called, must be avoided for true HIGH-FIDELITY recording and reproduction, although a small amount of it may be quite difficult to hear in practice.

Overmodulation A situation that occurs when the AMPLITUDE of a SIGNAL exceeds the limits of the broadcasting transmitter system. Broadcast stations almost always have limiters in the signal path to prevent overmodulation at the transmitter. The opposite of undermodulation.

The term only actually applies when true modulation of a carrier is involved; sometimes it is also used to mean "overloading" or "CLIPPING," which is not correct usage.

Overs The overloading of peaks in a digital audio signal, producing CLIPPING of the signal and, if severe, bursts of noise. Some software will attempt to count overs, and some CD replicators will reject masters that have excessive overs. In any event, an over in a digital system means DISTORTION, whether plainly audible or not.

Oversampling In reading or copying digital audio data, the signal may be sampled at a higher sampling frequency than was used in generating the digital signal in the first place. For instance, in some COMPACT DISC players, the nominal 44.1-KILOHERTZ SAMPLING FREQUENCY is raised to 176.4 kHz, or a factor of 4 higher. This means three artificial samples are created in between each pair of original samples. These samples are zero in level, and they do not change the information content of the original samples. DIGITAL filtering is then used for interpolation of the zero samples to values intermediate between the true 44.1-kHz sampled values. But because the sampling rate is now so much higher, a very gentle ANTI-ALIASING FILTER can be used rather than the BRICKWALL FILTER usually needed, resulting in much less PHASE DISTORTION of the signal. *See also* SAMPLING. Oversampling can occur at different multiples of the original sampling frequency, such as 8X or more.

Overshoot If a COMPRESSOR or LIMITER is subjected to a sudden large input signal level, its GAIN reduction circuitry may not be fast enough to prevent the output from being momentarily too high. This initial excessive level is called overshoot, and its severity depends on the speed of the device.

Also, imperfect transient response in an audio device will result in the WAVEFORM going past the desired value on fast signal transitions. This is also called overshoot and is frequently seen on square waves and impulse responses of CD players.

Overtones Overtones are tones produced by a musical instrument that are higher in FREQUENCY than the FUNDAMENTAL. They may or may not coincide with the frequencies of a HARMONIC SERIES.

All musical instruments produce complex sound WAVEFORMS that repeat at their fundamental frequency. Any complex periodic waveform such as this can be expressed as a collection of SINE WAVES of frequencies of integral multiples of the fundamental, or lowest frequency. These SINUSOIDAL components are called harmonics, or a harmonic series, the first harmonic being the fundamental. Generally, the harmonics excluding the fundamental are called overtones, the first overtone being the second harmonic, etc. Overtones are sometimes called PARTIALS.

Oxide The magnetic material in almost all analog magnetic tapes consists of the various oxides of iron and sometimes chromium. The business side of the tape is called the "oxide side." Debris that rubs off the tape and collects on the TAPE HEADS and guides is mostly oxide and binder, and the phenomenon is called oxide shed. Digital audio magnetic recorders usually use metal particle tapes that do not use oxides, but metallic particles encapsulated in a material to prevent their oxidation.

P

Φ The Greek letter phi, pronounced "fee" in Greek and usually "fye" in English. It is often used as an abbreviation for phase. Some control consoles have a small switch on their input modules labeled Φ that inverts the polarity of the signal in that channel. This is to allow all the signals being mixed together to have the same POLARITY regardless of wiring errors in patch panels and microphone cables and in the MICROPHONES themselves. *See also* PHASE INVERT.

The letter is also the physical symbol for magnetic flux.

PA Short for Public Address. An archaic term for a sound system used in auditoriums and other venues where people gather to listen to music or a speech.

Pack *See* TAPE PACK.

Pad A short name for attenuator, usually with a fixed amount of insertion loss. Pads are used between audio devices if there is a danger of the output of one device causing a signal OVERLOAD in the input of the other device. Some MICROPHONES have very high output voltages and will overdrive some PREAMPLIFIERS, so a pad of 10 to 20 decibels is inserted in the microphone line.

PAL, Phase Alternating Line The terrestrial ANALOG television broadcasting system used in most of Europe, (except France, which uses SECAM) is called PAL. The system uses 625 horizontal lines with interlaced scanning at the rate of 50 fields per second. The phase of the color portion of the video signal is reversed for each alternate line, so in one frame the alternating lines have alternating POLARITY. This improves the color quality because the reverse polarity compensates for unavoidable phase errors in the adjacent line caused by the transmission chain. PAL receivers, unlike those of the NTSC system, do not have tint controls because the colors are always true due to the color signal phase correction.

Pan To position the stereo image of an instrument or vocal across the stereo image. *See also* PANPOT.

Pancake A pancake is a 10½-inch reel of recording tape without the reel FLANGES. In other words, it is simply the tape wound onto a hub with no side supports. Recording studios often bought tape in this form and spooled it onto smaller empty reels to use. Spooling the tape off onto another reel is one thing, but it is quite another to try to spool it back onto the pancake. This usually results in a tangled disaster. One solution is to keep a pair of loose flanges around to sandwich the tape in when spooling the pancake.

P & Q Subcodes *See* SUBCODES.

Panotrope The Panotrope was the first phonograph that used electrical rather than mechanical means to extract the SIGNAL from the groove of the record. It had a magnetic CARTRIDGE, an AMPLIFIER using several TUBES, and a LOUDSPEAKER. It was made by the Brunswick company, introduced in about 1925, and sold for something like $650.

Panpot Short for panoramic POTENTIOMETER, which is two connected volume controls with a common knob, so wired that as one is turned "up," the other is turned "down." If the two STEREO channels are controlled by a panpot, the apparent position of the sound will move from left to right as the control is turned. The BALANCE control on most stereo AMPLIFIERS is actually a simple panpot.

Panpots are used in recording to place the apparent position of a sound, such as a soloist or other instrument, anywhere between the two LOUDSPEAKERS. Its operation relies on the ability of our ears to localize a sound by level differences heard by our two ears. *See also* BINAURAL. For a panpot to work properly, it must follow an accurately prescribed ATTENUATION curve. In many recordings, several instruments are given separate positions by using a panpot on each one when the final "mix" is made.

Assigning instrument locations by panpot is somewhat poor at best, because it assumes that the listener will be midway between the speakers. Otherwise, intensity CUES do not work very well, and the listener tends to localize the sound as coming from one speaker or the other, rather than being spread between them.

There exist multichannel panpots for use in motion picture sound tracks, where a sound may be "panned" across three channels as the source moves across the screen or from side to side using the surround speakers.

If a panpot were made that supplied small time and spectral differences between the channels as well as simple volume differences, it would be much more effective, although it would be complicated and expensive to implement.

Parabolic Microphone A MICROPHONE system consisting of a reflecting surface in the shape of a paraboloid and an otherwise conventional CARDIOID microphone mounted at its focus. Such microphones are extremely directional at high frequencies, making them well suited for picking up bird songs outdoors. The reflector is usually made of clear plastic, and may be from 18 to 36 inches in diameter. Parabolic microphones are often used by television crews at sporting events in order to capture dialogue (or monologue) on the field.

Parabolic microphones have somewhat limited FREQUENCY RESPONSE, and are not used where high-quality sound is required. However, they are much more directional and sensitive on-axis than SHOTGUN MICROPHONES.

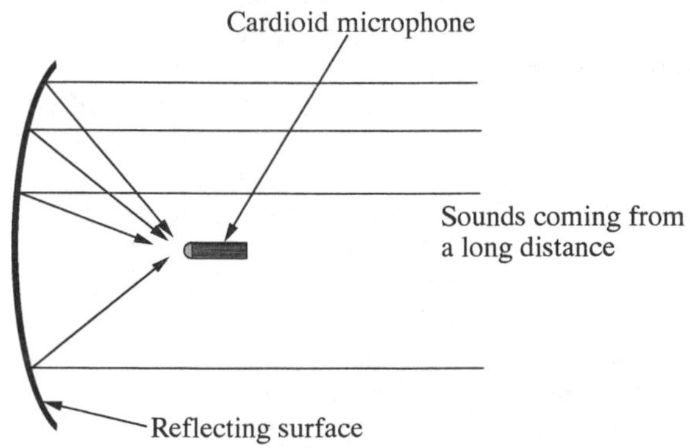

Parabolic Microphone

Paragraphic Equalizer A form of PARAMETRIC EQUALIZER that uses slider controls similar to GRAPHIC EQUALIZER controls rather than rotary knobs.

Parallel Electric CIRCUIT elements are said to be connected in parallel if the CURRENT divides at the connection point and part of it goes to each element. This is in contrast to a SERIES connection, in which all the current in each element is the same.

In a parallel circuit, the VOLTAGE across each element is always the same, but the current in each element depends on the individual IMPEDANCE of the element. As more elements are connected in parallel, the combined impedance is reduced. For this reason it can be difficult to drive many LOUDSPEAKERS in parallel from a single AMPLIFIER; the combined impedance can become so low that the amplifier cannot supply sufficient current to drive them.

In most ACTIVE audio devices, the INPUT IMPEDANCE is relatively high and the OUTPUT impedance relatively low so several devices can be connected or "paralleled" to the output of a single device with no problems.

Parameter *See* PARAMETRIC EQUALIZER.

Parametric Equalizer A parametric EQUALIZER has several "parameters" that can be varied. Typically there are several resonant CIRCUITS in such a unit, and they can accentuate or reduce selected FREQUENCY bands. They can be adjusted to be quite selective in frequency, operating in a very narrow BAND, or the response can be widened to cover a much wider band. So-called "sweepable" parametric equalizers are able to move the center frequencies of the equalization bands. Also sometimes called a "peaking equalizer." *See also* EQUALIZER.

Parasitic Oscillation A malfunction occurring in some audio devices, especially POWER AMPLIFIERS, in which the device will generate an ultra-high-frequency signal during a part of the audio signal. The oscillation is present only when the signal is present and occurs only during part of the audio WAVEFORM. Parasitic oscillation can burn out TWEETERS. Although the ULTRASONIC component is not directly audible, its existence causes audible distortion in the signal.

Partials The FREQUENCY components that make up musical sounds, also called OVERTONES or harmonics, although these terms are more specific. Harmonics are defined as integral multiples of a lowest, or FUNDAMENTAL, frequency of a sound, and they are precisely in tune with each other and the fundamental. Many musical instruments closely produce true harmonics, but many others, such as the piano, do not. Harmonics are numbered in succession from the fundamental, which is the first harmonic.

The term *partial* is defined as any component of a complex tone, whether it is in tune with the fundamental or not. Partials may be lower in frequency than the fundamental; then they are sometimes called subharmonics. Overtones are defined as the harmonics above the fundamental, but in common usage they are taken to mean any partials above the fundamental.

Certain instruments, such as bells and some drums, produce a collection of partials with little resemblance to a harmonic series. In the case of most bells, there is a strong partial at one-half the frequency of the perceived PITCH of the bell, and it is called the "HUM TONE." In many other percussive instruments there are strong out-of-tune partials that can be heard as distinct pitches bearing little or no relation to the perceived pitch of the instrument.

Pascal The SI unit of pressure, abbreviated Pa, equal to 1 newton per square meter. The name comes from the French scientist Blaise Pascal. The reference pressure equivalent to 0 dB SOUND PRESSURE LEVEL is 20 micropascals.

Passband The passband of a FILTER is the FREQUENCY span that the filter passes, or the range of frequencies not attenuated by the filter. The passband is usually measured between the points where the response is 3 DECIBELS down in AMPLITUDE relative to the maximum level.

Passive A device is called passive if it contains no amplification circuitry and a signal suffers a loss in power or level in passing through it. This loss is called INSERTION LOSS. Some passive devices, such as transformers, can increase the voltage or the current of a signal, but they all result in a power loss.

Many audio EQUALIZERS used to be passive, but most are active now. CROSSOVER NETWORKS inside loudspeaker cabinets are passive.

Passive devices in general do not add any appreciable NONLINEAR distortion or noise to the signal, but they may have so much insertion loss that additional amplification is needed, and this always contributes some noise and distortion. Passive devices can and do cause PHASE DISTORTION, however. There are many passive equalizer devotees among recording engineers who claim they sound better (or at least different from active ones) and they are often traded at high prices.

Passive Radiator A passive radiator is a device resembling a low-frequency LOUDSPEAKER (WOOFER), but it has no VOICE COIL or magnet assembly. It is a CONE with a flexible suspension. It is placed in some loudspeaker cabinets as a replacement for a PORT or DUCTED PORT. Such a system operates something like a BASS REFLEX system, but the extra mass of the passive CONE reduces the FREQUENCY of the resonance, allowing low frequency performance with a smaller cabinet than a true bass reflex would need. The passive radiator, however, has some other problems. The mass of the cone is relatively great and the resulting resonance is difficult to DAMP, and this can lead to bass HANGOVER and a "boomy" sound.

PA System *See* PUBLIC ADDRESS SYSTEM.

Patch Bay Generally, a group of connectors on a panel where PATCH CORDS are interconnected in various configurations to route audio signals. The most common design consists of modules of two rows of twenty-four ¼-inch jacks in a 1U RACK panel. This design dates from early telephone company use. As many modules as needed are added to form the full patch bay, although just one such module can be called a patch bay. Traditionally, outputs are wired to the top jacks, and inputs wired to the lower jacks. In order to avoid having to use patch cords at every jack, the input/output pairs that are normally used as-is are prewired such that the signal is already connected without the need for a patch cord. However, inserting a plug into the upper jack disconnects the prewired connection through a switching mechanism, sending the upper jack signal only to the inserted cord. Similarly, inserting a plug into the lower jack would disconnect the prewired connection, and allow only the inserted cord to be connected to that lower jack. This is called a normalled pair of jacks. Another configuration of jack pairs is called half-normalled. In this case, inserting a plug into the top jack does not disconnect the normalling, so that the output can be routed to 2 places—the normal jack below, and the inserted patch cord. However, inserting a plug into the lower jack does disconnect the normalling. Usually there are also provisions to have no normalling at all between jacks, and some designs allow easy changes between configurations. Although most patch bays present ¼-inch phone jacks on the front, the rear connections may be ¼-inch phone jacks, RCA jacks, punchdown terminals, or solder lugs. Many large mixing consoles use a smaller jack and patch cord known as the Tini-Tel. Television signal patch bays may look similar, but use a special high-frequency connector. *See also* PATCH CORD.

Patch Cord A relatively short AUDIO cable with connectors on each end is commonly called a patch cord. It is used for interconnecting various devices where the configuration must be changed from time to time. Recording studios make good use of patch cords.

The most common type of patch cord is probably the one using quarter-inch "phone" plugs on each end. This connector was first used by the telephone exchanges, hence the name. The telephone patch cord contains three conductors: two for the SIGNAL and a SHIELD. The connector also has three contacts, called tip, ring, and sleeve (thus, called TRS). The tip is always the "hot" side of the SIGNAL, the ring is the low side, or GROUND, and the sleeve is the shield. There also exist phone plugs that have only two conductors: tip and sleeve. They are common in nonprofessional audio equipment.

MICROPHONE signals should not be patched with phone plugs because the shield, or ground connection, is the last one to make contact, and loud pops and 60-Hz hum can result if a live microphone PREAMP input is patched with a TRS plug; rather, three-pin XLR-type plugs and jacks should be used. Pin number 1 in the XLR plug is always connected to the shield. The reason is that the connectors are so designed that pin 1 makes contact first, ensuring that the ground connection is made before the signal connection. This greatly reduces the TRANSIENT thumps and pops that occur when a CIRCUIT is patched with the power turned on. A group of similar receptacles (or "jacks") in an audio system is called a PATCH BAY, and the act of plugging and unplugging the cords is called patching. Recording consoles used in studios make extensive use of patch bays for ease of rerouting signals, especially microphone signals. *See* PHONE PLUG; TRS; XLR.

Patch Panel Another name for PATCH BAY.

PC Board *See* PRINTED CIRCUIT BOARD.

PCM Pulse Code Modulation (PCM) refers to any type of DIGITAL encoding and decoding of a SIGNAL. Some types of PCM are:

1. LINEAR PCM, where the VOLTAGE range of the ANALOG signal to be digitized is divided into a certain number of equal intervals. All the QUANTIZATION steps are the same size in such a system. This is the most common PCM for audio applications.

2. NONLINEAR PCM, wherein a COMPANDER is inserted before a linear PCM encoder. This will give the system better resolution at low signal levels at the expense of resolution at high signal levels. This system is desirable when the number of BITS for encoding is limited, and is widely used in telecommunications work.

3. Floating-point PCM. The floating-point converter produces an output digital word consisting of two parts: an exponent and a mantissa. The exponent represents the GAIN in a variable-gain AMPLIFIER that precedes a linear PCM encoder, which produces the mantissa. The GAIN is thus adjusted stepwise in order to best encode the variable-level input signal, and higher resolution is attained.

4. Differential PCM. A form of linear PCM where the difference between the present SAMPLE value and the previous sample value is encoded, rather than encoding the actual value of each sample. This has the advantage of requiring fewer bits than does straight linear PCM. If the encoding is done with only one bit, this special case is called DELTA-SIGMA MODULATION, originally called Sigma-Delta by its inventors.

Probably the most used schemes are linear PCM and Delta-Sigma differential PCM. However, when audio people speak of PCM, they invariably are referring to linear PCM, and Delta-Sigma is invariably explicitly called that.

PD *See* PRODIGI.

Peak Peak value is the maximum instantaneous excursion from zero of an audio WAVEFORM. The peak value of a sound is also the maximum instantaneous pressure excursion of the sound.

Usually, when measuring peak values of signals, a relatively short time interval is considered. For instance, the peak value of a recording of Beethoven's Ninth Symphony will, strictly speaking, be represented by a single value somewhere in the piece, but the peak value of the waveform of the symphony (determined over short time intervals of maybe a second or so) will vary with the dynamic level of the music at that particular time. *See also* RMS and CREST FACTOR.

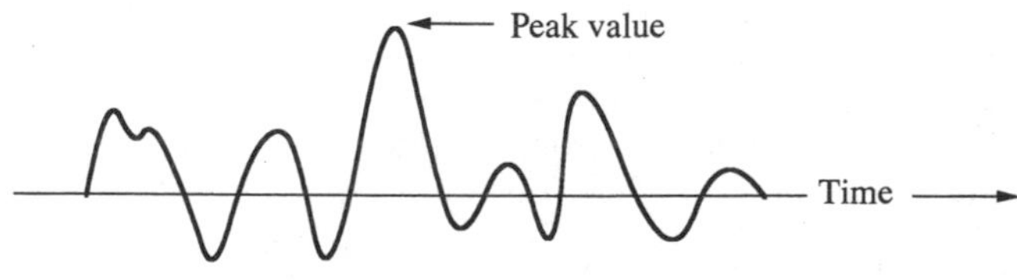

Peak Value of a Waveform

Peak Expansion A VOLUME EXPANDER can be adjusted so the expansion only occurs when the input signal is above a certain loudness level. This results in the expansion of the peaks in the program and does not affect the rest of the signal. Peak expansion can add "naturalism" to music that has been overly compressed.

Peak Hold A function of some volume indicators that indicates the peak level of the signal and holds that level until it is either exceeded by a higher peak or the indicator is reset by a time delay or manual reset button. *See also* PPM.

Peak Level Meter Same as peak program meter (PPM) and peak program indicator (PPI). *See* PPM.

Peak Limiter *See* LIMITER.

PEAQ, Perceptual Evaluation of Audio Quality PEAQ is an objective method for determining the perceived quality of wide-bandwidth audio. Its raison d'être is to eliminate the need for subjective evaluation of different types of audio signal processing and reproduction systems. Subjective evaluation of audio systems is time consuming, difficult, and expensive, because it uses a panel of human subjects for extended listening tests and relies on the subjects to explain what they heard using various statistical methods. Subjective evaluation tests are reliable when properly conducted, but they are not used very often due to their difficulty and expense. PEAQ was standardized by the International Telecommunications Union (ITU) in the document published as BS-1387. The standard was a joint effort by many workers in laboratories in Canada, the Netherlands, France, and Germany. The standard describes in detail how to objectively measure the quality of audio processing systems such as different CODECs associated with different sampling rates. Two methods are described in the standard, a basic and an advanced version. The advanced version is said to be more exactly repeatable in its results.

PEC/Direct In film re-recording, the act of switching between playback from the recorder (either off the play or record heads) and the console BUS. "PEC" stands for photoelectric cell and originates from when monitoring off optical photoelectric cell was as close as you could get to "playback."[22]

Pegged, Pegging When a strong signal connected to a meter, such as a VU meter on a tape recorder, causes the meter to reach its maximum possible level, the meter is said to be "pegged." The moving needle in the meter contacts a mechanical stop called the peg, hence the name. Pegging a VU meter is not a good idea because the needle may be bent or even broken by severe pegging. Of course, SOLID-STATE level indicators do not have moving needles, but they are still said to be "pegged" when overloaded.

Penthouse A metal housing containing the magnetic reproduce HEAD STACK for pickup of the sound from 35-mm and 70-mm motion picture film that has been SOUND-STRIPED. It is called a penthouse because it sits atop

22. This entry is copyright © 1999–2003 by Larry Blake and is reprinted with permission.

the movie projector, with the film going through it before entering the projector itself. Most digital readers now reside in the penthouse. There are a few readers called "basement" readers that are retrofits in the optical sound head.

Pentode A vacuum TUBE containing five active elements: the CATHODE, control GRID, screen grid, suppressor grid, and PLATE. The pentode has high gain and high efficiency and is used as a VOLTAGE amplifier stage in audio amplifiers. It has greater DISTORTION than the TRIODE, however.

The name comes from the Greek *hodos,* meaning "path," and *penta* meaning "five." Early pentodes were called "pentahodos."

%AlCons Percentage Articulation Loss of Consonants, a figure of merit for speech intelligibility in a room. A value of 10% loss or less is typically considered acceptable. In the 1950s, V. M. A. Peutz of the Netherlands conducted research using taped spoken words and human listeners, and determined that articulation loss of spoken vowel sounds did not correlate to intelligibility like consonants did. He determined a formula that correlated the %Alcons to measured room characteristics. Instruments such as the TEF analyzer can also calculate the %Alcons. %Alcons is popular in the U.S., but has shortcomings such as being limited to the 2-kHz band if the TEF analyzer is used. *See also* RASTI.

Perceptual Coding The digital audio coding scheme used on COMPACT DISCS (CDs) yields an amount of data often too immense to store or transmit economically, especially when multiple channels are required. As a result, new forms of digital audio coding, often known as "perceptual coding," have been developed to allow the use of lower data rates with a minimum of perceived degradation of sound quality. Perceptual coding schemes are "lossy," meaning the decoded signal is not identical to the original signal that was encoded because some of the data is discarded. But the losses are carefully designed so that they are essentially not audible. To perform this trick, the coder analyzes the input music signal and decides not to encode certain parts that would be inaudible due to MASKING in the ear, where loud sounds drown out softer sounds that are also present in the music. In a sense, a perceptual coder fools the ear into thinking it is hearing the entire music signal in its original form, and some are better than others at doing the job. Of course the acuity of the ear listening to the result varies also, adding to the complication. Dolby's audio-coding algorithm AC-3 is such a coder. *See also* CODEC.

Perfect Pitch *See* ABSOLUTE PITCH.

Perfs Slang for perforations in motion picture film, also called sprocket holes. Dolby Digital sound data on 35-mm film is located between the perfs.

Period In a WAVEFORM that repeats a particular pattern over and over, the time required for one repetition is called the period. The waveform is then called PERIODIC, and can be expressed as the summation of a series of SINE WAVES called HARMONICS. *See also* FOURIER ANALYSIS.

Periodic When the WAVEFORM of a SIGNAL repeats the same shape over and over, the waveform is said to be periodic, and the period is the time

The shape of the waveform repeats each period of time.

Periodic Waveform

required for one repetition. The repetition rate is called the FUNDAMENTAL FREQUENCY, and is equal to the reciprocal of the period, or $F = {}^1\!/_T$. If the period varies from repetition to repetition but still has the same general form, the signal is quasi-periodic. If there is no discernable repetition period, the signal is aperiodic. WHITE NOISE and PINK NOISE are examples of aperiodic signals.

Most musical instruments produce periodic, or nearly periodic, sounds, but some do not. Many percussion instruments produce sounds resembling random noise. *See also* FUNDAMENTAL.

Permalloy Permalloy is a special metallic alloy that has a very high magnetic PERMEABILITY. In other words, it is easy to establish a magnetic field in it. It is used in the pole pieces of analog TAPE HEADS and for the cores of some audio TRANSFORMERS.

Permeability The relative ease with which a magnetic field can be established in a medium is the medium's magnetic permeability. Of the common metals, iron has a high permeability; MUMETAL is a special alloy with very high permeability. Magnetic TAPE HEADS are designed with high-permeability cores to increase their SENSITIVITY, and magnetic SHIELDS are designed to have high permeability. The units of permeability are henrys per meter (H/m), and its symbol is the Greek letter μ (mu).

Perspecta Sound A type of single-channel magnetic sound recording system for motion pictures that used three subaudible tones (30, 35, and 40 hertz) mixed with the audio signal as control tones for varying the volume and placement of the sound image reproduced through three LOUDSPEAKER systems behind the screen. The tones were separated by BAND-PASS FILTERS and fed into the control inputs of variable GAIN amplifiers. You might well ask why the tones were considered subaudible; the reason was that the theater loudspeakers of the day were not able to reproduce such low frequencies at audible levels.

Perspecta sound was introduced in 1954 by the respected recording engineer Robert Fine, and was essentially an updated hi-fi magnetic version of the old VITASOUND optical system of the 1930s. Like Vitasound, it was COMPATIBLE in that a standard projection system with no control circuitry would simply reproduce the sound in a conventional way. Even though Perspecta sound was a MONAURAL system, it was said to produce pleasing and convincing audible effects in the theater.

PFL, Pre Fader Listen On a mixing console, the PFL button on an input allows monitoring of that input channel regardless of the input fader position.

PFX, Production Sound Effects Sound effects recorded on the production sound track during filming. PFX are kept separate during dialog editing and mixed with the music and Foley effects to create a complete sound track without the dialog. This track can then be mixed with any number of foreign language dialog tracks to create finished foreign language versions of the picture.

Phantom Center Channel A third LOUDSPEAKER placed between the two conventional loudspeakers in a stereo system to provide simulated three-channel stereo reproduction. The signal fed to the center channel is simply the sum of the two stereo channels. This technique was investigated at some length by Paul Klipsch (inventor of the famous KLIPSCHORN) in the late 1950s. The phantom channel does tend to reduce the effect of the HOLE IN THE MIDDLE but is not equivalent to true three-channel reproduction. The phantom signal can be derived simply by summing the two stereo channels with resistors and feeding this sum to a third amplifier and then to the speaker. If the power amplifiers have output transformers, as all tube-type amplifiers do, the phantom signal can be obtained by suitable connections to the transformer secondaries, avoiding the need for the extra amplifier.

Phantom Image A monophonic sound panned equally to both left and right stereo speakers. *See also* PHANTOM CENTER CHANNEL.

Phantom Power CONDENSER MICROPHONES require a PREAMPLIFIER to be close by due to the extremely high IMPEDANCE of the MICROPHONE itself. This preamplifier is in the housing of the microphone, and it needs a POWER source. Sometimes a battery is used, but more often a multiwire cable brings the audio signal from the microphone and brings the power from an external POWER SUPPLY to the preamp. This is a rather bulky and expensive arrangement. To eliminate the multiconductor cable, frequently a scheme called phantom powering is used, whereby the preamp power is carried by the same two wires that carry the SIGNAL. The key to its operation is the fact that the signal is ALTERNATING CURRENT and the power is DIRECT CURRENT, and they can be separated by the action of a transformer.

The direct-current path is from the power supply through two RESISTORS connected across the input transformer primary, through the microphone cable, and then through the secondary windings of the microphone output transformer and out through its center tap and to the preamp. The direct current in the transformer secondary does not magnetize the core because its direction in each half of the coil is such that it cancels itself out as far as the core is concerned. There is no direct current in the primary of the input transformer to the control console or tape recorder, even though the power supply VOLTAGE is present on it. This voltage causes no harm to the AUDIO signal.

Microphones and inputs without transformers separate the AC audio signal from the DC phantom power with blocking capacitors.

The voltage used for phantom powering is usually 48 volts, but it can vary from about 12 to 52 volts. Microphones that use the lower voltages have a regulator CIRCUIT to reduce the higher voltages so no harm is done when they are plugged into a 48-volt phantom power supply. The technical details of phantom power are given in the IEC standard 268-15.

Phase If a SINE WAVE signal is viewed on an OSCILLOSCOPE, the horizontal axis is time, and the shape of the wave is the same as the mathematical sine function, or SINUSOID, related to the geometry of a right triangle. The sine of an angle of a right triangle is the ratio of the length of the side opposite the angle to the hypotenuse and is a function only of the angle itself. The sine CURVE is thus a plot of this ratio versus angle, and the value of the angle is called phase.

In the SINUSOIDAL signal, time replaces angle in the graph, although it is convenient to speak of angle as well as time being the independent variable. A sinusoid goes through 360 degrees in one cycle, whereby it then returns to its starting point. The sine wave signal is also said to go through 360 degrees in one cycle; another way of saying the same thing is that the signal has gone through 360 degrees of phase angle, or phase change. The phase is actually a measure of time; 360 degrees equaling one PERIOD of the signal. The time represented by phase change of a certain number of degrees is thus dependent on FREQUENCY.

Phase Compensation In some analog tape recorders, there is a special EQUALIZER whose purpose is to make the PHASE response of the machine more LINEAR, i.e., to reduce relative PHASE SHIFT as FREQUENCY varies. The purpose of phase compensation is to improve the reproduction of TRANSIENTS, whose shape depends on the relative phase of the frequency components.

Phase Distortion Phase distortion in an AUDIO signal is relative PHASE SHIFT between various FREQUENCY components of the SIGNAL. Phase distortion causes TRANSIENTS to change in shape, but has a smaller effect on steady-state tones.

Most TRANSDUCERS, such as LOUDSPEAKERS and phono CARTRIDGES, produce significant phase distortion. *See also* PHASE.

Phase Invert A switch found on the inputs of many recording consoles that inverts the POLARITY of the signal in that input. Its purpose is to correct for cables that may be wired backward, microphones that may not be wired according to standard, or for a special effect such as to make a mic sound different in a mix by making the polarity inverted. The phase invert switch is commonly labeled with a circle with a forward slash through it, something like a Greek letter Phi (Φ). The term taken literally is meaningless, but nevertheless has come into popular use. Correct usage would be "polarity invert." *See also* Φ.

Phase Linear An audio device that will pass an audio signal without causing PHASE SHIFT at any FREQUENCY is said to be phase linear.

Phase-Locked Loop A phase-locked loop, or PLL, is an electronic CIRCUIT consisting of a VOLTAGE-controlled OSCILLATOR and a FREQUENCY DISCRIMINATOR connected in such a way that the output of the discriminator controls the oscillator. Such a system will "lock on" to an applied SIGNAL and will oscillate at that frequency. The PLL has some "inertia," and will not change its frequency instantaneously if the input frequency changes. It thus acts as a stabilizing influence, or a sort of frequency flywheel. PLLs are used in SERVO-control circuits, modulation, demodulation, phase modulation, frequency synthesis, and are frequently used as FM detectors, as they require no tuned circuits, and so do not require alignment.

According to Agilent Labs, "one can claim that PLLs are the most ubiquitous form of feedback systems built by engineers."

Phaser A phaser, or phase shifter, is a device that gives an effect similar to FLANGING, but with less depth. It works by shifting the PHASE of the SIGNAL and adding it back to the signal. This causes partial cancellation at frequencies where the phase shift approaches 180 degrees. Phasing is sometimes called skying in Britain.

Phase Shift Phase shift is a characteristic of a device and is the change in PHASE impressed on a SIGNAL that passes through the device.

An AUDIO device will always add a time delay to an applied signal. If this time delay is constant at all frequencies, the phase shift between the input and output of the device will be a LINEAR function of FREQUENCY. Such a system is called phase linear. (The term *phase linear* was used as a commercial trademark for some audio devices that were not actually phase linear in their performance.)

Very few devices are truly phase linear, and deviations from phase linearity are called phase shift. EQUALIZERS in particular exhibit large amounts of phase shift. In a complex WAVEFORM, phase shift will cause a DISTORTION of the waveform, even though the FREQUENCY RESPONSE curve may be perfectly flat. There is considerable controversy over whether the ear can detect this type of distortion, with many audio luminaries shedding more heat than light on the subject. It is definitely true that phase shift can be heard if it is large enough; and in agreement with most hearing phenomena, it is probably true that there is a threshold value below which it is inaudible and above which it is audible. The subject needs further study. DIGITAL audio systems in particular have large amounts of phase shift at very high frequencies.

Phasey, Phasiness Phasiness is a subjective term used to describe certain anomalies in the perception of STEREOPHONIC imaging, and it is difficult to define. The term is used to describe the subjective impression when the two ears hear similar sounds that differ significantly in PHASE.

If one hears exactly the same sound in each ear, either via headphones or LOUDSPEAKERS, the resulting image location will be centered. If the relative phase of one of the channels is shifted, the image will move one way or the other. If the phase is shifted more and more, a point is reached where the image is diffused and smeared, and finally the sound becomes unpleasant to listen to.

It is said that certain INTENSITY STEREO recordings and the AMBISONICS system sound less phasey than other types of stereo recording.

Phasing *See* PHASER.

Phasing Plug *See* COMPRESSION DRIVER.

Phlogiston "A hypothetical substance formerly supposed to exist in combination in all combustible materials and to be released in the process of combustion; the element fire, conceived as fixed in flammable substances." (*OED*) *See also* SMOKE.

Phon The phon is the psychological unit of LOUDNESS LEVEL and is defined as the SOUND PRESSURE LEVEL (SPL) of a 1,000-HERTZ PURE TONE that is judged to be the same loudness as the sound in question.

Because of the ear's complicated response versus FREQUENCY characteristics, it is no good to try to relate the perceived loudness of sounds directly to their sound pressure level as read on a SOUND LEVEL METER. The phon is therefore an attempt to relate perceived loudness to objective measurements of the sound. *See also* FLETCHER-MUNSON EFFECT; LOUDNESS.

Phonautograph The phonautograph was a device invented by Leon Scott in 1857 that recorded the WAVEFORM of sounds with a STYLUS on a rotating glass disc coated with soot by holding it over a smoking flame. It used a short HORN coupled to a diaphragm which in turn moved the STYLUS, and it is surely the most important precursor to the phonograph. The surprising thing is that it took Edison another twenty years to take the step from just recording the sound to being able to reproduce it.

Phone Patch A direct connection from an AUDIO device to a telephone line is called a phone patch if the audio SIGNAL is sent directly to the line. An example of the use of the phone patch is the sending of PROGRAM from the studio to a remote transmitter in radio broadcasting. In order to prevent extraneous noise and to avoid system damage due to component failure, the analog signal is sent through a TELEPHONE HYBRID rather than being directly connected to the telephone line. If the signal is DIGITAL data, a modem is used to interconnect with the telephone line.

Phone Plug One of the most used of audio connectors is the quarter-inch phone plug, which gets its name from its origin in the old telephone switchboards. Phone plugs come in two main varieties, the three-conductor type known as "tip, ring, and sleeve" (TRS), and the two-conductor "tip and sleeve" (TS). The sleeve is always the SHIELD or ground connection. When used on stereo headphones, the TRS plug may be called a stereo plug. There are several other smaller phone plugs common in audio. A .173-inch diameter version is often used in PATCH BAYS and is typically called by any of several trademarked names such as Bantam, TT, Tini-Telephone, Tini-Tel or miniature. Most references to a miniplug refer to a smaller plug used for audio circuits and in portable stereo headsets in the TRS version. The American version is traditionally .141 inches in diameter; however, some retailers refer to it as a ⅛ inch (.125 inch), or 3.5 mm (about .137795 inch). The international standard is 3.5 mm. Smaller still is the subminiplug, commonly seen on cellular phone earsets and some other audio and control devices where space is at a premium. The American version is traditionally .097 inches in diameter, however, some retailers refer to it as a 3⁄32 inch (.09375), or 2.5 mm (about .0984252 inch). The international standard is 2.5 mm. *See also* PATCH CORD; TRS.

Phonograph "An irritating toy that restores life to dead noises," according to Ambrose Bierce.

The term *phonograph* was used by Edison in his 1877 patent application for the first device capable of recording and reproducing sound, but the first known commercial use of the term was by the Englishman F. B. Fenby, who in 1863 patented the "Electro Magnetic Phonograph." His device, however, was for recording the keystrokes of a piano or other keyboard instrument, as the player piano. Later, others used different terms: "GRAMOPHONE" (Berliner's trademark for the first disc recorder/reproducer) and "Graphophone" (first used by Alexander G. Bell for his invention of a machine that he claimed was an improvement on the phonograph).

Edison's phonograph recorded the signal as a variable-depth groove, embossed, rather than cut, in a sheet of tin foil wrapped around a cylinder. It was a "hill-and-dale" modulation rather than the side-to-side, or lateral, modulation of the gramophone. There was a great controversy in the early years of the phonograph industry over the relative merits of the vertical and the lateral modulation. Edison continued to insist on the superiority of vertical, even in his "diamond disc" phonographs introduced after Berliner's Gramophone began to cut into the cylinder machine market. The Emerson Record Company introduced a disc system in 1916 that used modulation at 45 degrees to the surface, halfway between lateral and vertical! This was an early attempt at compatibility between the competing systems.

It is strange that Edison thought the greatest commercial value of the phonograph to be in dictating machines rather than in the recording of music. As far as the exploitation of the capabilities of his invention was concerned, it might be said that Edison barely scratched the surface.

Phonograph Cartridge *See* CARTRIDGE.

Phono Plug A small inexpensive coaxial connector used for interconnection of many audio devices, especially consumer devices. It was first used by RCA to connect the phonograph tone arm to the AMPLIFIER and is sometimes called an RCA plug or a "pin" plug. The mating JACK is called a phono jack, RCA jack, or pin jack. Phono plugs and jacks are notorious for becoming noisy and unreliable after a period of use. Some of the newer ones are gold plated, and this reduces the contact noise caused by corrosion or oxidation of the metal. The same plug is used for most consumer composite video connections and S/PDIF connections, although the cables for such should have 75-ohm characteristic impedance. *See also* RCA PLUG.

Picket Fencing The irregularly occurring distortion of FM broadcasts as picked up by a car radio in the presence of MULTIPATH DISTORTION. Multipath distortion comes about because of the relatively short wavelengths transmitted by FM and television transmitters. Because these wavelengths of FM signals are so short, sometimes moving the receiving antenna only a few feet will make the difference between a listenable and a completely garbled signal.

Pickup Alternative term for phonograph cartridge. *See* CARTRIDGE.

CONTACT MICROPHONES or other TRANSDUCERS used in electric guitars are sometimes called guitar pickups.

Piezoelectricity, Piezoelectric Piezoelectricity is an electric charge that occurs in some substances when they are squeezed or otherwise subjected to a mechanical stress. Quartz is one of the better known piezoelectric materials, and is commonly fabricated into small pieces, called "CRYSTALS," which are used for FREQUENCY standards. The crystal vibrates, similar to a miniature tuning fork, in response to an electric SIGNAL, and the frequency of vibration is very stable. Virtually all electronic watches use quartz crystals as frequency standards, and they can be very accurate.

A piezoelectric element was also sometimes used as the active part of a phonograph CARTRIDGE, although this use was restricted to inexpensive players. The STYLUS moving in the groove of the record causes the element to bend, and it generates an alternating VOLTAGE, which constitutes the signal. It is also possible to build MICROPHONES on the same principle, and many such were made in the past. They are characterized by low price and high IMPEDANCE, which limits their use because of the short cables required.

Pi-Filter A three-pole RIPPLE filter used in power supplies so called because of the resemblance of its SCHEMATIC drawing to the Greek letter π (Pi). It consists of a shunt CAPACITOR, a series INDUCTOR, and another shunt capacitor. A similar configuration in a multipole filter is called a PI-SECTION.

Pigtail The end of an AUDIO cable that simply has bare wires rather than any type of connector. Pigtails are used to connect cables to BINDING POSTS or screw terminals. Some fuses with bare leads are called "with pigtails."

Pilot A 19-KILOHERTZ tone transmitted along with stereo FM broadcasts in order to synchronize the local OSCILLATOR in the receiver to 38 kHz for the DETECTION of the STEREO subcarrier.

This 19-kHz tone can be troublesome even though it is above audibility for most people. If not filtered out of the receiver output, it can interact with the BIAS oscillator of a tape recorder, causing spurious tones to be recorded on the tape. It also can cause mistracking of COMPANDER systems such as Dolby, interfering with their ability to restore the proper dynamic level of high-frequency signals. *See also* FM STEREO.

Pilot Tone The pilot tone is a 60-HERTZ signal recorded on one track of an analog tape that is used for motion picture sound recording. The pilot tone SIGNAL is generated by the camera when the film is being shot, thus the FREQUENCY is an accurate measure of the camera speed. The tone, or "pilot," is then used later to synchronize the tape playback to the picture action.

This technique, which has many variations, allows movie sound to be recorded independently of the film, rather than being recorded directly on the film as it is shot. This is called "double system sound." Pilot tone systems have essentially been replaced by SMPTE TIME CODE, which records a digitally coded timing signal on the analog tape. The time code, when played back and decoded controls the speed of the playback machine to synchronize the picture and sound. Digital sound recorders are also used with SMPTE time code.

PIM Phase Intermodulation Distortion. PIM arises in AMPLIFIERS that have a nonlinearity such that one signal will cause phase modulation of another signal. Phase modulation is the same as FREQUENCY MODULATION but to a lesser degree. This is in contrast to ordinary INTERMODULATION DISTORTION, which is the amplitude modulation of a signal by another signal and is sometimes called AIM, for amplitude intermodulation distortion. For PIM to occur, a strong signal must modulate the BANDWIDTH of the amplifier, and this varying bandwidth varies the phase of another signal that is also being amplified. The measurement of PIM in audio devices is relatively new, but it has been known and measured in video amplifiers for some time, where it distorts the color rendition of the television picture.

The measurement of PIM is somewhat similar to the SMPTE method of measuring AIM. A high-frequency tone (7,000 hertz) is mixed with a low-frequency tone (60 Hz) of 4 times the amplitude and fed into the DUT. The DUT output is fed into a filter to remove the low-frequency tone, and the phase of the resulting high-frequency tone is compared with the phase of the input high-frequency tone. The unit of measurement is time, with the results usually expressed in nanoseconds as a function of signal level. PIM measurement techniques are not standardized, and there is no general agreement on its degree of audibility.

Pin 1 Problem An equipment condition coined by Neil Muncy in 1995. It refers to analog audio equipment with balanced connectors (e.g., XLR-3) where pin 1 (normally connected to the interconnecting cable shield) is connected to the audio circuitry ground inside the equipment, instead of being immediately tied to the CHASSIS and power ground. When the device is connected to other equipment in a system, any SHIELD currents on pin 1 can then modulate the audio ground, causing HUM and buzz problems that can be difficult to troubleshoot and eliminate. Such a problem does not show up on standard bench tests, although a simple modified AC transformer can be used to reveal a piece of equipment with the problem.

Pinch Effect Phonograph records are cut with a pointed, chisel-shaped cutting STYLUS and are played back with a circular, elliptical, or other suitably shaped stylus. Because the playback stylus has a finite width compared to the cutter's knife-edge, it will be squeezed upward during those times when the groove is narrowest. This is the pinch effect, and it causes HARMONIC DISTORTION in the reproduced SIGNAL. In the case of MONAURAL recordings, the pinch effect can be canceled by using a CARTRIDGE that is not sensitive to vertical motion of the stylus; but in the case of STEREO records, the

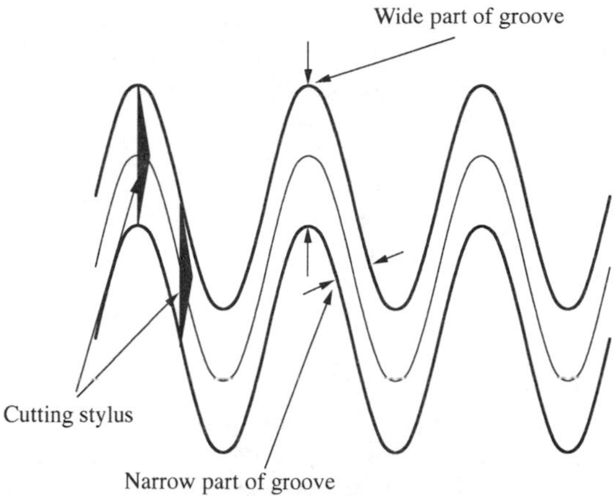

As the playback stylus traces the groove, it is forced upward at the narrow parts.

Pinch Effect

vertical component of stylus motion is where all the directional information is.

Pinch effect is minimized by using a playback stylus with very small radii on the sides. The elliptical stylus was the first of these, but there are several other designs.

Pinch Roller *See* PUCK.

Ping-Ponging Recording studio slang for OVERDUBBING. Also, the rapid panning of an audio track back and forth between extreme left and extreme right.

Pink Noise Pink noise is a type of random NOISE that has a constant amount of energy in each OCTAVE BAND, as opposed to WHITE NOISE, which has equal energy per HERTZ. Pink noise can be made from white noise by passing it through a FILTER with a 3 DECIBEL per octave ROLLOFF.

Because our ears tend to hear pitches on a logarithmic FREQUENCY scale, our perception of LOUDNESS correlates with the energy in constant percentages of BANDWIDTH. In experiments conducted many years ago, Harvey Fletcher, of Bell Telephone Labs, found that sounds within one "critical band" of frequency (about one-third of an octave) had a perceived loudness depending on the energy in that band of frequencies. Sounds separated in frequency by more than a critical band each had a loudness depending on its own energy content, and none influenced the loudness of another.

Because the critical bandwidth is a constant percentage of the center frequency of the band, as frequency rises, the critical bands become wider and wider in frequency. A third octave centered at 1,000 Hz is 230 Hz wide, but a third octave centered at 100 Hz is only 23 Hz wide. Our ears integrate the energy in these bands to determine perceived loudness. Therefore, pink noise, which has constant energy per percentage bandwidth, sounds as if it has relatively uniform loudness at all pitches. (It would sound equally loud at all pitches if it were not for the FLETCHER-MUNSON EFFECT.) This also means that white noise sounds very bright and lacking in low-frequency content.

Pink noise is a useful test signal for measuring frequency responses of audio equipment if the detecting instrument is a REAL-TIME ANALYZER (RTA) with octave band or one-third octave band response. The noise signal is input to the device under test, and the output is plugged into the real-time analyzer. Because the RTA has octave or one-third octave filters, it will show FLAT RESPONSE for pure pink noise. Any irregularities caused by the DUT will show up as deviation from flat response.

Pinna The outer ear, the visible part of our hearing mechanism. The shape of the pinna has a great deal to do with our ability to determine where a sound is coming from. *See also* BINAURAL.

Pirate Recording An unauthorized recording of a musical performance. Pirate recordings were often made with home-type equipment under poor conditions and the resulting quality was bad enough that it posed no threat to commercial recordings. On the other hand, with the advent of very small battery-operated DAT, MiniDisc, and MP3 recorders, pirate recordings can be made with great care and attention to quality. Even though unauthorized, sometimes these recordings can be of commercial value. There are reportedly some people who simply enjoy the challenge of planning, setting up, and doing pirate recordings of famous musicians without being detected, and would not sell the recordings or otherwise profit from the activity.

Pi-Section, π-Section A three-pole FILTER consisting of two shunt reactances and one series reactance. It is so called because of its schematic's physical resemblance to the Greek letter π. The π section has a flat frequency response in its PASSBAND and an 18 dB per octave slope in its STOPBAND.

Pitch The pitch of a musical sound is a subjective quality relating to where on a musical scale the sound is perceived to be. Pitch is closely related to TIMBRE, another subjective attribute of a musical sound.

Pitch is related to the FREQUENCY of a sound, but not in a simple way. In general, perceived pitch increases as the frequency rises, and the pitch will increase by one OCTAVE if the frequency is doubled. This is true for complex sounds that are not too close to the upper or lower frequency limits of our hearing. At frequencies above 4,000 HERTZ or so, the perceived pitch changes very little with frequency; and with SINE WAVE tones rather than COMPLEX tones, pitch perception is very inaccurate. It has been shown that at certain frequency ranges, two tones of different TIMBRE can be two octaves apart in frequency and still have the same pitch. This effect

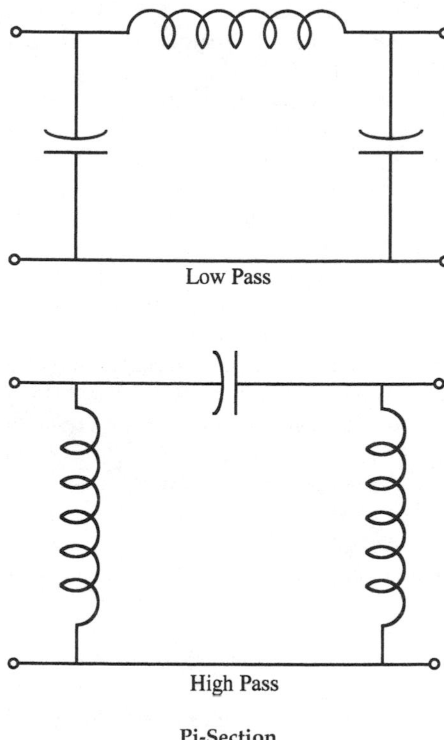

Pi-Section

was observed early—the French scientist and musician F. M. Mersenne noted in his *Harmonie Universelle* of 1636 that the bass recorder, a large flute-like instrument, sounds an octave lower than its actual frequency output would indicate. This has not been adequately explained to this day.

It is interesting that a person's two ears do not generally hear a sound as having the same pitch, especially in the case of sine waves. It is common to find differences of several musical half-tones in pitches of sine tones presented to each ear individually. For most people, the pitches fuse into a single pitch sensation if the two ears hear the tone simultaneously, but in some rare cases, a single note from a musical instrument will be perceived to be sounding two pitches at once. Such a hearing problem is of course a disaster for a musician.

Pitch also refers to the number of grooves per inch on the surface of a PHONOGRAPH record, CD, and DVD. *See also* VARIABLE PITCH. Incidentally, there is normally only one groove on each side of a phonograph record, and only one digital path on each layer of a CD or DVD. However, there exist some LP records with more than one groove on a side. An example is

Monty Python's *Matching Tie and Handkerchief* album. One side has two interlaced grooves, so you hear one of two programs on that side depending on how you hit the lead-in grooves.

Pitch Control A control that can vary the speed of a turntable or analog tape machine. Some digital devices, such as CD players, also have pitch control. *See also* VARISPEED.

Pitch Tracking A slightly misleading term meaning frequency-to-voltage conversion. PITCH is a subjective term, whereas FREQUENCY is a purely objective measure of a signal.

A pitch tracker will accept a complex periodic signal and extract from this the FUNDAMENTAL frequency. It will then convert this frequency into a direct VOLTAGE output that can be used as a control voltage in an electronic music synthesizer. Pitch tracking becomes more difficult as the input WAVEFORM becomes more complex, but practical devices are made that can handle most musical instruments, including the voice.

PIV Acronym for Peak Inverse Voltage, which is the maximum VOLTAGE a SEMICONDUCTOR DIODE can withstand in the reverse direction without damage. Also called PRV, or Peak Reverse Voltage.

Planar *See* LOUDSPEAKER.

Plate In an electron TUBE, the ANODE, or positive ELECTRODE, is called the plate.

Plate Dissipation The maximum power that the PLATE of a vacuum TUBE can dissipate without permanent damage to the tube. It is equal to the plate VOLTAGE times the plate current and is measured in watts. Some high-power tubes are so designed that the plate may be operated continuously in a red-hot condition without damage.

Plate Resistance The internal RESISTANCE of a vacuum TUBE, measured by the change in the plate voltage divided by the change in the plate current. The plate resistance depends on the potential of the control grid and is usually expressed as a family of curves taken at various values of grid BIAS. These are called CHARACTERISTIC CURVES.

Plate Reverberation One of the first synthetic REVERBERATION devices uses a steel plate that is under tension supplied by springs at the corners. The plate is vibrated in accordance with a SIGNAL from a loudspeaker-like device, and the vibration is sensed at another place on the plate with a CONTACT MICROPHONE of one type or another.

Plate reverberation has been used a great deal in the recording industry over the last forty years, even though it sounds very little like natural reverberation. The advantage of the plate is its small size and low cost compared to a reverberation room.

The advent of DIGITAL reverberation simulators has doomed the plate, even though they don't sound like real reverberation either.

PLL *See* PHASE-LOCKED LOOP.

Plosive A sudden puff of air emitted by the voice when pronouncing words containing the letter *p* and, to a lesser extent, *t*. *See also* POP FILTER.

Plug-in A piece of software designed for a specific audio task and designed to work from within another piece of software. For example, many companies produce plug-ins for Digidesign's ProTools editing program.

PM Permanent Magnet, normally an adjective, as in "PM speaker" for a loudspeaker with a permanent magnet.

PMCD Pre Master Compact Disc. Originally, master recordings for COMPACT DISCS were submitted on specially formatted ¾-inch "U-Matic" videocassettes made on Sony 1610 or 1630 digital recorders. With the advent of CD-R, the Sonic Solutions and Sony companies came up with an equivalent master format on a CD-R, which not only contained the audio but also special data tracks and special cues for the laser beam recorder (LBR). A special hardware/software combination was required for creating the CD-R, but an ordinary player could reproduce the audio for testing purposes. One could submit either a 1610/1630-style tape or a PMCD to be replicated into CDs.

The system has fallen by the wayside and today PMCD generally denotes an ordinary RED BOOK compliant audio CD-R that is ready for duplication exactly as is.

P-Mount A P-mount is a universal standard mounting arrangement for installing a phono CARTRIDGE in a TONEARM. In the P-mount system, the HEADSHELL is not needed—actually it is a part of the cartridge. P-mount cartridges are simply plugged into the end of the arm and are easily interchanged.

The P-mount ensures the correct placement of the STYLUS in relation to the record groove by using a standardized distance from the end of the arm to the stylus tip, and the angle of the stylus cantilever is accurately controlled.

PNdB "Perceived Noise DECIBEL," which is the unit of perceived noise level. It is equal to the SPL of the 1,000-HERTZ OCTAVE BAND of PINK NOISE, which is subjectively judged to be equally noisy as the noise under consideration. The PNdB is seldom used outside the psychology laboratory.

PNP Short for Positive-Negative-Positive. PNP refers to a type of TRANSISTOR that is constructed of three layers of semiconductor material that are positive-negative-positive. The manner of atomic doping of the SEMICONDUCTOR material determines whether it is P or N type. The emitter is a lead attached to a P layer, and in a circuit, its voltage is positive with respect to the collector lead, which is attached to other P layer. Signals to the base lead, attached to the N layer, control current flow. *See also* NPN.

Point Source A hypothetical sound source that is very small compared to the WAVELENGTHS of sound it is radiating, and that is radiating into free three-dimensional space.

True point sources do not exist, but some sound sources approximate point sources, especially if the listener is some distance away. A point source would radiate sound equally in all directions; it would be completely OMNIDIRECTIONAL. One school of thought says that a LOUDSPEAKER for music reproduction should behave like a point source, so it would radiate sound equally in all directions in the listening room. Such a loudspeaker would excite all the REVERBERATION in the room and would give the listener a maximum sense of ENVELOPMENT in the sound field. This assumes GOOD ACOUSTICS in the listening room.

Musical instruments, especially large ones like pianos, are far from point sources, and they radiate sound very nonuniformly into space, sending high frequencies in some directions and mid and low frequencies in other directions. This makes life difficult for the poor recording engineer, especially if he chooses to use CLOSE MIKING, for there is no one place that will pick up a representative sound of the entire range of the instrument. This is one reason that very close miked recordings do not sound the way the instruments actually sound in a room. For a more natural sound, the MICROPHONE must be at least one wavelength away from the instrument at the lowest FREQUENCY of interest. A room with good acoustics is required, however, because at the increased distance, the reverberation of the room becomes a more significant part of the sound that the microphone hears.

Polarity If the two wires to a LOUDSPEAKER are reversed, the SIGNAL is turned "upside down," that is, points on the WAVEFORM that moved the loudspeaker CONE outwards now move it inward. This is called a polarity reversal. It also is equal to a 180-degree PHASE SHIFT.

Many times, the term *out of phase* is used when a polarity reversal is meant. Out of phase is a matter of degree, whereas polarity defines the condition.

Recently there has been renewed interest in the "ABSOLUTE POLARITY" of an audio signal. It is thought that there should not be a polarity reversal anywhere between the MICROPHONE and the loudspeaker. In other words, SOUND PRESSURE in a positive direction at the microphone should result in a positive-going sound pressure at the listener's ears. Some experiments have been conducted to determine the ear's sensitivity to this polarity reversal, and indeed it seems that it is possible to tell the difference between a signal and its inverted brother. It is a different matter, however, to tell which one has the correct absolute polarity, and the matter has not been conclusively proven.

Polarize To place a constant (static) VOLTAGE across a device or CIRCUIT element is said to polarize it. An example is the CONDENSER MICROPHONE, which requires a polarization voltage to charge the capacitive element. Some electronic circuit elements, such as ELECTROLYTIC CAPACITORS, require a polarization voltage to allow them to operate in a LINEAR fashion.

Polar Pattern *See* POLAR RESPONSE CURVE.

Polar Response Curve The polar response curve, sometimes called the polar pattern, is a plot of the SENSITIVITY of an AUDIO device as a function of angle around the device. Thus, the polar response of a LOUDSPEAKER tells one the relative strength of signals radiated in various directions. To be meaningful, polar response plots must be measured at many frequencies, for no device will have the same polar curve over a wide FREQUENCY band.

Polar response curves of MICROPHONES are especially important because they tell the user how to point the microphone to optimize the frequency

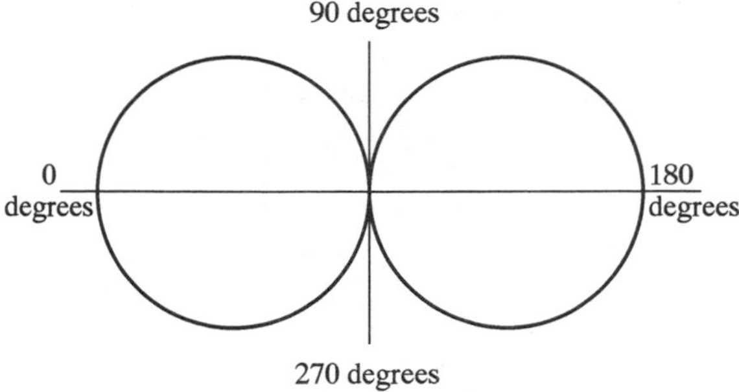

Sensitivity vs angle for a ribbon microphone. The curve is more flattened if plotted in decibels.

Polar Pattern

response. Ideally, polar curves would all be circles, indicating no discrimination due to direction, or at least they would all be parallel, indicating the same response at all frequencies.

Pole The part of the surface of a magnet where the magnetic field is most concentrated is called a pole. Any magnet has two poles; one is the "north-seeking" pole, or simply the north pole, and the other is the "south-seeking," or south, pole. These names are given because a suspended magnet will orient itself with the north pole pointing north. The earth is a giant magnet and thus also has north and south magnetic poles, but it follows that the magnetic pole in the northern hemisphere is actually a south pole and vice versa. *See also* POLE PIECE.

Also a mathematical condition where a polynomial has solutions that approach infinity, used in filter design and analysis.

Pole Cup A cylindrical hole in a speaker cabinet into which a pole is inserted to support or elevate the speaker.

Pole Piece A shaped piece of high-permeability metal, usually soft iron, which serves to concentrate and direct the magnetic field from a permanent magnet to maximize the efficiency of such devices as dynamic LOUD SPEAKERS, magnetic CARTRIDGES, and CUTTERHEADS. Pole pieces are needed because magnets are difficult to make in the complex shapes needed in such applications.

Pollywogs Tiny irregularities in the surface of the tape used in CASSETTES, caused by errors in the manufacturing process. Pollywogs cause momentary loss of contact between the tape and the head, producing DROPOUTS. The term is primarily British.

Polyester A type of strong, flexible plastic used as the backing for certain magnetic recording tapes. It was developed by DuPont, who called it Mylar. Mylar tape will last much longer than ACETATE tape but can be stretched if placed under too much tension, whereas acetate will break. It is possible to repair a broken tape but not a stretched tape! Some tapes are made from

Mylar that has been prestretched, or "tensilized," and they are much less likely to cause trouble.

Pop, Popping When a MICROPHONE encounters air currents, its diaphragm is jostled and the result is either a rustling noise or, if the wind is strong enough, explosive sounds called pops. Needless to say, this is not good for the microphone and thus must be avoided. Some microphones, especially ribbon types, are very sensitive to damage by air currents.

Most directional microphones will pop when a singer or speaker is at close range and utters plosive sounds, especially the letter *p*. *See also* POP FILTER.

Popcorn Noise A type of intrinsic noise produced by a defective piece of SOLID-STATE electronics. It resembles the sound of popping corn. Also a slang term in the motion picture sound world that refers to the ambient background noise in a movie theater. The audience eating popcorn is only one contributor to this kind of popcorn noise.

Pop Filter An acoustically transparent (transondent!) plastic foam material placed over a MICROPHONE that will reduce the effect of air currents and PLOSIVES ("pops") from the voice at close range. Such foam must be open-cell or "reticulated," that is, all the foam bubbles are open to each other. Closed-cell foam would block much of the sound. Some forms of pop filters are screens made of a metal ring several inches in diameter with a very fine nylon gauze (commonly made of panty hose material) stretched over it and placed in front of the microphone. Pop filters are sometimes built into the mesh ball in the business end of a vocal microphone. The pop filter also acts as one type of WINDSCREEN.

Port The opening below the LOUDSPEAKER in a BASS REFLEX system is sometimes called a port. *See also* DUCTED PORT.

Portamento A musical technique of sliding between two pitches. Sometimes called glissando. Synthesizers can make use of this under MIDI control.

Portastudio A trade name by the Tascam company for a small tape recorder that recorded four tracks on COMPACT CASSETTES. The unit would also provide basic studio functions such as overdubbing and mixing. The track format and speed was not compatible with regular stereo compact cassettes.

Port Noise At very low frequencies, the air movement in a bass ducted port of a loudspeaker cabinet makes a distinct sound or distortion. Of course, if you speak negatively about it, this is known as a "port noise complaint."

Post Simply means *after* as opposed to *pre*. In recording studio parlance it is used to indicate that the signal has already had the designated effect added, such as postequalization, posteffects, or postfader. Also used as an abbreviation for POSTPRODUCTION.

Post Echo *See* PRINT THROUGH.

Postfader In a mixing console, SENDS are either prefader or postfader. Postfader sends are affected by the position of the input fader, whereas prefader sends are not. An effects send is often postfader, so the level of the send to the effects device reflects the relative position of the input fader. In some cases, a send can be switched to be either pre- or postfader.

Postproduction Any work on a recording, film, or video that is done after the main recording session or filming is completed. Typical postproduction work can include EDITING, SWEETENING, and MIXDOWN.

Pot *See* POTENTIOMETER.

Potentiometer A variable resistor, usually controlled by a rotary knob, used extensively as a volume control, tone control, etc. The potentiometer has three terminals: one at each end of the resistor and the third connected to the movable contact, or "wiper." The term is also used for a step-type ATTENUATOR, although this is actually a multiple contact switch wired to a series of fixed resistors. The common slang term for potentiometer is pot. The SLIDE POT is a linear motion potentiometer used for FADERS.

POTS An acronym for Plain Old Telephone Service, meaning a traditional analog telephone line.

Poulsen, Valdemar Valdemar Poulsen invented the first working model of the magnetic recorder. He called his invention, made in 1899, the "Telegraphone," and it used a steel wire running at seven feet per second as a recording medium. He first thought of it as a device for recording Morse code telegraph transmissions for later transcription, and he also seems to have thought it might be used to record telephone conversations. However, he didn't hit on the idea of using it to record music.

Poulsen's model was preceded by eleven years by a description of a remarkably advanced concept for magnetic recording by Oberlin Smith, who wrote a letter to the editor of *Electrical World. See* SMITH, OBERLIN.

Power Power is defined as the rate of doing work and is measured in WATTS, 1 watt being 1 joule per second, which is equal to the power absorbed by 1 OHM of resistance when 1 AMPERE of CURRENT is in it. Power in an electrical CIRCUIT is calculated by the VOLTAGE squared divided by the RESISTANCE, the current squared times the resistance, or the voltage times the current.

The power rating of an AMPLIFIER is the maximum power it will deliver to a specific LOAD and is rated in watts of continuous power. The term *rms power* is a misnomer and should be avoided *(see* RMS). An amplifier will deliver its maximum power into only one value of load IMPEDANCE. Connecting a load of higher impedance will reduce the power output but will not cause any other problems; but connecting a lower than rated impedance to an amplifier will usually cause DISTORTION as well as reduced output.

Power-handling capacity of a LOUDSPEAKER is somewhat difficult to define. Any speaker will handle much more power when reproducing music than when reproducing a SINE WAVE test signal because of the large ratio of peak power in music compared to the average power. One of the limitations in speaker power handling is due to heating of the VOICE COILS, and another is mechanical damage due to large excursions of the moving parts. *See also* DECIBEL.

Power Amplifier An AMPLIFIER that accepts a low-level audio SIGNAL and strengthens, or amplifies, it to a suitable VOLTAGE and CURRENT level adequate to drive a LOUDSPEAKER or other LOAD.

Power Amplifier

The four key parts of a power amplifier are the input stage, driver stage, output stage, and power supply. The power supply provides the electrical power to drive the loudspeaker. Most modern amplifiers use SOLID-STATE electronics, and have a dual, or bipolar, power supply, one side providing positive voltage at fairly high current and the other side providing negative voltage at fairly high current.

The output stage, which is also usually bipolar, or "push-pull," acts as a controller and connects the positive and negative power supply outputs to the load in response to the audio signal. In a sense, the output stage acts as a pair of variable valves, gradually turning on and off the currents as required to duplicate the WAVEFORM of the signal. The British term valve for our vacuum tube is quite descriptive here. In actuality, it is the effective RESISTANCE of the output devices that is varied. One undesirable consequence of this state of affairs is that the output devices, which must pass all the current that enters the load, will dissipate heat because of their internal resistance. This heat is wasted energy and can cause problems such as premature failure of components.

The function of the driver stage is to control the output devices and usually to split the signal into two parts with opposite POLARITY, which is necessary to drive the positive-going and negative-going output devices. This function is also called phase splitting.

The input stage of the amplifier provides the needed voltage GAIN for the amplifier.

The design of the output stage has traditionally attracted the most attention, and many different designs have been developed to increase its efficiency and reduce its DISTORTION. Amplifiers can be categorized into several different classes as follows:

Class A: This was the first type of amplifier, and it is in theory the most LINEAR of the many types. Class A operation means the output devices are always conducting current, even when the signal level is zero. The instantaneous signal level modulates the current up and down, but the current never reaches zero. In fact, the average current is almost constant in a class A amplifier, regardless of the signal level. This means it is always dissipating a good deal of heat in the output stages, and it is therefore very inefficient. Efficiency is defined as the amount of power consumed by the amplifier in relation to the amount of power it delivers to the load.

The class A amplifier is capable of low distortion, even with small amounts of NEGATIVE FEEDBACK, but its low efficiency relegates it to fairly low output power capabilities. There are some people, however, who insist that the only amplifier fit for music is a class A amplifier, and some high-power class A amplifiers have been built that are so inefficient that they could be used as electric heaters.

Class B: The class B amplifier was developed to improve the efficiency of the class A designs. In it, each output device conducts current for only half of the waveform. One device handles the positive-going parts of the waveform while the other device handles the negative parts. In effect, the

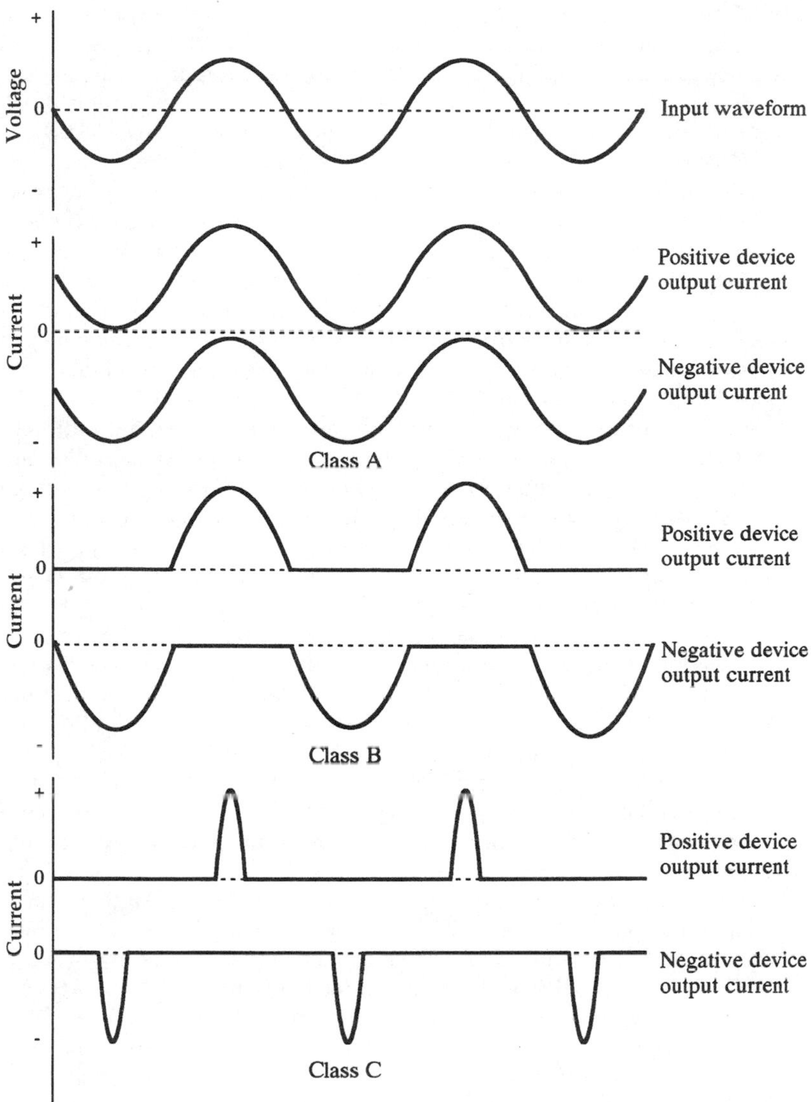

Class A, B, and C Amplifiers

signal is "handed off" to each output device in turn. This can work well from an efficiency standpoint, but there is a problem with the switching from one device to the other at very low signal levels. If switching is not done absolutely smoothly, a type of distortion called CROSSOVER DISTORTION occurs.

Class AB: Problems with crossover distortion in class B amplifiers led to a design in which both output devices conduct current when the signal level is very low. In effect, the amplifier operates in class A at very low levels and gradually becomes class B at higher signal levels. The result is much reduced distortion, but at the expense of lower efficiency than class B.

Class C: To further increase efficiency, although at the expense of a great deal of distortion, the output device of the class C amplifier conducts current only over a portion of the input waveform. The lower level parts of the waveform are not amplified at all, resulting in the very high distortion. Class C amplifiers are used in RF circuits to amplify narrow frequency bands. IF amplifiers in radio and television receivers are class C. The amplifiers are connected to sharply tuned resonant circuits tuned to the frequency of interest, effectively filtering out the distortion. The class C amplifier is not used as an audio power amplifier.

Class D: An interesting type of power amplifier in which the audio signal varies the width of a series of constant-amplitude pulses. The pulse repetition rate is much higher than the highest audio frequency. The average area under the pulses is equal to the instantaneous power level of the signal. The pulses are then passed through a LOW-PASS FILTER, which smooths, or integrates, them into an amplified replica of the input waveform. The phenomenon is called pulse width modulation (PWM); although this may appear to be a digital technique, it is not, for the formation and modulation of the pulses are done by purely analog means. The class D amplifier is very efficient because the output devices are operating either completely "on" or completely "off," neither condition dissipating any appreciable power in the devices themselves.

Some so-called switching power supplies operate very much like a class D amplifier. The width of the pulses is modulated to vary the output voltage or to maintain a constant output voltage under conditions of varying load current.

Class G: A type of power amplifier circuit somewhat similar to but more efficient than class B. In a class G amplifier, there are two bipolar power supply voltages that are selectively connected to the output stage in accordance with the signal level. When the signal is low, the supply voltages are low, providing good efficiency. When the signal levels are high, a higher voltage supply is switched in to allow the output devices to pass the extra power. Compared to class B, class G operation has several advantages: higher peak-power capability, reduced thermal problems, increased power output, and relatively low cost.

Class H: This type of power amplifier circuit is an extension of the class G design. In class H, the power supply voltage for the output devices is modulated so that it is always just above the signal level. This increases the efficiency of the amplifier because it is the excess power supply voltage that causes unnecessary power dissipation and heating in the output devices. The class H amplifier, like the class G, has two bipolar power supplies, but instead of switching back and forth between them as the signal level changes, the high-voltage supply is actually amplitude-modulated to keep it just above the instantaneous peak signal level. The class H amplifier has the same advantages as the class G but is even more efficient. *See also* TUBE.

Power Bandwidth The BANDWIDTH of an AUDIO device such as a POWER AMPLIFIER measured while delivering its full rated power output. This is limited by the SLEW RATE of the device and is always narrower than the SMALL SIGNAL BANDWIDTH.

Powered Mixer A mixer that also has a built-in POWER AMPLIFIER for driving passive LOUDSPEAKERS directly. This means you lug around one device instead of two.

Powered Speaker *See* SELF-POWERED SPEAKER.

Power Response A type of FREQUENCY RESPONSE where sound power versus FREQUENCY is plotted instead of the usual SOUND PRESSURE versus frequency. Power response is applicable to LOUDSPEAKERS because a simple SPL response curve is dependent on the angle between the speaker and the MICROPHONE. Most SPL measurements are made ON AXIS of the loudspeaker and at 1 meter distance. This does not provide any information on how the speaker's POLAR RESPONSE CURVE varies with frequency. The power response integrates all the energy produced by the speaker, regardless of angle. The rationale for measuring it is that in a real room, the listener hears sounds from all angles as the sounds reflect from the walls, etc., and therefore the perceived frequency response will be more like the power response than the SPL response.

However, there is a complication, as usual in ACOUSTICS. A corollary of the HAAS EFFECT says that the ear will judge the TIMBRE of a sound by the earliest sound it hears. The reflected sounds are later than the direct sound in a real room, so the SPL response of the speaker is what the ear hears first. Therefore, the SPL frequency response at the angle where the listener is located should be FLAT, as should the power response.

Power Supply *See* B-PLUS and SUPPLY RAILS.

PPI Peak Program Indicator. *See* PPM. Many radar screens are also called PPIs meaning Plan Position Indicators

PPM Short for Peak Program Meter, which is similar to a VU meter in appearance, but which responds to the peak, or maximum, level of the SIGNAL rather than the average level. The PPM is useful in applications where instantaneous overloads create large amounts of DISTORTION, such as DIGITAL audio devices. Any signal level above what a digital system can encode is CLIPPED at that level. A meter that reads the average level of a signal does not respond quickly enough to register the short TRANSIENT peaks that abound in music.

The PPM is often found in control desks/consoles, especially for broadcast, and in some ANALOG tape recorders and also in digital machines. It may take the form of a series of LEDs rather than a mechanical meter, but the function is the same. *See also* MODULOMETER.

Preamplifier, Preamp In an audio system, the first AMPLIFIER to accept the

SIGNAL from the TRANSDUCER is generally called a preamplifier. Examples are phono preamps, which amplify the output of the phono CARTRIDGE, and MIKE preamps, which amplify the signal from a MICROPHONE.

Preamplifiers usually must accept very low-level signals and amplify them without adding appreciable NOISE. Many preamps also contain appropriate EQUALIZATION (*see* RIAA), such as phono preamps and tape playback preamps. An exception is the PRE-PREAMPLIFIER, which is a specially designed low-noise preamplifier to be used with MOVING-COIL CARTRIDGES. It does not contain any equalization because its output is fed into an RIAA preamp.

The design of good quality preamplifiers is not easy, for they must be made to be immune to the introduction of many types of noise. Microphone preamps have BALANCED inputs for this reason. Also, preamps containing equalization, such as RIAA preamps, must handle a very wide DYNAMIC RANGE of input signals without overload DISTORTION. Often the noise input to preamps will be of very high frequency, such as in the case of radio or TELEVISION INTERFERENCE. If the preamp is NONLINEAR at these high frequencies, the signal may be DETECTED, and the interference enters the audible frequency range.

Precedence Effect *See* HAAS EFFECT.

Pre-Echo Sometimes when a record is being pressed and if the grooves are very close together, one groove may influence the shape of the adjacent one, causing the sound from the first one to be faintly heard in the second one. This is called pre-echo because it is usually heard at the very beginning of a record or record band as a soft precursor of the music to come.

In making records, the STAMPER has negative grooves, or hills, which form the grooves during pressing. When the soft vinyl flows out from the center as the press closes, it must flow over the interior hills on its way to the outer ones. Because of its molecular structure, it tends to remember its recent history, and it retains some of the shape of the previous hill as it settles into its final form. *See also* PRINT-THROUGH.

There is another, little-known type of pre-echo which sometimes occurs in DIGITAL audio systems. It arises from RIPPLE in the PASSBAND of the ANTI-ALIASING and ANTI-IMAGING FILTERS. In some low-pass filters, the AMPLITUDE response varies up and down at a regular rate along the FREQUENCY axis. This is called ripple and is usually held to a low value such as plus or minus ½ DECIBEL. This ripple, however, results in an IMPULSE RESPONSE of the FILTER, which has skirts both before and after the main response peak. (The impulse response of a system completely describes its frequency and PHASE response.) This means that if a short impulse is presented to the filter, there will be some output signal before the main burst of the impulse, and in reality it can be several milliseconds before the main burst. This results in a general muddying of musical TRANSIENTS.

There is presently no agreed-upon method of measuring this type of pre-echo, but it has been shown to be clearly audible. It seems that the dual-channel FFT ANALYZER is the best instrument to measure it, for it can produce a picture of the magnitude of the impulse response of a system.

Pre-Emphasis Pre-emphasis is a type of high-frequency boost applied to SIGNALS about to be broadcast on FM stations, or which are about to be recorded on tape or a phonograph record. The reason for the boost is to increase the level of the higher frequencies so they are well above the high-frequency noise generated by the transmission medium (i.e., radio broadcasting) or the recording medium (i.e., tape recorder or vinyl disc) to increase the apparent signal to noise ratio.

The long-term averaged SPECTRUM of most music has a maximum at about 500 HERTZ, and falls off above and below this range. In other words, there is much more energy in a music signal in the MID-RANGE than at the high and low frequencies. This means that the full DYNAMIC RANGE of the recording medium is not used at the extremes of the frequency range, and the SIGNAL-TO-NOISE RATIO is poorest there. The ear is much more sensitive to high-frequency noise than low-frequency noise due to the FLETCHER-MUNSON EFFECT. Pre-emphasis brings the high-frequency content of the music up to a level further above the ambient noise level of the recording medium.

In order to restore the proper balance of high and low frequencies to the reproduced music signal, the boost added by pre-emphasis must be removed by a complementary cut. This is called DE-EMPHASIS, and is applied to the signal when reproduced from the recording medium or received with an FM receiver. The de-emphasis reduces the strength of the high-frequency noise, just as if the TREBLE tone control is turned down. In other words, the noise reduction takes place in the de-emphasis, and the pre-emphasis is added to make the de-emphasized signal have FLAT FREQUENCY RESPONSE.

Pre-emphasis combined with de-emphasis is a very effective noise reduction technique, and has been in use for many years. Its effectiveness depends on the high-frequency signal handling capability of the medium, i.e., the greater the capacity of the medium, the greater the amount of pre-emphasis that can be used without adding too much DISTORTION.

In the case of early MONAURAL phonograph records, various manufacturers did not agree on the optimum amount of pre-emphasis, and pre-amplifiers had several different settings of high-frequency ROLLOFF to accommodate different records. The advent of the STEREO record in 1958 heralded the establishment of the RIAA standard pre-emphasis CURVE, and all records made after that date had the same pre-emphasis. At last, any phono preamp with the RIAA playback curve could play any record with correct EQUALIZATION. In a way, it is unfortunate that the RIAA standard calls for so much pre-emphasis, for the result is a very greatly exaggerated high-frequency signal on the record. This signal is difficult to track with the STYLUS, causing undue distortion and placing heavy demands on the first stage of the preamp, which must linearly amplify this signal. It is not feasible now to change the standard because of the great number of records and players in existence.

The opposite effect exists in the case of tape recorders. When the NAB set the standard pre-emphasis curve for tape recorders in 1954, the best tapes available then had relatively poor ability to accept strong high-frequency signals, and the amount of pre-emphasis was quite conservative. In the meantime, tape quality has increased markedly and much greater pre-emphasis could be used with no significant added distortion and with concomitant further reduced noise on playback.

An attempt was made by the Ampex company in the 1960s to introduce a more suitable curve, called the AME curve (for Ampex Master Equalization), but it was not universally adopted and fell into disuse. Stefan Kudelski introduced a different curve (the NAGRAMASTER curve) in his Nagra recorders in the 1970s, and it has enjoyed relative success in recording master tapes.

All this points up the complex problems entailed in standardization in disciplines where improvements in quality are constantly being made.

DAT and CD also have an optional pre-emphasis, with a signal bit (flag) to activate it or not. Unfortunately, not all devices have the deemphasis (particularly computer CD drives), so it is possible to have a DAT or CD with preemphasis and hear it undecoded on your system. However, it seems the vast majority of these tapes/CDs appear to be non-preemphasized.

Prefader In a mixing console, SENDS are either prefader or postfader. Prefader sends are unaffected by the position of the input fader, whereas postfader sends are. A MONITOR send is usually prefader, so the monitor continues to operate when the input fader is down.

Prepolarized Condenser Microphone *See* ELECTRET MICROPHONE.

Pre-Preamplifier A pre-preamplifier, in addition to being linguistically questionable, is a very low-noise AMPLIFIER designed to operate at extremely low SIGNAL levels.

Some modern MOVING COIL cartridges have such low output VOLTAGES that standard phono PREAMPLIFIERS have too little GAIN to achieve enough playback volume. MOVING MAGNET cartridges have several millivolts of output while moving coils may have only a few tenths of a millivolt. A step-up transformer can be used between the CARTRIDGE and preamp to increase the voltage gain, but transformers are difficult to shield against HUM, can cause DISTORTION, and may not have perfect TRANSIENT response.

The pre-preamplifier is usually preferred in this application. It is a LINEAR amplifier (i.e., it has flat response with no EQUALIZATION), and is designed to operate into the input of a standard RIAA preamplifier.

Presence Quite a few years ago, many home sound systems had a "presence switch" as a part of the PREAMPLIFIER or AMPLIFIER. It caused a rise in level in the FREQUENCY range between about 1 and 3 KILOHERTZ, which purportedly increased the illusion that the music was actually "present" in the room. The peak introduced in the FREQUENCY RESPONSE was, however, a DISTORTION; it was eventually recognized as such and fell into disuse.

The promotion and sale of the presence switch is further proof of the theory that in the audio business, you can sell anything. *See also* LOUDNESS CONTROL.

Pressing The common STEREO record is frequently called a pressing in audio circles, no doubt because it is manufactured by being pressed from a "biscuit" of soft vinyl in a large hydraulic press. CDs and all other optical discs are also pressed similarly, but no one seems to call them pressings.

Pressure Gradient Microphone A MICROPHONE that is sensitive to the variation of pressure over a distance rather than to the pressure itself. This pressure variation with distance, called pressure gradient, is proportional to the particle velocity. The particle velocity is the instantaneous velocity of the air molecules, and is not to be confused with the speed of sound, which is the velocity of propagation of a SOUND WAVE.

Pressure gradient microphones are of many different types, depending on the electroacoustic TRANSDUCER used. *See* GRADIENT MICROPHONE and VELOCITY MICROPHONE.

Pressure Microphone Any MICROPHONE that is sensitive to variations in the instantaneous air pressure surrounding it is called a pressure microphone. DYNAMIC and CONDENSER MICROPHONES in their simplest forms are pressure microphones. A perfect pressure microphone would be completely OMNIDIRECTIONAL because the sound pressure accompanying a sound wave is a scalar, or nondirectional, quantity, but practical designs depart from the ideal because of sound DIFFRACTION around them. The smaller the microphone body, the more ideal its response will be.

Pressure Pad On some analog tape recorders, usually of the inexpensive type, there is a small felt pad that presses the tape against the head during record or playback. This is to ensure good contact between the tape and the head; however, it causes more problems than it solves. Excessive head wear is one problem, and another is the introduction of SCRAPE FLUTTER to the tape motion. This problem is worse with higher tape speeds. The pressure pad is accepted as a necessary evil in the conventional cassette recorder, however Nakamichi 3-head cassette machines do not use them. They push the pad away and keep the tape against the heads by controlling the tape tension by using two CAPSTANS and PINCH ROLLERS.

Preview Head A preview head is a supplementary playback head on a tape recorder. It is designed for reproducing the master tapes for producing phonograph records. *See also* VARIABLE PITCH.

Primary The winding of a transformer to which the input SIGNAL or CURRENT is connected, as contrasted to the SECONDARY, which is the winding where the output signal or current is extracted.

Printed Circuit Board, or PC Board Most electronic CIRCUITS made today in mass production are constructed on epoxy fiberglass sheets, or boards, onto which the electric conductors have been applied. Originally, the electronic components were mounted to the board through small holes for the lead wires, which were then soldered to the conductors. Today most circuit components are surface mounted, and holes in the board are only used to establish electrical connections from one side of the board to the other.

The term "printed" circuit is a misnomer because the boards are not printed, but rather etched. Sometimes the correct term, "etched circuit board," is heard.

Print Through When analog tape recordings are wound tightly on the reel, the adjacent layers of tape sometimes influence one another so that the SIGNAL from one layer will magnetize or "print" onto the next layer. This causes a faint echo of the signal that may be heard as a PRE-ECHO, audible before the main signal. Print through is sometimes also called interlayer transfer.

Print-through is worse at high recorded signal levels, and some tape types are much more susceptible to it than others. Thin tapes are more prone to it than thick ones.

It is surprising, but print-through is much less obvious if the tape is not rewound after recording or playing, and is stored in a "tails out" condition. Print through on a "tails out" tape exhibits "Post Echo," since the printed signal is played after the fact instead of before. This may be the reason it is less audible and therefore, commercial and master analog tapes are stored tails out. Another reason for storage tails out is that the tape pack on the reel is very smooth and uniform, while it is quite ragged when fast rewound on most machines, making rewound tapes more susceptible to damage by abrasion or bent reels.

Processing In the manufacture of phonograph records from the master ACETATE, several steps are taken, and they are collectively called processing. In one-step processing, the acetate is first silvered and then electroplated with metallic nickel. When this plating is stripped away from the acetate, it is called a MATRIX and is a negative of the record, having hills where the record has valleys, etc. This matrix can be used to press records simply by using it as a mold in a record press. It is then called a STAMPER. About 500 to 1,000 records may be pressed from a stamper, after which it is worn to the point where high-frequency response will suffer and the NOISE level will increase.

If more records are required to be made from the same acetate, the negative of the master is again electroplated with nickel and the plating is stripped away. The result is a positive, or a replica of the acetate, which can be played like a regular record. It is called a "MOTHER," and it is in turn electroplated and stripped. This final plating is then used as the stamper. The mother may be repeatedly plated, making as many stampers as required. Also, the original negative can be replated to make more mothers. This whole procedure is called THREE-STEP PROCESSING.

ProDigi A digital audio format used in stationary-head multitrack digital tape recorders, similar to the DASH system. There were two formats, one for ¼-inch tape (up to 8 audio channels) and one for 1-inch tape (up to 32 audio channels). Various sampling rates were accommodated, and the format allowed editing of digital tapes by mechanical splicing with a reference analog track, and by PUNCH-IN recording. Abbreviated PD. PD was promoted by Otari, Mitsubishi, and AEG. The system has been abandoned.

Program In radio and television broadcasting, the main part of the SIGNAL from the mixing console or remote BOARD that will be broadcast is called program, as opposed to MONITOR, intercom, PA feed, etc. The program is always isolated from the other AUDIO outputs in order to prevent any interference or noise from the other connections affecting the broadcast signal.

Progressive Scan Video Rather than dividing each video frame into 2 fields as INTERLACE SCANNING does, progressive scanning "paints" complete frames on the screen at the frame rate, which can be 23.976, 24, 29.97, 30, 59.94 or 60 frames per second in the countries that conform to the ATSC standards. The result is much less visual flicker and increased picture sharpness. Certain DVD players provide progressive scanning, but the television set used must be "progressive-scan-ready" to be capable of handling it. Computer CRT monitors use progressive scan rather than interlaced, and they operate at various refresh rates such as 60, 75, and 120 per second. A computer's refresh rate means the same as the TV frame rate .

Project Studio A smaller recording studio setup, often in a home, to do recordings without the expense of going to a full-service studio. A project studio may be a precursor to going to a full studio, fleshing out a project first at home to save studio time and money. The distinction can sometimes blur, as some project studios can be better equipped than some full studios. The project studio has been popularized by modern technology that offers good quality multitrack studio equipment the average person can afford. This does not necessarily mean the average person can now make decent recordings, however.

Pro Logic™ Pro Logic is a matrix decoder developed by Dolby Laboratories that decodes the four channels of surround sound that have been encoded onto the stereo soundtracks of Dolby Surround program material such as VHS movies and TV shows. Dolby Surround is a matrix encoding process that in essence "folds" left, center, right, and surround channels onto stereo soundtracks. A Pro Logic decoder "unfolds" the four channels on playback (without a Pro Logic decoder, the encoded program plays in regular stereo). Such matrixing is sometimes called a 4-2-4 system, as four channels are encoded into two, transmitted, then decoded into four.

Pro Logic II™ Pro Logic II is a second-generation matrix decoder from Dolby Laboratories that derives five-channel surround (left, center, right, left surround, and right surround) from any stereo program material, whether or not it has been specifically Dolby Surround encoded. On encoded material such as movie soundtracks, the sound is more like Dolby Digital 5.1, while on unencoded stereo material such as music CDs the effect is a wider, more complex sound field. Pro Logic II provides two full-range surround channels, as opposed to Pro Logic's single, limited-BANDWIDTH surround channel. A software algorithm is available for use in certain Digital Audio Workstations (DAWS) to encode multichannel audio to provide

Pro Logic II surround sound in game software. Pro Logic II encoding can be decoded by virtually every DOLBY DIGITAL home theater system and is backward compatible with Dolby Pro Logic receivers and decoders.

Proscenium The part of the stage of a modern theater between the curtain or drop-scene and the auditorium, often including the curtain itself and the enclosing arch.

When the curtain is closed, the proscenium in a theater acts as a separation between the audience and the goings-on on the stage. The opening in the proscenium is called the "arch," even though it may be rectangular rather than arched. The part of the proscenium at the sides of and above the arch is frequently used for the installation of sound reinforcement speakers, usually without regard to their appearance. In new theaters, the speakers are usually recessed behind the surface of the proscenium walls.

ProTools™ A trademark for a family of software and hardware for audio production from the Digidesign company. The products so named have evolved over many years but essentially provide for multitrack recording and editing. Often referred to as PT.

Proximity Effect Proximity effect is the increase in low-frequency SENSITIVITY of a MICROPHONE when the sound source is close to the microphone. It is a characteristic of directional microphones, and some are much worse than others.

Proximity effect is a shortcoming, but sometimes it can be used to advantage. If a directional microphone is placed close to a bass instrument, the low tones will be enhanced, which could be advantageous for some music. A singer placed close to a directional microphone will sound much "bassier," an improvement in some voices, we suppose. Some of the early radio "crooners" and radio announcers used proximity effect to deepen and enrich their voices, and many frequently still do.

Proximity effect comes about because of the nature of the sound field close to a sound source. The magnitude of the velocity component of the sound wave near a sound source is a function of the WAVELENGTH as well as the distance from the source. At low frequencies, where the wavelength is long compared to the dimensions of the source, this velocity component rises as the distance decreases faster than the INVERSE SQUARE LAW would predict. Thus, any microphone that senses the velocity component (or the pressure gradient) will have increased low-frequency output compared to high frequencies.

The effect is described in mathematical detail in Leo Beranek's book *Acoustics,* which has been reprinted in paperback by the ASA (1986).

Pseudostereo The idea of multichannel listening has been around since at least 1881 (*see* ADER, CLEMENT), and many experiments since the 1920s have been conducted in stereophonic and binaural broadcasting and recording. It is surely inevitable that there would be many ideas put forth that attempted to realize similar results with only one transmission channel. F. M. Doolittle suggested in 1925 that a stethoscope could be substituted for the conventional earphones and that if one of its rubber tubes was longer than the other, a time delay would be introduced to one ear, providing a binaural effect. The effect was certainly audible but was hardly binaural. Then, also in 1925, the "Kluth system" from Berlin used an electric network to change the PHASE response in one ear, providing the listener with "plastic radio," as it was touted.

Then, the advent of commercial stereo recordings caused another flurry in the pseudostereo camp, avowedly for the purpose of updating the now-obsolete monaural recordings, which were so numerous. The STEREOPHONER of Hermann Scherchen was one result, as was the "3D converter" of Chernov. Holger Lauridsen of the Danish National Broadcasting System also worked on a pseudostereo system, as did Paul Weathers in the United States. All these systems rely on short time delays and/or phase shifts and EQUALIZATION to achieve their effects.

Another idea for improved spaciousness in monaural recordings was the addition of synthetic REVERBERATION, and one of the earliest devices for this purpose was the XOPHONIC built by Radio Craftsmen in the mid-1950s. The Xophonic contained a small LOUDSPEAKER connected to a coiled tube with a microphone in the other end. The delayed sound was then amplified and reproduced through another loudspeaker in the same cabinet. Used in conjunction with a conventional single-loudspeaker sound system, the Xophonic added a reverberant sound from another location. The coiled pipe had many resonances, and the frequency response of the system was far from uniform. The Xophonic died in the marketplace soon after its introduction. Nevertheless, there were several other synthetic reverberation devices soon placed on the market for home and automobile use, most of them using the spring reverberator patented in the 1930s by Laurens Hammond for the Hammond organ.

Psophometer A specialized instrument that measures NOISE in telephone CIRCUITS, radio transmissions, and other AUDIO-FREQUENCY communication systems. The thing that distinguishes it from a simple voltmeter is the addition of WEIGHTING FILTERS, which are designed to allow measurements that correlate well with subjective perception of noise. The CCIR (now ITU-R) formulated the applicable specifications for the psophometer, and the first commercially available psophometer was made by the Brüel & Kjaer company of Denmark.

Psychoacoustics Psychoacoustics is that discipline that treats the subjective, or psychological, aspects of acoustic phenomena. It is a branch of the larger field called psychophysics.

Psychoacousticians investigate such things as the ear's ability to localize sounds, the perception of PHASE SHIFT in AUDIO signals, the SENSITIVITY of the ear to various types and amounts of DISTORTION, etc. The field is relatively young, and a great deal remains to be learned in it.

Public Address System An old term, abbreviated PA or P.A., coined in the 1930s, probably by somebody at the Bell Telephone Laboratories, for sound reinforcement system. The term *sound reinforcement* was introduced in the 1960s to imply high quality and absence of DISTORTION compared with the older PA systems, many of which were notorious for unintelligibility. Of course, perfect intelligibility and absence of audible distortion are not very common characteristics of sound systems being built today. (We are frequently bemused by the various clicks, pops, spurious noises, and distortions present in the sound systems used in the lecture rooms at the national conventions of the Audio Engineering Society. Where would one expect to go to hear state-of-the-art sound systems if not at the AES meetings?) The term PA still seems to be preferred, especially among performers, even when referring to the most elaborate and complex sound reinforcement systems. Anyhow, it is easier to say.

Puck In a tape recorder, the tape is pressed against the CAPSTAN by a rubber wheel called a puck (or pinch roller). Possibly the name comes from its resemblance to a hockey puck.

Some record turntables are of the "rim drive" type, and they use a rubber wheel called a puck to engage and drive the rim at the proper speed.

Pulldown *See* 3:2 PULLDOWN.

Pumping Refers to the audible fluctuations in the NOISE level of a SIGNAL caused by poorly adjusted or unsuitable NOISE REDUCTION systems; also called noise pumping. Sometimes the term *breathing* is used synonymously. QUANTIZATION noise can also exhibit pumping.

Punch Block A type of TERMINAL STRIP, first used by the telephone companies. It uses small, metal, V-shaped terminals into which the wire is simply pressed with a special tool. No screws are used, and the wire insulation does not need to be stripped first, for the V groove cuts into the wire. Wiring up a punch block is much faster than making connections to a screw-type terminal strip. Connectors not requiring wire stripping are generally called IDCs, for Insulation Displacement Connectors.

Punch In The precise control of the onset of tape recording on one or more tracks in the midst of an already existing recording. For instance, a fluffed word or phrase by an announcer can be corrected by listening to the playback and punching in at the exact moment. Punching in requires considerable skill and also a tape recorder designed for it. *See also* PURC. Today, it is naturally much easier to do this on a digital editor.

PURC Pick Up Record Capability. This is a term coined by the Ampex company in the 1960s for the ability of a tape recorder to do PUNCH-IN recording.

Pure Tone A sound whose WAVEFORM is a SINE WAVE; or a SIGNAL with a single FREQUENCY and no HARMONICS. Pure tones have been used for much PSYCHOACOUSTIC research, and some of the phenomena discovered by using them do not apply to complex tones as are found in musical instruments or elsewhere in nature. For instance, the PITCH of a pure tone is found to vary with its AMPLITUDE, but this is only slightly true for complex tones. It is also difficult to apply the information from MASKING experiments using pure tones to real world complex tones.

Push-Pull Push-pull is a type of AMPLIFIER that originated in the days of TUBE-type POWER AMPLIFIERS and was patented by E. F. W. Alexanderson of General Electric in 1913. In a push-pull amplifier, there are two output tubes connected in such a way that while the CURRENT in one is increasing, it is decreasing in the other. In a sense, one tube "pushes" and the other "pulls" the current. The signals from the two tubes are combined in the output TRANSFORMER. The solid-state ANALOG of the tube push-pull CIRCUIT is the complementary symmetry CIRCUIT, where two TRANSISTORS operate in a similar manner.

There are several classes of operation of push-pull circuits. In CLASS A, both devices carry signal all the time, and there is no transition of the signal from one device to the other. This configuration produces relatively little DISTORTION. In CLASS B operation, one device is turned completely off during part of the cycle, and the other one carries the entire signal. The signal is thus traded back and forth between the tubes or transistors as it goes through the zero VOLTAGE point. This produces more distortion, but is more efficient, permitting more audio power output from the given devices than class A operation. To reduce the distortion in class B operation, relatively large amounts of NEGATIVE FEEDBACK are used. The different classes of operation are obtained by the amount of BIAS applied to the stages.

Because push-pull circuits are symmetrical with respect to the signal voltage and current, the distortion they generate has a symmetrical WAVEFORM, which means it consists only of odd-numbered HARMONICS. One difficulty in designing such circuits is to ensure that the signal is smoothly passed from one device to the other as it goes through zero. Otherwise, CROSSOVER DISTORTION is introduced, which is worse at low signal levels, where it represents a larger proportion of the signal. *See also* HARMONIC DISTORTION; POWER AMPLIFIER.

PWM Pulse Width Modulation. PWM is a method of encoding a SIGNAL by using the length of a pulse as a measure of the height of a sample of the WAVEFORM. PWM is not a DIGITAL encoding at all, but is all ANALOG. Some digital encoding systems use PWM as an intermediate stage between SAMPLING and ANALOG-TO-DIGITAL conversion. The video laserdisc system uses PWM coding of the video signal, and thus is not a digital system.

PZM™ A registered trademark for a type of commercial microphone, PZM stands for Pressure Zone Microphone. The PZM is a small ELECTRET CONDENSER MICROPHONE that is mounted very close to a small aluminum plate. It is meant to be placed on a large flat surface such as the floor or a wall. The PZM is 6 DECIBELS more sensitive than the same microphone would be if it were in free space. This is due to the pressure doubling, which occurs at a boundary when a SOUND WAVE is reflected from it.

This increase in SENSITIVITY is an advantage because it increases the SIGNAL-TO-NOISE RATIO of the microphone by the same amount. However, the primary advantage of a microphone at a surface is that it is not sensitive to PHASE cancellation of sound reflected from the surface and interfering with the direct sound. A free-standing microphone should never be placed closer than 5 or 6 feet from a surface to avoid this effect, which is a broad dip in the FREQUENCY RESPONSE curve at a frequency whose WAVELENGTH is twice the distance to the surface. Thus, a microphone 1 foot from a surface will have a dip centered at about 500 HERTZ, which is right in the middle of the audible range.

The PZM has hemispherical coverage if mounted on a surface large compared to the longest wavelength to be picked up. If it is mounted on a small surface, such as a square piece of plexiglass, the sensitivity will drop by 6 dB at low frequencies because the sound wave is simply diffracted around the barrier rather than being reflected from it. This results in an apparent treble BOOST.

PZMs are also somewhat sensitive to the vibration of the surface they are mounted on, causing nonuniform frequency response. A good close-miked piano sound can be obtained by placing such a microphone on the underside of a raised grand piano lid. (PZMs are excellent at picking up the sound of tap dancing.)

Although PZM is a recently introduced term, the technique of placing microphones very close to surfaces has been used for many years, especially by laying microphones on the lip of a stage for unobtrusive reinforcement of musicals, etc. If a CARDIOID microphone is laid on a floor, its directional pattern will be preserved, but with 6 dB greater GAIN. The true PZM always has a hemispherical pickup pattern and 6 dB higher gain than the microphone alone would have.

Q

Q In reference to a resonant mechanical or electrical CIRCUIT or a CAPACITOR, Q stands for "quality factor." In the case of a resonant system, Q is a measure of the sharpness of the resonant peak in the FREQUENCY RESPONSE of the system and is inversely proportional to the DAMPING in the system. EQUALIZERS that contain resonant circuits are rated by their Q value: the higher the Q, the higher and more well-defined the peak in the response. In a capacitor, Q is a measure of its efficiency and is defined as the ratio of its CAPACITIVE REACTANCE to its RESISTANCE at some specified high FREQUENCY. The Q of a capacitor is also called the power factor, and is the reciprocal of the dissipation factor.

In LOUDSPEAKER systems, Q is a measure of the directivity of the sound output. A Q of 1 means the system radiates energy equally in all directions, or into 360 degrees of solid angle. A Q of 2 means the speaker radiates only into a hemisphere, or 180 degrees of solid angle. Higher values of Q mean the speaker radiates into smaller and smaller angles, or in other words becomes more and more directional. Q is an important characteristic of sound reinforcement loudspeakers because the more directional the speakers, the less room reverberation will be excited by the sound system, increasing the clarity of the perceived sound.

Unfortunately, the Q of a speaker depends on frequency. It always increases at higher frequencies and is always near 1 at the lowest frequencies. This must be carefully considered by the sound system designer. *See also* DIRECTIVITY INDEX.

QAVC Quiet Automatic Volume Control. A type of AGC introduced about 1934 in radio receivers that reduced the sensitivity nearly to zero when no carrier was received, resulting in the SQUELCHING of interstation noise.

Q-Biphonic *See* BIPHONIC.

QS *See* QUADRAPHONIC SOUND.

Quadlet A 32-BIT digital data quantity.

Quad Microphone Cable A superior type of microphone cable consisting of four SIGNAL conductors and a SHIELD. The four signal wires are twisted together and opposite wires are connected together at each end of the cable, giving a double twisted pair configuration. Quad cable has significantly better rejection of 60-Hz "HUM" interference than conventional twisted pair cables.

Quadraphonic Sound A STEREOPHONIC system consisting of four channels, usually two in the front as in conventional two-channel stereo, and two in the rear, purportedly for the reproduction of reverberant sound. Quadraphonic sound, or "quad," enjoyed a brief period of popularity in the early 1970s and has experienced a gradual but inevitable death since then. The reason for its demise is that it did not provide the listener a convincing illusion of being immersed in a reverberant field; in short, it did not work. Perhaps any system that mixes Latin and Greek to invent its name is doomed from the start.

Throughout the history of AUDIO, there have been many techniques put forth that attempt to acoustically transport the listener to the room where the recording was made. Even in the earliest days of the cylinder phonograph, multiple reproducers were sometimes used to introduce small time delays when playing a record in an effort to produce greater REVERBERATION. Artificial reverberation has been added to recordings for many years, and synthetic reverberation devices have been promoted for home use to enhance the "spaciousness" of recordings. It has long been known that two channels are not sufficient to convey a realistic sound perspective to a listener-to-loudspeaker reproduction. Three-channel stereo, for instance, is much better at simulating the positions of instruments across a stage. *See also* STEREOPHONIC.

The advent of home-type, four-channel tape recorders helped to encourage the industry to produce four-channel recordings, and this was probably responsible for the birth of quadraphonic sound. Then someone discovered that four channels of audio could be combined in a special way (called MATRIXING) and recorded onto a two-channel disc. The composite SIGNAL, containing the four channels, is fed into a de-matrixing network, which recovers a reasonable facsimile of the original four channels. Thus, the matrixed format of recording quadraphony on discs was born. The initials QS and SQ referred to competing schemes, each requiring its own type of decoder, which the hapless consumer was expected to buy. Then, a multiplexing technique that used a high-frequency CARRIER MODULATED with the two rear channels and recorded on the disc along with the two standard stereo channels was born. This was called CD-4 and was advertised as "discrete" rather than "matrixed" quadraphony. Of course, a special demodulator was required to play it, not to mention a special CARTRIDGE and STYLUS assembly. The CD-4 system was too expensive and suffered from far too much background NOISE and DISTORTION to be considered HIGH-FIDELITY, and it was short-lived in the marketplace.

Probably, if P. T. Barnum had lived in the 1970s, he would have promoted a quadraphonic technique.

All these systems were rushed to the market, very often without sufficient engineering having been done. It was as if the manufacturers were using the public as a testing agency for the technology, constantly coming out with new "improved" models and expecting to sell them. Finally, the long-suffering public gave up in disgust. Who was it who said you cannot fool all the people all the time?

However, it must be said that today's multichannel surround sound systems found in most motion picture houses and many home theater setups are really a logical outgrowth of the now obsolete quadraphonic systems of the past. Of course, the systems of today are far more sophisticated and the construction of the multichannel sound tracks used with them is an art form in itself.

Quadrature Two SIGNALS which are 90 degrees out of PHASE with one another are said to be in quadrature. Also, a signal or a function such as IMPEDANCE will have a phase angle that varies with FREQUENCY or with time. This phase angle can be resolved into two components called the "real" and "imaginary" parts, which have a 90-degree phase difference. They are said to be in quadrature; or more commonly, the imaginary component is called the quadrature part. *See also* Appendix 11.

Quad Track Optical soundtrack negative, and release print made therefrom, which contains all three digital sound formats (DOLBY DIGITAL, DTS, and SDDS) plus a standard SVA analog track.[23]

Quantization The representation of a continuous VOLTAGE span by a number of discrete values. Quantization is inherent in any DIGITAL audio system, and it adds quantization error, NOISE, and DISTORTION to the SIGNAL.

The signal after quantization has a "staircase" shape rather than a continuous curve, and the difference between this and the original signal is quantization error. The amount of error will always be within one LSB; therefore, the smaller the LSB, the better. In the quantization of a SINE WAVE, whose frequency is a submultiple of the SAMPLING frequency, the error will have a definite pattern that repeats at the FREQUENCY of the SIGNAL. Thus, it will have a frequency content consisting of multiples of this frequency, and it can be considered HARMONIC DISTORTION rather than noise.

For music, however, the signal is constantly changing, and no such reg-

23. This entry is copyright © 1999–2003 by Larry Blake and is reprinted with permission.

ularity exists. The quantization error is then WIDEBAND noise, and is called quantization noise. Quantization noise is difficult to measure because it does not exist without a signal. A sine test signal is not good because sometimes this results in distortion, not noise. If the sine wave frequency is chosen so it is not a submultiple of the SAMPLING frequency, the quantization errors will be more nearly randomized and will resemble random noise.

Quantization Error *See* QUANTIZATION.

Quantizing Step *See* LSB.

Quarter-Track Quarter-track, sometimes called four-track, refers to most home-type, reel-to-reel analog tape recorders, which use one-fourth the width of the tape for each recorded track. This allows STEREO signals to be recorded in both directions, effectively doubling the recording time. The technique is simply to record two tracks in one pass of the tape, and then reverse the tape reels and record the other side on another pass of the tape. Professional stereo tape recorders use one-half of the tape for each track, which results in better quality and reduced noise level. Quarter-track tapes with both sides recorded cannot be edited by splicing the tape as can two-track tapes. Four-track usually refers to an open reel format with all four tracks recorded in one direction.

Quartz Control *See* SERVO.

Quiescent Current In TRANSISTOR and TUBE circuitry, the direct BIAS current is sometimes called the quiescent current because it still exists in the absence of a SIGNAL.

Quiescent Noise The residual NOISE produced by an AUDIO device at its output terminals when no SIGNAL is present.

Quieting The decrease in the noise level at the output of an FM receiver or tuner when tuned to an unmodulated CARRIER, as opposed to being tuned between stations. The quieting, expressed in DECIBELS, is one measure of the performance of the receiver or tuner.

Quietness

Quintophonic An unusual surround-sound system for motion picture use devised in Britain by the late John Mosely. It used both magnetic and optical sound tracks. Quintophonic sound never became a commercial success. *See also* COLORTEK.

R

Rack Many years ago, a standard method for mounting telephone equipment was devised that used steel frames spaced 19 inches apart. They were perforated with many tapped holes along the vertical axis, and equipment with FLANGES 19 inches apart could be bolted in place. These frames were originally called "relay racks." The same design is still widely used to mount commercial electronic equipment, including AUDIO components. Even some home-type components such as AMPLIFIERS and tuners are designed for rack mounting. Some components are adapted for rack mounting by the addition of "rack flanges," or "rack ears."

Rack Space *See* U.

Radiation Impedance The acoustic IMPEDANCE that acts as a load on a LOUDSPEAKER, opposing the motion of the CONE. The acoustic power output of a speaker, especially a low-FREQUENCY speaker, is greatly affected by the radiation impedance, and this depends on where the speaker is placed. In free space, with no nearby reflecting surfaces, the speaker will see the highest impedance and will radiate the least amount of power. If placed next to a large wall, it radiates into a hemisphere rather than a full sphere, cutting its radiation impedance in half and doubling its power output. The more restricted the volume the speaker sees, the more power it will radiate. This is the reason a loudspeaker system has such an increase in BASS response when placed in the corner of a room. The radiation impedance is also reflected back to the electrical input impedance of the speaker terminals, so the amount of power the speaker draws from the amplifier also varies with the speaker's location.

Radiation Pattern The graph of a LOUDSPEAKER's directional characteristics, usually plotted for several specific test frequencies. Also called the polar pattern. The term radiation pattern also applies to sound radiation of musical instruments.

Radio Frequency, RF An ALTERNATING CURRENT or VOLTAGE having a FREQUENCY above about 100 KILOHERTZ. It is so called because these frequencies are radiated as electromagnetic waves by radio (and now television) stations. Theoretically, RF could extend down into the audible range, and some special-purpose radio transmissions are at about 20 kHz, but RF is usually considered to be at least 100 kHz.

In radio and television broadcasting, the actual SIGNAL broadcast by the station is called the radio frequency, as opposed to the audio frequency (AF) or video frequency, which modulates it. The signal present at the receiving antenna terminals is also RF and remains so in the receiver until it is HETERODYNED or detected.

Radio Frequency Interference, RFI The noise that can be induced in audio systems due to radio and television broadcasting stations is called radio frequency interference. One might think that the extremely high frequencies radiated by broadcast stations would not cause problems at audio frequencies, but most audio circuits are NONLINEAR at these high frequencies, and this causes the interfering signals to be rectified, or DETECTED. The envelope of the RF signals can then be heard as the interference. RFI is a type of ELECTROMAGNETIC INTERFERENCE. *See also* TELEVISION INTERFERENCE.

Radiogram British terminology for radio-phonograph.

Radiophonics A term, coined by the BBC, referring to a type of electronic music made up of multiple recordings of natural sounds that have been copied and manipulated in various ways and spliced back together to make a collage of sound. The more usual term for this is *musique concrète.*

Rails *See* SUPPLY RAILS.

Random Incidence Correlator A mechanical accessory placed over an omnidirectional measurement microphone to improve its performance as a RANDOM INCIDENCE MICROPHONE.

Random Incidence Microphone An OMNIDIRECTIONAL microphone having essentially a constant sensitivity over a wide frequency range for sounds that arrive at the microphone from all directions with equal probability. Such a microphone will have a rising high-frequency sensitivity for sounds coming directly from the front. For recording A-B STEREO in a large auditorium, it is a good idea to use random incidence microphones, since the increased frontal high-frequency sensitivity tends to compensate for the high-frequency loss due to air absorption.

Raster The characteristic pattern of horizontal lines formed by the scanning beam of a television or computer monitor picture tube, or the resulting image.

RASTI Short for Rapid Speech Transmission Index, which is a technique for evaluating the intelligibility of speech in a given room. It is an objective measure that correlates well with the subjective articulation index of speech.

The RASTI system consists of a box that produces two OCTAVE bands of PINK NOISE that are AMPLITUDE MODULATED at frequencies corresponding to the fluctuations in level of human speech.

This SIGNAL is projected into a room at a spot where a talker would normally be placed. Then, a MICROPHONE and analyzer pick up the signal at a location where a listener would be. Room noise and REVERBERATION of the signal will reduce the amount of amplitude modulation. The analyzer translates this reduction in modulation into a number from 0 to 1, which is proportional to speech intelligibility.

The value of the system lies in the simplicity and rapidity with which many tests can be made in a building. It is useful for sound system evaluation, as well as for examination of ACOUSTICS.

Rated Bandwidth The FREQUENCY range, normally taken to be from 20 HERTZ to 20 KILOHERTZ for audio equipment, over which the performance of a device is rated with respect to characteristics such as power output, DISTORTION, etc.

Rated Characteristic A single value of a characteristic, such as power output, DISTORTION, etc., claimed as representative of the performance of the device and measured in conformance with standardized test procedures.

Rated Load The load IMPEDANCE into which a POWER AMPLIFIER is designed to operate, and upon which other characteristics such as power output, DISTORTION, etc., are based.

Ratio Detector A type of DETECTOR used in FM radios that is sensitive only to frequency modulation, as opposed to the frequency DISCRIMINATOR, which is also sensitive to amplitude modulation. Most of the interference heard by someone listening to FM is caused by amplitude modulation of the CARRIER. The ratio detector is insensitive to this type of interference.

Rayleigh, Lord Lord Rayleigh (John William Strutt, 1842–1919), an English mathematician and physicist, is considered the father of modern ACOUSTICS. He won a Nobel physics prize for the discovery of argon gas and published a monumental two-volume treatise titled *The Theory of Sound*, which is still the definitive work on the subject.

RC The magnitude of the TIME CONSTANT of a series RESISTANCE-CAPACITANCE circuit is the resistance in OHMS multiplied by the capacitance in farads.

RCA Plug, RCA Jack The most common type of AUDIO connector, next to the standard PHONE PLUG, is the "phono" connector designed by RCA many years ago. The input and output TERMINALS on almost all audio PREAMPLIFIERS are RCA jacks. The same jack is used for most consumer composite video and S/PDIF connections, although the cable for such should have 75 ohms characteristic impedance. They have the advantage of small size, shielded configuration, and low price, but the disadvantages of unreliability and lack of ruggedness. If you step on an RCA plug, you can usually forget about using it again; and with continued use, the outer "GROUND" connection is likely to lose its springiness and thereafter make poor contact, resulting in HUM and STATIC.

R-DAT Original name for the common audio DAT machine meaning Rotating-head DIGITAL Audio Tape. Since most common DAT machines are the rotating head type and S-DAT (stationary DAT) machines are referred to by format (DASH, ProDigi), the term R-DAT has fallen into disuse.

Reactance *See* CAPACITIVE REACTANCE; INDUCTIVE REACTANCE.

Reactive The term *reactive* describes an electronic component in an electronic CIRCUIT that has either CAPACITIVE REACTANCE or INDUCTIVE REACTANCE or both. Nonreactive components are sometimes called resistive. *See* CAPACITOR and INDUCTOR.

Read Only Memory A digital storage medium where the data cannot be erased or recorded. The original audio COMPACT DISC was a type of read only memory, as was the CD-ROM. ROMs are also silicon chips or modules that are an integral part of the computer, containing starting code that never will be changed.

Real-Time Analyzer A special type of SPECTRUM ANALYZER, which consists of a group of BANDPASS FILTERS, each having a constant percentage BANDWIDTH, such as one OCTAVE or one-third octave. All the FILTER inputs are connected to the input SIGNAL, and the outputs of each filter are passed through a DETECTOR and thence to an indicating device such as a CRT or, more commonly, an array of LEDs or an LCD. The display is a graph of AMPLITUDE of the signal versus FREQUENCY, which is a spectrum. The amplitude in each frequency band is almost always expressed in DECIBELS.

The real-time analyzer is so called because it does the entire frequency analysis simultaneously, or in "real time," as opposed to sweeping through the frequency range with a single filter. The real-time analyzer lacks resolution because the filters are too wide to separate narrowly spaced frequency components, but it is useful to indicate how a signal will sound subjectively, especially if the analyzer is a one-third octave type.

Real-Time Dubbing Duplicating an analog tape at its normal playing speed rather than at a higher speed. Real-time duplicating is generally of better quality than high-speed duplicating.

Receiver An audio component consisting of an AM-FM or FM-only tuner with a PREAMP and POWER AMPLIFIER all on one chassis. Nowadays receivers tend to be home theater oriented, with multiple amps (e.g., 6), several surround decoders, and AV switching as well as the aforementioned.

Recone To replace the cone of a dynamic LOUDSPEAKER. This involves replacing the VOICE COIL, SURROUND and SPIDER assemblies also. The magnet structure of a typical loudspeaker is the most expensive part, and this makes reconing of damaged units a practical proposition. When reconing a speaker, the original response characteristics will be regained only if the new parts used are the same as the originals!

Recording Horn A special HORN used to collect the sound to be recorded in the making of ACOUSTIC RECORDINGS. The recording horn somewhat resembled an ear trumpet and was actually an acoustic transformer, matching the acoustic IMPEDANCE of the air to that of the recording mechanism diaphragm. It thus greatly increased the efficiency of the recording process. Edison's first phonograph had a rudimentary short horn that was not very effective. It is said that one had to shout directly into it in order to make a playable recording. Edison quickly realized the importance of the horn, however, and he performed endless experiments to determine the best shapes and sizes. One Edison recording horn was reportedly 40 feet long.

It is interesting that all these early horns were conical in shape, and it was not until the mid-1920s that workers at the Bell Telephone Labs developed the mathematical theory of horns in general and determined that the EXPONENTIAL HORN is much more efficient than the conical.

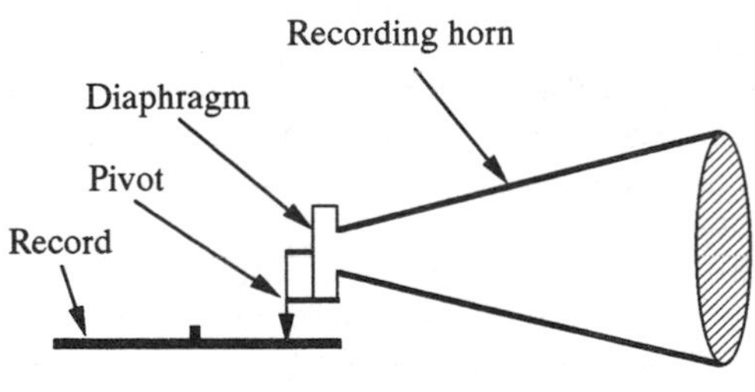

Recording Horn

Recording Lathe The recording lathe is the turntable assembly that is used in the recording of the ACETATE master, which is the first step in the making of phonograph records. The lathe is more than a turntable, however. It also includes the mechanism that advances the CUTTERHEAD across the record as it turns, and in so doing determines the spacing of the grooves or the PITCH of the record. The lathe must be accurate and stable in its motion, for any variations will show up in the final record. This means that the amounts of FLUTTER and WOW are very low, and the speed is very closely controlled.

Early recording lathes were driven by weights and mechanical speed governors because electric motors could not be made to have as stable a speed. In the 1950s, the RCA Victor Record Company in Camden, New Jersey, reportedly bought a manhole cover from the city of Camden and machined it into a turntable for a recording lathe in order to attain sufficient mass to ensure constant speed and negligible speed variations.

Although Edison chose 160 RPM as the speed of his 2-minute cylinder records and 80 rpm for his 4-minute cylinders and Diamond Disc records, the speed of 78.26 rpm was standardized about 1925 and used for many years before the 33⅓-rpm speed was adopted for MICROGROOVE records. You might well ask why the strange speed of 78.26 rpm was chosen. The various record manufacturers in the 1920s did not agree on the optimum speed for records to turn, and recording speeds varied from about 82 to 78 rpm. It was not considered a problem, because all phonographs were variable speed, and the listener simply adjusted each record to suit his own taste. In 1925, with the advent of electrical recording technology by the Bell Telephone Labs, it became necessary to standardize the speed. Victor Records was using 78 rpm at the time, and they were the largest record company of the day. Victor was also the first customer for the new electrical recording apparatus, so the Bell people settled on 78 rpm. However, it turns out that it is impossible to attain precisely 78 rpm with a synchronous motor driving a turntable through a worm gear. The worm gear is a very quiet drive mechanism compared to other types of gears. With a synchronous motor running at 3,600 rpm and a gear box with 46 to 1 ratio, the resulting speed is 78.26087. . . rpm, which is as close to 78 as possible with a gear drive.

The 33⅓-rpm speed also came about in 1925, this time through the efforts of the Western Electric Company, Inc. (a subsidiary of Bell Telephone). The first sound motion pictures had the sound track on a disc that was played in synchronization with the movie projector. This was called the Vitaphone system. A 1,000-foot reel of 35-mm motion picture film ran for 11 minutes, while the 10-inch standard 78-rpm record played for 3 minutes. In order to get 11 minutes playing time, a speed of about one-half of 78 rpm was sought. A worm gear of 54 teeth provides 33⅓-rpm at a 60-HERTZ line FREQUENCY driving a synchronous motor. Then the record diameter had to be increased to 20 inches to allow the needed time.

The Vitaphone system was used only a short time and was replaced by recording the sound track directly on the film, but the 33⅓ rpm format was retained for the purpose of recording radio broadcasts for delayed transmission. These "transcriptions" were used until the advent of the tape recorder in the early 1950s.

A third speed of 45 rpm was introduced about 1948 by RCA for their new microgroove records. One wag has suggested that the speed was a logical choice, since 78 less 33 equals 45.

Recordist A person (presumably) proficient in the art of making recordings of music. The person who operates the recording device during a recording session, who may also be called the machine operator.

Rectification The conversion of an ALTERNATING CURRENT to a DIRECT CURRENT. The AC of the power line is rectified in the power supply to provide DC for ACTIVE CIRCUIT devices. Rectification is also used to recover the signal from an AMPLITUDE MODULATED WAVEFORM. *See also* DETECTION; DETECTOR.

Rectify *See* RECTIFICATION.

Red Book A comprehensive manual published by Philips and Sony that sets out the complete standards defining the COMPACT DISC format. When buying a license to make CD players, a manufacturer obtains the rights to the applicable patents and also a copy of the Red Book. This ensures that all CD players will be compatible.

In like manner, the CD-ROM standards are contained in the Yellow Book, also published by Philips and Sony, but the file structure is not the same as in the Red Book CD. The CD-ROM file structure conforms to the ISO 9660 specifications, and this allows the CD-ROM to be read by many computer operating systems. The Orange Book covers CD-R. The Blue Book is the specification for CD-Plus, a multisession audio and data disc. The Green Book covers the CD-I standards and the White Book covers Video CD. The colors ostensibly come from the colors of the covers on the books.

Redundancy The transmission of more information (in a DIGITAL system, this means more BITS) than is necessary in order to improve the reliability of the transmission. It must, of course, be accompanied by appropriate decoding. ERROR CORRECTION bits are examples of redundant information.

Human speech is highly redundant by nature. This is the reason it is possible to understand what is said in the presence of large amounts of NOISE or DISTORTION. Music is also very redundant.

Reel Idler A rotating metal cylinder between the supply reel and the heads of a magnetic tape recorder. It is usually connected to a flywheel under the tape deck and thus serves to smooth out any irregularities in the tape motion caused by tape sticking in the supply pack.

Re-entrant Horn A type of HORN LOUDSPEAKER, usually made of metal, in which the sound path is folded back on itself to make the overall horn less bulky. Re-entrant horns (or re-entrant trumpets, as they are sometimes called) are characterized by poor low-frequency response, poor very high-frequency response, and many resonances in the audible range, making them sound "metallic" or "tinny." Their sole advantage is high efficiency, producing a lot of sound for a little input power. They are used only for low-cost paging systems. *See also* FOLDED HORN.

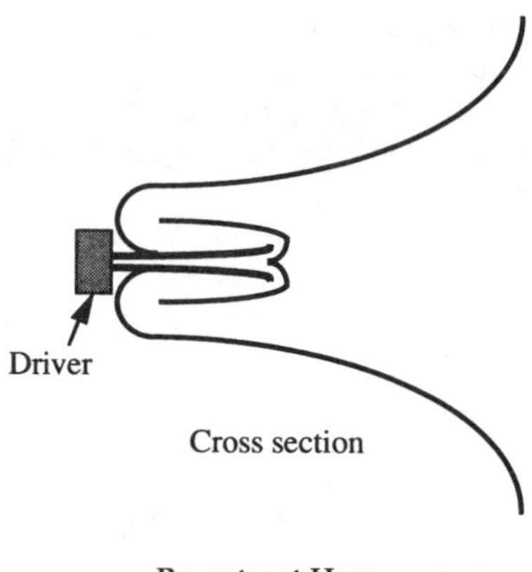

Re-entrant Horn

Reference Level The reference level in an audio device is a signal level near the maximum possible that the device can handle but low enough to ensure low DISTORTION. This difference is known as HEADROOM. In audio devices, it is desirable to attain the maximum SIGNAL-TO-NOISE RATIO, and to do this, one needs to know the signal level in the device in comparison to the maximum level possible without distortion. If the operator keeps the signal level as high as possible, the signal to noise ratio is maximized. Many devices will show the reference level as 0 dB with an LED or on a mechanical meter, and mark the onset of the maximum signal possible with a separate LED labeled "clip" or "overload." Meters are usually inadequate to show the maximum with any accuracy on program material because they are too slow in response. It is up to the operator to determine if factors such as the metering characteristics, or CREST FACTOR, DYNAMIC RANGE and spectral content of the audio signal warrant adjusting the signal level above or below the reference level. Operators may also interconnect devices and use each device's reference level indication to estimate these optimal operating conditions. Unfortunately, devices seldom agree on the desirable headroom, and this must be taken into account. *See* GAIN STRUCTURE. Headroom in many devices may be 24 dB or more, but you can get better signal-to-noise ratio numbers by reducing headroom.

In the case of digital devices, the important reference level is the maximum, known as 0 dBFS for decibels full scale. Program should be recorded to come as close to 0 as possible without ever going over. This is difficult to achieve in practice, as even peak reading meters cannot always display a brief level that is actually going over 0. Again, the operator must judge how far below 0 dBFS to adjust her program level to avoid ever going "over" and causing distortion. Some controversy exists over how many dB below 0 dBFS to record test tones intended to help subsequent analog equipment users set their levels. An accepted figure is 12–18 dB, but since there is no standard, a notation should be made for the benefit of the next user. Any decibel measurement requires a reference level that is 0 dB by definition. This reference level is typically not chosen for any reason involving optimizing signal to noise ratio as above.

In the case of analog tape recorders the term OPERATING LEVEL is used.

Reflex An early type of radio set that passed the RF signal through several amplifier tubes and then passed the audio signal after DETECTION through the same amplifier tubes again. In effect each tube does the work of two. Such sets usually had only one tuned circuit and were not very SELECTIVE, that is, they were likely to receive several strong stations at the same time. *See also* BASS REFLEX.

Regeneration A type of positive FEEDBACK in radio receivers invented and patented in 1913 by Major Edwin Armstrong. Lee DeForest contested the patent, claiming to have invented the same thing in 1912, although he didn't publicize it. There was a great court battle, and several decisions each way until finally the U.S. Supreme Court ruled in DeForest's favor and awarded him the patent in 1934.

The purpose of regeneration was to increase the gain of the RF AMPLIFIER in the receiver and thus increase the sensitivity of the receiver. Armstrong's patent used a "tickler" coil inside the main tuning coil and connected to the RF amplifier. The tickler could be rotated by a knob, varying the coupling between it and the coil and thus varying the feedback and the resultant gain of the stage. Too much regeneration would cause the set to oscillate, turning it into a miniature transmitter, to the consternation of the neighbors who might be trying to listen to their radios! One method of operation, called dead beat tuning, was to increase the regeneration to get the set to howl and then tune to a station. As the station was tuned in, the howl frequency would fall, and there would be a "bloop" sound when it was tuned in exactly. For this reason, these sets were also called bloopers.

Other methods of adding positive feedback were developed by different makers in order to get around Armstrong's patent, but most were inferior to the tickler coil. At least one maker built a set with a tickler coil that was short-circuited by a heavy wire. Attached to the wire was a large red tag cautioning the purchaser not to remove the wire under any circumstances, for this would result in patent infringement. However, the tag went on to extol the improved reception that would result if the wire were removed!

Regulation The ability of a POWER SUPPLY to maintain a constant VOLTAGE as varying CURRENT is being drawn from it. A "regulated" power supply is one that has a circuit specially designed to control the output voltage as the current drawn varies. A conventional power supply, without a regulator circuit, can have good regulation, in which case it may be called a brute force supply.

Relap To reshape analog tape recorder heads after they wear. For proper operation, a TAPE HEAD should have a smoothly curved surface where the tape makes contact with it. As the head wears with use, the surface will develop a "FLAT," and this reduces the pressure of the tape against the gap of the head, causing nonuniformity of the output.

The head can be restored to original performance by reshaping the curve by a process called relapping. This is another word for a very fine-grain grinding and polishing operation. Usually this can only be done once because the pole pieces in the head will wear too thin and the gap will increase in length. *See also* EDGE SLOTTING.

Release Agent A chemical additive to the vinyl COMPOUND used for pressing vinyl phonograph records to prevent them from sticking to the STAMPERS.

Remote A recording session that occurs at a location other than a recording studio, such as a concert hall or church.

Most classical music recordings are remotes, for the ACOUSTICS of the recording space are an important part of the musical experience. A remote recording requires a good deal of planning and a large amount of work compared to a studio recording, and unforeseen problems are always cropping up. An example of such a problem occurred in Seattle about forty years ago when a record company set out to record a large theater organ. MICROPHONE cables were strung, all the equipment was brought in and set up, and microphones were positioned for the first test recording. The technician, needing AC power, pulled the end of his long extension cord backstage and plugged it into what looked like a standard power outlet. The problem was that the theater was powered with DC rather than AC, and all the equipment instantly failed, some by blown fuses and some by burned-out power TRANSFORMERS.

Repeat Coil, Repeater Coil Another name for a one-to-one turns ratio transformer used in telephone and broadcasting applications in order to eliminate the requirement for the GROUND connection between two AUDIO devices or systems. GROUND LOOPS are thus eliminated, and certain noises such as HUM can be greatly reduced.

The repeat coil is typically designed for input and output IMPEDANCES of 600 OHMS. It is also sometimes called an ISOLATION transformer, although some isolation transformers are designed for use in the power line input of audio devices. These isolation transformers, however, are never called repeat coils.

Reproduce Alignment Tape *See* ALIGNMENT TAPE.

Resampling In DIGITAL audio systems, the changing of a SIGNAL encoded at one sampling rate to a different sampling rate is called resampling. The "brute force" way of doing this would be to convert the signal back to ANALOG with a DAC and then re-encode it with an ADC using a different sampling rate. This, however, subjects the signal to DISTORTIONS in the dual conversion processes, so it is much better to do the job completely in the digital domain.

If the two sampling rates are in a simple arithmetic ratio, it is relatively straightforward to do this, but it gets much more complicated, although it can still be done, when the two frequencies have a ratio of any real number. Because the COMPACT DISC system uses 44.1 KILOHERTZ as a sampling FREQUENCY, and the commonly used standard for master recording is 48 kHz, it can be seen that the resampling converter is a very useful device. Also known as sample rate conversion.

Residue pitch The perceived pitch of a complex tone. The residue pitch in many cases corresponds to a FREQUENCY that is not present in the complex tone. An example of this is the PITCH of a bell that is one OCTAVE higher than the lowest frequency component in the tone.

Resist The coating applied to an unetched PRINTED CIRCUIT BOARD in the places where the copper is to remain. The rest of the copper is then dissolved away in the etching process. *See also* PRINTED CIRCUIT BOARD.

Resistance Resistance is that characteristic of electric conductors which resists, or opposes, electric CURRENT. The unit of resistance is the OHM (symbol Ω, the Greek letter Omega), after Georg Ohm, who formulated OHM'S LAW. The reciprocal of resistance is CONDUCTANCE, which is measured in units that used to be called mhos, but today are called siemens, after Ernst von Siemens. Conductance is seldom used in practical applications. *See also* IMPEDANCE.

Resistor An electronic circuit component that has RESISTANCE but no appreciable INDUCTANCE or CAPACITANCE. Resistors are the most common type of circuit elements, and they are available in many different standardized resistance values. When an electric current exists in a resistor, a certain amount of random noise is added to the current, and different types of resistors contribute different amounts of noise. Carbon composition resistors are very inexpensive but are notorious for being noisy, whereas metal film and "wire wound" resistors are very quiet. There is a theoretical lower limiting noise that any resistor can produce, and this is the thermal noise, or JOHNSON NOISE, which is proportional to the resistance itself. Resistors are made in different sizes to handle different amounts of power. The resistance and tolerance values of the traditional axial resistors are generally not printed on the unit but are encoded by painted-on colored bands using an internationally agreed-upon code. The first two bands encode the first two digits of the resistance value, and the third band represents the multiplier in powers of ten, or simply the number of zeros to be appended to the first two digits. Surface mount and other forms will usually have the value printed in code.

Resonance A resonance is the tendency of a mechanical or electrical system to vibrate at a certain FREQUENCY when excited by an external force, and to keep vibrating after the excitation is removed. A bell is a good example. The Latin root of the word means to "sound again."

All mechanical structures have resonances at many frequencies. Resonances are most troublesome in audio TRANSDUCERS, where they "color" the sound by adding their own natural frequencies. LOUDSPEAKERS are offenders to a large degree. Ideally, one would design structures of TRANS-

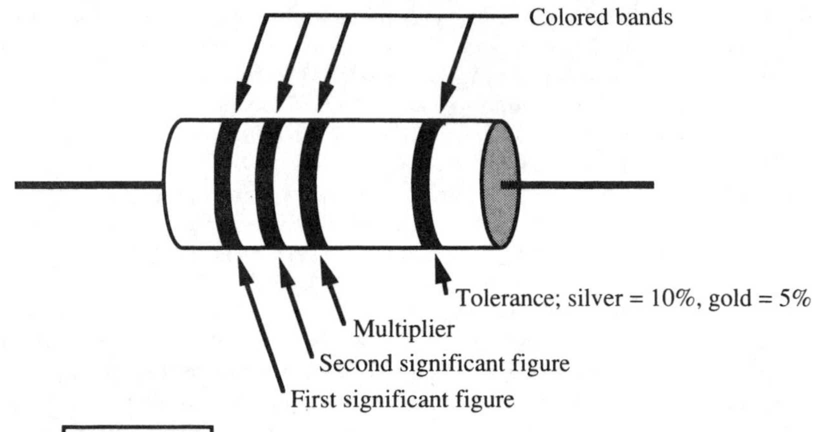

Color code:

0 = Black
1 = Brown
2 = Red
3 = Orange
4 = Yellow
5 = Green
6 = Blue
7 = Violet
8 = Gray
9 = White

Resistor

DUCERS so the resonances are outside the audible range, and this is done in the case of most MICROPHONES. It is not possible, however, for loudspeakers, so the resonances are DAMPED so that they will contribute as little DISTORTION as possible. Resonances in TWEETERS are probably the most insidious because the higher frequencies are where the ear is most sensitive to tone color, or TIMBRE, changes.

Some other mechanical resonances that cause problems are associated with record players. The resonance between the tonearm mass and the STYLUS stiffness can cause low-frequency distortion and mistracking.

Resonator An acoustic device that has a RESONANCE. The most common acoustic resonator is the HELMHOLTZ RESONATOR. Virtually all musical instruments have some sort of resonator as part of their tone-producing mechanisms.

Return *See* SEND.

Reverb Chamber Short for reverberation chamber or room. A specially designed room whose surfaces are all carefully designed with regard to placement and reflectivity, into which a speaker and MICROPHONE are placed for the purpose of creating controlled reverberation for adding to recordings. Dry recordings are played through the speaker and the microphone picks up the result created by the room, which can be judiciously mixed back into the original dry recording. The reverberation chamber preceded purely electronic devices, and is thought by some to still sound the best. Capitol Records in Hollywood has several famous reverb chambers under their parking lot. Curiously, a concrete stairwell can sometimes serve as a decent reverb chamber with the addition of the speaker and microphone, so long as no one uses the stairs.

Reverberant Field In a room with REVERBERATION, if a listener is close to a source of sound, the direct sound will predominate, and the listener is said to be in the direct field of the source. At greater distances, the reverberant energy will predominate, and this region is called the reverberant field.

In general, the purpose of sound reinforcement systems is to send direct energy into the reverberant field to increase intelligibility.

Reverberation The remainder of sound that exists in a room after the source of the sound is stopped is called reverberation, sometimes mistakenly called "ECHO." The time of reverberation is defined as the time it takes for the SOUND PRESSURE LEVEL to decay to one-millionth of its former value. This is a 60-DECIBEL reduction in level.

All rooms have some reverberation, and an important subjective quality of a room is its reverberation time, although other factors, such as ratio of direct to reverberant sound, are probably more important. In a real room, the sound heard by a listener is a mixture of direct sound from the source and reverberant sound from the room. Reverberant sound is diffuse, coming from random directions, and the direct sound allows us to localize the source of the sound. As we move farther from the source, the direct sound becomes weaker and the reverberant sound is relatively stronger. At a certain point, the two will be equal in strength, and this is sometimes called the CRITICAL DISTANCE. This distance is surprisingly small for most rooms. Even when we listen from distances greater than the critical distance, we can localize the sound because our hearing mechanism can distinguish the direct sound in the presence of stronger reverberation by BINAURAL hearing.

For good speech intelligibility, too much reverberation is a hindrance, and can be considered NOISE, although some reverberation helps intelligibility if the reverberation time is not too long. The objectively measured reverberation time of a room is not necessarily heard by a listener, for the reverberant sound may be high or low in level compared to the direct sound. For instance, a large cathedral with six seconds reverberation time does not sound reverberant to two people casually speaking inside it, but their speech in a small chamber, say twenty feet on a side, with six seconds reverberation would be inarticulate. In the large space, the reflections from the walls are much later in arriving at the listener, and are at a lower level than in the small rooms. For this reason, longer reverberation time is better tolerated in large buildings than in small ones; this also points up the fact that the reverberation time alone does not give very much information on how a room will sound to a listener.

Most music recordings have some reverberation recorded on them along with the direct sound, and this causes a sensation of room "AMBIENCE" to be present. Usually, recording studios are lacking in reverberation, and so synthetic reverberation is mixed with the music signal when making the master recording. This synthetic reverberation seldom sounds the same as real reverberation, but the music consumer seems to have gotten used to it.

Reverberator A device for the generation of synthetic REVERBERATION. *See also* PLATE REVERBERATION; SPRING REVERB.

Reverse Current The current in a DIODE or other SEMICONDUCTOR junction that is opposite to the normal direction. Reverse current is sometimes called leakage current and is usually extremely small, except in the case of the ZENER DIODE.

Reverse Resistance The actual RESISTANCE of a DIODE or other SEMICONDUCTOR junction when conducting current in the direction opposite to normal. Reverse resistance is normally very high, which causes reverse current to be very low. But when the reverse VOLTAGE reaches the breakdown, or avalanche, voltage, the resistance suddenly falls and the current increases. Some diodes have a very NONLINEAR reverse resistance when operating in the avalanche mode such that the voltage across them remains essentially constant regardless of the current. Such a diode is called a ZENER DIODE.

Reverse Voltage *See* REVERSE RESISTANCE.

RF, or R.F. *See* RADIO FREQUENCY.

RFI *See* RADIO FREQUENCY INTERFERENCE.

Rhythmicon A clever musical keyboard instrument built in 1930 by Leon Theremin, né Termen, the inventor of the THEREMIN, at the request of composer/theorist Henry Cowell. Each key of the Rhythmicon played a repeated tone, proportional in PITCH and rhythm to the overtone series (the second key played one OCTAVE higher in pitch [double the frequency of the first key] and twice as fast as the first key. The third key played three times higher in frequency and repeated three times faster then the first key, etc.). The instrument used electronic OSCILLATORS to produce the tones and a rotating disc with rows of holes in it at various spacing. The rhythm was generated by photoelectric cells on one side of the disc and neon light bulbs on the other side. When a hole let the neon light strike the photocell, a sound was produced, and the keyboard determined which lights were activated.

RIAA Short for Recording Industry Association of America. A long time ago, the RIAA was active in setting standards for recording and playback equalization of phonograph records. The universally used DE-EMPHASIS curve for stereo record playback was standardized by the RIAA, and is often referred to as the RIAA EQUALIZATION. In recent years, the RIAA is concerned with protecting musicians and music producers against copyright infringement by illegal copying and dissemination of original recordings. They also certify "gold record" status and present the awards for a gold record.

Ribbon Microphone *See* VELOCITY MICROPHONE.

Ribbon Tweeter The ribbon tweeter is a high-frequency LOUDSPEAKER that works like a RIBBON MICROPHONE in reverse. The audio SIGNAL is connected to the ribbon, which is a very thin metal (usually aluminum) strip suspended in a magnetic field. The CURRENT in the ribbon establishes another magnetic field, causing the ribbon to move in synchrony with the input signal WAVEFORM. The ribbon is a DIRECT RADIATOR of sound.

The ribbon tweeter, because of its small size, is only effective at very high frequencies, and must be used with a CROSSOVER above 5 KILOHERTZ or so. It is characterized by uniform output up to ULTRASONIC frequencies. A disadvantage is the very low IMPEDANCE of the ribbon, which usually requires that a step-down transformer be used with it. There have been some recent developments of fairly large ribbon tweeters, which are capable of response down to 1 kHz or so.

Rigging Points Special attachments on a LOUDSPEAKER cabinet designed to safely hang the cabinet. Speakers should not be hung from unapproved points, such as handles.

Ringing Any device, electronic or mechanical, is said to ring if it continues to produce a SIGNAL or to move after its input is stopped. Ringing is caused by too little DAMPING, and is particularly bothersome in audio TRANSDUCERS such as LOUDSPEAKERS and phono CARTRIDGES. Ringing of low-frequency loudspeakers is called HANGOVER. Ringing, of course, causes transient DISTORTION, and is to be avoided.

A FILTER with a very narrow BANDPASS or a very sharp CUTOFF will ring for a certain time if it is presented with a sharp TRANSIENT. This phenomenon is common and is to be avoided if possible. Unfortunately, the shape of the slopes of a filter is intimately connected to its inherent damping, and one cannot be changed without changing the other. This is the reason filters and EQUALIZERS should have as gentle a slope as possible, without extremely steep SKIRTS, especially if they are in the audible range.

ANTI-ALIASING and ANTI-IMAGING FILTERS in DIGITAL systems have very steep ROLLOFFS, and they ring when excited by a transient signal. The frequency at which they ring, however, is ULTRASONIC and so is not as bad as one would expect from looking at the picture. *See also* RESONANCE. OSCILLOSCOPE pictures of this ringing used to be published in equipment reviews. *See also* RINGING OUT.

Ringing Out One way to adjust a sound reinforcement system to maximize its GAIN before FEEDBACK is to raise the level of each band of a graphic EQUALIZER until the system begins to feed back, then to reduce its level by 2 or 3 dB. This usually does not result in an optimally adjusted FREQUENCY RESPONSE curve of the system but it is widely used in practice.

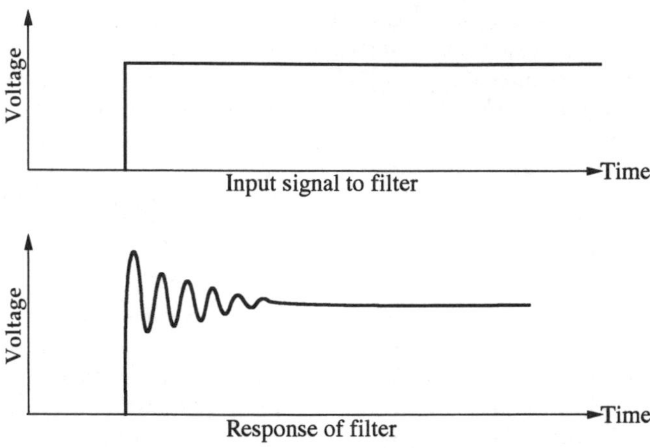

Ringing of a Sharp-Cutoff Low-Pass Filter

Ring Modulator A circuit that allows one signal to amplitude modulate another signal, resulting in a complex series of sum and difference frequencies between the input signal frequencies. The ring modulator introduces a gross nonlinearity and causes huge amounts of harmonic and intermodulation DISTORTION. It is sometimes used for special effects in the generation of electronic music, usually in conjunction with a low-pass filter, which reduces the high-frequency roughness of the resulting sound. It gets its name from its circuit configuration, which is a "ring" of four DIODES.

Ripping The extraction of audio tracks from CDs, or audio/video tracks from DVDs, onto a computer hard drive is called ripping. The process is more complex than one might expect, since the audio information is encoded with other data to enable ERROR CORRECTION when the CD is played. Also called "Grabbing."

Ripple Irregularities in the FREQUENCY RESPONSE of a FILTER that has nominally flat response in its PASSBAND. Irregularity in the value of direct VOLTAGE from a power supply is also called ripple.

In some filter designs, such as ELLIPTICAL and CHEBYSHEV, ripple in the passband is traded for steepness of the slope of the response above the CUTOFF frequency. Ripple is measured in DECIBELS, and is the maximum deviation from flat response, regardless of frequency.

Power supply ripple is mostly at 120 HERTZ, but it may contain significant HARMONICS of 120. Ripple is reduced by filters consisting of large CAPACITORS and RESISTORS and/or INDUCTORS in the power supply. Most power supplies in audio equipment today are electronically regulated, reducing ripple even further. Power supply ripple is measured in millivolts rms.

Rise Time The time required for a device to allow a signal waveform to rise from 10% of maximum amplitude to 90% of maximum amplitude, usually measured in microseconds. The shorter the rise time of a device, the higher in frequency its response will extend. To pass a full-level 20-kilohertz signal, the rise time must be less than 12 microseconds.

RLC Circuit A circuit usually found in EQUALIZERS or FILTERS that uses RESISTORS (Rs), INDUCTORS (Ls), and CAPACITORS (Cs).

RMS Root mean square (rms) is, literally, the square root of the mean of the squares.

To find the rms value of a SIGNAL, one must square the signal mathematically, then average it over a time period, and then take the square root of the average value. The result is a quantity which, when squared, is proportional to the energy content (or power) of the signal. The rms value of a SINE WAVE is .707 times the peak value, but it is not usually possible to deduce the rms value of an arbitrary WAVEFORM, especially a complex one like a music signal. Most common AC VOLTMETERS will not measure the rms value of any signal except sine waves. A meter that actually does the job is called a "true rms" voltmeter.

The term *rms power* is a misnomer. The rms value of the signal is used to calculate the average power, but the power is simply the power, in spite of misleading statements made by some manufacturers. A POWER AMPLIFIER rated as having "200 watts rms power" really puts out 200 WATTS of continuous sine wave power.

Rock and Roll Editing One way of EDITING analog tapes is by listening to the playback as the tape is slowly moved back and forth over the playback head to find the best edit point. To do this, the tape reels are grasped by hand and "rocked" back and forth, and the tape is "rolled" for short distances between the splice points. Although this is called rock and roll editing, it has nothing to do with the type of music being edited.

Roll off A FILTER that has a reduced output as the FREQUENCY is increased or decreased is called a roll off filter. Bass and treble tone controls are roll off filters when turned down. Sometimes the reduced high-frequency or low-frequency content of the SIGNAL itself is called roll off.

Roll Surround *See* SURROUND.

ROM See READ ONLY MEMORY.

Room Leakage In recording studio jargon, room leakage is unwanted transmission of sound from one room to the other.

Room Mode, Room Tone *See* EIGENTONE.

Router A multiple selector switch that can send any of several input signals to any of several outputs. The equivalent of a PATCH BAY. The actual switching mechanism in a router is sometimes called a crossbar switch from telephone exchange usage. A crossbar switch has the input circuits on a series of bars running at a right angle to a series of bars representing the output. To send any input to any output requires a connection between the bars where they cross. Modern routers are almost invariably electronic, rather than mechanical, switches. Special routers are also used for switching digital audio and video signals as well as computer network switching.

RPM Revolutions per minute, the standard unit for measuring rotation speed.

RTA *See* REAL-TIME ANALYZER.

Rub and Buzz Distortion A type of distortion found in some dynamic LOUDSPEAKERS caused by the VOICE COIL assembly rubbing against one of the magnetic POLE PIECES. The detection of rub and buzz is one of the quality control test procedures used by loudspeaker manufacturers. It is more likely to occur in high-efficiency speakers, where the distance between the coil and pole pieces is very small to maintain a strong magnetic field in the gap.

Rumble Turntables for the making and playing of phonograph records are designed to operate as smoothly and noiselessly as possible, but no matter how careful the design, the unit will exhibit some NOISE, caused by bearing irregularities, shaft and pulley eccentricities, belt inconsistencies, etc. This noise is mostly low-FREQUENCY, and is called "rumble." The frequency content affects the audibility of rumble, higher frequencies being more annoying than lower ones.

The advent of direct drive turntables did not eliminate rumble, but substituted a different kind, caused by motor vibration and irregularities, or "cogging," of the drive system. Rumble is measured by playing back a silent groove record, supposedly recorded without rumble, and measuring the low-frequency noise output of the phono CARTRIDGE. It is expressed as an RMS value in DECIBELS below a reference level.

S

Sabin The unit of acoustical absorption, equivalent to 1 square foot of a perfect absorber. An open window of 1 square foot would have 1 sabin of absorption. There are no perfect sound absorbers (other than open windows), and sound absorbers are rated in terms of their absorption as a percent of a theoretically perfect absorber. The sound absorption coefficient is actually this ratio. For instance, an absorber with a coefficient of .5 will absorb 50 percent of the sound that reaches it. Two square feet of this material will have a total absorption of 1 sabin. One square meter of absorption is called a metric sabin.

Absorption coefficients are used in the calculation of REVERBERATION times in rooms. The absorption of any material will differ at different frequencies, and acoustical materials are measured at many frequencies to determine their absorption characteristics.

The sabin is named after Wallace Clement Sabine, a Harvard professor of physics in the early 1900s. He is credited as being the first scientific acoustician. He defined reverberation time, developed methods to measure and predict it, and wrote extensively about architectural ACOUSTICS. He designed Symphony Hall in Boston, and this is considered to be the first music hall to be designed using scientific principles. It is regarded today as one of the finest halls in the world for symphonic music.

SACD, Super Audio Compact Disc™ SACD is a joint venture of Sony and Philips for a new format for CD recording. It uses one-BIT encoding of the audio signal at a sampling rate of 64 times 44.1 kHz or 2,822,400 samples per second. This encoding process is called DSD™. The high sampling rate does away with the need for an ANTI-ALIASING FILTER at the input and an ANTI-IMAGING FILTER at the output, eliminating the PHASE DISTORTION that these filters produce.

The SACD specification allows the discs to be encoded with both conventional CD encoding and SACD encoding by using two layers of data—the top layer is for conventional CD encoding and the bottom layer is for SACD encoding. The discs can be played on existing CD players (top layer only) as well as on SACD players. It is also possible to encode up to six-channel audio as well as conventional two-channel stereo on SACDs. *See also* DSD.

Sample and Hold The part of the ANALOG-TO-DIGITAL CONVERTER that actually does the job of SAMPLING the SIGNAL is called a sample and hold CIRCUIT. It measures the instantaneous signal VOLTAGE at a particular time and holds this level constant for the duration of the sampling interval. This level is meanwhile converted into a DIGITAL code of the sample BIT size (for example, 16 or 24 bits) before the sample and hold moves to the next sample. This code is a digital (arithmetic) expression of the signal level at that instant. Sample and hold circuits are subject to certain inaccuracies. The sample and hold function is much simpler in the case of delta-sigma encoding because each sample consists of only one bit. It can be positive, negative, or zero, but its magnitude is fixed and does not have to be translated into a digital word. *See also* APERTURE TIME ERRORS.

Sampler A device used in electronic music synthesis that digitizes and stores a short musical tone or phrase. The sampled signal may be the sound of an instrument played at a particular pitch, and it can then be subjected to various digital signal processing techniques to change its duration, pitch, timbre, etc.

Many of the sounds heard in electronic music productions are actually the sampled waveforms of actual instruments. There has been much legal turmoil in recent years about the use of even very short pieces of copyrighted material that has been sampled and used in otherwise unrelated commercial releases.

Sampling In a DIGITAL audio system, the analog audio SIGNAL must be fed into an ANALOG-TO-DIGITAL CONVERTER to be changed into a series of numbers for further processing by the system. The first step in this is sampling, where the instantaneous signal AMPLITUDE is determined at very short intervals of time. Sampling must be done very accurately to avoid adding DISTORTION to the digitized signal. The sampling rate, which is the number of samples per second, must be uniform and precisely controlled.

The choice of the sampling rate is somewhat complicated. For traditional, linear PCM, the Nyquist critieria states that the sampling rate must be twice the highest frequency of interest. For audio, this is considered 20 kHz, so the sampling rate must be at least 40 kHz.

Since perfect ANTI-ALIASING FILTERS can't be built, a slightly higher sampling frequency is needed as a practical matter.

There are many standard sampling rates in general use. The two most common for linear PCM are the "professional" sampling rate of 48 KILOHERTZ, which is often used for master recordings and digital sound with video. The "consumer" sampling rate is 44.1 kHz, as on the common compact disc.

This frequency was chosen because early recorders used videotape technology, which conveniently accomodated a 44.056 kHz sampling rate. 44.1 kHz was chosen for the compact disc merely because it is a "simpler" FREQUENCY. As a practical matter, recordings are often originated and processed at 44.1 kHz to eliminate having to convert the sample rate if the end product is a CD. *See also* OVERSAMPLING; DELTA-SIGMA MODULATION

As technology progresses, higher sampling rates and sample sizes are being used for better sound quality. Some would view this as odd considering the public's acceptance of reduced fidelity in the form of compressed digital audio from MP3s, DVDs, and motion pictures. To transfer a "professional" digital recording at the 48-kHz standard to CD is possible by purely digital means, and this process is called RESAMPLING. The other alternative is to convert the signal back to ANALOG and then pass it into another ADC operating at the new sampling rate. This is not a good solution, however, because the conversion from digital to analog and back to digital is a source of signal degradation.

Sometimes, the sampling rate will be notated as fs, as in frequency of sampling.

Sampling Rate *See* SAMPLING.

Sampling Rate Converter, SRC A somewhat complex digital device or computer program that accepts sampled inputs at one sampling FREQUENCY and converts them to sampled outputs of a different sampling frequency. It may seem that once a signal is sampled at a particular rate, it would not be possible to resample it at a different rate unless it were first converted back to an analog voltage, but it is theoretically possible to convert from any sampling rate to any other while still in the digital domain. Of course, the initial sampling will determine the maximum BANDWIDTH of the signal, and if the new sampling rate is lower than the original, the signal bandwidth will be reduced. The sampling rate converter is useful because there are several standardized sampling rates in use for various digital audio systems. *See* SAMPLING.

SAN Storage Area Network, a central, large, and high-speed digital data storage system used for audio and video workstations.

Sanders Theater Seat Cushion The first unit of acoustic absorption used by Wallace Sabine in his experiments in auditorium acoustics at Harvard University. He used the seat cushions from the Sanders theater to reduce the reverberation in the Fogg Art Museum and, along with organ pipes as sound generators and his ears as microphones, determined the reverberation time as a function of frequency and the amount of added absorption. Later, he defined the unit of absorption as 1 square foot of complete absorption, and this has become known as the SABIN in his honor.

Sand Filling A technique for increasing the mass and DAMPING of the panels of loudspeaker cabinets by forming the sidewalls from two panels separated by about an inch or so and filling the interior space with dry sand. It greatly reduces the amount of energy the sides of the cabinet radiate, reducing the COLORATION of the output sound. The technique was first used by Gilbert Briggs of Wharfdale Wireless Works in England. In recent times, other methods have been developed to add damping to the cabinet sidewalls.

SAP Acronym for Second Audio Program in the NTSC analog TV standard. SAP is a monophonic audio signal broadcast by a television station in addition to the standard television sound. One use is to broadcast the same program in a second language.

The SAP signal is FREQUENCY MODULATED onto a 78.67-kilohertz SUBCARRIER that is then added to the TV sound signal before the subcarrier modulates the 4.5-megahertz sound carrier. To receive the SAP, the TV receiver must be equipped with a device to select and demodulate the subcarrier. SAP is part of MTS, added to NTSC television in 1984.

Satellite Radio Systems that transmit radio-like channels of digital audio programming via satellites to receivers in automobiles or homes. In 1992, the FCC (Federal Communications Commission) allocated a spectrum in the 2.3-GHz band for nationwide broadcasting of satellite-based digital audio; CD Radio (now Sirius Satellite Radio) and American Mobile Radio (now XM Satellite Radio) are the two systems in operation in the U.S. Programs are beamed to three Sirius satellites and two XM satellites, which then transmit the signals to the ground, where your radio receiver tunes in to one of the channels within the signal. Signals are also beamed to ground repeaters for listeners in urban areas where the satellite signal cannot be received directly.

A third system called Worldspace is broadcasting now in Africa and Asia, and is planning to begin broadcasting in South America. All three systems require a subscription fee. *See also* DAB.

Saturation In MAGNETIC TAPE recording, saturation is the maximum magnetization that a tape can attain. In analog audio recording, actual recorded levels are less than saturation because DISTORTION is introduced if saturation is approached, especially at low frequencies. At high frequencies, it is not possible to reach tape saturation because the SIGNAL itself acts to partially erase itself as it is being recorded. This is called SELF-ERASURE, and limits the maximum level attainable in a tape recorder at high frequencies.

Some FM recording methods record to saturation in normal operation, and may be referred to as saturation recording.

The core of a transformer can also be saturated with magnetic flux by excessive signal level, and the result is severe distortion. For this reason, the maximum signal level that an audio transformer is capable of handling is part of its specification.

Saturation also applies to active audio devices such as TRANSISTORS or TUBES. A transistor is saturated if it is carrying as much CURRENT as possible with the given power supply VOLTAGE. In other words, an increase in current at the BASE will not result in any output current increase.

SAW Filter A type of high-frequency BANDPASS FILTER that uses surface acoustic waves on a small PIEZOELECTRIC crystal. SAW filters are very precise and can be designed for very flat bandpass and very steep SKIRTS. They are excellent for use as IF filters in FM receivers.

SCA Acronym for Subsidiary Carrier Authorization. In FM radio transmission, in addition to the 38-kilohertz SUBCARRIER used for stereophonic signals, an SCA subcarrier at 67 kHz can also be included and used for such things as foreign languages or background music. In 1955 the FCC authorized SCA channels working with mono FM, and FM STEREO with SCA was approved in 1961. *See also* MUSICASTING.

SCA Adapter A type of MULTIPLEX ADAPTER for use in decoding SCA broadcasts, such as MUSICASTING.

Schematic The wiring diagram of an electronic component or system is called a schematic. It has nothing to do with the physical location of the parts in the CIRCUIT, but is concerned only with their function. A drawing showing the physical parts layout of a circuit is called a "pictorial" diagram.

SCMS Acronym for Serial Copy Management System, often pronounced "scums." SCMS is a special circuit built into consumer digital recorders such as R-DAT, MINIDISC, and CD-R machines that are to be sold in the United States. The SCMS prevents unauthorized digital-to-digital replication of COMPACT DISCS. The RIAA, the IFPI, the EIA, and several manufacturers agreed to use the system in 1989.

The introduction of the R-DAT into the United States was delayed several years because of a dispute between the makers of the machines and the record industry regarding a circuit to inhibit multiple-generation copying of CDs, ostensibly to prevent copyright infringement. Several schemes were proposed by the record industry, but they were found to impair the quality of the resulting first-generation copies.

The SCMS allows a CD to be directly copied digitally onto the recorder, without using digital-to-analog conversion, filtering, copying, or analog-to-digital conversion.

The system deactivates the digital anti-copy FLAG in the CD, allowing it to be copied once. Another flag is inserted in the copy that prevents it from being copied; that is, second-generation copies cannot be made. The SCMS also prevents third-generation digital copying of R-DAT recordings originally made from the recorder's analog inputs.

The SCMS system is an outgrowth of the SOLO copy protection scheme, which was devised by Philips but never put into practice. SCMS is rendered impotent by computer drive audio extraction, also called "ripping," which ignores anti-copy bits. In addition, equipment designed for professional use does not have SCMS.

Scoring Stage A large recording studio equipped with interlocked film and video playback, in addition to audio recording equipment. Motion pictures and video production scores are recorded while the conductor watches the image and conducts the performers so the finished recording is synchronized properly with the video or film footage.

Scrape Flutter In an analog tape recorder, the tape must pass over several heads and tape guides on its way from the supply reel to the CAPSTAN, and it will sometimes vibrate something like a violin string due to friction from the heads and/or guides. This vibration is actually a high-frequency FLUTTER, and results in a FREQUENCY modulation of the recorded or reproduced SIGNAL. The frequency is too high to be heard as a PITCH variation, but is instead perceived as added noise to the signal. To combat this phenomenon, some of the better tape recorders place a small precision roller between the heads. This roller acts as a mechanical FILTER to reduce the vibration of the tape. The roller is called a "scrape flutter roller."

Scratch Filter A type of EQUALIZER that consists of a fairly sharp cutoff at high frequencies to reduce the effect of record surface noise; usually called a high-cut FILTER today. The name *scratch filter* was more appropriate in the days of SHELLAC 78-RPM records than it is today because of the much lower surface noise on vinyl compared to shellac.

Screen Grid In the TETRODE tube, a second grid is placed between the control grid and the PLATE. It is maintained at a high positive potential, and it increases the GAIN of the tube.

Scribe When the MASTERING engineer finishes cutting an ACETATE master record, he will scratch some identification letters on the uncut surface near the label area with a sharp stylus. This is called scribing, and it is used by the processing personnel to identify the record. The scribed code can also be seen on the finished record.

Scrub To scrub is to listen to a part of a recorded audio signal at a variable speed forward or backward under manual control to find the exact location in the music where an edit is to be made. In analog editing, the tape itself is "scrubbed" back and forth across the playback head, and in digital editing, a DAW is used.

Scrubbing Motion Relative back-and-forth motion along the record groove of the playback STYLUS as it plays an analog record. It is caused by a combination of the warp of the record raising and lowering the cartridge and the vertical pivot of the arm being located above the plane of the surface of the record. It causes a frequency variation of the music at the rate of the warp, which is called WARP WOW.

SCSI, Small Computer Systems Interface A family of parallel computer data interconnection formats. Many DAWS and computer audio users, especially Macintosh users, used SCSI hard drives for mass storage for many years because of its high performance. SCSI has since been eclipsed by other, cheaper systems such as FIREWIRE.

S-DAT Acronym for Stationary-head DIGITAL Audio Tape. *See* DAT; DASH; PRODIGI.

SDDS Sony Dynamic Digital Sound is a motion picture digital sound system capable of eight discrete digital channels. The sound track is on both edges of the film and is read optically by a device using a CCD (CHARGE COUPLED DEVICE) such as used in the late 1970s in the ill-fated COLORTEK 4-track optical film sound system. The soundtrack consists of an array of microscopic dots (or pixels) much like those recorded on a CD. Both edges are used to provide two continuous streams of data interleaved using a cross-redundant ERROR CORRECTION technique to further prevent dropouts from film damage or scratches. The ATRAC technique is used to reduce the bit rate of the digital data by as much as five to one. As the film runs, red LEDS are used to illuminate the SDDS soundtrack. CCDs read the SDDS data and convert the stream of dots on the film into digital information. This information is preprocessed in the reader and passed on to the SDDS decoder.

SDIF-2 Short for Sony Digital Interface-2. This is an interface format developed by Sony for digitally transferring audio signals between different Sony professional audio products. Each audio channel is transmitted over its own cable.

SDMI Secure Digital Music Initiative. A working group formed by the RIAA to develop a voluntary method for protecting copyrights of music distributed on the Internet. The SDMI's mandate is to legitimize music distribution and prevent copyright infractions. It is backed by the major labels. The similar group in England is called the Creative Industries Taskforce (CIT). *See also* DRM.

SDTV, Standard Definition Television Several formats for digital broadcast television have been put forth by ATSC, the Advanced Television Systems Committee. SDTV standards include 480 lines interlaced scan and 480 lines progressive scan, as compared to 1080 lines for high definition.

SECAM Système En Coleurs à Mémoir. The French standard for color television transmission. Sometimes it is referred to as "System Essentially Contrary to American Methods," which it is. The SECAM system is used in Hungary, Algeria, and the former USSR, besides France. It uses 625 lines in the picture and a frame rate of 25 per second.

Secondary In a transformer, the winding that supplies the output SIGNAL or CURRENT is called the secondary, whereas the input signal or current enters the PRIMARY winding. There is sometimes no fundamental difference in the two windings; either one can be used as a primary or secondary.

Secondary Emission In a TETRODE vacuum TUBE, the high-speed electrons striking the PLATE dislodge other electrons, which interfere with the action of the SCREEN GRID. This is called secondary emission, and its effect is reduced or eliminated by placing a third grid between the screen and plate.

This grid is at cathode potential and is called a suppressor grid. It is the defining element of the PENTODE tube.

Section *See* L-SECTION; PI-SECTION; T-SECTION.

Segue A quick, smooth switch from one musical selection to another without a gap; the absence of a CROSS-FADE. English speakers usually pronounce it, "seg-way."

SEL Acronym for Sound Exposure Level. The SEL of a noise event is the A-WEIGHTED SOUND PRESSURE LEVEL lasting 1 second that would have the same acoustic energy as the event itself. SEL is a way of comparing the noisiness of events that have different durations, such as airplane flyover noise or motorcycle passby noise.

Selectivity The ability of a radio receiver to tune to or "select" one station to the exclusion of others. A receiver with poor selectivity will pick up a very strong station even when tuned to another station. This is often noticed in car radios when driving near transmitting stations.

Self-Erasure The tendency of a high-frequency SIGNAL to erase itself while it is being recorded on an analog tape recorder. Self-erasure usually limits the maximum signal level that can be recorded on tape at high frequencies, and SATURATION of the tape cannot be achieved. The signal itself causes the record head to act like a tape DEGAUSSER, partially wiping out the recorded signal. *See* HX; HX PRO.

Self-Noise *See* NOISE FLOOR.

Self-Powered Speaker A loudspeaker system is called self-powered when it has its own POWER AMPLIFIERS inside the cabinet. This usually also implies that special circuitry for power limiting, crossover, and EQUALIZATION are included. The advantage is that the entire system of speakers, amplifiers, and processors can be optimized, and no power is lost in long speaker wires or passive crossovers. A line-level audio cable and AC power cable are simply attached to the speaker system.

Sel-Sync When the tracks of an analog multiple-track tape recording are recorded one after the other so as to build up a musical composite from several parts, one must listen to the previously recorded tracks while the next one is being recorded. If the standard tape playback HEAD is used for this, there will be a time delay between the tracks when played back because of the physical distance between the recording and playback heads in the machine. To solve the problem, the record head gaps of the previously recorded tracks are used as playback heads while the adjacent tracks are being recorded. Since all the record head tracks are in line, there will be no delay. This technique was developed by Ampex in the 1950s, and was first used commercially by Les Paul. Sel-Sync does not apply to digital recorders because new tracks are synchronized to played-back tracks digitally.

The term is short for "selective synchronization," and was invented at Ampex by Ross Snyder. The idea was trademarked, but not patented, and others have used the idea in their own recorders, using such names as "simul-synch."

Semicapacitor An electrical circuit whose IMPEDANCE is inversely proportional to the square root of FREQUENCY rather than inversely proportional to frequency itself has been called a semicapacitor. The PHASE of the current in a semicapacitor leads the VOLTAGE across it by 45 degrees, rather than the 90 degrees in a true capacitor. The proposed unit of semicapacitance is the semifarad. If a semicapacitor is connected in parallel with a SEMI-INDUCTOR, the impedance will have a broad peak rather than the sharp peak that results in an LC CIRCUIT. This broad peak can be called a semiresonance.

A resistive transmission line that has distributed shunt capacitance along its length exhibits semicapacitive behavior.

Semiconductor A semiconductor is technically any material whose electrical conductivity is somewhere between that of a conductor and an insulator. Semiconductors used for making SOLID-STATE electronic devices are the elements silicon and germanium. They are not semiconductors in their pure form but must be subjected to a complex procedure in which certain impurities are diffused into the pure crystals. This is called doping and increases the conductivity of the elements. Doping can add an excess of either positively charged ions or negatively charged ions to the pure material. These two types of doped elements are called P-type and N-type semiconductors. DIODES are made by combining P-type and N-type materials to form P-N junctions. TRANSISTORS are made in many forms by combining junctions in more complex ways, some of the simplest of which are PNP and NPN.

Although strictly speaking the materials involved are the semiconductors, some devices themselves, such as transistors and integrated circuits, are often collectively called semiconductors.

Semifarad *See* SEMICAPACITOR.

Semihenry *See* SEMI-INDUCTOR.

Semi-inductor A device in which the electrical IMPEDANCE is proportional to the square root of FREQUENCY rather than directly proportional to frequency. In a semi-inductor, the PHASE of the current lags the voltage by 45 degrees; whereas in a true inductor, the phase lag is 90 degrees. A semi-inductor is said to possess semi-inductance, and its units are semihenrys.

The concept of semi-inductance was developed by John Vanderkooy of the University of Waterloo, in Canada. It is useful in the analysis of the behavior of dynamic LOUDSPEAKERS. The current in the VOICE COIL induces EDDY CURRENTS in the iron magnetic structure around the coil, and these eddy currents modify the electrical impedance of the coil so it is dominated by a component proportional to the square root of frequency. The effect occurs much more strongly at high frequencies than at low frequencies, where the coil impedance becomes simply inductive.

The semi-inductive behavior of the coil is beneficial to the operation of the loudspeaker, for it reduces the rise in impedance at high frequencies, improving the high-frequency response.

Some manufacturers have inserted a copper or silver ring around the central magnetic POLE PIECE to increase these eddy currents and further reduce the high-frequency impedance. This works because copper and silver are much better electrical conductors than the iron of the pole piece. However, the conductive ring displaces some iron, and the magnetic field the VOICE COIL sees is reduced, so the overall sensitivity of the speaker is reduced somewhat.

Semiresonance *See* SEMICAPACITOR.

Semitone The musical interval one note in the chromatic scale. The interval from C to C sharp is a semitone, as is the interval between C sharp and D, etc. In the equal temperament system of tuning, all semitones are exactly the same interval, with a frequency ratio of the twelfth root of two, or slightly less than six percent in frequency. Equal temperament is almost universally used in the tuning of pianos world wide, but some instruments, such as harpsichords and organs, may be tuned to one of several systems of unequal temperament. These tuning schemes have interesting effects on the music being played. For instance, a selection played in the key of C will sound different than if it is played in the keys of D or G sharp. There is much discussion and sometimes even gnashing of teeth and wringing of hands among certain musicians over the desirability of using these temperaments, but that is another story. *See also* Appendix 8.

Send An output on a recording or sound reinforcement console for a signal to be sent to another device, such as a REVERBERATOR or EQUALIZER. The signal is returned to the console via the "return" connector. Typical consoles will have several sends and returns.

Sensitivity The minimum required SIGNAL at the input of an AUDIO device in order to produce the rated output is generally called the sensitivity of the device. The higher the sensitivity, the lower the signal required at the input.

The sensitivity is usually specified for a particular output. For instance, the sensitivity of a POWER AMPLIFIER is that input VOLTAGE that will result in the rated output power. In an FM tuner, the sensitivity is the input signal level which will result in a specified SIGNAL-TO-NOISE RATIO of the output signal.

Sometimes sensitivity is used in a relative way. A MICROPHONE may be said to be very sensitive, or a phono CARTRIDGE might have low sensitivity, without reference to numbers.

Sensurround A now obsolete motion picture sound system that used very strong, very low frequencies to simulate the effects of explosions, earthquakes, etc. Sensurround was developed by the sound engineers W. O. Watson and Richard Stumpf of Universal Studios in 1974 for the movie *Earthquake*. Sensurround essentially created SUBSONIC, low-frequency vibrations between 5 and 40 HERTZ at sound pressures of 110–120 DECIBELS, causing the audience to feel low vibrations during the main earthquake and dam collapse. The process was used for two subsequent films, *Rollercoaster* and *Midway*. The first film simply triggered a noise generator during the earthquake sequences, although later versions of Sensurround did record very low-frequency information on the film. The actual setup consisted of six speakers; four large speakers behind the screen, and two on a platform in the back of the theatre. To give you an idea for the size of the speaker cabinets, two featured Cerwin-Vega "Model W" horns 8 ft. long, 4 ft. wide, and 4 ft. high. The other two had Cerwin-Vega "Model C" horns 1 ft. wide and 5 ft. high. Each speaker was driven by a 1000-watt amplifier, which was controlled by a special optical control track in the film.

Sequencer A module in analog electronic music synthesizers that generate a repeating sequence of predetermined CONTROL VOLTAGES. These voltages can be used to control pitch, loudness, and timbre, etc., of the synthesized signals. The more common usage today refers to the MIDI sequencer.

Series An interconnection of CIRCUIT elements one after another in such a fashion that the CURRENT in all of them is the same; the VOLTAGE across each may be different, however. This is unlike PARALLEL connection, where the voltage across each element is the same, but the currents may be different. An example of series connection is the old-fashioned Christmas tree lights that all went out if one burned out. In some cases, LOUDSPEAKERS may be connected in series and then to a single power amplifier to ensure that the AMPLIFIER is driving an adequately high LOAD IMPEDANCE. However, as with the Christmas tree lights, if one fails, the others also stop working.

Servo Short for servomechanism, which is a control system that uses FEEDBACK of an output SIGNAL to compare to a reference signal. The difference between the two is an error signal, which is used to change the output signal in such a way as to reduce the error. In a servo system, if the reference is changed, the output will rapidly change to a new value, and so it is controlled by the reference.

Servo systems are of many different types and are quite common. One example of a mechanical servo is the power steering apparatus in a car. The steering wheel position is the reference and the mechanism moves the wheels so as to reduce the difference between this reference and the actual position of the wheels to zero.

The first servomechanism is generally thought to be the centrifugal flyball speed governor that James Watt built into his steam engine. The speed of the engine causes the flyballs to rise, which in turn reduces the steam input with a valve connected to the ball assembly. If the LOAD on the engine increases, the speed decreases a little, causing the valve to open more and speed up the engine. Thus, the speed will remain almost the same over varying loads.

This, however, was not the first servo, for organ builders had been using servos to control the wind pressure in an organ for centuries before Watt. The pressure in the windchest causes a bellows assembly to rise and close a valve from the air source. More demand for air, as when playing with more stops on, causes the bellows to fall a little, opening the valve more, restoring the pressure.

What has all this to do with audio, you ask? Servos are used to control speeds in tape recorders and record turntables, and are used to position the laser beam in COMPACT DISC players. Some speed servos use a vibrating quartz crystal as a reference, and they are often advertised as being "quartz controlled" or some other catch phrase. The quartz OSCILLATOR is very stable over long periods, and makes a good reference for speed control under varying loads.

The tape tension in some tape recorders is servo-controlled also, usually by means of a mechanical linkage that uses a spring tension as a reference. These servos prevent the tape recorder from running at different speeds with different amounts of tape on the reels.

Negative feedback in an AMPLIFIER is an example of an electronic servo.

ServoDrive™ A registered trademark for a novel SUBWOOFER system originally sold by Intersonics, and now by Sound Physics Labs and ServoDrive, Inc., which uses small rotary DC electric motors to drive the loudspeaker cones rather than VOICE COIL and magnet assemblies. The rotary motion of the motor is coupled to two CONES by a system of small belts in such a way that the cones move in opposite directions, canceling any reciprocating force on the motor shaft. The two cones are disposed on opposite sides of a closed cabinet so they radiate low-frequency sound in phase with each other. The motor is specially designed to have very little inertia and very high torque. The motor is driven directly by the AMPLIFIER output, and its alternating clockwise and counterclockwise motion follows the audio waveform; the belts resolve this motion into back and forth motion of the cones.

The advantage claimed for this system is an increase in linearity for very large cone excursions, allowing very high sound level output with low distortion. The frequency response extends uniformly from 25 to 100 hertz.

The name ServoDrive suggests that a servomechanism is used, which implies MOTIONAL FEEDBACK in the system. This is in fact not the case, for the designers believe the system is sufficiently linear that it does not need the FEEDBACK to reduce DISTORTION. In any case, this is an unfortunate and somewhat misleading choice of words (but not unprecedented in the audio business!).

SFX Shorthand for sound effects.

Sharp Higher in PITCH, as opposed to FLAT, which means lower in pitch. In reference to musical scales, sharp indicates one-half step higher; for example, F sharp is one-half step higher than F.

In HIGH-PASS, LOW-PASS, and BANDPASS FILTERS, sharp refers to the rapidity with which the response of the filter falls off in the filter STOPBAND. Very sharp filters have a very steep slope of decline in response. In general, the sharper the filter, the greater will be its PHASE SHIFT. The sharpness of a filter is commonly described in DECIBELS per OCTAVE. Six dB per octave of slope is a gentle filter, while 24 dB per octave is a sharp cutoff, and 96 dB per octave is a very sharp cutoff. Filter slopes usually work out to be multiples of 6 dB per octave because one filter SECTION provides this slope, and complex filters are made by cascading several sections, each adding ATTENUATION at 6 dB per octave.

Shellac An organic material excreted by certain tropical insects, shellac is used as the active ingredient in some varnishes and in "shellac." Shellac was the material used for making 78-RPM records. It is breakable and varies widely in quality. Pure shellac is quite smooth and fairly noise free when pressed into a record, but pure shellac is difficult to obtain. Most of the material used to make records contained significant impurities, including twigs, insect fragments, sand, etc. The introduction of vinyl chloride, which is the material currently used for records, was a great improvement, especially in uniformity.

It is interesting that Thomas Edison did much experimentation to find a suitable material for making records. For his Diamond Discs, he invented a plastic made from formaldehyde, which he called "densite." It was almost identical to Bakelite, a plastic invented by Dr. Leo Baekeland in 1907 and commercialized in 1909.

Shelving Sometimes an EQUALIZER is required wherein the response is flat above and below a certain transition FREQUENCY range and needs a gradual slope within the transition range. Such an equalizer is called a shelving equalizer or shelving control because of the resemblance of the response CURVE to a shelf. An example is a low-frequency reduction control for use when a person is speaking very close to a microphone. Such an equalizer might have a 20-DECIBEL "shelf," and a 6 dB per OCTAVE roll off below 200 HERTZ. *See also* PROXIMITY EFFECT.

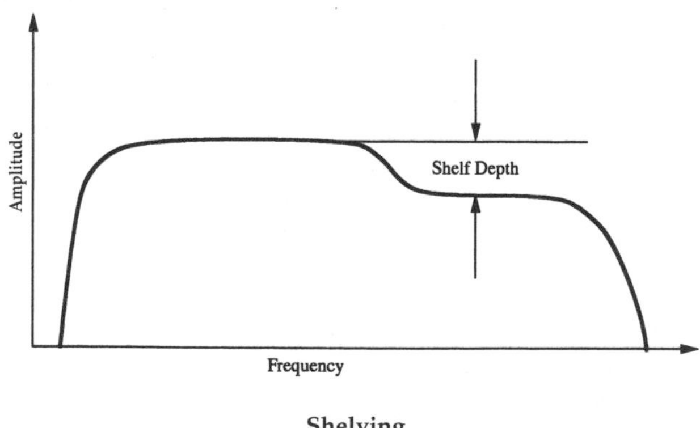

Shelving

Shibata An LP phono CARTRIDGE STYLUS that has a shape designed to reduce PINCH EFFECT and TRACING DISTORTION. Its edges that make contact with the record groove walls are sharply curved in the horizontal axis but are nearly straight lines in the vertical axis. This makes the area of contact almost a line along the groove wall, which reduces the wear on the groove as well as the stylus.

The shape was developed by the Japanese designer Shibata. It can be said to be a logical extension of the elliptical stylus shape.

Shield, Shielding A shield is an enclosure that protects its contents against the influence of magnetic fields or electrostatic fields or both. Some audio CIRCUIT elements, such as TRANSFORMERS and tape recorder heads, are sensitive to magnetic fields. A varying magnetic field induces CURRENTS in wires, and especially in coils of wires, at the FREQUENCY at which it is varying. The most common magnetic fields found in households are caused by the 60-HERTZ power line, and they are responsible for most of the 60-Hz HUM heard in audio systems. Some components, most notably power TRANSFORMERS, generate 60-Hz hum fields, and if a shield of soft iron, or other metal of high magnetic permeability, is placed around them, the fields are greatly reduced. This is one common type of magnetic shielding. The other type of shielding is placed around the sensitive circuit element. Thick shields are placed around tape heads to reduce induced hum.

Audio circuit elements are also sensitive to electric fields. The 60-Hz power lines also produce strong electric fields. Any electric conductor may be used as an electrostatic shield, and copper is generally used. One place where electrostatic shields are used is in signal cables between audio devices, such as MICROPHONE and phono CARTRIDGE cables and cables between PREAMPS and POWER AMPLIFIERS. These shields are usually of braided copper wire, and do not reduce magnetically induced HUM. To reduce magnetic induction, the shields would have to be of iron, and it is difficult to make such shields flexible. Other techniques such as twisting the signal wires together and using DIFFERENTIAL input amplifiers are used to reduce magnetic interference.

In general, all the CHASSIS and shields in any given audio system are connected together and sometimes are grounded to earth through a water pipe or other suitable connection. The actual connection to earth is not as effective an interference reducer as is generally supposed. More important is the integrity of the shield between devices and in cables. Sometimes connection to earth will cause a GROUND LOOP, which can increase induced noise rather then reduce it. *See also* BALANCED LINE.

Shift Register A type of INTEGRATED CIRCUIT time delay device in which a small quantity of electric charge is transferred, or shifted, along a series of small capacitors in response to a timing signal. The charges usually represent digital binary BITS rather than analog signal levels. *See also* BUCKET BRIGADE.

Shock Mount A flexible mounting arrangement for placing a microphone on a stand such that tapping or kicking the stand will not transmit mechanical shocks to the microphone, which would cause noise in the output. Shock mounts are made of rubber or some similar material or sometimes springs.

Some microphones are much more sensitive to shocks than others. OMNIDIRECTIONAL ones generally are much less sensitive than CARDIOIDS and VELOCITY MICROPHONES.

Vibration isolators used to reduce ACOUSTIC FEEDBACK in record-playing turntables are also sometimes called shock mounts.

Shock Switch A special switch found on some COMPACT DISC players that makes the unit less susceptible to losing the track in the disc due to mechanical shocks.

It is possible, with the formidable low-frequency performance of the compact disc system and some WOOFERS, that the vibration of the player caused by the reproduced sound itself can cause the laser to "lose its place" while tracking the series of pits on the disc. The shock switch tightens up the laser SERVO, making it "stiffer." It will then be less apt to lose track, but then if a sufficiently strong shock does occur, it will take a longer time to re-establish tracking.

This phenomenon is largely taken care of now by larger data buffers, such that some portable CD players can hold nearly a minute of sound during MISTRACKING.

Short Abbreviation for "short circuit," which is a direct connection between two points in an electric or electronic CIRCUIT. Shorts are usually undesirable and inadvertent, but sometimes a purposeful connection is called a short. A defective component, such as a TRANSISTOR or CAPACITOR, etc., is said to be shorted if its terminals are directly connected internally. Shorting is a common failure mode for many components.

Short Line An audio line, such as a telephone line, whose electrical length is shorter than the shortest audio wavelength to be transmitted. *See also* LONG LINE.

Shotgun Microphone *See* LINE MICROPHONE.

Shot Noise A type of random noise generated in nonmetallic media such as active devices like transistors or vacuum tubes. It is proportional to the current in the device and its load resistance. Shot noise arises because current in the device is made up of discrete charges and is thus somewhat "grainy" and not continuous and smooth. The total noise in the output of an active device is the sum of the shot noise of the device and the thermal noise, or JOHNSON NOISE, at its input. It is useless to reduce the input thermal noise if the shot noise overwhelms it. It turns out that different devices have different optimum input impedances: for vacuum tubes, about 1 megohm, and for most bipolar transistors, about 500 or 1,000 ohms.

Shuffler Circuit A type of MATRIXING circuit that includes EQUALIZATION of the sum and difference components. It allows the apparent width of a STEREO image to be varied as a function of FREQUENCY. It works on almost any stereo signal. Its invention is credited to the multitalented British engineer Alan BLUMLEIN in the 1930s, and was recently revived by Richard Kaufman and David Griesinger in the United States. *See also* M-S STEREO; BLUMLEIN, ALAN.

Shuttle To wind the tape on a tape recorder back and forth in order to locate a specific selection.

SI Système Internationale, or the INTERNATIONAL SYSTEM OF UNITS.

In the field of architectural ACOUSTICS, SI is also used, by Barron and Ando, among others, to indicate spatial impression, which is similar to ENVELOPMENT. SI is correlated with IACC.

Sibilance Vocal recordings, especially if made with very close MICROPHONES, are often characterized by excessive LOUDNESS of the voice sibilants, and this effect is sometimes called "sibilance." The most difficult sibilants to reproduce accurately are the sounds "s" and "sh." The effect is accentuated by high-frequency peaks in microphones and in many LOUDSPEAKERS; it is reduced by the use of a DE-ESSER.

Sibilant *See* SIBILANCE.

SID Short for Slew Induced Distortion. *See* TRANSIENT INTERMODULATION DISTORTION.

Sidebands When a SIGNAL of frequency F AMPLITUDE modulates a CARRIER of FREQUENCY C, the resultant WAVEFORM consists of the carrier and other frequency components at C minus F and C plus F. These added frequency components are called sidebands because in a graph of the spectrum they appear on the left and right sides of the carrier frequency.

The sum of the two sidebands and the carrier looks like a single frequency that is changing in AMPLITUDE at the modulation rate; however, it is actually the simple addition of the sidebands and carrier, with the carrier unchanged in any way. This means in an AM broadcast station, all the broadcast information is contained in the sidebands and none in the carrier. To maximize efficiency, the carrier can be suppressed and not transmitted at all, although it is much easier to recover the modulating signal in the receiver if the carrier is present.

The upper and lower sidebands of standard AM transmission contain the same signal information, but it is possible to modulate a carrier so that the upper and lower sidebands carry the left and right STEREO channels. This is the principle of one type of AM stereo broadcasting.

In the case of frequency modulation (FM), the situation is somewhat different. The FM sidebands extend farther from the carrier frequency and differ in PHASE from AM sidebands. In commercial FM transmission, only sidebands extending plus and minus 75 KILOHERTZ from the carrier are transmitted in order to prevent the transmissions from overlapping and interfering with each other. Thus more transmitters can operate within a given frequency band.

Side Tone *See* HYBRID TRANSFORMER.

Siemens The SI unit of CONDUCTANCE.

Sigma-Delta Modulation *See* DELTA-SIGMA MODULATION.

Signal A signal is an electrical phenomenon, usually a VOLTAGE but sometimes a CURRENT, that contains desired information, as opposed to noise, which is undesired. Audio signals are generally electrical ANALOGS of the corresponding sound WAVEFORMS. The SIGNAL-TO-NOISE RATIO (S/N) is the ratio in DECIBELS of the signal power to the noise power at a point in a CIRCUIT.

Signal Processing Signal processing is the modification of an AUDIO signal in a generally desirable way by any device inserted in the audio path. Examples of signal processing devices are REVERBERATORS, noise reduction units such as DOLBY, dbx, etc., and EQUALIZERS.

Signal-to-Noise Ratio Signal-to-noise ratio is the ratio of the signal power at a certain reference point in a CIRCUIT to the noise power that would exist there if the signal were removed. This ratio is expressed in DECIBELS. For instance, if an analog tape recorder has a signal-to-noise (S/N) ratio of 50 dB, the signal power at the output is 50 dB above the noise power.

Measurement of S/N ratio is complicated by several factors. In an analog tape recorder, for example, a signal is recorded at a high level, approaching the onset of audible DISTORTION, and its VOLTAGE is measured with a voltmeter. Usually the signal is a SINE WAVE. Then the signal is removed from the input, and the remaining noise consisting of tape noise, HUM, electronic noise, etc., is measured with the voltmeter. Because the noise will be mostly random in nature, the voltmeter should be a true RMS meter. The ratio of these two measurements expressed in dB is the signal-to-noise ratio. This measurement ignores any type of noise that is present only when the signal is present, such as MODULATION NOISE.

The subjective audibility of the measured noise will not be well correlated to the rms measurement of it because of our ears' varying SENSITIVITY to different frequencies. Therefore, a FILTER or WEIGHTING NETWORK is usually placed in the meter's input. The characteristics of this weighting network are not universally agreed upon, so when comparing noise specifications, as between European and American equipment, care must be taken to see that the measurements were similarly made.

In DIGITAL audio systems, the signal-to-noise ratio is defined as the ratio of the maximum possible sine wave signal power to the QUANTIZATION noise power, also expressed in dB. This is an unambiguous measure in LINEAR PCM systems; but in all other PCM schemes, the quantization noise depends strongly on the level of the signal being encoded. *See* PCM for a discussion of nonlinear PCM systems. *See also* DYNAMIC RANGE.

Silicon One of the more abundant chemical elements, with atomic number 14. Pure silicon (Si) is an insulator, but when it is "doped," or infused with small quantities of various impurities, it becomes a SEMICONDUCTOR and is the basic material from which almost all SOLID-STATE electronic devices are built.

Silicone Any one of a group of chemical compounds that contain silicon and oxygen, not to be confused with SILICON. Silicones are extremely varied in their properties; some are solids and some liquids. Most of the VISCOUS DAMPING fluids are silicones.

Simulcast The broadcasting of one program over more than one radio or television station at the same time. An example is broadcasting a live concert with MONAURAL sound on television and at the same time broadcasting the same concert in stereo from an FM station. The listener can thus watch the video on a television set with the volume turned down while listening to the program in FM stereo. Simulcasting has been rendered obsolete by the advent of television broadcasting with stereophonic sound.

Sine Wave The sine wave, or sinusoid, is the simplest possible periodic WAVEFORM. It consists of a single FREQUENCY and has a musical PITCH but a neutral TIMBRE or tone quality. It is called a sine wave because it has the same shape as the mathematical sine function, familiar to most of us from trigonometry.

Sine waves are commonly used as test signals for audio equipment because they consist of only one frequency. If a sine wave is passed through a device, it will always have some DISTORTION added to it, and this is detected by looking for other frequencies, such as HARMONICS of the original sine wave frequency. *See also* Appendix 5.

Single-Ended Single-ended can refer to an AMPLIFIER output CIRCUIT using a single vacuum TUBE or TRANSISTOR, as opposed to a PUSH-PULL circuit, which uses two active components operating in opposition to each other.

Single-ended more commonly means a circuit interconnection that is not BALANCED. Short lines interconnecting audio components are usually single-ended rather than balanced for simplicity, but low-level lines such as microphone cables are almost always balanced for reduced noise. Telephone lines are also balanced for the same reason.

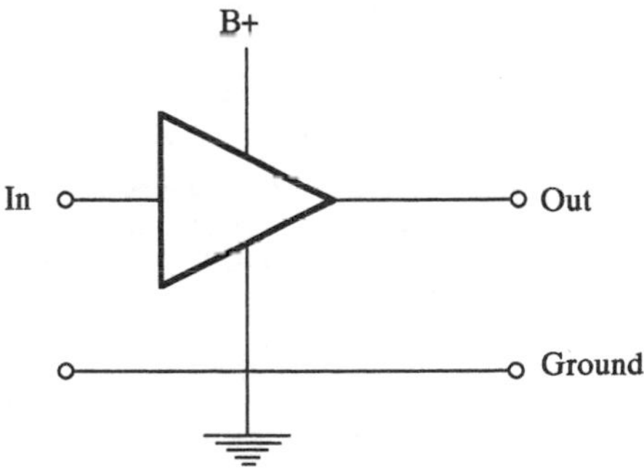

Single-Ended Amplifier

Single-System Sound A way of producing sound motion pictures where the sound is recorded directly onto the film in the camera at the time of shooting. This is the least expensive way to make sound movies, but is

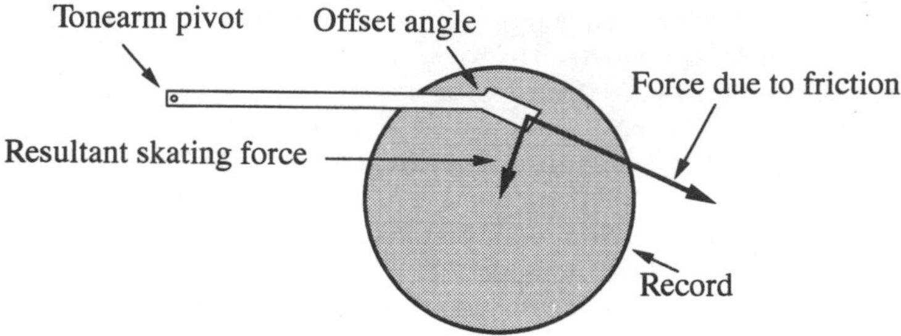

The offset angle of the cartridge headshell prevents the friction force from passing directly through the pivot point. This causes a resultant force toward the record center.

Skating Force

also much less flexible and of much poorer quality than DOUBLE-SYSTEM SOUND.

Sinusoid *See* SINE WAVE.

Sirius Satellite Radio *See* SATELLITE RADIO.

Skating Force The force on the STYLUS of a record player that causes the tonearm to move toward the center of the record. The skating force is caused by friction between the record and the stylus and is a result of the fact that the end of the arm is offset at an angle to the arm itself. Therefore, placing the stylus on a smooth surface to adjust anti-skating force is not quite right. The Johnny Winter LP *Second Winter* is somewhat famous for having a blank side 4, often used for this purpose. *See also* ANTI-SKATING DEVICE; OFFSET ANGLE.

Skew Skew is the motion of recording tape past a record or reproduce HEAD at an angle different from 90 degrees. Tape skew can be caused by loose or poorly adjusted tape guides, or it can be caused by the tape itself having been improperly slit during its manufacture. It causes high-frequency loss. *See also* AZIMUTH.

Skin Effect The tendency of high-frequency current to travel near the outside of an electric conductor rather than all through its cross section. Skin effect increases the effective RESISTANCE of a wire at high frequencies. It is not noticeable at audio frequencies but becomes troublesome at RADIO FREQUENCIES. There are certain people who believe the skin effect is actually audible at audio frequencies, but this has not been proven to be true.

Skirt The slope of a FILTER response CURVE outside its PASSBAND is sometimes called a skirt, especially in the case of a BANDPASS filter.

Slap Echo The single repetition of a signal at a fixed time delay to simulate an echo from a single reflecting surface, as opposed to a multiple echo from a time delay, where the delayed signal is repeatedly fed back into the delay input. Under certain acoustical conditions, a room can exhibit a similar sounding phenomenon when two walls are parallel and spaced apart by about ten to thirty or so feet apart. This is called a "flutter echo."

Slate To identify the various TAKES in a recording session by announcing the take numbers and recording them on one track of the tape. Slating and the notes taken at the time of recording are important once tape editing begins; it would be almost impossible to find any particular take otherwise.

Sometimes a low-FREQUENCY, high-level tone is recorded on ANALOG tapes before each take to aid in finding the beginning of the take when spooling the tape past the heads. The low frequency is heard as a beep even though the tape may not be contacting the playback head. This tone is called a slate tone and is usually about 20 or 30 Hz.

The term originated from motion picture usage, where a small chalkboard was photographed to identify the beginnings of various takes when filming. With the advent of motion picture sound, the "slate" became a "clapboard" when it acquired a hinged and striped appendage that is clapped against the board itself at the beginning of the take. During film editing, the sound of the clap is synchronized with the image of the clapper making contact. A slate at the beginning of a take is called a headslate. Sometimes another slate will be added at the end of a take to verify that sound synch has been maintained. This is called a tailslate and is made with the clapboard held upside down. In this way, the film editor can tell the beginning of a shot from the end. The advent of SMPTE TIME CODE has made the clapboard nearly obsolete, however its modern variant is still used to identify takes visually with written data, and to generate and display the timecode for the camera and sound recorders. In an emergency, the clapstick can still be used to synch sound and picture.

Slew Factor Defined originally by the IHF as the ratio of the highest FREQUENCY that can be applied to the input terminals of an AMPLIFIER at a SIGNAL level that produces rated output at 1 KILOHERTZ, and that can be reproduced at the output with acceptable linearity to 20 kHz.

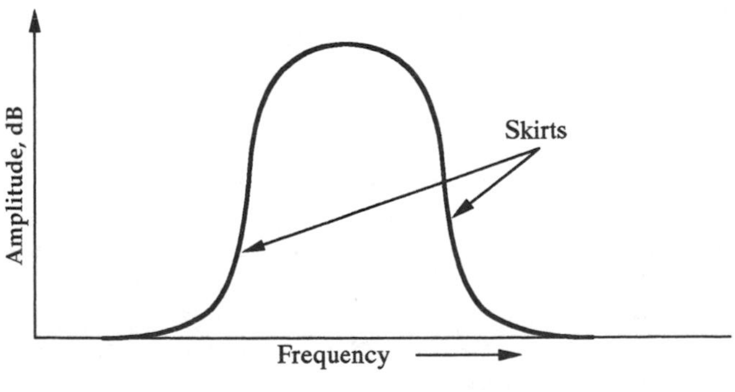

Skirts of a Bandpass Filter

For example, if an amplifier can produce a 10-kHz tone with acceptable linearity at the same level as the maximum it can produce at 1 kHz, its slew factor is ½. Slew rate is a measure of the high-level high-frequency performance of an amplifier. *See also* TIM.

Slewing, Slew Rate The slew rate of a SIGNAL in an audio device is the rate, usually expressed in VOLTS per microsecond, at which the signal is changing. It depends on the AMPLITUDE and FREQUENCY of the signal; high-amplitude, high-frequency signals have the highest slew rates. The slew rate also varies with time along the WAVEFORM, usually being the highest as the waveform passes through zero.

An audio device will have a maximum slew rate above which it cannot operate. This maximum slew rate limits the high-frequency power output of amplifiers and limits the high-level, high-frequency handling capacity of all audio devices. Too low a maximum slew rate results in slew-induced DISTORTION. *See also* TIM.

Slim Wire System *See* FAT WIRE SYSTEM.

Slip Cue A method of CUEing for records where the STYLUS is placed on the record at the beginning of a selection and the record is held stationary while it slips on the turntable. At the moment of truth, the record is let go, and it almost instantly comes up to the speed of the turntable. Slip cueing was done by radio disc jockeys merely to start songs on cue, but the modern club DJ takes slip cueing to new levels.

Slope The portion of the FREQUENCY RESPONSE curve of a FILTER or EQUALIZER that indicates the response is falling off as the frequency is increased or decreased. Filter slopes are characterized by their steepness and are usually 6, 12, 18, or some other multiple of 6 dB per octave. Filter slopes are sometimes called SKIRTS.

Slope Detector A primitive type of FM DETECTOR that uses a LOW-PASS or HIGH-PASS FILTER to convert the FREQUENCY-MODULATED signal into an AMPLITUDE-MODULATED signal. The CARRIER frequency is tuned to be on the SLOPE, or SKIRT, of the filter, and as the frequency varies with the modulating signal, the varying sensitivity of the filter passes more or less of its amplitude, resulting in the amplitude modulation. This modulation is then detected by a simple DIODE detector.

Small Signal Bandwidth The BANDWIDTH an audio device will exhibit at relatively small signal levels. Most audio devices will have a wider FREQUENCY range at low signal levels than at high signal levels because such effects as SLEW limiting occur at high frequencies and high levels.

In devices using TRANSFORMERS, high-level, low-frequency signals can be limited by SATURATION of the transformer core. In a POWER AMPLIFIER, the large signal bandwidth is called the POWER BANDWIDTH. The small signal bandwidth is important, but the power bandwidth of a device is far more so.

Smith, Oberlin In the September 8, 1888, issue of *The Electrical World*, a magazine published in New York at the time, Oberlin Smith wrote the first known description of magnetic sound recording under the title, "Some Forms of Phonograph."

In this article, Mr. Smith describes hypothetical magnetic recording on a steel wire using a telephone transmitter as a MICROPHONE. As an alternative to wire, he says a string or thread, suitably impregnated with iron filings or other small magnetic particles, might serve better. He also mentions illicit recordings of telephone conversations, an 1888 precursor to today's "bugging"!

It was eleven years later that Valdemar Poulsen built his telegraphone, which was a device for magnetic recording of telegraph messages, and which started the evolutionary process that led to the tape recorder.

Smoke, aka Magic Smoke From the PHLOGISTON theory of electronics: it is smoke that makes ICs (INTEGRATED CIRCUITS) and transistors work. The proof of this is self-evident because every time you let the smoke out of an IC or transistor it stops working—elementary. This has been verified through exhaustive testing, particularly regarding power amplifier ICs and transistors. (Incidentally, wires carry smoke from one device to another.) Origin unknown but classic.[24]

SMPTE Society of Motion Picture and Television Engineers. The SMPTE is a long-respected technical organization, and has been active in many aspects of audio engineering. Founded in 1916 in the U.S., SMPTE has spread throughout at least eighty-five countries worldwide.

The classical method of measuring INTERMODULATION DISTORTION was devised by the SMPTE.

SMPTE Time Code (TC) A digital code, standardized by SMPTE and the EBU, consisting of 80-bit digital words and recorded on a video recorder or film camera for identifying each FRAME. The time code is also recorded in audio recorders used for DOUBLE-SYSTEM SOUND and allows the synchronization and the precise editing of the program at any frame line with computer editors. Sometimes two multitrack audio recorders would be synchronized with TC to gain more audio tracks. The basic version of the code repeats in a 24-hour cycle, and within the 24-hour period, each frame is identified by an exact time (HH:MM:SS:Frames). There are many other specifications to accommodate analog and digital technologies and differences in film, video, and international standards. Originally used on analog video and audio recorders and film cameras, the code would be recorded on a special analog track on the video recorder, on a mag stripe or optical area on film, and on one track of a multitrack analog audio recorder or a special center track on a stereo audio recorder. This allowed recognition at faster than normal play speeds. A method called VITC (VERTICAL INTERVAL TC) inserts the TC data into the vertical interval of the television signal, which has some advantages and disadvantages over longitudinal TC (LTC). *See also* DROP-FRAME TIME CODE.

---

24. Thanks to Dennis Bohn, Rane Corp.

Snake A snake, or "mike snake," is a multiple-pair cable with several MICROPHONE connectors on each end. Snakes are used when several microphone cables must be run a fair distance, such as between a stage and the sound control console. The snake replaces an unwieldy collection of cables. The snake is also called a breakout cable.

Snake Track A special optical sound track on a test film for adjusting the alignment of the optical sound system in a motion picture projector equipped to reproduce SVA sound tracks. The snake track is a narrow sound track with a recorded tone. The entire track weaves back and forth over the width of a normal sound track, and the alignment is adjusted until the tone is heard alternately and equally loudly on the two output channels.

Soft Clipping A form of CLIPPING where the edges of the clipped WAVEFORM are rounded rather than sharp; compare to HARD CLIPPING. Soft clipping is much easier on the ears and on TWEETERS than hard, for it contains much less very high frequency energy. In the case of POWER AMPLIFIERS, ones using vacuum tubes tend to exhibit softer clipping when overloaded than do transistor amplifiers. Small signal amplifiers such as microphone PREAMPLIFIERS generally produce hard clipping, especially transistorized ones.

Some amplifiers and receivers exist with a switch to turn a "soft clipping" circuit on or off.

Soft Knee A term usually used to describe the response of a compressor/limiter when it begins to reduce the GAIN of the SIGNAL. The input vs. output graph of the compressor/limiter makes a bend (looking somewhat like a knee) when it starts to act. A soft knee characteristic smoothes this bend so the onset of compression or limiting is gradual instead of sudden and is not so harsh sounding.

Solder A metal alloy used to attach electrical conductors, such as electronic components to circuit boards and wires to connectors. The alloy is commonly 60% tin and 40% lead, but variations are seen as well as small amounts of other metals such as silver. The known toxicity of lead has given rise to other alloys as well. Solder has a fairly low melting point and certain flow characteristics that make it practical for electronic bonding. Electronic soldering uses a rosin material to clean the surfaces to be bonded, called rosin flux. If the solder is in the form of a wire, rosin flux is usually already inside the interior of the solder wire, and this is called rosin core solder. Acid fluxes exist but are never used in electronic work. Highly automated solder machines can solder an entire circuit board at once with a wave of solder. Hand soldering utilizes a heated stylus called a soldering iron, which the user wields to heat the desired joint just enough to melt the solder and allow it to cleanly flow around the joint. This can be quite a skill, and something quite useful when making or repairing circuits or connectors. Americans, at least, pronounce the material "sodder."

Solid State Solid state refers to electronic CIRCUITS that use TRANSISTORS and INTEGRATED CIRCUITS instead of vacuum TUBES as active elements.

Solo A special circuit configuration developed by Philips for use in DAT recorders that permits the recording of a perfect digital copy of a COMPACT DISC by simply copying the digital code from the disc directly, without going through the digital-to-analog conversion and subsequent filtering and other analog circuitry. The Solo system would insert in the DAT recording certain inaudible digital information (an anti-copy FLAG) that would not allow the recorder to make another digital copy of the DAT copy. The purpose is to prevent the unauthorized digital replication of CDs by unscrupulous persons, but it allows the consumer to make a DAT recording of various selections from CDs and still maintain the original quality. The RIAA, the British Phonographic Industry (BPI), the International Federation of the Phonographic Industry (IFPI), the EIA, and several Japanese and European manufacturers all agreed in mid-1989 to implement a system somewhat similar to Solo. *See also* SCMS.

Solo can also refer to certain buttons on recording consoles; most have a solo button associated with each console input. Pressing a solo button mutes the other channels and allows the recording engineer to hear only the signal from that channel over the MONITOR speakers while the recording or sound reinforcement program goes on unaffected.

Sone The subjective unit of LOUDNESS. A sound has a loudness of 1 sone if its loudness level is 40 PHONS. This means a sound of 1 sone loudness sounds equally loud as a 1,000-HERTZ sound whose SPL is 40 DECIBELS. A doubling of loudness corresponds to an increase of 10 sones.

Sonic An adjective meaning "of sound"; the audio equivalent of "visual." Sonic refers to any sound, not just audible sound. Outside the audio field, the term is used to mean the speed of sound in air. Thus supersonic is faster than the speed of sound, and subsonic is slower than the speed of sound. These terms are not to be confused with ULTRASONIC and INFRASONIC.

Sound Effects Filter A special-purpose BANDPASS FILTER. For creation of special effects for the stage and motion pictures, etc., sound effects filters are often used to modify the FREQUENCY RESPONSE of sound systems. An example is a steep high-frequency rolloff to simulate the sound of a telephone, or a voice on short-wave radio. Sound effects filters were very much used in the radio broadcasts of the 1940s and 1950s.

Sound Field Microphone *See* AMBISONICS.

Sound Head The sound-reproducing device in a motion picture projector. The traditional analog optical version consists of a roller over which the film passes, with one or two photocells inside. Associated with it is a lens assembly that focuses the light from the exciter lamp through the small area of the film sound track and onto the photocells. Newer units may use an LED and CCD devices. The commercial theater film projector sound head also usually includes the drive motor for the projector.

Sounding Vessels As described by the Roman architect VITRUVIUS, sounding vessels are large urn-like HELMHOLTZ RESONATORS placed in certain Roman theaters to improve the acoustics. Not much is known about ancient sounding vessels, and none survive to the present day. There is at least one Roman theater that has niches in the audience area that probably held sounding vessels. Also, in Saint Sophia's cathedral in Kiev, Ukraine, which dates from the thirteenth century, there are many Helmholtz resonators embedded in the interior walls, which were placed there to "amplify" sound, according to the local tour guide.

Of course the resonators, which are really resonant absorbers, cannot amplify sound but merely absorb energy at well-defined frequencies and then reradiate the energy later, effectively increasing the reverberation time of the room. Vitruvius's account of them implies that they were tuned to several notes of a musical scale, which would cause a musical chord to sound after being excited by a loud noise. If some sound-absorbing material is inside the resonator, it becomes a strong absorber at its resonant frequency. This type of specific absorber has been used in some modern auditoria.

An interesting use of Helmholtz resonators is in the "assisted resonance" system installed in the Royal Festival Hall in London. Many resonators, tuned to a broad range of frequencies in the lower musical registers, are placed above the ceiling of the auditorium. Each resonator has a small loudspeaker in it and a microphone associated with it. The microphone picks up sound at the resonant frequency and amplifies it into the speaker, prolonging the reverberation time of the resonator and thus prolonging the reverberation time of the auditorium itself. This is one of the few musically successful attempts to electronically alter the acoustical properties of an auditorium. A similar system was installed in the Hult Center auditorium in Eugene, Oregon.

Sound Intensity Sound intensity is defined as a measure of the net flow of acoustic energy in a sound field. The units are WATTS per square meter. Because the energy moves in a particular direction, sound intensity is a vector quantity, i.e., it has magnitude and direction. Sound intensity cannot be measured directly, and it should not be confused with SOUND PRESSURE LEVEL, which is what a sound level meter measures.

Some confusion exists about sound intensity because it used to be defined in terms of the energy content of a sound field, without regard to the movement of the energy. A much better concept for this is SOUND POWER.

It is interesting and important to note that there may exist a large sound pressure at a point, but the sound intensity may be very small, or even zero. This is the case for instance in standing waves, where the energy is sloshing back and forth within a distance of a half-WAVELENGTH or so, but does not progress through the medium.

A MICROPHONE always measures sound pressure, or sometimes it may measure the particle velocity, but it can never measure sound intensity directly.

Sound Level Meter A meter that measures SOUND PRESSURE LEVEL. It consists of a PRESSURE MICROPHONE, an AMPLIFIER, an RMS DETECTOR, a logarithmic amplifier, and a meter or other indicating device. It is battery-powered for portable use. Usually, it will contain at least one WEIGHTING FILTER to make its response more or less conform to the sensitivity of the human ear. *See also* A-WEIGHTING.

The microphone on a sound level meter is OMNIDIRECTIONAL, with wide and uniform FREQUENCY RESPONSE, and must be very stable in its SENSITIVITY to maintain accurate calibration. An accessory to the sound level meter is the acoustic calibrator, which presents the microphone with a known sound pressure level to check the sensitivity of the microphone and meter electronics.

A high-quality sound level meter will meet the ANSI and ISO specifications for frequency range, TIME CONSTANTS, microphone directivity, and filter response curve accuracy, and is always expensive. There are several very inexpensive meters available that masquerade as true sound level meters, but they seldom meet the standardized performance requirements for precise measurements. They may be useful for measuring relative levels, such as estimating the noisiness of a machine by measuring when it is running and comparing the noise level when it is turned off.

Sound-on-Sound A popular name for OVERDUBBING.

Sound Power Sound power is the amount of energy radiated by a sound source per unit time. Its units are joules per second, or WATTS.

Sound power is a measurement of a characteristic of a sound source, and has no direct relation to SOUND PRESSURE LEVEL (SPL). This is analogous to a light bulb, which may be rated at 100 watts. This does not tell how bright a room will be with the light bulb in it; that depends on the size and color of the room, etc. Thus, the SPL of a sound in a room is related to the sound power of the source in a complicated way, depending on the environment and microphone placement, etc.

Sound power measurements are made when the sources of sound are being investigated, for instance in noise control investigations, whereas SPL is measured if the effects of sound on a human subject are being studied.

Sound power cannot be measured directly, but must be calculated from a series of SPL or SOUND INTENSITY measurements and a knowledge of the environment. *See also* POWER RESPONSE.

Sound Pressure, Sound Pressure Level A sound wave progressing through air causes the instantaneous air pressure at any given point to vary above and below the barometric pressure in accordance with the WAVEFORM of the sound. This variation in pressure is used as a quantitative measure of the strength of the sound, and is called sound pressure. This is the quantity that a PRESSURE MICROPHONE measures, and if it is expressed on a DECIBEL scale and referred to a pressure of 20 micropascals, it is called sound pressure level. The reference pressure of 20 micropascals is 0 dB on the scale, and corresponds to the threshold of hearing at 1,000 HERTZ for a normal human ear.

Sound pressure level is what is measured by a sound level meter. *See also* LEVEL.

Sound Reinforcement The general term for a sound system designed to amplify the voice and/or music to improve its intelligibility to an audience. A sound reinforcement system always consists of at least one MICROPHONE, associated PREAMPLIFIERS, CONTROL CONSOLE, AMPLIFIERS, and LOUD-

SPEAKERS. The old term for such a system is "PA" system, standing for public address, and it is still in common use.

Traditionally, sound systems have been MONAURAL, i.e., they have had only one independent channel of AUDIO. In recent years, there has been a strong interest in STEREOPHONIC sound reinforcement, and when properly designed and operated, these systems offer a large degree of naturalness. The best stereo reinforcement systems have three or five independent channels or more. It is possible to perform multichannel stereo reinforcement of classical music programs for very large audiences in such a way that the reinforcement itself is not noticed by the audience, although this is rarely attained in practice.

The advent of large rock concerts has spawned the development and refinement of very high power sound reinforcement systems, and they can be extremely complex and expensive, in addition to being very loud. Such systems are really part of the musical ensemble, and the operator often has as much musical talent as the performers.

The primary problem that has to be overcome in any sound reinforcement system is acoustic FEEDBACK, which is an OSCILLATION of the system due to the microphone picking up the amplified sound and the system amplifying it again into a continuous howl. To minimize feedback, directional microphones and loudspeakers are used, and much attention is paid to their placement in the room and their proximity to the performers. EQUALIZATION is often used to reduce the system GAIN at frequencies where the acoustic gain may be high due to peculiarities in the room acoustics, the loudspeakers, and/or the microphones. *See also* SOUND SYSTEM EQUALIZATION.

Sound Stage A theatrical stage for filming motion pictures or video productions that is specially treated for the simultaneous recording of dialogue or music. A sound stage must have a low level of background noise and a low reverberation time. The cameras and other equipment used must be specially designed for quiet operation.

Sound Stripe A narrow strip of magnetic sound recording material applied to motion picture film for recording of the sound track, in the manner of a tape recorder. In the case of Super-8 and 16-mm film, two stripes were used, one for the sound and one just to balance the thickness so the film would wind smoothly on the reels. 35-mm magnetic stripe prints could have multiple tracks and stripes on both sides of the film, as well as the traditional optical sound track. 70-mm release prints of motion pictures exclusively used magnetic sound tracks until recent digital systems became available. 35-mm "mag" prints are essentially obsolete and are rarely seen.

Sound System Equalization The EQUALIZATION of a SOUND REINFORCEMENT system, either to increase its amount of GAIN before FEEDBACK, or to make its overall FREQUENCY RESPONSE more nearly FLAT. Sound system equalization is a complex and tricky business, because the

ACOUSTICS of the room, as well as the frequency responses of all the audio devices, are involved, in addition to the characteristics of the MICROPHONE being used. Actually, it is only possible to attain a given frequency response CURVE at one place in an auditorium and for a narrow range of microphone locations at a time. Therefore, many curves are measured and an average is made to represent the best compromise to the desired curve. Equalization requires measuring the frequency response while the equalizer is being adjusted, and this requires the use of a REAL-TIME ANALYZER (RTA) or an FFT ANALYZER.

Some years ago, it was thought by some audio people that if a sound system had a series of very narrow band NOTCH FILTERS, each tuned to a frequency at which the system would be likely to go into ACOUSTIC FEEDBACK, the available gain would be increased. This is true to a certain extent, but it would only work for a single microphone location, and also the DISTORTION of the tonal quality by the phase shift introduced by the filters is disturbing to many listeners.

Quite a few years ago the idea of putting a frequency shifter that increased the frequency of the signal by a few hertz in the sound system was tried to reduce the tendency for feedback. The theory was that the amplified sound picked up by the microphones would not be at the same frequency as the original sound that was being amplified, and therefore, with repeated trips through the microphones, amplifiers, and speakers, would not build up energy in the room at a specific frequency. Unfortunately, it was soon found that instead of conventional feedback, the sound system would emit "chirps" when the gain was increased to high levels. This was as obnoxious as feedback, and these systems met a rapid demise.

Today the narrowest frequency BAND in common use for fixed sound system equalization is one-third OCTAVE, or about 23 percent of the center frequency. There is a relatively new technique, however, which uses a dual-channel FFT analyzer to continuously measure the frequency response of the entire system, including the room, and using live music as the test SIGNAL. Equalization in narrow bands can be performed in "real time" during the progress of a concert without the audience knowing about it. The advantage of this is that no matter where the system is used, and no matter where the microphones are, the optimum equalization is rapidly achieved. An example of this real-time approach is the popular Sabine FBX Feedback Eliminator *See also* FEEDBACK.

Source One terminal of a FIELD EFFECT TRANSISTOR, the other two of which are the GATE and the DRAIN. Also, some tape recorders with "3 heads" or "confidence heads" have a switch labeled "Source/Tape" for switching the output between the "source" of the signal and the playback from the recorded tape. "Source" is sometimes labeled "input" in that you monitor the input signal, as opposed to the recorded playback. Video people refer to source as "EE" for Electronics to Electronics."

Source Follower A CIRCUIT element configuration, usually using an OPAMP, which has a GAIN of 1 (unity). The INPUT IMPEDANCE of a source follower is very high, and the OUTPUT IMPEDANCE is very low. This makes the circuit useful for driving AUDIO lines and other low impedance devices. The source follower is similar in its action on signals to the CATHODE FOLLOWER and EMITTER FOLLOWER.

Spaced Microphone Stereo *See* A-B STEREO.

Spaced Omnis *See* A-B STEREO; OMNIDIRECTIONAL.

Spaciousness A subjective quality of reproduced music that is related to ENVELOPMENT in room ACOUSTICS. Spaciousness comes from the ability of the recording to capture the acoustical effect of the room in which the music was being played.

SPARS Acronym for Society of Professional Audio Recording Studios. This group is responsible for the so-called SPARS code. The three-letter SPARS code appears on records and COMPACT DISCS and indicates whether the original recording, the editing, and the final production were done by analog or digital means. For instance, AAD means the original recording was analog, the editing was done before digitizing, and the final product was digitally mastered. The use of the SPARS code has come under fire in recent years, usually because it does not accurately indicate the number of A to D and D to A conversions the signal has undergone in its travels from microphone to mixing console to tape recorder to the CD mastering facility. The Society of Professional Audio Recording Services met during an Audio Engineering Society conference and decided to recommend that the SPARS code be discontinued. They issued a statement that said, in part, "But by that time, the digital/analog technical scene had become so cluttered with conversions and algorithms for interface as to resemble rocket science, and many felt the SPARS code too simple to carry enough information to be meaningful." SPARS withdrew endorsement of the code in 1991. But many labels continued to use it, and the organization renewed its endorsement of the code in 1995.

Spatializer™ A proprietary digital signal processor that modifies a stereo input signal to simulate a stereo image wider than the speaker spacing, developed by Desper Products, Inc., a subsidiary of Spatializer Audio Labs, Inc. Widely licensed in both the consumer audio and multimedia computing markets, the Spatializer process is normally used as a postprocessor. It claims to place sounds in front of the listener in an arc of 180 degrees, with excellent imaging and fidelity.

S/PDIF Sony/Philips Digital Interface or Sony/Philips Digital Interface Format, a serial digital audio interconnection scheme found on consumer equipment. It uses RCA plugs and jacks with 75-ohm coaxial cable, or fiber optics. The format was eventually recognized as IEC958, and later as IEC 60958-3 when other formats such as AES3 (IEC 60958-4) were included by the IEC specification.

SPDT Single Pole Double Throw. This refers to a switch that has a single current path but is capable of routing the input to either of two outputs.

Speaker *See* LOUDSPEAKER.

Speaker Sensitivity A number that quantifies the efficiency of a speaker or speaker system, usually expressed as SPL (SOUND PRESSURE LEVEL), produced by the speaker at one meter directly in front of the speaker when driven by one watt of input power. The higher the number, the louder it will sound at a given volume control setting. Speaker sensitivity is not a measure of the quality or FIDELITY of a speaker—it only refers to the speaker's loudness.

Speakon™ A trademark for a high-power audio connector from the Neutrik company used for loudspeakers. The previous lack of a good solution has led to wide industry acceptance. Speakons can have several contact options, allowing for easy BIAMPING for example, and a locking collar.

Spectral Contamination A sensitive technique, developed by Gary Sokolich and the late Deane Jensen in the 1980s, for measuring cross-modulation products produced by nonlinearities in a DUT that is passing many frequencies at once. The DUT is excited at many simultaneous well-defined frequencies, and the distortion components are measured at frequencies where no excitation energy exists. Their method detects distortion components as low as 110 dB below the level of the signal.

The test signal can have many forms but is usually a collection of evenly spaced sine waves spread over a broad frequency range. One signal of this type has frequency components from 10 kHz to 25 kHz spaced 120 Hz apart. All these frequencies interact in the DUT to produce energy in the 0-Hz to 10-kHz band, where no test signal existed. This frequency band in the output of the DUT is passed into an FFT analyzer for spectrum analysis.

It is interesting that this technique is able to separate linear errors, such as frequency response, magnitude, and time delay errors, from the nonlinear errors. The results are said by the inventors to correlate well with listening tests. At present, there are no established standards for spectral contamination measurement.

Spectral Recording, SR A somewhat complex type of COMPANDER system invented and marketed by Dolby Laboratories that achieves a greater degree of noise reduction than Dolby A, B, or C systems and also results in reduced DISTORTION in most cases. The system was described by Ray Dolby at the Audio Engineering Society convention in November 1986. It is intended for use with professional-quality analog recording media, such as tape recorders and motion picture sound, rather than digital systems, whose low distortion and wide DYNAMIC RANGE are already adequate to the task of recording music.

In the SR system, low-level components in the music signal are compressed in a frequency-selective way during recording, and high-level parts of the signal at the very high and very low frequencies are attenuated. The attenuation of the signals at the frequency extremes reduces the distortion added by the recording medium, and the compression of low-level signals increases their SIGNAL-TO-NOISE RATIO. In playback of the recorded signal, these effects are reversed in order to restore the original dynamics to the signal.

For the system to operate properly, the signal levels in the encoding and decoding sections must be matched, and this is cleverly accomplished by the encoder generating a calibration tone for signal level and a band of PINK NOISE for frequency response matching. The SR system is very well conceived and engineered, and probably represents the state of the art in compander systems.

Spectrum When a time-varying SIGNAL is subjected to FREQUENCY analysis, it is transformed from the "time domain" to the "frequency domain." The frequency-domain representation of the signal is called the spectrum, and the time-domain representation is called the WAVEFORM. The two quantities contain the same information, and one can be converted into the other by a mathematical operation called the FOURIER TRANSFORM.

Spectrum analysis, frequency analysis, and Fourier analysis are synonymous.

Spectrum Shifter *See* FREQUENCY SHIFTER.

Specular According to the *OED*, "Having the reflecting property of a mirror; presenting a smooth, polished, reflective surface; of a brilliant glassy or metallic luster." In acoustics, specular reflection is a discrete reflection of a sound where the angle of reflection is equal to the angle of incidence. An example is an ECHO reflected off a large plane surface like a wall. In general, specular reflections are avoided in rooms designed for music listening or recording. *See* Appendix 4 for more details. The opposite of specular reflection is diffuse reflection, where the reflected sound is scattered in all directions.

Speech Coil The same as VOICE COIL. This is primarily British usage.

Speech-Music Switch A special type of EQUALIZER that adds a low-FREQUENCY reduction to the SIGNAL when in the speech position. The reason is that most broadcast and recorded speech has too much low-frequency content because of too-close MICROPHONE position and PROXIMITY EFFECT when directional microphones are used.

Speech-music switches are often found on SOUND REINFORCEMENT system PREAMPLIFIERS. The low-frequency cut usually amounts to 6 DECIBELS per OCTAVE below 100 HERTZ or so.

Speed Word yelled by the production sound mixer when the production recorder is in record and up to speed (indicated by "flags" on a Nagra), indicating to the camera crew and the assistant director that he or she is recording. While Nagras get up to speed quickly, and digital machines are always "at speed," the term derives from older Hollywood technology in which a common motor system drove cameras and film sound recorders (originally optical, and later either 17½-mm or 35-mm mag) and sometimes even turntables for music playback.[25]

---

25. This entry is copyright © 1999–2003 by Larry Blake and is reprinted with permission.

Spider The assembly that holds the VOICE COIL of a DYNAMIC LOUDSPEAKER centered in the magnetic gap. The spider is a corrugated circular piece of specially treated fabric. The name comes from the early days of LOUDSPEAKERS when it was made of a plastic material that resembled the legs of a spider.

SPL Common abbreviation for SOUND PRESSURE LEVEL.

Splatter A type of DISTORTION of an audio signal caused by hard CLIPPING of the WAVEFORM, usually because of the OVERLOAD of a device. The term *splatter* is most often used for the distortion caused by overmodulation of AM transmitters. *See also* ASYMMETRICAL LIMITER.

Splice In reference to magnetic recording tape, a splice is a discontinuity in the tape itself occasioned by cutting the tape and pasting it back together with thin adhesive "splicing tape" in a different sequence. If carefully done, splices can be inaudible.

Splicer A mechanical device for cutting and taping together magnetic recording tape. Many designs have been produced, some with various attachments for cutting the tape and applying splicing tape. There was a guillotine-type tape splicer on the market for quite a few years that had a pair of curved blades that trimmed the tape on both sides at the vicinity of the splice to make the spliced tape a little narrower than ¼ inch. The purpose of this was to assure that no sticky splicing tape would overlap the tape edges and gum up the guides and heads in the tape recorder. The splicer was called the Gibson Girl, by analogy to the "hour glass" figure of the Gibson Girl style. The *OED* defines Gibson Girl as follows: "A girl typifying the fashionable ideal of the late 19th and early 20th cents. as represented in the work of Charles Dana Gibson."

While splicing analog audio tape is quite effective and was essential until computer editing, it doesn't work very well on videotape due to the way the signal is recorded and the nature of the video signal.

Splicing Block A small rectangular block of aluminum, or sometimes plastic, which has a shallow groove designed to hold MAGNETIC TAPE while it is being cut and spliced. The splicing block also has a slot to guide the razor blade used to cut the tape.

Splicing Tape Sticky tape for holding together splices in analog AUDIO tape. Splicing tape comes in different widths to accommodate tapes of 2-inch, 1-inch, ½-inch, ¼-inch, and ⅛-inch widths. Splicing tape is slightly narrower than the tape it is designed to join, and has a special adhesive that is designed not to slide or "bleed" out of the area where it is applied. This is very important; it is not advisable to use standard Scotch tape for splicing MAGNETIC TAPE for this reason. Unfortunately, over decades, all splicing tape seems either to dry up or ooze anyway.

Splitter A small device used in recording studios to accept a SIGNAL from one device, usually a MICROPHONE, and "split" the signal and feed it to two or more other devices. Splitters are also used for connecting several television sets to a single COAXIAL cable. The simplest type of splitter is the so-called Y-cord, but most splitters contain series resistors in the signal paths to avoid excessive loading of the device being split. This causes the split signals to be about 6 dB lower in level than the signal being split.

Spot Microphone A microphone purposely aimed toward a certain subject, like a spotlight. Usually the spot mic augments a stereo microphone array such as when recording an orchestra. A soloist or soft instrument may get a spot mic. The concept is essentially foreign in the MULTITRACK, close microphone world.

Spring Reverb A type of synthetic REVERBERATOR that uses a vibrating spring as the reverberating element.

The first commercial artificial reverberator was introduced in the late 1930s by the Hammond Organ company. It used a somewhat complex series of springs that were driven by the vibration of a LOUDSPEAKER VOICE COIL that was connected to the organ's PREAMPLIFIER output. This vibration was sensed by a TRANSDUCER similar to a phonograph CARTRIDGE whose output was mixed with the organ signal as it entered the POWER AMPLIFIER. The reverberation of the springs was thus added to the organ signal. The vibration of the springs was DAMPED by their ends being submerged in a bath of oil.

This system was improved over the years by the Hammond Organ company, and was the subject of several patents. Later spring reverberators applied a twisting, or torsional, motion to the springs, which made them much less sensitive to external vibrations.

Springs are among the least expensive types of synthetic reverberators, and they do not sound very much like real reverberation—but no synthetic reverberation really does. *See also* PLATE REVERBERATION.

Sprocket A toothed wheel found in motion picture cameras and projectors to control the motion of the film. The teeth in the sprocket interlock with holes in the film in the manner of a sprocket and chain of a bicycle. At one time, audio portions of a film soundtrack were transferred to sprocketed audio film known as "fullcoat" or "magstock." This allowed editing while keeping synch with the picture. Sprocketed magstock players were used for the sound in theater systems such as Cinerama. Occasionally a sprocketed audio recorder would be used just for audio recording, a technique championed and used by the late recording engineer Bert Whyte, owner of Everest Records.

Sprocket Run Sometimes the film in a motion picture projector can become misaligned such that the sprockets punch a series of holes in the film alongside the sprocket holes, damaging the optical sound track. The audible result of this is a 96-Hz buzz superimposed on the sound. Such a film is beyond repair.

SPST Single Pole Single Throw. This describes a switch that has only one current path through itself and only "on" or "off" positions.

Sputter Microphone diaphrams are often made of polyester (trademarked "Mylar" by DuPont) coated with gold a few molecules thick. Gold is used because of its inert nonoxidizing character and its ductility. The coating

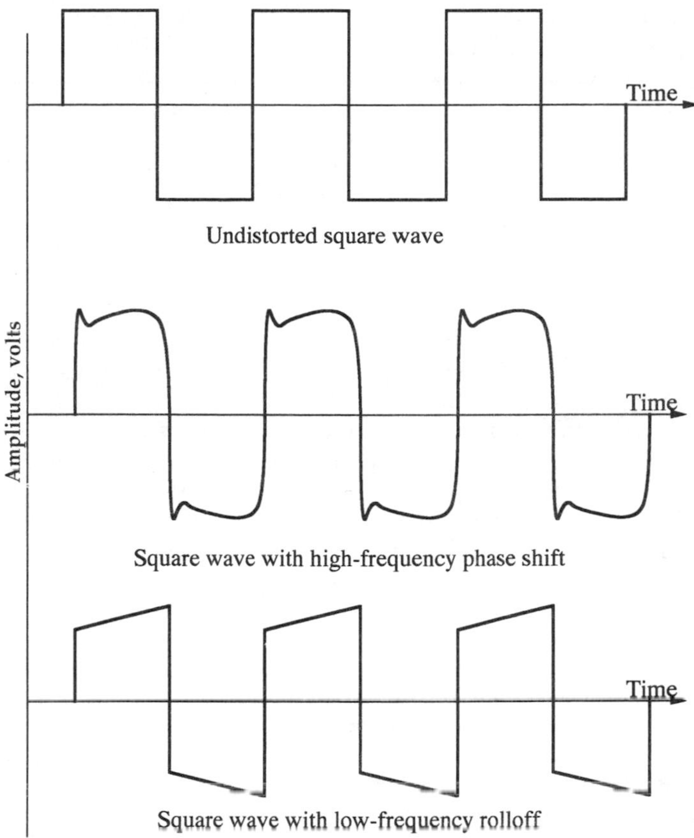

Square Wave

process is called sputtering, and the result is a sputtered diaphragm. The Mylar is placed in a vacuum chamber, and a small piece of pure gold is heated until its atoms boil off and impinge on and stick to the Mylar.

SQ *See* QUADRAPHONIC SOUND.

Square Wave A square wave is a PERIODIC WAVEFORM that consists of a FUNDAMENTAL and all the odd-numbered HARMONICS. The harmonics gradually decrease in AMPLITUDE as FREQUENCY rises, and they are in PHASE with the fundamental.

The square wave, along with the SINE WAVE, is one of the classic test signals used for evaluating audio device performance. It contains energy up to at least the twentieth harmonic, so an AMPLIFIER that passes a 1,000-HERTZ square wave without DISTORTION has a BANDWIDTH of at least 20 KILOHERTZ. Because the shape of the wave is sensitive to the phase of the harmonics, the phase accuracy can also be determined. The square wave is a good test signal because it exercises the device at many frequencies at the same time, as does music.

Squawker An unflattering name sometimes given to mid-range LOUDSPEAKER units in three-way or more systems.

Squelch A circuit, commonly found in two-way radio systems, that mutes the audio signal when the RF CARRIER is not present. This prevents noise from being received when the transmitter is not operating. Squelch circuits are also used in some audio devices to reduce the output noise in the absence of an input signal. *See also* MUTING.

SR *See* SPECTRAL RECORDING.

SRC Stereo Reception Control, a proprietary system used in Mitsubishi FM car radios in which the stereo separation is reduced in response to noise and DISTORTION caused by multipath reception.

Because of the short wavelengths used in FM broadcasting, and the fact that radios in cars are in motion, reflected signals cause rapid variations in received noise, or PICKET FENCING. The SRC circuit senses the noise level and gradually blends the stereo channels into monaural as the noise increases. Several other manufacturers use somewhat similar techniques. *See also* SAMPLING RATE CONVERTER.

SSFS Stereophonic Sound Film System, developed during the 1930s by Harvey Fletcher and others at the Bell Telephone Laboratories and first publicly demonstrated in New York in 1937 and 1939. *See also* FANTASOUND.

The SSFS was an extremely innovative experimental system, using four optical tracks on a separate 35-mm film. Three of the tracks carried stereophonic sound. The fourth, or control, track controlled the GAIN in the sound tracks. This was done by recording a mixture of different-frequency tones on the control track and, in playback, separating these tones with filters and using their individual levels to vary the amplification in the appropriate channel. The system was thus a three-channel COMPANDER and was able to deliver a dynamic range of 80 dB. The optical track itself was only capable of about 50-dB dynamic range. The original stereo tracks were compressed in the recording process to compensate for the later expansion.

SSFS was a remarkably good system considering when it was developed. It was capable of 20 Hz to 14 kHz response with quite low distortion.

Stage In an amplifier CIRCUIT, a unit of amplification, such as provided by a TRANSISTOR or vacuum TUBE, is called a stage, or sometimes a GAIN stage. There is no fixed amount of amplification provided by a single stage; some stages may provide 40 DECIBELS of gain, while others may provide less than 1 dB.

Stamper The stamper is the master record from which records are pressed. The stamper can be made by direct plating onto the ACETATE master but is usually made from a MOTHER in the technique known as THREE-STEP PROCESSING. About four or five hundred records can be pressed with one stamper if it is not damaged. After this number, wear on the stamper decreases the quality of the pressings. Normally, only one good-quality stamper can be made from an original acetate, so if more than five hundred records are to be made, three-step processing must be used.

Standards In order to ensure interchangeability of such components as records among record players, tapes among tape recorders, etc., they must conform to certain shared characteristics. Examples are record turntable speeds, tape speeds, tape widths, tape track widths, and playback EQUALIZATION curves.

Many of these standardized values are not significant in themselves; the only important thing is the existence of the conformity between manufacturers. For instance, record RPM might just as well be 30 rpm or 35 rpm as 33⅓ rpm and no difference in the quality would be noticed. Other types of standards, however, are selected to optimize the performance of certain types of products or processes, and they no longer apply when the product or process has become obsolete. An example is the standard NAB recording and playback equalization curve for tape recorders, which was adopted by the NAB in 1954. It made optimum use of the then-available recording tape, but new technology has revolutionized tape formulation since 1954. A new equalization scheme would greatly improve the SIGNAL-TO-NOISE RATIO in tape recorders, but it would make all existing recorders and tapes obsolete.

This points up the perennial problem of standardization. Standards should be set early to allow exploitation of the technology, but they should be set late to take maximum advantage of that technology. Some feel that standards are set too early in many cases. With the public crying for improved technology, and the manufacturers anxious to take advantage of the new market, the temptation is to standardize early and rush to market with new products, even before the engineering is completed. Probably the worst case of poor planning in this regard was the birth and quick death of commercially available QUADRAPHONIC SOUND, where products, both hardware and software, were heavily promoted while the industry was in the midst of great turmoil over standardization. Even the basic theory of SURROUND SOUND was not well established, as system after system was promoted, sold, and made obsolete almost overnight. Another example is the standardized SAMPLING RATES of DIGITAL audio systems, which are thought by many to be too low for optimum performance.

American organizations interested in the determination of standards are the ANSI (American National Standards Institute), the FTC (Federal Trade Commission), the NAB (National Association of Broadcasters), the SMPTE (Society of Motion Picture and Television Engineers), the AES (Audio Engineering Society), and the ASA (American Standards Association). There are correspondingly many such groups in Europe. With so many standardization groups, there is inevitable overlap and disagreement in some areas.

Standard Tuning Frequency The internationally agreed upon standard for musical instrument tuning is 440 Hz for the note A4. The frequencies for the equal tempered scale based on A-440 are shown in the following table.

Note	Frequency	Note	Frequency	Note	Frequency
B2	123.47	B5	987.77	B8	7,902.10
#	116.54	#	932.33	#	7,458.60
A2	110.00	A5	880.00	A8	7,040.00
#	103.83	#	830.61	#	6,644.90
G2	97.999	G5	783.99	G8	6,271.90
#	92.499	#	739.99	#	5,919.90
F2	87.307	F5	698.46	F8	5,587.70
E2	82.407	E5	659.26	E8	5,274.00
#	77.782	#	622.25	#	4,978.00
D2	73.416	D5	587.33	D8	4,698.60
#	69.296	#	554.37	#	4,434.90
C2	65.406	C5	523.25	C8	4,186.00
B1	61.74	B4	493.88	B7	3,951.10
#	58.27	#	466.16	#	3,729.30
A1	55.00	A4	440.00	A7	3,520.00
#	51.91	#	415.30	#	3,322.40
G1	49.00	G4	392.00	G7	3,136.00
#	46.25	#	369.99	#	2,960.00
F1	43.65	F4	349.23	F7	2,793.80
E1	41.20	E4	329.63	E7	2,637.00
#	38.89	#	311.13	#	2,489.00
D1	36.71	D4	293.66	D7	2,349.30
#	34.68	#	277.18	#	2,217.50
C1	32.70	C4	261.63	C7	2,093.00
B0	30.87	B3	246.94	B6	1,975.50
#	29.14	#	233.08	#	1,864.70
A0	27.50	A3	220.00	A6	1,760.00
#	25.96	#	207.65	#	1,661.20
G0	24.50	G3	196.00	G8	1,568.00
#	23.13	#	185.00	#	1,480.00
F0	21.83	F3	174.61	F6	1,396.90
E0	20.60	E3	164.81	E6	1,318.50
#	19.45	#	155.56	#	1,244.50
D-0	18.35	D3	146.83	D6	1,174.70
#	17.32	#	138.59	#	1,108.70
C0	16.35	C3	130.81	C6	1,046.50

Standing Wave A phenomenon in room ACOUSTICS whereby a sound is reflected back and forth between two parallel surfaces, such as two sidewalls. The sound waves interfere with one another to produce a series of places where the SOUND PRESSURE LEVEL (SPL) is high and another series of places between them where the SPL is very low. It is as if a sound wave were stationary in the space between the surfaces.

A standing wave exists between surfaces only when the FREQUENCY is such that the distance between the walls is an integral multiple of one-half the WAVELENGTH. For a given distance, there will be many frequencies that will generate standing waves, each an integral multiple of the lowest, or FUNDAMENTAL, frequency. Standing waves are created by "room modes," which are modes of vibration of the air in a room.

Standing waves are always detrimental to the acoustics of a room, and are avoided by careful design in music listening rooms. They are the cause of irregularities in the bass response of most home sound systems. In recording studios, special constructions called BASS TRAPS are sometimes used to add low-frequency absorption in order to prevent or reduce the formation of standing waves. *See also* EIGENTONES.

All musical instruments with strings or columns of air operate on the principal of standing waves. They set up standing waves that cause vibrations of the instruments and radiation of sounds at all the resonant frequencies of the standing waves.

State-Variable Filter A type of ACTIVE filter that uses RESISTORS, CAPACITORS, and three OPAMPS to provide simultaneous low-pass, high-pass, and BANDPASS functions of the input signal. The state-variable filter has the advantage that the Q and the cutoff frequency are independently adjustable by varying resistance values in the circuit. It is a simple matter to arrange voltage control of these two parameters, and this is often done. The state-variable filter exactly simulates the response of an equivalent RLC filter and has been used for some time in analog computer circuitry.

Static Any high-frequency intermittent noise is called static. The term comes from the early days of radio broadcasting when distant lightning strokes caused such noise in reception.

Static is distinct from such continuous noises as HUM or buzz, and can be difficult to diagnose because of its intermittent quality. It can be caused by loose or oxidized connections in audio devices as well as from RFI.

It is curious that it was called static in as much as it is a dynamic type of noise.

Stems The three or more final components of a stereo film mix, usually comprising three multichannel mixes, one each of dialog, music, and sound effects that, combined, make up the final mix of a film. Minimal (hopefully no) additional level changes, EQUALIZATION, etc., should be needed to create a printmaster, although of course a 6-track printmaster will sometimes have different requirements than a print master for stereo analog uses.

The separation of elements afforded by stems allows Music and Effects (M&E) mixes to be easily derived from the original stereo mix. For this reason, dialog stems are sometimes comprised of multiple centers.

The word "stem" should not be used for any other element prior to the final mix masters; it is a common mistake to refer to the various premixes as stems.[26]

Ster-Bin A CIRCUIT that converts a STEREOPHONIC signal into a quasi-BINAURAL signal to make it more suited to listening via HEADPHONES.

If conventional stereo music is heard through headphones, the subjective effect is usually one of great spaciousness and exaggerated DYNAMICS and stereo separation. The effect may be pleasant with some types of music, but is not at all natural; that is, it does not resemble the sound of live music. Binaural recordings, on the other hand, are eminently suited to headphone listening by their very nature. In order to simulate binaural from stereo, CROSSTALK that varies with FREQUENCY combined with a time delay must be introduced between the signals. When listening to LOUDSPEAKER reproduction of stereo, each ear hears both channels, but the right-channel SIGNAL heard by the left ear is modified by DIFFRACTION of the sound about the head. This causes a relative time delay between the left and right ears' hearing of the signal, and also causes a modification of the FREQUENCY RESPONSE of the left ear signal compared to the right.

The Ster-Bin circuit introduces this frequency-dependent crosstalk and time delay. Stereo recordings heard through the Ster-Bin sound more compact and realistic, and cause less listener fatigue than if it is not used, although they do not sound as realistic as true binaural recordings. Some simple systems have been built that introduce crosstalk between the channels without the EQUALIZATION and time delay, and they are sometimes called "cross-feed" circuits. Their effect is not nearly as convincing as that of the Ster-Bin.

The Ster-Bin was invented by Benjamin Bauer of CBS Laboratories, and was marketed for a time by the Jensen company. Improvements in the system were suggested by M. V. Thomas of Boston University. There seems to be little interest in it today.

Stereo *See* STEREOPHONIC.

Stereophoner A commercially unsuccessful device invented in the late 1950s by the eminent orchestra conductor Hermann Scherchen for producing a PSEUDOSTEREO effect from monaural recordings. It embodied time-delay and EQUALIZATION networks to derive two different signals from the single source. It was intended to provide a means for improved listening to the vast number of monaural recordings in existence at the time that commercial stereo records were being introduced.

Stereophonic In common usage, "stereo" has come to mean any sound system with two LOUDSPEAKERS. "Stereophonic," however, refers to a sound system that provides the listener with an illusion of directional realism, regardless of how many channels are used.

Probably the first large-scale test and demonstration of stereophonic reproduction of music was carried out by Harvey Fletcher and his cowork-

26. This entry is copyright © 1999–2003 by Larry Blake and is reprinted with permission.

ers at the Bell Telephone Labs in 1933. In this historic experiment, the Philadelphia Orchestra, playing in Philadelphia, was picked up by three MICROPHONES carefully placed in front of the proscenium. The microphone SIGNALS were amplified and sent over telephone lines to Constitution Hall in Washington, D.C., where they were further amplified and sent to three specially designed high-power loudspeaker systems on the stage. Leopold Stokowski was the conductor of the orchestra, but on this occasion, he was in Constitution Hall, where he controlled the volume of the three reproduced channels. In this way he controlled the musical DYNAMICS of the performance in a way he could not do simply by conducting the orchestra.

As part of the demonstration, a number of experiments were performed by Dr. Harvey Fletcher, who had charge of the development work. On the stage in Philadelphia, a carpenter hammered and sawed, while conversing with his helper; a soloist sang as she walked across the stage; and finally a trumpeter in Philadelphia played antiphonally with another trumpeter on the opposite side of the stage in Washington. It was only when the curtain that hid the loudspeakers was raised that the audience in Washington could believe that what they had heard had not happened on the stage before them.

To present this demonstration in 1933 was a monumental task, for suitable AMPLIFIERS and loudspeakers did not exist, and had to be designed and built just for the event. Great care was taken to ensure high-quality reproduction, and I am sure the standards of excellence set then are seldom equaled today. In any event, the experiment established the fact that three independent microphones, amplifiers, and loudspeakers are sufficient to provide a convincing illusion of spatial perspective.

So successful was this production that when a few years later Dr. Stokowski was asked to direct a local orchestra in the Hollywood Bowl, he insisted that a stereophonic system be installed to reinforce the music. The Bell Laboratories had pioneered the development of sound reinforcement systems and, with the assistance of Electrical Research Products, Inc., undertook this project as a further research in that art. Again, the results were successful; some 25,000 people in the open air were able to hear a program of vocal and instrumental music with ease.

The fact that present-day stereo consists of only two channels is simply due to cost considerations and the relative ease of recording two channels of sound in the single groove of a record. With the advent of the digital COMPACT DISC, there is no such theoretical limitation, and the design could have been done so that three channels rather than two could be recorded. This would have resulted in a true improvement in the realistic reproduction of music in the home, rather than the marginal improvement provided by using DIGITAL technology with only the two channels of conventional stereo.

Stereophonizer A device introduced by Kintek that converts a monaural signal into a 3-channel stereo effect. It is used in certain movie theater sound systems to add width and depth to the sound field in the theater.

Stereophony A term coined by Western Electric Corporation, first used in the 1920s to mean the transmission of sound from one place to another by a STEREOPHONIC system. Stereophonic audio transmission actually dates from 1881. *See also* ADER, CLEMENT.

Stereosonic A term, mostly used in Britain, for INTENSITY STEREO, especially the technique of using two coincident FIGURE-8 MICROPHONES.

The term was also used in 1950 by Murray Crosby for a multiplex FM-stereo system of broadcasting. *See also* FM STEREO.

Sticky Shed A malady that affects certain magnetic tapes, especially those with back coatings and urethane binders. When stored for many years, the binder that holds the magnetic oxide material together becomes soft and sticky, and when the tape is played, some of the oxide rubs off onto the tape recorder tape guides and heads. The oxide adhering to the heads prevents the tape from contacting the head near and over the gap causing the high-frequency response to be degraded and the tape to squeal, and leaving the sticky material on everything that touches the tape. The problem has been studied for some years, and luckily, it was discovered that if the tape is roasted in a 130-degree oven for several hours, the binder regains its integrity and the tape behaves almost as if it were new for a month or so.

Stinger In motion picture music, a short emphasized passage that calls attention to an important event in the story.

Stomp Box A floor-mounted effects device for use in the cable between a guitar and an AMPLIFIER. It has foot-operated switches to turn the effects on and off.

Stopband The FREQUENCY band that is not passed by a FILTER is called the stopband, as opposed to the PASSBAND. A filter can have more than one stopband; for instance a BANDPASS filter will have a high stopband and a low stopband, above and below the filter's passband, respectively.

Storage Cell Any type of electric CELL that can be recharged after being discharged. Examples are the NICKEL-CADMIUM CELL and the LEAD-ACID CELL.

Strapping The interconnection of transformer windings is often referred to as strapping. In many AUDIO and some POWER TRANSFORMERS, there are several primary and secondary windings. They can be connected in SERIES to increase the IMPEDANCE or they can be connected in PARALLEL to reduce the impedance. These connections are frequently made by short pieces of wire between the screw terminals of a terminal strip. The wires are called straps, hence the term strapping.

LINE LEVEL inputs and outputs of professional audio devices often have transformers with two windings. When connected in series, the impedance is 600 OHMS, and when connected in parallel, the impedance will be 150 ohms. This offers the user the choice, depending on application. Power transformers sometimes have a similar arrangement so they can be strapped for 120 VOLTS or 240 volts input.

Streaming Transmission of digital audio or video data to a client (the listener or viewer) in a way that requires it to be monitored in real time as it arrives. An example is listening to a "radio station" via the internet. If the stream of data stops, so does the program. The alternative is to require the client to download the entire media file first. Streaming, however, can be more efficient at distributing the media to many clients at the time of their own choosing, and affords some copy protection.

Strike To remove sets, props, etc., from a theater stage or sound stage. Simply put, it means to clear the stage in preparation for the next act or next production. The term is also used to refer to a single or several items in the set, like "strike the piano."

Stroboscopic Disc A disc made of cardboard or other plastic typically with three circles of dots or bars around the periphery. When the disc is placed on a record-playing turntable and the disc illuminated with fluorescent or neon light, one of the circles of dots appears stationary if the turntable speed is correct. The light flashes at the rate of 120 flashes per second and the time between flashes is just enough for each dot to move one space to take the place of the previous dot. The three circles are for 78.26 rpm, 45 rpm, and 33⅓ rpm, and they contain 92, 159, and 216 dots, respectively. Some turntables have the stroboscopic circles of dots on their underside, with a small observation mirror and neon lamp.

If the turntable has variable speed (which means it is probably never running at the correct speed), the stroboscope is a real help in setting it. If the turntable does not have variable speed, the stroboscope can be used to determine if it is defective or needs lubrication.

In most European countries, the power line frequency is 50 Hz rather than our 60 Hz, and the stroboscopes have fewer dots.

This strobe principle works whenever the light and rotation rates are known, and at least one tape recorder, the Nagra 4 series, had stroboscopic marks on the top of one the rotating tape rollers.

Stylus The business end of the phono CARTRIDGE is the stylus. It consists of a small arm called the CANTILEVER and the stylus tip, which makes contact with the record groove. The ideal shape for a stylus tip is a subject of much controversy. The first styli were conical, with a spherical section at the end.

The conical stylus does not do a perfect job of tracing the stereo record groove due to the PINCH EFFECT, and it has a very small area of contact with the groove. The ELLIPTICAL stylus was introduced to reduce this effect. The top of the elliptical stylus is narrower in the front-back direction than in the side-to-side direction, so it fits better into the groove. The elliptical stylus, however, also has a very small area of contact with the groove, causing relatively rapid wear.

The SHIBATA stylus is somewhat like an elliptical, except the shape is such that the contact area on each side of the groove is a small line rather than a point. It is capable of excellent high-FREQUENCY RESPONSE, and was in fact developed for use in playing CD-4 QUADRAPHONIC records, which had a high-frequency CARRIER signal that had to be picked up. Since that time, several styli have been developed with quite complex shapes, each claiming to be the best compromise for low DISTORTION, low wear, and best frequency response. One of these that was popular was known as the Van den Hul stylus after its inventor.

There is a certain (small) group in the audio field who insist the old conical stylus is best.

Subcarrier In MULTIPLEX radio broadcasting, the subcarrier is an ULTRASONIC signal MODULATED by another signal and then used to modulate the transmitted CARRIER along with the main modulating signal. The subcarrier is normally frequency modulated, but could also be amplitude modulated. *See also* FM STEREO.

Subcode In digital audio systems, particularly CD and R-DAT, additional data are interleaved with the audio information, which carry synchronization and user information such as tags and comments that are independent of the audio data. CD subcodes consist of digital data included on the CD that contains such information as track numbers, track playing times, copyright information, and copy inhibit codes, etc. In the COMPACT DISC format, eight additional bits (one BYTE) containing no AUDIO information are added to each frame of data. This means a byte of information is available from the disc every 136 microseconds. Each bit in the added byte is given a one-letter name: P, Q, R, S, T, U, V, and W. Thus eight separate subcodes can be recorded on and recovered from the CD. So far, only subcodes P and Q are used; the P subcode is used for the pause signal between musical tracks and at the end of the last track and the Q subcode tells the player if the recording is two- or four-channel. (No QUADRAPHONIC player is yet available, however.) The Q subcode also contains timing information about the tracks and identifies the country of origin and date of the recording. The P and Q control bytes also contain the timing information that allows the CD player to cue instantly to the beginning of each selection, display the selection's number and running time, and provide a continuous display of elapsed time. No standard has been defined for the use of the other six sub codes.

The three main types of DAT subcodes are Start IDs that mark the beginning of each song, Program Numbers that are the ordinal numbers assigned to each Start ID, and Skip IDs that cause a player to skip the current Start ID and go to the next one.

Subgroup A term used in mixing consoles where several input channels can be grouped together and their output levels controlled by one gain control that is called a Submaster.

Subharmonic A submultiple, usually one-half, of a fundamental FREQUENCY. Sometimes subharmonics are produced by LOUDSPEAKERS that have poorly controlled CONE resonances. The audible effect is a DISTORTION component one OCTAVE lower than the input signal frequency.

Submaster A control on a recording or sound reinforcement console that controls the level of a mixture, or SUBGROUP, of signals. Several submasters may be fed into a MASTER control for final level control of the console output signal. The use of submasters makes it easier to handle a large number of input signals.

Submini Plug A very small version of the phone plug, with a diameter of 2.5 mm. It is commonly seen on cellular phone earsets and some other audio and control devices where space is at a premium.

Submix The mixture of signals fed into a SUBMASTER control in a recording or sound reinforcement console. The submix is usually a mix of signals that remains constant over a period of time, and it is convenient to control it as a single signal.

Subsequent Reverberation Time Similar to the classic REVERBERATION time except it is measured from the time of arrival of the first reflected sound rather than from the time the sound source is stopped.

Subsonic Literally, "under sound." Actually, subsonic means slower than the speed of sound, but it is often misused to mean sound having frequencies below the human hearing range. The proper term for this is INFRASONIC.

Subtractive Synthesis The technique of generating a desired musical timbre by filtering complex signals generated electronically. Typical WAVEFORMS used in this way are the square wave and the sawtooth wave, both of which sound bright and raucous before filtering to subtract, or attenuate, some of the upper harmonics.

Subwoofer A LOUDSPEAKER system designed to reproduce the very low frequencies from about 16 HERTZ to 100 Hz or so. A subwoofer must be capable of large amounts of POWER output because of our ears' relative insensitivity to low frequencies. Use of a subwoofer also allows using stereo speakers with modest bass response, and our insensitivity to directionality of low bass means only one subwoofer is needed and placement is not stereophonically sensitive.

Super-Cardioid A modification of the CARDIOID microphone to reduce SENSITIVITY to sounds coming from the sides. It is something like a cross between a cardioid and a FIGURE 8 in that it has a somewhat large rear lobe. Its advantage is that it reduces the apparent REVERBERATION by about 1.3 DECIBELS if placed at the same location as a true cardioid. It will pick up the same direct-to-reverberant ratio as an OMNIDIRECTIONAL microphone when it is 1.9 times as far away from the source.

Like all directional microphones, it suffers from PROXIMITY EFFECT.

Superheterodyne A revolutionary type of radio receiver, invented in the late 1920s by Major Edwin F. Armstrong, who also developed FM broadcasting much later. *Superheterodyne* is a contraction of *supersonic heterodyne,* which is actually a misnomer; it should have been called *ultrasonic heterodyne.* In the standard AM superheterodyne ("superhet") receiver, the RADIO FREQUENCY signal is combined with a local OSCILLATOR signal in a "mixer" to produce a beat FREQUENCY of 455 kHz. The 455-kHz signal is called the intermediate frequency (IF) and is always the same regardless of the station being tuned in. This is because the local oscillator is tuned such that the difference frequency between it and the indicated broadcast frequency is 455 kHz. The IF is then amplified through several stages and is detected by a standard DETECTOR of one sort or another. The mixer stage (also call the "first detector") is not a linear mixer as is implied but actually performs a multiplication of the two signals, similar to AMPLITUDE MODULATION. One of the resulting SIDEBANDS is at 455 kHz and is the IF signal. The actual signal detector is called the second detector.

All modern radios, AM and FM, and analog television sets use the superhet principle. The IF in a standard FM receiver is 10.7 MHz rather than the 455 kHz used in AM receivers. The main advantage of the superhet design is that the AMPLIFIER stages always operate at the same frequency and so can be optimized for GAIN and SIGNAL-TO-NOISE RATIO performance.

Supersonic Faster than the speed of sound, as in supersonic aircraft. The term is sometimes mistakenly used to mean sound higher in frequency than the audible range; the correct term for this is ULTRASONIC.

Supply Rails The output terminals of the POWER supply in an AUDIO device are commonly called rails. Each STAGE of the device is connected to the rails via some sort of DECOUPLING circuit. Most modern devices utilize two supply rails, one at a positive (B+) VOLTAGE, and one at a negative (B-) voltage, although there may be several rails at different voltages in certain devices. The common, or GROUND, terminal of the power supply is called a ground BUS rather than a rail.

Supply Reel The reel on a magnetic tape recorder from which is unwound the tape to be recorded or played back. It normally resides on the left-hand side of the machine. The other reel is the TAKEUP REEL.

Supraaural Literally, "on top of the ear." This term refers to headsets that rest on the outer ear, or PINNA. These headsets are necessarily light in weight, and do not exclude external sounds very well. *See also* CIRCUMAURAL.

Surface Mount An electronic circuit board construction technology, using specially formed electronic components such as RESISTORS, CAPACITORS, and INTEGRATED CIRCUITS. The components are designed to have their electrical contacts soldered directly to the surface of the circuit board, as opposed to the traditional method of wire leads going into holes in the board. This technique greatly decreases manufacturing cost as it is highly automatable, and greatly increases component density on circuit boards.

Surround The mechanical suspension that holds the outer edge of the CONE of a dynamic loudspeaker is called the surround. Loudspeaker cone surrounds can be made of many different materials, such as corrugated cloth or paper, polyurethane or other plastic foam, and rubber, and some, called roll surrounds, have a single large semicircular corrugation. Roll surrounds allow a greater amount of cone motion and are relatively linear in their springiness, reducing DISTORTION. Most surrounds are treated with some type of DAMPING material to reduce the effects of cone resonances. *See also* SPIDER.

Surrounds In many modern motion pictures, the sound tracks will include some sound intended to come from behind or beside the viewer. These channels are called surround channels, and the LOUDSPEAKERS are called surround speakers, or simply "surrounds." They are also found in many home theater setups.

One of the aims of QUADRAPHONIC SOUND was to create "surround" sound for the listener.

Surround Sound The sound effects in motion pictures that come from the sides and/or rear of the theater. In the case of the original analog Dolby optical sound tracks, the surround sound was recorded on the film by MATRIXING the sound effects signal into the two stereo channels using the QS technique. In the theater the signal was decoded and sent to the rear and side speakers after passing through a time delay device. The time delay makes the resulting effect sound more distant, although one also needs to take the physical distance of the surround speakers into account. Dolby Stereo movies that were transferred to laserdisc or video tape may contain the original coded sound track intact, although DVDS usually have the sound tracks remixed for home use.

In the case of stereophonic magnetic and digital sound tracks for movies, there have been several schemes employed over the years. Some of these sound tracks were encoded like the Dolby optical sound tracks, but some, especially 70-mm presentations and all the digital systems, have been recorded with at least two independent surround tracks, allowing true stereophonic surround sound. The current 5.1 type surround systems in theaters and DVD all provide for true stereo surround.

Suspension In a dynamic LOUDSPEAKER, the SPIDER and the SURROUND are collectively called the suspension, or suspensions, because they effectively suspend the VOICE COIL in the gap of the magnet.

SVA, Stereo Variable Area A motion picture sound track on film system consisting of two closely spaced optical VARIABLE-AREA sound tracks. SVA sound tracks have existed since the 1930s, but were never a commercial success until Dolby Laboratories applied their type A COMPANDER system to the two tracks, greatly improving the SIGNAL-TO-NOISE RATIO and reducing the distortion. The Dolby system also includes MATRIXING to synthesize a third, or center, channel for three-loudspeaker reproduction and a fourth channel for ambience, or SURROUND SOUND effects. Most modern movies with analog stereo sound tracks employ the Dolby SVA system with their SR companding. *See also* DOLBY DIGITAL.

S-VHS, Super Video Home System An improved videocassette recorder that will record a horizontal resolution of 400 lines, whereas the standard VHS recorder only manages 250 lines. S-VHS accomplishes this with wider video BANDWIDTH and by separating the chrominance (the part of the video signal that carries the color information) and the luminance (the part of the video signal that carries the brightness information), and records them on separate tracks.

The video cassette recorder (VCR) for home use was pioneered by Sony and introduced in 1975 as the Betamax system, and the Japan Victor Company introduced the VHS system in 1976. S-VHS was introduced several years later. Both Betamax and VHS systems used ½-inch recording tape, but were not compatible with each other, which is not surprising. There ensued a battle for market dominance, which VHS finally won, even though the Betamax system was believed to have superior quality by many aficionados.

S-VHS tape has slightly different magnetic characteristics than ordinary VHS tape and has a sensing hole in the bottom of the cassette which S-VHS machines use to determine standard or S-VHS mode. The popular ADAT MDM recorders use S-VHS tape for digital audio. All S-VHS machines include the VHS HI-FI FM analog audio system as well as a linear audio track. Ordinary VHS machines can use S-VHS tape to no detriment, however they cannot play back an S-VHS tape unless specially equipped with a special conversion circuit and then, only at standard resolution.

Swarf British usage for the CHIP of acetate material removed from the surface of the acetate disc during the cutting process.

Sweep When a test tone (usually a SINE WAVE tone) is smoothly varied in FREQUENCY from low to high, or vice versa, it is called a "frequency sweep" or simply a "sweep."

The use of the sine sweep is the classical method for measuring the FREQUENCY RESPONSE of a device.

Sweepable EQ An equalizer section whose center frequency can be adjusted. *See also* EQUALIZER; PARAMETRIC EQUALIZER.

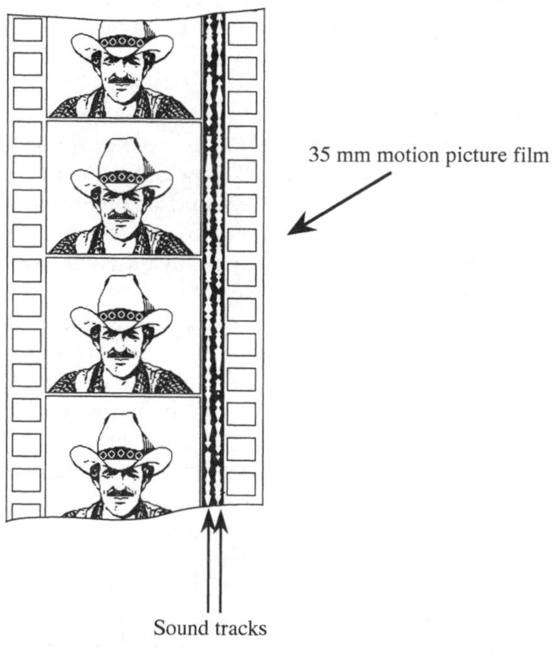

SVA

Sweetening A recording session in which a previously made recording is augmented by the addition of other instruments, usually strings or a vocal chorus. The original recording will have lead vocals and instruments as well as the rhythm tracks. The requirements for sweetening are less demanding on the musicians, and the sweetening can usually be done in a shorter time at a later date. *See also* OVERDUB.

Sweet Spot The listener position in front of stereophonic loudspeakers that provides the optimum listening conditions for tonal balance, stereo separation, etc. In the case of TRANSAURAL systems, which allow loudspeaker listening to BINAURAL recordings, the sweet spot is likely to be very precisely defined, with essentially no binaural effect to be heard at other locations.

In the case of 2-channel stereo, the sweet spot is generally located equidistant from the two speakers and preferably directly in front of each speaker, implying that the speakers should be "toed in" so each one points directly to the listener in the sweet spot.

Swinger An analog phonograph record that has been pressed either with the center hole not exactly centered or with the center hole too big. When played, such a disc will introduce a WOW component at about .5 HERTZ. As small an error as .1 mm will cause audible wow to careful listeners.

Swinging Choke An iron-core INDUCTOR designed so that its inductance varies inversely with the amount of current it passes. Swinging chokes are used as RIPPLE filters in power supplies that are subjected to various load currents. The varying inductance maintains better regulation of the output voltage.

Switched-On Bach An album of the music of J. S. Bach arranged for electronic SYNTHESIZER, produced in 1969 by Wendy Carlos, neé Walter Carlos. This album was probably the most influential of any electronic music recording, for it was the first purely electronic album of "real" music. It had a tremendous popularity and greatly assisted in the promotion of synthesizers as serious instruments.

Synchronous Refers to a type of motor used in many tape recorders and some turntables. A synchronous motor is locked to the 60-HERTZ (U.S.) power line FREQUENCY and always runs at a constant speed, regardless of any VOLTAGE fluctuations. Early AC-powered electric clocks operate with synchronous motors for this reason. Many European turntables and electric clocks also use synchronous motors, but with different gear ratios to run at the correct speed for 50-Hz power.

Synthesizer Strictly speaking, a purely electronic musical instrument which can be used to imitate many different conventional instruments. The accuracy of the imitation varies from synthesizer to synthesizer.

The first synthesizer was built by RCA Research Labs in the 1950s, was called the Mark II, and is a very large affair, using multitudes of vacuum TUBES. Although primitive in terms of the capabilities of today's SOLID-STATE machines, the original synthesizer established the feasibility of music synthesis by electronic means, and it has an interesting characteristic sound. It is still used by some composers to write serious music. It was donated by RCA to the Columbia-Princeton electronic music laboratory in New York many years ago, where it still resides.

Modern solid-state synthesizers are seldom used to imitate natural sounds; it has been demonstrated adequately that in most cases, synthetic imitations of musical instruments are rarely convincing. Synthesizers are used much more for generating special musical sounds that could not be made by conventional instruments. They are also used to modify the TIMBRE of existing instruments, for instance the singing voice.

DIGITAL audio technology has been applied to synthesizers, and some of these units are able to sample or "digitize" the sound from an actual instrument by use of an ANALOG-TO-DIGITAL CONVERTER. In digital form, the sound can then be manipulated in a great many ways, which would be impossible in the ANALOG domain. Digital synthesizers are very popular, and have essentially replaced analog models.

Syntony The principle of tuning a radio receiver to the same FREQUENCY as that of the transmitter. The concept of syntony was first explained by Sir Oliver Lodge before 1900, but Guglielmo Marconi perfected and patented the technique in 1900 for use in wireless telegraphy, as radio was called then. This is one of the most important patents in the history of radio. It may seem obvious now, but it was a revolutionary idea at the time, for it allowed a receiver to select between several transmitting stations. Up to that time, all stations broadcasting were received at once!

T

Tails Out A tape that has not been rewound after being played is said to be "tails out." In general, it is a good idea to store tape recordings tails out and rewind them just prior to playing them. This helps to reduce the effects of PRINT-THROUGH.

Take A recorded performance, or part of a performance, that is to be kept for possible use rather than being recorded over is a take. The various takes are then EDITED into a complete composite performance. In the case of solo performers, it is not unusual to record several hundred takes during the course of a single piece of music.

Take Sheet A sheet of paper on which the recording engineer makes notes about each take as it is recorded. The notes are useful to speed up the editing process.

Take-up Reel On a reel-to-reel tape recorder, the tape moves from the left-hand reel, called the SUPPLY REEL, to the head stack to the CAPSTAN and PINCH ROLLER and then onto the take-up reel.

Talkback Microphone A microphone in the control room of a recording studio or by the control console in a sound reinforcement system to allow the engineer to talk to the performers.

Tangency The orientation of an analog magnetic tape head such that the tape contacts the head for an equal distance on either side of the gap. Poor adjustment of tangency causes uneven head wear on the sides of the gap.

Tape *See* MAGNETIC TAPE.

Tape Head In an analog tape recorder, the TRANSDUCERS that magnetize the tape in response to the input signal and reconvert the magnetization into an electrical signal are called the tape heads. For each track, a tape head consists of a small two-part core of soft iron or other suitable ferro-magnetic material with a COIL of wire wound around it. Between the two parts of the core is a very short gap, over which the tape is moved. CURRENT in the coil causes the tape near the gap to be magnetized in proportion to its strength. Record and reproduce heads are similar in construction, except that the reproduce head has a narrower gap and many more turns of wire in the coil. This increases the SENSITIVITY of the head in picking up signals recorded on the tape.

Another type of tape head is the ERASE HEAD, which is similar to a record head, but has a wider gap. The erase head is fed with a very high FREQUENCY, high-amplitude SIGNAL, usually derived from the bias OSCILLATOR, which effectively demagnetizes the tape just before it reaches the record head. This eliminates any previously recorded signals from the tape.

Some early tape recorders used a permanent magnet as an erase head, and although it did a good job of erasing the signal on the tape, it left the tape in a magnetized condition that greatly increased the noise level of the subsequent recording. Some inexpensive small portable cassette recorders still use permanent magnet erase heads.

Helical-scan recorders such as video, ADAT and R-DAT have several small heads placed near the surface of the rotating aluminum head drum. These small heads, or "POLE PIECES," write and read the magnetization on the

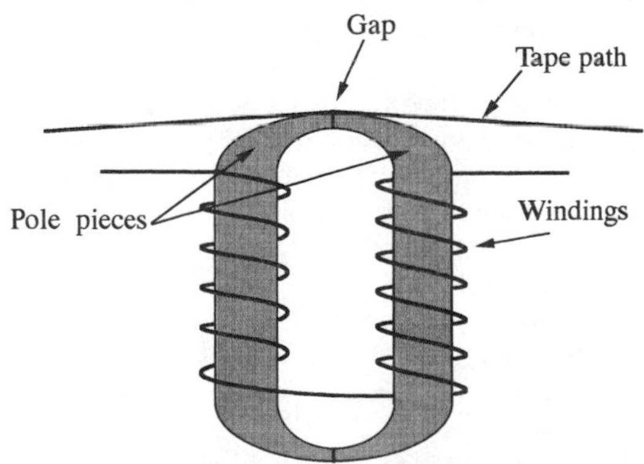

Windings will have many more turns than shown

Tape Head

tape in slanted tracks. Digital recorders have no erase heads, merely overwriting old data at tape saturation level. Video recorders usually have a very traditional analog erase head, but some have a so-called "flying erase head" that is mounted in the rotating head drum and allows accurate erasing and editing.

Tape Hiss The residual NOISE of a blank tape being played; also the tape noise of a recorded tape.

In general, the tape hiss of a blank tape will be less than that of a recorded tape because the recording process, including BIAS and erase, adds some noise to the tape. Tape hiss is distinguished from MODULATION NOISE. The primary cause of tape hiss is the BARKHAUSEN EFFECT.

Tape Lifter A device in an analog reel tape recorder that lifts the tape from the heads during rewind and fast forward to decrease the head wear and sound output. The magnetic coating on tape usually consists of iron oxide, which is an abrasive and will wear the tape heads, especially at high speeds. Audio cassettes move an assembly of all heads and the pinch roller away from the tape during the fast wind modes. R-DAT type recorders don't bother lifting the tape, leaving it on the head drum (with a bit less tension) to enable enough data pickup to provide timecode or ABS time readings.

Tape Pack The smoothness with which magnetic recording tape is wound onto the hub of a reel is called the tape pack, or simply the pack. If the tape wanders around when being wound, the exposed edges of tape are subject to damage, especially if left in this condition for an extended time. This is one reason it is desirable to store tapes "tails out" without rewinding. Most poor tape pack occurs with high-speed winding.

Tape Speed In analog tape recorders, the velocity with which the tape moves across the TAPE HEAD is the tape speed. It is measured in inches per second (IPS) in English-speaking countries, and in centimeters per second elsewhere. Quite important for analog recorders, the actual tape speed is often obscured to the consumer for digital devices in preference for running time.

It is interesting that the tape speed in the first successful commercial tape recorder, the German Magnetophon from the 1930s, used a tape speed of 78.5 centimeters per second, which is close to 30.9 ips. This came about by the use of a CAPSTAN motor turning 1,500 RPM (a four-pole motor operating at 50-HERTZ line FREQUENCY), and a capstan diameter of 1 centimeter. (According to Friederich Karl Engel, of BASF AG in Germany, the Magnetophon motor was not SYNCHRONOUS, and its actual speed was about 1,470 rpm. This gave an actual tape speed of about 30.2 ips.) When Ampex made the first American-built tape recorder (the model 200, introduced on April 25, 1948), they chose 30 ips in order to use English units and still be close to the German practice, which was known to work well. In a similar situation, the German machine used tape of 6.5 millimeters width, and this is very close to ¼-inch, so Ampex and the 3M company chose ¼-inch as a standard width, and it has remained so ever since.

As tape was improved in quality and as Ampex gained expertise in tape recorder electronics and tape head design, they found the same FREQUENCY RESPONSE could be obtained at half the speed, so the next production machine operated at 15 ips. It also was able to operate at 7.5 ips and give acceptable results for noncritical use. The NAB, feeling it was about time to set some standards for tape recording, adopted the 15-ips tape speed and the Ampex-designed DE-EMPHASIS curve as standards. At this time the rest of the world followed suit; European and Japanese machines were also standardized at 15 ips and 7.5 ips, although they did not copy the NAB de-emphasis curve.

With continued improvement in tape formulation and tape head design, comparable performance in frequency response was attainable at 3¾ ips and even 1⅞ ips. The Philips company, in setting the standards for the cassette recorder, chose 1⅞ ips as the speed, and so it remains to this day.

It is important to note that although the successive halvings in tape speed allowed the frequency response to be maintained, other parameters such as HEADROOM (especially at high frequencies) suffered and DISTORTION increased. For this reason, professional-quality analog tape recording is done almost exclusively at 15 ips, with some manufacturers returning to 30 ips.

In analog audio tape recording, the tape speed must be very accurately controlled so the reproduced pitch of the music is the same as the pitch of the source, and the uniformity of the speed is also very crucial (*See* FLUTTER and WOW). In digital audio recording, the actual tape speed is not nearly as important because the audio signal is reconstructed from the digital data on the tape, and is not directly related to the speed of the tape. *See also* HEAD BUMP.

Tape Tension Tension is pulling force, and in any tape recorder, tension on the tape is a critical operating factor. Tension must be just right to maintain proper head contact and mechanical control of the tape. Elaborate mechanical and electronic means have been employed to control tape tension.

Tape Weave An improper gradual up and down motion of magnetic tape as it passes over the TAPE HEADS in a tape recorder, causing tape SKEW. It is usually caused by the tape not having been properly slit, but it can also result from worn tape guides.

TDFD *See* TOTAL DIFFERENCE FREQUENCY DISTORTION.

TDS *See* TIME DELAY SPECTROMETRY.

TEF Originally a trademark of the Crown company that stands for Time-Energy-Frequency and refers to a measurement instrument based on TIME DELAY SPECTROMETRY.

It is possible to display a family of curves that graph the relationship of three different parameters of a SIGNAL. A familiar FREQUENCY RESPONSE CURVE plots two parameters: magnitude of the signal as a function of frequency. If a series of these curves are plotted next to each other on a page, and if each one is measured at a slightly different time, the relationship of frequency, response, and time can be visualized. The curves merge into a three-dimensional surface that is represented in perspective on the paper.

If instead of simply plotting AMPLITUDE response versus frequency and time, the actual energy content of the signal is plotted, the TEF surface is obtained. Such a representation of a signal reveals much information to the trained eye. The performance of a LOUDSPEAKER during the time just after a signal is applied to it is an example of the use of TEF, and these measurements of loudspeakers reveal that various frequencies are produced at different times; in other words, the time delay inherent in a loudspeaker is a function of frequency.

It is also possible to obtain the TEF measurement by means of a dual-channel FFT ANALYZER.

Telephone Hybrid A device designed to couple the audio of a telephone line to a broadcast or recording system, while keeping them electrically isolated and protected from each other. *See also* PHONE PATCH.

Telescope "A device having a relation to the eye similar to that of the telephone to the ear, allowing distant objects to plague us with a multitude of needless details. Luckily, it is unprovided with a bell summoning us to the sacrifice."—A. Bierce.

Television Interference, TVI Analog television broadcast stations transmit very large amounts of energy in the form of synchronizing pulses that are used by the TV receiver to determine when each field of the picture is to start. These "synch" pulses, as they are called, occur at almost exactly 60 per second in NTSC, the same as the AC power line FREQUENCY. (Actually, the line frequency is a little different from the synch frequency, but it is very close.)

If the transmitted TV SIGNAL is picked up by AUDIO equipment, usually by wires and cables leading to AMPLIFIER inputs and outputs, and if the signal is "detected," or rectified, by the first TRANSISTOR or tube it encounters, the audio signal will be contaminated by the synch pulses and will be heard as a 60-HERTZ buzz. Very often, the amount of buzz heard is dependent on the exact location of the cables, which act like antennas. If such a buzz occurs in a sound system, and it changes with movement of the cables or with a person walking about in the room, you can be sure the cause is TVI.

There are many cases where "HUM" exists in sound systems and is blamed on the sound system components resulting in heroic efforts to eliminate it, but elimination of TVI can be very difficult. It involves filtering out the RF signal before it reaches any active component like a transistor. The signal can enter the equipment through the output wires or the power cord, as well as through the input wires.

Telharmonium The first purely electrical musical instrument, invented by Thaddeus Cahill in 1903. It worked on the same principle as the Hammond organ, introduced in 1935, using a group of alternators or AC generators, that produced all the frequencies of the musical scale. Unlike the Hammond organ, which used conventional AMPLIFIERS and LOUDSPEAKERS to produce the sound, the Telharmonium had no amplifiers. (The triode vacuum TUBE was not invented until 1906.) The tones were produced at kilowatt levels by the alternators. These signals were controlled by a keyboard, and switches allowed various tones to be mixed together to make complex WAVEFORMS. Cahill's idea was to transmit the resulting music over telephone lines to subscribers, but he had few takers and eventually went bankrupt.

Temperament In the tuning of a musical instrument to a scale, temperament is the deliberate mistuning of pure or JUST intervals so the various frequency ratios between notes of the scale are compatible with perfect OCTAVES. *See* Appendix 8.

Temporary Threshold Shift, TTS An upward shift in the THRESHOLD OF HEARING caused by exposure to a loud sound. The human ear is remarkably tolerant of abuse, and it has several ways of protecting itself from damage from very loud sounds. One of these is to reduce its SENSITIVITY, causing the hearing threshold to shift upward. If the ear is repeatedly exposed to very loud sounds over a period of years, the temporary shifts will become permanent, and this is permanent hearing loss, or a permanent threshold shift.

Tennis Shoe Remote In the making of some REMOTE recordings, especially of classical music, often the MICROPHONES must be hung from the ceiling, or from some superstructure over the stage. This requires much running back and forth and up and down, stringing microphone cables, suspension cords, and power cords, etc. Such a recording session is called a tennis shoe remote.

Tension Ring Many microphones use a round diaphram of thin plastic or metal, that must be precisely stretched and held taut and stable. The tension ring is the circular piece that uniformly draws the diaphram down over a cylinder, then holds it in position.

Terminal The point at which the SIGNAL either enters or leaves an AUDIO device is a terminal. Strictly speaking, terminals are screws under which wires are placed, but all types of audio connectors are also commonly referred to as terminals

Terminal Impedance Terminal impedance is the impedance seen from either the output or the input terminals of an audio device such as an EQUALIZER when connected to their rated impedance. The device is said to be terminated when connected to the impedance it was designed to work with; sometimes the terminal impedance matches the source impedance, but more often not. *See also* IMPEDANCE; Appendix 11.

Terminal Strip A series of connections, usually screw terminals, arranged in a line to permanently connect multiple audio lines to such devices as recording or broadcast consoles. It is essentially obsolete today in favor of faster methods. When many lines are connected to the same terminal strip, the individual wires are often laced together with linen lacing cord in such a way that they are "fanned" out between the lacing to match the distance between the terminals. Sometimes the terminal strip was called a fanning strip for this reason.

Termination A transmission line is said to be terminated if it is connected to an IMPEDANCE equal to its characteristic impedance. Under these conditions, the SIGNAL will enter the terminating impedance as if it were an infinitely long extension of the line, and no energy will be reflected. If the termination is not correct, a reflection of the signal will occur, and this effect was sometimes heard as an ECHO in old analog long-distance telephone conversations. In the case of television, it is important that the antenna lead-in wire be terminated to prevent reflections that will be seen as ghosts on the screen. Video lines in closed-circuit television systems also need to be properly terminated for the same reason. The termination is frequently a RESISTOR of the proper value, usually 600 OHMS for analog telephone lines, 300 ohms for TV antennas using twin lead, and 75 ohms for video signals using coaxial cables.

There exists a certain amount of confusion about the need for termination of audio transmission systems such as microphone lines. Generally, it is not desirable to terminate a microphone line with an impedance matching the OUTPUT IMPEDANCE of the microphone, because the SIGNAL-TO-NOISE RATIO will suffer. This is because the termination loads the line and reduces the signal VOLTAGE level, which is what the microphone PREAMPLIFIER is sensitive to. If the microphone line were many miles long, it would be necessary to terminate it to prevent reflections, but in relatively short lines and at audio frequencies, reflections do not cause any trouble. *See also* BALANCED LINE; MATCHING.

The term termination is also (mis)used to indicate the proper resistance to which an audio device is intended to be connected. The 47,000-ohm input resistance of phono preamps is an example. The phono CARTRIDGE requires the 47,000 ohms for proper DAMPING, but this is not the same thing as a line termination.

Terrestrial The word "terrestrial" as used by TV people means conventional wireless TV transmission. This is to differentiate it from satellite or cable transmission.

Tertiary A third WINDING in an output transformer, in addition to the normal PRIMARY and SECONDARY, sometimes used in POWER AMPLIFIERS to provide a NEGATIVE FEEDBACK signal. The classic McIntosh tube amplifiers were some of the first to use tertiary winding.

Tesla, Nikola A Serbian-American scientist who conducted many experiments in the transmission of high-frequency radio waves. Had he added a DETECTOR to his apparatus, he would be credited as the inventor of radio. He invented the Tesla coil and many other electrical devices and spent many years of his life attempting to transmit electric power over long distances without wires. He was a great champion of alternating-current power distribution as opposed to direct current, which Edison favored. Tesla is responsible for the establishment of 60 Hz as the standard frequency for power distribution in the United States. He also invented the induction motor, which is the type of motor used today almost to the exclusion of all other types. In his honor, the unit of magnetic flux density is called the tesla. It is equal to 10,000 gauss, which is the older unit of measure.

Tetrode A vacuum TUBE containing four elements, as opposed to the TRI-

ODE, which contains three. The extra element in the tetrode is a screen grid placed between the control GRID and the PLATE. The screen has a high positive voltage on it, and it increases the efficiency of the tube, but at the expense of higher DISTORTION and a higher plate IMPEDANCE. Most modern power output tubes used in audio amplifiers are tetrodes with added beam-forming plates. *See* BEAM POWER TUBE.

THD *See* HARMONIC DISTORTION.

Theremin An unusually clever electronic musical instrument invented in 1919 by Leon Termen, a Russian émigré and engineer living in New York. He changed his name to Leon Theremin in the 1920s. The Theremin had two antennas, and it was played by moving one's hands nearer to and farther from them. One antenna controlled the volume of the sound produced by the instrument, and the other varied the musical PITCH. The pitch was continuously variable, and the sound had a somewhat eerie, other-worldly character. It attracted the attention of a few serious performers for a while, and the idea was brought up to date by Robert Moog with his modular synthesizer.

The Theremin was the subject of a fascinating documentary movie titled *Theremin: An Electronic Odyssey* made in 1993, directed by Steven Martin. Mr. Theremin lived into his nineties and died shortly after the documentary was released.

Thermal Noise *See* JOHNSON NOISE.

Thermionic Emission The process by which the CATHODE in a vacuum TUBE emits electrons by being heated to a red-hot temperature. In Britain, tubes are sometimes called thermionic valves.

Thiele-Small Parameters Characteristics of DIRECT RADIATOR loudspeakers that can be used to predict the low-frequency performance of the LOUDSPEAKER under various conditions of baffling (*see* BAFFLE).

Australian researchers Neville Thiele and Richard Small identified several parameters that can be used in the analysis of both closed-box and ported loudspeaker systems. These parameters can be deduced from two IMPEDANCE measurements of the loudspeaker itself, one in open air and one with the DRIVER mounted in a closed box of known volume.

The Thiele-Small parameters are: DC resistance of the driver, resonant FREQUENCY of the driver, the impedance at RESONANCE, the mechanical Q of the driver, the electrical Q of the driver, the total Q of the driver, the equivalent volume of the compliance of the driver, the acoustic compliance of the driver suspension, the acoustic mass of the driver diaphragm assembly, the acoustic resistance of the driver suspension, the product of the magnetic flux density and coil length, and the acoustic efficiency.

Third Octave Filter Commonly heard corruption of ONE-THIRD OCTAVE FILTER.

Three-Step Processing *See* PROCESSING.

3:2 Pulldown A clever method of matching the 24 per second frame rate of motion pictures to the 30 per second frame rate of NTSC television. Simply put, 24 frames of film must be "stretched out" to fill 30 frames of video. This is equivalent to stretching 4 frames of film onto 5 frames of video. This

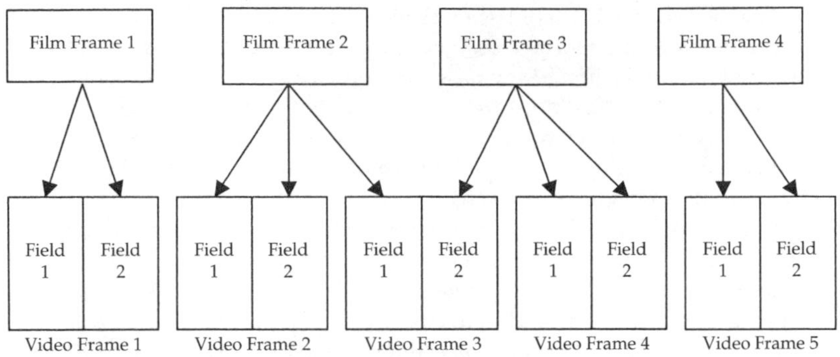

3:2 Pulldown

is possible because 30 frames of video contain 60 interlaced fields. Here is the procedure:

The first and second frames of film are used for both fields of the first two video frames. So far, so good. Video frames 3 and 4 are treated differently, as follows: Field 1 of video frame 3 is taken from the film frame 2, BUT field 2 of video frame 3 is taken from film frame 3. Then, field 1 of video from 4 is taken from film frame 3 and field 2 of video frame 4 is taken from film frame 4. Then, both fields of video frame 5 are from film frame 4.

So, film frames 1 and 4 are translated directly to video frames 1 and 5, and film frames 2 and 3 are combined to make frames 2, 3, and 4 of video, or "3:2 pulldown."

This is cheating, of course, because film frames 2 and 3 are different, so the video frames derived from both of them is garbled a little, depending on how fast the motion is moving. The actual result is that some artifacts are present in the video presentation, such as some "fluttering" of motion and a visible horizontal line once in a while.

Threshold of Hearing The softest sound that a normal human ear can detect is called the threshold of hearing, and it varies in absolute strength at different frequencies. The threshold for 1,000 HERTZ is taken as a SOUND PRESSURE of 20 micropascals, and this is the zero DECIBEL point of the SOUND PRESSURE LEVEL scale. The threshold for 3,000 Hz is several dB lower than this, our ears being more sensitive in this FREQUENCY range. As the frequency goes down, the threshold gradually rises, until at 30 Hz it is some 40 dB higher than at 1,000 Hz. *See also* FLETCHER-MUNSON EFFECT; MINIMUM AUDIBLE FIELD.

THX™ or THX Ltd. A company originally formed in 1983 as a division of Lucasfilm Ltd. Tomlinson Holman was hired by Lucasfilm to design a higher quality motion picture theater sound system for their dubbing stages. The THX division was formed to license the design to movie theaters and verify that the licensed theaters hold to the THX specifications. The theory was that if studios used THX dubbing stages to mix their movies, and consumers heard them in THX-approved theaters, everyone would hear the same high quality sound. The letters ostensibly stand for Tom Holman's eXperiment, but note also that one of George Lucas's early films was titled THX-1138. THX Ltd. was spun off into its own company in 2002, although reportedly a majority of it is still owned by Lucasfilm.

THX has expanded into activities such as certifying home audiovisual equipment and car audio systems, quality control of commercial laserdiscs, videotapes, and DVDs, cinema and studio consulting, and studio mixing equipment. They market no hardware of their own except for the loudspeaker crossover network in the commercial movie theater system. THX is not a form of encoding or a delivery system. A THX theater can play analog, digital, mono, stereo, Dolby, DTS, etc., to their quality specifications. In order to be licensed as a THX theater, special care must be taken in all aspects of the sound system design and installation, including such things as the acoustics of the room and even the building materials used in the space behind the screen.

Tight The low-FREQUENCY performance of a LOUDSPEAKER is said to be "tight" if it is relatively free of HANGOVER, or in other words, is well DAMPED. A recording using CLOSE MIKING is described as "tight." Conversely, sometimes poorly damped systems are said to sound "loose."

TIM *See* TRANSIENT INTERMODULATION DISTORTION, also called Dynamic Intermodulation (DIM).

Timbre Timbre, pronounced tamber, refers to the subjective quality or "tone color" of a sound. It is not related to PITCH or LOUDNESS. It is timbre that allows us to tell the difference between musical instruments. The timbre of a sound depends on many factors, including the strength and number of PARTIALS present.

The character of the beginning and ending TRANSIENT sounds of a tone has more to do with the timbre of the tone than its HARMONIC content. For instance, if a tape recording of a piano is played backward, it sounds very much like a harmonium, although the OVERTONE structure is unchanged. This illustrates the importance of the shape of beginning transients, or "attacks," of the sound. A harmonium recording played backwards does not sound like a piano, but still sounds like a harmonium. There have been experiments performed where the attack of one instrument is spliced onto the steady-state sound of another instrument, and in almost all cases, the sound is identified as the instrument that supplied the attack. For instance, an oboe attack spliced onto a violin steady-state sounds much more like an oboe than a violin.

It is commonly said that the piano gets its characteristic timbre from the fact that its partials are all out of tune with the FUNDAMENTALS, an effect called "stretching." If this were the case, it would still sound like a piano when played backward, for the tuning of the partials is the same each way.

There are many unanswered questions about timbre. For example, the flute sounds as if it has a simple tone with few if any harmonics, but a SPECTRUM ANALYZER shows the flute to produce a complete array of harmonics. It is the attack which determines the timbre of the flute, for even if a flute attack is spliced onto a clarinet steady-state, the resulting timbre is very much like the flute.

Some instruments produce a pitch one would not expect from the frequencies of the sounds produced. For instance, the bass recorder sounds an OCTAVE lower than it should, and the human whistle sounds one or even two octaves lower that its frequency would indicate. *See also* PITCH; FUNDAMENTAL TRACKING.

Time Alignment In a multiple-driver LOUDSPEAKER system, it is important that the time delay of each DRIVER and its associated CROSSOVER NETWORK be the same to preserve accurate TRANSIENT response. In other words, the high frequencies and the low frequencies must reach the listener's ear at the same time. A system that meets this criterion is said to be "time aligned."

Unfortunately, drivers differ in their time delays, WOOFERS generally having more than TWEETERS. Crossover networks also have different delays depending on the FREQUENCY range they cover. One way to correct this is to place the tweeter farther from the listener than the WOOFER, and this is done in some systems. Another way is to specially design the crossover network to add suitable electrical delay to the high-frequency SIGNAL.

The term "time-align" in this regard is copyrighted as a trademark by Edward Long.

Time Code A special nonaudio SIGNAL used to record elapsed time on a tape track. A time code is useful in allowing later synchronization of the audio tracks with another tape recording or with a motion picture that was shot at the same time as the recording was made. *See also* SMPTE TIME CODE.

Time Constant In an EQUALIZER CIRCUIT consisting of a RESISTOR and a CAPACITOR, the time constant is the product of the two values, or RC. The time constant determines the FREQUENCY RESPONSE of the equalizer, even though the values of the R and C may be different in different circuits. It is only the product of the two that determines the CUTOFF FREQUENCY.

Many PRE- and DE-EMPHASIS circuits are specified in standards by their time constants because this is simpler than specifying the frequency response CURVE. Thus, a 70-microsecond curve in a tape recorder specifies a certain de-emphasis curve, and the manufacturer can choose his Rs and Cs at will in order to attain it.

Time Delay Spectrometry, or TDS A method for measuring the FREQUENCY RESPONSE of a device. In essence, TDS is the measurement of the response of a device over a certain time interval after the excitation of the device occurs. This allows measurement of such TRANSDUCERS as LOUDSPEAKERS in real rooms, excluding from the measurement the sound reflections from the room's surfaces. The basic technique has been around for many years, but the late Richard Heyser resurrected it and greatly refined it for use in AUDIO testing.

TDS of a loudspeaker is accomplished by using a LINEAR SINE-WAVE SWEEP as an excitation SIGNAL. The response of the device is picked up by a precision MICROPHONE at some distance from the speaker, and this response signal is passed through a sweeping BANDPASS FILTER whose sweep rate matches that of the excitation sine wave source. The sweep of the filter is delayed in time, or "offset," in order to compensate for the propagation time of the sound from the test speaker to the microphone. The signal from the speaker will arrive at the microphone just in time to get through the filter, but other signals, such as background noise and reflections from the room walls, will arrive at the microphone too late to get through because the filter will be tuned to a new FREQUENCY by that time. Thus the SIGNAL-TO-NOISE RATIO of a TDS measurement can be very large, and measurements can be obtained in quite noisy environments.

It might seem that TDS is a magical technique, allowing measurements to be made that could never be done by any other technique. To some extent this is true, but a careful analysis shows that the increase in signal-to-noise ratio is accompanied by a decrease in frequency resolution, and that the size of the room (and the speed of sound) determines the ultimate frequency resolution attainable.

An important benefit of the TDS technique is the ability to generate TEF, or Time-Energy-Frequency, curves.

Tin Ear A "Tin Ear" is someone who is unable to appreciate the fine points of quality sound reproduction, sometimes by his or her own admission, but usually not. The typical Tin Ear probably has no physiological problems with the hearing mechanism, but simply lacks interest or experience. The poor fellow, however, is much disdained by the GOLDEN EAR.

Tip, Ring, and Sleeve, TRS A type of PHONE PLUG found on PATCH CORDS used for balanced audio signals. It makes three separate contacts. On the balanced line, the tip is the "hot,"or "signal +"; the ring is the "low," or "signal –" side. The sleeve is connected to the SHIELD of the cord; the tip and ring are connected to the twisted pair of wires enclosed within the shield. The plug is designed so it does not cause a momentary SHORT between the high and low sides of the signal. The most common TRS design is ¼-inch in diameter, but there are other sizes.

The tip, ring, and sleeve plug dates from the early days of telephone exchanges and is still in wide use today. The telephone or MIL spec design of the real TRS plug is not quite the same as that of the commonly seen commercial stereo phone plug, for the tip and ring are smaller in diameter. Some stereo phone jacks will make connections with a standard TRS plug. All similar versions may be called TRS plugs, and sometimes stereo plugs since commercial TRS plugs are used on stereo headphones. The similar commercial TS plug looks nearly the same, but has only two contacts, the tip and the sleeve.

TOC Table of contents (TOC) is the inner track of a COMPACT DISC, and contains information about the disc such as number of tracks, their position on the disc, the timing, and disc identification number.

TOGAD Tone-operated gain-adjusting device. The TOGAD was the control circuitry in the FANTASOUND system that responded to the tones recorded on the control track for the purpose of varying the apparent location and volume of the stereophonic sound image. It was used for the roadshow performances of the movie Fantasia in 1940 and 1941. A similar technique was pioneered by Harvey Fletcher and his co-workers several years earlier in their Stereophonic Sound Film System (SSFS).

Tone Tone refers to a SIGNAL that has a particular and usually steady PITCH. The simplest of tones are SINUSOIDS, or sine waves, and they are used a great deal as test signals for AUDIO equipment. The signals recorded on tape recorder ALIGNMENT TAPES are called tones and are sine waves of several frequencies.

Tone also refers to TIMBRE, or quality of a musical sound. Tone can be described by many different analogies, such as "bright," "mellow," "harsh," "tubby," "muddy," etc. *See also* TONE CONTROL.

Tonearm The mechanical assembly in a phonograph that contains the CARTRIDGE and allows it to move in such a manner that the STYLUS makes contact with the record groove at the proper angle and with the proper forces. The tonearm is much more important than it would seem at first glance, and its design has a great deal to do with the way the record will sound and the wear it will experience.

The tonearm must be pivoted in both horizontal and vertical directions in order to allow proper freedom of motion for the stylus. In most tonearms, the entire mass of the arm and cartridge must be dragged across the record by a force on the stylus and cantilever as the record is played. This results in a greater force and consequently greater wear on the outside of the groove wall than on the inside. (But *see also* ANTI-SKATING DEVICE.) Therefore, the friction in the arm pivots must be very low: friction in the vertical pivot causes undue vertical forces on the stylus, and friction in the horizontal pivot causes undue horizontal forces. Sometimes these forces can be so great that the stylus will skip from one groove to the next.

The tonearm must also shield the SIGNAL from the cartridge to the wiring leading to the PREAMPLIFIER input, and this must not add significant friction or noise. For this reason, the tonearm is almost always made of conductive material, and is grounded to the amplifier CHASSIS.

The geometry of the tonearm can be optimized by such design features as making the cartridge form an angle with the arm itself. This is called "offset," and minimizes the tracking angle error. The vertical pivot should be placed in the plane of the record so that a warped record will not result in any back-and-forth motion of the stylus in the groove. This "scrubbing" action of the stylus causes audible WARP WOW.

Although most tonearms are pivoted, i.e., they cause the stylus to swing in an ARC as it plays the record, this does not provide the ideal geometry as far as the stylus and groove are concerned. The record is cut on a RECORDING LATHE where the cutting stylus is carried across the record in a straight line, so that it makes a constant angle with the surface of the record and with the groove itself. The pivoted arm causes the playback stylus angle to vary constantly as the record is played, and this causes a certain amount of record wear and a small amount of DISTORTION as well. Some tonearms are designed to move the cartridge in a straight line to match that of the cutter in order to eliminate these effects. Some such designs work very well, while others introduce other problems such as mechanical RESONANCE and/or more friction. *See also* TONEARM RESONANCE.

Tonearm Resonance The STYLUS of a phono CARTRIDGE is fastened to a springy cantilever, and the tonearm-cartridge assembly has mass. This forms a spring-mass RESONANCE system similar to a weight hanging on a spring. The stiffness of the cantilever is directly proportional to the resonant FREQUENCY: the greater the stiffness, the higher the resonant frequency. The mass of the system is inversely proportional to the frequency: the greater the mass, the lower the resonant frequency. (The stiffness of the cantilever is seldom specified, but, instead, the compliance is usually specified by the cartridge manufacturer. The compliance is the reciprocal of stiffness, or 1 divided by the stiffness.)

If the frequency of the resonance in question is in the audible range, it will be excited by the motion of the stylus as it traces the groove, and an increase in output at that frequency will occur, resulting in a PEAK in the response CURVE. If the resonance is very strongly excited, it can result in the stylus leaving the groove entirely, causing skipping. For this reason, the resonance is kept below the lowest frequency recorded on the record. But it should not be so low that it would be excited by other disturbances, such as eccentricity of the record or warps in the record. The best frequency for the resonance to have is about 10 HERTZ. To attain this with high compliance cartridges requires arms with very low mass. Unfortunately, the needed information to determine the resonance frequency is usually not available to the consumer, complicating the selection of tonearms and cartridges.

In some tonearm systems, attention is paid to the DAMPING of this resonance, and this is a good idea. Tonearm damping acts like the shock absorbers on a car, reducing the amount of motion at the resonance and making the entire system more stable, especially from floor vibrations, etc.

Tone Burst A test SIGNAL composed of several cycles of a SINE WAVE. The tone burst is a TRANSIENT signal, with FREQUENCY content above and below the frequency of the sine wave itself.

Tone bursts have been used as test signals for LOUDSPEAKERS for many years, where they show the effects of HANGOVER. The frequency of the burst can be chosen to match that of a mechanical resonance, and the amount of hangover is a measure of the DAMPING of the RESONANCE.

Tone Control One or more knobs on an audio AMPLIFIER or PREAMPLIFIER that modify the relative balance between the treble (high-frequency) tones and the bass (low-frequency) tones. Tone controls are actually EQUALIZERS, and they change the FREQUENCY RESPONSE curve of the

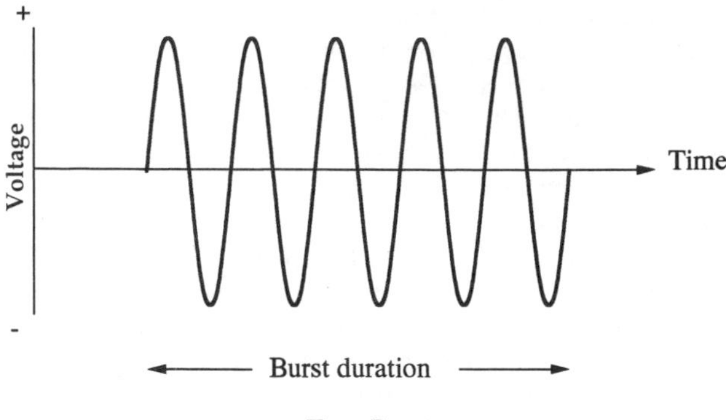

Tone Burst

device containing them. Mixing consoles will refer to the tone controls collectively as EQ.

Tone controls vary a great deal in their design and in the effects they have on the SIGNAL. The earliest tone controls were simply variable LOW-PASS FILTERS, designed to reduce the effect of noisy 78-RPM records and noisy AM radio reception.

By far the most common configuration today is the familiar bass and treble controls. They are designed so that in midrotation they have no effect, yielding FLAT FREQUENCY RESPONSE. Leftward rotation reduces the bass or treble, and rightward (clockwise) rotation increases the level of the applicable frequency range. The ostensible purpose of tone controls is to compensate for minor irregularities in individual loudspeaker systems, or to compensate for less than ideal placement of the loudspeakers. Some designs work very well for this, causing only subtle changes in the sound of the system, while other designs allow gross DISTORTION of the frequency response to be made. Some home-type equipment even contains GRAPHIC EQUALIZERS for tone controls, and they must be used with discretion to avoid such distortion.

Because of the prevalence of the exaggerated effects mentioned above, some audio aficionados have come to believe that no tone controls are any good, and they refuse to use them at all, thinking any modification of the tonal BALANCE must be a distortion. This, however, is wishful thinking, for there is no such thing as a perfectly flat recording/reproducing chain, especially when MICROPHONES, records, amplifiers, CARTRIDGES, COMPACT DISC players, and LOUDSPEAKERS, etc., are available from such a great number of different manufacturers, each deciding what the optimum tonal balance is.

We have rarely heard a sound system that did not benefit from at least the subtle application of tone controls.

Tonic The reference pitch on which a musical scale is built; the "do" of the familiar "do-re-mi-. . . ." It is defined in terms of the musical note rather than in terms of absolute FREQUENCY. If one changes the key of a musical selection from C to A flat, this is a change of the tonic from the note C to the note A flat.

Top A term for the uppermost octave or so of the response of a LOUDSPEAKER or other audio device. The term is used more in Britain than in the United States.

Top Hat A plastic disc about 10½ inches in diameter with a 5⁄16-inch hole and a handle in the center, designed for placing over a PANCAKE of audio tape on a tape recorder. The top hat takes the place of the upper reel FLANGE and allows the smooth WINDING of tape. Sometimes called simply a hat.

Topology Topology is a branch of geometry that deals with the way points in a plane or in space are connected to each other, without regard to the actual distances or angles between them. It is sometimes called "rubber sheet geometry." In topology, a circle and an ellipse are equivalent, a sphere and an ellipsoid are equivalent; but a plane, a Möbius strip, and a torus (donut) are very different from one another.

In an electronic CIRCUIT containing RESISTORS, CAPACITORS, and TRANSISTORS, etc., the actual geometry of the circuit is less important than the topology; the order in which the components are connected is much more important than their physical layout. (The physical layout can also be very important in some circuits because of capacitive and magnetic COUPLING, and this must be taken into account when designing the circuit.) Circuit designs are thus sometimes called "topologies."

Toroidal Sometimes TRANSFORMERS are wound on cores shaped more or less like donuts (or toroids, as the mathematicians would have us call them).

Toroidal transformers are very efficient because they retain almost all the magnetic field inside the toroidal shape. There is little leakage of the field away from the assembly, and therefore toroidal power transformers cause less induced 60-HERTZ HUM in nearby CIRCUITS. They are difficult to wind, however, and are more expensive than conventional "E-core" transformers.

TOSLINK A consumer fiber-optic connector used to convey an optical S/PDIF digital audio data stream. It is short for Toshiba Link, for the company that invented it.

Total Difference Frequency Distortion, TDFD A method of measuring NONLINEAR distortion proposed by the IEC in 1982 and based on a suggestion first published in JAES by A. N. Thiele in 1975.

The test is a type of INTERMODULATION measurement scheme where two low-distortion sine tones of frequencies F1 and F2 are passed through the device under test (DUT), and the amount of energy at the intermodulation frequencies is measured. The tones are almost but not exactly a musical fifth apart (a FREQUENCY ratio of 2:3). The IEC recommendation is 8 KILOHERTZ for F1 and 11.95 kHz for F2. This gives rise to two intermodulation products, F2 – F1 and 2F1 – F2, which lie 100 HERTZ apart in frequency about an OCTAVE below F1 on a piano. These tones are quite easy to isolate from the test tones with a FILTER. The total energy in these tones is expressed as a percentage of the energy in the parent tones, something like the way total HARMONIC DISTORTION (THD) is expressed. One advantage of TDFD is that it is much more sensitive than THD and much lower quantities of distortion can be measured. This is because THD measurements are contaminated by WIDEBAND noise in the DUT output; whereas with TDFD, all the distortion is in the two closely spaced components, and it is measured through a narrowband filter that discriminates against the noise. It is said that distortion of less than 0.0001 percent (one part per million) can be measured accurately with this technique.

The method is applicable to measurements on PREAMPS, AMPLIFIERS, LOUDSPEAKERS, and tape recorders.

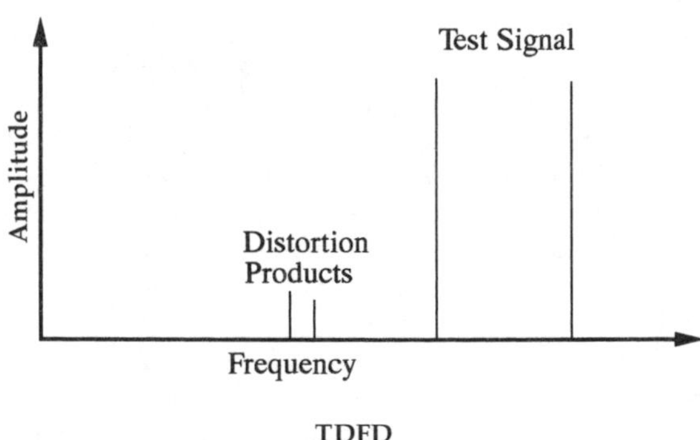

TDFD

Total Harmonic Distortion, or THD *See* HARMONIC DISTORTION.

Totem Pole Gyrator A type of GYRATOR circuit that uses four RESISTORS, a CAPACITOR, and two OPAMPS in a configuration that looks on paper something like a totem pole.

T-Pad A type of ATTENUATOR typically consisting of three resistors arranged schematically in the form of the letter T. It can have a fixed amount of attenuation or can be variable, in which case, the three resistors are replaced with POTENTIOMETERS that are GANGED together. The variable T-pad presents constant input and OUTPUT IMPEDANCES to its associated circuitry regardless of the attenuation and was often used as a master gain control in passive audio consoles. See figure at ATTENUATOR for schematic.

Trace A term sometimes used for the copper conductors on etched circuit boards. *See also* FOIL.

Tracing Distortion Records are cut with a chisel-shaped cutting STYLUS with a very sharp point, and this point accurately follows the audio WAVEFORM being recorded. The record is reproduced, however, with a stylus having a round cross section with a finite radius. This means that the reproduced waveform will be distorted because the playback stylus cannot follow precisely the curve of the groove bottom.

This can be visualized by considering the chisel-shaped cutter moving side to side as it cuts the groove. The groove will be narrower when the cutter is moving sideways the fastest, and will be wider when the cutter is at the extremes of its motion. The groove thus will become narrower in its midpoints and wider at its extremes. The playback stylus will be forced upwards in the narrow parts and will fall downwards at the wider parts. In other words, it is "pinched" out of the groove periodically. This is sometimes called the PINCH EFFECT.

Because the stereo CARTRIDGE is sensitive to vertical as well as horizontal motion, this pinched motion adds to the SIGNAL, and is manifested as HARMONIC DISTORTION. The smaller the tip radius, the smaller the effect; and an elliptical stylus, with smaller side radii, minimizes it. There are other special stylus shapes designed to have even smaller side radii than an elliptical, and they do reduce tracing distortion.

It is possible to "pre-distort" the signal fed to the cutter in such a way as to cancel out tracing distortion, but it can only work for one playback tip radius. Because these tip radii exist in many different sizes and shapes, this is only a compromise at best.

Track and Hold *See* SAMPLE AND HOLD.

Track-at-Once, TAO A CD-R production method in which one or more tracks are recorded at a time and a link is written between the tracks. This method is often used to create multisession CD-RS. A disadvantage of track-at-once recording is that gaps between tracks must be at least two seconds in length. *See also* DISC-AT-ONCE.

Tracking When producing a modern multitrack recording, the first step is usually to record the separate instruments and vocals on their own audio tracks, but with less regard to the later MIXDOWN. This is called tracking.

Many types of tape transports using rotary head technology, such as DAT, videotape, and ADAT, must control the tape motion and synchronization of the rotating head with the track location in the tape. This is also called tracking. In most such systems a SERVO system detects tracking pulses recorded on the edge of the tape and automatically makes required small adjustments in the tape speed. In most video recorders, there is also a knob labeled tracking that adjusts for differences in the machine geometry of different machines when playing a tape made on another machine. Once adjusted manually the servo will take over and maintain alignment.

Tracking Error Because the TONEARM of a record player is pivoted at the stationary end, the STYLUS moves across the record in an ARC and meets the groove at an ever-changing angle. The cutting stylus, however, moves in a straight line, always 90 degrees to the groove direction. This condition is called tracking error. If the CARTRIDGE is mounted to the end of the arm at a suitable angle (called the offset angle), the error can be made to be zero at two places on the record and only a few degrees in the worst case. Several schemes for straight-line tracking have been developed over the years, some with greater success than others. Some of these "tangential" tracking arms are quite complex, with motor-driven SERVO systems moving the cartridge across the record. Most people consider the slight improvement in tracking to be not worth the effort and expense involved.

Trank *See* TRANSCRIPTION.

Transaural Stereo A technique of recording and playback where a BINAURAL head is used to make the recording, but instead of listening to it via headphones, two loudspeakers are used. In order to simulate binaural hearing conditions using loudspeakers, the two signals must be specially processed to cancel the CROSSTALK between the channels caused by the fact that each ear hears both loudspeakers. In a true binaural listening situation, each ear hears only the sound from its corresponding microphone in the dummy head. In a transaural system, the crosstalk signal heard in each ear is canceled by inserting an inverted replica of that signal in the opposite channel. If the inserted signal is an exact replica of the crosstalk signal, it will completely cancel at the ear of the listener, giving the effect of true binaural listening. The problem is to determine what the crosstalk signal actually is and then to generate it. There are several schemes available for doing this, one of which was patented by Atal and Schroeder in 1966. The schemes enjoy varying degrees of success. It should be noted that every listener has a unique physiology, and the correct cancellation signal for one person will not be correct for another. However, exact cancellation is not required for a convincing effect, and the listener is relieved of the burden of wearing a headset, contributing to the sense of realism. *See also* BINAURAL RECORDING.

Transconductance In vacuum TUBES, transconductance is the ratio of a small change in PLATE current to a small change in GRID voltage. It is expressed in units of CONDUCTANCE, originally micromhos but now microsiemens. The transconductance of a tube is closely related to its voltage GAIN.

Transcription Before the advent of the tape recorder, 16-inch ACETATE discs were used to record radio broadcasts for later playback at a more suitable time, usually in another time zone. Some transcriptions were cut from the inside out, and some used vertical groove modulation rather than lateral. A typical standard transcription would play for a half-hour per side—in fact, many were only recorded on one side. A smaller version also existed that was 12 inches in diameter and played for 15 minutes. These transcriptions, originally thought to be needed for one playing only, are the only records of old radio programs in existence and are quite valuable now as collector's items.

In the vernacular of radio station personnel, transcriptions were called "tranks" or ETs (ET standing for "electrical transcription").

Transducer A transducer is a device that converts mechanical, magnetic, or acoustic energy into electrical energy, or vice versa. Examples of transducers are MICROPHONES, phono CARTRIDGES, LOUDSPEAKERS, TAPE HEADS, and disc cutting heads. In general, the transducers are the weakest links in an AUDIO chain, and cause most of the DISTORTION. The primary problem with electromechanical transducers is that they are NONLINEAR except for relatively small ranges of signal FREQUENCY and AMPLITUDE. In other words, they have a limited DYNAMIC RANGE compared to music, which has energy spread over at least a 90-DECIBEL range. This is a factor of 1 billion in power!

Transformer A transformer is a device consisting of two or more coils of wire wound on a common core of soft iron or other magnetically permeable material. The number of turns in one coil divided by the number of turns in the other one is called the turns ratio. An alternating VOLTAGE across one coil will appear across the other coil multiplied by the turns ratio.

Some transformers are designed to operate at 60 HERTZ and to handle a large amount of CURRENT. They are called power transformers, and are found in almost all electronic equipment to change the 110-volt line voltage to suitable values. A large version of this type of transformer is found on utility poles by your house.

Audio transformers are designed to operate at audible frequencies, and are used to step audio voltages up and down and to send signals between devices such as MICROPHONES and tape recorders, etc., while maintaining electrical isolation. *See also* BALANCED LINE.

The turns ratio of a transformer always determines the relative voltages at the input (primary) and output (secondary) terminals, but the IMPEDANCE ratio of a transformer is equal to the square of the turns ratio because the INDUCTANCE of a coil is proportional to the square of the number of turns. Because the power in the signal is conserved between the input and output of a transformer, it can be shown that a 2:1 step-up transformer will have a 4:1 impedance ratio. A 100-OHM resistor across the secondary of a 2:1 transformer will be reflected at the primary as 25 ohms. Usually, audio transformers are rated by their impedance ratios rather than their turns ratios. A microphone input transformer might be rated as 150 ohms to 15,000 ohms. Such a transformer will have a turns ratio of the square root of 100:1, or 10:1. One millivolt generated by the microphone will be transformed into 10 millivolts at the secondary, and a 15,000-ohm impedance connected to the secondary will look like 150 ohms to the microphone.

Transformers are nice because they can provide voltage GAIN without

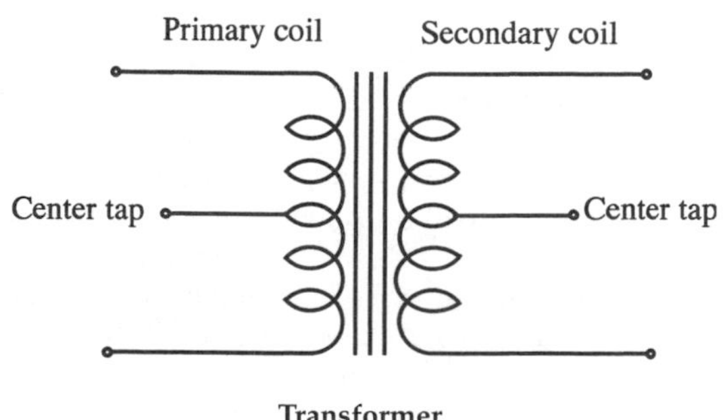

Transformer

significant NOISE increases, but they do add a certain, although small, amount of DISTORTION. In recent years, much effort has been expended in refining transformer design, and much progress has been made. Today, one can find audio transformers with very wide FREQUENCY RESPONSE and uniform PHASE response, along with very low distortion.

Transient A transient is a nonperiodic, or nonrepeating, sound WAVEFORM or electrical SIGNAL. Music contains many transients, such as the attacks of musical instruments, especially percussion instruments. The consonants of speech are transients.

Transients are more difficult to record and reproduce without DISTORTION than are steady-state sounds. A TRANSDUCER or AMPLIFIER with perfect transient response must have uniform FREQUENCY RESPONSE, but also must have uniform PHASE response. Transients in music are often of much higher AMPLITUDE than the average amplitude level, and they can cause OVERLOAD of devices with too little HEADROOM. How an amplifier or other device recovers from a momentary overload has a great deal to do with its sound quality.

The achievement of adequate transient response in all parts of an audio recording and reproducing system is an ongoing quest.

Transient Intermodulation Distortion, TIM A type of dynamic INTERMODULATION DISTORTION that occurs in FEEDBACK amplifiers and is caused by NONLINEAR operation of the GAIN stages within the FEEDBACK LOOP. It occurs when the input signal VOLTAGE contains a very rapid change. In essence, the cause of TIM is that an AMPLIFIER has a finite transit time for a signal going through it, and this means the feedback is a little late in its ability to reduce distortion. A rapidly changing signal gets through the amplifier before the feedback can control it. TIM is also called "slew-induced distortion." *See* SLEW RATE. There is no standard for measuring TIM, and several methods are used by different investigators. TIM affects the sound of very high frequency, high-level sounds, such as that of a cymbal crash at short range, and the result is the addition of low frequencies, causing a muddying or "thickening" of the sound. To reduce TIM, amplifiers are used that have a very wide OPEN LOOP BANDWIDTH, which is another way of saying that their transit time is very short. Early forms of INTEGRATED CIRCUIT OPAMPS are notorious for large amounts of TIM.

DIGITAL audio systems are also capable of a type of slew-induced distortion. In DAC theory, it is assumed that the DAC output moves instantaneously from one level to another, creating a "staircase" WAVEFORM with vertical transitions. The actual steepness at the output of a practical DAC-DEGLITCHER combination will be determined by the slew rate of the output amplifier. If the slew rate is too low, small triangular pieces will be cut out of the staircase, causing an error or distortion that is a nonlinear function of the input signal. This is slew-induced distortion, and the problem does not stop at the output of the deglitcher. The signal at this point still contains voltage transitions that are too fast for many audio processing devices to handle. The ANTI-IMAGING FILTER must be carefully designed to see that it is not driven into slew limiting by these transitions.

Transient Response *See* TRANSIENT.

Transistor The transistor is the basic SOLID-STATE amplifying element used in almost all audio equipment today, having almost completely replaced the vacuum TUBE.

The transistor is NONLINEAR in its amplification of electric CURRENTS, and to make it usable in amplifiers, great pains must be taken to make it behave in a LINEAR fashion and so to reduce its DISTORTION.

The transistor is a three-element device consisting of two terminals to pass the signal CURRENT and a third terminal for controlling the signal current. In this it resembles the TRIODE tube, although the triode is much more linear and has other desirable characteristics such as a very high INPUT IMPEDANCE.

Conventional transistors pass current in one direction only and are called BIPOLAR. (Logic would dictate that they should be called unipolar.) There are two types, NPN and PNP, and each carries current in the opposite direction.

In addition to bipolar transistors there exist FIELD EFFECT TRANSISTORS (FETs), which behave much more like triode tubes. They also are of two types, called P-channel and N-channel. FETs are suitable for high-quality audio devices, but they are only recently available with sufficiently high current-carrying capacity to be used in high-power amplifier outputs. *See also* SEMICONDUCTOR.

Transondent Possessing the ability to freely transmit sound, analogous to transparent in reference to light. The grill cloth covering a LOUDSPEAKER must be transondent for obvious reasons. The term is believed to have been coined by the late Paul Veneklasen, a respected acoustician in the Los Angeles area.

Trap A band reject FILTER designed to eliminate a particular frequency from a desired signal. *See also* BIAS TRAP; BASS TRAP.

Treble That portion of the audio spectrum that encompasses the frequencies from about 2,000 HERTZ to 20 KILOHERTZ, as opposed to BASS and MID-RANGE.

TRF Acronym for Tuned Radio Frequency. A type of radio receiver invented and patented by the U.S. Navy in the mid-1920s that used resonant circuits in the GRID or PLATE circuits of one or more RF AMPLIFIER tubes. The resonant circuits were tuned by variable capacitors or inductors, that were connected to the tuning dials, one for each stage. Thus several dials had to be tuned to the station frequency for reception. TRF receivers were superseded by the SUPERHETERODYNE sets.

Tri-amplification A system used in some loudspeaker systems where a three-way CROSSOVER NETWORK is used before three POWER AMPLIFIERS, each amplifier handling only its limited part of the total frequency range. It is an extension of BIAMPLIFICATION.

Trigger An instantaneous voltage pulse generated from a synthesizer keyboard when any key is depressed. The trigger is used to initiate the action of some other device, such as an ADSR.

In analog CRT OSCILLOSCOPES, the horizontal sweep is initiated at a particular instantaneous signal level, and this is called a triggered sweep.

Trim Generally refers to a small adjustment, analogous to TWEAK. Small controls such as GAIN controls operated by screwdrivers are called "trimpots" or "trimmers," and are used for such things as adjusting PRE-EMPHASIS and DE-EMPHASIS in tape recorders, etc. Some recording consoles label the fine-adjust microphone preamplifier gain control a "mic trim."

Trimmer A variable CAPACITOR whose value can be adjusted by means of a small screwdriver. Trimmers are meant to be adjusted only rarely and are commonly found in EQUALIZATION circuits, where they are finely tuned to achieve a particular frequency response characteristic. *See also* TRIM.

Also, a control knob that has a relatively subtle effect, such as the fine volume control on a recording console input module, is called a trimmer or a gain trimmer.

Trimpot A small POTENTIOMETER whose setting is usually adjusted by a small screwdriver. Trimpots are designed to be adjusted only rarely and are used in sensitive circuits such as EQUALIZERS, where they can be finely adjusted and left for long periods. *See also* TRIM.

Triode The three-element vacuum TUBE in which the elements are the CATHODE, the GRID, and the PLATE. The triode is probably the most common type of tube and is used primarily as an AMPLIFIER stage and as a CATHODE FOLLOWER. The triode was invented and patented by Lee DeForest in 1906, and this is one of the fundamental patents in the history of electronics. It is interesting to note that DeForest thought of the triode as a DETECTOR of radio signals, not an amplifier. As a detector, it was inferior to other detectors of the time, including the FLEMING VALVE, which was the first DIODE detector. It was the quick-witted engineers at the Bell Telephone Laboratories who first hit on the idea of using the triode as an amplifier, and they obtained a license to build it from DeForest very early and immediately started using it as an amplifier in long-distance telephone circuits. They also started manufacturing triodes for commercial sale under the Western Electric brand.

TRS *See* TIP, RING, AND SLEEVE.

T-Section A filter, or part of a filter, that has two series and one shunt REACTIVE components. Its name derives from its schematic resemblance to the letter T. The T-section has a flat response in its PASSBAND and an 18 dB per octave slope in its STOPBAND.

TTS *See* TEMPORARY THRESHOLD SHIFT.

Tube Short for vacuum tube. The tube is the forerunner of the TRANSISTOR. The first tube used for amplification of signals was the AUDION invented by Lee DeForest. In England, tubes are called "valves," a carryover from the FLEMING VALVE, which was the first two-element tube, or

DIODE. In actuality, Edison invented the diode but did not exploit it for any practical use. Fleming, an Englishman, used it as a DETECTOR of radio signals, and patented it for this use.

Tubes generally contain the CATHODE and ANODE of the diode, with the addition of one or more GRIDS that control the CURRENT between cathode and anode, and are relatively LINEAR in their amplification of signals. The primary disadvantages of tubes compared to transistors is that they are much larger and they generate much more heat. They are thus much less efficient. Some applications require tubes, such as X-ray equipment and high-power radio and television transmitters.

The natural linearity of tubes, as compared to transistors, is much admired by some audio people, who insist that tube equipment sounds more musical than equipment using transistors. Although a great deal of nonsense has been written about this subject, sometimes by people who ought

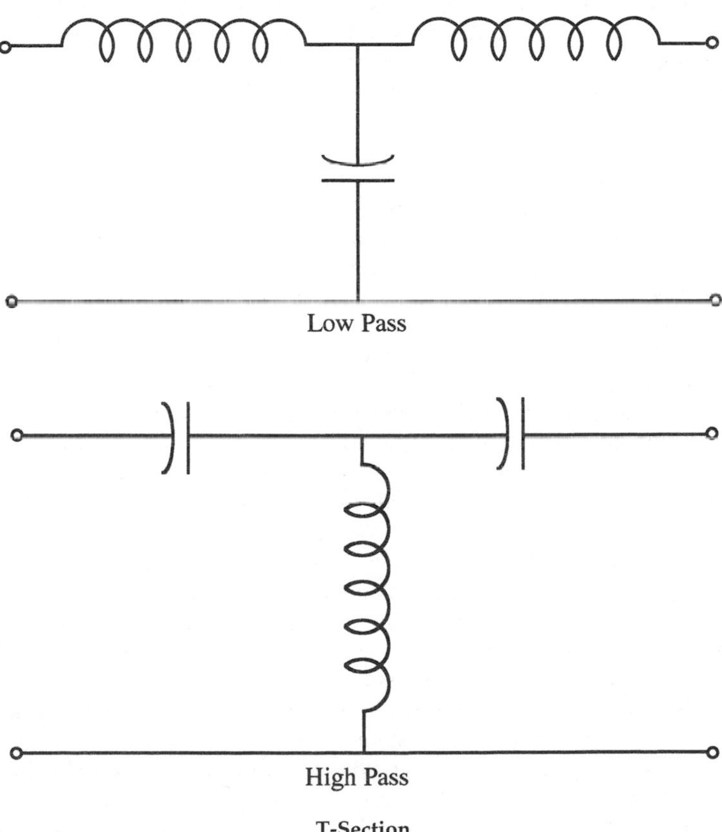

T-Section

to know better, it is true that there is a difference in the sound produced by the two systems, especially when SIGNAL levels are high and likely to drive the system into OVERLOAD. Generally, tube equipment produces more even-order HARMONIC DISTORTION, while transistors tend to produce more odd-order harmonics. Even-order harmonics are associated with "loud," "brassy," etc., timbres, while odd-order harmonics produce a more "covered" or "closed" sound. Tube equipment usually overloads more gradually, causing the signal to begin to sound loud and bright before CLIPPING occurs. With transistor equipment, HARD CLIPPING starts at the instant of overload, and it generates large quantities of high-order distortion.

There is a viable market for very expensive, hand-built tube-type audio equipment, and most of this market is, maybe surprisingly, in Japan. The Japanese are masters at large-volume production of high-quality electronics, and they lead the world in the manufacturing of audio components. But they are not so much interested in the limited production of high-quality handmade components, and most of the world's production of this esoteric equipment is in the United States. Curiously, tube manufacturing is now mainly in China and eastern Europe.

Tuchel Connector Some European and, to a lesser extent, American audio equipment uses cable connectors that conform to the German DIN standard for pin locations. These DIN-standard connectors are made in large quantities by the German manufacturer Tuchel, and this name is commonly used for all of them, regardless of manufacture. DIN connectors are relatively inexpensive, and the standard dictates not only the locations of the pins, but also what the pins are connected to. For instance, input and output signals might use the same connector, but would use different pins. Alas, not all manufacturers conform to the letter of the standard, causing some confusion.

Tuning Condenser A variable CAPACITOR, usually consisting of two groups of aluminum plates that gradually intermesh as a shaft is turned. It is the component used to change the FREQUENCY of maximum sensitivity of conventional radios, allowing different stations to be tuned in. In some small radios, the tuning knob is connected directly to the shaft of the tuning condenser.

Turnover In the recording of phonograph records, the turnover frequency is that FREQUENCY below which the recording is done at CONSTANT DISPLACEMENT and above which it is CONSTANT VELOCITY. Before the RIAA standardized the playback EQUALIZATION curve for stereo records, different record manufacturers used different turnover frequencies, and PREAMPLIFIERS had adjustable controls to select various CURVES.

Turntablism A musical form based on the real-time manipulation of musical sounds recorded on vinyl LP stereo discs. The Berklee Press, a subsidiary of the Berklee College of Music in Boston, publishes books and LP records for turntablism.

Turntablist A musical performer who uses two or more phonograph turntables and records (usually stereo LPs) along with a mixing console to control the resultant musical effect; a highly specialized Disk Jockey. One tool used by turntablists is the cross-fader, a type of mixer that fades from one stereo source to a different one.[27]

TVI *See* TELEVISION INTERFERENCE.

Tweak, Tweak Up "Tweak" is technicians' slang for a delicate adjustment procedure. Often the performance of AUDIO components can be improved over the original manufacturer's specifications by judicious tweaking up of the adjustments, or by making small changes in certain component values.

Some audio buffs spend a good deal more time tweaking up than listening to their sound systems. *See also* ALIGNMENT.

Tweek A trade name of Sumiko for an electrical contact enhancer fluid sold to the home audio market, much praised by some audiophiles. It is otherwise known as Stabilant 22 from D. W. Electrochemicals, Ltd., of Canada.

Tweeter In a multiway LOUDSPEAKER system, the small speaker that emits the high frequencies is sometimes called a tweeter.

Twin-Tone Intermodulation Distortion A method of measuring INTERMODULATION DISTORTION by passing two sinusoidal tones of equal amplitude through the DUT and examining the output signal to see the amplitude of the difference FREQUENCY. The two tones, which differ in frequency by a fixed amount, usually 50 hertz, are swept through the audible range and often into the ultrasonic range. Even though the ultrasonic signals themselves are not audible, the difference frequency is in the audible range.

Twist-Lock™ A trademark of the Hubbell Corporation for a family of locking AC power connectors. For years, many sound companies used them for LOUDSPEAKER to AMPLIFIER connectors, but since they were also often used for mains power distribution, the obvious disaster often occurred. Recently, the Neutrik Speak-On connector has become popular for loudspeakers.

U

U Abbreviation of unit, as in modular unit or rack unit, which is the standard unit of height measurement of rack-mounted equipment. One modular unit is 1¾ inches, and all rack-mounted components measure an integral number of modular units high. Thus, a device might be described as occupying 3U of rack space, or 5¼ inches. The standard width of 19 inches is assumed. The Modular Unit standard was agreed upon by the EIA and ANSI.

UDF, Universal Disk Format™ A trademarked name for an optical disc

27. Thanks to Dennis Bohn, Rane Corp.

file format defined by OSTA, the Optical Storage Technology Association. It complies with the ISO 13346 standard (volume and file structure of write-once and rewritable media using nonsequential recording for information interchange), and its use facilitates compatibility among computers of different operating systems.

UHJ Abbreviation for Universal H J matrix, a method of encoding three or four channels of audio onto two channels. "H" and "J" are simply code letters adopted by the BBC, and have no other meaning. *See also* AMBISONICS.

UL Short for Underwriters' Laboratories, which is a standards and testing laboratory financed by the insurance industry. The purpose of UL testing is to ensure fire safety of electrical equipment. UL approval has nothing to do with the audio quality of any apparatus.

Ultrasonic Having frequencies above the normal range of human hearing. Not to be confused with SUPERSONIC, which means faster than the speed of sound. Ultrasonic signals can cause DISTORTION in audio components that is in the audible range. *See also* TRANSIENT INTERMODULATION DISTORTION.

U-Matic A ¾" helical scan video cassette tape recorder format developed by Sony for professional use. It was the world standard for industrial and semipro videotape productions for a long time. This format was also used in conjunction with a Sony PCM 1610 or PCM 1630 encoder to record digital audio destined for release on CDs.

Una Corda Italian for "one string." Notation used in printed piano music to indicate the use of the soft pedal, which shifts the keyboard so the hammers only hit one or two of the three strings per note.

Unbalanced Line Any transmission line in which the ground conductor completes the electrical circuit and serves as a shield. *See also* Appendix 6.

Underhung Coil One way to increase the linearity and reduce the DISTORTION of a dynamic loudspeaker is to design the VOICE COIL so it is relatively short compared with the length of the magnetic gap in the POLE PIECES. This means the coil sees a uniform magnetic field strength regardless of its position in the gap, reducing the nonlinear distortion. This does not reduce the EFFICIENCY of the loudspeaker, but it does increase the cost, because a larger magnet must be used. *See also* OVERHUNG COIL.

Uni-axial Microphone A UNIDIRECTIONAL MICROPHONE that has maximum SENSITIVITY in the axial direction, or along the main axis of the microphone.

Unidirectional Microphone A microphone that is more sensitive to sounds coming from one particular direction than those coming from other directions; sometimes called simply "directional microphone." There are many degrees of directionality, and there is no such thing as a perfect unidirectional microphone. *See* CARDIOID; SUPER-CARDIOID; SHOTGUN; LINE MICROPHONE; and HYPER-CARDIOID.

Unidyne™ The first directional MICROPHONE to use a single active transducing element was the Unidyne, invented by Benjamin Bauer in 1937. The name comes from unidirectional dynamic, and it was a dynamic microphone that was modified to allow sound to reach the rear of the diaphragm through a time-delay network. This caused the PHASE cancellation of sounds coming from the rear. Today the principle is used in many dynamic microphones having CARDIOID or similar POLAR PATTERNS. Unidyne is a trademark of Shure.

Prior to the Unidyne, directional microphones were made with two elements whose outputs were added. Typically, a bidirectional VELOCITY MICROPHONE element and a dynamic PRESSURE MICROPHONE were used. The rear lobe of the ribbon element was canceled by the rear response of the pressure microphone, as the two were of opposite polarity.

Unity Gain A device that does not attenuate or amplify a signal is said to be a unity gain device. In other words, the GAIN is 1. Most SIGNAL PROCESSING devices have unity gain, which means they can be inserted into an audio system at various places without upsetting the overall gain of the system.

USB Universal Serial Bus, a medium BANDWIDTH serial digital data interconnection standard, commonly used for keyboards, mice, and other peripherals, including some digital audio gear. Even though the newer USB 2 may appear fast enough, FIREWIRE/IEEE 1394 is usually preferred for digital audio and video work.

UUT Acronym for Unit Under Test. *See* DUT.

V

VA Short for Volt-Ampere, or the product of the voltage times the current. In a resistive circuit, the VA will be equal to the wattage, for a watt is 1 volt x 1 ampere. In an inductive circuit, or device such as an electric motor, however, the current will not be precisely in phase with the voltage, and the average current times the average voltage will be greater than the actual power absorbed by the device. Also short for VARIABLE AREA.

Vacuum Tube *See* TUBE.

Valve British terminology for vacuum TUBE. The first tube was a DIODE introduced by Ambrose Fleming in 1904, and he called it the FLEMING VALVE. It was used as a DETECTOR of radio signals. *See also* EDISON EFFECT.

Van den Hul A specially shaped STYLUS tip for reduced DISTORTION and wear and increased high-FREQUENCY performance in playing phonograph records. *See also* STYLUS.

Varactor A special semiconductor DIODE used as a variable CAPACITOR. The capacitance varies as a function of an applied DC potential. Varactors are sometimes used as TUNING CONDENSERS in certain radio receivers. They are also sometimes called varicaps.

Variable Area The most common type of analog OPTICAL SOUND TRACK used in motion pictures. The variable area track is a transparent line in a

Variable Area

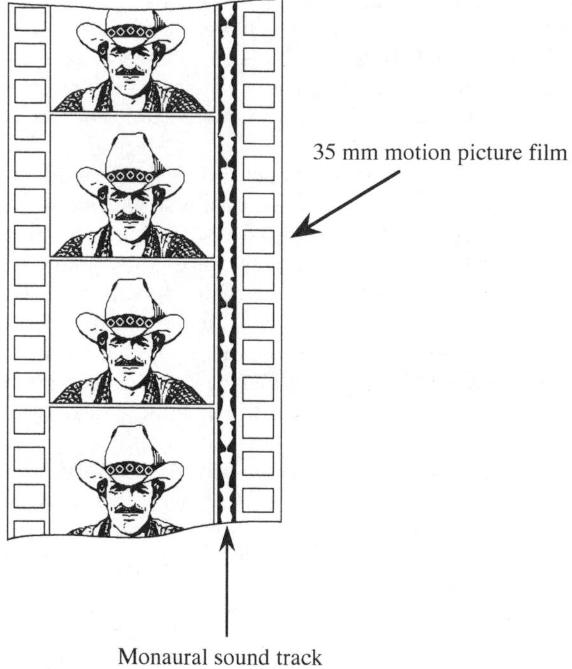

Variable Area

black background. The relative width of the transparent part (strictly speaking, not the area) is varied in accordance with the sound WAVEFORM. To produce the sound in the projector, a thin flat beam of light is passed through the film and onto a photocell, which generates an electric current in response to the amount of light transmission.

Most analog movie sound tracks today consist of two parallel variable area tracks, and this makes it possible to record stereophonic sound. *See* SVA. The track is recorded on the unexposed film by a special optical device known as a light valve.

Another type of early variable area film recorder was a Dutch invention called Philips-Miller (see illustration below). It had a special mechanical cutter, and was used in the 1930s for recording radio transcriptions in Europe and in the 1950s for a few television productions made on 16-mm film. The film had a thin opaque coating over the sound track area, and a small pointed plow-shaped stylus was used to cut a furrow through the coating into the film. As the depth of cut was varied according to the audio waveform being recorded, the furrow varied in width in like manner, resulting in a sound track that could be read by conventional optical sound heads.

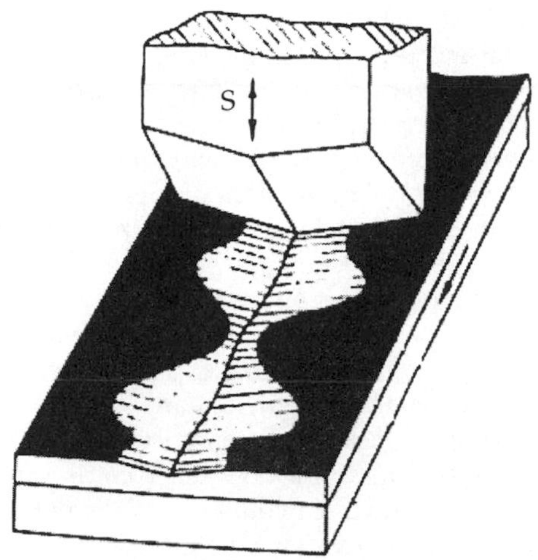

The Philips-Miller cutter

Variable D™ A trademark of Electro-Voice for a series of dynamic directional microphones introduced in 1954. The term stands for "variable delay," and refers to three sound entry ports on the side of the microphone. Each port incorporates a different time delay for sound entering it and then reaching the back side of the diaphragm. The time delays for rear entering sounds effectively shift the phase of the sound by 180 degrees so they cancel the sound entering the front of the microphone. The longest delay extends the phase cancellation to lower frequencies reducing the PROXIMITY EFFECT.

Variable Density A type of OPTICAL SOUND TRACK used for motion picture sound for many years until the advent of the VARIABLE AREA sound track. The variable density sound track is a narrow gray strip between the picture frames and the sprocket holes of the film. In recording the track, the audio WAVEFORM is used to AMPLITUDE MODULATE a thin, narrow light beam that exposes the film. The resulting film density, or light transmissibility, varies in accordance with the variations in the waveform. To reproduce the sound in the projector, a tiny beam of light is passed through the film and onto a photocell, which generates an electric current proportional to the amount of light transmitted, thus reproducing the waveform. The track resembles a modern bar code that uses shades of gray.

Variable density recording is plagued with problems, one of the worst of which is a high noise level caused by the inherent graininess in the film. The photographic process is NONLINEAR and this causes a relatively high DISTORTION. These problems led to a great deal of research in the 1930s, much of it done by the Bell Telephone Laboratories, and the result was the introduction of the much-improved variable area system.

Variable Pattern Microphone A microphone that can be adjusted to achieve different directional characteristics, or POLAR PATTERNS. Some of the earliest variable pattern microphones were the 77 series of RIBBON MICROPHONES introduced in the 1930s by Harry F. Olson of RCA. Most variable pattern microphones made today consist of two CONDENSER MICROPHONE elements placed back to back with their output voltages combined in different ratios and polarities. This configuration was originally developed by H. J. Von Braunmuhl and Walter Weber in Germany and has been gradually refined over the years.

Variable Pitch The pitch of a phonograph record has nothing to do with musical PITCH; it is defined as the groove density in grooves per inch.

If a record is cut with low pitch, i.e., with widely spaced grooves, the recorded volume can be large with no danger of the grooves inter-cutting one another. Low pitch, however, means less recorded time on the record, and we see there is a trade-off between recording time and volume or AMPLITUDE of the SIGNAL. Of course, music is not uniformly loud, and recording time can be increased if the grooves are packed together more closely during soft passages and spread wider apart on louder passages. This is variable pitch recording.

In order to record a disc with variable pitch, the recording LATHE must sense what the signal level is in order to adjust the spacing accordingly. This is done with a PREVIEW HEAD, which is another playback head on the tape machine that plays the master tape into the record cutter. The preview head is placed so it hears the signal before the main playback head does so, and this negative time delay allows the pitch control system to start spacing the grooves wider apart before a loud passage comes along. A digital delay can also be used to delay the signal feeding into the cutter.

Variometer A type of RF transformer where one coil is wound on a spherical form and placed inside the other coil. By rotating the inner coil, the amount of coupling between the coils is varied. Variometers were used in the 1900s to add positive feedback to the RF stages of radio receivers. *See also* REGENERATION.

Vari-Speed™ Vari-speed is a means of changing the speed at which an analog tape recorder runs in order to change the PITCH of a recorded tape or to change the time duration of the recording. In most modern tape machines, a SERVO-controlled CAPSTAN is used, and frequently the speed may be varied by changing the reference FREQUENCY of the servo.

Vari-speed historically consisted of an OSCILLATOR coupled to a POWER AMPLIFIER that had enough power output to drive the synchronous CAPSTAN MOTOR of the tape recorder. As the oscillator frequency is varied from the nominal 60-HERTZ line frequency, the capstan motor will change speed accordingly, changing the tape speed. The first commercial tape recorder speed control system used a 60-hertz tuning fork as a standard and was introduced by the Ampex company in the 1950s. It was not meant to control the speed over a broad range, but only to provide a steady 60 Hz reference for use when the tape recorder had to be operated from power lines other than the normal 60 Hz. The exact term "vari-speed" was trademarked by Superscope (Superscope distributed Sony recorders in the U.S. at the time) in the 1970s.

Varistor A semiconductor circuit component whose resistance is a function of the voltage applied across it. Its resistance drops nonlinearly with increasing voltage, with a steep decrease at its rated voltage. Varistors are used as surge protectors in equipment sensitive to overvoltage conditions.

VCA *See* VOLTAGE-CONTROLLED AMPLIFIER.

VCF *See* VOLTAGE-CONTROLLED FILTER.

VCO *See* VOLTAGE-CONTROLLED OSCILLATOR.

Velocity Microphone A type of microphone that has a POLAR PATTERN shaped like a FIGURE 8. This pattern is also called a COSINE PATTERN because the cosine function gives this CURVE when plotted in polar coordinates. The first velocity microphone was the ribbon microphone, invented about 1931 by Harry F. Olson of RCA Research Laboratories.

The ribbon microphone uses as an active element a small corrugated strip of very thin aluminum ribbon hanging loosely in a strong magnetic field. The ribbon is moved by the action of air molecules, which are set in motion by the SOUND WAVE. The resonant FREQUENCY of the ribbon is very low, below the audible range, so the motion of the ribbon is "mass controlled," or is proportional to the velocity of the air particles. For this reason, it is called a "velocity" microphone.

The ribbon is most sensitive to sound approaching it either at normal incidence or perpendicular to the plane of the ribbon because this causes it to execute maximum motion. As the angle of incidence of the sound changes, the motion of the ribbon is reduced and the output VOLTAGE from the microphone is reduced, until it is zero when the angle of incidence is 90 degrees. This is like a window shade, which is easily moved by air currents perpendicular to it, but is not moved by wind blowing across its surface.

The ribbon was the first commercially successful directional microphone, and found instant acceptance in the motion picture and radio broadcasting industries. It is still in use for many purposes, although it has numerous disadvantages compared to modern microphone types, especially CONDENSER MICROPHONES. It is characterized by very smooth sound, much appreciated by brass players for recording. It suffers from PROXIMITY EFFECT, however, making it less than ideal as a vocal microphone. It is also quite sensitive to air currents and wind, making it useless outdoors, unless a good WINDSCREEN is used.

In recent years, special condenser microphones have been designed with the cosine pattern. They are compound microphones, consisting of two CARDIOID microphones placed back-to-back and connected in PHASE opposition.

VF-14 A vacuum TUBE made in the 1950s by Telefunken in Germany. The VF-14 was used as a PREAMPLIFIER in the famous U-47 CONDENSER MICROPHONE. The U-47 has a pronounced high-FREQUENCY peak, and

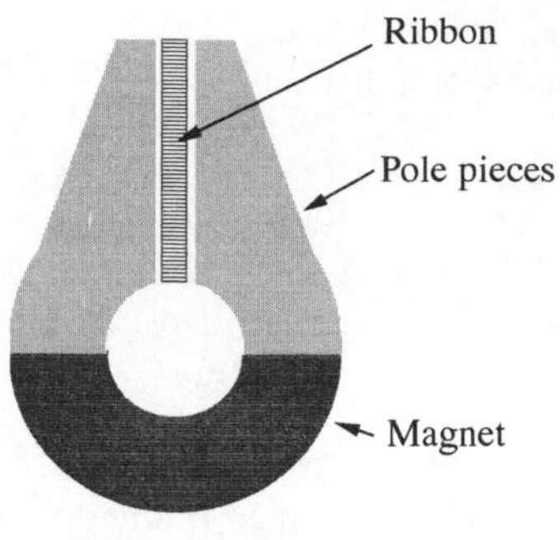

Front view

Top view

Velocity (Ribbon) Microphone

recordings made with it have a characteristic sound much praised by many recording engineers.

The VF-14 has been obsolete and out of production for many years, and most U-47s have been converted to FET preamplifiers. However, many people believe the tube sounded better, and the price of used VF-14s has reached astronomical values. There is now a company making replica Telefunken microphones that has the rights to the Telefunken name in the U.S. They will supply various tubes including NOS VF-14s.

VFO Acronym for Variable Frequency Oscillator. Audio-frequency VFOs are used in the generation of electronic music and for generating test signals for audio equipment. Radio-frequency VFOs, also called local oscillators, are used in SUPERHETERODYNE AM and FM tuners and television sets to generate signals for mixing with the received signal to produce the INTERMEDIATE FREQUENCY.

VHS Hi-Fi A method of very high-quality AUDIO recording using a VHS video cassette as the recording medium. The audio recording is a companded frequency modulation process, and the carrier is recorded onto the tape at a very high level so the recording penetrates into the magnetic coating. The recording still exists after the video track is recorded over it, a trick called "depth multiplexing." VHS Hi-Fi was introduced after Sony's BETA HI-FI, and has similar performance specifications, but is not compatible with it.

Vibration Switch *See* SHOCK SWITCH.

Vibrato The FREQUENCY MODULATION of the sound of a musical instrument, especially the singing voice. The vibrato also includes AMPLITUDE MODULATION, but the frequency modulation is more apparent to the listener.

Most solo instruments are able to produce the vibrato, although some, most notably the piano, cannot. The combined vibratos in a string section help give rise to the "chorus" effect.

Victrola Victrola was the trade name from 1906 for phonographs made by the Victor Talking Machine company, of Camden, New Jersey. It soon became a generic name for the record player. Victor also introduced the famous little fox terrier named Nipper sitting in front of the Victrola listening to "His Master's Voice" as a trademark in the United States.

Video Literally "I see" in Latin. Video is to television what audio is to radio.

Virtual Pitch *See* RESIDUE PITCH.

Viscous Damping The DAMPING of a mechanical resonance by the viscosity of a thick, oily fluid. The fluid used today is usually a type of silicone oil. Some early CUTTERHEADS were viscous damped, and many record-playing tonearms have been viscous damped. One advantage of viscous damping is that the amount of damping can be adjusted by the amount of the damping fluid used or by the viscosity of the fluid. Disadvantages of viscous damping are the fact that the amount of damping is temperature dependent, and it can be messy to deal with the fluid.

Vitaphone A corporation formed in 1926 by Western Electric and Warner Bros. for the purpose of manufacturing and installing sound motion picture equipment. The Vitaphone system was designed by Maxfield and Harrison of the Bell Telephone Laboratories and used a 33⅓-rpm, 16-inch diameter disc record coupled to the movie projector mechanism. This was the first recording medium to use a speed of 33⅓ rpm and was the first successful commercial sound system for movies in the United States. *The Jazz Singer*, starring Al Jolson and released in 1927, was the first to movie use it.

One problem with the Vitaphone was the inconvenience of handling the large records, one for each reel of film. There were also synchronization problems, especially if the film had broken and had been spliced. The Vitaphone system was supplanted in the 1930s by optical sound tracks recorded on the film.

Vitasound A short-lived type of motion picture OPTICAL SOUND TRACK system developed by Warner Bros. in the late 1930s. It used a single conventional VARIABLE AREA sound track in the usual place on the film and two more, smaller variable area tracks along the sprocket holes of the other side of the film. These two control tracks, as they were called, controlled the GAIN of variable gain AMPLIFIERS connected to LOUDSPEAKERS strategically located around the theater. By properly encoding the control tracks, the source of the sound could be effectively moved around the room. Of course, this is no substitute for stereophonic sound, but it was capable of spectacular sonic effects. The system was "compatible" in that a standard projector would sense only the standard sound track and ignore the control tracks.

Vitruvius A Roman architect who lived about 50 B.C. He is the earliest known writer about ACOUSTICS, having described in some detail the acoustical characteristics of Greek and Roman theaters. Among other things, he said that theater acoustics would be improved if SOUNDING VESSELS tuned to the pitches of the musical scale were placed around the seating area. His *Ten Books on Architecture* has been translated and is fascinating to read today.

Vocoder An electronic device similar to a music synthesizer that is used to synthesize the human voice and modify a voice spoken or sung into it. It is used for special effects like changing the PITCH of a voice, adding VIBRATO, replacing the voiced pitch with a noise signal, etc.

Voice Coil In a dynamic LOUDSPEAKER, the CONE is caused to move by a COIL of wire which is wound around a cylindrical "former" attached to its center. The coil is called the voice coil, a quaint reminder of the early days of audio.

The voice coil is immersed in a strong magnetic field emanating from a permanent magnet. CURRENT in the coil causes another magnetic field to be developed, and the two fields interact to cause the force on the coil. Current in one direction moves the coil one way, and current in the other direction moves it the other way. Thus, the coil (and attached cone) will move in a way analogous to the WAVEFORM of the SIGNAL applied to it.

Voice coils may be wound with relatively more or less wire of any of several diameters. In this way, the IMPEDANCE of the coil is determined. The impedance is a combination of the RESISTANCE of the wire and the INDUCTANCE of the coil. The motion of the coil in the magnetic field creates another component of the impedance, called the motional impedance. This reflects the dynamic characteristics of the moving system, including the mass of the cone assembly, the springiness of the suspension of the cone, and the acoustic LOAD on the speaker. It is possible to determine a great deal about the loudspeaker itself by examining and testing the impedance versus FREQUENCY.

It is desirable to minimize the resistance of the coil because it wastes energy, simply turning it into heat. Therefore, the more copper that can be placed in the magnetic gap, the more efficient the unit will be, with less power lost to heat. Sometimes voice coils are wound with flat wire placed edgewise on the former in order to get more copper in the gap.

The Voice of the Theatre™, VOTT A trademark of the Altec Lansing company for their family of horn-loaded loudspeakers used in movie theatres. Their popularity was unmatched for many decades, and they were widely used for music and sound reinforcement.

Voice-Over A voice sometimes present in motion pictures and video presentations without the person speaking being visible, i.e., a narration.

Voice Processor, Vocal Processor A device that includes several audio processors designed to economically replace a battery of outboard processors commonly used to record a human voice or vocal signal, although any signal can be used. It may include a mic PREAMP with PHANTOM POWER, a compressor/limiter, a DE-ESSER, a multiband EQUALIZER, and other processors in one small package.

Volt, Voltage The voltage is the electrical potential difference between two points; it is defined in terms of the work required to move a unit charge (1 COULOMB) from one point to the other. The unit of voltage is the volt, named after Alessandro Volta, and is numerically equal to 1 joule per coulomb.

The voltage of an audio SIGNAL is usually measured in terms of the RMS value of the signal, but sometimes the peak or average voltages are measured. The rms voltage squared is proportional to the amount of POWER the signal carries.

Voltage-Controlled Amplifier, VCA An AMPLIFIER whose GAIN is adjusted, or controlled, by the application of an external direct VOLTAGE. One of the most common uses of VCAs is in electronic music SYNTHESIZERS, where they are used to generate the ENVELOPE of generated signals. They are also used in COMPRESSORS, LIMITERS, and COMPANDERS.

Voltage-Controlled Filter, VCF A FILTER whose frequency is controlled by the application of an external direct VOLTAGE. VCFs exist in many forms, including low pass, high pass, BANDPASS, and band reject. Not only the tuning of the filter but also its Q can usually be voltage controlled. VCFs are very important components of electronic music SYNTHESIZERS, where they offer amazing control over the TIMBRE of signals passed through them.

Voltage-Controlled Oscillator, VCO An electronic OSCILLATOR whose output frequency is controlled by the application of an external direct VOLTAGE. VCOs are used extensively to generate musical signals in electronic music SYNTHESIZERS. The ease with which their frequency can be controlled makes them very suitable for FREQUENCY MODULATION and the generation of very complex sounds. *See also* PHASE-LOCKED LOOP.

Voltage Gain The output voltage of a device divided by its input voltage. Most PASSIVE devices have a negative voltage gain, and most ACTIVE devices, especially AMPLIFIERS, have a positive voltage gain. A negative voltage gain is sometimes called a loss or an INSERTION LOSS. Voltage gain, by definition, is a ratio of two voltages and is therefore a dimensionless number.

It is common practice to express voltage gains, especially of amplifiers, in terms of DECIBELS, using the following formula:

$$Gain = 20 \log_{10} \frac{V_{output}}{V_{input}}$$

However, this formula is valid only if the input and output impedances are the same, and this is seldom true in practice. The problem arises because the decibel is defined as 10 times the logarithm of a power ratio. The square of a voltage ratio is a power ratio if the impedances across which the voltages of the numerator and denominator are measured are the same, and this allows us to express power ratios from voltage measurements by multiplying the logarithm by 20 instead of 10.

It is our contention that voltage gains should be simply stated as pure ratios, with no reference to decibels. An amplifier with "60 dB" of gain then would be said to have a gain of 1,000, which would be true regardless of the loading conditions on the input and output.

Voltaic Cell Any type of electric CELL, which normally cannot be recharged, such as the LECLANCHE cell.

Volume Expander A device for increasing the DYNAMIC RANGE and reducing the apparent NOISE of a SIGNAL. *See also* COMPANDER. A volume expander decreases the system GAIN as the signal level decreases, making soft signals softer still. This results in an apparent noise decrease because the relative level between the softest and loudest sounds is greater. If the noise level is already low enough that the signal will MASK it in the loud passages, the expansion will put the low end of the dynamic range at a point where the ear has reduced SENSITIVITY, making the noise less audible. *See also* PEAK EXPANDER.

VOM Short for Volt-Ohm-Milliammeter, which is a portable device for measuring AC and DC VOLTAGE, RESISTANCE, and electric CURRENT. The VOM was the basic and venerable instrument for the electronics technician for many years, but it has essentially been replaced by the ubiquitous DIGITAL MULTI METER (DMM) even though the DMM is almost useless when trying to measure a changing voltage or current. *See also* VTVM.

VST™, Virtual Studio Technology A proprietary digital computing system to perform the various tasks performed in a recording studio, such as limiting, compression, EQUALIZATION, REVERBERATION, etc. The virtual studio can also act as the recording machine by digitizing the audio signals and writing them directly to a hard disc where they can be recalled and manipulated as desired. VST is a registered trademark owned by Steinberg Media Technologies GmbH, a member of Pinnacle Systems, since December 2002,

VTVM Short for Vacuum Tube Volt Meter, which was an electronic, or active, version of the passive VOM. This allowed a very high INPUT IMPEDANCE, so it did not disturb the CIRCUIT being measured nearly as much as did the VOM, and it allowed higher sensitivity. The VTVM was eventually made with TRANSISTORS and integrated circuits rather than vacuum TUBES as AMPLIFIERS, but the acronym still hangs on. The VTVM has been made obsolete by the DIGITAL MULTI METER. *See also* VOM.

VU VU is the abbreviation for Volume Unit, which is a measure of SIGNAL level on a meter with a DECIBEL scale and accurately controlled rate of response to a signal. The reference power for the volume unit is delivered to a 600-OHM LOAD when the VOLTAGE is 0.775 volts RMS. This is zero on the meter, or 0 VU. Signal levels are generally less than this value, and are read as negative decibel values.

The VU was first used as a measure of signal level in radio broadcasting, but it has been used for many years in other areas, especially tape recorders. It is interesting to note that a true VU meter is somewhat complex in that its speed of operation (ballistics) is closely controlled. Most meters on home-type tape recorders are calibrated in decibels, but are not true VU meters.

W

Wall Wart Slang for a power transformer/power supply that plugs directly into the power outlet on the wall, usually covering both outlets.

Warp Wow If the vertical pivot of a TONEARM is above the surface plane of the record being played, a warp in the record that causes the STYLUS to move up and down will also cause it to move a little forward and backward along the groove. Sometimes this motion along the groove is called "scrubbing." This motion is added to the relative velocity of the groove with respect to the stylus, and it causes a small variation in FREQUENCY that is called warp wow. Longer tonearms have less of a problem than shorter ones, and the closer the vertical pivot to the plane of the record, the better.

Watermarking The addition of unique digital data to an existing digital file, in order to identify it. The user need not be aware at all of the extra data, but it can identify files such as photos or music and would be used to detect piracy. The term comes from the paper industry technique of embossing a unique design into moist paper during manufacture.

Watt The watt is the metric unit of power and is defined as 1 joule per second. The joule is a unit of energy, so power is the rate of energy transfer, or the rate of doing work. In electrical CIRCUITS, power can be calculated in three ways: CURRENT squared times the real part of IMPEDANCE, VOLTAGE squared divided by the real part of impedance, or voltage multiplied by current.

The unit is named for James Watt, the developer of a practical steam engine and inventor of the speed governor. Incidentally, it is commonly thought that Watt's speed governor was the first FEEDBACK control system, but this is not true. Organ builders have been using a feedback control mechanism to regulate wind pressure since the thirteenth century.

WAV The Windows file extension that indicates Microsoft's audio file format. .WAV files can include mono or multichannel audio at 8-bit or 16-bit resolution at several sampling rates up to 48 kHz.

Waveform The waveform of a SIGNAL is a graph of the instantaneous VOLTAGE versus time. The familiar SINE WAVE is an example. The picture seen on an OSCILLOSCOPE is a waveform.

Wavelength In a sound wave in air, the distance between two successive pressure maxima or minima is called the wavelength, and it is equal to the speed of sound divided by the FREQUENCY. In air at standard conditions of temperature and pressure (STP), sound travels at about 340 meters per second, so the wavelength of a 10,000-HERTZ sound is 340/10,000 meters, or about 3.4 centimeters. The wavelength in air of a 34-Hz sound (low C sharp of a 16-foot organ pipe) is thus 340/34 = 10 meters. *See also* PARTIALS. Audio signals travel in cables and wires much faster than sound travels in air. This means the wavelengths of the electrical signals is far longer than their equivalent sounds in air. The actual speed of transmission depends on the characteristics of the transmission line.

Wavelet Transform A type of mathematical transform from the time domain to the frequency domain, somewhat analogous to the FOURIER TRANSFORM. Whereas the Fourier transform decomposes a time WAVEFORM into a series of sinusoidal components that are infinite in extent, the wavelet transform decomposes the time signal into a series of "tone bursts." One disadvantage of the Fourier transform is that discrete events in the time domain are "smeared" over a wide frequency range when transformed, and discrete frequencies are spread throughout infinite time when transformed back. For this reason, nonstationary signals, which contain rapid changes and transients, are not efficiently handled. The frequency domain representation of them does not encode their placement in time. The wavelet transform, on the other hand, also encodes the placement of changes in the waveform along the time axis. For this reason, it is thought to be more suitable for analysis of speech and music waveforms.

There are many possible variations of the wavelet transform, and they are being investigated at present by many workers to determine their most suitable forms. Today we have available a few wavelet analyzers to complement our overworked frequency analyzers.

Weighting Weighting is a standardized frequency-variable discrimination against a measured quantity of something, usually to make it more nearly descriptive of the subjective perception of the quantity. An example is the A-WEIGHTING curve applied to many measurements of SOUND PRESSURE LEVEL in order to correlate the measurements better with our loudness perception. Another example is the weighting applied to measurements of FLUTTER and WOW. The weighting curve takes into consideration which frequencies are the most annoying to human listeners, and attenuates other frequencies. In this way the measured level of the flutter will correlate well with the annoyance of the flutter.

Wet Wet refers to a recording or a sound that has significant REVERBERATION present, as opposed to DRY sound. The output of an effects device is 100 percent wet when only the output of the processor itself is being heard, with none of the unprocessed signal.

Whistle Filter A LOW-PASS FILTER with a CUTOFF FREQUENCY of 10 kilohertz found in AM tuners and receivers. Its purpose is to eliminate the 10-kHz tone that would otherwise be audible if there were another station broadcasting on an adjacent channel. The FCC has stipulated that the frequencies for AM broadcasting be 10 kHz apart, and if a receiver has response above this frequency, the adjacent channel carrier frequency will be detected. When the FCC made the frequency allocations many years ago, the maximum frequency response of receivers was considered to be 5 kHz, and many of them then did not exceed 3 kHz.

White Noise White noise is a special type of random noise where the energy content is the same at each FREQUENCY. Strictly speaking, true white noise would have energy extending from DC, or zero frequency, to infinitely high frequency. In practice, we see only BAND-LIMITED white noise. The sound heard when an FM receiver is tuned between stations is quite close to white noise over the audible frequency range.

Because of our ears' peculiar method of determining LOUDNESS of sounds, white noise sounds as if it has more energy at high frequencies than at low. *See also* PINK NOISE.

White Van Speaker Perhaps an urban myth, such loudspeakers look very impressive, may have a brand name on them and sell for an unbelievably low price from a street vendor in an unmarked automobile. However, when later examined, the product turns out to be very low quality and the vendor has disappeared.

Whizzer Cone A small supplementary cone attached to the VOICE COIL of a dynamic LOUDSPEAKER for the purpose of radiating high frequencies more efficiently than the regular cone. The whizzer cone is unsupported at the outer edge, being simply glued to the voice coil at the point where the regular cone is attached. If a whizzer cone is to work, there must be some COMPLIANCE between the coil and the regular cone so at high frequencies the regular cone is decoupled from the coil so as not to restrain the motion of the whizzer cone.

Whizzer cones were popular in the 1950s but have fallen into disfavor because it has been determined that they add COLORATION due to the nonlinearity of the added compliance. Some other loudspeaker units featured a decoupling compliance partway up the cone. One of these was the Biflex of Altec Lansing. These have receded into oblivion for the same reasons.

Whole Step The musical interval of a major second in a DIATONIC scale. The frequency ratio between the notes of a major second in JUST INTONATION is 8/9, and in equal temperament it is the 6th root of 2, or about 12%. *See* Appendix 8.

Wideband *See* BROADBAND.

Wild Sound A sound recorded for a motion picture where there is no attempt to synchronize the sound recorder to the camera, generally because no visual synchronization is needed. An example might be the sound of crickets for a night scene. *See also* DOUBLE-SYSTEM SOUND; SINGLE-SYSTEM SOUND.

Williamson Amplifier A famous POWER AMPLIFIER designed in Britain by D. T. N. Williamson in the 1950s. It used all TRIODE tubes, with PUSH-PULL CLASS A output circuitry and a specially designed OUTPUT TRANSFORMER. It had a single FEEDBACK loop from the output transformer secondary to the input tube CATHODE. The original Williamson put out only about 8 watts of power, but it had a smooth and "musical" sound much appreciated at the time. There were many variations of the basic circuit devised by other designers, probably the most famous of which was David Hafler's "Ultra Linear" configuration, which used a different output transformer with taps on the primary winding being returned to the output tube screen GRIDS. This increased the power output and efficiency with not too much penalty in added DISTORTION.

Winding The wire coils that compose the PRIMARY and SECONDARY of a TRANSFORMER are called windings.

Windscreen Although most microphone diaphragms are protected by perforated metal or a mesh of some sort, these do little to prevent a blast or wind or breath from overloading the diaphragm. Therefore, various devices can be added to a microphone to prevent this. The first level of protection may be built into the structure of the microphone, especially a hand-held vocal microphone, as a POP or BREATH FILTER, and is usually a piece of open-cell foam. A ball of such foam can be fitted over most mics if needed. Another tactic, especially with studio mics, is to place a ring with gauze-like material stretched over it between the vocalist and the microphone. Recording outdoors is especially tricky from a wind standpoint, and a device resembling, and called, a blimp or zeppelin is fitted over the entire microphone, with several inches of airspace between the mic and the blimp shell. The blimp may be lined with acoustic foam and mesh, and for very serious air movements, the blimp may be covered with a porous synthetic fur. *See also* POP FILTER.

Wiper The movable contact in a POTENTIOMETER is called the wiper or, sometimes, the arm.

Wireless Microphone A microphone with a miniature radio transmitter built in. The wireless is used with a remote receiver that picks up the SIGNAL. Wireless microphones are a good choice when a cable would be troublesome, such as when performers must move over a considerable area, or when the microphone must be concealed.

The quality of wireless systems is improving, but there are still problems with their use. Interference with other broadcast signals, such as citizens' band equipment and radio-dispatched taxicabs, can be an embarrassment. Also, the signal is subject to MULTIPATH DISTORTION in some cases where the RADIO FREQUENCY can be reflected around inside a building. Many of these problems are much improved by the use of a DIVERSITY RECEIVER.

Woofer The woofer is the low-FREQUENCY loudspeaker, or DRIVER, of a multiway LOUDSPEAKER system. Sometimes if frequencies below 30 or 40 HERTZ are to be produced, it is called a SUBWOOFER. Woofers generally are quite large, usually 12 or 15 inches in diameter, or sometimes 18 or even 24 inches. At one time, Electro-Voice made a giant woofer of 40-inch diameter.

Sheer size, however, is not the most important attribute of a woofer. A loudspeaker CONE does not vibrate as a simple piston at all frequencies; it "breaks up" into several modes of vibration, each one associated with a different frequency. Normally, the cone would not be operated at frequencies above the second mode of vibration, because its FREQUENCY RESPONSE and directional characteristics are quite irregular and unpredictable in this region. The larger the cone, the lower the frequency of the second mode and the lower the upper CUTOFF FREQUENCY must be to avoid these problems.

One of the most important developments in low-frequency reproduction with low DISTORTION was the "acoustic suspension" principle invented by Harry Olson of RCA Research Laboratories and first commercialized in 1954 by the Acoustic Research company. This system uses a relatively small woofer cone (8 to 12 inches in diameter) with the capability of very large AMPLITUDE of vibration. The cone is made quite massive and very loosely suspended. The box behind the cone is sealed, and the springiness of the air in the box is the major contributor to the force that returns the cone to the rest position. This air spring is LINEAR, and allows the cone to move relatively great distances without DISTORTION. The box is filled with a damping material such as fiberglass or mineral wool, partly to DAMP internal reflections of sound and partly to further linearize the air spring.

This invention was the first to permit excellent low-frequency performance from relatively small enclosures. The compromise in this type of system is that the EFFICIENCY is reduced from that of larger systems, meaning that more AMPLIFIER power is needed for the same output sound level. *See also* BASS REFLEX.

Word Clock The digital timing reference signal that is the same frequency as the sampling rate being used. In digital audio and video facilities with many digital devices, a single master word clock generator may be used as the timing reference for all devices, minimizing timebase jitter that might occur if the separate digital devices all used their own clocks for timing reference. There are also digital system clocks that are multiples of word clock, with claims for higher accuracy. *See also* HOUSE SYNCH.

Wow Wow is a relatively slow variation in FREQUENCY of reproduced sound caused by slow speed variations in records, tape recorders, etc. PITCH fluctuations of one or two per second or fewer are classed as WOW, while faster variations are called FLUTTER.

The term was first used during the early days of sound motion pictures. When threading a movie projector with the SOUND HEAD activated, moving the film by hand makes a sound something like the word "wow."

Wrap In an analog magnetic tape recorder, the tape wrap angle is the angle made by the tape as it approaches and leaves the TAPE HEAD. Wrap is actually a measure of the distance along the face of the head where the tape makes contact. This distance has an effect on the low-frequency response of the playback head. *See also* HEAD BUMP.

X-Copy An identical copy of pre-existing audio or video material used in movie editing.

X curve Extended curve. In the motion picture sound industry the X curve, also known as the wide-range curve, is a specification for the acoustic response curve of a movie theater. It is defined by ISO Bulletin 2969, which specifies at the listening position in a dubbing situation or two-thirds of the way back in a theater that the acoustic FREQUENCY RESPONSE be flat to 2 kHz, rolling off at 3-dB/OCTAVE above that. The input signal is specified as PINK NOISE. The small-room X curve is designed to be used in rooms with less than 150 cubic meters, or 5,300 cubic feet. This standard specifies flat response to 2 kHz, and then rolling off at a 1.5 dB/octave rate of ROLL OFF. Some people use a modified small-room curve, starting the roll off at 4 kHz, with a 3-dB/octave roll-off rate. The X curve replaced the old Academy Curve, and the X curve is meant to be used for monaural and Dolby Stereo analog sound tracks. The X Curve must be met in all theaters that are certified to the THX specification.

Xformer Abbreviation for TRANSFORMER.

XLR Connector In its three-conductor form (XLR-3), a common audio connector, widely used in balanced professional audio applications and for the AES3 (AES/EBU) digital interface. The XLR connector was a trademark of the Cannon company, but usage has made it a generic term and an international standard (as IEC 268-12), and many manufacturers make such connectors. Pin number 1 in the XLR plug is always connected to the shield. The reason is that the connectors are so designed that pin 1 makes contact first, ensuring that the ground connection is made before the signal connection. This greatly reduces the TRANSIENT thumps and pops that can occur when a CIRCUIT is patched with the power turned on. IEC standards now specify that pin 2 is wired to the "high" or plus (+) wire of a balanced pair, and pin 3 to the "low" or minus (–) wire. Unfortunately, there was no standard several years ago, and one still finds items wired with "pin 3 hot." The XLR connector is called a QG connector by one manufacturer, for "Quick Ground."

XM Satellite Radio *See* SATELLITE RADIO.

Xmtr Short for TRANSMITTER.

Xophonic An artificial reverberation device for the home made by Radio Craftsmen in the 1950s. The Xophonic was a box that looked about like a bookshelf LOUDSPEAKER. It contained an analog time delay device in the form of a small loudspeaker connected to a coil of tubing about 50 feet long with a MICROPHONE in the other end, producing a time delay of about 50 milliseconds. The incoming signal from the AMPLIFIER of the sound system was fed to the time delay unit and to a mixer, which combined it with the delayed signal from the tube microphone. A power amplifier and loudspeaker were included to amplify and radiate this combined signal into the listening room.

The Xophonic was probably the first signal processing device intended for home use. It enjoyed a brief popularity, and then quietly fell into oblivion, aided by the advent of the stereophonic record.

X-over Short for crossover. *See* CROSSOVER FREQUENCY; CROSSOVER NETWORK.

Xtal Abbreviation for CRYSTAL.

XYL Amateur radio operator slang for "wife." The term was popular in the 1950s and earlier, when ham radio was dominated by males. *See also* YL.

X-Y Stereo *See* INTENSITY STEREO.

Y

Yagi An early type of directional receiving antenna, mostly used for television reception, invented by Hidetsugu Yagi in 1928.

Y-Cord A Y-cord consists of two short AUDIO cables with similar connectors on one end that are joined to a single connector, usually of similar type but different gender. The Y-cord, or Y-connector as it is sometimes called, is used to create "split feeds," where the same signal is sent to two different places at the same time. Sometimes a Y-cord is used as a mixer to SHORT the two channels of a STEREO SIGNAL together to make a MONAURAL signal. This can lead to problems in low-IMPEDANCE circuits, because each output circuit LOADS the other one. The solution is to place a series RESISTOR in each signal path.

Also, a Y-cord can never be used to connect two channels of DIGITAL data together!

Yellow Book *See* RED BOOK.

YL Amateur radio operator slang for "girlfriend"; YL stands for "young lady."

Z

Z The symbol for IMPEDANCE.

Zener Diode The zener diode is a SOLID-STATE silicon DIODE that is "reverse biased" to such an extent that it conducts CURRENT backward. It is then said to be operating in the "avalanche" mode, and is sometimes called an avalanche diode. Under these conditions, the VOLTAGE across it will be very nearly constant over a range of current values. This constant voltage property is exploited by using it as a voltage regulator or voltage reference in power supply circuits. Zener diodes are available in a wide range of voltage values.

Zenith The angle that the face of the TAPE HEAD in an analog tape recorder makes with the top plate of the machine. The zenith should be 90 degrees, and if it is not, the head will not wear uniformly. Zenith angle is adjustable on some machines.

Zero Reference A standard SIGNAL level, usually recorded on an ALIGNMENT TAPE, used to set the reproduce GAIN control on a tape recorder. This level may or may not result in a zero VU reading on the tape recorder meter, depending on the philosophy espoused by the recording engineer. *See also* REFERENCE LEVEL.

Zipper Noise Audible artifacts or LOUDNESS steps heard in the audio when being changed by a digital system. Digital controllers have a finite number of discrete steps when controlling a signal parameter such as loudness, and under certain circumstances they can be heard. Some companies claim to use smoothing techniques to eliminate the problem. It is compared to the sound of the clothing fastener of the same name.

Zobel Network An R-C network consisting of two resistor-capacitor series circuits connected in parallel. The network is connected across the input terminals of a LOUDSPEAKER, where the impedance of the network is designed to "cancel" the inductance of the speaker voice coil. The result is a more nearly resistive LOAD on the CROSSOVER, smoothing the high-FREQUENCY amplitude and PHASE response of the crossover-speaker combination. In a two-way system, the WOOFER and TWEETER can be corrected with a Zobel network associated with each DRIVER.

Zoom Microphone A type of microphone system consisting of three CARDIOID microphone elements and a special PHASE correction and EQUALIZATION circuit. By varying the position of a control knob, the microphone outputs are combined in such a way that the directivity of the array changes from OMNIDIRECTIONAL through CARDIOID to SUPER-CARDIOID. The control can be synchronized with the control of a zoom lens on a video or motion picture camera so that the auditory perspective changes with the visual perspective.

Appendix 1
The Art and Science of Good Acoustics

The systematic study of musical acoustics existed as early as the first century B.C., as documented by Vitruvius in his *Ten Books on Architecture*. Great strides in understanding were achieved in the nineteenth century, especially with the work of Hermann Helmholtz. The twentieth century has spawned a near explosion in the field, as witnessed by the great number of recent publications on all fields of acoustics.

Research in physical acoustics has produced theories leading to improvements in the design of musical instruments and has greatly influenced the design of concert halls built in the last 100 years. Research in psychoacoustics has likewise influenced instrument design and auditorium acoustics.

One might expect that all this activity would have produced better instruments, better music, and happier musicians. This appendix attempts to show that this has not always happened. Some observations on the reasons for this are presented, along with some suggestions for further research. The areas considered are (1) auditorium acoustics, (2) psychoacoustics, and (3) musical instrument design.

Fads in the Design of Auditoriums

The first truly scientific architectural acoustician was Wallace Clement Sabine, professor of physics at Harvard University. He is credited with the acoustical design of Symphony Hall, built in Boston in 1900. Sabine investigated the measurement of reverberation time and devised the first formula to predict reverberation time from the dimensions of a room and the amount of sound absorption in it. He invented the concepts of acoustical absorption coefficients and absorption units, now called sabins. (One sabin is defined as one square foot of total sound absorption. The absorption of a given area of a material may be predicted by multiplying its absorption coefficient by its area in square feet.) Sabine also did much work on the measurement of absorption coefficients of many materials. He was probably the first to suggest that materials be manufactured for the express purpose of sound absorption, in effect making him the father of acoustical tile.

Symphony Hall has been universally claimed by musicians and audiences to possess superlative acoustics. Many would agree with the 1950 opinion of Rudolf Elie, music critic of the *Boston Herald*, "It is very clear to me now that Symphony Hall is the most acoustically beautiful hall in the United States. It is to the orchestra what a Stradivarius is to the great violinist in providing a sound box of the utmost brilliance and sensitivity."

While Sabine deserves credit for many of the hall's acoustic features, he was also very lucky that even though all of the hall's design features were not planned specifically for acoustic reasons, they contributed positively to the hall's qualities. Examples are the basic shape of the space, the large amount of sound-diffusing surfaces that are relatively broadband in action, and the well-placed natural frequencies of the wall and ceiling surfaces.

Later in the century, as a sequel to Sabine's work, the measurement of reverberation time in halls became fashionable, and along with this came the ability to control the reverberation time by the use of special sound-absorbing materials. The "control" of reverberation rapidly attained the status of an architectural fad. Existing auditoriums and all types of public buildings were "corrected" by liberal applications of acoustical tile, or acoustical plaster. Many architects, acousticians, and especially acoustic tile salesmen were convinced that all manner of acoustical defects could be cured simply by the liberal application of sound-absorbing material. Books on architecture and musical acoustics began to appear, nearly all citing reverberation time as the most significant aspect of the acoustics of a room, in spite of such an authority as Vern Knudsen writing in 1963, "A felicitous shape is a requirement of the highest priority. Unfortunately, many architects believe that faulty shapes can be corrected by covering the offending surfaces with highly absorptive materials and by adjusting the reverberation time. Thus deluded, they adopt a fashionable construction method, such as a concrete shell, and produce a building that is an acoustical perversion. A bad shape is a permanent liability."

It became apparent very early that reverberation time could be made to have different values at different frequencies. It was noted that many existing buildings had much longer reverberation at low frequencies than at high frequencies. The reaction to this observation was to introduce selective absorption so that the reverberation would be nearly constant with frequency, the rationale being that the overall tonal quality would be more uniform over the musical pitch range. It was thought that longer low-frequency reverberation caused the music to sound "muddy" and ill-defined and that uniform reverberation vs. frequency would improve musical clarity and definition.

The result of this thinking was the construction of many new music auditoriums with very hard, crisp, or "tinny" sound with very little warmth and solidity. In a few cases the trend was carried to such an extreme that the high-frequency reverberation time actually exceeded that of low frequencies. Of course the musicians knew better all the time and acousticians and architects began to be held in contempt.

In the November 5, 1955, issue of the *New Yorker,* Joseph Wechsberg wrote, "Most of the people who have set themselves up as consultants on matters of acoustics contend, not unnaturally, that by applying certain laws of physics and using certain testing devices they can determine in advance how hospitable to sound a new auditorium will be. The fact is, however, that several auditoriums built in Europe recently under the guidance of consultants who presumably applied the laws of physics and using the testing devices have turned out to have dreadful acoustics."

The eminent American acoustician Leo Beranek read these words and was forced to admit that most modern auditoriums were not free of criticism. Beranek then undertook a systematic study of fifty-four concert halls located in various parts of the world. He identified several acoustical characteristics other than reverberation that contribute in large measure to the acoustics of halls. One of these measures is the Initial Time Delay Gap, or ITDG as Beranek called it. The ITDG is defined as the time interval between a listener's hearing of the direct sound from a source and the earliest reflected sound from the walls or ceiling. It is a measure of the subjective "intimacy" of a music hall, a shorter ITDG corresponding to the subjective impression of smaller rooms and vice versa. Beranek reasoned that a large concert hall must have a high ceiling to attain sufficient reverberation, but should have a low ceiling to provide a sufficiently short ITDG for subjective intimacy. The two requirements being mutually exclusive, led Beranek to the invention of relatively small sound-reflecting panels (called acoustical clouds) suspended from the true ceiling and forming a second lower but partially acoustically-transparent sound ceiling. The reasoning was that sounds reflecting from the clouds would provide a short ITDG, while sounds passing between the clouds would excite the reverberation of the entire room volume.

Leo Beranek was the acoustician for Philharmonic Hall at Lincoln Center in New York, completed in 1962. His well-written and researched book, *Music, Acoustics, and Architecture,* published in 1962, tells the story of the hall's design in painstaking detail. The book is fascinating, both in regard to its technical completeness and in respect to the complex fate of Philharmonic Hall since its opening. As is well known, the hall was subjected to criticism from all areas of music from its opening, and several expensive attempts to correct it were made, ending in a $750,000 remodeling in 1969. This remodeling purportedly eliminated the clouds but retained the same shape. Even after this, musicians and music lovers were not happy with the acoustics and finally the building was gutted and a completely new concert hall constructed within the four walls at a cost of $17,000,000. The new auditorium was named Avery Fisher Hall in honor of the man who donated most of the needed funds. The new hall, designed by the acoustician Cyril Harris, is similar in shape to Symphony Hall in Boston, the hall the New York Philharmonic Society had asked Beranek to emulate in the first place (letter from George Judd, Jr., to Max Abramovich, dated April 20, 1959, quoted in Beranek, *op. cit.).* At last the controversy over Philharmonic Hall seems to have ended, but the obvious question is, "What went wrong?" Beranek is in every sense a respected and accomplished acoustician and it is obvious from his book that he did his homework. The answer must come from psychoacoustics: the study of our perception of what we hear.

There is an excellent, but relatively unknown, book by Georg von Békésy called *Sensory Inhibition* (Princeton University Press, 1967), that summarizes much of Békésy's research spanning many years. There are some strong clues to why the clouds at Lincoln Center did not behave as expected. Békésy points out that an array of acoustical clouds will reflect high frequencies while permitting low frequencies to pass through and be reflected from the true ceiling above. This means the high frequency portion of complex musical sounds reach the listener earlier than the lower frequency components of those sounds. Békésy had established earlier that sounds arriving in quick succession at the ear result in complex nervous system processing whereby a part of the response is inhibited. He called this phenomenon auditory inhibition. He states, "In the concert hall the low frequencies will lose their effectiveness in brief pulses of sound heard by a listener. These tones are physically present but are inhibited because they are delayed in arrival at the listener's ears. This type of distortion may be called 'room acoustics phase distortion' and represents an interesting new field. The construction of auditoriums and the subsequent discovery of these distortions represent very expensive experiments on inhibition." Békésy then points out that this type of phase distortion is not noticed if it is slight, but when it is increased, a threshold is reached where suddenly the unexpected happens. Such thresholds exist also for other sensory phenomena. "These sensory thresholds present barriers that often prevent technical extensions into what otherwise might be unlimited fields."

The lesson from this is that architectural acousticians must be mindful of psychoacoustics and sensory inhibition and must be wary of extrapolating known designs into larger scales. Also, perhaps a different point of view should be sought. Siegmund Levarie and Ernst Levy bemoan the fact that architectural acoustics is still thought of in terms of reverberation and absorption of sound. In other words geometrical acoustics, or ray acoustics, has been used because of its ease of theoretical simplification and measurements. When addressed from the standpoint of volume resonance and wave theory, room acoustics measurements seem much better correlated to what a person hears with his complex auditory mechanism. There has been recent work, much of it instigated by Manfred Schroeder of Gottingen, on the importance of strong side wall reflections and diffused ceiling reflections in concert halls; this work appears promising. New auditoriums designed to provide strong reflection from the side walls across the audience have been designed recently by some acousticians, notably Paul Veneklasen of Los Angeles; these rooms are praised by musicians and audiences alike. The Japanese acoustician Yoichi Ando, in collaboration with Manfred Schroeder, has done much work to place a firm theoretical formulation under this concept. In this work the somewhat simplistic ITDG is being replaced by the IACC, or Interaural Cross Correlation function, which is a mathematical measure of the "sameness" of the sounds reaching the two eardrums. Ando has been able to establish a connection between the IACC function and the degree of preference expressed by listeners to different sound fields. Perhaps this will allow innovative concert halls to be designed and still attain acceptance by musicians.

Appendix 1

Psychoacoustics, Hearing Threshold, Critical Bands, and Earphones

In efforts to determine how our auditory system works, a great many experiments have been performed that effectively isolate various hearing phenomena. One of the best known of these was the measurement of equal loudness contours by Harvey Fletcher and W. A. Munson in the early 1930s. By presenting pure tones of many frequencies and intensities to various subjects, it was shown that the ear's sensitivity varies with the frequency of the test tone. Most notably, tones of low frequencies must be many times more intense than high frequency tones to be judged equally loud. Also the auditory threshold, or least intensive sounds that can be heard at a given frequency, is drastically higher at low frequencies and at very high frequencies compared to the most sensitive region of about 3000 Hz. Any sound must be above the threshold in intensity at its frequency to be heard at all and presumably any sounds below threshold will not be heard.

This observation holds true, of course, for single pure tones, but when the ear is subjected to more than one tone at a time, things get complicated quickly. It has been shown that the presence of any tone that is above threshold will raise the auditory threshold for other frequencies. In other words the presence of a single relatively intense tone can cause a less intense tone of another frequency to be inaudible. This phenomenon is called masking; masking contours have been plotted that show under what conditions of frequency and intensity tones can be heard. These masking contours have different shapes for masking tones of different frequencies and intensities, making the situation somewhat complicated.

Examination of this masking data leads one to believe that many instances occur in common experience when sounds cannot be heard even though they are known to exist. This has been the case in the field of electronic reproduction of music, known popularly as "high fidelity." Music reproducing equipment always adds some spurious signals to the music in the form of distortion of various kinds. Distortion has been reduced as equipment has become more sophisticated, especially in the case of amplifiers. Some amplifier manufacturers claim the distortion added by their equipment is inaudible because of its extremely low intensity and its being masked by the music itself. Many people have been skeptical of these claims, believing that they could easily tell differences between various amplifiers all having very low distortion.

An interesting study was performed in Finland and reported in the *Journal of the Audio Engineering Society* in 1978 (cf. Petri-Larmi, Otala, and Lamurasniemi). A special machine was built to introduce controlled amounts of Transient Intermodulation Distortion to recorded musical examples. One surprising result was that the detection threshold was .003% rms distortion for piano recordings. The authors acknowledge that this is "difficult to explain" because the distortion components are so low in intensity as to be below the hearing thresholds of the subjects! In other words, adding certain sounds that are so low in intensity that they are inaudible by themselves to a piano recording will result in a detectable difference in the piano sound. Clearly more work needs to be done in audibility of low intensity sounds, and the Fletcher-Munson curves do not predict the audibility of some complex sounds.

Generally, psychoacoustic testing is performed with earphones rather than loudspeakers in order to facilitate exact control of the signals reaching the ears. Audiometric testing is always done with earphones, presumably for the same reason. But earphones present formidable problems in standardizing sound levels at the eardrum and in attaining standardized frequency response with different listeners. The seal between the phone and the head greatly affects the low frequency response and the shape of the listener's pinna greatly affects the middle and high frequency response. Greater than 10 dB frequency response discrepancies between subjects using the same earphones have been reported (Sank, *op. cit.).* Also the presence of the earphone on the ear increases the audibility of the listener's own physiological processes. This is somewhat akin to hearing the ocean roar when holding a seashell to one's ear. Those extraneous noises can act as masking signals and could, it would seem, invalidate audiometric testing. Is it possible that critical bands and loudness contours are artifacts caused by using earphones? In any case it is obvious that earphone listening is an unnatural condition for our hearing mechanism, and it seems that insofar as possible, psychoacoustic testing should be done under free field conditions using both ears.

Problems can occur when trying to apply the results of psychoacoustic testing to musical experiences. Most experiments aimed at investigating our hearing ability have used sine waves (pure tones) as independent variables. One phenomenon that was noticed early is that the perceived pitch of a tone varies with intensity and is not directly correlated with its frequency (Stevens, *op. cit.).*

Low pitches are made subjectively lower with increasing intensity and high pitches are made subjectively higher with greater intensity. One might expect this to explain out-of-tune playing among orchestra members, but it happens that according to some researchers the effect disappears with complex tones! However, this has not been shown to be true under all conditions and more studies need to be done. In summary we think it would be desirable if psychoacoustic research could be conducted with sounds that more clearly imitate natural sounds, and the use of earphones should be approached with caution.

Instrument Design – Piano and Stringed Instruments

It has been known for many years that the overtones present in the sound of the piano are not accurately tuned to the frequencies of the harmonic series, but are in fact higher in frequency. This sharpening of the overtones increases with the order of the overtone. Because the piano is tuned in octaves up and down from a central temperament octave, the piano will be tuned progressively sharp in the treble octaves and progressively flat in the bass. On the surface it would appear that this is a defect in the piano. As long ago as 1949, F. Miller proposed that if small masses were applied to the strings near their ends, the inharmonicity could be cancelled. He proposed that the piano could be improved by this method, but there seemed to be essentially no interest among piano makers to adopt the improvement. Then in 1962, Harvey Fletcher, *et al.*, reported that synthesized piano tones without inharmonicity were not preferred by listeners over synthetic tones that did contain inharmonicity. The non-stretched tones were described as dull, uninteresting, and not piano-like. After a series of similar listening experiments, the Conn company came to a similar conclusion. Thus it turns out that a "defect" in the piano tone, as discovered by physical measurement of the sound, is actually an important factor in the quality of the instrument.

Stringed instruments such as the violin, viola, cello, and bass viol have been built for so many years that one would expect their design to have been optimized by now. Many people have studied most aspects of stringed instruments and the consensus has been that the violin has been optimized insofar as its size and shape in relation to its pitch are concerned. Acoustically the violin has its resonances properly placed to ensure a uniform tonal output and its size allows relative ease of playing. The cello is also close to an ideal size for its pitch range. The viola and string bass, however, are too small physically to radiate optimally in their pitch range. Carleen Hutchins of the Catgut Acoustical Society has studied this situation and has proposed new designs for the viola and bass that nearly optimize their size and shape to their respective ranges. Because of its larger size, the Hutchins viola must be played vertically in the manner of the cello. According to one violinist who has mastered the instrument, this is not an important advantage. The so-called Great Bass is significantly larger than its double bass cousin, making it somewhat awkward to play, at least by persons of normal size. These instruments are characterized by a greater production of the fundamental frequencies, especially in the lower register. The difference is quite striking.

Hutchins envisioned the use of the new instruments in orchestras where their greater strength in the low register would be welcome. Perhaps at last the viola section could compete on a more equal basis with the violins, and perhaps the Great Basses would finally provide the rich, strong support in the low frequencies that has been lacking in symphony orchestras. However, sufficient time has passed that these instruments should have made definite inroads in orchestra makeup if they are going to do so. The Great Bass in particular was praised by Leopold Stokowski; this alone should have encouraged its introduction and use, but no such revolution has occurred. The initial interest and excitement has seemingly dissipated.

Can this fact be attributed to a simple inertia and unwillingness on the part of musicians to try something new? Is it simply a matter of time before we see vertical violas and Great Basses in all our symphony orchestras? We think not. We believe that even though the new instruments may be optimized from the standpoint of their acoustical performance in some sort of absolute sense, they are not necessarily well suited to performance of the existing body of symphonic music. It must be remembered that composers have had to work around the so-called inadequacy of existing instrument design, and the structure of the music has been designed to exploit the tonal characteristics of existing instruments. The introduction of a relatively new and different sound to the performance of this music must be expected to meet with significant resistance. Innovations in instrument design probably should not exhibit great differences in tone quality if they are to be accepted by the musical community. An example is the transverse flute designed by Theobald Boehm in the nineteenth century. Boehm's work resulted in greater ease of playing and improved tuning in both the flute and clarinet, and musicians readily accepted the changes. The basic sound of the instruments was changed very little. Perhaps our research efforts should be aimed at greater ease of performance and tuning stability of instruments rather than at the creation of new sounding instruments that "correct" the deficiencies of existing instruments as measured by scientific instrumentation and techniques.

References

Beranek, Leo. *Music, Acoustics, and Architecture.* New York: John Wiley & Sons, 1962.

Fletcher, Harvey, *et al.* "Quality of Piano Tones." *Journal of the Acoustical Society of America,* Vol. 36.

Hutchins, Carleen. "Founding a Family of Fiddles." *Physics Today,* Vol. 20, February 1967.

Knudsen, Vern O. "Architectural Acoustics." *Scientific American,* Vol. 209, No.5, November 1963.

Levarie, Siegmund, and Ernst Levy. *Tone: A Study in Musical Acoustics.* Kent, OH: Kent State University Press, 1968.

Miller, F., Jr. "Proposed Loading of Piano Strings for Improved Tone." *Journal of the Acoustical Society of America,* Vol. 21, 1949.

Petri-Larmi, M., M. Otala, and J. Lamurasniemi. "Psychoacoustic Detection Threshold of Transient Intermodulation Distortion." *Journal of the Audio Engineering Society,* Vol. 28, No. 3, February 1980.

Roederer, Juan. *Introduction to the Physics and Psychophysics of Music.* Heidelberg, Germany: Heidelberg Science Library, 1975.

Sank, J. R. "Improved Real-Ear Tests for Stereophones." *Journal of the Audio Engineering Society,* Vol. 28, No.4, April 1980.

Stevens, S. S. "The Relation of Pitch to Intensity." *Journal of the Acoustical Society of America,* 1935.

Terhardt, E. "Influence of Intensity of the Pitch of Complex Tones." *Acustica,* Vol. 33, 1975.

Appendix 2
Some Frequently Used Symbols and Units

Table 1

Prefixes		
Prefix	**Multiple**	**Symbol**
deka	ten times	d, or da
hecto	hundred times	h
kilo	thousand times	k
mega	million times	M
giga	billion times	G
tera	trillion times	T
deci	tenth part	d
centi	hundredth part	c
milli	thousandth part	m
micro	millionth part	μ
nano	billionth part	n
pico	trillionth part	p

Appendix 2

Table 2

Symbols and Names of SI Units

Name	Quantity	Symbol	Unit
kilogram	mass	kg	
meter	length, distance	m	
second	time	s	
ampere	electric current	A	coulombs/s
coulomb	electric charge	C	
farad	capacitance	F	
henry	inductance	H	
hertz	frequency	Hz	cycles/s
joule	work, energy	J	newton-meters
newton	force	N	
pascal	pressure	Pa	newtons/m^2
siemens	electric conductance	S	
tesla	magnetic flux density	T	
volt	electric potential	V	
watt	power	W	joules/s
weber	magnetic flux	Wb	
ohm	electric resistance	Ω	volts/ampere

Appendix 2

Table 3

Decibel Values

Power Ratio	Voltage Ratio	Decibel Value
1	1	0 dB
2	1.4	3 dB
4	2	6 dB
10	3.16	10 dB
100	10	20 dB
1,000	31.6	30 dB
10,000	100	40 dB
100,000	316	50 dB
1,000,000	1000	60 dB

By memorizing Table 3, one can easily approximate calculations involving decibels and power and voltage ratios.

Adding decibels is equivalent to multiplying power ratios. For instance, adding 3 dB to a power level multiplies it by 2, and adding 6 dB multiplies it by 4. Therefore, 36 dB (30 dB + 6 dB) is equivalent to a power ratio of 4,000 (1,000 x 4); and 23 dB (20 dB + 3 dB) equals a power ratio of 200 (100 x 2), etc.

Adding decibels is also equivalent to multiplying voltage squared ratios. Thus, 26 dB is equivalent to a voltage ratio of 20 (10 x 2), and 43 dB equals a voltage ratio of 140 (100 x 1.4), etc.

Appendix 3
How to Subdue a Hi-Fi Salesperson

Who has not innocently walked into a stereo store to listen to certain components in a leisurely manner, only to be inundated with technical jargon (or pseudo-technical jargon) by a salesperson who is seemingly intent on minimizing the contents of your pocketbook, with apparent disregard for your sonic requirements and desires? What is the best way to handle such a situation? How can one make meaningful comparisons of loudspeakers, amplifiers, record players, etc., in the presence of such a confusing array of equipment, almost each component of which represents a "breakthrough" in technology? Well, we believe it is possible to make some sense out of a seemingly hopeless situation.

- Loudspeaker Evaluation. The first thing your salesperson is likely to say is that you must compare the sounds of various loudspeakers switching between them while playing a recording of some sort. Surely you will be told that everybody hears differently and what sounds accurate to you may seem inaccurate to others, and supposedly you will be able to select the most "natural" sounding unit easily. However, this has been shown many times over to be untrue. Comparing the sounds of loudspeakers might allow you to select the most pleasant-sounding one with that particular CD, but this has almost no relation to absolute accuracy.

  Accuracy in reproduction is not a subjective effect, but is objective—not a characteristic of perception, but an actual characteristic of sound itself. How, then, can you select the most accurate loudspeaker out of a group? You must compare the sounds of the speakers to a live sound with which you are familiar. A good test sound is a male voice. If possible, arrange to record the voice of a friend whose voice you know well, preferably a male friend. The recording should be done either in a very large space or outdoors, and the microphone must be of as high a quality as possible. Be sure the microphone is at least three feet from the talker to avoid recording proximity effect on the tape. A good quality cassette recorder is adequate for this. Then, accompany your friend to the stereo store, hand the salesman the recording and ask to hear it through various loudspeakers. Have your friend stand near the loudspeaker in question, have him speak, and then adjust the loudness of the reproduced sound of his voice to match the loudness of the live voice. This is important. You will very quickly find that almost none of the speakers sound natural.

Listen particularly to the low-frequency tones and note the resonant "boominess" projected by many systems. Then listen to the sibilant sounds, and note the great differences in the way they are handled by the various speakers. At the start of the test, the tone controls in the amplifier should be set for "flat" response, and you can experiment with different settings to increase the naturalness of the sound. You will find, however, that many speaker systems will not sound natural, no matter what the tone control settings are.

While it may seem that a voice will not exercise the full frequency range of a loudspeaker system, and this is true in the strict sense, the male voice does cover the part of the frequency range most important to music. It is interesting to note that this is a much more severe test than simply to tune in a radio announcer you may be used to hearing and use this voice as a test signal. The latter is not good for two reasons: you are familiar with the sound of the voice heard over the radio and not in person; and radio broadcasters nearly always use directional microphones at short range to pick up announcers, causing very large increase in bass response due to proximity effect. Some have called this the "Jolly Green Giant" effect, and it makes this a hopeless test signal.

If you are not able to do this test, another simple experiment is enlightening. Simply tune an FM tuner in the store to a point between stations and listen to the random noise thus produced. (Be sure the tuner used does not have interstation muting, or turn the muting off.) This random noise is devoid of any musical pitch, being made up of a collection of all frequencies mixed in a completely chaotic manner. It exercises the loudspeaker in all frequency ranges simultaneously, allowing you to hear anomalies over the whole audio range. The noise should have no perceived musical pitch at any pitch level. Switching between speakers will immediately show up those that have peaks, or resonances, in the audible range. Listen especially at very high frequencies and very low frequencies. It takes practice to learn how to listen to random noise. (It always must be reproduced by some sort of loudspeaker to be heard, and none are perfect.) Nevertheless, this is a very easy task to perform, and it will tell you a great deal about the frequency responses of loudspeakers. Also, it is fun to watch the expression on the salesperson's face.

- Phono cartridge evaluation. Probably the most objective way to evaluate a cartridge is to use a special test record that contains a recording of "pink noise," which is random noise that has been equalized so it contains equal energy in each octave band of frequency. (The noise heard between FM stations is not pink noise, but it is an approximation of it. True pink noise is somewhat difficult to generate.) Some dealers may have such a test record. Simply play the record with different cartridges, using the most neutral-sounding speaker system, selected from the previous test. Listen for any signs of definite pitch, especially in the very high frequencies. Also, play various records and listen in particular to the timbre of the music. In general, classical music is best for this type of evaluation because popular music is usually highly compressed in dynamic range and also greatly "equalized."

Listen to the tone color of percussion, especially cymbals. Note if the tone color is similar when playing various records, or whether each record sounds individual, as it should. Similarities in tone color are due to the cartridge, which has characteristic timbre of its own that it impresses on the reproduced music. Find the cartridge which seems to have the least influence on the tone color of various types of music. One type of music which will show up high-frequency anomalies is the massed strings of a symphony orchestra. These comments also apply to loudspeaker evaluation, so when listening to cartridges, use only one speaker.

These tests are aimed at the transducers, the devices which alter the sound more than other audio components. Evaluation of CD players, amplifiers, tape recorders, etc., is more difficult but also less important, most such units sounding quite similar. Perceptual encoding recorders and players can be a different matter.

There are some ways to evaluate CD players, whose digital to analog converters can vary in quality, and whose error correction and concealment systems differ. Try the pink noise test described above for phono cartridges, using a test CD. In addition pay particular attention to the very soft sounds, and sounds fading into silence, using headphones if necessary. Avoid a player that makes fading sounds just above silence seem to splatter, or sound like "static."

The error correction and concealment characteristics of players differ widely. The sounds players emit when confronted with increasing data error rates can be remarkable, with one player sounding fine and another playing heavy static. This can be a problem not only with dirty and damaged CDs, but with poor CD-R burns. You can approximate an error test CD by using a fine point alcohol-based marker, such as a Sharpie, and putting about a 1-mm dot on the underside of the CD. CDs play from the inner diameter to the outside, so putting the dot about the 4 mm from the beginning of the data area avoids the TOC and should affect the music a few minutes from the start. Some players will skip, and some may sound fine. The dot cleans off easily with a issue moistened with alcohol.

Devices using perceptual coding such as MP3 devices and MiniDisc are carefully designed to disguise their performance limitations when playing music. They should be considered a step down in fidelity from the CD, and it is usually relatively easy to get poor

> sound from them. Be sure to compare the same data rates or disc play times. Like most digital systems, it is usually in the softest sounds where these systems show weakness.

By the time these tests are completed, the salesperson may be stunned into silence, or possibly will have understood what you are doing and have helped you through the process, thereby learning something as well.

Appendix 4
Good Acoustics in Small Rooms and Auditoria

1. Small Room Acoustics

In this section, we will try to demystify the subject of the acoustical properties of a small room, and we will offer suggestions on how to optimize the performance of the loudspeakers in your listening environment. Information presented here will be useful to recording engineers, but should be of interest to serious audiophiles as well.

We will study some of the acoustical principles involved and the behavior of sounds of different frequencies in small rooms in order to get a better understanding of what we hear. By a small room, we mean a room the size of a typical recording studio control room or a home living room. (By this definition, a shower stall is a very small room, albeit one with interesting acoustical properties. We will return to the shower stall a little later.)

It is interesting that the acoustics of a small room are quite different from the acoustics of a large room such as an auditorium. It is also quite well known that a given loudspeaker will sound very different in a small room compared to how it would sound in an auditorium.

We will look into the reasons for these differences, and will explain the principles at work in such a way that you can understand them, even if you do not happen to have a Ph.D. in acoustical engineering. With these general facts in mind, you will be able to make valid decisions about the placement of the speakers, the placement of the listeners, and the adjustment of the speakers in order to achieve the most agreeable listening experience. We will try to inform you what to do if your room seems to be impossible to configure for good sound, even if, in the extreme case, only a stick of dynamite will serve to correct the situation. Fortunately for all involved, this extreme case is seldom encountered in practice.

It will be interesting to think about the philosophy of loudspeakers recording engineers use in recording studio control rooms for evaluating microphone types and placement and the monitoring of the final mix of recordings. After all, the recording engineer makes his living with his ears, and they must not deceive him. (The serious but nonprofessional music listener will also benefit from this.)

There is a long history of the various types of speakers used in monitoring recordings. In former times, very large theater speakers were often used, the idea being that everything should be accentuated and reproduced bigger than life so the slightest defect in the recording would be painfully obvious.

Appendix 4

The sound levels used in monitoring often came close to deafening the engineer, making him insensitive to the subtleties in the reproduced sounds.

Today, we know better. We understand the effect of very high-intensity sounds on human hearing, such as threshold shifts and auditory fatigue. We believe the monitoring levels should not be much greater than the levels that will be used in the final reproduction in the user's environment. We believe the monitor speakers should be as neutral sounding as possible, that they should have no discernable acoustic character or tone color. Simply put, they should just convert the electrical signal fed to them into sound without adding or subtracting anything. All the sounds that emanate from the monitor speakers have their origin elsewhere in the recording chain. If the engineer hears something he does not like, he knows that it is not a distortion or coloration introduced by the speakers. He is therefore able to track it down and correct it and then be able to hear the difference.

However, speaker systems are not used in a vacuum. They must be located in rooms that will modify their sounds in complex ways, as we shall see shortly. Therefore, we must find the best way to see to it that the placement in the room and the characteristics of the room itself do not destroy the purity and linearity of the sounds the loudspeakers are capable of producing.

The typical small room is unfortunately not ideal for listening to live music, and is also not ideal for listening to reproduced music. There are many reasons for this, and most of them boil down to the fact that the wavelengths of the sounds produced by music vary from about 40 feet for the lowest bass notes to about ½ inch for the highest notes in the treble. The wavelengths of the sounds of the fundamental pitches of a piano are shown in figure 1, below. (The harmonics of these pitches extend to much higher frequencies and much smaller wavelengths.) Large auditoriums that are designed for listening to music can handle this huge range of sound wavelengths well, mostly because even the longest waves are short compared to the dimensions of the room. The large room swallows up these long waves, and allows them to bounce

Frequency	Pitch	Wavelength
27.5 Hz	Bottom A	40 feet
55 Hz	Low A	20 feet
110 Hz	Tenor A	10 feet
220 Hz	Middle A	5 feet
440 Hz	A 440	2.5 feet
880 Hz	6th A	1.25 feet
1760 Hz	7th A	7.5 inches
3520 Hz	8th A	3.6 inches

Figure 1

around freely and to be diffused by the reflections from the distant walls so they can attain a proper balance with the higher pitched tones. The small room, however, is not able to cope with these long sound waves in a manner that satisfies the musical ear.

The typical small room does not have enough space to permit this diffusion of the longer waves, and they bunch up, interfere with one another, and generally raise havoc with the musical balance. This is bad enough when real musicians with conventional instruments are performing in a small room, but the situation is worse when you try to reproduce the music with loudspeakers. This is because the speakers are the sources for all the musical sounds, rather than having the music come from many different locations in the room.

Sound waves are actually pressure disturbances that travel at a nearly constant speed (the speed of sound, about 1,100 feet per second) through the air. They carry energy as they travel, or in other words they convey power from the sound source to the sound receiver. The molecules of the air do not travel from the source to the receiver but simply vibrate, transmitting energy from one to another, somewhat analogous to a series of upright dominoes each one of which will fall due to being pushed by its neighbor. Each domino does not move very far, but the energy it took to topple the first one is transmitted all along the path of the domino "wave." See figure 2.

Figure 2

When a source of sound is radiating into three-dimensional space with no barriers present, the energy emitted by the source will flow outwards in all directions in the form of compression waves in the air. The waves will expand in spheres ever increasing in size, and this will go on ad infinitum if the waves do not encounter any barriers or objects. This is called a free-field condition, and the sound level you would sense at any location in the sound field would be dependent on the strength of the source and the distance between you and the source. See figure 3.

Since the waves are expanding in area as they move out from the source, each doubling of the distance results in a reduction of the sound energy by a factor of four. (The area of a sphere is proportional to the square of its diameter.) In more precise terms, the sound level is said to obey the inverse square law. For instance, the sound power you would sense at 1 foot will be four times the power at 2 feet, and nine times the power at 3 feet. A factor of four in sound energy level is a 6-decibel (6 dB) change, so we say the sound level falls off at 6 dB for each doubling of distance.

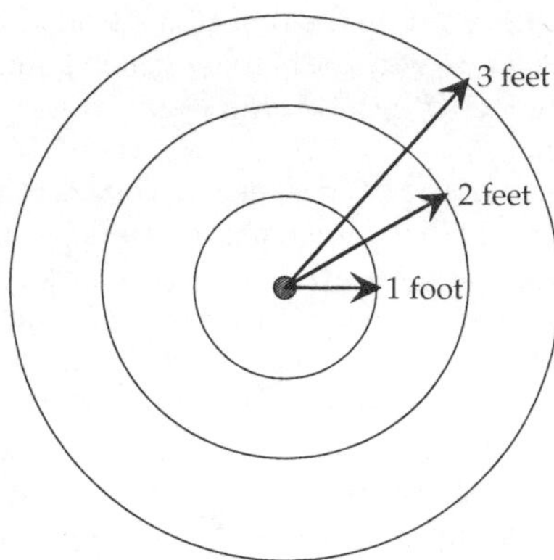

Figure 3

True free-field conditions are almost never met in practice since there are always barriers and objects in the path of the sound waves, but under certain conditions, there can exist a good approximation of a free field. We will return to this concept a little later.

When a sound wave encounters a large barrier, such as a wall, part of it will be reflected from the wall and the wall will absorb part of it. The amount of the energy in the wave that is absorbed is dependent on how much the wall moves in response to the pressure exerted by the wave. If the wall is very solid, i.e., made of concrete or solid uranium a foot thick, the wall will not move appreciably and almost all of the energy in the wave will be reflected back into the room. The amount of energy reflected by the wall also depends on the surface condition of the wall, and on the wavelength of the sound. If the wall is covered with a soft material, such as egg cartons, fiberglass, cloth tapestries, or old undershirts, sounds with short wavelengths will be absorbed more efficiently than sounds with long wavelengths. This is the reason that most rooms will have a longer reverberation time at low frequencies than at high frequencies. Of course most rooms are not made of uranium and they do flex when they are struck by sound waves, and this absorbs energy, reducing the strength of the reflected sound.

In large rooms where the smallest dimension is about 50 feet, the waves from the sound sources expand in spheres as if in a free field until they meet the surfaces. Then they are reflected in such a way that they continue to spread out after they are reflected. This allows the reflected sounds to become randomized on multiple reflections, and the interference patterns are so complex and overlapped that they are scarcely noticeable.

In a large room, the sounds of all wavelengths get reflected many times and in all directions as they meet the surfaces of the room. They finally reach a condition called diffusion, which means the waves are moving in unpredictable directions as they gradually die away from being partially absorbed at each reflection. In a diffused sound field, you are not able to tell where a sound is coming from. You are immersed in an ocean of uniform sound coming from all directions at once. Complete diffusion is not possible in practice, but in some very reverberant spaces, it is approached. For listening to music, however, you do not want the sound field to be too diffuse, since the musical line would be blurred, and the structure of the melody and harmony would be difficult to discern at best. For this reason, concert hall designers strive to achieve a pleasing balance between the diffuse reverberation in the room and the direct sounds coming from the musical instruments.

The acoustics of large rooms can be wonderful for live music, but they often present problems for amplified sound. The sound system designer must be careful to see that the speakers direct the amplified sounds to the listener's ears before they reflect from the walls or other surfaces. Otherwise, the sound heard by the listener would be too reverberant and "muddy." Also, the microphones used in sound reinforcement systems must be close to the performers so they don't pick up the reverberant sound of the room.

In a small room, the situation is different. The small room has reflecting surfaces that are close enough to the source of sound that there is not sufficient space for the long-wavelength sound waves to diverge, and they strike the surfaces almost as plane waves rather than spherical waves. Therefore the long wavelengths of the lower frequencies prevent them from being able to diffuse smoothly throughout the room. The main reason for this is the phenomenon called "interference." Interference is a condition where two sound waves occupy the same space; their sound pressures add together when they are in phase with each other and they subtract (partially cancel) when they are out of phase with each other. This is called constructive and destructive interference.

A special case of constructive and destructive interference is the dreaded "standing wave," sometimes called the "stationary wave." A standing wave occurs when two large parallel surfaces have a sound source between them operating at certain specific frequencies. To form a standing wave, the sound waves must be of a frequency where one half a wavelength is a submultiple of the spacing between the surfaces. In other words, an integral number of ½ wavelengths of the sound must fit between the two surfaces.

In the example shown in figure 4, there are five ½ wavelengths between the wall surfaces. As the sound energy bounces back and forth between the walls, the sound pressures successively add together and cancel, causing a series of locations of maximum loudness and minimum loudness to exist. (This example shows complete cancellation and zero sound pressure at the minima, but this never happens in practice.) Note that there is always a pressure maximum at the wall surfaces. The locations of maximum sound pressure are called "antinodes," and the locations of minimum sound pressure are called "nodes." Of course, the locations of the nodes and antinodes depend on the wavelengths involved and the spacing between the walls. The two surfaces will generate standing waves at every frequency at which the wall spacing is divisible by ½ of the wavelength. Each of these standing wave patterns is

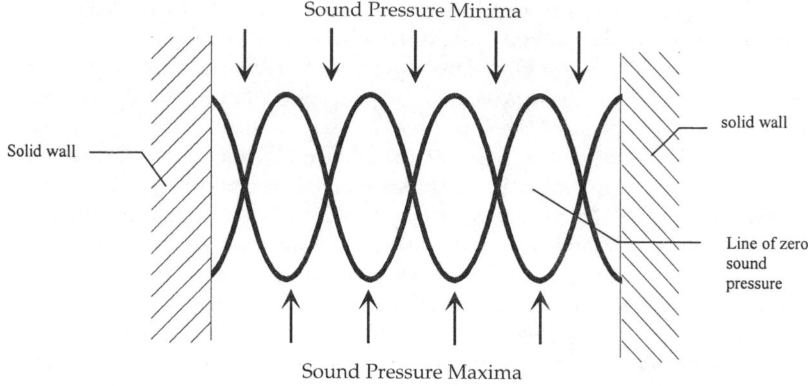

Figure 4

known as a "room mode" or simply a "mode," not to be confused with a node. A room mode is similar in many ways to a mode of vibration of a mechanical structure, such as a violin string. It is seen that there are theoretically an infinite number of possible modes between two surfaces; however the wavelengths of sounds above about 500 Hz are short enough that they form spherical waves that tend to become diffused very quickly.

A standing wave pattern like the one shown above obviously creates a very nonuniform sound level as you move around between the surfaces. For instance, if you are standing at the location of a pressure minimum, the sound will be very soft, even inaudible, but when you are near a pressure maximum, the loudness can be very great. Needless to say, this is not a desirable state of affairs in which to listen to music!

It gets worse. The problem is that in any room that has parallel walls, floor, and ceiling, there will be a whole slew of standing wave patterns that exist between the two front-rear walls, the two side walls, and the floor and ceiling. The worst possible case would be a room that is shaped like a cube, with all the linear dimensions the same. This kind of a room would have three sets of equal standing wave frequencies, which would add together to produce extremely nonuniform distribution of sound pressure in the room. There are also other families of standing waves that occur in rectangular rooms. One such is caused by reflections back and forth between the diagonal corners of the room. These diagonal modes are the lowest frequency modes possible in a room, since the distance between the diagonal corners is greater than any wall spacing.

For an illustration of a prominent standing wave phenomenon, consider a shower stall for a moment. It is generally about 7 feet high, and has hard, reflective walls. The lowest frequency standing wave that such an enclosure can produce is at that frequency where 7 feet is ½ wavelength. This turns out to be about 157 Hz, which is not far from the fundamental frequency of the average male speaking voice. The voice thus excites this room mode, and the person's voice and ears are near the upper end of the enclosure, which is close to the upper antinode, so the room mode is heard as a strong reinforcement of the voice's fundamental tone. This is no doubt the reason that men, especially basses, often are pleased by their own performance of singing in the shower!

Since parallel surfaces are a major source of standing waves, designers have learned that it is not a good idea to design music rooms with parallel walls, floors, and ceilings. This is not as easy as it sounds, because you still have to have corners (unless the room is round), and they will generate their own standing wave pattern. Not only that, but the walls have to be very significantly out of parallel to prevent standing waves to build up between them. The walls would have to be at fairly large angles to appear nonparallel to a sound wave with a 10- or 20-foot wavelength. Nonparallel walls do prevent standing waves from being much of a problem at higher frequencies, i.e., at frequencies above 200 Hz or so.

Another thing that has been tried is to treat the wall surfaces with suitable materials that absorb the sound rather than reflect it. This is also easier said than done, for long wavelengths are notoriously difficult to absorb. It takes very thick layers of absorptive material (about ¼ of the wavelength you want to absorb) in order to be effective. This is not only unsightly and expensive, but it reduces the useful size of the room. Another way to reduce the strength of the room modes is to make the walls flexible rather than massive. A room lined with ½-inch sheet rock on 2x4 studs spaced at 16 inches is quite flexible at low frequencies, and it absorbs these frequencies much better than a solid wall of brick or concrete. However, thin flexible walls will also let more sound pass through them, possibly waking up Aunt Minnie, or worse.

Resonant Absorbers

There do exist so-called resonant absorbers (sometimes called "bass traps") of fairly small size that will absorb energy at specific frequencies. They can take the form of rectangular Helmholtz resonators, which are resonant cavities than can be built behind the walls with holes in the walls connecting to them. Another form of resonant absorber looks like a cylinder several feet long with a hole in the end about a foot in diameter. These devices have been used to help in reducing the effects of troublesome low-frequency standing waves. Again, they are expensive, unsightly, and they have to be tuned fairly accurately to the frequency being absorbed. See figure 5.

Instead of, or in addition to, placing sound absorbent material on the walls of the room, it is a good idea to cover them with fairly large irregular surfaces. There are many different forms that diffusing surfaces can take, and to describe them all is beyond the scope of this appendix. In general, the irregularities in diffusers must be of sizes comparable to the wavelengths they are to diffuse. This means they must be of varying size in order to attain diffusion over a frequency range from 40 Hz to over 500 Hz or so.

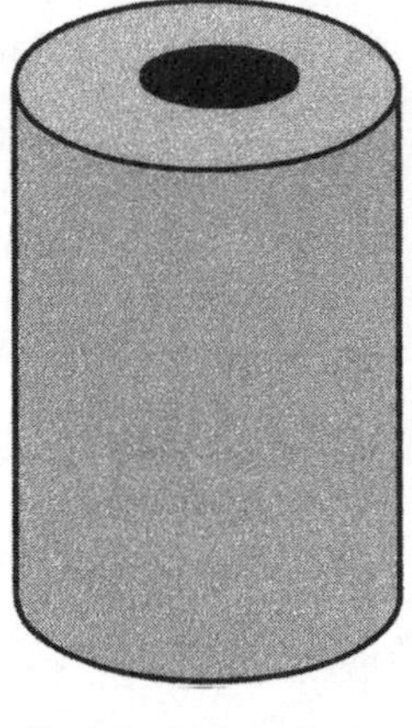

Cylindrical Helmholtz resonator

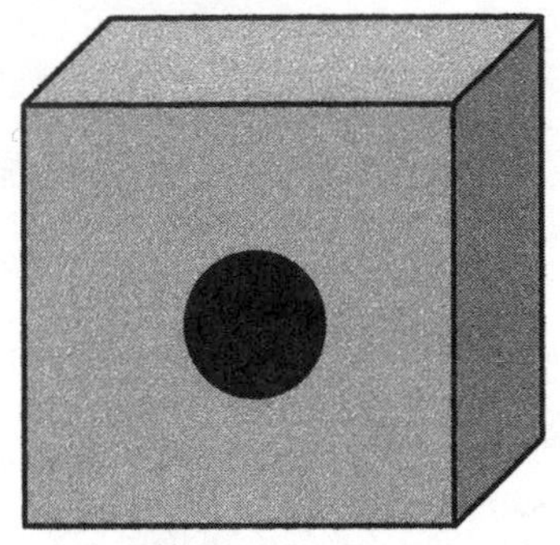

Rectangular Helmholtz resonator

Figure 5

One thing that is commonly overlooked in the design of music listening rooms is the need for good diffusion of sounds reflected from the ceiling. Diffused ceiling reflections are very important if you desire good stereo imaging. This is because a specular reflection from the ceiling produces an audible image above the speaker, and the sound from the image interferes with the direct sound from the speaker. Figure 6-A shows the effect of a flat ceiling, and figure 6-B represents a diffusing ceiling. Note that here the listener is not hit with the first reflection

Interestingly enough, specular reflections from the walls are much less annoying than the ones from the ceiling and provide a certain amount of widening of the stereo image. This does not sound unnatural, while widening of the image in a vertical direction does not correlate well with our everyday experience.

All in all, experience over many years has taught us that no matter how carefully a room is designed, it will still contain a collection of room modes that will produce nonuniformity in its distribution of sound energy. It is hopeless to try to design a space that will have no room modes. We must live with this fact, and we must seek other ways to reduce the effect of the troublesome room modes on the quality of the musical sound that we experience in a room.

That is the subject we will consider in the next section.

Before you attempt to set up a loudspeaker system in a room, you should first determine what types of problems the room has, and how severe the problems are. Only then can you meaningfully attack the situation and realize a satisfactory result.

As we have seen, there is no such thing as a room without room modes, so forget trying to find one. But there are huge variations in the frequency and amplitude distribution of the modes that exist in different rooms. As a

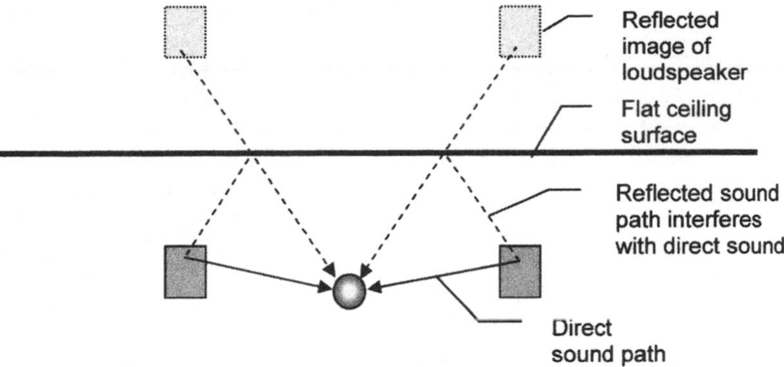

Figure 6-A

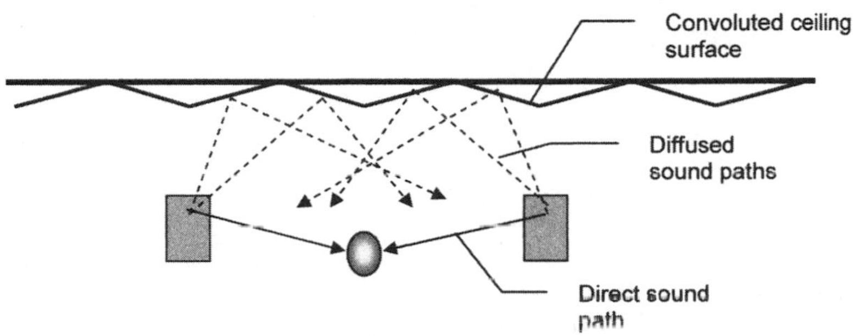

Figure 6-B

general guideline, you do not want different modes to produce nodes and antinodes that are in the same location in the room at the same frequencies. These are called overlapping modes. Therefore, the room should not have dimensions that are simple multiples of each other. For instance, the room height and width should not be multiples of each other, or multiples of any common factors. Ideally, the ratios of height, length, and width should be irrational, like the square root of three (1.73 . . .), or the Golden Mean.[1] It is impor-

1. The Golden Mean, also called the golden ratio, is a relationship discovered by the ancients that occurs frequently in nature, and has a numerical value of about 0.618. It was intensely studied by many people involved in number theory and artistic endeavors. It has been said that a rectangle with length and width proportional to the golden mean is more pleasing to the eye than any other rectangular shape. An ordinary 3 x 5-inch card conforms very closely to the golden mean.

tant that the ceiling height of the listening room not be too low, as discussed in the section on stereo imaging.

If at all possible, the walls should not be simple plane surfaces, but should be broken up with furniture, windows, tapestries, paintings, etc. to reduce the efficiency of the standing wave patterns. The walls should not be parallel if possible for the same reason, and they should not be extremely rigid, such as concrete or brick. A good compromise construction is ½-inch gypsum wallboard (sheet rock) on 2x4 wooden studs. The ceiling should not be parallel to the floor, or else should be deeply coffered or have irregular surfaces on it.

Carpeted floors are in general good for listening rooms because they reduce reverberation and also tend to break up floor-to-ceiling standing waves.

The room where you will install your monitor speakers will have a series of room modes that will be more or less severe depending on the shape and construction of the room. Placing a loudspeaker in the room will not affect the pattern of room modes, and moving the loudspeaker around to different locations in the room will not change the room modes either. However, different locations of the speaker will affect how strongly the speaker will excite the various modes. This means the room will affect the perceived frequency response of the loudspeakers, as discussed next.

While frequency response problems may not generally be considered "distortion" in the strict sense of the word, the frequency response produced by a sound system is extremely important in the perceived tone quality of the reproduced sound. Poor frequency response is a linear type of distortion rather than a nonlinear distortion, but it still is distortion and is annoying like any other type of distortion.

When different frequency components of a reproduced sound are produced at sound pressure levels different from the levels that existed in the recording venue, the result is frequency response distortion. If all frequencies are reproduced at their original relative levels, the frequency response of the system is said to be "flat." Irregularities in frequency response cause the tone color, or timbre, of the sound to be different from the original sound, and this is probably the most common and noticeable problem heard in music reproducing systems.

The frequency response of a music system is a curve that plots frequency versus the sound pressure level, or "response," produced by the system. The response is normally scaled in dB, and the frequency is normally plotted on a logarithmic scale, where octave bands all span the same distance on the horizontal axis. The ideal frequency response curve is a straight horizontal line, indicating no accentuation of sound pressure level at any frequency, nor any attenuation at any frequency. This is why it is called a "flat response."

It is possible to have a great many different types of variations in frequency response, and they have quite different effects on the perceived sound. Probably the most disagreeable type of irregular frequency response is the existence of peaks. High frequency peaks sound harsh and bright, while low-frequency peaks will sound "boomy" or "honky," depending on the frequency where the peaks occur. Your loudspeakers are generally designed to produce the most flat and uniform frequency response possible when radiating sound into a free field, i.e., into a field where there are no standing waves. However, the monitors are at a loss to correct for frequency response anomalies contributed by the room.

For instance, if there were a prominent room mode between the front and rear walls at 50 Hz, this mode would result in a maximum in sound pressure at both wall surfaces when a 50 Hz tone was sounded in the room. It will also produce a minimum in sound pressure at ¼ wavelength away from the walls. Now, if you place the speaker against the front wall where the sound pressure from that mode is a maximum, the speaker will excite that mode to its maximum degree. Only a small amount of acoustic energy at 50 Hz will produce very strong sound levels at all the antinodes. If, on the other hand, you move the speaker out from the wall and place it in the location of a node (minimum) of the 50 Hz mode, that mode will not be excited to any great degree. It is as if the room will not accept any energy at this frequency at that particular location. Of course, there may be other modes near 50 Hz that exist between the side walls or the floor and ceiling that would not have minima at that same location, and these modes would be excited by the speaker, producing significant sound pressure at that point.

The whole process of determining the best location for the speakers and the listeners in a room is simply to find the location where the speakers are placed so they do not excessively accentuate any room modes that are in the musical range. Also, the listeners must not be located at minima of these modes. In other words, the most prominent room modes must not be excited to a large degree, and the other modes should be excited to the same moderate degree.

If the room is quite reverberant (live), the listener should be fairly close to the speakers for increased clarity of the sound. For critical monitoring of music sources in most typical medium-sized rooms, a good speaker to listener distance would be somewhere around 4 to 6 feet. For dead rooms this could be a little farther, and for very live rooms, a little closer.

It might seem intuitive to most people that the loudspeakers in a stereo listening set up should be symmetrically disposed with respect to the centerline of the room. This, however, is frequently not the case. If you are listening to stereo in a small room, and if the room is symmetrical and the speakers equidistant from the side walls your two ears essentially hear similar sounds. A sound that comes from both speakers equally, i.e., from an instrument centered in the stereo field, will be reflected from the sidewalls, and the reflections will arrive at your ears with the same delay time. It has been shown that under these conditions, the stereo balance is less pleasant to the listener than if there is some asymmetry in the acoustic field. This increases the complexity and subjective spaciousness of the sound field. So, don't worry about exact symmetry in the setup. You may be happier being a little to the left or right of center. (Of course, for proper stereo imaging you must be located at the same distance from each speaker.)

Appendix 4

The proper location of a speaker in a room involves two essentially different tasks; optimizing the low-frequency performance and optimizing the high-frequency performance. The low-frequency performance is almost exclusively determined by the interaction between the speaker and the room modes, while the high-frequency performance is essentially immune to the mode structure of the room. High-frequency characteristics are affected by reflecting surfaces near the speakers and by the relative liveness of the room at the higher frequencies.

Low-frequency behavior is the most difficult to control, so we will tackle it first. One fairly easy, but somewhat tedious, way to minimize the effect of the room modes on the response of the speakers in a room uses an omnidirectional microphone of good quality.[2] The microphone must have smooth frequency response at low frequencies, and it can be connected to each monitor (one at a time) through a recording console or tape recorder set to monitor mode. The microphone should be placed very near a corner of the room, and fairly close to the floor or ceiling. This will assure that the microphone will respond to all the room modes with equal sensitivity.[3] A convenient way to mount it is to simply tape it to the wall. Do not change the microphone location during these tests; you want to have as few variables as possible. See figure 7.

Start with the volume at minimum with the speaker located in the room at the height at which it will be used. This is usually ear height. Then very slowly bring up the volume control and listen carefully to the sound just as the system begins to go into feedback. Do not turn up the volume to produce a roar or shriek; just listen to the first onset of a feedback tone. You will find the feedback starts at a specific frequency and this will usually be the frequency of one of the most prominent of the room modes.

Then, with the volume turned down, move the speaker to another position and repeat the process. Listen to find out if the same frequency tone is activated. Keep repeating this until the onset of feedback occurs at several different frequencies at the same time. If, in repeating this process, the feedback always occurs at high frequencies, roll off the treble response of the speaker, and/or roll off the microphone sensitivity at high frequencies with an equalizer.

You will find that in some cases, moving the speaker only a few inches will make a big difference in the tones that are activated at feedback. If at all possible, place the speaker where it excites the maximum number of different frequencies at the same time. Sometimes in good rooms this will turn out

2. If you do not have an omnidirectional microphone, a suitable one can be purchased from most audio electronic parts houses, such as Radio Shack, for a few dollars. The smaller the physical size of the microphone the better. You are only concerned about its low-frequency response, so you do not have to have an expensive microphone.

3. If the microphone is placed away from the walls, its response will depend on its location relative to the room modes. If it is near the corner, it will be at a maximum (antinode) for all the room modes.

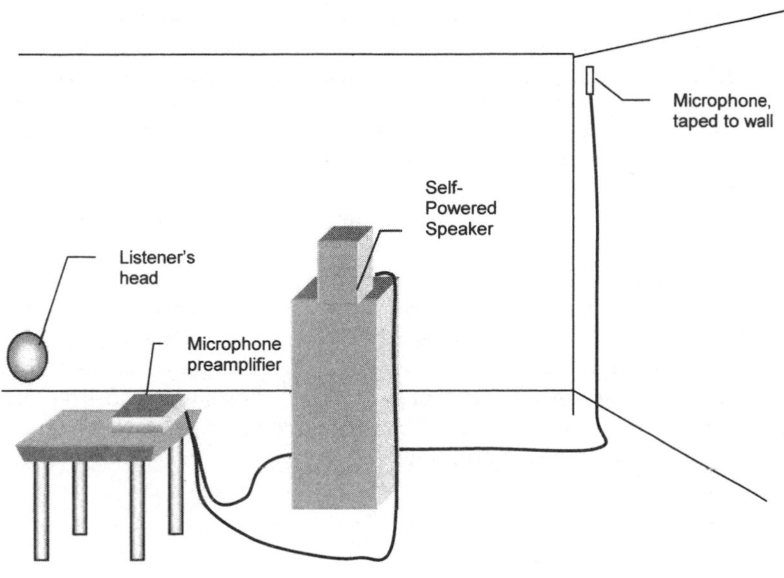

Figure 7

to be as many as four or five different tones. When you have achieved this situation, the speaker is exciting several room modes equally, with none standing out over the others. This will be close to the best you can do in that room, and you should bolt the speaker in place. The process must be repeated with the other speaker, and hopefully, its ideal location will be such that the two of them make a good stereo pair.

When you discover this magic location, you will have located the speaker so that it excites the most prominent of the room modes to a nearly equal degree. You will find that music heard over the speakers will sound as neutral as is possible in that particular room. Listen critically to the speakers with several different types of music. The room modes will still be there, and if you walk around the room, you will hear different degrees of low frequency response, but the variations will be minimized.

Incidentally, this same process can be used to find the location for a microphone in a recording studio to minimize the effects of the room modes. Place the speaker in the corner to excite all the modes, then move the microphone around for the greatest number of tones at feedback. You will discover that a recording made with this microphone location will sound more balanced and neutral than if you had placed the microphone at random. Of course, you will have to position the instruments to be recorded to suit the microphone rather than vice versa, but this is generally a small price to pay.

The control of high frequencies in a room is usually just a matter of equalization to establish the correct balance between the mid-range and the treble. The high-frequency balance must be adjusted for the listening position. It will be found that reduced high-frequency levels will be required for closer listening than for more distant listening. This is because most rooms have a greater amount of high-frequency absorption than low-frequency absorption.

The level of the highs will also be affected by the presence of reflecting surfaces near the speakers. In general, there should be no hard flat surfaces near the speakers (within several feet or so) to prevent sounds reflected from them from reaching the ear. This not only would change the balance of the high-frequency energy, but also would compromise the stereo imaging produced by the speakers.

In recording studios, it is not uncommon to find that high-frequency reflections off the mixing console adversely affect the tonal balance and stereo imaging heard by the mixing engineer. To avoid, or at least minimize this effect, the speakers should be placed so the working surface of the console is at least a few feet from the tweeter, and that the console work surface does not produce a reflected image of the speaker that can be heard by the listener. The angle of reflection of the sound is equal to the angle of incidence. See figure 8 for more detail.

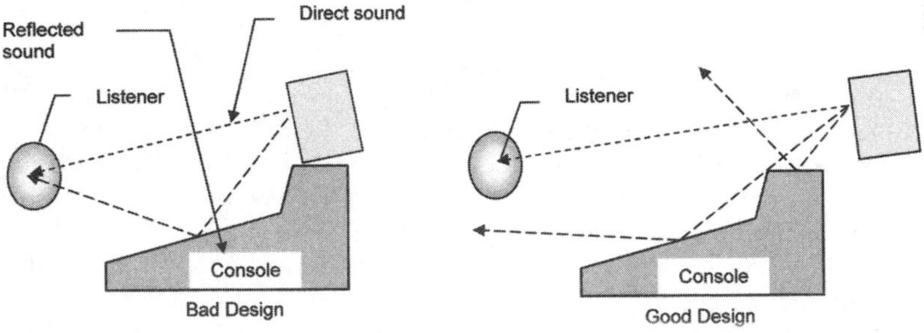

Figure 8

It has been known for a long time that precise imaging of the location of the musicians in a two-channel stereo sound system is difficult at best and even impossible under some conditions. For good imaging, the phase and amplitude vs. frequency characteristic of each channel must be very closely matched, and this includes the entire recording chain from microphones through recording consoles and speakers. At the playback end of this chain, the loudspeakers must be matched in frequency response, sensitivity, and phase. These characteristics are accurately controlled in the high-quality studio monitors, so you shouldn't worry about that.

Stereo imaging is almost totally controlled by high-frequency cues that the ear interprets as source location information. The high-frequency amplitude and phase response must, at all costs, be identical in the two speakers, and the acoustic paths between the speakers and the ears must also have identical characteristics. To attain acceptable imaging with two-channel stereo, you must be very careful to eliminate short time-delayed reflected sounds from reaching your ears from the loudspeakers. This means the speakers should be placed at least five feet or so from any reflecting surfaces such as walls or large objects. If this is unavoidable, then the surfaces or objects must be irregular enough that the reflected sound is diffuse. A smooth flat surface acts like an acoustical mirror and sound reflected from such a surface is called a "specular" reflection. A specular reflection will create an image of the sound source (the speaker) that appears to be behind the offending surface, and this image behaves like a delayed source of the sounds the speaker produces. This added delayed sound would confuse the ear and lead to poor imaging, as well as poor frequency response due to interference. See figure 8 for an example of bad reflections from flat surfaces.

For optimum performance, the vertical and horizontal angles the monitors make with respect to the listener's ears need to be considered. If the monitors are to be placed very much above ear level (a practice that is not recommended for best performance), then the cabinets should be tipped toward the listener at the top so the line of sight to the center of the speakers is at a vertical right angle to the faces of the cabinets. See figure 9.

The horizontal dispersion of sounds of different frequencies is very well controlled by the speakers, and while the speakers should each be "toed in" to face directly to the listener, a horizontal angular error of up to 10 degrees should not be audible under normal operation.

As was mentioned earlier, the ceiling can be a troublesome source of specular reflections. If the ceiling above the monitors is closer than about 5 or 6 feet from the speakers, then it should have a convoluted shape to avoid specular reflections. Alternatively, the ceiling can be treated with acoustical absorbent material, but adequate absorption is difficult to achieve at long wavelengths.

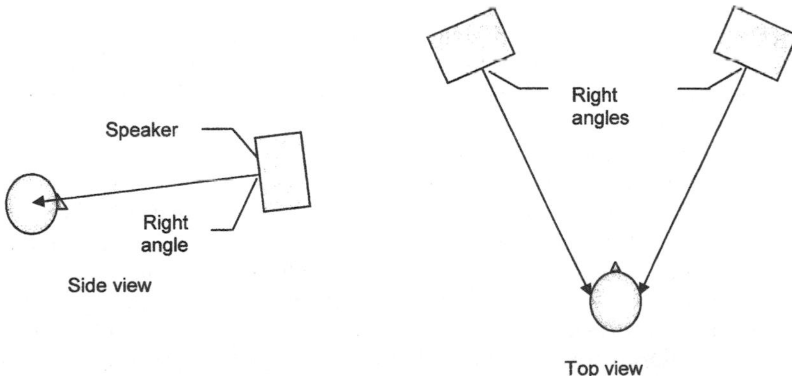

Figure 9

Appendix 4

2. Auditorium Acoustics

Among the definitions presented in this book are several references to "good acoustics." Although many people seem to be able to tell good acoustics from "bad" acoustics, it is quite another matter to adequately describe what actually constitutes acceptable acoustics, especially in any quantitative way. It is always risky to try to relate subjective impressions to objectively measured data, as has been abundantly proved by some acousticians who thought they designed the "perfect" concert hall only to have it condemned wholesale by the public and critics.

Charles Garnier, the architect for the Paris Opera, wrote a book in 1871 on theater design titled *Le Theatre.* Here are some excerpts from the chapter on acoustics:

> For two years at least, I kept this question of the elements of acoustics before me. I read all the books dealing with it; I looked over almost all the theaters built, hoping to discover for myself some clear rules which the literature failed to reveal. In short, I left no stone unturned to find a way, a means, a bit of factual, helpful information. . . .
>
> But what can we conclude? Halls almost identical in shape, arrangement, and dimensions vary a great deal. This one is good; that one is bad. One hall quivers at the slightest sound from a stringed instrument. This is an excitable, nervous hall. Another doesn't even vibrate under the influence of the entire orchestra. That is a lifeless, soulless hall. Then, an echo may be heard during the day which disappears in the evening, or one is heard in the evening but disappears during the day when the hall is empty. And the notes one takes on these observations, the comparisons, the thorough research—all these data tend to merge into an endless mass, an inextricable maze where the end of the string cannot even be located.
>
> Dissatisfied, one then inquires of others. Buildings are examined and other works are consulted with the hope of at least finding someone to guide, but none turns up. The terrain is unknown, the guides do not know the way, and each one goes on blindly in his own way. This one wants a long hall; that one a wide hall. This one a low ceiling; and someone else a lofty one. . . . The end result is simply confusion with nothing converging toward the adoption of any fixed rules. . . .
>
> After sound quality, the matter of resonance again emerges to complicate matters. The walls of the hall for some writers must be constructed of stone and have rigid partition walls. Following the direction of others, it should be made of wood or of a light elastic material. One German wants a dome of masonry; another German might want it padded with wool.
>
> And Lord knows what else! In the final analysis everybody wants something, but nobody agrees on the choice. Reconciling all these par-

ticulars is impossible. The science of theater acoustics is still in its infancy and its outcome uncertain.

In view of the spotty track record of certain modern halls, it seems that Garnier's *tristesse* might be echoed by contemporary theater architects and that his conclusions are basically as valid today as they were in 1871.

But all this notwithstanding, let us at least take a cursory look at some of the acoustical measurements we can perform and try to correlate them with our aesthetic senses.

Reverberation time is probably the most discussed acoustical parameter and, as we shall see, is also probably the most misunderstood. The concept of reverberation time was developed by Wallace Clement Sabine, of Harvard University, around 1900. He called it the "duration of audibility of residual sound." Reverberation is easily heard and its concept is easy to grasp. Sabine quantized the measurement and prediction of reverberation time by defining it as the time in seconds it takes for a sound to decay in level by 60 decibels after the source of the sound is stopped. He also developed a formula for predicting what this value will be based on: the volume of the room, the surface area of all the boundaries, and the amount of sound absorption these boundaries provide. It should be clear that for most materials the absorption of sounds of different frequencies will not be the same, leading to a reverberation time that varies with frequency.

It is generally recognized that long reverberation times cause musical phrases to overlap and become indistinct; in other words, clarity, or intelligibility, suffers. On the other hand, short reverberation times allow excellent intelligibility and very little blurring of musical passages while at the same time sounding "dry" and lifeless. Thus one might think that it would be easy to define an optimum reverberation time that would be acceptable for all rooms. This, however, is a gross oversimplification.

Consider the subjective impression of being in a very large reverberant space, such as Chartres cathedral in France, which has a reverberation time at midfrequencies which exceeds 10 seconds. Two people engaged in conversation in such a building are scarcely aware of any reverberation at all. Only if they suddenly raise their voices to a shout or loudly clap their hands do they consciously hear the sound die away after what seems a very long time. Intelligibility between them is excellent so long as they are relatively close together. This is because the reverberation, although very long-lasting at 10 seconds, is very low in level compared with the direct sounds of the voices, and the individual sound reflections that make up the reverberation are quite late compared with the direct sound because of the large distances to the walls and ceiling.

Now, consider a small room, say 20 feet square, which has very hard walls and a 10-second reverberation time. The reverberation versus frequency curve of this room could be made to be the same as the large cathedral if desired. Would the two spaces sound the same? Decidedly not! The small room would have nearly zero intelligibility because the reverberation would start out at almost the same level as the direct sound, and the reflections would be much more densely spaced in time. The result would be extensive masking of the direct sound.

From this we see that a large space can have much more reverberation than a small space for the same perceived acoustical clarity. In fact the apparent reverberation time will depend on the level of the reverberant sound immediately after the arrival of the direct sound, and it decreases with room size for a given reverberation time.

The variation in decay time for different frequencies is also very important. Most intelligibility is transmitted by the high-frequency content of a sound, the lower frequencies contributing to the timbre, or tone color, of the sound. Therefore, one can tolerate much longer reverberation time at low frequencies than at high. Real rooms naturally provide this, for high frequencies are much more readily absorbed than low, especially in large rooms. If a room is constructed so it does not have this reduction of decay time as frequency rises, it will definitely sound strange and will be shunned by musicians.

Another acoustical parameter related to reverberation is diffusion, which is a measure of the randomness of the directions in which reverberant energy is moving. In a perfectly diffuse space, the sound at any point is equally likely to come from any direction; in other words, sound is arriving from all directions at once, and a listener cannot localize a sound source. (The degree of diffusion is independent of the reverberation time and cannot be inferred from reverberation measurements alone.) The opposite extreme is no diffusion at all, which is the condition in a free field, such as out of doors or in an anechoic chamber. In a free field, all the energy is moving in the same direction, and source localization is easiest. A free sound field would be described by a listener as completely dead and lifeless.

How much sound diffusion is desirable in a room? This is a very good question. The Hungarian physiologist and acoustician Georg Von Békésy has shown that the human hearing mechanism is somewhat directional and that sounds arriving from the frontal angles of less than 60 degrees from straight ahead attract much more attention from us than sounds coming from the sides and rear, and we are much more able to ignore sounds coming from the sides and rear. The Japanese acoustician Yoichi Ando has conducted experiments to show that listeners prefer reflected sounds to come from within this plus and minus 60-degree angle. In other words, our preference is for reflected sounds to come from the direction in which we pay the most attention. Ando also found that our preference is for directions that maximize the difference in the sounds heard by the two ears. In other words we prefer to listen to sounds that have a maximum of stereophonic information. The objective measure of this difference in sounds is the so-called interaural cross-correlation (IACC), which can be found by using a dummy binaural head and suitably analyzing the signals from the two microphones.

From all this, it can be determined that in a music-listening room, the reverberation decay curve must be steep enough and the reverberant level must be low enough so as not to obscure the clarity or intelligibility of the music. Also, and even more important, the reflections that make up the early reverberation should come from fairly wide horizontal angles, preferably about 60 degrees off axis, and there should not be strong reflections from the ceiling. Ceiling reflections result in increased IACC and are not preferred. This means the reflection from the ceiling should be diffuse, and reflections from the sidewalls should be discrete and should be aimed laterally across the room. A room meeting these criteria is said to have a large degree of envelopment. An excess of diffusion of the early sound is undesirable because it reduces our ability to localize sources. For this reason, it is not desirable to place strongly diffusing surfaces near the performers in an auditorium.

It is important that the early reflections reaching the ear contain the full frequency range, which means reflecting surfaces must be quite large. Otherwise only high frequencies will be reflected and the tone quality will be perceived as "thin." Some music auditoriums have been designed with small reflecting surfaces spaced out from the walls or hung some distance from the ceiling, and they distort the tonal balance by their frequency-selective reflections.

In a music room, it is important to avoid echoes, which are discrete strong reflections occurring at times later than about 60 milliseconds or so after the direct sound reaches the listener. Echoes can be difficult to avoid in large rooms. A similar problem, but one that occurs more often in small rooms, is that of standing waves, which are the result of sound bouncing back and forth between two parallel surfaces. Standing waves accentuate certain frequencies and distort the tonal balance of music as well as alter the uniformity of decay of the reverberant energy in a room.

Most of these comments apply to rooms for listening to recorded music as well as to rooms for live music, although such rooms will be relatively small and consequently less reverberant.

Appendix 5
Some Notes on Audio Measurements

In order to improve and refine the performance of audio equipment, the engineer must undertake considerable research and development and, in so doing, has a vast array of measuring instruments available. This instrumentation for audio measurements has become very sophisticated in recent years, drawing on the discoveries and techniques of many scientific disciplines.

In a way, it is surprising that the 1920s through 1940s brought forth so many audio inventions when one considers how primitive most of the measuring techniques and instruments were. For instance, measurements of distortion and frequency response were difficult and time-consuming and were of necessity of limited range. But this pre–World War II era saw the invention of all the microphone types in use today, as well as the exponential horn with compression driver, the introduction of negative feedback in amplifiers, and the development of stereophonic recording and reproduction. Most of the impetus for all this invention came from the motion picture industry. In Alan Blumlein's famous 1933 patent disclosure, where he puts forth the ideas of intensity stereo and the stereophonic record, he never mentions commercial products for home use, but discusses in detail the applications of his invention to motion picture sound. The same may be said of the many inventions by the Bell Telephone Laboratories of the period.

In this section, we would like to review the measurement techniques in use today in an attempt to "demythologize" them, if our editor will let us get away with this word. But first, a word about the philosophy of audio testing: Our friend Henning Møller likes to make an analogy between listening to a sound system and looking at an attractive work of art such as a statue. When listening to reproduced music, the mind integrates the sensory input from the ears into a "global" experience; the sum of the parts is appreciated at once without reference to the various "local" parts such as frequency response, stereo imaging, distortion, etc. Similarly, when first looking at the statue, it takes only a few seconds to sense its overall beauty—we do not consciously (at least at first) evaluate its individual features and textures in order to reach the conclusion.

Now, suppose we wish to describe the beautiful statue to someone objectively, and do so in such a way that the person could sense the global effect we experienced on seeing it. The key word is "objectively," for it is easy to fall into subjective descriptions of local details, but they would not help if the person were trying to build up analytically a total image of the work of art.

The audio designer's plight is similar, for he must assemble his transistors, voice coils, styli, capacitors, etc., to optimize their performance in reproducing music in an attempt to produce a subjective global experience for the listener. To do this, he must make measurements and tests, always trying to see that they are measuring and testing the correct local parameters—the ones that make a difference. The making of a recording of a musical performance is something like taking a photograph. A picture of our statue will convey a large amount of its character to the viewer, even if the color is off, the lens not sharp, or the perspective incorrect. The viewer is able to see "through" the photograph and imagine what its true appearance is. The same is true of the listener to the recording. He is able to listen "through" the medium and to build in his imagination a replica of the performance. Incidentally, this ability of listeners to overlook the medium is a great stroke of luck for audio designers, for there is often precious little in common between the original performance and the reproduction of it! It behooves the audio person to train himself to listen to the medium rather than to the music.

For many years there has been an antipathy between certain audio critics and audio designers. Many times an equipment reviewer believes the audio device designer is measuring the wrong parameters, for even though there may be minuscule distortion and near zero noise, etc., the device may sound very bad when reproducing music. The designer, on the other hand, is sure the reviewer is crazy because the measurements "prove" the component is nearly perfect.

For instance, harmonic distortion is a local parameter that can be reduced to almost unmeasurable amounts. If this is done by the indiscriminate use of negative feedback, the result can be the introduction of large quantities of transient intermodulation distortion, which does not show up in steady-state distortion measurements at all. The device, however, will sound bad with music. On the other hand, analog tape recorders typically produce several percent of harmonic distortion when signal levels are relatively high. But the tape recorder does not sound bad from a musical standpoint—the distortion it produces is more "musical" in character.

This is only one example of measurements being at odds with what our ears tell us. The ear is after all the final arbiter, and when properly trained, it can be a very sensitive instrument indeed. It is interesting that the ear is at once extremely forgiving and tolerant of gross distortions (witness the popularity of the miniature transistor radio) and also is the most sophisticated measurement instrument available when properly educated and experienced. The noncritical ear finances the audio industry, and the critical ear keeps the designers forever busy and frustrated.

Now let us define some relevant measurements and then look at some techniques for performing them. The mechanical engineer has a certain advantage over his electrical colleague in that he can see and feel the various parts of a machine and easily visualize the way in which they interact. The electronic designer cannot directly sense the workings of his circuit, that is, he is unable to see the charges moving around being resisted and impeded. Therefore, he must use instruments to transform the operating parameters of the circuit into a form he can sense. This necessary use of instruments places the observer another level of abstraction away from the actual device under observation, and this contributes to the sense of mystery that the uninitiated feel. A true understanding of instrumentation and what it can and cannot do is probably the most important body of knowledge the electronics person can have.

The most fundamental of audio measurements is frequency response, or more accurately, amplitude response versus frequency. Electronic device frequency response is measured in a straightforward manner to be sure that all frequencies are amplified by the same amount. The frequency response of transducers is quite another matter, for here the environment in which the measurements are made influences the result, requiring much more sophisticated techniques.

The next important measurement to be made is phase response, for frequency response alone does not tell us much about the handling of transients. Frequency and phase response together allow us to predict the transient response of any device or system.

The third class of measurements is of distortions and noise, of which there are a great many. Some are far more detrimental to reproduced sound than others, and some are very difficult to measure.

The fourth class of measurements is of those applicable to the evaluation of digital audio systems and devices. Digital systems produce different types of distortions than analog systems do, and their measurement can be tricky.

Many audio measurements use a sine wave as a test signal, but the sine wave does not occur naturally in music, and it does not resemble music in any statistical or spectral way. Statistically, the sine wave spends much more time at the upper and lower extremes of its voltage swing than does music, which spends most of the time nearer to zero voltage. The sine wave thus does not exercise the dynamic range of an audio device the same way a musical signal does. Spectrally, the sine wave consists of a single frequency with zero bandwidth. Music is always a broadband signal, consisting of many frequency components at once. Moreover, it is almost always characterized by a continuous spectrum, where energy is distributed over a frequency band, rather than by a discrete spectrum, where energy is concentrated at specific frequencies. Pink noise has a much closer resemblance to music from a technical standpoint (and maybe to some music from the aesthetic standpoint also) than does a sine wave, and therefore it is in some cases a more appropriate test signal for audio devices.

Electrical Frequency Response and Signal-to-Noise Ratio

A straightforward method for testing frequency response is to apply a constant amplitude sine-wave signal to the input of a device, measure the output of the device with a voltmeter or a recorder that plots the amplitude on a chart, and then vary the input frequency over the applicable range. The audible range may be from 20 hertz to 20 kHz, but response curves are usually made over a much wider frequency range, sometimes up to 200 kHz or so. This is because the out-of-band response affects other parameters such as distortion.

Figure 1 shows a typical classical frequency response measurement setup. Measurements of this type are time-consuming to perform because the frequency must be slowly swept over a wide range for each measurement. The measurements are repeated at various levels to evaluate the amplitude linearity of the device under test (DUT).

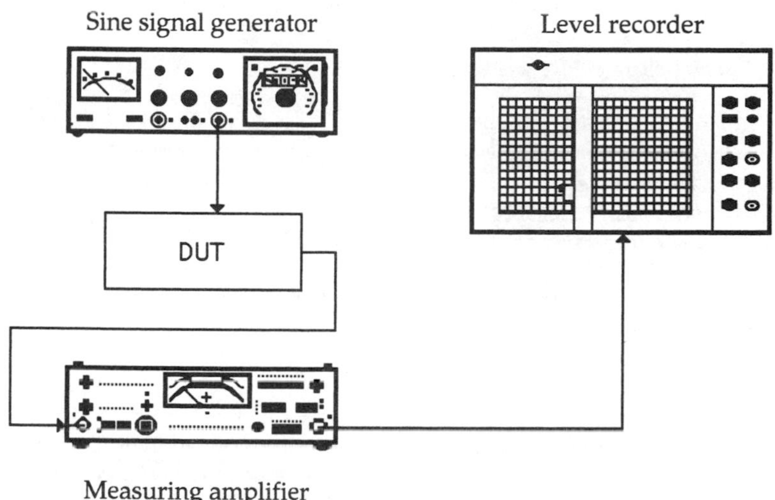

Figure 1

Another way to do a similar test is to input a random noise signal (pink noise or white noise) to the DUT and examine the output signal with a spectrum analyzer. Random noise is a combination of all frequencies at once, and it exercises the entire bandwidth of the device at the same time, unlike sine-wave testing, which presents only a single frequency at a time. Random noise is a better simulation of music than a sine wave for this reason.

The spectrum analyzer can be an FFT analyzer, which can provide extremely high resolution over the frequency range of interest. It effectively divides the audio band into 400 or 800 spectral "lines," giving amplitude information every 50 or 25 Hz. It is important in this type of test that the input spectrum have uniform output level at all frequencies, and this is not particularly easy to achieve. In any case, the test signal being random, meaning its long-term average is flat with frequency and amplitude, requires that the output spectrum be averaged over a time period. This allows the fluctuations in the signal to be smoothed out. The FFT analyzer does this time averaging.

A newer faster method for doing the same test is to use a dual-channel FFT analyzer (figure 2). This unit looks at the input and output signals at the same time and calculates the frequency response by dividing the output spectrum by the input spectrum. This allows much shorter averaging times to achieve accurate results. An added advantage is that this analyzer also calculates the phase angle of the output versus the input at all frequencies and displays a phase versus frequency plot. Also, the noise generator is built into the analyzer, making the setup quite simple.

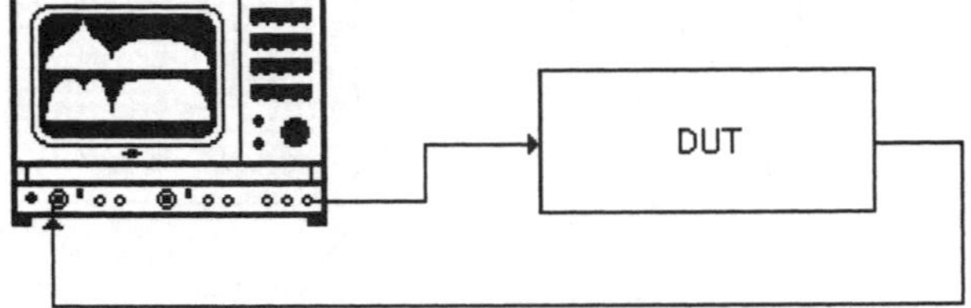

Figure 2

Signal-to-noise ratio is also measured with the setup of figure 1. First, the output level is measured with the voltmeter at a mid-frequency, and the input level is adjusted until the output begins to show an overload. This is the maximum output level, and it is noted. Then, the input signal is removed and the residual noise at the output is measured with the voltmeter. The ratio of the two measurements, expressed in decibels, is the signal-to-noise ratio. The FFT analyzer also can measure S/N ratio and has the advantage of showing the frequency distribution of the noise.

Acoustical Frequency Response

To measure frequency response of a loudspeaker requires a setup similar to that of figure 1, with the addition of a power amplifier and a microphone. Figure 3 illustrates the setup. The loudspeaker and the microphone must be in an anechoic room to eliminate the influence of sound reflections. Alternatively, the testing can be performed outdoors if the background noise is low. The microphone and power amplifier are also in the signal path and are measured as well, so it is necessary to ensure that they have flat frequency response so as not to distort the measurement. By making several measurements with the loudspeaker at different angles, it is possible to plot its polar response pat-

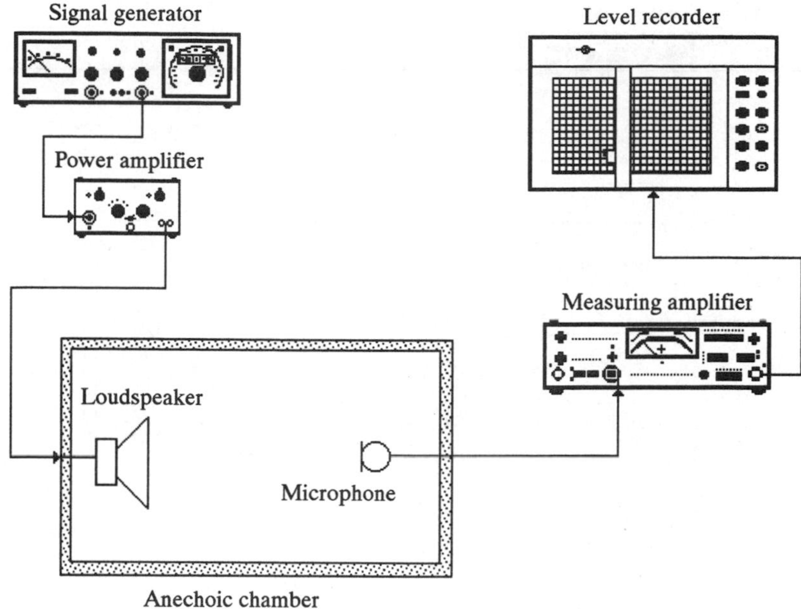

Figure 3

tern, or its response versus angle. This measurement is very important in assessing the subjective effect of a given loudspeaker, for off-axis sounds excite the reverberation of the listening room, coloring the perceived sound adversely if they are not of uniform strength.

This same measurement is easily made with the dual-channel FFT analyzer. One channel looks at the signal at the loudspeaker terminals and the other channel looks at the microphone output. See figure 4. If the time delay between the two signals (due to the finite speed of sound) is taken into account, the phase versus frequency of the speaker can be measured as well. The analyzer will do the time compensation. The dual-channel FFT approach is a great timesaver, and polar plots and response plots at various levels are quickly made.

It is possible to make "anechoic" or free-field measurements in real time by using a time-gating technique, or time delay spectrometry (TDS). The signal from the microphone is passed through a sweeping bandpass filter whose sweep rate is the same as that of the signal generator. The instantaneous frequency of the filter is offset from that of the generator by a constant amount. This frequency offset is equivalent to a time offset because of the propagation time between the speaker and the microphone. By the time the microphone receives the signal, the generator is emitting a different frequency. Thus, the filter in the microphone circuit is effectively looking at a different time,

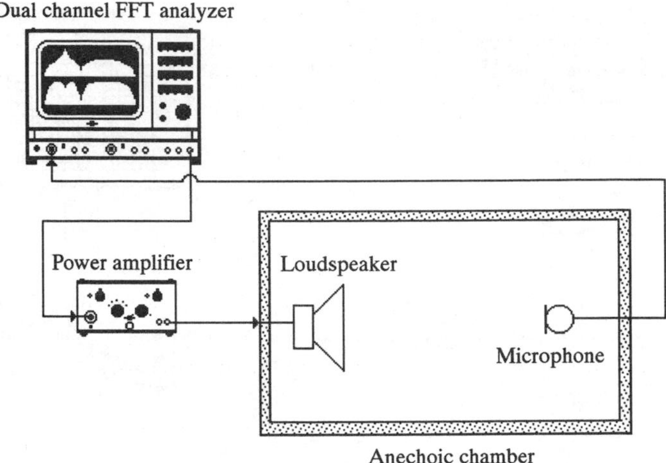

Figure 4

and it ignores signals arriving later. The length of this "time window" is a function of the filter bandwidth. The room reflections reaching the microphone are at different frequencies because of their time delays, and so are not measured.

TDS is a powerful and complex technique that can be used to separate signals closely spaced in time. For example, the sound reflected from the rear of a loudspeaker cabinet and coming through the speaker cone a little later can be measured. The dual-channel FFT analyzer is able to do a similar measurement by "gating" the signal to the loudspeaker; in other words by using short bursts of random noise and opening the time window of the analyzer so as to hear the direct sound and ignore the reflected sounds. The impulse response of the speaker is also measured with this instrument. This measurement will show that sounds from the loudspeaker do not all arrive at the listener at the same time, there being various reflections from parts of the cabinet, and there being frequency-dependent time delays in the loudspeaker drivers and crossover.

Harmonic Distortion

In the classic technique for measuring harmonic distortion, a single-frequency signal is input to a device and the output signal is passed through a notch filter tuned to that test frequency. The notch eliminates the input frequency from the measurement, and all that is left are the harmonics and any residual noise. This residue is measured with a voltmeter and expressed as a percentage of the input signal level.

Sometimes a tunable bandpass filter is used to look at the residual output signal in order to determine which harmonics are present and to reduce the contribution due to the noise. A faster and more meaningful way to measure harmonic distortion is to use an FFT analyzer. The spectrum of the output will show the input frequency and all the harmonics, which can each be accurately noted in terms of level. Also, any noise in the output is effectively excluded from the measurement. See figure 5.

Harmonic distortion of a phono cartridge is measured using a test record that has a sine-wave sweep recorded on it. The signal is replayed through a sweeping filter that is offset to track the second or third harmonic of the test signal rather than the fundamental. If the fundamental is tracked, the frequency response of the cartridge is measured. If the test frequency on the record goes to very low frequencies (typically 1 or 2 Hz), the effect of the tonearm resonance can be measured.

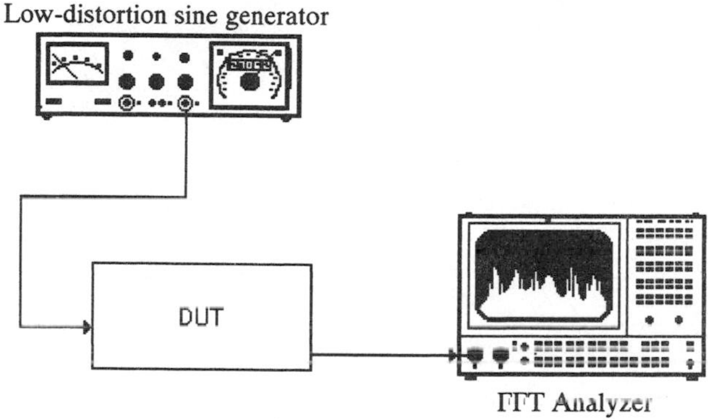

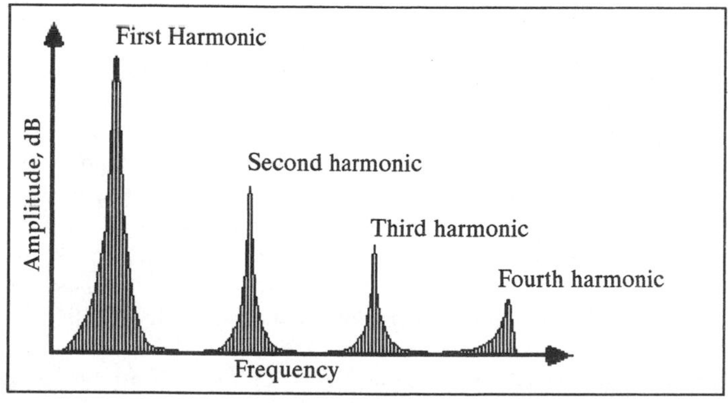

Harmonic spectrum

Figure 5

Appendix 5

Intermodulation Distortion

Intermodulation can be measured by inputting two simultaneous sinusoidal signals to the DUT. The amount of residual energy at the difference frequency between the two signals is then measured. See figure 6. A relatively new intermodulation test sweeps the two input signals over a wide frequency range while keeping the analyzer at the output tuned to the difference frequency, which is held constant. Many audio devices are found to have easily audible intermodulation even when the two test frequencies are outside the audible range. This causes trouble, for instance in phono preamps where ultrasonic noise from the record causes intermodulation products in the audible range.

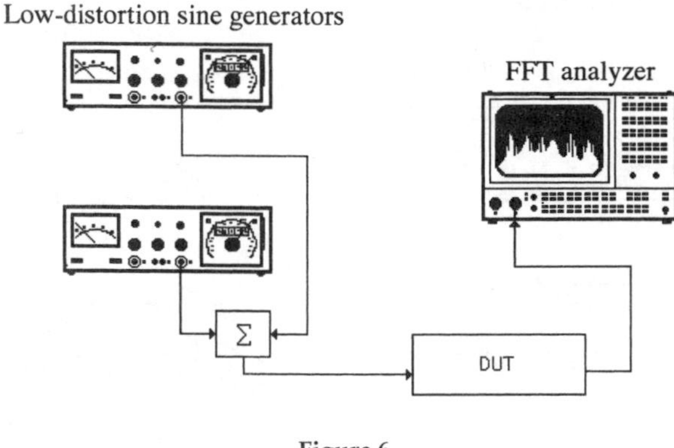

Figure 6

Transient Intermodulation Distortion (TIM)

From Fourier analysis we know that the performance of any linear system is completely described by its frequency and phase responses, provided they are measured over a wide enough frequency range. Unfortunately, this is *only* true for linear systems, and it is nonlinearities that create distortion. Transients can drive an otherwise linear system into a nonlinear range, and the behavior of the system is not predicted by classic theory.

The cause of TIM is the finite time delay inherent in an electronic circuit that has feedback around it. This time delay means the feedback arrives at the input too late to reduce the distortion of very high frequencies. The slew rate of an amplifier, or how fast its output will move from one voltage to another, is related to its susceptibility to TIM.

There is no generally agreed-upon method for quantitatively measuring TIM, although several schemes have been proposed. One of these is to use a test signal consisting of a band of pink noise with a one-third octave wide notch in it. The notch is placed in the mid-frequency range, where our hearing is most acute. When the signal is passed through the DUT, any residual signal in the notch is due to TIM. The problem with this method is that intermodulation and harmonic distortion will also result in energy in the missing band.

Another suggested approach is to use a square wave mixed with a high-frequency sine wave as a test signal. TIM will cause the high-frequency part of the signal to be amplitude modulated at twice the square wave frequency because of ineffective feedback while the device is slewing from one side of the square wave to the other. A spectrum analysis of the signal will reveal sidebands around the high-frequency signal caused by the modulation. There is no standard that specifies the frequencies or their levels or how to state the result in numbers.

A third method of measurement is to use the previously discussed twin-tone intermodulation test at very high frequencies, above the audible range. Again, there is no standard procedure.

We do not know the complete answer to TIM problems, but we do know that listening tests confirm its audibility. It seems safe to say that measurements in the past were confined to too narrow a frequency range to adequately investigate TIM.

Frequency Response of the Listening Room

As was mentioned before, the acoustics of the listening room will influence the frequency response of loudspeakers. If a playback system is to be optimized, then this influence must be measured. One of the best ways to do this is to play a test recording that has one-third octave bands of pink noise recorded on it. The recording is played and the sound pressure level (SPL) is measured with a sound level meter at the listening position. Ideally, if the overall frequency response is flat, all the bands of noise will be at the same SPL. This is a simple test to conduct and involves a minimum of instrumentation.

It might seem that third octaves are too broad in frequency to give adequate resolution to the measurement. It has been shown, however, that the ear is not very sensitive to deviations in frequency response as long as they are less than one-third octave apart and if they are not too extreme in amplitude.

This is a good test to perform to determine the best loudspeaker position in a room. Large changes in low-frequency performance will be seen for different locations, and the one giving the most uniform response can be chosen (consistent with domestic harmony, of course). Most listening rooms will be plagued with standing waves, which result in uneven distribution of low frequency level around the room. Moving the loudspeaker to various places will not change this, contrary to some opinions; but moving the loudspeaker *will* change the relative level at which the standing wave pattern will be excited, and can result in more uniform response in at least one listening position.

This test will also allow one to adjust the tone controls of the sound system for optimum performance, but some care must be exercised. It is not true that the acoustic response of the listening room should be equalized to be flat to 20 kHz. There should be a gradual roll-off above 2,000 Hz or so, amounting to about 10 dB at 15 or 20 kHz. The reason for this is that the measuring meter is sensitive to the sound from the reverberant energy of the room, as well as to the level of the direct sound from the loudspeaker. Our ears, however, are much more sensitive to the direct sound than to the reverberation. Also, the loudspeaker will always be more directional at the high end than at mid and low frequencies. This means the reverberant field of the room is less excited at high frequencies than at low. The room also has much greater sound absorption at high frequencies compared to low. These effects mean that if the reverberant level is equalized to be flat, the direct sound will be grossly accentuated.

In recent years, it was in vogue to equalize playback systems by placing one-third octave graphic equalizers in them, performing the above-described test, and adjusting the response to be flat. This is a questionable practice for two reasons: the first is the reverberant effect just discussed, and the second is the fact that the equalizer will introduce phase anomalies and ripple in the response. Poor phase response is especially bad in the upper and middle ranges, where it degrades stereo imaging. At least the phase response in the two channels should be the same for proper stereo. The upper frequency ranges are best modified with conventional tone controls, which have very gentle slopes and relatively smooth phase curves. At the low-frequency end, where much of the irregularity in response will be found, it is easier to justify narrowband equalization.

Theoretically, it makes more sense to equalize the sound power output of the loudspeakers to be flat than to equalize the reverberant field. This can be approximated by measuring the speaker output at close range rather than at the listening position. In this way, the actual signal input to the room is made more uniform as a function of frequency. The room will modify the response, of course, but it will do so in the same way it modifies any other sound source in the room, such as a live musical instrument. If a violin were to be played in a room, there would be no attempt made to "equalize" its response at the listener's position! It is true that some rooms are very "bright" and others very "dull." Subtle adjustments of the tone controls can assist in these cases.

In any case, it is important to remember that the ear is the final measuring instrument, and it must be satisfied in the end. We were once asked to listen to a newly installed sound system and to comment. The sound was extremely bright, harsh, and unpleasant. When we pointed this out to the owner, he said, "Yes, but I have equalized the system and it is absolutely flat to 18 kHz just where you are standing."

Measurements of Digital Audio Systems

All the techniques discussed above can be and are used to evaluate digital audio systems. However, digital systems frequently produce noise and distortion in such small amounts that conventional instruments may not be able to measure them. For instance, to measure harmonic distortion of a device down to .001 percent requires a sine-wave test generator with significantly less distortion than that. Such generators are rare.

In the measurement of digital systems, sometimes the frequency of the test signal will influence the measured result. If the test signal is a submultiple of the sampling frequency, or is related to the sampling frequency by a rational factor, quantization noise (or quantization error) will be added to it in exactly the same "phase" each cycle of the signal. The output waveform will be periodic, and the error will show up as harmonic distortion. If, on the other hand, the test frequency is not related to the sampling frequency, the quantization error will show up as broadband noise because the individual cycles of the signal will be sampled at random times. These two types of quantization error will sound very different, even though the only difference in the input signal is a slightly different frequency.

For measurement of noise, harmonic, and intermodulation distortion of digital systems, some sort of DSP (digital signal processing) device is probably best. An example of such a test device is the high-resolution FFT analyzer. But the analyzer itself, being also a digital device, suffers from the same types of limitation that the devices under test exhibit. An example is phase shift in the anti-aliasing filters. It so happens that these filters are not needed if the input signals are band-limited to below the Nyquist frequency of the analyzer and so they may be switched out. This is normally possible when measuring digital devices, for the anti-imaging filter in the device under test will effectively band-limit the output signal.

The FFT analyzer, however, analyzes signals of different frequencies in different ways. If an integral number of periods of the test signal fit into the time window of the analyzer, the analysis will be correct. But if the period of the test signal is such that the analyzer time window truncates part of the signal waveform, the phenomenon of "leakage" will occur, and the frequency resolution of the analyzer will be reduced. Therefore, test signal frequencies, such as are found on compact discs designed for testing CD players, should be chosen carefully and the type of analyzer to be used kept in mind.

A test signal suitable for measuring the response and phase characteristics of the anti-aliasing and anti-imaging filters of CD players is the impulse. An impulse can be made by setting all the bits of the PCM code to 1 (maximum amplitude) for one sample, and thereafter setting all the bits to 0 (no signal amplitude). The spectrum of such an impulse is perfectly flat in amplitude and phase over the entire bandwidth of the CD player, so a measurement of the output spectrum of the player will be the response of the system, including the anti-imaging filter. The impulses on the test disc should be spaced far enough apart so that the filter will stop ringing from one impulse before the next one arrives. This allows evaluation of the time response of the filter.

When digital audio signals are recorded on videotape recorders or compact discs, the PCM code is arranged into "frames" occurring at 30 per second in order to simulate a video signal, and 1 every 136 microseconds in the case of the compact disc. On playback, the frames of data must be put back together into a continuous code so the audio signal will be continuous. Because of uncertainty in the timing of the beginning of each frame, there will be a time jitter introduced onto the signal. This is like a high-speed flutter, or phase modulation, and cannot be easily measured with conventional flutter meters. But it is still a type of distortion of the signal, and is thought to be audible under certain conditions. (It could be the cause of the "roughness" or "graininess" some people say they hear in digital systems.) It should be measured, although no standard method is available.

Appendix 6
The Balanced Line

In order to transmit power from one place to another by electrical means, two conductors are required; e.g., a light bulb needs two wires, one for the current to enter and one for the current to leave. Likewise, in order to send signals, which are alternating electric currents, two conductors are also required. It was found in the early days of the telegraph industry that the earth could be used as one of the conductors, meaning that only a single wire was needed to send telegraph signals. See figure 1.

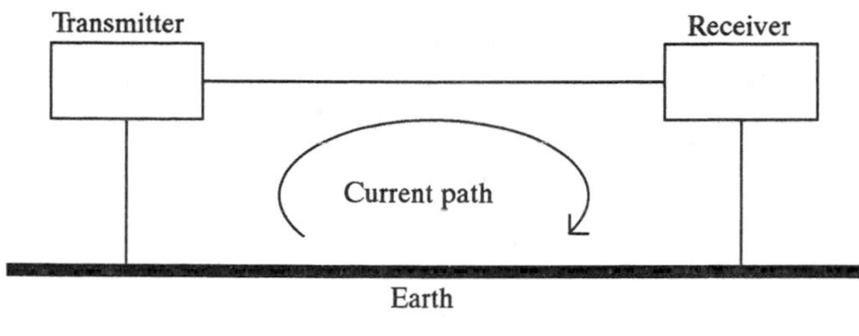

Figure 1

The use of the earth as a conductor is only useful if small amounts of power are to be transmitted, because the high resistance of the ground results in large power losses and low efficiency. This is the reason your electric utility runs two wires to your house rather than using the earth as a return path.

In electronic equipment, such as audio amplifiers, it is convenient to connect one terminal of the power supply to the chassis of the device. This simplifies internal wiring somewhat. The chassis is called the "ground" side of the power supply, in keeping with the telegraph tradition.

As can be seen from figure 2, one terminal of the signal is common to one terminal of the power supply. By connecting this terminal to the chassis, the chassis is made to act as a shield around the circuits and thus reduce the interference due to external fields, such as 60-Hz hum from the power lines. In nearly all audio circuits, this chassis connection is continued in the form of a shield in the cables which interconnect devices. The shield isolates the inner conductor from electrostatic hum fields and also serves as one of the conductors for the audio current. This type of interconnection, where the shield carries signal current, is called "single-ended" or "unbalanced." Single-ended circuits are fine for almost all short cable runs that carry relatively high signal voltages.

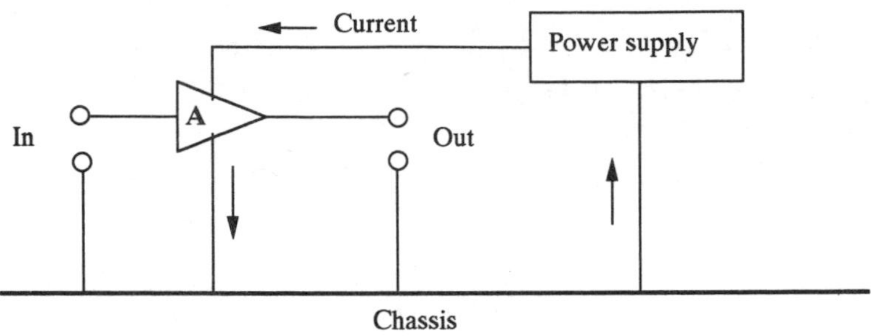

Single-ended amplifier circuit

Figure 2

However, if a situation arises where the shield has induced in it a noise current, such as a 60-Hz current due to a ground loop or magnetic induction from a power transformer, the noise will be added to the signal, causing an audible hum. If any two devices whose chassis are not at exactly the same potential are connected, the shield will carry 60-Hz current as well as signal current, and the signal-to-noise ratio will be degraded.

The way to avoid this possibility is to arrange things so that the shield does not carry any signal current, and any currents induced in the shield will not be added to the signal. One way to do this is to place a transformer at the input of the receiving device. See figure 3. One secondary terminal is connected to the chassis, but neither primary terminal is so connected because the two windings are insulated from one another. This configuration is called an "isolated" or "floating" input. The transformer input exhibits another very important characteristic called common-mode rejection. The transformer is only sensitive to current passing through its primary winding, and the only way to establish such a current is to apply a voltage difference to the input terminals. If the two terminals are at the same voltage at the same time, even though it may be a varying voltage, there will be no current in the winding and no resultant output from the transformer. This arrangement is also called a "differential input" or "balanced input."

A long audio cable, such as a microphone cable, will have noise induced in it by stray magnetic and electrostatic fields. The same voltage will be induced in both conductors of the two-wire cable, and if these two wires are connected to the transformer primary, the induced noise will not be sensed by the transformer because it has the same voltage in both conductors. The noise is said to be common-mode voltage, and the transformer rejects it. This is common-mode rejection. The microphone, on the other hand, generates a differential voltage in the wires, causing currents that are equal and of the opposite direction in each wire, and the input transformer is sensitive to this. Such an arrangement is called a "balanced line."

Further Refinements: This long balanced line is still susceptible to hum

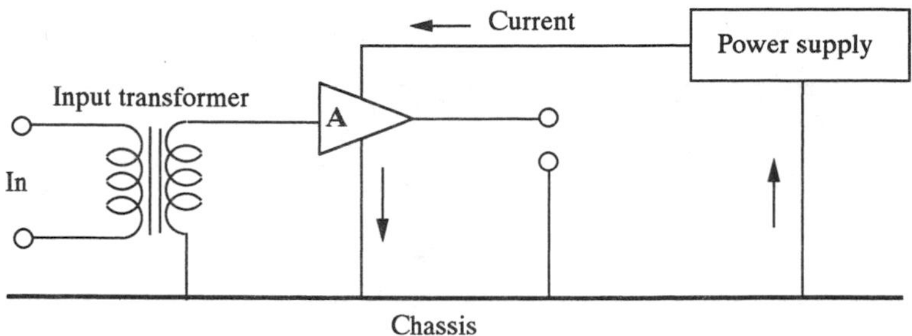

Balanced Amplifier Circuit

Figure 3

induced differentially in the conductors if there is any appreciable area between them through which a magnetic flux can pass. Therefore, the two wires must be kept as close together as possible. The best way to do this is to twist them together, forming a "twisted pair." All long audio lines are of this type. The twisting also helps in another way because the current induced in each half twist is in the opposite direction to that induced in the next half twist. Over the length of the cable, the induced currents tend to cancel. Multiple twisted pairs can be run alongside each other for long distances without crosstalk.

Another refinement is to place a shield around the twisted pair and connect it to the system ground. This prevents very large common-mode voltages from building up, reducing the noise even further. This shield is less important than the shield on a single-ended circuit, which is absolutely essential because it carries signal current. Telephone lines are an example of balanced twisted pairs that are not shielded.

It is very important that the shield on a balanced line not be connected to either of the signal wires. To do so will throw the line out of balance. It is also important that the shield not carry any current, especially any 60-Hz power-line-induced current. For this reason, sometimes the shield will be connected to ground on one end only, the chassis being connected by a separate wire. *See also* PIN 1 PROBLEM. There is one exception to this rule, and that is the case of the "phantom powering" of some condenser microphones, where the shield carries the preamplifier DC power current. This is a small current, however, and it is direct current, so it normally causes no problems. In long microphone lines, if the ground connectors on the cables are not in good condition, a poor shield connection can cause intermittent phantom current, resulting in noise.

Nowadays, transformers used for balanced lines are falling into disuse, and are being replaced by electronic circuits that mimic the transformer. Such circuits have the advantages of lower cost, lighter weight, and superior performance.

Appendix 7
Some Notes on Digital Audio

Digital audio is a very wide-ranging subject that can be described in general terms as the application of digital computer-based technology to the processing, recording, and reproduction of music. For details on how this works, see the many dictionary entries on digital audio devices.

In all digital systems, the audio signal is reduced to a series of numbers that are then manipulated with computer-like techniques to effect time delays, reverberation, equalization, editing, etc., and/or storage.

The first commercially available digital audio equipment was the digital time delay system, used for flanging, phasing, and artificial reverberation. The next was the digital tape recorder, which stores the signal in digital form on magnetic tape. One advantage of digital storage is that copies can be made with theoretically no degradation in quality. A copy of a digital tape is an exact replica of the original digital tape (provided no "bits" are lost and no noise is added in the copying process). In practice some bits will be lost in copying, and any of several error correction schemes can be used to restore the signal to a reasonable facsimile of what it was. Generally, these error correction processes work well and the corrected signal usually cannot be distinguished by ear from the original, but if multiple copies of a signal are made, each requiring error correction, obvious signal degradation will be the result.

Some advantages of digital storage of music signals are extremely wide dynamic range and freedom from noise, very wide and flat frequency response, and very low distortion. The first practical truly digital medium available to the consumer was the compact disc, which uses an optical, rather than magnetic, coding of the signal. In this, it was extremely innovative. The compact disc had the highest density of information storage of any available medium when it was introduced and is replayed by shining a tiny laser beam onto the disc surface, which contains microscopic pits that alternately reflect and cancel the beam. Because there is no physical contact involved, there is no wear on the disc, and no degradation of sound with repeated playings, assuming the disc is not scratched, contaminated with foreign material, or otherwise deformed.

At the time of its introduction, the compact disc was probably the highest quality medium for reproducing sound ever offered to the public, and this fact was much ballyhooed by the press and the manufacturers. The SACD and the DVD are significant techical advances over the CD. The SACD provides an improvement in signal-to-noise ratio and distortion, and the DVD is used for either audio or video or both. It offers much longer playing time than the CD or SACD and the capability of multichannel audio.

Digital audio, and in particular, compact discs, have been heralded as the last word in quality, the ultimate state of the art in sound reproduction beyond which there can be no improvement. This, of course, is nonsense. While digital systems do offer much reduced noise and distortion compared to analog systems, they still do have noise and distortion. The types of distortion are quite different from those of analog systems, and their objective measurement and subjective evaluation are difficult. For instance, certain digital systems usually had large amounts of high-frequency phase shift and group delay distortion, but this has been much improved in much of today's equipment.

The nonlinear distortion in digital systems tends to increase as the signal level decreases, meaning soft passages are more distorted than loud ones. As signals become very small, the energy in the fundamental components of the sounds becomes distributed into the harmonics, and this is a timbre change. This also amounts to dynamic expansion, for the level of the fundamentals is proportionally too small as signal levels are reduced. There is good reason to question the 44.1-kilohertz sampling rate used in the CD system, which was chosen for easy compatibility with already-existing video tape recorders. A higher sampling rate, such as the 48 kHz chosen for professional digital tape recorders, would allow less steep anti-alias and anti-image filters, with consequently reduced phase distortion. The problem is that it would be very difficult to change now, for compatibility with discs and players in present use would be destroyed. This is the universal problem with early standardization.

There is no doubt that digital audio systems sound different from the best analog systems, and it is easy to convince most people that they sound better. However, quite a few listening tests where digital and high-quality analog master tape recordings of the same performance are played side by side to a panel of listeners have been conducted, and in many of these the analog recordings are judged as being more "musical" and pleasant, even though they are admittedly a little more noisy. Extended critical listening of CDs reveals that there are certain problems in some areas, such as tonal balance and a sense of ambience or spaciousness.

Appendix 8
Musical Scales and the Tuning of Musical Instruments

The tonal space in which music exists is defined by the subjective pitches of the notes of musical scales, which are almost exclusively determined by the objective frequencies of these pitches. If one examines the musical scales that are used in various cultures around the world, a large variety is found, consisting of quite distinct pitch intervals. However, there is one universal interval that is always recognized as a fundamental basis for musical expression, and that interval is the octave. It seems that a part of being human is the recognition of the octave not as an interval like any other but as an overriding sense of pitch or tonality. Octave transpositions are frequently unnoticed by musicians, as if all the notes spaced apart by octaves have the same pitch.

The familiar "do re mi fa sol la ti do" notes of the diatonic scale arise naturally from the fact that the overtones of musical instruments consist of frequencies that are integral multiples of their fundamental frequency. Let us investigate this situation and attempt to understand how this musical scale is logically built.

The octave, the most musically consonant interval, is simply a frequency ratio of 2 to 1. The second harmonic of a musical sound has a frequency and a pitch one octave above that of the fundamental. Two simultaneously sounding notes one octave apart blend together extremely well, for the higher one has the same frequency as the second harmonic of the lower one. Each harmonic of the lower one will have a harmonic of the higher one at the same frequency.

The next most consonant interval is the perfect fifth, which has a frequency ratio of 1.5 to 1, or 3 to 2. The second harmonic of the higher tone will have the same frequency as the third harmonic of the lower tone, and the two tones blend together extremely well. The musical interval between the second and third harmonics of a musical sound is a fifth.

The musical interval between the third and fourth harmonics is a perfect fourth, with ratio of 3 to 4, and the interval between the fourth and fifth harmonics is a major third, with a ratio of 5 to 4. The next two harmonics, numbers five and six, span a musical interval of a minor third.

All these harmonic frequencies can be transposed downward in octaves until they are in the octave just above the fundamental, or "tonic." If this is done, and if we consider the tonic to be C, the third harmonic becomes G, called the "dominant." The transposed fourth harmonic is F, the "subdominant," and the fifth harmonic becomes E, or the "mediant." The C-E-G together form the major triad, a very important chord in music. If we start from G and form another major triad above it, the notes are G-B-D, giving us the "leading tone" B and the "second" D. In like manner, we can start from the subdominant F and build a major triad on it. This produces the "submediant" A and brings us back to C. All eight notes of the diatonic scale in the key of C are now present, and they are tuned to the perfect intervals known as "just intonation." These intervals produce chords that have no beats and sound perfectly smooth.

This construction of a just scale by taking various harmonic frequencies of the tonic C is illustrated in musical terminology in figure 1.

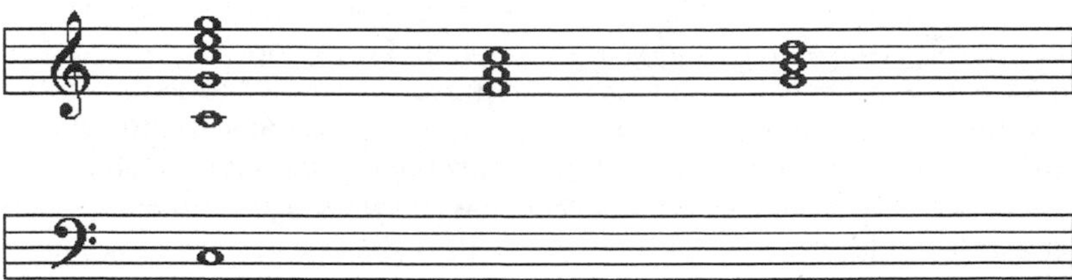

Figure 1

It is tempting to think that the just system of tuning the scale would be an ideal basis for music and that if a musician had a free choice of frequency for each note, she would always play in just intonation. Surprising as it may seem, however, this is impossible, for the diatonic scale and these perfect intervals are not compatible. To illustrate this, consider the sequence of chords shown in figure 2, which contains ascending intervals of a sixth and a fourth, and then descending intervals of two fifths. Refer to the black notes in figure 2. Let f be the frequency of the tonic C. The first sixth produces A, with a frequency of $(5/3)f$. In going to D, an interval of a fourth is required, and this is a frequency ratio of $4/3$, so its frequency will be $4/3$ of A, which is $5/3$ of f, or $(4/3)(5/3)f$, which is $(20/9)f$. The descending fifth gives G, at a frequency of $(2/3)(20/9)f = (40/27)f$. The last fifth brings us back to the tonic C, with a frequency of $(2/3)(40/27)f = (80/81)f$. But this is not the same frequency f we started with. This error interval, with a frequency ratio of $80/81$, is called the syntonic comma, and amounts to about one fourth of a semitone. This means that after this simple five-chord progression, our tonic is no longer at the same frequency at which it started.

Many players, especially string and brass players, think that when playing together without keyboard instruments, they play all perfect beatless intervals in just intonation. As we have just seen, this is impossible without allowing the pitch of the tonic to wander about—and this is never allowed in music.

Another way to look at this situation is to consider twelve ascending perfect fifths (the "circle of fifths"), followed by seven descending octaves. The pitch discrepancy between the starting note and the ending note is called the

Figure 2

diatonic comma or the comma of Pythagoras, after its most famous investigator, and amounts to a little over 1%, or about one sixth of a semitone.

It is surprising that this state of affairs should exist, for it seems that since our basis for musical harmony is the naturally occurring harmonic series of overtones consisting of simple frequency ratios of small integers, they should all be commensurate with each other, and there shouldn't be such glaring errors as the syntonic and diatonic commas. It seems that the octave, which is really a single pitch percept, is incompatible with the simple frequency ratios of the intervals of the diatonic scale. Another way of saying this is that the following integer equation must be false for all integers:

$$\left(\frac{X}{Y}\right)^{n} f = 2^{mf}$$

where *X*, *Y*, *n*, and *m* are integers, and *f* is the frequency of the tonic. The left-hand side of the equation represents successive steps of musical intervals, and the right-hand side represents octave transpositions.

It can be shown with elementary number theory that this equation cannot in fact ever be satisfied, except for the trivial case where the left-hand side also represents an octave, and therefore, it is true that the octave percept is not a subset of the harmonic, or intervalic, percept. The two percepts are independent of one another, like the *X* and *Y* coordinates of the Cartesian plane. Moreover, it can also be easily shown that intervals of major thirds are not commensurate with perfect fifths, the difference being the syntonic comma.

Any system of tuning a musical scale, especially in the case of a keyboard instrument or fretted instrument, must contend with this basic difference between the concept of the octave and the noncommensurability of musical intervals with respect to the octave. We must introduce some sort of compromise in tuning, and this compromise is called a temperament, of which there are theoretically an infinite number.

One of the earliest known schemes used for tuning keyboard instruments was the so-called Pythagorean intonation. Strictly speaking, this is not a temperament, for it is based on pure perfect fifths. It consists of eleven perfect fifths starting on E flat and ending on G sharp. The fifth between these last two notes is one comma too small, and the interval is so discordant as to be unusable. This poorly tuned fifth is called the wolf, presumably because it howls so.

Pythagorean tuning also has very poor thirds, most of which are too wide. It sounds better when used melodically rather than harmonically, and those keys must be avoided where the wolf would occur. Pythagorean tuning was probably used for keyboard instruments until near the end of the fifteenth century.

An early attempt to improve Pythagorean tuning was the so-called meantone temperament, in which the thirds are tuned pure, and all the fifths are ¼ comma too narrow. The circle of fifths cannot be closed, and the wolf, between E flat and G sharp, amounts to 1¾ comma and is even worse than the wolf in Pythagorean tuning. Meantone temperament produces very rich and satisfying harmony in keys near C major because of the pure thirds. All the whole tones are equal and are precisely half a major third, hence the name meantone.

Much effort was expended in trying to modify meantone tuning to reduce the size of the wolf in order to make more keys available and still keep most of the beautiful pure thirds. This led to hybrid Pythagorean-meantone, or "baroque," temperaments. One such system tunes four of the fifths ¼ comma narrow and all the others pure, eliminating the wolf by spreading the comma over four fifths. The thirds range from pure to Pythagorean. Andreas Werckmeister designed several such tunings around 1690, his number III being the best known. In this variation, the keys with the fewest accidentals have the best thirds and sound the purest, whereas keys with the most accidentals sound the wildest or most "brutal." Incidentally, Werckmeister said this shouldn't be a problem because "the ordinary organist can't play in those keys anyway"(!). Nevertheless, it was theoretically possible to play in all keys, and this led to these temperaments being called "wohl temperirt," or well tempered, and it is probable that J. S. Bach wrote his famous *Well-Tempered Clavier* with one of these tunings in mind, although there are those who believe that he favored equal temperament.

From about 1800, the most used type of tuning has been equal temperament, in which the comma of Pythagoras is evenly divided among the twelve half-steps of the octave. Although the idea of equal temperament predates Bach, it was not generally used in the baroque era because it was thought to be boring. All the half-steps are of equal size and are exactly one twelfth of an octave. They span a frequency ratio of the twelfth root of 2, which is about 6 percent. In equal temperament, all the intervals are the same regardless of the key in which one is playing, and none except the octave is perfectly tuned. This makes it very easy to modulate from one key to another, although the keys lose their individuality because they all have equal intervals.

Many theorists complain about the fact that the intervals in equal temperament are all impure, but in fact the fourths and fifths are within 0.001% of just intervals—so close that most musicians have a hard time telling them apart. The thirds, however, are not very satisfying, being about 0.01% away from pure thirds, and they have annoying audible beats. And of course all the thirds in all keys are equally bad.

With the advent and almost universal use of equal temperament, music today lacks the variety and richness that it had when many different systems of tuning were in common use. Of course, we must live within the capabilities of the musical instruments we have, such as the piano with only twelve keys per octave and its equal temperament. But electronic music has no such tuning limitations. A composer could define any number of intervals within an octave, even one thousand or more, and this is within the range of even relatively simple synthesizers. One can only hope that the vast variety and richness of intonation that is readily available to us will be recognized more fully and exploited by our musicians. They have only to look into the past for countless inspirational examples.

Appendix 9
Some Notes on the History of High Fidelity

The roots of high-quality sound reproduction lie not in the early days of radio broadcasting and receiving but in the sound motion picture industry, which has its beginning about 1930. A great many of the principles that govern music recording and reproduction today were discovered and developed in the thirties, with World War II putting an effective damper on further exploitation during the decade of the forties. Most of the breakthroughs that occurred in this fertile decade were the direct result of research at the Bell Telephone Laboratories under Harvey Fletcher and at the RCA Research Laboratories under Harry Olson. It was Fletcher and Munson who discovered and quantized the very nonlinear behavior of the human hearing mechanism about 1933 (the famous Fletcher-Munson effect), and this represents the beginning of psychoacoustic research, at least in this country.

The Bell Labs had an interest in this type of research and development partly because they were interested in the perfection of the telephone and partly because the manufacturing arm of the Bell company (Western Electric) was interested in building sound systems for movies and also for "public address" use. The equipment built during this time by Western Electric included microphones, amplifiers, preamps, phonograph reproducers, radio broadcasting equipment, and loudspeakers, and was of excellent quality. In fact much of this venerable gear is in great demand today and is eagerly sought after by many aficionados. The feedback amplifier, the moving-coil phono cartridge, the exponential horn loudspeaker, the compression driver for high-frequency loudspeakers, the crossover network, the compander, SVA sound-on-film recording, stereophonic recording and reproduction, and many more techniques and devices were introduced by Western Electric and the Bell Telephone Laboratories people in the thirties.

Alan Blumlein, chief engineer at EMI in England, carried out much research in audio and also developed a two-channel stereo system for motion picture sound. It seems that he and Bell Labs were unaware of each other's work.

Harry Olson, the director of the RCA acoustics research laboratory for many years, was responsible for over one hundred patents relating to audio, most notably pertaining to directional microphones and many improvements to loudspeaker designs, including acoustic suspension.

The consumer began to get interested in high fidelity after World War II, but had very little to choose from because the major radio manufacturers paid no attention to what they thought was far too small a market. An interesting article in *Fortune* magazine of October 1946 stated that according to research by CBS, the public did not prefer wide-range sound reproduction, and musicians especially advocated the deliberate limitation of high-frequency response to below 5 kHz, even when they could have had response to 10 kHz at the time. Hi-fi enthusiasts had to buy equipment from commercial sources, such as theater equipment dealers and broadcast equipment suppliers, and had to build their own systems.

But it was not long before small companies began to spring up to service the growing hi-fi market, and the 1950s saw the birth of the consumer audio business. One of the early entries into consumer audio was the Altec Lansing company, which had originally been formed as the All Technical Service Corporation and which had acquired all the Western Electric patents and designs for theater sound systems. Western Electric had left the theater sound business just before the start of World War II. The Lansing Manufacturing company, which had been making commercial loudspeakers, merged with All Technical, and the name was shortened to Altec Lansing company. James B. Lansing went on to form JBL about 1946 and was considered by many to be the preeminent consumer loudspeaker maker of the time. Lansing himself became despondent over business indebtedness and tragically committed suicide in 1949.

Another pioneer in consumer audio was Avery Fisher, after whom Avery Fisher Hall in New York is named. He founded the Fisher Radio company and became one of the first manufacturers to produce a complete high-fidelity system, including even the cabinet. Fisher also built components, and his receivers were especially well respected.

The modern microgroove LP record was introduced by Columbia in 1948, and it was an immediate success. Of course, Edison had a long-playing record as early as 1929, so Columbia's innovation was not exactly new. It did establish 33⅓ rpm as a standard. (This was also borrowed from Western Electric, which first used that speed for the Vitaphone motion picture sound system.) Before the Columbia engineers announced the LP publicly, they approached RCA, hoping to get an agreement from them to join them in making LPs, but RCA did not do so. RCA then introduced the 7-inch microgroove 45-rpm disc and player in 1949, thus initiating the famous "battle of the speeds." The rationale was that the most popular musical selections were no more than 5 minutes long, and the 7-inch disc was easier to handle than a 12-inch disc! The loser in the battle of the speeds was of course the consumer, for he now had to buy another turntable, or at least a two-speed model.

The introduction of the quiet vinyl microgroove records made existing 78-rpm record players obsolete, and the reduced distortion and noise levels attainable placed much higher demands on existing amplifiers and preamps, initiating a new wave of improved components. Around this time, stereophonic sound was becoming known, and some two-channel tape recorders were becoming available, along with prerecorded stereo tapes. Emory Cook, one of the pioneers in LP technology, introduced a stereo LP record that had two separate grooves and was played by two cartridges in a double-headed tonearm made by Livingston. It was not commercially viable, for it was impossible to preserve anything like correct phase relationships between the two channels.

The stereophonic LP record was introduced in 1958, and it was again an outgrowth of stereophonic experiments conducted in the 1930s by Western Electric. About this same time, FM stereo broadcasting began. These developments of course made existing sound systems obsolete, for now two preamps, amplifiers, and loudspeakers were needed; so another revolution in components was born.

In the field of loudspeakers, one notable development was the introduction of the Bass Reflex principle by the Jensen company in the 1930s. This was the first of the "vented" loudspeaker systems and resulted in extending the low-frequency limit about one-half octave below what was common for that day. Another significant loudspeaker development was the Klipschorn, patented by Paul W. Klipsch in 1941. This system had a folded low frequency horn designed to fit into the corner of a room so that the walls and floor of the room effectively extended the horn. It was characterized by prodigious low-frequency output for its day and also had very high efficiency. Its high-frequency section was a straight horn coupled to a high-efficiency compression driver. Even though the Klipschorn was good at radiating low frequencies, it also had a series of resonances in the mid-bass range, causing it to sound hollow and cavernous, especially on voices. A true revolution in loudspeaker design occurred in 1954 when Edgar Villchur introduced the acoustic suspension principle in the form of the AR-1. This bookshelf-sized system was capable of smooth, highly damped, and extended low-frequency response, and it outperformed almost all other speakers of the day. Villchur had tried to interest several speaker makers in his idea, but none would accept it, so he and three other people started the Acoustic Research Corp. It is interesting that in the late 1950s, the courts ruled that Villchur's patent on acoustic suspension was invalid because of a disclosure by Harry Olson much earlier. Had RCA elected to commercialize the idea in the thirties, the course of future loudspeaker development would have been far different! Today, a great many loud speaker systems use the acoustic suspension principle or variations of it to attain good low-frequency performance from relatively small boxes. In the 1970s, Thiele and Small undertook a theoretical analysis of the vented loudspeaker box, greatly adding to the understanding of the principles involved. This work led to the ability to optimize the performance of systems of different sizes and further led to the introduction of many small-sized systems with excellent low-frequency performance by many different manufacturers.

While the principle of magnetic recording was described as early as 1888 by the American Oberlin Smith, the professional tape recorder as we know it today was developed by the Magnetophon company in Germany just before World War II. John Mullin brought back two of these machines after the war, and he, along with promised financing by Bing Crosby, convinced Alexander M. Poniatoff of the Ampex Electric company to build the first commercial American machine. Col. Richard Ranger built a copy of the Magnetophon in 1947, which he then used for motion picture sound recording. He had developed a synchronizing technique, called Rangertone, which allowed the tape to run in synch with the movie camera.

The first commercial Ampex machine was the model 200, and it outperformed the Magnetophons. It gained instant acceptance as a recorder for delaying radio broadcasts. The Brush Development company had in 1946 made a home-type tape recorder called the Soundmirror, which used DC bias. Tape for the machine was being made by the Minnesota Mining and Manufacturing company (3M). The German machines used tape made by the Bayrische Analin und Soda Fabrik (BASF), some of which was brought back by John Mullin and used by Ampex in the development of their machine. From this point, the development of the reel-to-reel tape recorder progressed rapidly. But the audio compact cassette is by far the most important tape medium for the consumer. It is the noise reduction systems that have made the cassette format acceptable for recording music. When originally conceived by Philips in the 1950s, the audio cassette was never meant to be anything more than a format suitable for voice dictation, and the strict standards under which Philips licensed manufacturers prevented true high-fidelity response. This was especially true of stereo, where the two tracks are side by side, very narrow, and very close together.

Although the compander principle of noise reduction had been used much earlier in motion picture sound, it was Ray Dolby who introduced the Dolby A noise reduction system for master tapes in the 1960s and who deserves credit for its modern exploitation. Henry Kloss, one of Edgar Villchur's original partners, who started KLH Corporation and Advent Corporation, convinced Ray Dolby to let him market a simplified Dolby compander for use with audio cassette machines. Dolby has been modifying and improving companders for many years, and his company produces Dolby A and SR for professional use and Dolby B, C, and S for home use. Other manufacturers of compander systems have come forward, but the Dolby systems are dominant.

The compact disc system, jointly developed by Philips and Sony, is unquestionably the highest quality sound reproduction system for the consumer for a long time, but improvements have become recently available. The Super Audio Compact Disc (SACD), introduced by Sony and Philips, is noticeably better in reproducing stereo music and DVD Audio, derived from the video DVD system can present music in a variety of formats, from two or three-channel stereo to 5.2 channel with surround sound.

Appendix 10 Some Notes on Decimal and Binary Arithmetic as Used in Computer Terminology

Computers and data processing machines use binary numbers in their calculations rather than decimal numbers because it greatly simplifies the handling of data. The binary number system uses only 0s and 1s to represent numbers of any size. The 0s and 1s are the "bits" (short for "binary digits") of information. When talking about computer data quantities, memory sizes, and storage medium capacities, many thousands, millions, or trillions of bits are involved.

The International System of measurements (SI) long ago standardized arithmetical prefixes to indicate multiples of numerical quantities. For instance, it is well known that *kilo* means a multiple of 1000 and that *mega* is one million times, etc. The SI prefixes most commonly used in "computerese" are these two plus *giga,* standing for one billion, and sometimes *tera,* for one trillion. So, according to the SI, one kilobit is 1000 bits, and a megabit is 1,000,000 bits.

So far, so good.

Binary arithmetic, which is used in computers almost exclusively, is based on powers of 2, contrasted with the decimal system, which is based on powers of 10.

Computer professionals realize that 2^{10} is equal to 1024, which is only about 2% greater than 1000, and since this is quite a small error, they started calling 2^{10} bits (1024 bits) a "kilobit" and calling 2^{20} bits (1,048,576 bits) a "megabit." This was acceptable practice before the advent of data storage for gigabytes, and even terabytes, but the storage devices were not constructed on binary arithmetic, which meant that, for many practical purposes, binary arithmetic was less convenient than decimal arithmetic. When discussing computer memory, most manufacturers use megabyte to mean 2^{20} = 1,048,576 bytes, but the manufacturers of computer storage devices usually use the term to mean 1,000,000 bytes. Some designers of local area networks have used megabit per second to mean 1,048,576 bit/s, but all telecommunications engineers use it to mean 1,000,000 (10^6) bit/s. The result is that today "everybody" does not "know" what a megabyte is.

Floppy disk manufacturers are even more confusing. The prefix *M* means (1000 × 1000) in SI, and (1024 × 1024) in standard computing. However, the standard "1.44 MB" floppy holds (1.44 × 1000 × 1024) bytes.

In 1999, the International Electrotechnical Commission (IEC) published Amendment 2 to "IEC 60027-2: Letter symbols to be used in electrical technology–Part 2: Telecommunications and electronics." This standard, which had been approved in 1998, introduced the prefixes *kibi, mebi, gibi, tebi, pebi, exbi,* to be used in specifying binary multiples of a quantity. The names come from shortened versions of the original SI prefixes and *bi* which is short for binary. It also clarifies that, from the point of view of the IEC, the SI prefixes only have their base-10 meaning and never have a base-2 meaning.

New IEC Standard Prefixes

Name	Abbr	Factor
kibi	Ki	2^{10} = 1024
mebi	Mi	2^{20} = 1 048 576
gibi	Gi	2^{30} = 1 073 741 824
tebi	Ti	2^{40} = 1 099 511 627 776
pebi	Pi	2^{50} = 1 125 899 906 842 624
exbi	Ei	2^{60} = 1 152 921 504 606 846 976

As of 2004 this naming convention has not yet gained widespread use. The IEC did not give names for the prefixes beyond *exa-*, but if they had given them names, they would probably be *zebi* and *yobi*.

Appendix 11
Some Notes on Impedance and Frequency Response

The definition of impedance (pronounced im-**peed**-ents), according to the International Standards Organization (ISO), is the "ratio of the harmonic excitation of a system to its response (in consistent units), both of which are complex quantities, and both of whose arguments increase linearly with time at the same rate. The term applies to linear systems only and the terms and definitions relating to impedance apply to sinusoidal conditions only."

Let us take a closer look at this definition and attempt to clarify it. First, it is very important to note that impedance is a characteristic of a device or system and is not dependent in any way on the input signal to the system. We are concerned here with electrical impedance, although a similar treatment can be given to mechanical systems, and mechanical impedance is a perfectly legitimate and useful concept.

The term "harmonic excitation" means a sinusoidal voltage, or a sine wave, is applied to the device whose impedance we wish to investigate. The response is the electric current in the device that is a result of the excitation voltage. That this excitation voltage and the response current are "complex" means that we are to be concerned with their phase as well as their magnitude. In other words, the impedance will let us know if the device will apply a time delay to the excitation signal, and if so, how long a delay. The statement about both arguments increasing linearly with time means that the ratio of excitation to response is to be measured as a function of frequency. This implies that the impedance will be different at different frequencies, and this will be true for nearly all cases.

The fact that the concept of impedance applies to linear systems only simply means that a nonlinear system or device cannot be said to have an impedance. A nonlinear system behaves differently at different excitation levels, and its response is not generally predictable from its excitation. Ideal audio systems and components would be truly linear, but we know that real devices suffer from certain nonlinearities, and these nonlinearities cause most of the various distortions that we struggle to reduce. Because audio systems are at least conceptually linear, and also because they approach true linearity, we are justified in defining their impedances, even though the definition of impedance would strictly speaking preclude it. In some cases—for instance, when a loudspeaker is overdriven into nonlinearity—we could say that its impedance varies with drive level.

The definition says that impedance is only meaningful with sinusoidal excitation and response conditions, but this does not mean that we cannot apply the concept of impedance to systems that are excited by complex waveforms such as music. The definition simply means that to measure the impedance, we must consider the ratio of excitation to response at each frequency independently, and this implies sinusoidal voltage and current signals. Once the impedance is known as a function of frequency, the behavior of the system with complex waveform excitation will be predictable, because the system is essentially linear.

Because impedance has three dimensions—magnitude, phase, and frequency—it is difficult to graph on two-dimensional paper. One solution is to graph the magnitude of impedance versus frequency on one plot, and to graph the phase versus frequency on another plot.

The three-dimensional impedance curve can be thought of as the locus of a vector that extends from the frequency axis a distance proportional to the magnitude of the impedance. The angle the vector makes with a fixed coordinate system is the phase angle of the impedance. This curve will in general be some sort of spiral extending along the frequency axis. The shape of this curve can be resolved by projecting it onto two planes that intersect along the frequency axis. One of these planes extends in the zero phase angle direction from the frequency axis, and the other one extends in the 90-degree phase angle direction. See Heyser Spiral for graphic details. Mathematically, if a vector is multiplied by $\sqrt{-1}$ (abbreviated "i" by mathematicians and "j" by engineers), it is rotated 90 degrees with respect to its coordinate system or in other words is simply given a 90-degree phase shift. These two projections of the curve are called, respectively, the "real" and the "imaginary" parts of the impedance. The real part is that part of the impedance that is in phase with the excitation, and the imaginary part is that part that is 90 degrees out of phase with the excitation. The actual phase at any frequency can be determined mathematically by taking the arctangent of the real part divided by the imaginary part. The term "imaginary" is unfortunate, for it is a perfectly valid concept. A more descriptive term for it is the quadrature part, and this term is preferred. The term "imaginary" comes from the early mathematicians, who could not quite believe that the square root of negative 1 could exist.

Another scheme is the so-called Nyquist plot, in which a rectangular coordinate system is used to represent magnitude of impedance as the distance from the origin and positive phase as a rotation to the right from vertical, with negative phase as a rotation to the left from vertical. The Nyquist plot is useful for identifying resonances, because the phase of the impedance will smoothly vary from zero degrees below the resonance frequency to 90 degrees at the resonance frequency to 180 degrees above the resonance frequency. The Nyquist graph of the impedance of such a resonance will be a circle, and a system with several resonances will have a circle for each one in the Nyquist plot. The diameter of the circle is an indication of the magnitude of the impedance at the resonant frequency and is thus a function of the damping of the resonance. The Nyquist plot is often used to represent the impedance of loudspeakers, where resonances can readily be identified.

Appendix 11

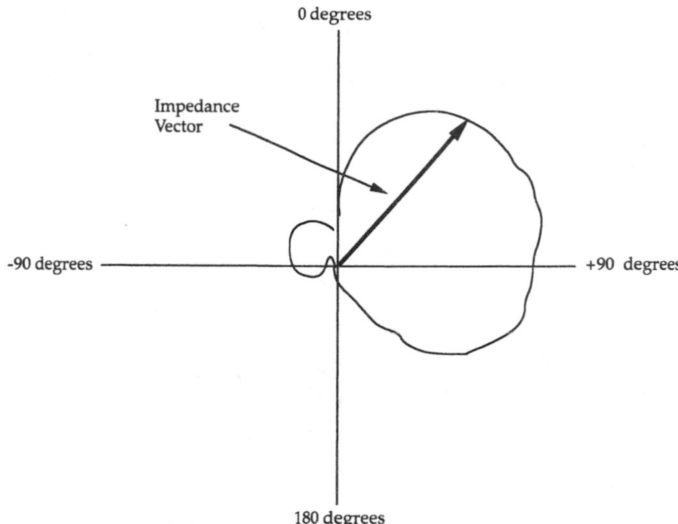

Nyquist diagram showing two resonances

The Nyquist plot does not identify the frequency of resonances; in a sense it is like looking at the three-dimensional impedance curve by sighting down the frequency axis.

The phase of the current will be shifted either positively or negatively depending on whether the impedance is capacitive or inductive. If the phase is not shifted, the impedance is said to be resistive. The phase of the impedance of a real circuit or device will generally vary from positive to negative, and it is called inductive if the current lags the voltage and capacitive if the current leads the voltage.

As mentioned above, mechanical impedance can be treated in a manner similar to electrical impedance, and is often used in loudspeaker analysis. The excitation can be a sinusoidal force, and the response can be a resulting motion. In a dynamic loudspeaker, inductive motional impedance means the cone motion lags behind excitation and acts like a mass (or is "mass-controlled"), whereas capacitive motional impedance means the cone motion leads the excitation and acts like a spring (or is "stiffness-controlled"). If the impedance looks resistive (zero phase angle), it means the system is controlled by friction. At resonance, the mass and stiffness effectively cancel each other and the phase angle is 90 degrees and the impedance magnitude is controlled by the damping (friction) of the system.

Another type of mechanical impedance is the so-called acoustic impedance, which is defined as the complex ratio of the sound pressure at a point in a medium to the complex acoustic volume velocity at the same point. Acoustic impedance is thus a complex quantity, meaning it can be resistive and reactive, having phase angles between pressure and velocity that are zero, leading, or lagging. Acoustic impedance considerations are important in loudspeaker design, for the impedance is what provides the loading for the speaker. For instance, the horn in horn-type loudspeakers acts as an impedance transformer to better match the driver impedance to the impedance of the air in the room.

Impedance is expressed as the symbol Z and has units of ohms.

The frequency response function is closely related to the impedance function; in fact they are reciprocals, for frequency response is defined as the complex ratio of the output signal of a device or system to the input signal. It is also a three-dimensional quantity, having magnitude, phase, and frequency, and it is often displayed in the same ways as impedance, such as in Nyquist plots or real and quadrature parts versus frequency.

In audio devices, such as amplifiers, sometimes it is useful to define two types of impedance—input impedance and source impedance. If measured at the input terminals of the device, it is defined as input impedance, and if measured at the output terminals, it is source impedance, or sometimes output impedance. However, output impedance usually means the impedance the output of the device is designed to be connected to. An example is the output of an audio power amplifier that is labeled "8 ohms" or "16 ohms." This means the amplifier will work best whan connected to speakers with input impedances of 8 or 16 ohms, respectively. The source impedance of the amplifier, however, will be very much lower than the speaker impedance, usually in the neighborhood of less than a tenth of an ohm. This is to increase the efficiency of the power transfer to the speaker.

Bibliography

Some of the books listed here are out of print and may be difficult to obtain, even in public libraries, but we have included them because of their importance at their time of publication. Many of them offer valuable practical information today, and all are of historical interest.

Books and Articles

Ando, Yoichi. *Concert Hall Acoustics.* New York: Springer Verlag, 1985.

A very detailed mathematical study of concert-hall acoustics, this book represents a distillation or summary of Ando's considerable research into the subject. In many ways, it represents the state of the art, but it is not easy reading. The introduction by Manfred Schroeder is well written and entertaining. Ando's discussion of the interaural cross-correlation function and its importance is first-rate.

Ballou, Glen, ed. *Handbook for Sound Engineers.* Boston: Focal Press, 2002.

This very large (1,552 pages) book is the replacement for the similar-sized *Audio Cyclopedia* of Howard Tremaine, which has been out of print for many years. The third edition drops the Audio Cyclopedia part of the title. It covers many subjects, such as acoustical design, transducers, audio electronic circuits, sound system design, electronic components, and audio measurements. It is primarily for the audio professional but contains plenty of information of interest to the hobbyist.

Békésy, Georg Von. *Sensory Inhibition.* Princeton: Princeton University Press, 1967.

This important compact book by the Nobel-Prize-winner Von Békésy describes a series of experiments and draws conclusions from them that apply to many aspects of our hearing. The author is extremely ingenious in his experimental technique, and his findings help to explain such phenomena as masking and precedence effect. He also points out many basic similarities between hearing and our other senses.

Benade, Arthur H. *Fundamentals of Musical Acoustics.* New York: Oxford University Press, 1976.

This introductory text uses a minimum of mathematics and describes many acoustic phenomena in somewhat unconventional ways. It covers a lot of ground but is a little jumbled in its organization, and some explanations are difficult to understand.

Bibliography

Blesser, Barry A. "Digitization of Audio: A Comprehensive Examination of Theory, Implementation, and Current Practices." *Journal of the Audio Engineering Society*, October 1978.

An excellent overview of the pros and cons of PCM, delta modulation, etc. Blesser has written many good articles in the popular press on digital audio.

Blesser, Barry; Bart Locanthi; and Thomas Stockham. *Digital Audio.* Collected papers from the premier conference of the Audio Engineering Society, June 1982.

A very advanced volume of 270 pages dealing with basics, converters, measurements, rate conversion, recording formats, error correction, manufacturing, and applications.

Bohn, Dennis. *Rane Pro Audio Reference.* Mukilteo, Wash.: Rane Corp., 2002.

A 320-page large-format paperback with a large glossary and several good technical tutorials; with CD-ROM.

Burroughs, Lou. *Microphones: Design and Application.* New York: Sagamore, 1974.

This well-written and interesting book contains a great deal of practical and useful information about microphones and their use in recording and broadcasting. The emphasis is on professional-quality dynamic microphones, although other types are also discussed.

Chamberlin, Hal. *Musical Applications of Microprocessors.* 2d ed. Indianapolis: Howard Sams & Company, 1985.

This is an expanded and revised version of Chamberlin's classic original. It is more up to date in its coverage of new technology and describes commercial music synthesis products in some detail. It also contains program listings for doing computerized spectrum analysis.

Colloms, Martin. *High Performance Loudspeakers.* London: Pentech Press, 1978.

This is a very detailed book on the design and construction of loudspeakers. It is intended for the professional and knowledgeable engineer rather than for the beginner, but the casual reader will find much of interest nevertheless. It is well illustrated and well written, and it covers the subject with unusual thoroughness.

Eargle, John. *Sound Recording.* New York: Van Nostrand Reinhold Co., 1976.

A good book covering most aspects of sound recording from a somewhat theoretical viewpoint, although it does not rely heavily on mathematics. There is a good chapter on psychoacoustics. Digital recording and signal processing are not covered.

Bibliography

Eargle, John, ed. *Stereophonic Techniques.* New York: Audio Engineering Society, 1986.

This anthology of reprints of articles on stereophonic techniques is divided into five parts: historical papers, analysis and experimentation, studio technology, broadcasting, and the consumer interface. The historical section begins in 1881, which actually seems to be the first time a stereophonic sound was transmitted. The writings of many famous people are to be found here, and it is enlightening to read about key audio developments in the words of the developers themselves.

Fletcher, Harvey. *Speech and Hearing.* New York: Van Nostrand, 1929.

This is a classic work on speech and hearing by one of the most important investigators in psychoacoustics.

Hall, Donald E. *Musical Acoustics, An Introduction.* Belmont, Calif.: Wadsworth, 1980.

A good introductory textbook on the subject that uses mathematical formulas sparingly. There are chapters on physical acoustics, how musical instruments work, hearing, and sound reproduction.

Helmholtz, Hermann von. *On the Sensations of Tone.* New York: Dover, 1974.

This is a reprint of an English translation of the monumental German publication of 1863. Helmholtz was an accomplished scientist and also a physician, and he performed many truly ingenious experiments in the investigation of the human hearing mechanism. He was one of the first to show that complex sounds are made up of component parts, or harmonics, and he devised a method for hearing these partials via special resonators of his design. He also made a mechanical model of the human speech mechanism, and it was able to intone vowel sounds. Today, the book is of historical interest and is a good source for anyone interested in the scientific method and its application to basic research. His sections on music and harmony are very well done.

Huber, David M. and Robert E. Runstein. *Modern Recording Techniques.* 5th ed. Boston: Focal Press, 2001.

This is an enlarged and more up-to-date version of Robert E. Runstein's original *Modern Recording Techniques* (1974). It covers digital audio technology quite well.

Isom, Warren Rex, ed. *The Phonograph and Sound Recording After 100 Years.* New York: Journal of the Audio Engineering Society, Centennial Issue, October 1977.

This greatly expanded issue of the AES journal commemorates the 100th anniversary of the invention of the phonograph and is full of historical information on all aspects of phonograph record production and recording. The section on the manufacturing of records is particularly complete. There is an interesting article on digital audio by Tom Stockham.

Langford-Smith, F. *Radiotron Designer's Handbook.* Harrison, N.J.: Radio Corporation of America, 1953.

This is a comprehensive handbook (over 1,400 pages), primarily on the applications of vacuum tubes to audio. Although it may seem outdated, there is a great deal of useful information here. Such subjects as equalizers, transformers, harmonic analysis, tuned circuits, distortion, loudspeakers, oscillators, etc., are treated in detail. Lately, there has been an increased interest in the use of tubes for audio, and this work is the most complete we know of on this subject.

Mathews, Max V. *The Technology of Computer Music.* Cambridge, Mass.: MIT Press, 1969.

A good overview of the generation of computer-realized and computer-composed music.

Miyaoka, Senri. "Digital Audio Is Compact and Rugged." *IEEE Spectrum,* March 1984.

A short but precise description of the optical aspects of the compact disc concept, by the leader of the development staff at Sony.

Olson, Harry F. *Modern Sound Reproduction.* 1972. Reprint, New York: Robert E. Krieger, 1978.

An interesting book by one of the giants of electroacoustics, who headed the RCA Research Laboratories for many years. The book is outdated now, but contains much historical information.

Philips Technical Review. Vol. 40, No. 6, 1982, published by Philips in the Netherlands.

A very good and extensive (180 pages) general description of the technical aspects of the compact disc format.

Pierce, John R. *Almost All about Waves.* Cambridge, Mass.: MIT Press, 1974.

While not specifically directed toward audio, this well-written little book describes waves in a good deal more detail than almost any other. It is not for the beginner, requiring as it does an understanding of mathematics through calculus, but it offers the careful reader a most clear and penetrating insight into wave motion, vector and complex notation, polarization, diffraction, and radiation, etc.

Pierce, John R. *The Science of Musical Sound.* New York: Scientific American Library, 1983.

This is a fascinating book from John Pierce, who consistently addresses technical subjects with fresh insight and penetrating powers of observation. The book comes with two small phonograph records that illustrate various topics that are discussed.

His chapter on sound reproduction has some interesting history, but it is not very complete. The sections on the ear and hearing are detailed and first-rate, and are written in a way that makes this difficult subject easy to understand.

Pohlmann, Ken C. *Principles of Digital Audio.* 4th ed. New York: McGraw-Hill Professional, 2000

This is one of the first popular books on digital audio by a well-known columnist on the subject. Pohlmann writes in an amusing and easy-to-read style, and the book is well illustrated. The first chapter, on the basics of sound and acoustics, has some inaccuracies, but the rest of the book is very informative and quite complete.

Read, Oliver. *The Recording and Reproduction of Sound.* 2d ed. Indianapolis: Howard W. Sams, 1952.

This classic volume, even though not up to date, contains a wealth of information on all aspects of audio, and it makes fascinating reading today. It is well illustrated and covers the entire subject with fine detail.

Read, Oliver, and Walter L. Welch. *From Tin Foil to Stereo.* 2d ed. Indianapolis: Howard W. Sams, 1976.

This fact-filled book is the most complete history of the acoustic phonograph from its invention by Edison up through the development of stereophonic recording. It is biased heavily toward acoustic recording, and perhaps reveres Edison unduly, but it is a fascinating anecdotal history of the many events, inventions, patent fights, etc., that constituted the development of audio recording and reproduction.

Rossing, Thomas D. *The Science of Sound.* Reading, Mass.: Addison-Wesley, 1982.

This is a fine if conventional text on musical acoustics, covering perception and measurement of sound, how musical instruments work, etc. Its best features are the chapters on electrical production of sound, which cover electronic circuitry, and a fair amount of detail on audio devices. Electronic music and digital sound are also covered.

Schubert, Earl D., ed. *Psychological Acoustics.* Stroudsburg, Penn.: Dowden, Hutchinson, and Ross, 1979.

A collection of previously published papers, providing a fascinating chronology of major discoveries from 1876 to 1970.

Sinclair, Ian R., ed. *Audio Electronics Reference Book.* Boston: BSP Professional Books, 1989.

This interesting technical book from Britain includes 20 chapters written by various experts in their respective fields and contains a wealth of information on most aspects of audio electronics. Emphasis is given to British audio products and developments. It also covers elementary acoustics and psychoacoustics as related to sound reproduction. The compact disc system and tape recording are well represented, as are loudspeakers, loudspeaker enclosures, and automobile audio.

Woram, John M. *The Recording Studio Handbook.* Commack, N.Y.: Elar Publishing Co., 1983.
An interesting, quite well-illustrated book covering most aspects of recording studio operations. It is detailed and accurate in its descriptions of audio equipment, although it does not cover digital equipment.

Periodicals

Audio Media. IMAS Publishing Group, 5827 Columbia Pike, Third Floor, Falls Church, VA 22041 (monthly).
A magazine with several world region editions, it aims for sound professionals in various fields, especially recording studios. Many reviews of equipment, facility showcases, and general articles of audio production topics. It is free to qualified individuals.

EQ. United Entertainment Media, P.O. Box 0532, Baldwin, NY 11510-0532 (monthly).
A recording magazine suited for the project studio owner and recording musician, it features articles on recording and studio techniques, equipment reviews and several well-known columnists. It is free to qualified individuals.

Journal of the Audio Engineering Society (JAES). 80 East 42nd Street, New York, NY 10165 (monthly).
A technical journal, containing detailed articles on all aspects of audio engineering. Many of the articles are manuscripts of papers presented at the semi-annual Audio Engineering Society conventions and represent the most up-to-date information available. The journal is intended for the professional in audio, and the articles are on an advanced technical level, with a good deal of mathematics included. The AES also publishes occasional anthologies or collections of papers on various subjects such as loudspeaker design and digital audio. The journal is included with paid membership in the AES.

Mix. Mix Publications, Inc., 6400 Hollis Street, Suite 12, Emeryville, CA 94608 (monthly).
This relatively large magazine is somewhat similar to *RE/P* and *db,* but reflects a more popular approach. It includes semi-technical articles on most

aspects of audio and studio techniques, some articles on video, and reviews of studio equipment. Like *S&VC*, it is heavily supported by advertising. It is free to qualified individuals.

Sound & Video Contractor (S&VC). Primedia, Inc., 6400 Hollis Street, Suite 12, Emeryville, CA 94608 (monthly).

Distributed free to qualified professionals in sound reinforcement and closed-circuit video system contracting. There are articles on theater sound, signal processing equipment and techniques, digital equipment for sound reinforcement and semi-technical articles on the operation of audio devices such as loudspeakers. The magazine is heavily supported by advertisers.

Periodicals No Longer Published

The following periodicals all ceased publication since the last edition. Many issues contained articles of merit and still make good reading when taken in historical context

Audio. 1515 Broadway, New York, NY (monthly).

This was one of the oldest magazines devoted to audio, and was aimed at the knowledgeable consumer. It contained semi-technical articles on a wide range of subjects of interest to the stereo enthusiast, and also contained reviews of consumer audio equipment as well as reviews of records, tapes, and compact discs. One of its most endearing features was the monthly article by the late Edward Tatnall Canby, which ran continuously since the early 1950s.

db, The Sound Engineering Magazine. Sagamore Publishing Co., Plainview, L.I., NY (bi-monthly).

An interesting magazine for the recording engineer and studio operator, including reviews of professional and semi-professional audio products. The continuing column on digital audio by Barry Blesser was very well written and informative.

Recording Engineer/Producer (RE/P). P.O. Box 2449, Hollywood, CA (monthly).

This semi-technical magazine was aimed at the recording studio operator and engineer, and also had articles of interest to the recording musician. Articles covered a wide range of subjects, from historical pieces to digital recording and motion picture sound. The emphasis was always on practicality, and much useful information is included. A typical issue ran to over 200 pages.

Studio Sound and Broadcast Engineering. Link House Publications, Croydon, England (monthly).

This publication was available free to audio professionals, and was considered very important. Although published in England, it was still relevant to American readers interested in all aspects of audio, with emphasis on the recording studio and its operation. One of its most valuable features was the equipment review section, where professional audio devices were subjected to extensive testing and reporting. They included high-level articles on new and little-known techniques, and the letters to the editor make interesting reading. It seemed the British have raised the writing of such letters to an art form, and it was well represented here.

The Internet

One should approach information on the internet with caution, as much advice is ill-informed. One should seriously evaluate the authority of the source of information. It is, however, a practical form of give and take communication.

Usenet Newsgroup "Rec.Audio.Pro," also known as "RAP"

An unmoderated newsgroup where participants post questions and replies, and chat. Read the FAQ (Frequently Asked Questions) which generally answers many beginner's questions about audio production reasonably well. The "noise" or useless chatter can be daunting, but many front-line audio workers post questions and answers. Very few well-known authorities make their presence, if any, known.

Live Audio Board (LAB) at <www.prosoundweb.com/forums> or <www.live-audio.com>

A favorite of many in the sound reinforcement field. The prosoundweb.com site has other forums for recording and stage lighting. There is advertising to support the site, but no fees for users.